Privacy and Data Protection in Business: Laws and Practices

Jonathan I. Ezor

ISBN: 9781422490969

Library of Congress Cataloging-in-Publication Data

Ezor, Jonathan
    Privacy and data protection in business : laws and practices / Jonathan I. Ezor.
      p. cm.
    Includes index.
    Looseleaf ISBN 978-1-4224-9096-9
    1. Business records--Law and legislation--United States. 2. Data protection--Law and legislation--United States. 3. Privacy, Right of--United States. 4. Computer networks--Access control--United States. 5. Digital communications--United States. I. Title.
      KF1357.5.E96 2012
      346.73'065--dc23
 	
                            2012028733

NOTE TO USERS
To ensure that you are using the latest materials available in this area, please be sure to periodically check the LexisNexis Law School web site for downloadable updates and supplements at www.lexisnexis.com/lawschool.

Editorial Offices
121 Chanlon Rd., New Providence, NJ 07974 (908) 464-6800
201 Mission St., San Francisco, CA 94105-1831 (415) 908-3200
www.lexisnexis.com

MATTHEW◆BENDER

Acknowledgments

This book would not have been possible without a number of people to whom I express my deep appreciation. First and foremost, I wish to thank my wife Stacy and our children Avi, Eitan and Elisheva, for their support, encouragement, and feedback.

Next, my friends and Touro College Jacob D. Fuchsberg Law Center colleagues Gary Shaw and Linda Howard Weissman, who co-founded and remain active in building the Institute for Business, Law and Technology at Touro which I have headed since 2003. Touro Law Dean Emeritus Howard A. Glickstein and Dean Lawrence Raful have provided valued leadership, both institutional and personal, and the Touro Law faculty has always supported me and the Institute's programs. My Touro students have learned from and with me about privacy and many other business technology law subjects, and teaching law students remains one of my sweetest pleasures. This work in particular would not have been possible without the enthusiastic and capable research assistance of Touro Law students Stephanie Rapp and Scott Richman, for which I am grateful.

I also want to acknowledge the attorneys and other professionals of the IBLT Advisory Board, on whose sage guidance I have relied for many years; Andrew Lustigman and Adam Solomon and their Olshan colleagues; and Andrew Lupu, Jules Polonetsky, and the other business privacy thought leaders and practitioners from whom I have learned so much in my career.

Finally, this book is dedicated to my mother Rita Ezor, "star of stage, screen and language arts." She has always been my best example of how writing and teaching are most effective when done with an appreciation of audience and purpose, and a desire to engage, not just inform, one's students.

TABLE OF CONTENTS

TABLE OF CONTENTS

TABLE OF CONTENTS

TABLE OF CONTENTS

TABLE OF CONTENTS

TABLE OF CONTENTS

TABLE OF CONTENTS

Chapter 1

INTRODUCTION: THE MEANING OF PRIVACY AND THE VALUE OF INFORMATION

I. STARTING POINT: WHAT IS "PRIVACY"?

Privacy means many things to many people. It can encompass everything from thought to action to location to identity to association to one's very body. It is described as if it were physical; privacy can be "breached," "lost," "violated" or "protected," even though it is not itself tangible. The earliest known uses of the English word "privacy" itself are from the 16th Century, potentially via a misspelling of the earlier "privity".[1]

The term's very broadness makes it a challenging one to understand and use especially in the context of law and compliance. In U.S. law, the word "privacy" does not appear anywhere in the Constitution; the idea of a "right to privacy" is generally attributed to future Justice Louis D. Brandeis and his co-author Samuel D. Warren in their 1890 Harvard Law Review article of that title.[2] In that groundbreaking article, Brandeis and Warren ascribe the growing need for this new right to the rise of business and technology:

> *Recent inventions and business methods call attention to the next step which must be taken for the protection of the person, and for securing to the, individual what Judge Cooley calls the right "to be let alone." Instantaneous photographs and newspaper enterprise have invaded the sacred precincts of private and domestic life; and numerous mechanical devices threaten to make good the prediction that "what is whispered in the closet shall be proclaimed from the house-tops." For years there has been a feeling that the law must afford some remedy for the unauthorized circulation of portraits of private persons; and the evil of the invasion of privacy by the newspapers, long keenly felt, has been but recently discussed by an able writer. The alleged facts of a somewhat notorious case brought before an inferior tribunal in New York a few months ago, directly involved the consideration of the right of circulating portraits; and the question whether our law will recognize and protect the right to privacy in this and in other respects must soon come before our courts for consideration.[3]*

---

[1] *Privacy Definition*, Oxford English Dictionary, http://www.oed.com/view/Entry/151596 (last visited May 7, 2012).

[2] Samuel D. Warren & Louis D. Brandeis, *The Right to Privacy*, 4 Harv. L. Rev. 193, 195–96 (1890).

[3] *Id.* (notes omitted).

In the more than a century since the publication of the Brandeis and Warren article, a succession of Supreme Court cases have gleaned and defined a "right to privacy" arising from a number of the Constitution's provisions, notably the Fourth, Fifth and Fourteenth Amendments, beginning with *Griswold v. Connecticut*:

> *By Pierce v. Society of Sisters, supra, the right to educate one's children as one chooses is made applicable to the States by the force of the First and Fourteenth Amendments. By Meyer v. State of Nebraska, supra, the same dignity is given the right to study the German language in a private school. In other words, the State may not, consistently with the spirit of the First Amendment, contract the spectrum of available knowledge. The right of freedom of speech and press includes not only the right to utter or to print, but the right to distribute, the right to receive, the right to read (Martin v. City of Struthers, 319 U.S. 141, 143, 63 S.Ct. 862, 863, 87 L.Ed. 1313) and freedom of inquiry, freedom of thought, and freedom to teach (see Wieman v. Updegraff, 344 U.S. 183, 195, 73 S.Ct. 215, 220, 97 L.Ed. 216)-indeed the freedom of the entire university community. Sweezy v. State of New Hampshire, 354 U.S. 234, 249–250, 261–263, 77 S.Ct. 1203, 1211, 1217–1218, 1 L.Ed.2d 1311; 81 Barenblatt v. United States, 360 U.S. 109, 112, 79 S.Ct. 1081, 1085, 3 L.Ed.2d 1115; Baggett v. Bullitt, 377 U.S. 360, 369, 84 S.Ct. 1316, 1321, 12 L.Ed.2d 377. Without those peripheral rights the specific rights would be less secure. And so we reaffirm the principle of the Pierce and the Meyer cases.*

> *In NAACP v. State of Alabama, 357 U.S. 449, 462, 78 S.Ct. 1163, 1172, we protected the 'freedom to associate and privacy in one's associations,' noting that freedom of association was a peripheral First Amendment right. Disclosure of membership lists of a constitutionally valid association, we held, was invalid 'as entailing the likelihood of a substantial restraint upon the exercise by petitioner's members of their right to freedom of association.' Ibid. In other words, the First Amendment has a penumbra where privacy is protected from governmental intrusion. In like context, we have protected forms of 'association' that are not political in the customary sense but pertain to the social, legal, and economic benefit of the members. NAACP v. Button, 371 U.S. 415, 430–431, 83 S.Ct. 328, 336–337. In Schware v. Board of Bar Examiners, 353 U.S. 232, 77 S.Ct. 752, 1 L.Ed.2d 796, we held it not permissible to bar a lawyer from practice, because he had once been a member of the Communist Party. The man's 'association with that Party' was not shown to be 'anything more than a political faith in a political party' (id., at 244, 77 S.Ct. at 759) and was not action of a kind proving bad moral character. Id., at 245–246, 77 S.Ct. at 759–760.*

> *Those cases involved more than the 'right of assembly'-a right that extends to all irrespective of their race or idealogy. De Jonge v. State of Oregon, 299 U.S. 353, 57 S.Ct. 255, 81 L.Ed. 278. The right of 'association,' like the right of belief (West Virginia State Board of Education v. Barnette, 319 U.S. 624, 63 S.Ct. 1178), is more than the right to attend a meeting; it includes the right to express one's attitudes or philosophies by membership in a group or by affiliation with it or by other lawful means. Association in that context is a form of expression of opinion; and while it is not expressly included in the*

First Amendment its existence is necessary in making the express guarantees fully meaningful.

The foregoing cases suggest that specific guarantees in the Bill of Rights have penumbras, formed by emanations from those guarantees that help give them life and substance. See Poe v. Ullman, 367 U.S. 497, 516–522, 81 S.Ct. 1752, 6 L.Ed.2d 989 (dissenting opinion). Various guarantees create zones of privacy. The right of association contained in the penumbra of the First Amendment is one, as we have seen. The Third Amendment in its prohibition against the quartering of soldiers 'in any house' in time of peace without the consent of the owner is another facet of that privacy. The Fourth Amendment explicitly affirms the 'right of the people to be secure in their persons, houses, papers, and effects, against unreasonable searches and seizures.' The Fifth Amendment in its Self-Incrimination Clause enables the citizen to create a zone of privacy which government may not force him to surrender to his detriment. The Ninth Amendment provides: 'The enumeration in the Constitution, of certain rights, shall not be construed to deny or disparage others retained by the people.'

The Fourth and Fifth Amendments were described in Boyd v. United States, 116 U.S. 616, 630, 6 S.Ct. 524, 532, 29 L.Ed. 746, as protection against all governmental invasions 'of the sanctity of a man's home and the privacies of life.' We recently referred in Mapp v. Ohio, 367 U.S. 643, 656, 81 S.Ct. 1684, 1692, 6 L.Ed.2d 1081, to the Fourth Amendment as creating a 'right to privacy, no less important than any other right carefully and particularly reserved to the people.' See Beaney, The Constitutional Right to Privacy, 1962 Sup.Ct.Rev. 212; Griswold, The Right to be Let Alone, 55 Nw.U.L.Rev. 216 (1960).

We have had many controversies over these penumbral rights of 'privacy and repose.' See, e.g., Breard v. City of Alexandria, 341 U.S. 622, 626, 644, 71 S.Ct. 920, 923, 933, 95 L.Ed. 1233; Public Utilities Comm. v. Pollak, 343 U.S. 451, 72 S.Ct. 813, 96 L.Ed. 1068; Monroe v. Pape, 365 U.S. 167, 81 S.Ct. 473, 5 L.Ed.2d 492; Lanza v. State of New York, 370 U.S. 139, 82 S.Ct. 1218, 8 L.Ed.2d 384; Frank v. State of Maryland, 359 U.S. 360, 79 S.Ct. 804, 3 L.Ed.2d 877; Skinner v. State of Oklahoma, 316 U.S. 535, 541, 62 S.Ct. 1110, 1113, 86 L.Ed. 1655. These cases bear witness that the right of privacy which presses for recognition here is a legitimate one.

The present case, then, concerns a relationship lying within the zone of privacy created by several fundamental constitutional guarantees. And it concerns a law which, in forbidding the use of contraceptives rather than regulating their manufacture or sale, seeks to achieve its goals by means having a maximum destructive impact upon that relationship. Such a law cannot stand in light of the familiar principle, so often applied by this Court, that a 'governmental purpose to control or prevent activities constitutionally subject to state regulation may not be achieved by means which sweep unnecessarily broadly and thereby invade the area of protected freedoms.' NAACP v. Alabama, 377 U.S. 288, 307, 84 S.Ct. 1302, 1314, 12 L.Ed.2d 325. Would we allow the police to search the sacred precincts of marital bedrooms for telltale signs of the use of contraceptives? The very idea is repulsive to the notions of privacy surrounding the marriage relationship.

We deal with a right of privacy older than the Bill of Rights-older than our political parties, older than our school system. Marriage is a coming together for better or for worse, hopefully enduring, and intimate to the degree of being sacred. It is an association that promotes a way of life, not causes; a harmony in living, not political faiths; a bilateral loyalty, not commercial or social projects. Yet it is an association for as noble a purpose as any involved in our prior decisions.[4]

This "right" has been evoked in cases involving the permissibility of banning medical procedures such as abortion,[5] border searches of computers,[6] and other contexts, and is often evoked in the context of attempted governmental action.

Brandeis and Warren, though, showed true insight in recognizing that it was the confluence of technological development and economic growth that would be at the heart of the debate over whether a person should have the right "to be let alone." For them, the most serious affront was the rise of the popular press and its publication of gossip:

Of the desirability — indeed of the necessity — of some such protection, there can, it is believed, be no doubt. The press is overstepping in every direction the obvious bounds of propriety and of decency. Gossip is no longer the resource of the idle and of the vicious, but has become a trade, which is pursued with industry as well as effrontery. To satisfy a prurient taste the details of sexual relations are spread broadcast in the columns of the daily papers. To occupy the indolent, column upon column is filled with idle gossip, which can only be procured by intrusion upon the domestic circle. The intensity and complexity of life, attendant upon advancing civilization, have rendered necessary some retreat from the world, and man, under the refining influence of culture, has become more sensitive to publicity, so that solitude and privacy have become more essential to the individual; but modern enterprise and invention have, through invasions upon his privacy, subjected him to mental pain and distress, far greater than could be inflicted by mere bodily injury. Nor is the harm wrought by such invasions confined to the suffering of those who may be made the subjects of journalistic or other enterprise. In this, as in other branches of commerce, the supply creates the demand. Each crop of unseemly gossip, thus harvested, becomes the seed of more, and, in direct proportion to its circulation, results in a lowering of social standards and of morality. Even gossip apparently harmless, when widely and persistently circulated, is potent for evil. It both belittles and perverts. It belittles by inverting the relative importance of things, thus dwarfing the thoughts and aspirations of a people. When personal gossip attains the dignity of print, and crowds the space available for matters of real

---

[4] Griswold v. Conn., 381 U.S. 479, 482 (1965).

[5] Roe v. Wade, 410 U.S. 959 (1973).

[6] U.S. v. Cotterman, 637 F.3d 1068 (9th Cir. 2011).

interest to the community, what wonder that the ignorant and thoughtless mistake its relative importance. Easy of comprehension, appealing to that weak side of human nature which is never wholly cast down by the misfortunes and frailties of our neighbors, no one can be surprised that it usurps the place of interest in brains capable of other things. Triviality destroys at once robustness of thought and delicacy of feeling. No enthusiasm can flourish, no generous impulse can survive under its blighting influence.[7]

The inherent definition of "privacy" here is one of behavior, and its invasion or breach occurs when an individual's behavior is monitored and then reported via popular press. There are two drivers: the "prurient" interest of the consumer public, and the desire for businesses to increase revenues by feeding that interest. To the extent that the individuals whose behavior is being reported have any competing interest (as Brandeis and Warren assert), that personal interest in "privacy" may not be able to counterweigh the others, especially if there is no legal support for the aggrieved party to complain.[8] In their analysis of existing cases, they see a gap where traditional property and contract rights fail to explain how courts have prohibited certain types of disclosure and publication, and suggest that this implies (and requires) a separate right to privacy that should be formally recognized by the law.

There is, though, a second major meaning of "privacy" that is relevant for businesses in particular, which was not explicitly discussed in Brandeis and Warren's piece: the collection and use of information relating to an individual's identity, otherwise known as "personally identifiable information" or PII. The types of data that can constitute PII are quite varied. Certainly, specific data that refer to unique individuals (or at most a small group) are generally included: name, street address, telephone number, Social Security and similar identification numbers, and biological features (called biometrics) such as fingerprints, retinal patterns, voiceprints, and even DNA. PII, though, may encompass even those features and elements that are not particularly unique, such as occupation, hair or eye color, age, nationality, religion and family status, if these data in combination serve to identify a unique individual. As a fanciful example, consider these unrelated data points: male, 6'2" in height, black hair, blue eyes, grew up in Kansas. While there could hypothetically be many men who fit this description, adding a few more separate data points (newspaper reporter,

---

[7] 4 Harv. L. Rev. 193, 196 (1890).

[8] To the extent that reported gossip is untrue, there might well be recourse in defamation laws, which were well established by Brandeis and Warren's time, and are understood to be an exception to the right to free speech set forth in the First Amendment. *See, e.g.,* Chaplinsky v. N.H., 315 U.S. 568, 571 (1942):

> Allowing the broadest scope to the language and purpose of the Fourteenth Amendment, it is well understood that the right of free speech is not absolute at all times and under all circumstances. There are certain well-defined and narrowly limited classes of speech, the prevention and punishment of which has never been thought to raise any Constitutional problem. These include the lewd and obscene, the profane, the libelous, and the insulting or 'fighting' words-those which by their very utterance inflict injury or tend to incite an immediate breach of the peace. It has been well observed that such utterances are no essential part of any exposition of ideas, and are of such slight social value as a step to truth that any benefit that may be derived from them is clearly outweighed by the social interest in order and morality. 'Resort to epithets or personal abuse is not in any proper sense communication of information or opinion safeguarded by the Constitution, and its punishment as a criminal act would raise no question under that instrument.' Cantwell v. Conn., 310 U.S. 296, 309, 310, 60 S.Ct. 900, 906, 84 L.Ed. 1213, 128 A.L.R. 1352.

superhero), themselves not unique (at least in the comic books), yields a single individual's identity (or, perhaps secret identity): Clark Kent, aka Superman.

II.   THE BUSINESS VALUE OF INFORMATION

For businesses, both user behavior and user identity can have substantial value. Companies sell more to customers when the offerings are better aligned with the customers' preferences demonstrated through their shopping pattern. For that matter, knowing what a customer does and buys outside one's own store can be tremendously helpful in enticing that customer into the store. Broader demographic information about potential customer populations can also assist companies in their strategic planning and advertising; this is why so many industries have sought to add specific queries to the decennial U.S. census:

> *For much of American history, business interests have shaped questions in order to capture marketing data from the census. For instance, the 2000 census long form asked numerous questions about home and consumption habits. Even in the late 19th Century, business associations have played a strong role in the creation of specific census questions. Rather than just including the original questions of race, age, sex, the census grew to include complex socioeconomic questions. Various statistical associations along with the Chairperson of the Board of the American Marketing Association appoint the members of the official Census Advisory Committee of Professional Associations . . . .*[9]

Knowing the identity of current customers means that companies can offer a faster, more tailored experience, providing those goods or services the customer has previously or regularly purchased in a more prominent location, or being ready to give the customer "her usual." Knowing who one's *potential* customers are enables more effective sales pitches and solicitations; as much as consumers may be jaded when it comes to "personalized" messages in this database age, such messages are still more likely to catch their attention than those without the consumers' names on the envelope or e-mail subject line.

Companies have also long understood that their customer records may have value to *other* firms, and have sought to monetize that value. Whether through sharing, renting or selling customer lists, or by sending third-party solicitations to one's own customers, businesses are able to lower costs and generate revenue well outside their ordinary operations through data mining and marketing, at times beyond the earnings potential from their core businesses. Just as auto manufacturers have at times made more from their financing divisions than their dealerships, companies with detailed, high-worth customer lists can substantially boost their bottom lines without ever selling a single actual product to those customers. The same data may represent a substantial part of the value of the company as a whole to acquirers, financiers, and investors, whether directly or as a driver of the company's success (through the ability

---

[9] Electronic Privacy Information Center, EPIC, THE CENSUS AND PRIVACY, *http://epic.org/privacy/census/ (last visited May 7, 2012).*

to better target the advertising whose sales are the company's revenue source). Ultimately, in an economy driven by knowledge and information, knowing more things, about more people, will always be an asset. Absent any countervailing pressures, businesses and institutions would therefore continue to maximize their acquisition and exploitation of information about their customers (and even their own employees).

III.   COMPUTERS AND DIGITAL MEDIA: THEIR IMPACT ON PRIVACY

Historically, one major countervailing pressure reducing organizations' pursuit and use of behavioral and personal information as assets was the cost and difficulty of the effort. Observation of individuals often required dedicated personnel to track them, and manual record keeping was slow. The records themselves took up space, especially when the volume of records mounted, and sorting and sifting the records for useful data was also slow and expensive. Sharing the information required either giving up the original record or making a copy (which took almost as long as creating the original), and the copies were only as portable as the available transportation for them could handle: a warehouse worth of records required as much effort to move as a warehouse worth of goods.

Beginning in the 19th Century, though, new technologies sharply and permanently reduced the time, cost, and effort needed to create and share collections of data about individuals, steam engines powering land (railroad)[10] and sea (steamships)[11] vehicles meant that interstate and international travel and cargo carriage was both more reliable and could carry greater volumes of materials (including ledgers and other data records). Remote wired and wireless communications methods (from the telegraph[12] to facsimile[13] to the telephone[14] and teletype[15] and beyond) allowed for sharing of data with distant recipients. Handwritten records gave way to typewritten ones, manual duplication was superseded by carbon paper, mimeography, and photocopying[16], and written notes were replaced by punched cards.[17]

---

[10]   *See, e.g.*, Library of Congress, HISTORY OF RAILROADS AND MAPS, http://memory.loc.gov/ammem/gmdhtml/rrhtml/rrintro.html (last visited May 7, 2012).

[11]   *See, e.g.*, Bureau of Ocean Energy Management, 19TH CENTURY STEAMSHIPS, http://www.boem.gov/Environmental-Stewardship/Archaeology/19th-Century-Steamships.aspx (last visited May 7, 2012).

[12]   *See, e.g.*, Library of Congress, SAMUEL F. B. MORSE PAPERS TIMELINE, http://memory.loc.gov/ammem/sfbmhtml/timeline02.html (last visited May 7, 2012).

[13]   John H. Lienhard, THE FAX NEWSPAPER, http://www.uh.edu/engines/epi1433.htm.

[14]   Alexander Graham Bell filed for his patent on the telephone in March of 1876. National Archives, ALEXANDER GRAHAM BELL'S TELEPHONE PATENT DRAWING AND OATH, 03/07/1876 http://research.archives.gov/description/302052 (last visited May 7, 2012).

[15]   R.A. Nelson, HISTORY OF TELETYPE DEVELOPMENT, http://www.rtty.com/history/nelson.htm (last visited May 7, 2012).

[16]   *See, e.g.*, Xerox Corporation, CHESTER CARLSON AND XEROGRAPHY, http://www.xerox.com/innovation/chester-carlson-xerography/enus.html (last visited May 7, 2012).

[17]   Priya Ganapati, *July 7, 1752: Jacquard's Loom Will Weave a Durable Web*, WIRED (July 7, 2009), http://www.wired.com/thisdayintech/2009/07/dayintech_0707/.

These technologies, though, tended to be one-to-one in nature (one sender to one recipient; one original to one copy at a time), and also were prone to data corruption and loss. Each copy made was of lower quality than the original, making copies from copies accelerated the quality loss, and the original itself could be damaged by too-frequent copying. Transmission of records was also limited by the speed and quality of the connection. Further, even with methods for compressing information into machine-readable records like punch cards, the amount of storage required for a single set of records could be daunting, and each copy of the set required the same amount of storage. To copy a warehouse full of customer records, one needed enough boxes and trucks to move the contents of the warehouse, and a second warehouse to store the copy. These conditions placed practical limits on the amount of information any single organization could and would collect, and the extent to which that information could and would be shared with others.

IV.   THE ROLE (AND RULE) OF LAW

With the ubiquity of computers, high-speed data networks and large-capacity storage, all at low and ever-lowering costs, organizations of every size collect, use, and share more data about users and their activities than ever before. Consumer awareness of, and concern about, this reality are also at historic highs. While market forces may exert some pressure on businesses to moderate their data collection and use practices (or at least to disclose them), they are insufficient, especially when the rewards for businesses for more and broader data exploitation are so great. Even where consumers may complain individually or in a group, they are rarely successful in engineering change in one organization, let alone many.

Just as Brandeis and Warren posited, the most effective way to set and enforce any limitations on privacy breaches by companies and other organizations is through the legal system. Legislation and regulation can (ideally) act to reflect the standards of the community, extend those standards to new situations, and ensure that those standards are met, and the context of privacy is no exception. Proactively (through establishing permissible and prohibited data collection and use) and reactively (via enforcement authorities and private rights of action in the courts), the law creates the structure for whether and how businesses may monitor, or learn more about, their users and customers.

The law focuses as well on many other privacy contexts, of course. Two in particular have close parallels to questions about businesses and their customers' information: the collection and use by companies of their employees' private information, and the acquisition and exploitation of individuals' PII and activities by governments and their agencies. In both of these other cases, actual and feared abuses, and the inability for either market forces or personal objections to ensure proper conduct, once more make the law a better avenue for change.

Neither legislation nor litigation, however, are the most efficient or rapid processes. The former is frequently subject to political process as well as legislators' subject matter expertise (or lack thereof), and the latter to barriers of cost and access to overburdened courts. For some types of risks and disputes, these real-world delays are acceptable; when it comes to privacy issues driven by constantly changing technology, though, they can render the remedies all but useless.

V. CHALLENGES FOR THE RISK MANAGER

Risk is a key element in any venture or initiative. Risks cannot and should not be avoided; the key to successful growth of any initiative is to *identify* and *manage* the risks rather than letting them get out of control. Proper management in turn requires access to relevant information, and understanding the information and its context.

Given the complexity of privacy and data protection generally, and the particular impact of digital technologies on them, managing the related risks can be similarly complex for a few reasons. First, because the information needed for risk management may not be readily available. Even in a sole proprietorship, the owner and operator may not be completely aware of all personal information flowing into and out of the company, especially when the information is collected through automated processes or as a secondary effect. When a customer makes a payment by a personal check, the check itself may contain not only the customer's bank and account number, but home address and even the name of the customer's spouse or other joint account holder. The business may not have asked for that information, but it is presented with it just the same. Fax headers may include the sender's name and fax number, single-line e-mail messages may have long signature blocks filled with personal information automatically inserted at the bottom, and so on. Internet-based communications come with their own set of automatically included information that can include arguably personal data. For example, any Web page request, instant message transmission or e-mail will include the sender's IP address, which some courts and jurisdictions treat as personally identifiable information.[18]

Even less obvious a source of personal information is the *referrer*, a standard feature of Web browser software through which every Web page request is accompanied by a report of the page *last visited*. Most Web servers will collect and store that information in their log files. Ordinarily, referrer information does not contain personally identifiable information, but because of the way some Web sites construct their URLs, it *can*, which can have significant and unexpected legal consequences. Imagine a user who searches for references to himself via the Google search engine. Google search result pages include the query within their URLs. If his search was, for example, *Jonathan Ezor*, the first result page has this URL:

http://www.google.com/search?q=Jonathan%20Ezor

The next page the user visits, then, will receive as the "referrer" that Google search URL, *including the user's first and last name.* If the site retains the referrer data in its logs, it is thereby collecting and storing the user's personal information, *even if it didn't intend to.* The privacy implications of referrer data have been raised in contexts

---

[18] *See, e.g.*, Joshua J. McIntyre, Balancing Expectations Of Online Privacy: Why Internet Protocol (IP) Addresses Should Be Protected As Personally Identifiable Information, 60 DePaul L. Rev. 895 (Spring 2011).

including the Tracking Protection Working Group of the World Wide Web Consortium, the standards body for the Web.[19]

This is not just hypothetical. In one case, *In re Pharmatrak, Inc.*,[20] a company that provided Web site analytical services to pharmaceutical companies was sued for collecting personal information of users in violation of its stated practices. The company did not *intend* to collect the data; rather, its methodology enabled referrer data to be collected and saved, and those data were discovered to include personal information for a small percentage of site visitors. Out of the myriad visitors to the site, [fewer than 200] users' personal information was discovered among the referrer and similar information in the user logs, but that was sufficient to expose Pharmatrak to class action liability for breaching its privacy disclosure.

A similar situation arose involving the unintentional *release* of personally identifiable information. On August 6, 2006, AOL publicly released a database containing 20 million search queries from 658,000 "anonymized" users, as a research tool. While there were in fact no names or other expressly personal information provided, the database included numerical identifiers that allowed legitimate researchers (and anyone else) to group the searches by user. Given that many people tend to search terms relevant to their personal lives, reporters from the New York Times were able within two days to group, analyze, and positively identify a set of queries as coming from a specific individual:

From "A Face Is Exposed for AOL Searcher No. 4417749"

Buried in a list of 20 million Web search queries collected by AOL and recently released on the Internet is user No. 4417749. The number was assigned by the company to protect the searcher's anonymity, but it was not much of a shield.

No. 4417749 conducted hundreds of searches over a three-month period on topics ranging from "numb fingers" to "60 single men" to "dog that urinates on everything."
. . . There are queries for "landscapers in Lilburn, Ga," several people with the last name Arnold and "homes sold in shadow lake subdivision gwinnett county georgia."

It did not take much investigating to follow that data trail to Thelma Arnold, a 62-year-old widow who lives in Lilburn, Ga., frequently researches her friends' medical ailments and loves her three dogs . . . ."[21]

Although AOL had already publicly withdrawn the data within a day of its being made available due to complaints,[22] the database was already mirrored around the

---

[19] ISSUE-122: SHOULD WE HAVE USE LIMITATIONS ON REFERRER DATA? - TRACKING PROTECTION WORKING GROUP TRACKER, http://www.w3.org/2011/tracking-protection/track/issues/122?changelog (last visited Jul 27, 2012).

[20] In re Pharmatrak Privacy Litig., 220 F. Supp. 2d 4 (D. Mass. 2002), *rev'd*, 329 F.3d 9.

[21] Michael Barbaro & Tom Zeller Jr., *A Face is Exposed for AOL Searcher No. 4417749*, THE NEW YORK TIMES (Aug. 9, 2006), http://www.nytimes.com/2006/08/09/technology/09aol.html.

[22] Michael Arrington, *AOL: "This Was a Screw Up,"* TECHCRUNCH (Aug. 7, 2006), http://techcrunch.com/2006/08/07/aol-this-was-a-screw-up/.

world, and remains available for diligent searchers as of August 2011.[23] The incident was both embarrassing (the two key researchers responsible for the database's release were terminated and the company's Chief Technology Officer resigned,[24] while Business 2.0 magazine called the publication of the database one of the "101 Dumbest Moments in Business for 2006"[25]) and legally problematic (a class action suit was pursued in California,[26] and the Electronic Frontier Foundation filed a complaint with the FTC).[27]

VI. THE APPROACH OF THIS BOOK: PRACTICAL UNDERSTANDING AND A PATH TO BEST PRACTICES

These situations highlight the unique challenges of digital privacy and the law: effective compliance and risk management requires not only knowledge of applicable laws and regulations, but at least a basic understanding of relevant technologies and the processes of the company or other organization that is collecting and/or using the personal information or monitoring behavior. Accordingly, the remaining chapters of this book are structured to provide a framework for law and other students to both learn the law and place it in the necessary technological and practical context, divided into topic areas such as children's privacy, health information, governmental requirements, employee data, and more. The examples and best practices, study questions, and links to additional materials for each chapter (and supplemented through dedicated Web-based content) should be approached by readers not only as aids to understanding the law, but as guides for future counseling and decisionmaking.

---

[23] *See, e.g.*, http://www.atrus.org/hosted/AOL-data.tgz (last visited May 7, 2012).

[24] THREE WORKERS DEPART AOL AFTER PRIVACY UPROAR — CNET News, http://news.cnet.com/Three-workers-depart-AOL-after-privacy-uproar/2100-1030_3-6107830.html (last visited May 7, 2012).

[25] 101 DUMBEST MOMENTS IN BUSINESS — SORRY ABOUT THAT. BUT IF YOU DON'T QUIT WHINING ABOUT IT, WE'LL TRANSFER YOU OVER TO JOHN IN CUSTOMER RETENTION . . . (57) — Business 2.0, http://money.cnn.com/galleries/2007/biz2/0701/gallery.101dumbest_2007/57.html (last visited May 7, 2012).

[26] *See, e.g.*, Doe 1 v. AOL, LLC, 552 F.3d 1077 (9th Cir. 2009).

[27] EFF: AOL'S DATA VALDEZ, http://w2.eff.org/Privacy/AOL/ (last visited May 7, 2012).

Chapter 2

CONSUMER PRIVACY: BALANCING VALUE TO CONSUMERS WITH VALUE OF CONSUMERS

Consumer privacy is both a general descriptor of privacy-related ideas (covering health, finance, commerce, and many other areas) and a more specific term. In its limited aspect, it refers to the collection, use and sharing by businesses of the personally identifiable information of (or about) potential or actual customers, whether in connection with a transaction or otherwise. Unlike many of the other areas of data privacy discussed in this book, there is currently no overall federal statute mandating specific business practices with regard to consumer privacy. Instead, it is left to companies to essentially police themselves via self-regulation, although as will be seen, enforcement authorities and the courts stand ready to take action if this self-regulation fails.

I. WHY CONSUMER PRIVACY MATTERS: A LESS THAN CHEERY SCENARIO

While there is a significant amount of discussion and attention on general consumer privacy, it may be somewhat difficult to understand why, when compared to areas of seemingly greater risk such as children's privacy and the protection of financial and health information. To illustrate the potential concerns arising out of consumer privacy, consider the classic television sitcom "Cheers," named for the fictional eponymous Boston bar where most of the "action" took place. The title of the show's theme song, "Where Everybody Knows Your Name" by Gary Portnoy,[1] was reflected in the way the main characters (the bar's staff and the regular customers) knew about and got involved in each other's lives. For the regulars, it was a given that they would be greeted by name and served their preferred drink as soon as they mounted the bar's stools.

Imagine, though, a new customer named Fred walks into Cheers for the first time and discovers that everybody in fact knows his name and the bartender pours his favorite brand of beer without his even having to order it. Next, imagine this same customer traveling from Boston and encountering identical familiarity at every new bar into which he walks anywhere in the country, except that after the third week, every bartender insists the man's name is Murray, and only serves him dry martinis. Even worse, at a few of the bars, he is welcomed with a bill for the three rounds of drinks he has told he has already purchased for the patrons before even walking through the door. On returning home and heading to his local pharmacy, the

---

[1] GARY PORTNOY.COM, http://www.garyportnoy.com/ (last visited May 7, 2012).

pharmacist hands him an unasked-for bottle of ibuprofen for the headache he "must have after visiting so many bars," and his mailbox is stuffed with coupons and offers from other brands of alcoholic beverages, who want him to switch away from his preferred beer. Would this situation be a problem? After all, our hypothetical bar visitor has been given the same type of favored service that Norm and Cliff enjoyed at Cheers. The crucial difference is that the visitor did not get a chance to choose to share (or withhold) his name, his drink preference, his travel history with the establishments in which he entered. Rather than feeling pampered, he is likely to be at best disturbed and at worst quite paranoid about the unwanted invasion into his identity and preferences.

II. CONSUMER INFORMATION COLLECTION AND THE RISE OF E-COMMERCE

Concerns such as those arising in the above hypothetical have informed discussions about best practices in consumer privacy for decades, especially in connection with computers and other information technologies. One of the most influential analyses of consumer privacy is *Records, Computers and the Rights of Citizens* (the "HEW Report"), prepared by the U.S. Department of Health, Education and Welfare (now Health and Human Services) in July 1973, particularly in its Section III:

A Redefinition of the Concept of Personal Privacy

Our review of existing law leads to the conclusion that agreement must be reached about the meaning of personal privacy in relation to records and record-keeping practices. It is difficult, however, to define personal privacy in terms that provide a conceptually sound framework for public policy about records and record keeping and a workable basis for formulating rules about record-keeping practices. For any one individual, privacy, as a value, is not absolute or constant; its significance can vary with time, place, age, and other circumstances. There is even more variability among groups of individuals. As a social value, furthermore, privacy can easily collide with others, most notably free speech, freedom of the press, and the public's "right to know."

Dictionary definitions of privacy uniformly speak in terms of seclusion, secrecy, and withdrawal from public view. They all denote a quality that is not inherent in most record-keeping systems. Many records made about people are public, available to anyone to see and use. Other records, though not public in the sense that anyone may see or use them, are made for purposes that would be defeated if the data they contain were treated as absolutely secluded, secret, or private. Records about people are made to fulfill purposes that are shared by the institution maintaining them and the people to whom they pertain. Notable exceptions are intelligence records maintained for criminal investigation, national security, or other purposes. Use of a record about someone requires that its contents be accessible to at least one other person-and usually many other persons.

Once we recognize these characteristics of records, we must formulate a concept of privacy that is consistent with records. Many noteworthy attempts to address this need have been made.

Privacy is the claim of individuals, groups, or institutions to determine for themselves when, how, and to what extent information about them is communicated to others.

this is the core of the "right of individual privacy" — the right of the individual to decide for himself, with only extraordinary exceptions in the interests of society, when and on what terms his acts should be revealed to the general public.

The right to privacy is the right of the individual to decide for himself how much he will share with others his thoughts, his feelings, and the facts of his personal life.

As a first approximation, privacy seems to be related to secrecy, to limiting the knowledge of others about oneself. This notion must be refined. It is not true, for instance, that the less that is known about us the more privacy we hive. Privacy is not simply an absence of information about us in the minds of others; rather it is the control we have over information about ourselves.

The significant elements common to these formulations are (1) that there will be some disclosure of data, and (2) that the data subject should decide the nature and extent of such disclosure. An important recognition is that privacy, at least as applied to record-keeping practices, is not inconsistent with disclosure, and thus with use. The further recognition of a role for the record subject in deciding what shall be the nature and use of the record is crucial in relating the concept of personal privacy to record-keeping practices.

Each of the above formulations, however, speaks of the data subject as having a unilateral role in deciding the nature and extent of his self-disclosure. None accommodates the observation that records of personal data usually reflect and mediate relationships in which both individuals and institutions have an interest, and are usually made for purposes that are shared by institutions and individuals. In fact, it would be inconsistent with this essential. characteristic. of mutuality to assign the individual record subject a unilateral role in making decisions about the nature and use of his record. To the extent that people want or need to have dealings with record-keeping organizations, they must expect to share rather than monopolize control over the content and use of the records made. about them.

Similarly, it is equally out of keeping with the mutuality of record-generating relationships to assign the institution a unilateral role in making decisions about the content and use of its records about individuals. Yet it is our observation that organizations maintaining records about people commonly behave as if they had been given such a unilateral role to play. This is not to suggest that decisions are always made to the disadvantage of the record subject; the contrary is often the case. The fact, however, is that the record subject usually has no claim to a role in the decisions organizations make about records that pertain to him. His opportunity to participate in those decisions depends on the willingness of the record-keeping organization to let him participate and, in a few .instances, on specific rights provided by law.

Here then is the nub of the matter. Personal privacy, as it relates to personal-data record keeping must be understood in terms of a concept of mutuality. Accordingly, we offer the following formulation:

> **An individual's personal privacy is directly affected by the kind of disclosure and use made of identifiable information about him in a record. A record containing information about an individual in identifiable form must, therefore, be governed by procedures that afford the individual a right to participate in deciding what the content of the record will be, and what disclosure and use will be made of the identifiable information in it. Any recording, disclosure, and use of identifiable personal information not governed by such procedures must be proscribed as an unfair information practice unless such recording, disclosure or use is specifically authorized by law.**

This formulation does not provide the basis for determining a priori which data should or may be recorded and used, or why, and when. It does,, however, provide a basis for establishing procedures that assure the individual a right to participate in a meaningful way in decisions about what goes into records about him and how that information shall be used.

Safeguards for personal privacy based on our concept of mutuality in record-keeping would require adherence by record-keeping organizations to certain fundamental principles of fair information practice.

- *There must be no personal-data record-keeping systems whose very existence is secret.*

- *There must be a way for an individual, to find out what information about him is in a record and how it is used.*

- *There must be a way for an individual to prevent information about him obtained for one purpose from being used or made available for other purposes without his consent.*

- *There must be a way for an individual to correct or amend a record of identifiable information about him.*

- *Any organization creating, maintaining, using, or disseminating records of identifiable personal data must assure the reliability of the data for their intended use and must take reasonable precautions to prevent misuse of the data.*

These principles should govern the conduct of all personal-data record-keeping systems. Deviations from them should be permitted only if it is clear that some significant interest of the individual data subject, will be served or if some paramount societal interest can be clearly demonstrated; no deviation should be permitted except as specifically provided by law.[2]

From the early 1970s, though, computers and networks expanded in functionality and ease of use (and dropped in cost), and spread from the largest corporations and

---

[2] RECORDS, COMPUTERS AND THE RIGHTS OF CITIZENS (1973) III. SAFEGUARDS FOR PRIVACY, *http://aspe.hhs.gov/datacncl/1973privacy/c3.htm (last visited May 7, 2012).*

organizations to the smallest sole proprietorship. As a result, the definition of "record-keeping organization" evolved, and the quantity and diversity of those organizations increased far beyond what the drafters of the HEW Report may have assumed. When customer records were stored on paper, creating and managing them required significant physical space and manpower, and large-scale copying could take hours or days. With personal computers' entry into businesses, file rooms, and archive warehouses were replaced with hard drives, and copying could be done with a click. With the addition of Internet connectivity, records could be shared and copied remotely, in bulk, by someone in another office or another country. This meant that every company could potentially market its customer list to other firms, and there were now many more sources of information about consumers for businesses to access and utilize.

While the revolution in customer data collection and use occurred in all types of companies, the broad adoption of the Internet by consumers revived a form of commerce that had been less popular for decades: mail order purchases via online storefronts. Historically, mail order had once been a key retail channel for the many rural communities that could not support larger shops;[3] throughout the 20th Century, the archetypical Wells Fargo wagon and rural free delivery gave way to department stores anchoring shopping malls and big box retailers,[4] with mail order becoming largely the province of specialty products and direct marketing (including "infomercials"). This trend began to reverse with two otherwise unrelated developments at around the same time: the invention of the World Wide Web protocol by Tim Berners-Lee at the CERN physics lab in 1989–90[5] and the withdrawal of the ban on commercial use of the Internet previously contained in the National Science Foundation's Acceptable Use Policy for the Internet.[6] As the now-commerce friendly Internet offered a growing series of retailing Web sites, as shoppers got Internet connections both at home and at work to access them, and as encryption technologies such as Secure Sockets Layer ("SSL")[7] were added to Web browser programs to increase both security and consumer confidence, mail order once again became a standard method for buying even products commonly available in local brick-and-mortar stores. Those same traditional offline retailers, seeing the new competition[8] (and seeking to reduce the real estate and staffing-related costs of doing business), themselves created or

---

[3] *See, e.g.*, PRINTING FOR THE MODERN AGE: COMMERCE, CRAFT AND CULTURE IN THE R.R. DONNELLEY ARCHIVE>, http://www.lib.uchicago.edu/e/webexhibits/PrintingForTheModernAge/MailOrderCatalogs.html (last visited May 7, 2012).

[4] *See, e.g.*, International Council of Shopping Centers, A BRIEF HISTORY OF SHOPPING CENTERS, http://www.icsc.org/srch/about/impactofshoppingcenters/01_briefhistory.pdf (last visited May 7, 2012).

[5] THE ORIGINAL PROPOSAL OF THE WWW, HTMLIZED, http://www.w3.org/History/1989/proposal.html (last visited May 7, 2012).

[6] NIFTY 50: THE INTERNET, http://www.nsf.gov/od/lpa/nsf50/nsfoutreach/htm/n50_z2/pages_z3/28_pg.htm (last visited May 7, 2012).

[7] SSL was developed by then-leading browser software publisher Netscape in 1994. IBM, HISTORY OF SSL, http://publib.boulder.ibm.com/infocenter/iseries/v5r3/index.jsp?topic=%2Frzain%2Frzainhistory.htm (last visited May 7, 2012).

[8] *See, e.g.*, E-COMMERCE MORE THAN JUST A PASSING FAD STRATEGY, http://strategyonline.ca/1999/02/15/24514-19990215/ (last visited May 7, 2012).

enhanced their mail-order and other online shopping resources. All of these online retailers, whether new or existing, were collecting much more information from and about consumers than would be true for most offline purchases: full names and delivery addresses, telephone numbers, credit card billing addresses, e-mail addresses for confirmation, and so on. The collection was not just to facilitate the transactions and reduce the chance of fraud: the retailers saw both research and resale value in the customer data.[9]

III. CONSUMER PRIVACY AND CONSUMER PROTECTION: THE FTC

With the expansion of collection and use of consumers' PII came the expansion of abuse potential. Consumer protection agencies such as the FTC and state Attorney General sharply expanded their monitoring and reporting of information practices, with the FTC in particular issuing a stream of reports and guidance for both Congress and businesses. The overall authority for the FTC's activities regarding privacy protection arises from Section 5 of the Federal Trade Commission Act,[10] the statute (originally enacted in 1914) which established and empowered the FTC as the federal agency responsible for consumer protection:

Unfair methods of competition unlawful; prevention by Commission

(a) Declaration of unlawfulness; power to prohibit unfair practices; inapplicability to foreign trade

(1) Unfair methods of competition in or affecting commerce, and unfair or deceptive acts or practices in or affecting commerce, are hereby declared unlawful.

(2) The Commission is hereby empowered and directed to prevent persons, partnerships, or corporations, except banks, savings and loan institutions described in section 57a(f)(3) of this title, Federal credit unions described in section 57a(f)(4) of this title, common carriers subject to the Acts to regulate commerce, air carriers and foreign air carriers subject to part A of subtitle VII of Title 49, and persons, partnerships, or corporations insofar as they are subject to the Packers and Stockyards Act, 1921, as amended [7 U.S.C.A. § 181 et seq.], except as provided in section 406(b) of said Act [7 U.S.C.A. § 227(b)], from using unfair methods of competition in or affecting commerce and unfair or deceptive acts or practices in or affecting commerce.

(3) This subsection shall not apply to unfair methods of competition involving commerce with foreign nations (other than import commerce) unless —

---

[9] *See, e.g.*, Baohong Sun, HOW TO PROFIT FROM CONTINUOUS ACQUISITION OF CUSTOMER INFORMATION, available at http://tepper.cmu.edu/faculty-research/research-centers/center-for-marketing-technologies-and-informat ion/center-fellows-scholars/baohong-sun/download.aspx?id=8696.

[10] 15 U.S.C. §§ 41–58.

(A) such methods of competition have a direct, substantial, and reasonably foreseeable effect —

(i) on commerce which is not commerce with foreign nations, or on import commerce with foreign nations; or

(ii) on export commerce with foreign nations, of a person engaged in such commerce in the United States; and

(B) such effect gives rise to a claim under the provisions of this subsection, other than this paragraph.

If this subsection applies to such methods of competition only because of the operation of subparagraph (A)(ii), this subsection shall apply to such conduct only for injury to export business in the United States.

(4)(A) For purposes of subsection (a) of this section, the term "unfair or deceptive acts or practices" includes such acts or practices involving foreign commerce that —

(i) cause or are likely to cause reasonably foreseeable injury within the United States; or

(ii) involve material conduct occurring within the United States . . . .[11]

In its 1998 "Privacy Online — A Report to Congress,"[12] the FTC sets forth a detailed description of the "Fair Information Practice Principles" that it views as underlying responsible data collection:

Fair Information Practice Principles Generally

Over the past quarter century, government agencies in the United States, Canada, and Europe have studied the manner in which entities collect and use personal information — their "information practices" — and the safeguards required to assure those practices are fair and provide adequate privacy protection. The result has been a series of reports, guidelines, and model codes that represent widely-accepted principles concerning fair information practices. Common to all of these documents [hereinafter referred to as "fair information practice codes"] are five core principles of privacy protection: (1) Notice/Awareness; (2) Choice/Consent; (3) Access/ Participation; (4) Integrity/Security; and (5) Enforcement/Redress.

1. Notice/Awareness

The most fundamental principle is notice. Consumers should be given notice of an entity's information practices before any personal information is collected from them. Without notice, a consumer cannot make an informed decision as to whether and to what extent to disclose personal information. Moreover, three of the other principles discussed below — choice/consent, access/participation, and enforcement/redress —

---

[11]   15 U.S.C. § 45.

[12]   FTC, Privacy Online — A Report to Congress (1998), http://www.ftc.gov/reports/privacy3/priv-23a.pdf.

are only meaningful when a consumer has notice of an entity's policies, and his or her rights with respect thereto.

While the scope and content of notice will depend on the entity's substantive information practices, notice of some or all of the following have been recognized as essential to ensuring that consumers are properly informed before divulging personal information:

identification of the entity collecting the data;

identification of the uses to which the data will be put;

identification of any potential recipients of the data;

the nature of the data collected and the means by which it is collected if not obvious (passively, by means of electronic monitoring, or actively, by asking the consumer to provide the information);

whether the provision of the requested data is voluntary or required, and the consequences of a refusal to provide the requested information; and

the steps taken by the data collector to ensure the confidentiality, integrity and quality of the data.

Some information practice codes state that the notice should also identify any available consumer rights, including: any choice respecting the use of the data; whether the consumer has been given a right of access to the data; the ability of the consumer to contest inaccuracies; the availability of redress for violations of the practice code; and how such rights can be exercised.

In the Internet context, notice can be accomplished easily by the posting of an information practice disclosure describing an entity's information practices on a company's site on the Web. To be effective, such a disclosure should be clear and conspicuous, posted in a prominent location, and readily accessible from both the site's home page and any Web page where information is collected from the consumer. It should also be unavoidable and understandable so that it gives consumers meaningful and effective notice of what will happen to the personal information they are asked to divulge.

2. *Choice/Consent*

The second widely-accepted core principle of fair information practice is consumer choice or consent. At its simplest, choice means giving consumers options as to how any personal information collected from them may be used. Specifically, choice relates to secondary uses of information — i.e., uses beyond those necessary to complete the contemplated transaction. Such secondary uses can be internal, such as placing the consumer on the collecting company's mailing list in order to market additional products or promotions, or external, such as the transfer of information to third parties.

Traditionally, two types of choice/consent regimes have been considered: opt-in or opt-out. Opt-in regimes require affirmative steps by the consumer to allow the collection and/or use of information; opt-out regimes require affirmative steps to prevent the collection and/or use of such information. The distinction lies in the default rule when no affirmative steps are taken by the consumer. Choice can also involve more than a binary yes/no option. Entities can, and do, allow consumers to tailor the nature of the information they reveal and the uses to which it will be put. Thus, for example, consumers can be provided separate choices as to whether they wish to be on a company's general internal mailing list or a marketing list sold to third parties. In order to be effective, any choice regime should provide a simple and easily-accessible way for consumers to exercise their choice.

In the online environment, choice easily can be exercised by simply clicking a box on the computer screen that indicates a user's decision with respect to the use and/or dissemination of the information being collected. The online environment also presents new possibilities to move beyond the opt-in/opt-out paradigm. For example, consumers could be required to specify their preferences regarding information use before entering a Web site, thus effectively eliminating any need for default rules.

3. Access/Participation

Access is the third core principle. It refers to an individual's ability both to access data about him or herself — i.e., to view the data in an entity's files — and to contest that data's accuracy and completeness. Both are essential to ensuring that data are accurate and complete. To be meaningful, access must encompass timely and inexpensive access to data, a simple means for contesting inaccurate or incomplete data, a mechanism by which the data collector can verify the information, and the means by which corrections and/or consumer objections can be added to the data file and sent to all data recipients.

4. Integrity/Security

The fourth widely accepted principle is that data be accurate and secure. To assure data integrity, collectors must take reasonable steps, such as using only reputable sources of data and cross-referencing data against multiple sources, providing consumer access to data, and destroying untimely data or converting it to anonymous form.

Security involves both managerial and technical measures to protect against loss and the unauthorized access, destruction, use, or disclosure of the data. Managerial measures include internal organizational measures that limit access to data and ensure that those individuals with access do not utilize the data for unauthorized purposes. Technical security measures to prevent unauthorized access include encryption in the transmission and storage of data; limits on access through use of passwords; and the storage of data on secure servers or computers that are inaccessible by modem.

5. Enforcement/Redress

It is generally agreed that the core principles of privacy protection can only be effective if there is a mechanism in place to enforce them. Absent an enforcement and redress mechanism, a fair information practice code is merely suggestive rather than prescriptive, and does not ensure compliance with core fair information practice principles. Among the alternative enforcement approaches are industry self-regulation; legislation that would create private remedies for consumers; and/or regulatory schemes enforceable through civil and criminal sanctions.

a. Self-Regulation

To be effective, self-regulatory regimes should include both mechanisms to ensure compliance (enforcement) and appropriate means of recourse by injured parties (redress). Mechanisms to ensure compliance include making acceptance of and compliance with a code of fair information practices a condition of membership in an industry association; external audits to verify compliance; and certification of entities that have adopted and comply with the code at issue. A self-regulatory regime with many of these principles has recently been adopted by the individual reference services industry.

Appropriate means of individual redress include, at a minimum, institutional mechanisms to ensure that consumers have a simple and effective way to have their concerns addressed. Thus, a self-regulatory system should provide a means to investigate complaints from individual consumers and ensure that consumers are aware of how to access such a system.

If the self-regulatory code has been breached, consumers should have a remedy for the violation. Such a remedy can include both the righting of the wrong (e.g., correction of any misinformation, cessation of unfair practices) and compensation for any harm suffered by the consumer. Monetary sanctions would serve both to compensate the victim of unfair practices and as an incentive for industry compliance. Industry codes can provide for alternative dispute resolution mechanisms to provide appropriate compensation.

b. Private Remedies

A statutory scheme could create private rights of action for consumers harmed by an entity's unfair information practices. Several of the major information practice codes, including the seminal 1973 HEW Report, call for implementing legislation. The creation of private remedies would help create strong incentives for entities to adopt and implement fair information practices and ensure compensation for individuals harmed by misuse of their personal information. Important questions would need to be addressed in such legislation, e.g., the definition of unfair information practices; the availability of compensatory, liquidated and/or punitive damages; and the elements of any such cause of action.

c. Government Enforcement

Finally, government enforcement of fair information practices, by means of civil or criminal penalties, is a third means of enforcement. Fair information practice codes have called for some government enforcement, leaving open the question of the scope and extent of such powers. Whether enforcement is civil or criminal likely will depend on the nature of the data at issue and the violation committed.[13]

The FTC continued to monitor and report to Congress on the progress (or lack thereof) of privacy protection for electronic commerce in its 1999 report *Self-Regulation and Privacy Online.*[14] As summarized by the FTC at the time:

> *. . . . The report describes the growth of electronic commerce, explains how Web sites collect information about consumers, explores consumers' concerns about online privacy, and analyzes the state of online privacy self-regulation. The report states that "the Commission believes that legislation to address online privacy is not appropriate at this time. We also believe that industry faces some substantial challenges. Specifically, the present challenge is to educate those companies which still do not understand the importance of consumer privacy and to create incentives for further progress toward effective, widespread implementation." It goes on to outline an agenda to address online privacy issues that includes a number of public workshops, task forces and an online survey, to reassess progress in Web sites' implementation of fair information practices.*

> *The report discusses the results of two studies of commercial Web sites conducted by Georgetown University Professor Mary Culnan, and the efforts of the Online Privacy Alliance, TRUSTe, BBBOnline, and others. "We continue to believe that effective self-regulation is the best way to protect consumer privacy on the Internet, and I am pleased that there has been real progress on the part of the online industry," Chairman Pitofsky said. "Because of that progress, I do not believe legislation is necessary at this time. But this is not the occasion to declare victory. There is more to protecting consumer privacy than simply publishing notices on Web sites. We intend to monitor what we hope and expect will be continuing progress in development of privacy protection programs, as well as efforts to develop effective enforcement mechanisms. Responsible elements in the online business community have accomplished a great deal in a short time, but there is a considerable distance to go before consumers can feel secure from privacy invasions in their dealings on the Internet."*

> *In analyzing the state of online privacy self-regulation, the report emphasizes that "self-regulation is the least intrusive and most efficient means to ensure fair information practices, given the rapidly evolving nature of the Internet and computer technology." Professor Culnan's studies, the report*

---

[13] *Id. at 7–11 (notes omitted).*

[14] FTC, SELF-REGULATION AND PRIVACY ONLINE (1999), available at http://www.ftc.gov/os/1999/07/privacy99.pdf.

*points out, "suggest that the majority of the more frequently-visited Web sites
are implementing the basic Notice principle by disclosing at least some of
their information practices." The report notes, however, that only a relatively
small percentage of these sites are disclosing information practices that
address all four substantive fair information practice principles: Notice,
Choice, Access and Security. It also states that the privacy seal programs
underway encompass only a small minority of all Web sites. "The self-
regulatory programs described . . . reflect industry leaders' substantial effort
and commitment to fair information practices," the report states.* [15]

By the next year, however, the FTC had changed its official stance on self-
regulation, requesting that Congress enact general online privacy protection legislation:

> *. . . . Based on the past years of work addressing Internet privacy issues,
including examination of prior surveys and workshops with consumers and
industry, it is evident that online privacy continues to present an enormous
public policy challenge. The Commission applauds the significant efforts of
the private sector and commends industry leaders in developing self-
regulatory initiatives. The 2000 Survey, however, demonstrates that industry
efforts alone have not been sufficient. Because self-regulatory initiatives to
date fall far short of broad-based implementation of effective self-regulatory
programs, a majority of the Commission has concluded that such efforts
alone cannot ensure that the online marketplace as a whole will emulate the
standards adopted by industry leaders. While there will continue to be a
major role for industry self-regulation in the future, a majority of the
Commission recommends that Congress enact legislation that, in conjunction with continuing self-regulatory programs, will ensure adequate protection of consumer privacy online.*

> *The proposed legislation would set forth a basic level of privacy protection
for consumer-oriented commercial Web sites. Such legislation would establish
basic standards of practice for the collection of information online, and
provide an implementing agency with the authority to promulgate more
detailed standards pursuant to the Administrative Procedure Act.*

> *Consumer-oriented commercial Web sites that collect personal identifying
information from or about consumers online would be required to comply
with the four widely-accepted fair information practices:*

> *(1) **Notice** — Web sites would be required to provide consumers clear and
conspicuous notice of their information practices, including what information they collect, how they collect it (e.g., directly or through non-obvious
means such as cookies), how they use it, how they provide Choice, Access, and
Security to consumers, whether they disclose the information collected to
other entities, and whether other entities are collecting information through
the site.*

---

[15] FTC, Self-Regulation and Privacy Online, *http://www.ftc.gov/opa/1999/07/report1999.shtm (last visited May 7, 2012).*

*(2) **Choice** — Web sites would be required to offer consumers choices as to how their personal identifying information is used beyond the use for which the information was provided (e.g., to consummate a transaction). Such choice would encompass both internal secondary uses (such as marketing back to consumers) and external secondary uses (such as disclosing data to other entities).*

*(3) **Access** — Web sites would be required to offer consumers reasonable access to the information a Web site has collected about them, including a reasonable opportunity to review information and to correct inaccuracies or delete information.*

*(4) **Security** — Web sites would be required to take reasonable steps to protect the security of the information they collect from consumers.*

The Commission recognizes that the implementation of these practices may vary with the nature of the information collected and the uses to which it is put, as well as with technological developments. For this reason, a majority of the Commission recommends that any legislation be phrased in general terms and be technologically neutral. Thus, the definitions of fair information practices set forth in the statute should be broad enough to provide flexibility to the implementing agency in promulgating its rules or regulations.

Finally, the Commission notes that industry self-regulatory programs would continue to play an essential role under such a statutory structure, as they have in other contexts. The Commission hopes and expects that industry and consumers would participate actively in developing regulations under the new legislation and that industry would continue its self-regulatory initiatives. The Commission also recognizes that effective and widely-adopted seal programs could be an important component of that effort.

For all of these reasons, a majority of the Commission believes that its proposed legislation, in conjunction with self-regulation, will ensure important protections for consumer privacy at a critical time in the development of the online marketplace. Without such protections, electronic commerce will not reach its full potential and consumers will not gain the confidence they need in order to participate fully in the online marketplace . . . .[16]

Notwithstanding the FTC's request, however, Congress did not pass and has not to date passed overall information privacy legislation for electronic commerce, leaving privacy protection subject to self-regulation; that is, depending on companies to "do the right thing" with consumer information. What that entails, as per the FTC's reports, has come to be known as a privacy policy.

---

[16] Prepared Statement of The Federal Trade Commission Before the Committee on Commerce, Science, and Transportation United States Senate Washington, D.C. May 25, 2000, PRIVACY ONLINE: FAIR INFORMATION PRACTICES IN THE ELECTRONIC MARKETPLACE, *http://www.ftc.gov/os/2000/05/testimonyprivacy.htm (last visited May 7, 2012) (notes omitted).*

IV. ANATOMY OF A PRIVACY POLICY: THE FAIR INFORMATION PRACTICE PRINCIPLES IN ACTION

The term "privacy policy" is actually somewhat confusing; it isn't so much an establishment of a policy for the company but rather a *disclosure* of the existing information collection and use practices of the company. The practices themselves should track the Fair Information Practice Principles in order for the company to be self-regulating as described by the FTC,[17] with particular attention required for the first of the principles notice and awareness:

a. Notice/Awareness: Spreading the (Accurate) Word

At the core of the FTC's potential willingness to accept self-regulation over legislative mandates is the requirement that those from whom information is to be collected must be aware of the collection and the purposes to which the information will be put, including with whom else it may be shared. Such awareness may not be assumed, but requires notice of the practices to be at least available to the individual prior to the collection. The "privacy policy" placed on a Web site is the generally accepted form of such notice.

One aspect of making notice available is its presentation: how prominent and easy to obtain and read is the privacy policy? Is it linked from every page, just the home page, or some combination? Is the link obvious and properly labeled? Is it on a separate page, or a pop-up which might be blocked by some browser programs? Is the language clear or confusing legalese? Is it formatted for different sized devices? The more prominent, clear, and accessible the privacy policy is, the more likely it would pass muster with the FTC and other enforcement bodies.

Having a legible privacy policy, however, is far from the only or even most important aspect of notice. Where too many organizations err, and where the FTC and other enforcers have been very willing to exercise their authority, is in the requirement that the privacy policy above all be *accurate*. An inaccurate privacy policy, one which does not correctly describe the data collection and use practices of the site posting it, can yield liability for the siteowner, even if both what the policy describes and what the site is doing are both *legal*, because the inaccuracy means that the consumer was not actually given notice.

---

[17] In February 2012, the Obama Administration released its "Consumer Privacy Bill of Rights," which included an updated statement of the Fair Information Practice Principles encompassing:

Individual control over what personal data organizations collect from them and how they use it
- Transparency that allows consumers to easily understand information about privacy and security practices
- Respect for the context in which consumers provide data
- Security and responsibility in the way companies handle personal data
- Access to personal data in usable format and an ability to correct errors
- Reasonable limits on the personal data that companies collect and retain
- Accountability as to how companies handle personal data.

White House Office of Science and Technology Policy, Feb. 24, 2012, INTERNET PRIVACY: PROTECTING CONSUMERS, BUILDING TRUST, CREATING JOBS | THE WHITE HOUSE, http://www.whitehouse.gov/blog/2012/02/24/internet-privacy-protecting-consumers-building-trust-creating-jobs (last visited May 7, 2012).

Among the most common inaccuracies in privacy policies is some version of the following reassuring statement:

We do not share your personal information with any third parties.

This is essentially *never* true, if only because of how the Internet functions. There are so many third parties involved in connecting the sender and recipient of content (whether an e-mail message, a Web page, or something else), and so many other third parties specifically involved in the process of commerce, that some portion of the consumer's personal information will inevitably be shared with one or more of those third parties. Again, this may not be illegal, and may even be what the consumer wants, but the privacy policy's inaccurate statement can nevertheless expose the publisher of the policy to liability.

Consider the following illustration describing a hypothetical e-commerce site, CuteFuzzyBears.com:

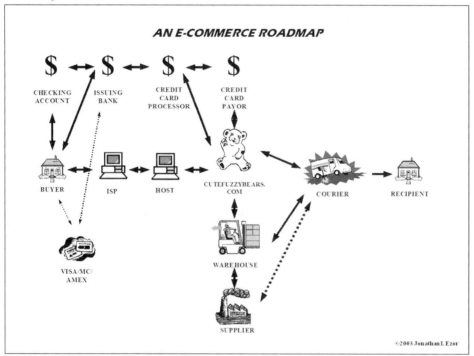

As with many other such companies, CuteFuzzyBears does not maintain its own warehouse, but outsources the picking, packing, and shipping of its bears to another company, which maintains a relationship with a home delivery courier service. CuteFuzzyBears also contracts with a manufacturer in China to make and ship bears as needed; the warehouse maintains the inventory and reports low levels to Cute-FuzzyBears, which then orders new merchandise to be sent directly to the warehouse. CuteFuzzyBears works with one vendor to process credit card information and a different one to manage the flow of funds from the card issuers (a typical situation). Finally, CuteFuzzyBears uses a Web development and hosting firm to create, operate, maintain, and update its site.

In the illustration, a sender wishes to buy a teddy bear and have it sent as a gift to a friend. The sender accesses CutefuzzyBears.com, skims through the available bears, and decides to order one. Thanks to a real-time inventory report from the outside warehouse, the site shows that the desired bear is in stock. The sender clicks to place an order, and is presented with a form in which to enter payment and delivery information, including the sender's billing address and credit card data and the recipient's name and address. The sender types in the data and presses "Submit," after which he is shown a confirmation page with all the entered data. Once he confirms the information, he clicks once more to actually place the order.

Once the order is accepted, CuteFuzzyBears asks its credit card processor to pre-authorize the transaction; that is, to verify the account and billing information and ensure that there is sufficient credit available to pay for the bear once it's ready to ship. The processor communicates with the issuing bank and, if the credit is available, places a temporary "pre-authorization hold" on that amount of credit to keep the purchaser from using it for more than one purchase. The processor reports back to CuteFuzzy-Bears that the credit is available, and CuteFuzzyBears notifies the warehouse to pick, pack, and ship that particular bear to the recipient's address. The warehouse gets the shipment ready, hands it off to the courier, and transmits a tracking number to CuteFuzzyBears indicating that it has shipped. CuteFuzzyBears then notifies the credit card processor that it has earned payment, after which the processor communicates with the issuing bank and instructs it to transfer the payment amount through CuteFuzzyBears' payment processing (or merchant account) company (this is called "settlement"). CuteFuzzyBears gets paid (minus processing fees and other possible charges), the bear gets delivered to the recipient, and when the credit card comes due for payment, the buyer, issuing bank, and the bank holding the buyer's savings collaborate to pay the bill. (The dotted lines on the illustration to "VISA/MC/Amex" indicate the policies of the credit card brand owners that govern how issuing banks and customers may utilize the cards bearing their marks.)

In order to fulfill the order that the buyer wishes to place, CuteFuzzyBears must transmit personal information from the buyer to its Web host, the buyer's ISP (on its way to the buyer), the credit card processing and payment firms, the issuing bank, and (if the buyer's identity will be placed on the package) the warehouse and courier, not to mention the recipient. Even without purchases and shipments, the mere act of repeating back the information the buyer has provided passes that information through CuteFuzzyBears' Web hosting company and the buyer's ISP at a minimum. Each of those is a "third party" with which CuteFuzzyBears is "sharing" the buyer's personal information, and this type of "sharing" is inevitable for any Web site operator, making those general "comforting" statements red flags of inaccuracy.

Other inaccuracies arise because many site owners (and even, regrettably, their attorneys) copy and paste language from a "good policy" published by another site for their own privacy statement. Unfortunately, unless by some miraculous coincidence the source site's data collection and use practices are *identical* to those of the site copying the language, the policy will be at least somewhat incorrect in its description, and therefore will not be providing the required notice and enabling awareness.

One further source of inaccuracy (or at least incompleteness) is lack of knowledge on the part of the siteowner's employees about the actual data practices of the company. Those responsible for drafting the policy, even if they do so from scratch, may not know all the ways personal information comes in, is utilized, and leaves the organization. For example, the policy may state that the company "only" collects personal information via a form on a Web site. That may well be one inbound channel, but if the company receives and logs telephone calls, e-mails, faxes or other communications from the customer, those represent additional ways the company collects information that must also be disclosed. The same goes for how data are used and shared; even if the company is not selling its customers' personal information to marketers, it may be storing the data in a third-party, offsite backup facility (which is thus being "provided" with the information).

b.   Choice/Consent: Getting Informed Permission

Assuming that the notice was accurate and effective in communicating the company's data practices to the consumer, self-regulation next requires that the consumer agree to participate in the data collection and use. The agreement may not have to be explicit (i.e., a signature on a contract), but it should be possible for the consumer to consent, or choose not to, *before* the information is collected. Ideally, there should also be a method for the consumer to subsequently withdraw previously granted consent.

What happens, however, when the business wishes to change its information practices, especially if it intends to broaden its use or sharing beyond that to which consumers have already consented? In such circumstances, the company may prefer not to request permission for the new use from its existing customers, since the request may draw unwanted scrutiny to its plans and generate consumer discomfort or withdrawals of consent. One option is to segregate the data into "before" and "after" files, and only change the practices for the "after" customers. This, though, may reduce the value to the company of the new uses (for example, if it is looking to share its customer list with another marketer; segregation could substantially reduce the quantity of names and addresses being provided).

The other alternative would be to merely provide notice of the change, and offer consumers the opportunity to opt out of the added or changed uses of their personal information. This may, however, not be deemed sufficient by consumer protection agencies or the courts, as discovered by Amazon.com after it sought to change its information use practices in 2000:

May 24, 2001 Letter from FTC Bureau of Consumer Protection to Junkbusters Corp and Electronic Privacy Information Center

. . . . On December 4, 2000, Junkbusters Corp. and the Electronic Privacy Information Center filed a joint petition requesting that the Federal Trade Commission ("FTC") investigate whether Amazon.com ("Amazon") deceived consumers in its representations about privacy and the circumstances under which Amazon might disclose information about its customers.

In reviewing the petition, FTC staff considered whether Amazon, under its revised privacy policy, changed its practices with respect to its collection and use of personal information in a way that was deceptive or unfair in violation of Section 5 of the Federal Trade Commission Act ("FTC Act"), 15 U.S.C. § 45. Based upon information we received from Amazon concerning its actual information disclosure practices, including correspondence attached to this letter as Exhibit A, staff believes that Amazon's revised privacy policy does not materially conflict with representations Amazon made in its previous privacy policy and that it likely has not violated Section 5 of the FTC Act.

*Amazon's previous privacy policy stated that "Amazon.com does not sell, trade, or rent your personal information to others. We may choose to do so in the future with trustworthy third parties, but you can tell us not to by sending a blank e-mail message to never@amazon.com." Exhibit B at 2. You are concerned that under its revised privacy policy, Amazon may now disclose personal information about consumers who previously selected "never." Amazon has assured us that, despite the ambiguity of its revised policy on this issue, it will not disclose to third parties any personal information concerning consumers who previously selected "never." Moreover, Amazon has informed the FTC that it has never sold, traded, or rented the personal information of any of its customers, even those customers who did **not** e-mail never@amazon.com, and it will not do so without notice to its customers and an opportunity for them to choose not to have their information shared. Exhibit A at 2–3.*

Although Amazon's revisions to its privacy policy are subject to various interpretations, Amazon's letter describes its actual practices. It thus does not appear that Amazon has violated Section 5 of the FTC Act by making material changes in its previously disclosed information collection and disclosure policies. We would expect that in the event of a material change to its stated privacy practices, Amazon would provide adequate notice to customers as well as a mechanism to obtain consumers' consent to the change with respect to information already collected from them. In addition, we of course would urge Amazon and others developing their privacy policies to make their policies clear and understandable to consumers.

We appreciate your bringing this matter to our attention. Petitions from groups such as yours are a helpful means of reviewing possible unfair or deceptive practices, and we hope you will continue to bring to our attention any practices that you believe may violate the FTC Act.[18]

A key point from this letter is the FTC's view that in the event of a "material change" to a stated privacy policy, Amazon (or any other collector) would be required not only to provide "adequate notice" of the change, but to obtain "consumers' consent to the change with respect to information already collected from them." That is, if a business makes a material change (however that might be defined) to its practices, it must obtain an opt-in from customers whose information was previously collected before applying the change to those data. Otherwise, it could face enforcement for unfair or deceptive practices. For clients whose businesses, and privacy practices, may

---

[18] AMAZON.COM, *http://www.ftc.gov/os/closings/staff/amazonletter.shtm (last visited May 7, 2012) (notes omitted).*

evolve over time, it is essential that they are aware of this obligation.

Note as well that it is not merely changes in practices that might trigger this opt-in obligation, but to the statement of those practices contained in a privacy policy. To the extent that a company has published an *inaccurate* privacy policy, and seeks to correct it, the correction itself could be deemed a "material change" requiring affirmative consent from those from whom the company has previously collected personal information. This can offer significant challenges for businesses and their counsel seeking to improve their compliance with self-regulatory principles.

c.   Integrity/Security: Keeping Data Safe and Unaltered

A business' obligations regarding personally identifiable information collected from consumers are not solely connected with the use and sharing of those data. Companies are also required under the Fair Information Practice Principles to take steps to protect the security and integrity of the information. These are related but not identical concepts. Security represents the methods, both physical and electronic, to prevent unauthorized access to the data both during transmission and when stored. Integrity refers to the business' obligation to protect the data from being edited, changed, damaged, or deleted other than by those permitted to do so. A company that fails to maintain either the security or integrity of the data entrusted to it could expose both itself and its customers to risks including identity theft, reputational damage, financial loss, and others.

As previously stated, there is as of yet no federal general privacy law for consumer information, nor is there an industry-neutral statutory obligation regarding either data security or integrity.[19] This has not, however, prevented the FTC from taking action against companies for their failures to maintain security and integrity for consumer data, whether or not the companies' privacy policies promised specific protection:

BJ'S Wholesale Club Settles FTC Charges Agency Says Lax Security Compromised Thousands of Credit and Debit Cards

BJ's Wholesale Club, Inc. has agreed to settle Federal Trade Commission charges that its failure to take appropriate security measures to protect the sensitive information of thousands of its customers was an unfair practice that violated federal law. According to the FTC, this information was used by an unauthorized person or persons to make millions of dollars of fraudulent purchases. The settlement will require BJ's to implement a comprehensive information security program and obtain audits by an independent third party security professional every other year for 20 years.

Natick, Massachusetts-based BJ's operates 150 warehouse stores and 78 gas stations in 16 states in the Eastern United States. Approximately 8 million consumers are currently members, with net sales totaling about $6.6 billion in 2003.

---

[19] There are, however, requirements connected with specific industries such as health and financial privacy. For more discussion of these, see Chapter 5 and Chapter 6 of this book respectively.

"Consumers must have the confidence that companies that possess their confidential information will handle it with due care and appropriately provide for its security," said Deborah Platt Majoras, Chairman of the FTC. "This case demonstrates our intention to challenge companies that fail to protect adequately consumers' sensitive information."

According to the FTC's complaint, BJ's uses a computer network to obtain bank authorization for credit and debit card purchases and to track inventory. For credit and debit card purchases at its stores, BJ's collects information, such as name, card number, and expiration date, from the magnetic stripe on the back of the cards. The information is sent from the computer network in the store to BJ's central datacenter computer network and from there through outside computer networks to the bank that issued the card.

The FTC charged that BJ's engaged in a number of practices which, taken together, did not provide reasonable security for sensitive customer information. Specifically, the agency alleges that BJ's:

- *Failed to encrypt consumer information when it was transmitted or stored on computers in BJ's stores;*

- *Created unnecessary risks to the information by storing it for up to 30 days, in violation of bank security rules, even when it no longer needed the information;*

- *Stored the information in files that could be accessed using commonly known default user IDs and passwords;*

- *Failed to use readily available security measures to prevent unauthorized wireless connections to its networks; and*

- *Failed to use measures sufficient to detect unauthorized access to the networks or to conduct security investigations.*

The FTC's complaint charges that the fraudulent purchases were made using counterfeit copies of credit and debit cards used at BJ's stores, and that the counterfeit cards contained the same personal information BJ's had collected from the magnetic stripes of the cards. After the fraud was discovered, banks cancelled and re-issued thousands of credit and debit cards, and consumers experienced inconvenience, worry, and time loss dealing with the affected cards. Since then, banks and credit unions have filed lawsuits against BJ's and pursued bank procedures seeking the return millions of dollars in fraudulent purchases and operating expenses. According to BJ's SEC filings, as of May 2005, the amount of outstanding claims was approximately $13 million.

The FTC alleges that BJ's failure to secure customers' sensitive information was an unfair practice because it caused substantial injury that was not reasonably avoidable by consumers and not outweighed by offsetting benefits to consumers or competition. The settlement requires BJ's to establish and maintain a comprehensive information security program that includes administrative, technical, and physical safeguards. The settlement also requires BJ's to obtain an audit from a qualified, independent, third-party professional that its security program meets the standards of the order, and to comply with standard book keeping and record keeping provisions.

The Commission vote to accept the proposed consent agreement was 5-0. The FTC will publish an announcement regarding the agreement in the Federal Register shortly. The agreement will be subject to public comment for 30 days, beginning today and continuing through July 16, 2005, after which the Commission will decide whether to make it final. Comments should be addressed to the FTC, Office of the Secretary, Room H-159, 600 Pennsylvania Avenue, N.W., Washington, D.C. 20580. The FTC is requesting that any comment filed in paper form near the end of the public comment period be sent by courier or overnight service, if possible, because U.S. postal mail in the Washington area and at the Commission is subject to delay due to heightened security precautions.

Copies of the complaint and consent agreement are available from the FTC's Web site at http://www.ftc.gov and also from the FTC's Consumer Response Center, Room 130, 600 Pennsylvania Avenue, N.W., Washington, D.C. 20580. The FTC works for the consumer to prevent fraudulent, deceptive, and unfair business practices in the marketplace and to provide information to help consumers spot, stop, and avoid them. To file a complaint in English or Spanish (bilingual counselors are available to take complaints), or to get free information on any of 150 consumer topics, call toll-free, 1-877-FTC-HELP (1-877-382-4357), or use the complaint form at http://www.ftc.gov. The FTC enters Internet, telemarketing, identity theft, and other fraud-related complaints into Consumer Sentinel, a secure, online database available to hundreds of civil and criminal law enforcement agencies in the U.S. and abroad.[20]

*   *   *

ValueClick to Pay $2.9 Million to Settle FTC Charges

Online advertiser ValueClick, Inc., will pay a record $2.9 million to settle Federal Trade Commission charges that its advertising claims and e-mails were deceptive and violated federal law. The agency also charged that ValueClick and its subsidiaries, Hi-Speed Media and E-Babylon failed to secure consumers' sensitive financial information, despite their claims to do so . . . .

The FTC . . . charged that ValueClick, Hi-Speed Media, and E-Babylon, misrepresented that they secured customers' sensitive financial information consistent with industry standards. The FTC alleged the companies published online privacy policies claiming they encrypted customer information, but either failed to encrypt the information at all or used a non-standard and insecure form of encryption. The agency also charged that several of the companies' e-commerce Web sites were vulnerable to SQL injection, a commonly known form of hacker attack, contrary to claims that the companies implemented reasonable security measures . . . .

The settlement . . . bars ValueClick, Hi-Speed Media, and E-Babylon from making

---

[20] FTC Press Release, June 16, 2005, BJ'S Wholesale Club Settles FTC Charges, *http://www.ftc.gov/ opa/2005/06/bjswholesale.shtm (last visited May 7, 2012). See also FTC Press Release, March 25, 2010, Dave & Buster's Settles FTC Charges it Failed to Protect Consumers' Information, http://www.ftc.gov/opa/2010/ 03/davebusters.shtm (last visited May 7, 2012).*

misrepresentations about the use of encryption or other electronic measures to protect consumers' information, and about the extent to which they protect personal information. The order also requires the companies to establish and maintain a comprehensive security program, and obtain independent third-party assessments of their programs, for 20 years . . . .[21]

d. Enforcement/Redress: Remedies for Wrongs

Self-regulation does not preclude the possibility of problems arising; in fact, the FIPP mandates that organizations collecting personal information provide some level of user remediation in the event of issues with their practices. As discussed above,[22] consumers may and ideally will have access to internal (company-specific), private external (trade associations; alternative dispute resolution bodies) and governmental channels for both enforcement and redress. Businesses that are members of industry groups and associations should be particularly aware of any enforcement and other privacy-related mandates that may be imposed upon them as members, both in order to comply with the mandates and to be prepared for any group-driven enforcement they may face.[23]

One more potential avenue of redress for consumers is through the activities of advocacy organizations such as the Electronic Privacy Information Center,[24] the Electronic Frontier Foundation,[25] and others. These groups monitor, inform, and actively litigate on behalf of digital privacy rights, often prompting FTC and other enforcement action through their initiatives.[26]

V. OTHER FEDERAL LAWS INVOLVING CONSUMER PRIVACY

While there remains no general federal Internet privacy law, there are federal statutes and regulations that nevertheless impose specific consumer privacy-related obligations. One is the Video Privacy Protection Act.[27] This statute was originally enacted following the use of Judge Robert Bork's personal video rental records in the Senate confirmation hearing as part of the effort to derail his (ultimately unsuccessful)

---

[21] FTC Press Release dated March 17, 2008, VALUECLICK TO PAY $2.9 MILLION TO SETTLE FTC CHARGES, http://www.ftc.gov/opa/2008/03/vc.shtm (last visited May 7, 2012).

[22] *See supra* note 38.

[23] *See, e.g.*, the Direct Marketing Association's Guidelines for Ethical Business Practices (available at http://www.dmaresponsibility.org/guidelines), enforced through the DMA's Ethics Committee (http://www.dmaresponsibility.org/CaseReport/).

[24] EPIC - ELECTRONIC PRIVACY INFORMATION CENTER, http://epic.org/ (last visited May 7, 2012).

[25] ALL EFF's LEGAL CASES | ELECTRONIC FRONTIER FOUNDATION, https://www.eff.org/cases?tid=540 (last visited May 7, 2012).

[26] *See, e.g., Federal Trade Commission Announces Settlement in EPIC Google Buzz Complaint*, EPIC press release, Mar. 30, 2011, available at http://epic.org/press/EPIC_Buzz_Press_Release_03_30_11.pdf.

[27] Video Privacy Protection Act, 18 U.S.C. § 2710 (1988).

nomination to the U.S. Supreme Court.[28] The statute provides in relevant part:

(b) Video tape rental and sale records. — (1) A video tape service provider who knowingly discloses, to any person, personally identifiable information concerning any consumer of such provider shall be liable to the aggrieved person for the relief provided in subsection (d).

(2) A video tape service provider may disclose personally identifiable information concerning any consumer —

(A) to the consumer;

(B) to any person with the informed, written consent of the consumer given at the time the disclosure is sought;

(C) to a law enforcement agency pursuant to a warrant issued under the Federal Rules of Criminal Procedure, an equivalent State warrant, a grand jury subpoena, or a court order;

(D) to any person if the disclosure is solely of the names and addresses of consumers and if —

(i) the video tape service provider has provided the consumer with the opportunity, in a clear and conspicuous manner, to prohibit such disclosure; and

(ii) the disclosure does not identify the title, description, or subject matter of any video tapes or other audio visual material; however, the subject matter of such materials may be disclosed if the disclosure is for the exclusive use of marketing goods and services directly to the consumer;

(E) to any person if the disclosure is incident to the ordinary course of business of the video tape service provider; or

(F) pursuant to a court order, in a civil proceeding upon a showing of compelling need for the information that cannot be accommodated by any other means, if —

(i) the consumer is given reasonable notice, by the person seeking the disclosure, of the court proceeding relevant to the issuance of the court order; and

(ii) the consumer is afforded the opportunity to appear and contest the claim of the person seeking the disclosure.

If an order is granted pursuant to subparagraph (C) or (F), the court shall impose appropriate safeguards against unauthorized disclosure.

(3) Court orders authorizing disclosure under subparagraph (C) shall issue only with prior notice to the consumer and only if the law enforcement

---

[28] Adam Clark Estes, WHY ROBERT BORK (INDIRECTLY) KEPT NETFLIX OFF FACEBOOK — TECHNOLOGY — THE ATLANTIC WIRE, http://www.theatlanticwire.com/technology/2011/07/why-robert-bork-indirectly-kept-netflix-facebook/40408/ (last visited May 7, 2012).

agency shows that there is probable cause to believe that the records or other information sought are relevant to a legitimate law enforcement inquiry. In the case of a State government authority, such a court order shall not issue if prohibited by the law of such State. A court issuing an order pursuant to this section, on a motion made promptly by the video tape service provider, may quash or modify such order if the information or records requested are unreasonably voluminous in nature or if compliance with such order otherwise would cause an unreasonable burden on such provider.

(c) Civil action. — (1) Any person aggrieved by any act of a person in violation of this section may bring a civil action in a United States district court.

(2) The court may award —

(A) actual damages but not less than liquidated damages in an amount of $2,500;

(B) punitive damages;

(C) reasonable attorneys' fees and other litigation costs reasonably incurred; and

(D) such other preliminary and equitable relief as the court determines to be appropriate.

(3) No action may be brought under this subsection unless such action is begun within 2 years from the date of the act complained of or the date of discovery.

(4) No liability shall result from lawful disclosure permitted by this section.

(d) Personally identifiable information. — Personally identifiable information obtained in any manner other than as provided in this section shall not be received in evidence in any trial, hearing, arbitration, or other proceeding in or before any court, grand jury, department, officer, agency, regulatory body, legislative committee, or other authority of the United States, a State, or a political subdivision of a State.[29]

Recent developments in technology, both in the method for delivering rented videos (DVDs and now downloadable and streaming video) and providing consent have posed challenges to the understanding and applicability of the Video Privacy Protection Act. On the delivery side, the definition of "video tape rental service" contained in the statute can still be read to encompass other media and delivery mechanisms:

the term "video tape service provider" means any person, engaged in the business, in or affecting interstate or foreign commerce, of rental, sale, or delivery of prerecorded video cassette tapes or similar audio visual materials, or any person or other entity to whom a disclosure is made under subpara-

---

[29] *Id. Sections (b) through (d).*

graph (D) or (E) of subsection (b)(2), but only with respect to the information contained in the disclosure . . . .[30]

The requirement for "written consent," however, may not include current online methods for consumer consent, whether directly provided to the rental/streaming site or via a partnership with another site such as Facebook. A bill introduced in the 112th Congress[31] sought to broaden the permissible methods of consent accordingly:

Section 2710(b)(2) of title 18, United States Code, is amended by striking subparagraph (B) and inserting the following:

'(B) to any person with the informed, written consent (including through an electronic means using the Internet) in a form distinct and separate from any form setting forth other legal or financial obligations of the consumer given at one or both of the following times —

'(i) the time the disclosure is sought; and

'(ii) in advance for a set period of time or until consent is withdrawn by such consumer;'.[32]

Companies must also consider privacy-related obligations coming from other areas of law. One notable example arises in federal bankruptcy law, addressing the possibility that personal information could be found among the assets that may be sold to help repay creditors in a bankruptcy. Depending on the details of the proposed sale, it could violate the terms of a privacy policy under which the information was originally collected. In such a circumstance, the court-appointed trustee must follow additional procedures to address privacy concerns:

§ 332. Consumer privacy ombudsman

(a) If a hearing is required under section 363(b)(1)(B),[33] *the court shall order the United States trustee to appoint, not later than 7 days before the*

---

[30] *Id. § 2710(a)(4) (2006).*

[31] HR 2471 as enrolled by the House, available at http://www.gpo.gov/fdsys/pkg/BILLS-112hr2471eh/pdf/BILLS-112hr2471eh.pdf.

[32] *See supra note 54.*

[33] 11 U.S.C. § 363(b) states:

(b)(1) The trustee, after notice and a hearing, may use, sell, or lease, other than in the ordinary course of business, property of the estate, except that if the debtor in connection with offering a product or a service discloses to an individual a policy prohibiting the transfer of personally identifiable information about individuals to persons that are not affiliated with the debtor and if such policy is in effect on the date of the commencement of the case, then the trustee may not sell or lease personally identifiable information to any person unless —

(A) such sale or such lease is consistent with such policy; or

(B) after appointment of a consumer privacy ombudsman in accordance with section 332, and after notice and a hearing, the court approves such sale or such lease —

(i) giving due consideration to the facts, circumstances, and conditions of such sale or such lease; and

(ii) finding that no showing was made that such sale or such lease would violate applicable nonbankruptcy law.

commencement of the hearing, 1 disinterested person (other than the United States trustee) to serve as the consumer privacy ombudsman in the case and shall require that notice of such hearing be timely given to such ombudsman.

(b) The consumer privacy ombudsman may appear and be heard at such hearing and shall provide to the court information to assist the court in its consideration of the facts, circumstances, and conditions of the proposed sale or lease of personally identifiable information under section 363(b)(1)(B). Such information may include presentation of —

(1) the debtor's privacy policy;

(2) the potential losses or gains of privacy to consumers if such sale or such lease is approved by the court;

(3) the potential costs or benefits to consumers if such sale or such lease is approved by the court; and

(4) the potential alternatives that would mitigate potential privacy losses or potential costs to consumers.

(c) A consumer privacy ombudsman shall not disclose any personally identifiable information obtained by the ombudsman under this title.

Section 332 was added to the federal bankruptcy law in 2005[34] in response to cases such as that of *Toysmart*, in which an Internet retailer undergoing an involuntary liquidation sought to sell its customer lists as part of the bankruptcy proceedings. The FTC objected, based upon the language of Toysmart's privacy policy:

Through its Web site, Toysmart collects detailed personal information about its visitors, including name, address, billing information, shopping preferences, and family profiles, which include the names and birthdates of children. Since September 1999, Toysmart has posted a privacy policy which states that information collected from customers will never be shared with third parties.

That policy states that:

Personal information, voluntarily submitted by visitors to our site, such as name, address, billing information and shopping preferences, is never shared with a third party.

The policy continues:

When you register with toysmart.com, you can rest assured that your information will never be shared with a third party.[35]

Toysmart subsequently settled with the FTC over many of these privacy policy issues

---

11 U.S.C. § 363(b)(1) (2010).

[34] PL 109-8, April 20, 2005, 119 Stat. 23.

[35] FTC Press Release, July 10, 2000, FTC SUES FAILED WEBSITE, TOYSMART.COM, FOR DECEPTIVELY OFFERING FOR SALE PERSONAL INFORMATION OF WEBSITE VISITORS, *http://www.ftc.gov/opa/2000/07/toysmart.shtm (last visited May 7, 2012).*

(although COPPA-related children's privacy claims were not included in the settlement):

> . . . . *Under the settlement agreement, Toysmart will file an order . . . in Bankruptcy Court ("Bankruptcy Order"), prohibiting Toysmart from selling the customer list as a stand-alone asset. The settlement only allows a sale of such lists as a package which includes the entire Web site, and only to a "Qualified Buyer" — an entity that is in a related market and that expressly agrees to be Toysmart's successor-in-interest as to the customer information.*
>
> *The Qualified Buyer must abide by the terms of the Toysmart privacy statement. If the buyer wishes to make changes to that policy, it must follow certain procedures to protect consumers. It may not change how the information previously collected by Toysmart is used, unless it provides notice to consumers and obtains their affirmative consent ("opt-in") to the new uses.*
>
> *In the event that the Bankruptcy Court does not approve the sale of the customer information to a Qualified Buyer or a plan of reorganization within the next year, Toysmart must delete or destroy all customer information. In the interim, Toysmart is obligated to abide by its privacy statement.*
>
> *After the Bankruptcy Order is approved, the FTC will also file a stipulated consent agreement and final order before the U.S. District Court, Massachusetts ("District Court Order"), enjoining the unlawful practices alleged in the Complaint, prohibiting Toysmart from making any false or misleading statements about the disclosure of personal information to third parties, and prohibiting Toysmart from disclosing, selling, or offering for sale to any third party any customer information, except as provided for in the Bankruptcy Order.*[36]

VI.   STATE CONSUMER PRIVACY LAWS: LOCAL LEGISLATION, WIDE-RANGING IMPACT

Even as the federal government has declined to enact general legislation mandating the publication and form of digital privacy disclosures, states have stepped up to do so. While the jurisdiction of state law is limited to a state's borders by the so-called negative or dormant Commerce Clause of the U.S. Constitution, which understands as exclusive Congress "[p]ower . . . to regulate [c]ommerce with foreign [n]ations, and among the several [s]tates, and with the Indian [t]ribes . . . .,"[37] the essentially borderless nature of the Internet, and the intertwined nature of modern business, mean that almost any state's enforcement power may potentially stretch to a company located in another state.[38]

---

[36] FTC Press Release, July 20, 2001, FTC ANNOUNCES SETTLEMENT WITH BANKRUPT WEBSITE, TOYSMART.COM, REGARDING ALLEGED PRIVACY POLICY VIOLATIONS, *http://www.ftc.gov/opa/2000/07/toysmart2.shtm#N_1_ (last visited May 7, 2012).*

[37] U.S. Const. art. I, § 8.

[38] The cross-border nature of the Internet, and its potential extension of state law enforcement beyond the state's borders, can be seen in the growth of so-called "Amazon tax" legislation in a number of states,

One significant example of a state privacy law with interstate influence is California's Online Privacy Protection Act of 2003,[39] which specifically mandates disclosure of online data collection and use practices affecting California residents:

Cal. Bus. & Prof. Code § 22575. Commercial Web site operators; posting of privacy policy; violation of subdivision for failure to post policy; policy requirements

(a) An operator of a commercial Web site or online service that collects personally identifiable information through the Internet about individual consumers residing in California who use or visit its commercial Web site or online service shall conspicuously post its privacy policy on its Web site, or in the case of an operator of an online service, make that policy available in accordance with paragraph (5) of subdivision (b) of Section 22577. [40] *An operator shall be in violation of this subdivision only if the operator fails to post its policy within 30 days after being notified of noncompliance.*

---

starting with New York. Following the U.S. Supreme Court's guidance in *Quill Corp. v. North Dakota*, 504 U.S. 298 (1992) and related cases, states have been limited under the Commerce Clause in their power to levy sales taxes to those transactions where the seller maintains a "substantial nexus," a significant presence, in the state. This presence has been understood to include elements such as physical offices and/or employees, including sales personnel, based in the state. In recent years, given the resurgence of mail order online sales as a major stream of commerce (and the resulting loss of easily collectible sales taxes from the local retailers whose potential customers may be shopping online instead), states are attempting to extend the definition of "nexus" to include some Internet-based sales. One popular method of doing so is via a focus on the commission-based referral methods known as "affiliate programs," through which independent Web site publishers can refer potential customers to an online retailer through unique Web links, and receive commissions if the referrals result in sales. *See, e.g.*, Affiliate Marketing Definition | Small Business Encyclopedia | Entrepreneur.com, http://www.entrepreneur.com/encyclopedia/term/82092.html (last visited May 7, 2012). Although the so-called "affiliates" are not employees of the retailer, and often join these programs through automated, non-negotiated clickthrough agreements, states are broadening their definition of taxable sales transactions to include referrals from in-state affiliates to out-of-state retailers that result in sales back to state residents. The non-resident retailers will therefore be obligated to collect, and remit, sales taxes on those transactions, and enforcement can potentially occur against any assets or financial resources of the retailers that may pass through the enforcing state. Amazon.com, being the most prominent retailer whose affiliate marketing program (which Amazon calls its Associates Program) is affected by these laws, has both provided the unofficial name used to describe the new statutes and has mounted legal challenges (so far unsuccessfully) to the constitutionality of the efforts. *See, e.g.*, Andrew B. Lustigman and Jonathan I. Ezor, New York affiliate tax complicates affiliate marketing programs — Mobile Marketer — Columns (Aug. 18, 2008), http://www.mobilemarketer.com/cms/opinion/columns/1547.html (last visited May 7, 2012); Jonathan I. Ezor, Split Decision in Appeal of NY "Amazon Tax" Case | New York Advertising Attorneys Blog (Nov. 5, 2010), http://www.advertisinglawblog.com/2010/11/split-decision-in-appeal-of-ny-amazon-tax-case.shtml (last visited May 7, 2012).

[39] Cal. Bus. & Prof. Code § 22575 (2005).

[40] § 22577(b) states,

(b) The term "conspicuously post" with respect to a privacy policy shall include posting the privacy policy through any of the following:

(1) A Web page on which the actual privacy policy is posted if the Web page is the homepage or first significant page after entering the Web site.

(2) An icon that hyperlinks to a Web page on which the actual privacy policy is posted, if the icon is located on the homepage or the first significant page after entering the Web site, and if the icon contains the word "privacy." The icon shall also use a color that contrasts with the background color of the Web page or is otherwise distinguishable.

(b) The privacy policy required by subdivision (a) shall do all of the following:

(1) Identify the categories of personally identifiable information that the operator collects through the Web site or online service about individual consumers who use or visit its commercial Web site or online service and the categories of third-party persons or entities with whom the operator may share that personally identifiable information.

(2) If the operator maintains a process for an individual consumer who uses or visits its commercial Web site or online service to review and request changes to any of his or her personally identifiable information that is collected through the Web site or online service, provide a description of that process.

(3) Describe the process by which the operator notifies consumers who use or visit its commercial Web site or online service of material changes to the operator's privacy policy for that Web site or online service.

(4) Identify its effective date.

California further protects its citizens' data privacy rights through its so-called "Shine the Light" law, most notably its mandated notice of consumer access to information about data sharing with marketers:

Excerpt from Cal. Civ. Code § 1798.83: Personal Information; Disclosure to Direct Marketers

(a) . . . . [I]f a business has an established business relationship with a customer and has within the immediately preceding calendar year disclosed personal information that corresponds to any of the categories of personal information set forth in paragraph (6) of subdivision (e) [41] *to third parties, and if the business knows or*

---

(3) A text link that hyperlinks to a Web page on which the actual privacy policy is posted, if the text link is located on the homepage or first significant page after entering the Web site, and if the text link does one of the following:

(A) Includes the word "privacy."

(B) Is written in capital letters equal to or greater in size than the surrounding text.

(C) Is written in larger type than the surrounding text, or in contrasting type, font, or color to the surrounding text of the same size, or set off from the surrounding text of the same size by symbols or other marks that call attention to the language.

(4) Any other functional hyperlink that is so displayed that a reasonable person would notice it.

(5) In the case of an online service, any other reasonably accessible means of making the privacy policy available for consumers of the online service.

[41] The categories include:
  (i)   Name and address.
  (ii)   Electronic mail address.
  (iii) Age or date of birth.
  (iv)   Names of children.
  (v)   Electronic mail or other addresses of children.
  (vi)   Number of children.
  (vii) The age or gender of children.
  (viii) Height.

reasonably should know that the third parties used the personal information for the third parties' direct marketing purposes, that business shall, after the receipt of a written or electronic mail request, or, if the business chooses to receive requests by toll-free telephone or facsimile numbers, a telephone or facsimile request from the customer, provide all of the following information to the customer free of charge:

(1) In writing or by electronic mail, a list of the categories set forth in paragraph (6) of subdivision (e) that correspond to the personal information disclosed by the business to third parties for the third parties' direct marketing purposes during the immediately preceding calendar year.

(2) In writing or by electronic mail, the names and addresses of all of the third parties that received personal information from the business for the third parties' direct marketing purposes during the preceding calendar year and, if the nature of the third parties' business cannot reasonably be determined from the third parties' name, examples of the products or services marketed, if known to the business, sufficient to give the customer a reasonable indication of the nature of the third parties' business.

(b)(1) A business required to comply with this section shall designate a mailing address, electronic mail address, or, if the business chooses to receive requests by telephone or facsimile, a toll-free telephone or facsimile number, to which customers may deliver requests pursuant to subdivision (a). A business required to comply with this section shall, at its election, do at least one of the following:

(A) Notify all agents and managers who directly supervise employees who regularly have contact with customers of the designated addresses or numbers or the means to obtain those addresses or numbers and instruct those employees that customers who inquire about the business's privacy practices or the business's compliance with this section shall be informed of the designated addresses or numbers or the means to obtain the addresses or numbers.

(ix)   Weight.
(x)   Race.
(xi)   Religion.
(xii)   Occupation.
(xiii)   Telephone number.
(xiv)   Education.
(xv)   Political party affiliation.
(xvi)   Medical condition.
(xvii)   Drugs, therapies, or medical products or equipment used.
(xviii)   The kind of product the customer purchased, leased, or rented.
(xix)   Real property purchased, leased, or rented.
(xx)   The kind of service provided.
(xxi)   Social security number.
(xxii)   Bank account number.
(xxiii)   Credit card number.
(xxiv)   Debit card number.
(xxv)   Bank or investment account, debit card, or credit card balance.
(xxvi)   Payment history.
(xxvii)   Information pertaining to the customer's creditworthiness, assets, income, or liabilities.

Cal. Civ. Code § 1798.89(e)(6) (2010).

(B) Add to the home page of its Web site a link either to a page titled "Your Privacy Rights" or add the words "Your Privacy Rights" to the home page's link to the business's privacy policy. If the business elects to add the words "Your Privacy Rights" to the link to the business's privacy policy, the words "Your Privacy Rights" shall be in the same style and size as the link to the business's privacy policy. If the business does not display a link to its privacy policy on the home page of its Web site, or does not have a privacy policy, the words "Your Privacy Rights" shall be written in larger type than the surrounding text, or in contrasting type, font, or color to the surrounding text of the same size, or set off from the surrounding text of the same size by symbols or other marks that call attention to the language. The first page of the link shall describe a customer's rights pursuant to this section and shall provide the designated mailing address, e-mail address, as required, or toll-free telephone number or facsimile number, as appropriate. If the business elects to add the words "Your California Privacy Rights" to the home page's link to the business's privacy policy in a manner that complies with this subdivision, and the first page of the link describes a customer's rights pursuant to this section, and provides the designated mailing address, electronic mailing address, as required, or toll-free telephone or facsimile number, as appropriate, the business need not respond to requests that are not received at one of the designated addresses or numbers.

(C) Make the designated addresses or numbers, or means to obtain the designated addresses or numbers, readily available upon request of a customer at every place of business in California where the business or its agents regularly have contact with customers.

The response to a request pursuant to this section received at one of the designated addresses or numbers shall be provided within 30 days. Requests received by the business at other than one of the designated addresses or numbers shall be provided within a reasonable period, in light of the circumstances related to how the request was received, but not to exceed 150 days from the date received. [42]

Note that while the definition of "Customer" used here is limited to California residents, [43] the word "business" in this section includes companies both within and outside the state:

> *"Business" means a sole proprietorship, partnership, corporation, association, or other group, however organized and whether or not organized to operate at a profit, including a financial institution organized, chartered, or holding a license or authorization certificate under the law of this state, any other state, the United States, or of any other country, or the parent or the subsidiary of a financial institution. The term includes an entity that disposes of records.* [44]

---

[42] Cal. Civ. Code § 1798.83(a) (2006).

[43] " 'Customer' means an individual who is a resident of California who provides personal information to a business during the creation of, or throughout the duration of, an established business relationship if the business relationship is primarily for personal, family, or household purposes." Cal. Civ. Code § 1798.83(e)(1) (2006).

[44] *Id. § 1798.80(a).*

As one measurement of the actual impact of California's statute on companies located beyond its borders, a Google search for the phrase "Your California Privacy Rights," [45] one of the required headings for the marketing disclosure, yields literally millions of results, including the privacy policies for explicitly non-California businesses such as WTVY, a television station in Dothan, AL whose parent company, Gray Television, Inc., is based in Albany, GA. [46]

Another state which has enacted its own privacy policy-related statute is Pennsylvania. In contrast to the affirmative disclosure obligation imposed by California, Pennsylvania includes within its definition of "deceptive or fraudulent business practices" a situation in which a person "knowingly makes a false or misleading statement in a privacy policy, published on the Internet or otherwise distributed or published, regarding the use of personal information submitted by members of the public." [47] Such a provision clarifies and potentially expands the liability for inaccurate privacy policy statements beyond general consumer protection concerns into the realm of criminal law.

VII. CONCLUSION: BEST PRACTICES START WITH ACCURATE DISCLOSURE

Given that, in the realm of consumer privacy law, the overarching principle is informed consent, best practices in connection with consumer information must incorporate a mechanism for obtaining this consent. In order to do this, though, the company must itself be informed not only about relevant law where applicable, but also the complete path and scope of consumer data it may be collecting, using and sharing. This is not always a simple process, since organizations both large and small, may have different business units each of which has some knowledge of the company's information practices. Unfortunately, those professionals who are made responsible for drafting and promulgating a company's privacy policy are often not fully aware of their colleagues within the organization (or, if the policy is being drafted by outside counsel all of personnel within the client organization) who "touch" consumer data. It's therefore critical both for effective policy drafting and in preparation for defending any enforcement action claiming any improper information use that the people in charge of creating the consumer information document known as a privacy policy collect the relevant information about company process in an organized, detailed fashion.

One useful tool in this process is a questionnaire. A properly drafted questionnaire will list the full range of relevant issues for privacy policies encompassing not only the type and channels of collection for consumer information but also general corporate details that may be of relevance in both the disclosure and in identifying and managing privacy risks. For example, the location of any out of state or foreign offices in which

---

[45] "YOUR CALIFORNIA PRIVACY RIGHTS" — GOOGLE SEARCH, https://www.google.com/search?q=%E2%80%9C Your+California+Privacy+Rights (last visited May 7, 2012).

[46] GRAY TELEVISION, INC. PRIVACY POLICY AND YOUR PRIVACY RIGHTS, http://www.wtvy.com/unclassified/ 34218884.html (last visited May 7, 2012).

[47] 18 Pa.C.S.A. § 4107(a)(10) (2005).

company employees or strategic partners may exist is extremely relevant for consumer privacy management given the broad range of diverse often contradictory privacy laws and regulations to which a multijurisdictional organization may be subject. Understanding the off-line process as to how consumers connect with the company (e.g., through faxes, telephone calls, postal letters, etc.) will inform the policy's disclosure of consumer information collection. Knowing of other business units, whose operations may nominally be separate from that for which the policy is being drafted, will help the professional crafting the policy to determine if there are more sensitive areas of law that could, in the future, become relevant if information will be shared with those other business units. Finally, asking about the organization's membership and trade associations and any existing enforcement (whether privacy related or not) may raise questions about consent orders, self-enforcement policies, and other matters with which the IT professionals within the organization may not be immediately familiar.

Another benefit of a question-based process for drafting consumer disclosure is that it enables research. An attorney discussing privacy policies with a client may ask all of the right questions, but that particular individual may not have all of the answers immediately at hand. With a questionnaire, though, all of the relevant personnel within the company can be given a chance to do all of the relevant research to track down a more complete set of answers to the questions. The questionnaire will further sensitize those in the company who answer it to the kinds of potential pitfalls that arise in the context of consumer privacy, such as those described in this chapter.

Once the questionnaire has been fully answered, any uncertainties addressed and the drafter made aware of the current practices of the organization with regard to consumer information, the process can go much more smoothly. However, there are both strategic and risk-related considerations that arise in the choice of language and provision in the privacy policy itself beyond merely accurate reflection of the company's practices. One is flexibility. A well considered privacy policy will not merely disclose the company's current data uses, but will provide sufficient flexibility so that some future uses, which may not yet be contemplated by the company, will fall within the privacy policy without the language having to be revised.

Chapter 3

SOCIAL MEDIA PRIVACY: NOT (NECESSARILY) AN OXYMORON

Social media (and the similar term "social networks") are not a new concept either in the analog or digital world. At their heart, social media are many where members of a community can express themselves, and respond to others' statements, whether one at a time or as part of a group. Subway trains and overpasses covered with different taggers' graffiti and the stereotypical public bathroom wall are (perhaps extreme) examples of offline social media. Party lines (telephone lines shared by more than one household, before individual lines became available and affordable), single-line college dorm suites, and pay-per-minute "chat lines" (often with sexually explicit conversations) were social media as well, using the telephone wires as their conduit. While television production and distribution costs made social television unfeasible (most individuals did not and could not build their own television stations), the lower cost and greater accessibility of radio meant that communities could develop using that medium: ham operators would chat worldwide via voice or even Morse code, while citizen band radios became popular for conversations among both truck drivers and others in the 1970s and early 1980s.

On the Internet, social media have formed a major part of the framework since the earliest days. Network users could send each other short text messages via UNIX "write" or "talk" commands,[1] Usenet hosted message boards on thousands of different topics, Internet Relay Chat ("IRC") servers across the Internet enabled real-time, multi-user chat, and Internet-based multi-user dungeons ("MUDs") combined text-based virtual "worlds" with live interaction among players through the characters whose actions they controlled (known as avatars). Similar socially driven programs ran on private dial-up bulletin board systems (BBSes) and proprietary online systems like GEnie, Prodigy, and CompuServe. These communities, while at times incredibly vibrant and ongoing, were accessed by a tiny fraction of society, mainly technologists, hobbyists, and those in university communities which provided Internet access to some or all students.

Beginning in the early-to-mid '90s, and especially since the turn of the millennium, Internet-based social networks have expanded in numbers and market penetration. As the skills needed to access social networks lessened, and the user base diversified, hundreds of millions of people around the world have become regular users of social networks from the earlier MySpace to Facebook, Twitter, LinkedIn and many more. In doing so, they have joined a culture of relationships and sharing that raises

---

[1] UNIX Commands Guide, http://www.cs.brown.edu/courses/bridge/1998/res/UnixGuide.html (last visited May 7, 2012).

significant and diverse privacy issues, in terms of what information is shared, by whom, with whom, and how it can be accessed. Some of these issues are under control of the person to whom the information pertains, but most may not be. Service providers, other users, and third parties may have control, and resulting legal obligations, with regard to the personal and behavioral information relating to social media services, in addition to the other laws and regulations that generally cover digitally stored private information.

I.   THE ELECTRONIC COMMUNICATIONS PRIVACY ACT: THE KEY FEDERAL STATUTE

The Electronic Communications Privacy Act ("ECPA") is the major federal statute which determines whether and how social media posts and data about them may be shared, at least to the extent that the issue involves something that falls under one of the statutory definition of electronic communications to which the statute applies:

> *"electronic communication" means any transfer of signs, signals, writing, images, sounds, data, or intelligence of any nature transmitted in whole or in part by a wire, radio, electromagnetic, photoelectronic or photooptical system that affects interstate or foreign commerce, but does not include —*
>
> *(A) any wire or oral communication;*
>
> *(B) any communication made through a tone-only paging device;*
>
> *(C) any communication from a tracking device (as defined in section 3117 of this title); or*
>
> *(D) electronic funds transfer information stored by a financial institution in a communications system used for the electronic storage and transfer of funds . . . .*[2]

Assuming it does, the next question to be answered is whether the requesting party, the disclosing party, or both are considered governmental actors: police or other law enforcement officials, public education facilities, government agencies, etc. If so, the provisions of ECPA that apply to governmental acts apply. Otherwise, one looks to those requirements and restrictions for private entities and individuals.

Two more key distinctions under ECPA are (1) whether the information being collected and sought is from the content or other portions of the communications, and (2) whether the disclosure is of communications as they are being sent or of stored communications after the fact. Depending on the answer to these two questions, different portions of ECPA may apply:

---

[2]   18 U.S.C. § 2510(12) (2002).

	As message is being transmitted	After message is received
Content (i.e. what is being said/written)	Wiretap Act[3]	Stored Communications Act[4]
Non-content (e.g., who sent it to whom; when was it sent; other identifying and addressing information)	Pen Register Statute[5]	

Further, ECPA distinguishes between two types of service providers: an electronic communications service ("ECS")[6] and a remote computing service ("RCS").[7] Each has its own unique requirements and restrictions in terms of what information it may disclose, under what circumstances, to whom, and the documentation required to authorize the disclosure.

II.   SOCIAL MEDIA SHARING: THE FOUR WS

Perhaps the most surprising element of social media from a privacy perspective is the sheer scope of how much and what types of information can be obtained from and about users. It may be helpful to frame the discussion via a concept borrowed from journalism: the five Ws and an H. Reporters are trained to answer six crucial questions in a story: "who," "what," "where," "when," "why," and "how." While "why" and "how" are not specifically privacy-related, the other four W questions are precisely on point.

a.   Who: Identity, Anonymity and Pseudonymity Online

From the earliest days of online communities, users were given a choice that they rarely had in most off-line, real-world contexts: whether to use their real identities, remain anonymous, or take the middle ground of creating and using a pseudonym. Certainly, anonymity was actually possible in real-world interactions, but it required hiding one's face and voice; so did taking on a pseudonym. While fiction was full of successful anonymous or pseudonymous interactions (e.g., the superhero's "secret identity" or Alexander Dumas' "Man in the Iron Mask"), there were few real life situations where an individual could not be quickly and easily identified. By contrast, online communities very quickly provided identifiers that could be different from one's real name. E-mail addresses or network logins could technologically use words other than the user's identity, with limits only in available characters or the policy of the network owners. As networks offered more sophisticated, software-based games, chat

---

[3]   18 U.S.C. §§ 2510–22.

[4]   18 U.S.C. § 2701–11.

[5]   18 U.S.C. §§ 3121–27.

[6]   " '[E]lectronic communication service' means any service which provides to users thereof the ability to send or receive wire or electronic communications." *Id.* § 2510(12).

[7]   "[T]he term 'remote computing service' means the provision to the public of computer storage or processing services by means of an electronic communications system." 18 U.S.C. § 2711(2).

rooms, and message boards, the opportunities to create or hide one's true name expanded. At a whim, or perhaps for more nefarious reasons, a user could utilize a different name, age, gender, or even species, limited only by the programming of the particular software being run and/or rules and policies created by the community itself.

Excerpt from *"A Rape in Cyberspace"* by Julian Dibbell

The facts begin (as they often do) with a time and a place. The time was a Monday night in March, and the place, as I've said, was the living room — which, due largely to the centrality of its location and to a certain warmth of decor, is so invariably packed with chitchatters as to be roughly synonymous among LambdaMOOers with a party. So strong, indeed, is the sense of convivial common ground invested in the living room that a cruel mind could hardly imagine a better place in which to stage a violation of LambdaMOO's communal spirit. And there was cruelty enough lurking in the appearance Mr. Bungle presented to the virtual world — he was at the time a fat, oleaginous, Bisquick-faced clown dressed in cum-stained harlequin garb and girdled with a mistletoe-and-hemlock belt whose buckle bore the quaint inscription KISS ME UNDER THIS, BITCH! But whether cruelty motivated his choice of crime scene is not among the established facts of the case. It is a fact only that he did choose the living room.

The remaining facts tell us a bit more about the inner world of Mr. Bungle, though only perhaps that it wasn't a very cozy place. They tell us that he commenced his assault entirely unprovoked, at or about 10 p.m. Pacific Standard Time. That he began by using his voodoo doll to force one of the room's occupants to sexually service him in a variety of more or less conventional ways. That this victim was exu, a Haitian trickster spirit of indeterminate gender, brown-skinned and wearing an expensive pearl gray suit, top hat, and dark glasses. That exu heaped vicious imprecations on him all the while and that he was soon ejected bodily from the room. That he hid himself away then in his private chambers somewhere on the mansion grounds and continued the attacks without interruption, since the voodoo doll worked just as well at a distance as in proximity. That he turned his attentions now to Moondreamer, a rather pointedly nondescript female character, tall, stout, and brown-haired, forcing her into unwanted liaisons with other individuals present in the room, among them exu, Kropotkin (the well-known radical), and Snugberry (the squirrel). That his actions grew progressively violent. That he made exu eat his/her own pubic hair. That he caused Moondreamer to violate herself with a piece of kitchen cutlery. That his distant laughter echoed evilly in the living room with every successive outrage. That he could not be stopped until at last someone summoned Iggy, a wise and trusted old-timer who brought with him a gun of near wizardly powers, a gun that didn't kill but enveloped its targets in a cage impermeable even to a voodoo doll's powers. That Iggy fired this gun at Mr. Bungle, thwarting the doll at last and silencing the evil, distant laughter.

These particulars, as I said, are unambiguous. But they are far from simple, for the simple reason that every set of facts in virtual reality (or VR, as the locals abbreviate it) is shadowed by a second, complicating set: the "real-life" facts. And while a certain tension invariably buzzes in the gap between the hard, prosaic RL facts and their more fluid, dreamy VR counterparts, the dissonance in the Bungle case is striking. No hideous clowns or trickster spirits appear in the RL version of the incident, no voodoo dolls or wizard guns, indeed no rape at all as any RL court of law has yet defined it. The actors in the drama were university students for the most part, and they sat rather undramatically before computer screens the entire time, their only actions a spidery flitting of fingers across standard QWERTY keyboards. No bodies touched. Whatever physical interaction occurred consisted of a mingling of electronic signals sent from sites spread out between New York City and Melbourne, Australia. Those signals met in LambdaMOO, certainly, just as the hideous clown and the living room party did, but what was LambdaMOO after all? Not an enchanted mansion or anything of the sort — just a middlingly complex database, maintained for experimental purposes inside a Xerox Corporation research computer in Palo Alto and open to public access via the Internet.

To be more precise about it, LambdaMOO was a MUD. Or to be yet more precise, it was a subspecies of MUD known as a MOO, which is short for "MUD, Object-Oriented." All of which means that it was a kind of database especially designed to give users the vivid impression of moving through a physical space that in reality exists only as words filed away on a hard drive. When users dial into LambdaMOO, for instance, the program immediately presents them with a brief textual description of one of the rooms of the database's fictional mansion (the coat closet, say). If the user wants to leave this room, she can enter a command to move in a particular direction and the database will replace the original description with a new one corresponding to the room located in the direction she chose. When the new description scrolls across the user's screen it lists not only the fixed features of the room but all its contents at that moment — including things (tools, toys, weapons) and other users (each represented as a "character" over which the user has sole control).

As far as the database program is concerned, all of these entities — rooms, things, characters — are just different subprograms that the program allows to interact according to rules very roughly mimicking the laws of the physical world. Characters may not leave a room in a given direction, for instance, unless the room subprogram contains an "exit" at that compass point. And if a character "says" or "does" something (as directed by its user-owner via the say or the emote command), then only the users whose characters are also located in that room will see the output describing the statement or action. Aside from such basic constraints, however, LambdaMOOers are allowed a broad freedom to create — they can describe their characters any way they like, they can make rooms of their own and decorate them to taste, and they can build new objects almost at will. The combination of all this busy user activity with the hard physics of the database can certainly induce a lucid illusion of presence — but when all is said and done the only thing you really see when you visit LambdaMOO is a kind of slow-crawling script, lines of dialogue and stage direction creeping steadily up your computer screen . . . . [8]

---

[8] Julian Dibbell, A RAPE IN CYBERSPACE, *http://www.juliandibbell.com/articles/a-rape-in-cyberspace/ (last visited May 7, 2012).*

From a practical perspective, the anonymity or pseudonymity of a particular user can be limited by a number of factors. First, of course, is whether the user (accurately) discloses her true identity within the online community, either intentionally or otherwise. As was pointed out earlier in the book,[9] identity can be effectively disclosed through combination of facts that individually do not serve as identifiers. Even if the user member never explicitly mentions her name, address, or other typical pieces of personally identifiable information, others within the community can "put the pieces together" and figure out the user's actual identity.

Human nature can also play a part in de-anonymizing social media users. Often, a user may use the same word or phrase, by itself or in connection with a meaningful number such as an age or birth date, as his user name for multiple communities or services. If so, the fact that the user hid his identity on one message board may be meaningless, if a quick search of his "pseudonym" turns up another site or service where his personal identity is more easily found. The more unique the chosen identifier, especially in combination with other information provided by the user, the greater the chance of such discovery, as occurred when the Wikileaks mass information release was traced to intelligence specialist Bradley Manning, born in 1987, who used the online name "Bradass87" while discussing his occupation and position:

Excerpt from "Afghanistan War Logs: Story Behind Biggest Leak in Intelligence History"

. . . On 21 May, a Californian computer hacker called Adrian Lamo was contacted by somebody with the online name Bradass87 who started to swap instant messages with him. He was immediately extraordinarily open: "hi . . . how are you? . . . im an army intelligence analyst, deployed to eastern bagdad . . . if you had unprecedented access to classified networks, 14 hours a day, 7 days a week for 8+ months, what would you do?"

For five days, Bradass87 opened his heart to Lamo . . . . On 26 May, at US Forward Operating Base Hammer, 25 miles outside Baghdad, a 22-year-old intelligence analyst named Bradley Manning was arrested, shipped across the border to Kuwait and locked up in a military prison . . . .[10]

Whatever other users may discover about an anonymous or pseudonymous user, though, identifying information is almost certainly known by (and potentially obtainable from) various service providers, at least from a technical perspective. First, to the extent the particular social medium requires registration before use, the user may have had to provide a verifiable real identity and/or payment information to the service host. Even if the service provider did not require pre-registration, or was given false

---

[9] *See* discussion at Chapter One, note 20.

[10] Nick Davies, Afghanistan war logs: Story behind biggest leak in intelligence history | World news | The Guardian, http://www.guardian.co.uk/world/2010/jul/25/wikileaks-war-logs-back-story (last visited May 7, 2012). Comedian Jon Stewart, host of The Daily Show, highlighted the weakness of Mr. Manning's pseudonym for concealing his identity. Jon Stewart | Wikileaks | Bradass87 | Mediaite, http://www.mediaite.com/online/best-leak-ever-jon-stewart-mocks-media-coverage-of-wikileaks-controversy/ (last visited May 7, 2012).

information, one piece of data is embedded in every communication sent via the Internet, including through social networking communities: the IP address of the sender. The service host can associate a unique IP address with every message, and that IP address will in turn be assigned to a unique individual or account at that particular date and time by the ISP or network owner from whose blocks of addresses that specific one comes. While an IP address cannot by itself identify a person, it can be traced to an account, a device, or other unique location to which a limited number of people may have access.

At times, the IP address' use and ownership is publicly accessible: in August 2007, Wired Magazine wrote of tracing the IP address used to excise negative information about Diebold voting machines from a Wikipedia article to an IP address registered to Diebold itself.[11] In that instance, the IP address itself was shown on Wikipedia, and its ownership was searchable via the Arin.net Web site. Similar methods, along with a broader analysis of geography and similar word choices, helped bloggers identify the so-called "Fake Steve Jobs" as reported by The New York Times the same month.[12] While technologies do exist to enable IP address hiding, spoofing and other conceal-ment techniques,[13] the vast majority of Internet users connect without such methods and via traceable IP addresses.

When social media or other communications, or the information about by whom and when they were sent, are not publicly viewable, however, relevant statutory and case law along with internal policies may determine whether and how the service providers with the information may share it.

Beyond the formal legal prohibitions and requirements for disclosure, the service provider's own internal and published policies will have an impact. Internally, the service provider must initially decide whether it will be collecting, and verifying, user information; such a decision will be driven both by relevant law and the interests of the desired membership and the provider itself. In some contexts, a service provider may be required to collect and archive user information and communications because of its industry or the type of discussions that occur.[14] In others, as with COPPA,[15] the service provider may be discouraged from collecting user identity information because of the substantial requirements for such collection.

Other concerns such as marketing and reputation come into play as well in the establishment of a service provider's internal policies. Some services require users to publicly utilize their actual names, and may even verify them, to provide accountability and retain a decorum in the discussions.[16] Others will verify only some users, such as

---

[11] John Borland, *See Who's Editing Wikipedia - Diebold, the CIA, a Campaign*, WIRED (Aug. 14, 2007), http://www.wired.com/politics/onlinerights/news/2007/08/wiki_tracker (last visited May 7, 2012).

[12] Brad Stone, THE TRIAL OF FAKE STEVE JOBS - NYTIMES.COM (AUG. 5, 2007), http://bits.blogs.nytimes.com/2007/08/05/the-trial-of-fake-steve-jobs/ (last visited May 7, 2012).

[13] *See, e.g.*, TOR PROJECT: ANONYMITY ONLINE, https://www.torproject.org/ (last visited May 8, 2012).

[14] *See, e.g.*, 17 CFR § 240.17a-4(b)(4) (SEC retention requirements for broker-dealers).

[15] See discussion on COPPA in Chapter 4: The Special Case of Children.

[16] Google's Google Plus service requires that members use real rather than fanciful names: "To help fight spam and prevent fake profiles, use the name your friends, family or co-workers usually call you. For

celebrities, to reduce the risk that imposters may take famous names and fool other users.[17] Intermediaries like auction, payment, and dating sites may enable public pseudonymity, but will retain and utilize verified personal information to facilitate and improve the reliability of the desired transaction or introductions.

By contrast, there are service providers which seek to enable anonymity for their users, for a variety of reasons including but not limited to:

- Providing a forum for unpopular or dissident political discussions;

- Performing or supporting illegal activity;

- Granting access to socially sensitive content (e.g., sexually explicit discussions or materials); and

- Otherwise giving those who fear reprisal or danger from disclosing their identities a tool for communicating without risking doing so.

If providers wish to offer true anonymity, they must consider both technical and legal issues. Technically, even if the provider does not itself request or retain other identifying information, it may still be logging IP addresses which can be obtained and utilized by authorities or others to identify the otherwise anonymous service users, as occurred in 1995 to the well-known and relied-upon anon.penet.fi automated remailer:

EXCERPTED FROM THE CUTTING EDGE: The Helsinki Incident and the Right to Anonymity BY DANIEL AKST

. . . . *Anon.penet.fi is basically a computer in Helsinki, Finland, whose purpose is to allow e-mail users all over the world to send anonymous messages, both to individuals as private e-mail and to Internet newsgroups, as the Net's 10,000-plus discussion forums are known. You message anon.penet.fi and it strips off your identity, substituting a code number. Responses at your anon.penet.fi address get routed back to you. There are many "anonymous remailers" like anon.penet.fi, but probably none is as stable or widely used. Its operator, a selfless computer networking specialist named Johan (Julf) Helsingius, supports the server to the tune of $1,000 a month and has developed a reputation for integrity. Helsingius has rules: He won't disclose the name behind an anonymous ID, but every message explains how to send him complaints. Abuse anon.penet.fi and you'll probably find yourself locked out of the system. During previous incidents in which he was pressured to disclose the identity of a user, Helsingius stood firm. Then the inevitable happened: He was faced with a search warrant served by Finnish police . . . .* [18]

---

example, if your full legal name is Charles Jones Jr. but you normally use Chuck Jones or Junior Jones, either of those would be acceptable." POLICIES & PRINCIPLES - GOOGLE, http://www.google.com/intl/en/+/policy/content.html (last visited May 8, 2012).

[17] *See, e.g.*, Twitter, TWITTER HELP CENTER | FAQS ABOUT VERIFIED ACCOUNTS, https://support.twitter.com/groups/31-twitter-basics/topics/111-features/articles/119135-about-verified-accounts# (last visited May 8, 2012).

[18] Daniel Akst, HELSINKI INCIDENT | THE CUTTING EDGE?: THE HELSINKI INCIDENT AND THE RIGHT TO ANONYMITY - LOS ANGELES TIMES, *http://articles.latimes.com/1995-02-22/business/fi-34831_1_anonymous-remailers (last visited May 8, 2012).*

As the anon.penet.fi incident shows, a social network or other service may be legally obligated to disclose personal information it retains, whether or not it promises anonymity. This highlights a second potential area of legal exposure: the promise itself. Just as sites generally may be held liable under consumer protection laws for unkept promises or other misstatements in their privacy policies, a service that promises unlimited anonymity but is required to disclose could face civil exposure from its no-longer anonymous members. In this context, as with privacy policies generally, it's important to include exceptions to any commitment to protect identities. Alternatively, the service may choose not to preseve logs of IP addresses (assuming it is otherwise not legally required to do so), so that it cannot disclose them because it does not actually have them. While this does enhance its ability to detect identities, it removes the service's ability to identify and seek redress from users who abuse or damage the service itself. Further, while the service may decline to keep logs, its real-time connections could be tapped to obtain IP addresses as the communications are made.

b. What: Content as Disclosure

The informality of social media, along with potentially confusing settings from various social media services regarding who can or cannot see a particular user's postings, can result in content being posted that is at best embarrassing, and at worst may violate legal obligations such as confidentiality requirements, whether contractual or arising out of a particular industry's requirements.[19]

From an inbound information collection perspective, companies that are covered by statutory or regulatory obligations discussed elsewhere in this volume (for example, COPPA for information collection from children, HIPAA for health-related businesses, and the various requirements for financial service providers) may not be exempt from those rules merely because the channel through which they are collecting personal information is a social network rather than their own Web sites or other internal resources. Similarly, if the organization is prohibited from or faces restrictions on its disclosing of personal information, those restrictions may or will include disclosure via social media. Unfortunately, customers who are *not* covered by the same restrictions may be able to tweet or post about the company, even falsehoods that might damage the company's reputation, with the only available response being a costly and uncertain defamation lawsuit.

Some industries and professions face formal confidentiality obligations beyond those arising of privacy regulations. Attorneys, for example, are required by the ethical rules of the state(s) in which they are admitted to practice to maintain client confidences,[20] which is as true of social media posts as casual conversations in elevators and other public places:

Note that the obligation for attorneys goes beyond information that may be generally thought of as personal identifiable information or even confidential information, to encompass all "information relating to the representation of a client."

---

[19] *See, e.g.*, discussions of health privacy in Chapter 5; financial privacy in Chapter 6;, and the ethical obligations of confidentiality for attorneys in Chapter 11.

[20] See discussion of attorney confidentiality obligations at Chapter 11, note 1.

This broad requirement can be breached not only through express revelations, but through implicit ones as well. For example, a corporate attorney from New York City who checks in on Foursquare at a hotel in Bentonville, Arkansas (well-known as the home of Walmart's corporate headquarters) could effectively be disclosing that her client has some business or other relationship with Walmart, even if that information is not otherwise public. Consider as well the actual litigator who tweeted that he was in a settlement meeting at his opponent's office. While this might seem a casual message rather than an ethical breach, this is not so clear. Although the attorney did not name either the case or the opposing attorney, and regardless of the fact that the existence of settlement discussions is inadmissible,[21] a juror from the case who was following that attorney (as many non-sequestered jurors are now in the habit of doing) would be made aware that settlements were being discussed (or might believe so, even though the attorney could have been discussing settling a *different* case) and could share that information with other jurors or otherwise allow it to impact on the verdict.

A further privacy-related legal issue for businesses is the confidentiality obligations they may face based upon their contractual relationships. Companies can all too easily violate a non-disclosure provision or agreement regarding a business relationship or even the name of the contracting parties through an injudicious tweet or blog posting, especially if the employee who tweets is not aware of the obligation in the first place. When Apple was preparing to launch its first-generation iPad in February 2010, it showed pre-release units to technology journalists under strict non-disclosure obligations. A deputy managing editor for The Wall Street Journal tweeted during such a meeting that he was using the iPad; the tweet later was deleted, but was later reported by BusinessWeek.[22] At times, social media can facilitate unauthorized disclosure even when the posting doesn't contain any obvious information, confidential or otherwise, solely due to *how* various technologies function. In one instance, a well-known technology blogger inadvertently leaked the not-yet-public 5 megapixel camera resolution of the pre-release Palm Pre 2 smartphone he was apparently given to test, when he posted his photo of an old stereo system[23] via the photo-sharing service img.ly. While the contents and caption of the photo ("Vintage from the 90s. I'm old.") were unremarkable, the photo's digital file contained standardized EXIF (Exchangeable Image File Format)[24] information clearly indicated that it had a resolution of 2576 x 1928 pixels (that is, 5 megapixels) and that it was taken with a "Palm Pre." Since no then-available Palm Pre phone had a 5 megapixel camera, the blogger had inadvertently disclosed a specification upgrade that the company itself had not yet confirmed, *merely by posting a photo to a social media service.*

Even if the revelation of information does not violate laws or contracts, it can still be detrimental to the business, whether due to embarrassment or loss of competitive

---

[21] *See, e.g.,* Fed R. Evid. 408.

[22] Douglas MacMillan, Apple Swears iPad Partners to Secrecy — BusinessWeek, http://www.business week.com/technology/content/mar2010/tc20100318_833402.htm (last visited May 8, 2012).

[23] Joshua Topolsky, Vintage from the 90s. I'm old. — img.ly, http://img.ly/2gxT (last visited May 8, 2012).

[24] Standard of Japan Electronics and Information Technology Industries Association, exif22_1, http://www.digicamsoft.com/exif22/exif22/html/exif22_1.htm (last visited May 8, 2012).

advantage.

From "A Twitter Code of Conduct" by Douglas MacMillan

During a recent tour of interactive ad agency Tocquigny's Austin (Tex.) headquarters, Chief Executive Yvonne Tocquigny was confronted by her guest, an executive from a large energy company who was a potential client. The visitor had recently learned that Tocquigny was wooing one of his company's competitors — by seeing a message that one of Tocquigny's employees had posted to Twitter "It took me by surprise," says Tocquigny. "I realized that we needed to be more cautious about what we throw out there in to the universe . . ."

Twitter can be a great business tool. But as use of the Web site for 140-character messages spreads to workplaces around the world, companies are also discovering the risks. Now, instead of just worrying about a dubious blog post or an embarrassing photo of the boss being posted to Facebook, employers have to contend with staffers shooting off frequent blasts of personal insight into a public and traceable sphere. "The concept of [workers] posting inappropriate material that could be harmful has been around for a while, but Twitter accelerates the problem because of its immediacy and volume," says Mark Rasch, a former head of the U.S. Justice Dept.'s computer crime unit who now consults with companies on creating policies to address employees' use of technology.

To prevent sensitive information leaks, blemishes on a reputation, and other potential liabilities of a Twittering workforce, companies are drafting new employee codes of conduct and educating workers about what they should and shouldn't say on the site. The basic rule: Don't be stupid . . . .[25]

c.   When: Time as a Key Element of Identity

While an IP address may be a unique identifier, it may also be shared among numerous users either sequentially or simultaneously. Either way, in order to specifically identify a user, the investigator will require the *exact* date and time of each relevant communication; that is, to answer the question of *when*.

This is due to two technical factors. The first is that, because IP addresses in their current format (consisting of four sets of three digits between 0 and 255, separated by periods; e.g., 192.168.1.1) are a large but finite resource,[26] they can be allocated in both dynamic as well as static methods. In a dynamic IP environment, the network operator or service provider maintains a set of IP addresses it controls. As a new user signs into the network or service, the user is assigned an available IP address from the set, and whenever the user signs off the network, that IP address becomes

---

[25] Douglas MacMillan, A TWITTER CODE OF CONDUCT — BUSINESSWEEK *(May 8, 2009), http://www.businessweek.com/managing/content/may2009/ca2009058_089205.htm (last visited May 8, 2012).*

[26] For a discussion of the issues involving the exhaustion of available IPv4 numbers, and the need to transition to the far-more-plentiful IPv6 structure, see IEEE-USA White Paper, Next Generation Internet: IPv4 Address Exhaustion, Mitigation Strategies and Implications for the U.S. (2009), available at http://www.ieeeusa.org/policy/whitepapers/IEEEUSAWP-IPv62009.pdf.

available for reuse either by the same or another user upon signon to the network. A dynamic IP address environment is similar to the way telephone numbers are assigned within a particular area code or other geographic region: new customers may be given telephone numbers that could have been used by previous customers who have moved or otherwise discontinued service. In the telephone system, numbers may be kept inactive for some period between assignments to reduce the chance of newer customers receiving calls properly dialed but intended for the previous assignee of the number. For dynamic IP addresses, however, very little time is required between assignments, since the infrastructure of the Internet is not designed to assume that IP addresses will remain fixed, and each communication will include a "lookup" to obtain the latest IP address for the indended recipient.

The second technical matter has to do with how networks route communications. Modern local area networks ("LANs") will likely utilize the same type of IP address-based communications as the broader Internet. The difference, however, is that while every device communicating with the Internet must have an IP address that is unique throughout the world, locally connected devices will be issued internal IP addresses that must only be unique within the local network, but could be identical to those assigned to any number of devices connected to other local networks, just as numerous corporate telephone systems could use the same set of numbers for their internal extensions without conflicting with each other.

In order for internal networked computers to communicate with the Internet, however, the network must provide a router, a device which will redirect Internet-bound communications from internal machines out to the Internet, and then receive and distribute any replies back to the internal machines to which the replies are being sent. In order for this to work properly, the router will be assigned a single public IP address, which will be associated with every communication and request from every user coming from that router's internal network, just as the caller ID from callers within a corporation may be reported as the main number of the corporation, since the internal corporate telephone system routes outbound calls from its local extensions through its available public lines.

As with dynamic IP addresses, an exact date and time is needed in order to identify the particular user from which a communication utilizing a router's public IP address has come. With those data, the network's administrator may be able to trace the communication back to the specific internal network user who connected to the Internet through the router at that moment. Given how many internal users may be sharing the router, however, this identification can be more difficult than simply associating a dynamic IP address with its then-current assignee. Without the time information, though, it can be almost impossible absent additional evidence to identify a user behind a shared router's public IP address.

Even if one has the date and time a particular IP address was used, that will not necessarily lead to positive identification. First, one must be sure that the clocks of the sending and receiving networks are identical; if not, it is vital to correct for any discrepancies, since failing to do so could likely lead to inaccurate identification. Second, even when the network operator is provided with the correct information, it could report back inaccurate identification, leading to embarrassment or worse.

From "Faulty IP address data leads to Shaq attack on innocent family"

Anyone who follows the slate of lawsuits against music fans is cognizant of the crucial role that IP addresses play in attempts to cow suspected file sharers. But as we have seen time and time again, IP addresses are not consistently reliable means of identifying users. Law enforcement officials and a family in Gretna, Virginia and learned that lesson the hard way after their home was searched by a law enforcement team that included Miami Heat center Shaquille O'Neal, according to a law enforcement official.

The spectre of an angry, uniform-wearing Shaq, let alone an entire team of deputies and federal marshalls would be enough to turn one's knees to jelly. That's the sight apparently witnessed by farmer A.J. Nuckols, his schoolteacher wife, and three children last month when their home was raided and their computers, DVD, video tapes, and other belongings were confiscated after they were connected to an IP address reportedly used to access child pornography on the Internet.

It turned out to be a case of mistaken identity. Nine days after the raid, an investigator told Nuckols that "the wrong IP address had been identified" and that he and his family would not be charged in the investigation . . . .[27]

One more caveat about obtaining identity via social media: at best, the unique identifiers used (IP addresses, account names, etc.) can be connected to an account or specific computer or device rather than the specific person using the device or operating the device. Further investigation may be necessary to definitively match the IP address to the human utilizing it, as in legal proceedings with particular evidentiary standards or burdens of proof.

### d.	Where: Location-Based Information

For most of the history of networked communications, geography was both irrelevant (as long as there was a wire or a signal) and difficult to determine, especially when the communicator wished to hide her location. In the analog world, while the central offices would likely know and could potentially report the physical location of wired telephone lines, each participant in the call might not automatically know where the other caller was located, beyond general information from the telephone number. For example, the old Hotel Pennsylvania in New York City had the telephone number "Pennsylvania 6-5000," memorialized by the Glenn Miller Orchestra in a song;[28] the "Pennsylvania" in the number (later updated to PE6-5000 and currently in use with the Manhattan 212 area code by the hotel as 212-736-5000[29]) was the telephone exchange of that part of Manhattan, named for the nearby

---

[27] Eric Bangeman, Faulty IP Address Data Leads to Shaq Attack On Innocent Family (Updated), *http://arstechnica.com/tech-policy/news/2006/10/8062.ars (last visited May 8, 2012).*

[28] Michael Sigman, Pennsylvania 6-5000: A Hotel, A Phone Number and a Song | LA Progressive, http://www.laprogressive.com/pennsylvania-6-5000/ (last visited May 8, 2012).

[29] Midtown Manhattan New York Hotel Accommodations | New York's Hotel Pennsylvania, http://www.hotelpenn.com/ (last visited May 8, 2012).

Pennsylvania Railroad Station.[30] Anyone calling Pennsylvania 6-5000, or any number beginning with Pennsylvania, would know the other party was likely in the region of Pennsylvania Station on the West Side of midtown Manhattan. Telephone exchanges (and, once the number of phones in use exceeded the available quantity of telephone numbers, area codes appended to the exchanges) continued to provide rough geographic data about caller location at least until call forwarding and mobile telephones disconnected the caller from a particular place. Today, little can be definitively determined about the physical location of a caller from the telephone number the caller uses; even the country may be unknowable.[31]

With computer networks, the issue of geographical location became even more irrelevant, at least at first. The TCP/IP protocol on which all Internet communication is carried was designed to be tolerant of breaks in the network, by routing messages (actually, by breaking messages into packets of information that would be reassembled at their final destination to once again represent the complete message) via any available connection, no matter the geographical location. While a particular connection might not be the most direct from a physical perspective (i.e., the shortest length of wire), it could be the one that happened to have the least congestion and therefore most availability at the moment a packet needed to be sent. While the initial wires that carried Internet traffic were mainly within the United States (as part of the original ARPAnet), as the network spread and other countries' internal networks were interconnected through multiple paths, national borders turned porous to network traffic. It was only those countries whose international telecommunications services were routed through a single, controllable connection where Internet traffic could generally be "stopped at the border." As for the transmitted information itself, it was identified only by a numerical IP address, which theoretically could be assigned to any computer without regard to its physical location; while domain names often included geographic designations (e.g., .uk as a "country code" for systems based in the United Kingdom), IP addresses did not. There were no equivalents of international calling codes, or postal codes, assigned to computers.

As a result, social media services would generally have no inherent knowledge of their members' geographical location, unless the members provided the information to the services either voluntarily or as a condition for gaining access to the service itself. The most frequent situation in which a service provider *would* have information about a member's location (or at least mailing address) was when the service required payment in some way, or the member required or requested physical materials to be sent from the service. Payments made by check or credit card would connect a location to the member account, as would mailing instructions or any correspondence sent by the member to the service for whatever reason.

Paid services, therefore, would need to consider how they would protect the location information as part of their overall privacy policies, where free services had less need to do so (except when the information was volunteered by the member).

---

[30] The Telephone Exchange Name Project, http://ourwebhome.com/TENP/TENproject.html (last visited May 8, 2012).

[31] *See, e.g.*, Online Number — Online Business Number with Voicemail — Skype, http://www.skype.com/intl/en-us/features/allfeatures/online-number/ (last visited May 8, 2012).

They could also, however, face potential liability based upon their imputed knowledge of their members' locations, especially when those locations' laws were violated by the activities of the service.

From "Virtual Community Standards"

. . . . *[I]n the law-enforcement community and in the mainstream press, the prospect of online obscenity is still an eyegrabber . . . . This factor does much to explain the hoopla surrounding the obscenity prosecution of Robert and Carleen Thomas of Milpitas, CA. At first glance, the case may seem little different from the average obscenity prosecution. Sure, there's a computer bulletin-board system (BBS) involved, but there's nothing new about prosecuting pornography distributors in conservative states like Tennessee, is there?*

Except that this BBS wasn't in Tennessee. It was in California. But that didn't stop Tennessee prosecutors from going after it . . . .[32]

More recently, a technology called "geolocation" has made it substantially easier for social media service providers to know (or at least have a strong likelihood of knowing) where a particular user might be. One method of geolocation involves the creation and maintenance of a database matching IP addresses to physical locations based upon a variety of source information (domain name records, ISP and corporate office addresses, and others); once the databases are compiled, they can be queried by Web site and social media service owners each time a user connects to the service. This can enable the service to provide location-specific content (e.g., advertising for local businesses) or, alternatively, *block* content which the service may not legally provide in the location in which the user is believed to be. Even when the accuracy of the databases may not be complete, the service provider may nevertheless make decisions about the information they provide.

From "Geo-Location Technologies and Other Means of Placing Borders on the 'Borderless' Internet"

If a Web site operator can know the location of those who access the Web site, he/she can, due to the reactive nature of Web servers, control what material is presented, and indeed, accessible to each access-seeker. In addition to business advantages, such as targeted advertisement, a structure allowing for geo-identification has the advantage of providing the Web site operator with the means to comply with local regulations . . . .

A Web site operator with the ability to determine the geographical location of those who access his/her Web site would be in a good position to avoid minimum contact being established between him/her and undesirable locations . . . . [A]s long as states apply conflict of laws rules that focus on the location of the effect rather than on the location where the defendant acted, there is a need for Web site operators to take steps

---

[32] Mike Godwin, VIRTUAL COMMUNITY STANDARDS, *http://w2.eff.org/legal/virtcom_standards.article.txt (last visited May 8, 2012). See also U.S. v. Thomas, 74 F.3d 701 (6th Cir. 1996).*

to limit the geographical spread of their content . . . .[33]

While the currency and accuracy of geolocation databases may vary depending on their source materials and collection methodologies, the expansion of global positioning system ("GPS") technology in cellphones, smartphones, laptops, and other devices enables social networks and other Web sites to receive extremely accurate[34] location information for each user. In fact, a growing number of social media services are either based directly upon[35] or have added supplemental features[36] arising out of GPS-enabled location reporting.

Along with the enhanced scope and accuracy of knowledge of users' location, social media services are facing increased legal exposure as well, particularly on the privacy front. First, they must disclose whether they know the user's location and how they use that information, within their general privacy policy. As with all such disclosures, failing to do so, or failing to be accurate in the disclosure, can open up a site to

---

[33] Dan Jerker B. Svantesson, *Geo-Location Technologies and Other Means of Placing Borders on the "Borderless' Internet,* 23 J. Marshall J. Computer & Info. L. 101, 102–03 (2004).

[34] As stated in the Executive Summary of the official standard document for the U.S. government's Global Positioning System,

> *The U.S. Global Positioning System (GPS) Standard Positioning Service (SPS) consists of space-based positioning, navigation, and timing (PNT) signals delivered free of direct user fees for peaceful civil, commercial, and scientific uses worldwide. This SPS Performance Standard (SPS PS) specifies the levels of SPS performance in terms of broadcast signal parameters and GPS constellation design. The U.S. Government is committed to meeting and exceeding the minimum levels of service specified in this SPS PS and this commitment is codified in U.S. Law (10 U.S.C. 2281(b)).*

> *Since GPS initial operational capability (IOC) in 1993, actual GPS performance has continuously met and exceeded minimum performance levels specified in the SPS PS and users can generally expect improved performance over the minimum levels described here. For example, with current (2007) Signal-in-Space (SIS) accuracy, well designed GPS receivers have been achieving horizontal accuracy of 3 meters or better and vertical accuracy of 5 meters or better 95% of the time. A number of U.S. agencies continually monitor actual GPS SPS performance, including the Federal Aviation Administration (FAA) which publishes quarterly Performance Analysis Reports at its National Satellite Test Bed (NSTB) web site (http:// www.nstb.tc.faa.gov/). Interested readers are encouraged to refer to this and other sources for updated GPS performance.*

U.S. Dept. of Defense, Global Positioning System Standard Positioning Service Performance Standard, http://www.pnt.gov/public/docs/2008/spsps2008.pdf, page v.

[35] *See, e.g.,* foursquare, https://foursquare.com/ (last visited May 8, 2012).

[36] When the social media service Facebook added Facebook Places in August 2010, product manager Michael Eyal Sharon introduced the feature via a blog posting:

> *If you're like me, when you find a place you really like, you want to tell your friends you're there. Maybe it's a new restaurant, a beautiful hiking trail or an amazing live show.*

> *Starting today, you can immediately tell people about that favorite spot with Facebook Places. You can share where you are and the friends you're with in real time from your mobile device.*

> **Checking In with Friends**

> *Ever gone to a show, only to find out afterward that your friends were there too? With Places, you can discover moments when you and your friends are at the same place at the same time . . .*

> . . . .

Michael Eyal Sharon, (20) Who, What, When, and Now . . . Where, https://www.facebook.com/blog/blog.php?post=418175202130 (last visited May 8, 2012).

consumer protection actions.

Next, social media services may be subject to subpoenas and other formal process from law enforcement officials and litigants with regard to the location of particular individuals. This information can be relevant in the context of investigating crimes (whether to find an accused perpetrator or to verify or establish an alibi), in divorce cases (e.g. tracking the location of a spouse accused of having an affair), and in essentially every other situation where the physical whereabouts of an individual social media user may be relevant.

One key question is what *type* of legal process is required to obtain location information. ECPA distinguishes between content and non-content information, for both in-process and stored communications.[37] Both those seeking the information and those being asked to provide it must be sure that the proper process is used, in order to avoid exposure for improper access or disclosure. While one might assume that location information is non-content and generally subject to lesser requirements and standards for disclosure, this may not be true. Consider that some social networks are based upon sharing location information; for those services, the location could be defined as content whose disclosure would be governed by the more stringent requirements within ECPA, especially for monitoring non-published current and previous "check-ins" or other location reports by users.

One further potential area of exposure, whether legal or otherwise, arises from the *consequences* of enabling location sharing and disclosure. If, for example, a user is robbed or injured as a result of reporting her location via a social media service, the service itself could theoretically find itself the subject of a liability lawsuit. Even without legal action, though, such incidents could substantially harm the reputation and business prospects of a social media service:

From "Please Rob Me: The Risks of Online Oversharing"

Think before you tweet. You might not be aware of how much information you're revealing.

That's the message from the founders of Please Rob Me, a website launched on Tuesday that illustrates just how easy it is to rob people blind on the basis of the information they're posting on the Web. The site uses streams of data from Foursquare, an increasingly popular location-based social network that is based on a game-like premise. Players use smart phones or laptops to "check in" to a location, recording their position on a map for friends using the service to see. The more often you check in, the better your chances of being declared the mayor of a particular location, be it a restaurant, bar, office or even your own home.

The problem comes when users also post these locations to Twitter, says Boy van Amstel, one of the founders of Please Rob Me. Then the information becomes publicly available, making it theoretically possible for a robber (or anyone else) to keep tabs on when you say you're in your home or not.

---

[37] See discussion of ECPA at Chapter 3:I.

"We saw people checking in at their home addresses, or even worse, those of their friends and family," van Amstel says. "Which we just thought was very wrong."

Van Amstel is no expert hacker, and Please Rob Me isn't a complicated website; it's simply a dressed-up page of Twitter search results that monitors the latest posts of users sharing their locations via Foursquare. And there are a lot of results — thousands of people willingly broadcast when they're not at home (it's rarer for users to post to Foursquare when they return). A select, misguided few broadcast their address or those of unknowing and disapproving friends or family. This makes the site more useful at proving a point than an actual tool for robbers to exploit . . .[38]

* * *

From "Facebook 'Friend' Suspected in Burglary"

Everyone you consider a "friend" on Facebook, may not have the friendliest intentions. That was the hard lesson homeowners in New Albany, Ind., believe they learned after their home was ransacked by two men.

Keri McMullen and Kurt Pendleton left a status update on Facebook Saturday night that said they wouldn't be home because they were going to a concert in nearby Louisville at 8 p.m.

At 8:42 p.m., two burglars entered their house, using a screwdriver to force open a back door. However, luckily for McMullen and Pendleton, they had recently installed a surveillance system in their home. The cameras caught the entire episode on tape.

The video shows the two men going through McMullen's purse, stealing electronics — more than $10,000 worth — including a plasma television right off the wall. The burglars are then seen driving away with a laundry basket filled with the stolen goods.

After posting images of the suspects on Facebook, McMullen realized one of them had "friended" her about six months ago. She says he grew up across the street from her and hasn't seen him in more than 20 years . . . .[39]

III. CONCLUSION: SOCIAL MEDIA PRIVACY: SIGNIFICANT CHALLENGES AND BEST PRACTICES

As the number and adoption of social media services increase, organizations and their advisors must consider how issues of privacy law and policy impact on how they and their affiliates use social media. For companies that host social media services, the primary legal challenges involve customer behavior and personal information (that is, the Four Ws discussed above). Whether the service is focused upon common user characteristics or locations (e.g. location-based services such as Foursquare, or topic-driven communities based upon occupations or hobbies), the company must

---

[38] Dan Fletcher, PLEASE ROB ME: SITE SHOWS DANGERS OF FOURSQUARE, TWITTER — TIME (Feb. 18, 2010), http://www.time.com/time/business/article/0,8599,1964873,00.html (last visited May 8, 2012).

[39] FACEBOOK "FRIEND" SUSPECTED IN BURGLARY — CBS NEWS *(Mar. 25, 2010), http://www.cbsnews.com/ stories/2010/03/25/earlyshow/main6331796.shtml (last visited May 8, 2012).*

decide what kind and quantity of information it will be collecting, as it designs both its software and its marketing materials. It must further identify necessary (and potential future) uses of the information it collects, as well as with whom and how it may (or must) share the data. The preceding is true of all companies collecting personal information; what makes a social network different is that it is *expected* to share the information in some ways, and that its business requires users to provide more information than they otherwise might to a third-party vendor. Once those parameters are determined, the service must ensure that *all* of its disclosures are accurate, and that it has procedures for circumstances in which it may be legally compelled to produce otherwise private user information.

Social networks must also consider the culture they wish to create among their users, or that may arise organically from the most frequent users of the service amongst themselves,[40] when deciding what kind and how much information they will collect and share. When Google launched its Buzz social network in February 2010, its integration with other Google services and poorly structured privacy controls resulted in new users sharing more their Buzz use than they had intended to with their Gmail contacts and others. This in turn led to rapid condemnation by users and journalists,[41] congressional inquiries, and FTC legal action,[42] and Buzz was quickly discontinued by Google. By contrast, Google's follow-up effort Google Plus was much easier to control with regard to privacy issues, and has met with substantially more positive reactions.

Even when disclosure may be technically accurate and data collection within legal parameters, social media services may still face legal and reputational challenges as to their privacy practices. Facebook, for example, is explicit in its terms of service[43] and signup procedures that children under 13 are not permitted to use the service, in order to avoid compliance issues under COPPA and likely to minimize other unwanted situations such as pedophiles "friending" underaged Facebook users.[44] Nevertheless, a May 2011 survey published by Consumer Reports found that 75 million Facebook users were under the age of 13, exposing it to potential liability.[45]

For the companies that are using social media in their operations, or whose employees (whether identified or *identifiable* as coming from the company) are doing so personally, it is crucial to establish and communicate clear guidelines as to both the acceptable uses of social media for business purposes, and the risks of improper use. If there are specific laws or regulations that apply to the company because of its industry, the guidelines must be consistent with those as well. Businesses should keep

---

[40] *See, e.g.*, discussion of LambdaMOO at Chapter 3, note 8.

[41] Molly Wood, GOOGLE BUZZ: PRIVACY NIGHTMARE | MOLLY RANTS — CNET NEWS (Feb. 10, 2010) http://news.cnet.com/8301-31322_3-10451428-256.html (last visited May 8, 2012).

[42] FTC Press Release, FTC CHARGES DECEPTIVE PRIVACY PRACTICES IN GOOGLE'S ROLLOUT OF ITS BUZZ SOCIAL NETWORK (Mar. 30, 2011), http://www.ftc.gov/opa/2011/03/google.shtm (last visited May 8, 2012).

[43] (20) FACEBOOK, https://www.facebook.com/legal/terms (last visited May 8, 2012).

[44] For more on COPPA, see Chapter 4.

[45] Press Release, CR SURVEY: 7.5 MILLION FACEBOOK USERS ARE UNDER THE AGE OF 13, VIOLATING THE SITE'S TERMS?: CONSUMER REPORTS HTTP://PRESSROOM.CONSUMERREPORTS.ORG/PRESSROOM/, (May 10, 2011), http://pressroom.consumerreports.org/pressroom/2011/05/cr-survey-75-million-facebook-users-are-under-the-age-of-13-violating-the-sites-terms-.html (last visited May 8, 2012).

in mind, though, that while they *prohibit* unauthorized or inappropriate social media use by employees in the workplace, they can likely not *prevent* such use; unless the company's offices are in a cellular deadzone, employees whose internal networks block connection to social media services can simply access them on their cellphones, smartphones, or other mobile devices. Instead of relying on firewalls, organizations should use education and policy to reduce their risks of privacy and related breaches through social media use.

Chapter 4

THE SPECIAL CASE OF CHILDREN

The law has long given special consideration to children, and offered them additional protection beyond that for adults. Children are presumed to be less capable of protecting their own best interests, and more vulnerable to exploitation from known individuals and strangers alike. Ancient Jewish law prohibited parents from sacrificing their children to idols, a prohibition needed at a time when neighboring cultures in fact did engage in child killing for some rituals. The same legal code required parents to teach their children to swim, and even extended compassion to youthful animals.[1] More modern cultures have enacted laws against child labor or at least limited their work hours, and even when the children have significant earnings potential of their own, have required their wages to be kept in trust away from the predation of their parents.

At the same time that the law is protecting children, though, it is affording them fewer rights than adults have. Children (of varying ages depending on culture) have been deemed incapable of consenting to contracts, to marriage, to sexual activity. In school settings, children may have fewer rights to free speech, and more exposure to searches by school and law enforcement officials. In the work arena, the flip side of the protection of child labor laws is a restriction on the number of hours youthful employees may work even if they'd prefer to do more, in order that they don't harm their education or health. Child actors, while having their earnings sheltered, are required to continue their education on set, even if they'd rather be out enjoying their celebrity.

At the heart of both the additional protection and fewer rights for children are a number of factors, one of which is a belief that children lack the capacity for judgment that adults (hopefully) have. This lack may arise from biological factors (neurological development and sophistication continues throughout childhood) as well as experiential ones (most children have had fewer negative experiences from which to learn "life lessons" than have adults). The belief of the lack of understanding by children of the world around them, and particularly its risks, is embedded within our language: when an adult seems unaware of what's going on around her, she is called naive, a term derived from a French term meaning "just born."

In the realm of privacy, although (as stated above) children in schools may have fewer rights when it comes to searches (at least by governmental actors), the belief that they are less sophisticated and therefore more vulnerable has informed the laws and regulations regarding the collection of personal information from them. Children can be tremendous sources of information, not only about themselves but about their

---

[1] *Exodus* 23:19.

families, and they may not understand the consequences of sharing the information with third parties. On a prosaic level, young children who are alone at home must be taught that they should not tell callers or people knocking at the door how old they are or that their parents are not present, so that they don't expose themselves to criminal activity. Similarly, whether online or offline, children and teenagers may be targeted by pedophiles who prey on their naiveté to draw them into dangerous situations. On a more extreme level, children may not fully understand the implications of actions they are asked to take, leading to some unlikely results. In January 1965, comedian Soupy Sales, the host of a daytime variety show for children on local television in New York City, told his young audience to go to their parents' wallets and purses, take the green pieces of paper, and send them to him at the station. At least some of them did, prompting audience outrage and the suspension of Mr. Sales' show.[2]

Marketers and advertisers have long understood that children are a ripe target for both outgoing sales pitches and inbound information collection, both because they have more time to consume the media through which the pitches and requests are made, and because children will actively seek to influence their parents' purchasing behavior. Popular children's entertainment properties are sponsored (financially supported) by consumer products companies,[3] and create opportunities for children to partcipate in promotions and thereby provide valuable demographic information to the sponsors. Manufacturers pay to place their goods within the actual entertainment content [i.e. think of Reese's Pieces in the movie E.T.], or even develop entertainment products based on and intended to sell the products. It is not just children who are subject to these types of marketing pitches; the term "soap opera" arose from the creation by consumer products companies like Procter and Gamble of radio and then television dramas whose content drew mainly homemaker women into regular listening and watching, during which they would be subjected to advertisements for the companies products. Children, though, are less likely to perceive and perhaps doubt the sponsors message, or at least to separate the sales pitch from the show. For their part, manufacturers and marketers have little internal pressure to limit their use of access to children and their preferences.

---

[2] SNOPES.COM: SOUPY SALES "GREEN PIECES OF PAPER," http://www.snopes.com/radiotv/tv/soupy1.asp (last visited May 8, 2012).

[3] This is by no means a new development. For example, popular Little Orphan Annie radio serial of the early Twentieth Century was sponsored by chocolate drink maker Ovaltine (Raymond William Stedman, AND A LITTLE CHILD SHALL LEAD THEM, http://thenostalgialeague.com/olmag/annie.htm (last visited May 8, 2012)), and the long-running Superman radio was presented by Kellogg's (Andrew Belonsky, WHEN SUPERMAN FOUGHT THE KKK: HOW KELLOGG'S HELPED SHAPE THE MAN OF STEEL'S "AMERICAN WAY" | DEATH AND TAXES, http://www.deathandtaxesmag.com/179040/when-superman-fought-the-kkk-how-kelloggs-helped-shape-the-man-of-steels-american-way/ (last visited May 8, 2012)).

I.   LAW AND SELF-REGULATION TO PROTECT CHILDREN'S PRIVACY

a.   Self-Regulation: The CARU Guidelines

One quasi-legal avenue through which children's exposure to advertising-embedded content has been moderated is via self-regulation, most notably the Children's Advertising Review Unit of the Better Business Bureau known as CARU. CARU has published and revised a series of guidelines for advertisers seeking to sell their wares to or through children, adjusting them as new methodologies such as interactive media came to the fore.[4] The guidelines, which generally seek protect children under 12 years of age, direct advertisers to separate advertising from content, clearly tell children what is advertising, and disclose and limit any personal information collection from the children. The section on interactive electronic media was first added to the Guidelines in 1996 and then amended to conform to COPPA (see below). The 2003 edition[5] provided the following guidance for "Interactive Electronic Media":

Making a Sale

Advertisers who transact sales with children online should make reasonable efforts in light of all available technologies to provide the person responsible for the costs of the transaction with the means to exercise control over the transaction. If there is no reasonable means provided to avoid unauthorized purchases of goods and services by children, the advertiser should enable the person responsible to cancel the order and receive full credit without incurring any charges. Advertisers should keep in mind that under existing state laws, parents may not be obligated to fulfill sales contracts entered into by their young children.

Children should always be told when they are being targeted for a sale.

If a site offers the opportunity to order or purchase any product or service, either through the use of a "click here to order" button or other on-screen means, the ordering instructions must clearly and prominently state that a child must have a parent's permission to order.

In the case of an online means of ordering, there should be a clear mechanism after the order is placed allowing the child or parent to cancel the order.

Data Collection

The ability to gather information, for marketing purposes, to tailor a site to a specific interest, etc., is part of the appeal of the interactive media to both

---

[4] CARU - Children's Advertising Review Unit, http://www.caru.org/guidelines/index.aspx (last visited May 8, 2012).

[5] CARU - Children's Advertising Review Unit, http://web.archive.org/web/20031009060622/http://www.caru.org/guidelines/#media (last visited May 8, 2012).

the advertiser and the user. Young children however, may not understand the nature of the information being sought, nor its intended uses. The solicitation of personally identifiable information from children (e.g., full names, addresses, email addresses, phone numbers) triggers special privacy and security concerns.

Therefore, in collecting information from children under 13 years of age, advertisers should adhere to the following principles:

In all cases, the information collection or tracking practices and information uses must be clearly disclosed, along with the means of correcting or removing the information. The disclosure notice should be prominent and readily accessible before any information is collected. For instance, in the case of passive tracking, the notice should be on the page where the child enters the site. A heading such as "Privacy", "Our Privacy Policy", or similar designation which allows an adult to click on to obtain additional information on the site's information collection and tracking practices and information uses is acceptable.

When personal information (such as email addresses or screen names associated with other personal information) will be publicly posted so as to enable others to communicate directly with the child online, or when the child will be able otherwise to communicate directly with others, the company must obtain prior verifiable parental consent.

When personal information will be shared or distributed to third parties, except for parties that are agents or affiliates of the company or provide support for the internal operation of the Website and that agree not to disclose or use the information for any other purpose, the company must obtain prior verifiable parental consent.

When personal information is obtained for a company's internal use, and there is no disclosure, parental consent may be obtained through the use of email coupled with some additional steps to provide assurance that the person providing the consent is the parent.

When online contact information is collected and retained to respond directly more than once to a child's specific request (such as an email newsletter or contest) and will not be used for any other purpose, the company must directly notify the parent of the nature and intended uses of the information collected, and permit access to the information sufficient to permit a parent to remove or correct the information.

In furtherance of the above principles, advertisers should adhere to the following guidelines:

The advertiser should disclose, in language easily understood by a child, why the information is being requested (e.g., "We'll use your name and email to enter you in this contest and also add it to our mailing list") and whether the information is intended to be shared, sold or distributed outside of the collecting advertiser company.

If information is collected from children through passive means (e.g., navigational tracking tools, browser files, etc.) this should be disclosed along with what information is being collected.

Advertisers should encourage the child to use an alias (e.g., "Bookworm", "Skater", etc.), first name, nickname, initials, or other alternative to full names or screen names which correspond with an email address for any activities which will involve public posting.

If the information is optional, and not required to engage in an activity, that fact should be clearly disclosed in language easily understood by a child (e.g., "You don't have to answer to play the game"). The advertiser should clearly disclose what use it will make of this information, if provided, as in #2 above, and should not require a child to disclose more personal information than is reasonably necessary to participate in the online activity (e.g., play a game, enter a contest, etc.).

The interactivity of the medium offers the opportunity to communicate with children through electronic mail. While this is part of the appeal of the medium, it creates the potential for a child to receive unmanageable amounts of unsolicited email. If an advertiser communicates with a child by email, there should be an opportunity with each mailing for the child or parent to choose by return email to discontinue receiving mailings.

In the 2011 version,[6] the differentiation between interactive and off-line activities has been reduced, given how ubiquitous online communication is to all marketing. There is, however, a specific section discussing online privacy protection:

3. Part II: Guidelines for Online Privacy Protection

This Part addresses concerns about the collection of personal data from children and other privacy-related practices on the Internet. Its provisions are consistent with the Children's Online Privacy Protection Act of 1998 (COPPA) and the FTC's implementing Rule, which protect children under the age of 13. Online data collection from children poses special concerns. The medium offers unique opportunities to interact with children and to gather information for marketing purposes. Young children however, may not understand the nature of the information being sought or its intended uses, and the medium makes it easy to collect such data directly from children without the supervision or permission of their parents or guardians. The solicitation of personally identifiable information from children (e.g., full names, addresses, email addresses, phone numbers) therefore triggers special privacy and security concerns. The guidelines below address those concerns by providing guidance on specific issues involving online data collection and other privacy-related practices by Website operators that target children under 13 years of age or that know or should know that a visitor is a child under 13 years of age.

---

[6] *Children's Advertising Review Unit*, Council of Better Business Bureau, Inc., http://www.caru.org/guidelines/guidelines.pdf (last visited Dec. 30, 2011).

(a) Data Collection

1. In collecting information from children under 13 years of age, advertisers should adhere to the following guidelines: Advertisers must clearly disclose all information collection and tracking practices, all information uses, and the means for correcting or removing the information. These disclosures should be prominent and readily accessible before any information is collected. For instance, on a Website where there is passive tracking, the notice should be on the page where the child enters the site. A heading such as "Privacy," "Our Privacy Policy," or similar designation is acceptable if it allows an adult to click on the heading to obtain additional information on the site's practices concerning information collection, tracking and uses.

2. Advertisers should disclose, in language easily understood by a child, (a) why the information is being requested (e.g., "We'll use your name and email to enter you in this contest and also add it to our mailing list") and (b) whether the information is intended to be shared, sold or distributed outside of the collecting company. Violations of this guideline may be brought to the attention of the relevant rating entity.

3. Advertisers should disclose any passive means of collecting information from children (e.g., navigational tracking tools, browser files, etc.) and what information is being collected.

4. Advertisers must obtain prior "verifiable parental consent" when they collect personal information (such as email addresses, screen names associated with other personal information, phone numbers or addresses) that will be publicly posted, thereby enabling others to communicate directly with the child online or offline, or when the child will be otherwise able to communicate directly with others.

5. For activities that involve public posting, advertisers should encourage children not to use their full names or screen names that correspond with their email address, but choose an alias (e.g., "Bookworm," "Skater," etc.) or use first name, nickname, initials, etc.

6. Advertisers should not require a child to disclose more personal information than is reasonably necessary to participate in the online activity (e.g., play a game, enter a contest, etc.).

7. Advertisers must obtain prior "verifiable parental consent" when they plan to share or distribute personal information to third parties, except parties that are agents or affiliates of the advertiser or provide support for the internal operation of the Website and that have agreed not to disclose or use the information for any other purpose.

8. When an advertiser collects personal information only for its internal use and there is no disclosure of the information, the company must obtain parental consent, and may do so through the use of email, coupled with some additional steps to provide assurance that the person providing the consent is the parent.

9. When an advertiser collects and retains online contact information to be able to respond directly more than once to a child's specific request (such as an email newsletter or contest) but will not use the information for any other purpose, the advertiser must directly notify the parent of the nature and intended uses of the information collected, and permit access to the information sufficient to allow a parent to remove or correct the information.

10. To respect the privacy of parents, advertisers should not maintain in retrievable form information collected and used for the sole purpose of obtaining verifiable parental consent or providing notice to parents, if consent is not obtained after a reasonable time.

11. If an advertiser communicates with a child by email, there should be an opportunity with each mailing for the child or parent to choose by return email or hyperlink to discontinue receiving mailings.

(b) Age-Screening/Hyperlinks

1. On Websites where there is a reasonable expectation that a significant number of children will be visiting, advertisers should employ age-screening mechanisms to determine whether verifiable parental consent or notice and opt-out is necessitated under the Data Collection provisions above.

2. Advertisers should ask screening questions in a neutral manner so as to discourage inaccurate answers from children trying to avoid parental permission requirements.

3. Age-screening mechanisms should be used in conjunction with technology, e.g., a session cookie, to help prevent underage children from going back and changing their age to circumvent age-screening.

4. Since hyperlinks can allow a child to move seamlessly from one site to another, operators of Websites for children or children's portions of general audience sites should not knowingly link to pages of other sites that do not comply with CARU's Guidelines.

These guidelines are influential, both on major companies and on regulators, but they are ultimately neither binding or judicially enforceable on their own. A marketer that does not care about Better Business Bureau approval or membership may disregard the CARU guidelines as well as complaints filed with the joint arbitration board operated by the Better Business Bureau's National Advertising Review Council[7] without legal or direct financial penalty.

Another self-regulatory method that has become more popular, particularly with the rise of the consumer Internet is the "privacy policy."[8] Essentially, the privacy policy is a public disclosure of the site owner's practices for collecting, using, and sharing personal information. The idea behind the privacy policy is that consumers can

---

[7] ADVERTISING INDUSTRY SELF-REGULATION, http://www.asrcreviews.org/ (last visited May 8, 2012).

[8] For a more detailed examination of privacy policies and the role of self-regulation in privacy, see Chapter 2.

and will make informed decisions with regard to which Web sites they frequent, and what information they provide, utilizing the information in the policy to provide the knowledge required to make good choices. In practice, this idea often falls short in a number of ways. First, consumers may not read the policies at all, making whatever information they may provide irrelevant to the choices the consumers make. Second, the policies and the disclosure they contain may simply be incomplete or inaccurate, so that even when consumers intend to make an informed choice, they cannot effectively do so. It is this latter situation, quite common in the privacy policy arena, that led to the passage of the first major federal privacy legislation focused on consumer Internet use: COPPA.

b. The Origins of COPPA

Beginning in the mid-1990s, approximately the same time that CARU was revising its guidelines to address interactive marketing children, the FTC reformed a number of annual reviews of Web sites targeting children, to compare the information in the sites were collecting with the disclosure they were providing to children. The results, unfortunately, were less than satisfactory to the FTC.[9] In the reports that the FTC issued, the Commission bemoaned the insufficient and often inaccurate disclosure that the sites provided to their youthful users. Advertising was not properly distinguished from non-advertising content, and when the sites did provide privacy policies, which wasn't always, the disclosure did not match the actual activities of the sites:

> *The Mini-Surf [a one-day review on October 14, 1997] of 126 child-oriented Web sites] was not intended to be a comprehensive survey, but a quick "snapshot" to see what child-oriented Web sites are doing to inform parents about their information gathering practices. Approximately 86 percent of the sites surveyed were collecting personally identifiable information from children — names, e-mail addresses, postal addresses and telephone numbers. Fewer than 30 percent of those sites collecting this personal data posted either a privacy policy or a confidentiality statement on their Web site. Four percent of those sites collecting personally identifiable information required parental authorization for the collection of the information.*

In addition to general reports, the Commission issued an opinion letter in July 1997[10] responding to a request by the Center for Media Education to investigate the practices of a Web site called KidsCom:

> *. . . . On May 13, 1996, the Center for Media Education (CME) filed a petition requesting that the Commission investigate and bring a law enforcement action for alleged deceptive practices in the operation of an Internet Web site called "KidsCom," then operated by SpectraCom, Inc. The site is now operated by an affiliated entity, The KidsCom Company (hereinafter, both are referred to as KidsCom). Our review of this matter indicates that certain of*

---

[9] Press Release, Federal Trade Commission, *FTC Surfs Children's Web Sites to Review Privacy Practices* (Dec. 15, 1997), http://www.ftc.gov/opa/1997/12/kids.shtm (last visited May 8, 2012).

[10] FTC: CENTER FOR MEDIA EDUCATION (July 15, 1997), http://www.ftc.gov/os/1997/07/cenmed.htm (last visited May 8, 2012).

KidsCom's practices likely violated Section 5 of the Federal Trade Commission Act. For several reasons, including the fact that KidsCom has modified its conduct, we have decided not to recommend enforcement action at this time. To provide guidance in this area, however, we are providing our analysis of the practices involved in this Web site, and are setting forth several broad principles we believe apply generally to online information collection from children.

BACKGROUND

KidsCom is a Web site that describes itself as "[a] Communications Playground for kids ages 4 to 15." Children with a computer, a modem, and a Web browser can access KidsCom through the Internet.(2)

At the time of your petition, when children first accessed the KidsCom site, they were required to register by completing the "Who Do You Wanna Be?" survey, which requested them to answer a number of questions about themselves, including their name, sex, birthday, e-mail address, home address, number of family members, and grade.(3) They then had access to the rest of the site, which consisted of a number of connected activity sections including, among others, "Find A Key Pal," which matched children for e-mail "pen pal" correspondence; the "Graffiti Wall," a chat room for children; "KidsKash Questions," which provided an opportunity to earn KidsKash points used to redeem prizes at the "Loot Locker;" and "New Stuff For Kids," which provided information about various new products. In the "KidsKash Questions" portion of the site, children were asked to provide their full name and e-mail address and to answer questions about their product and activity preferences.

This letter addresses two issues raised by CME's petition with regard to KidsCom's practices. First, the petition alleges that the KidsCom site was used to solicit personal information from children in a deceptive manner. It charges that KidsCom failed to fully and accurately disclose the purpose for which it collected the information and the uses that it made of it. Second, the petition asserts that KidsCom deceptively portrayed KidsCom as independently and objectively endorsing products, when in fact the "endorsements" were essentially disguised advertising.

THE COLLECTION OF PERSONAL INFORMATION

The staff has conducted an investigation of KidsCom's collection and use of children's personal information through the KidsCom Web site,(4) and concluded that certain of KidsCom's information practices may have violated Section 5 of the Federal Trade Commission Act.

Deception

The "KidsKash Questions" area of the Web site awarded "KidsKash" to children who answer surveys containing detailed questions regarding, among other things, their preferences with respect to specific products. These surveys were optional. Information collected from some of these surveys was provided to private companies on an aggregate, anonymous basis.(5)

As you know, Section 5 of the Federal Trade Commission Act ("FTC Act"), 15 U.S.C. 45, prohibits unfair and deceptive practices that are in or affecting commerce. A representation, omission or practice is deceptive if it is likely to mislead reasonable consumers in a material fashion.(6) When KidsCom collected information at the KidsKash Questions area, it represented that the information collection would enable the children to earn premiums, but did not also disclose the marketing uses of this information. It is a deceptive practice to represent that a Web site is collecting personally identifiable information from a child for a particular purpose (e.g., to earn points to redeem a premium), when the information will also be used for another purpose which parents would find material,(7) in the absence of a clear and prominent disclosure to that effect.(8)

Moreover, in order to be effective, any disclosure regarding collection and use of children's personally identifiable information must be made to a parent, given the limited ability of many children within the target audience to comprehend such information. While the KidsCom site, from time to time, did feature notices advising children to seek parental consent before participating in KidsCom or completing surveys, we agree with petitioner that these disclosures were inadequate to notify children or parents that the personally identifiable information solicited was intended for marketing research purposes.

An adequate notice to parents should disclose: who is collecting the personally identifiable information, what information is being collected, its intended use(s), to whom and in what form it will be disclosed to third parties, and the means by which parents may prevent the retention, use or disclosure of the information.(9)

Unfairness

On the KidsCom site, the "Who Do You Wanna Be?" registration survey asked questions about children's preferences and was mandatory for gaining access to most other portions of the site. Some of the information collected at this area of the site was used in the site's Key Pal (online pen pal) program, if the child wanted to participate in that activity. Thus, a child's first name, age, e-mail address and areas of interest were made available to other registrants, in order that they could become "key pals."(10)

A practice is unfair under Section 5 if it causes, or is likely to cause, substantial injury to consumers which is not reasonably avoidable and is not outweighed by countervailing benefits to consumers or competition.(11) We believe that it would likely be an unfair practice in violation of Section 5 to collect personally identifiable information, such as name, e-mail address, home address or phone number, from children and sell or otherwise disclose such identifiable information to third parties without providing parents with adequate notice, as described above, and an opportunity to control the collection and use of the information. As we learned at the recent Privacy

Workshop, the release of children's personally identifiable information to third parties creates a risk of injury or exploitation of the children so identified.(12) The release of children's information through the KidsCom Key Pal program, without providing parents with adequate notice and an opportunity to control the information, raised just such risks. For example, it is possible that an adult posing as a child could have used the Key Pal program to contact a child directly. In such a circumstance, we believe that before releasing individually identifiable data about children, the company should obtain parental consent.

PRODUCT ENDORSEMENTS

CME's petition also alleges that the "New Stuff for Kids" section of KidsCom contained deceptive product endorsements. In that section, KidsCom posted information about various products along with the following statement:

KidsCom kids said that they want to know about new things just for kids . . . So we will post updates for you here as we get them. And, if you want us to do some investigative snooping on something of interest to you . . . [j]ust e-mail us . . . and we will do our best to find it out for you.

The petition asserts that KidsCom represented that the information contained in New Stuff for Kids constituted an independent and objective endorsement of the featured products. In fact, according to the petition, KidsCom solicited new product press releases from manufacturers for this section, and required manufacturers to donate products valuing at least $1,000 to obtain the "endorsement." It appears that the donated products may have been used as prizes purchased by children with the KidsKash they earned.

The passing off of an advertisement as an independent review or endorsement is a deceptive practice under Section 5 of the FTC Act. This is based on the common sense notion that independent product evaluations are material to consumers, i.e., that consumers reading what appears to be an independent review or news report about a product are likely to give it more credence than they would give what they know to be an advertisement.(13) KidsCom's practice of portraying the product information in the New Stuff for Kids section as stemming from an independent appraisal, and its failure to clearly and conspicuously disclose in a manner understandable to children that the information was solicited from the manufacturers and printed in exchange for in-kind payment, was likely to mislead reasonable consumers.

CONCLUSIONS

Notwithstanding our belief that the practices identified above likely violated Section 5, we are not recommending that the Commission take enforcement action at this time. This decision is based on several factors.

First, KidsCom has modified its Web site in significant respects. KidsCom now sends an e-mail to parents when children register at the site, providing notice of its collection practices. Parents are provided with the option to object to release of information to third parties on an aggregate, anonymous basis. Most importantly, KidsCom does not release personally identifiable information (in the form of Key Pal information) to third parties without prior parental approval. KidsCom currently requires that parents return by facsimile or postal mail a signed authorization. KidsCom also now discloses to the site visitor the purposes for which it is collecting the information. With regard to the deceptive endorsements, KidsCom has eliminated the statement quoted in the previous section regarding the product evaluations and expressly states (when this is the fact) that the products' descriptions are obtained from the manufacturer. Additionally, KidsCom has introduced The Ad Bug™, a cartoon icon, which together with other textual material is designed to identify the presence of advertising in the New Stuff for Kids section and other site locations.

Second, there is no evidence that KidsCom at any time released any personally identifiable information to third parties for commercial marketing or any other purposes (other than for the Key Pal program). Such practices would have been of particular concern in light of the absence of adequate disclosure and prior parental consent.

Third, the collection of information from children on the Internet is widespread. Thus, the legal principles implicated here have broader application to other marketers. In light of the rapidly growing technological development and commercial expansion on the Internet, we believe that it is appropriate to issue this letter to provide notice of our interpretation of the relevant legal standard.

In light of the foregoing, the staff has determined not to recommend that the Commission initiate a law enforcement action against KidsCom at this time. We will continue to monitor KidsCom, as well as other commercial Web site operators, to ascertain whether they may be engaged in deceptive or unfair practices. Hereafter, staff may recommend law enforcement proceedings against marketers who engage in deceptive information practices, or who unfairly use personally identifiable information collected from children.

We encourage your continued participation in developing the issues and solutions to protecting privacy online. Petitions from groups such as yours are a helpful means of reviewing possible unfair or deceptive practices, and we hope you will continue to bring to our attention any advertising or marketing campaign that you believe may violate the FTC Act.

In its first few reports, the Commission suggested strongly that should the sites not improve their information collection and disclosure practices, the Commission would request of Congress legislation to mandate such improvement. Ultimately, that's exactly what the FTC did: in its June 1998 report to Congress, "Privacy Online,"[11] the Commission described yet another survey of Web sites, including those oriented

---

[11] TABLE OF CONTENTS, http://www.ftc.gov/reports/privacy3/toc.shtm (last visited May 8, 2012) [notes omitted].

toward children, and their information practices. In the report's conclusion, the FTC made new recommendations for legislation:

A medical clinic's online doctor-referral service invites consumers to submit their name, postal address, e-mail address, insurance company, any comments concerning their medical problems, and to indicate whether they wish to receive information on any of a number of topics, including urinary incontinence, hypertension, cholesterol, prostate cancer, and diabetes. The online application for the clinic's health education membership program asks consumers to submit their name, address, telephone number, date of birth, marital status, gender, insurance company, and the date and location of their last hospitalization. The clinic's Web site says nothing about how the information consumers provide will be used or whether it will be made available to third parties.

An automobile dealership's Web site offers help to consumers in rebuilding their credit ratings. To take advantage of this offer, consumers are urged to provide their name, address, Social Security number, and telephone number through the Web site's online information form. The Web site says nothing about how the information provided will be used or whether it will be made available to third parties.

A mortgage company operates an online prequalification service for home loans. The online application form requires that each potential borrower provide his or her name, Social Security number, home and business telephone numbers, e-mail address, previous address, type of loan sought, current and former employer's name and address, length of employment, income, sources of funds to be applied toward closing, and approximate total in savings. The online form also requires the borrower to provide information about his or her credit history, including credit card, car loans, child support and other indebtedness, and to state whether he or she has ever filed for bankruptcy. The application form requires the borrower to agree that the mortgage company may disclose his or her "credit experiences" to third parties, but the Web site says nothing else about how the mortgage company might use all of the information provided or whether that information will be made available to third parties.

A child-directed site collects personal information, such as a child's full name, postal address, e-mail address, gender, and age. The Web site also asks a child extensive personal finance questions, such as whether a child has received gifts in the form of stocks, cash, savings bonds, mutual funds, or certificates of deposit; who has given a child these gifts; whether a child puts monetary gifts into mutual funds, stocks or bonds; and whether a child's parents own mutual funds. Elsewhere on the Web site, contest winners' full names, age, city, state, and zip code are posted. The Web site does not tell children to ask their parents for permission before providing personal information and does not appear to take any steps to involve parents. Further, the Web site says nothing about whether the information is disclosed to third parties.

Another child-directed site collects personal information to register for a chat room, including a child's full name, e-mail address, city, state, gender, age, and hobbies. The Web site has a lotto contest that asks for a child's full name and e-mail address. Lotto contest winners' full names are posted on the site. For children who wish to find an electronic pen pal, the site offers a bulletin board service that posts messages, including children's e-mail addresses. While the Web site says it asks children to post messages if they are looking for a pen pal, in fact, anyone of any age can visit this bulletin board and contact a child directly. The site also has an area where children can submit stories online. The Web site posts the stories along with children's full names, ages, and e-mail addresses. The Web site does not tell children to ask their parents for permission before providing personal information and does not say that it takes steps to involve parents. The Web site says nothing about whether the information is disclosed to third parties.

*   *   *

The practices of these Web sites demonstrate the real need for implementing the basic fair information practices described in this report. The World Wide Web provides a host of opportunities for businesses to gather a vast array of personal information from and about consumers, including children. The online environment and the advent of the computer age also provide unprecedented opportunities for the compilation, analysis, and dissemination of such information. While American businesses have always collected some information from consumers in order to facilitate transactions, the Internet allows for the efficient, inexpensive collection of a vast amount of information. It is the prevalence, ease, and relative low cost of such information collection that distinguishes the online environment from more traditional means of commerce and information collection and thus raises consumer concerns.

The federal government currently has limited authority over the collection and dissemination of personal data collected online. The Federal Trade Commission Act (the "FTC Act" or "Act") prohibits unfair and deceptive practices in and affecting commerce. The Act authorizes the Commission to seek injunctive and other equitable relief, including redress, for violations of the Act, and provides a basis for government enforcement of certain fair information practices. For instance, failure to comply with stated information practices may constitute a deceptive practice in certain circumstances, and the Commission would have authority to pursue the remedies available under the Act for such violations. Furthermore, in certain circumstances, information practices may be inherently deceptive or unfair, regardless of whether the entity has publicly adopted any fair information practice policies. As discussed above, Commission staff has issued an opinion letter addressing the possible unfairness inherent in collecting certain personal identifying information from children online and transferring it to third parties without obtaining prior parental consent. However, as a general matter, the Commission lacks authority to require firms to adopt information practice policies.

The Commission has encouraged industry to address consumer concerns regarding online privacy through self-regulation. The Internet is a rapidly changing marketplace. Effective self-regulation remains desirable because it allows firms to respond quickly to technological changes and employ new technologies to protect consumer privacy. Accordingly, a private-sector response to consumer concerns that incorporates widely-accepted fair information practices and provides for effective enforcement mechanisms could afford consumers adequate privacy protection. To date, however, the Commission has not seen an effective self-regulatory system emerge.

As evidenced by the Commission's survey results, and despite the Commission's three-year privacy initiative supporting a self-regulatory response to consumers' privacy concerns, the vast majority of online businesses have yet to adopt even the most fundamental fair information practice (notice/ awareness). Moreover, the trade association guidelines submitted to the Commission do not reflect industry acceptance of the basic fair information practice principles. In addition, the guidelines, with limited exception, contain none of the enforcement mechanisms needed for an effective self-regulatory regime. In light of the lack of notice regarding information practices on the World Wide Web and the lack of current industry guidelines adequate to establish an effective self-regulatory regime, the question is what additional incentives are required in order to encourage effective self-regulatory efforts by industry. The Commission currently is considering this question in light of the survey results, monitoring self-regulation efforts since the survey was completed, and assessing the utility and effectiveness of different courses of action. This summer, the Commission will make recommendations on actions it deems necessary to protect online consumers generally.

In the specific area of children's online privacy, however, the Commission now recommends that Congress develop legislation placing parents in control of the online collection and use of personal information from their children. Such legislation would set out the basic standards of practice governing the online collection and use of information from children. All commercial Web sites directed to children would be required to comply with these standards . . . .

In making this recommendation, the Commission has drawn on its extensive experience in addressing business practices affecting children, as well as its three-year study of online privacy issues. The Commission has already taken some steps, particularly the release of the staff opinion letter, to address online information practices involving children that may violate Section 5 of the Federal Trade Commission Act. Moreover, the Commission has recognized a growing consensus reflected in consumer survey evidence and some industry self-regulatory guidelines that parental involvement is necessary in the collection and use of information from children. Nonetheless, Section 5 may only have application to some but not all of the practices that raise concern about the online collection and use of information from children. The Commission does not believe, for example, that Section 5 necessarily authorizes it to require parental notice and involvement across the board for all commercial Web sites engaged in information collection from children. Accordingly, the Commission concludes that as a matter of policy additional steps should now be taken to ensure adequate online privacy protections for children.

Children's privacy legislation also would recognize that a marketer's responsibilities vary with the age of the child from whom personal information is sought. In a commercial context, Congress and industry self-regulatory bodies traditionally have distinguished between children aged 12 and under, who are particularly vulnerable to overreaching by marketers, and children over the age of 12, for whom strong, but more flexible protections may be appropriate. In each case, the goal of legislative requirements should be to recognize the parents' role with respect to information collection from children.

Accordingly, the Commission recommends that Congress develop legislation to require commercial Web sites that collect personal identifying information from children 12 and under to provide actual notice to the parent and obtain parental consent as follows:

Where the personal identifying information would enable someone to contact a child **offline**, *the company must obtain prior parental consent, regardless of the intended use of the information (opt-in);*

Where the personal identifying information is **publicly posted or disclosed to third parties**, *the company must obtain prior parental consent (opt-in);*

Where collection of an e-mail address is necessary for a child's participation at a site, such as to notify contest winners, the company must provide notice to parents and an opportunity to remove the e-mail address from the site's database (opt-out).

Where the personal identifying information is collected from children over 12, the Commission recommends that:

Web sites must provide parents with notice of the collection of such information and an opportunity to remove the information from the site's database (opt-out).

The development of the online marketplace is at a critical juncture. If growing consumer concerns about online privacy are not addressed, electronic commerce will not reach its full potential. To date, industry has had only limited success in implementing fair information practices and adopting self-regulatory regimes with respect to the online collection, use, and dissemination of personal information. Accordingly, the Commission now recommends legislation to protect children online and this summer will recommend an appropriate response to protect the privacy of all online consumers.[12]

With the input of the Commission, Congress enacted COPPA, 15 U.S.C. §§ 6501–6508, in October 1998, with the law going into effect 18 months later.

II. REQUIREMENTS OF COPPA

COPPA and its accompanying regulations[13] prohibit, as an unfair practice, collecting personally identifiable information from children under the age of 13 without "verifiable parental consent." What is more difficult, and what has gotten even large, sophisticated companies into expensive trouble, is how"verifiable parental consent" is defined, since the statute itself expressly does not dictate the means:

> *The term "verifiable parental consent" means any reasonable effort (taking into consideration available technology), including a request for authorization for future collection, use, and disclosure described in the notice, to ensure that a parent of a child receives notice of the operator's personal information collection, use, and disclosure practices, and authorizes the collection, use, and disclosure, as applicable, of personal information and the subsequent use of that information before that information is collected from that child.*[14]

In its regulations implementing COPPA,[15] the FTC expanded somewhat on the means through which site owners could obtain verifiable parental consent:

> *. . . (b) Mechanisms for verifiable parental consent.*
>
> *(1) An operator must make reasonable efforts to obtain verifiable parental consent, taking into consideration available technology. Any method to obtain verifiable parental consent must be reasonably calculated, in light of available technology, to ensure that the person providing consent is the child's parent.*
>
> *(2) Methods to obtain verifiable parental consent that satisfy the requirements of this paragraph include: providing a consent form to be signed by the parent and returned to the operator by postal mail or facsimile; requiring a parent to use a credit card in connection with a transaction; having a parent call a toll-free telephone number staffed by trained personnel; using a digital certificate that uses public key technology; and using e-mail accompanied by a PIN or password obtained through one of the verification methods listed in this paragraph. Provided that: Until the Commission otherwise determines, methods to obtain verifiable parental consent for uses of information other than the "disclosures" defined by § 312.2*[16] *may also include use of e-mail*

---

[12] CONCLUSION, *http://www.ftc.gov/reports/privacy3/conclu.shtm (last visited May 8, 2012).*

[13] 16 C.F.R. § 312 (2000).

[14] 16 U.S.C. § 6501(9) (2003).

[15] 16 C.F.R. § 312 et seq.

[16] As defined in that regulation,

coupled with additional steps to provide assurances that the person providing the consent is the parent. Such additional steps include: sending a confirmatory e-mail to the parent following receipt of consent; or obtaining a postal address or telephone number from the parent and confirming the parent's consent by letter or telephone call. Operators who use such methods must provide notice that the parent can revoke any consent given in response to the earlier e-mail.

(c) Exceptions to prior parental consent. Verifiable parental consent is required prior to any collection, use and/or disclosure of personal information from a child except as set forth in this paragraph. The exceptions to prior parental consent are as follows:

(1) Where the operator collects the name or online contact information of a parent or child to be used for the sole purpose of obtaining parental consent or providing notice [of its privacy practices] under § 312.4. If the operator has not obtained parental consent after a reasonable time from the date of the information collection, the operator must delete such information from its records;

(2) Where the operator collects online contact information from a child for the sole purpose of responding directly on a one-time basis to a specific request from the child, and where such information is not used to recontact the child and is deleted by the operator from its records;

(3) Where the operator collects online contact information from a child to be used to respond directly more than once to a specific request from the child, and where such information is not used for any other purpose. In such cases, the operator must make reasonable efforts, taking into consideration available technology, to ensure that a parent receives notice and has the opportunity to request that the operator make no further use of the information . . . immediately after the initial response and before making any additional response to the child. Mechanisms to provide such notice include, but are not limited to, sending the notice by postal mail or sending the notice to the parent's e-mail address, but do not include asking a child to print a notice form or sending an e-mail to the child;

(4) Where the operator collects a child's name and online contact information to the extent reasonably necessary to protect the safety of a child participant on the website or online service, and the operator uses reasonable

---

Disclosure means, with respect to personal information:

(a) The release of personal information collected from a child in identifiable form by an operator for any purpose, except where an operator provides such information to a person who provides support for the internal operations of the website or online service and who does not disclose or use that information for any other purpose . . .; or

(b) Making personal information collected from a child by an operator publicly available in identifiable form, by any means, including by a public posting through the Internet, or through a personal home page posted on a website or online service; a pen pal service; an electronic mail service; a message board; or a chat room.

efforts to provide a parent notice . . . , where such information is:

(i) Used for the sole purpose of protecting the child's safety;

(ii) Not used to recontact the child or for any other purpose;

(iii) Not disclosed on the website or online service; and

(5) Where the operator collects a child's name and online contact information and such information is not used for any other purpose, to the extent reasonably necessary:

(i) To protect the security or integrity of its website or online service;

(ii) To take precautions against liability;

(iii) To respond to judicial process; or

(iv) To the extent permitted under other provisions of law, to provide information to law enforcement agencies or for an investigation on a matter related to public safety.

A number of groups, including CARU, have successfully sought the FTC's designation[17] as "safe harbors," through which the groups' own certification programs are deemed sufficient to demonstrate COPPA compliance. The vast majority of sites, however, have not taken advantage of these safe harbors, and even large corporations have been sued and fined by the FTC for failing to fulfill COPPA's "verifiable parental consent" requirement. Such enforcement began soon after COPPA went into effect in 2000:

April 22, 2002 News Release: FTC Protecting Children's Privacy Online

. . . . The Ohio Art Company, manufacturer of the Etch-A-Sketch drawing toy, will pay $35,000 to settle Federal Trade Commission charges that it violated the Children's Online Privacy Protection Rule by collecting personal information from children on its www.etch-a-sketch Web site without first obtaining parental consent. The settlement also bars future violations of the COPPA Rule. This is the FTC's sixth COPPA law enforcement case.

The FTC alleges that The Ohio Art Company collected personal information from children registering for "Etchy's Birthday Club." The site collected the names, mailing addresses, e-mail addresses, age, and date of birth from children who wanted to qualify to win an Etch-A-Sketch toy on their birthday. The FTC charged that the company merely directed children to "get your parent or guardian's permission first," and then collected the information without first obtaining parental consent as required by the law. In addition, the FTC alleged that the company collected more information from children than was reasonably necessary for children to participate in the "birthday club" activity, and that the site's privacy policy statement did not

---

[17] *Safe Harbor Program: BCP Business Program*, Federal Trade Commission, Safe Harbor Program | BCP Business Center, http://business.ftc.gov/content/safe-harbor-program (last visited May 8, 2012).

clearly or completely disclose all of its information collection practices or make certain disclosures required by COPPA. The site also failed to provide parents the opportunity to review the personal information collected from their children and to inform them of their ability to prevent the further collection and use of this information, the FTC alleged.[18]

Even after a number of well-publicized cases involving major consumer brands in the subsequent years (including $1,000,000 fines paid by social networking site Xanga.com in 2006[19] and Sony BMG Music in 2008[20]), the FTC has continued to identify and punish COPPA violations, including against apparel marketer Iconix in October 2009:

Iconix Brand Group Settles Charges Its Apparel Web Sites Violated Children's Online Privacy Protection Act Company Will Pay $250,000 Civil Penalty

Iconix Brand Group, Inc. will pay a $250,000 civil penalty to settle Federal Trade Commission charges that it violated the Children's Online Privacy Protection Act (COPPA) and the FTC's COPPA Rule by knowingly collecting, using, or disclosing personal information from children online without first obtaining their parents' permission.

Iconix owns, licenses, and markets — both offline and online — several popular apparel brands that appeal to children and teens, including Mudd, Candie's, Bongo, and OP. Iconix required consumers on many of its brand-specific Web sites to provide personal information, such as full name, e-mail address, zip code, and in some cases mailing address, gender, and phone number — as well as date of birth — in order to receive brand updates, enter sweepstakes contests, and participate in interactive brand-awareness campaigns and other Web site features. Since 2006, Iconix knowingly collected and stored personal information from approximately 1,000 children without first notifying their parents or obtaining parental consent, according to the FTC's complaint. On one Web site, MyMuddWorld.com, Iconix also enabled girls to publicly share personal stories and photos online, according to the complaint.

"Companies must provide parents with the opportunity to say 'no thanks' to the collection and disclosure of their children's personal information," said FTC Chairman Jon Leibowitz. "Children's privacy is paramount, and Iconix really missed the boat by denying parents control over their kids' information online."

COPPA requires operators of Web sites directed to children under 13 years old that collect personal information from them — and operators of general audience Web

---

[18] *FTC Protecting Children's Privacy Online, Federal Trade Commission (Apr. 22, 2002),* COPPA ANNIVERSARY, *http://www.ftc.gov/opa/2002/04/coppaanniv.shtm (last visited May 8, 2012).*

[19] Press Release, Federal Trade Commission, XANGA.COM TO PAY $1 MILLION FOR VIOLATING CHILDREN'S ONLINE PRIVACY PROTECTION RULE (Sept. 7, 2006), http://www.ftc.gov/opa/2006/09/xanga.shtm (last visited May 8, 2012).

[20] Press Release, Federal Trade Commission, SONY BMG MUSIC SETTLES CHARGES ITS MUSIC FAN WEBSITES VIOLATED THE CHILDREN'S ONLINE PRIVACY PROTECTION ACT (Dec. 11, 2008), http://www.ftc.gov/opa/2008/12/sonymusic.shtm (last visited May 8, 2012).

sites that knowingly collect personal information from children under 13 — to notify parents and obtain their consent before collecting, using, or disclosing any such information. One requirement of the COPPA Rule is that Web site operators post a privacy policy that is clear, understandable, and complete.

The Commission's complaint also charges Iconix with violating both COPPA and the Federal Trade Commission Act by falsely stating in its privacy policy that it would not seek to collect personal information from children without obtaining prior parental consent, and that it would delete any children's personal information about which it became aware. According to the FTC complaint, Iconix knowingly collected personal information from children without obtaining prior parental consent and did not delete it.

The settlement order requires Iconix to pay a $250,000 civil penalty. The order also specifically prohibits Iconix from violating any provision of the FTC's COPPA Rule, and requires the company to delete all personal information collected and maintained in violation of COPPA. The company is required to distribute the order and the FTC's "How to Comply with the Children's Online Privacy Protection Rule" to company personnel. The order also contains standard compliance, reporting, and record-keeping provisions to help ensure the company abides by its terms.

To provide resources to parents and their children about COPPA and about children's privacy in general, the order requires the company to link to the Commission's www.OnGuardOnline.gov Web site on any Iconix Web site that collects or discloses children's personal information, and on any Iconix site that offers the opportunity to upload writings or images, to create publicly viewable user profiles, or to interact online with other Iconix site visitors . . . .[21]

III.   COPPA, THE FTC, AND THE EVOLUTION OF NEW TECHNOLOGIES

From the outset, COPPA was designed to be as technology-neutral as possible, not only in the requirements for "verifiable parental consent" but in its definitions of the media to which it applies:

(6) Internet

The term "Internet" means collectively the myriad of computer and telecommunications facilities, including equipment and operating software, which comprise the interconnected world-wide network of networks that employ the Transmission Control Protocol/Internet Protocol, or any predecessor or successor protocols to such protocol, to communicate information of all kinds by wire or radio . . . .

(10) Website or online service directed to children

---

[21] Press Release, Federal Trade Commission, Iconix Brand Group Settles Charges Its Apparel Web Sites Violated Children's Online Privacy Protection Act *(Oct. 20, 2009), http://www.ftc.gov/opa/2009/10/ iconix.shtm (last visited May 8, 2012).*

(A) In general

The term "website or online service directed to children" means —

(i) a commercial website or online service that is targeted to children; or

(ii) that portion of a commercial website or online service that is targeted to children.

(B) Limitation

A commercial website or online service, or a portion of a commercial website or online service, shall not be deemed directed to children solely for referring or linking to a commercial website or online service directed to children by using information location tools, including a directory, index, reference, pointer, or hypertext link.[22]

As flexible as these definitions are, they may still not be sufficient to cover new technologies, or new uses of then-existing technologies such as the Internet or cellular phones. To address this reality and other changing circumstances, the FTC has undertaken periodic reviews of COPPA, as required by statute[23] as well as its own standard practice regarding its regulations. In the case of COPPA, though, the FTC accelerated its usual every-10-year-review:

An Examination of Children's Privacy: New Technology and the Children's Online Privacy Protection Act

. . . . In 2005, the Commission commenced a statutorily required review of its experience in enforcing COPPA. Specifically, Congress directed the Commission to evaluate: (1) operators' practices as they relate to the collection, use, and disclosure of children's information, (2) children's ability to obtain access to the online information of their choice; and (3) the availability of websites directed to children. At the same time, the Commission sought public comment on the costs and benefits of the Rule, including whether any modifications to the Rule were needed in light of changes in technology or in the marketplace.

After completing that review, in 2007 the Commission reported to Congress that, in keeping with the legislative intent, the Rule: (1) played a role in improving operators' information collection practices and providing children with greater online protections than in the era prior to its implementation; (2) provided parents with a set of effective tools for becoming involved in and overseeing their children's interactions online; and (3) did not overly burden operators' abilities to provide interactive online content for children. Accordingly, the Commission concluded that there was a continuing need for those protections, and that the Rule should be retained without change. At that time, the Commission also acknowledged that children's growing embrace of mobile Internet technology and interactive general audience sites, including social networking sites, without the concomitant development of suitable

---

[22] 16 U.S.C. § 6501 (2003).

[23] 15 U.S.C. § 6506(1) (1998).

age-verification technologies, presented challenges for COPPA compliance and enforcement.

Although the Commission generally reviews its rules approximately every ten years, the continued rapid-fire pace of technological change, including an explosion in children's use of mobile devices and participation in interactive gaming, and the possibility of interactive television, led the agency to accelerate its COPPA review by five years, to [2010]. Accordingly, on March 24, 2010, the Commission announced the start of a public comment period aimed at gathering input on a wide range of issues relating to the COPPA Rule, including:

- *The implications for COPPA enforcement raised by mobile communications, interactive television, interactive gaming, and other similar interactive media and whether the Rule's definition of "Internet" adequately encompasses these technologies;*

- *Whether operators have the ability, using persistent IP addresses, mobile geolocation data, or information collected from children online in connection with behavioral advertising, to contact specific individuals, and whether the Rule's definition of "personal information" should be expanded accordingly;*

- *How the use of centralized authentication methods (such as OpenId) will affect individual websites' COPPA compliance efforts;27*

- *Whether there are additional technological methods to obtain verifiable parental consent that should be added to the COPPA Rule, and whether any of the methods currently included should be removed; and*

- *Whether parents are exercising their rights under the Rule to review or delete personal information collected from their children, and what challenges operators face in authenticating parents.*[24]

Unsurprisingly, among the comments the FTC received during this review were those from major online communities which argued against the need for additional or revised COPPA standards:

July 12, 2010 Comments by Facebook, Inc. on COPPA Review

. . . . Facebook started in 2004 as a social networking site for college and university students. Over time, our users grew to include teens and adults. While you must be 13 years of age or older to join Facebook, we take our responsibility to safeguard the Internet's youngest users seriously, and built the service with COPPA in mind. Accordingly, we require those attempting to enter Facebook.com for the first time to type in their age on the very first screen. This birth date field prevents children who indicate that they are under the age of 13 from establishing an account, and the technology places a persistent cookie on the device used to attempt to establish an account, preventing the user from modifying their birth date on a subsequent attempt.

---

[24] Federal Trade Commission, An Examination of Children's Privacy: New Technology and The Children's Online Privacy Protection Act *(Apr. 29, 2010), http://www.ftc.gov/os/testimony/100429coppastatement.pdf.*

When Facebook becomes aware of accounts established by children under 13, we terminate those accounts and delete all the information uploaded by that account holder. Facebook has also participated in many online safety initiatives around the world, such as the US State Attorneys General Internet Technical Task Force, the UK Home Office Task Force on Child Safety, the EU Safer Internet initiative, the Australia Attorney General's Online Safety Working Group and others.

In enacting COPPA, Congress sought to "enhance parental involvement in a child's online activities" to protect their privacy and safety online "in a manner that preserves the interactivity of children's experience on the Internet and preserves children's access to information in this rich and valuable medium." The Rule respects and promotes the Congressional goal of enhancing child safety on the Internet without undermining interacting, constraining content creation, or chilling innovation, and should be retained in its current form. In our experience, the current Rule gives the Commission sufficient flexibility to respond to changes in technology that affect online privacy and safety. Material expansion of the Rule, in particular, by expanding coverage to teens, imposing liability based on a "constructive knowledge" standard, or by stretching the definition of personal information to encompass the use of non-personally identifiable information to provide an anonymous but tailored user experience — would both be inconsistent with the intent of Congress and likely to undermine the goals of COPPA by discouraging ongoing private sector innovation to identify new and better ways to promote child online safety and privacy. Rather, Facebook encourages the Commission to use this Rule review to promote responsible exploration of new ways to enhance parental involvement, secure parental consent, and educate children and parents about online privacy and safety. Further, Facebook encourages the Commission to use this Rule review to incentivize the creation of more effective privacy safeguards for the online environment and to facilitate the introduction of innovative mechanisms for acquiring parental consent when required by the statute . . . .[25]

By contrast, others suggested that substantive changes were needed. Given the global reach of the Internet, some of these suggestions came from outside the United States, even though the FTC's regulations and federal law do not directly apply outside our borders.

European NGO Alliance for Child Safety Online Submission to the FTC Review of the COPPA Rule

The internet is not what it was

When the COPPA Rule was first formulated the internet was still an edgy arriviste. Today in many countries broadband is spoken of as the fourth utility, essential to modern living in the same way as access to gas, electricity and running water.

Moreover it is now apparent that the demand for internet access and services has moved into and become a permanent feature of a highly diverse range of markets.

---

[25] COMMENTS OF FACEBOOK IN RESPONSE TO FTC REQUEST FOR COMMENTS ON COPPA RULE REVIEW *(Jul. 12, 2010), http://www.ftc.gov/os/comments/copparulerev2010/547597-00079.html (last visited May 8, 2012).*

Some of these markets are not obvious or easy bedfellows. It is becoming increasingly difficult to imagine how they can continue to be governed by the same set of rules and expectations.

An obvious and potentially useful line of demarcation is between internet connectivity and internet services which are sold into or are used in overwhelmingly adult environments e.g. at work or within Universities or research institutes, and those which operate largely in domestic settings where families with children are perhaps the largest segment. Very often in both environments one will be accessing services or sites where the age of the person is completely irrelevant. But in others it will be relevant. That is where the unresolved difficulty still lies.

So how did we get here?

When the COPPA rule was first formulated there were comparatively few policymakers or public commentators around, mainstream journalists and the like, in the USA and elsewhere, who felt they understood the internet sufficiently to question some of the then rapidly evolving, rapidly changing practices associated with the emergence of the new medium. No one really wanted to jump in with strict or close regulation for fear of choking off growth in the brave new world that seemed to be opening up. Fewer still felt confident enough to challenge the powerful, rich companies and their highly technically literate spokespeople who were assiduously promoting the internet, marketing it as a democratic agent of liberation, a symbol of modernity, an endless source of fun and games, culture, knowledge, even wisdom. The internet was the ultimate in cool. Doubters, critical questioners were dismissed or marginalized as fuddy duddy Luddites or spoilsports who just didn't get it. We were dazzled by the sheer scale, ambition and evident financial success of the new technological behemoths that were clearly on a fast track to Master of the Universe status.

Today the halo that hovered over Silicon Valley hasn't entirely evaporated but it's a lot thinner than it was. Many aspects of how the internet works are more settled, even if innovation around the edges continues apace. Certainly there are lots more people, particularly in the public policy space, who can now disentangle the hype from the reality, who understand the technology and are more ready to query the claims and the business practices of internet companies, just as they would do any other industrial or commercial sector.

In 2010 the internet is many different things but part of it is unquestionably a consumer commodity. Individual online services and internet connectivity packages are frequently promoted by advertisements in mainstream family media, often linked to such things as cable TV packages, sometimes sold or presented in brightly coloured eyecatching boxes in shops on the High Street, displayed on shelves next to kettles and radio alarm clocks. We need to start thinking about the internet and online services in those terms.

Above all we need to stop thinking about the internet as if it were, essentially, an adult medium for which special (meaning "irritating") provisions need to be made to take account of the fact that children will use it from time to time. Children and young people are a large, persistent and permanent group of internet users. They need to be central to all of our thinking about how we evolve policy across the whole of the space.

The internet is now more akin to a modern city. In the modern city we have planning and zoning laws to govern who can do what, and where and when they can do it. We have laws about who can buy and consume different products and services. We need to put much more effort into developing cyber equivalents. We need to embrace the internet wholeheartedly as a social place, populated and used by many different interests of which families with children are one, and not the least one.

It is pointless and dispiriting for internet company executives and Government officials to continue repeating the mantra about how everyone accepts that what is legal in the real world is legal in the online world, and what is illegal in one is equally illegal in the other when we have hitherto so very obviously failed to match that rhetoric with the reality.

A new legal obligation?

In our view every technology company should be put under a legally binding, explicit obligation to carry out a child safety audit prior to the launch of any new product or service which they propose to release on to the internet, particularly (not exclusively) where it is proposed to supply it "free" to the end user. This is because we know from very long experience that on the "free" internet there is a high probability that children will be able to access and use the product and there are also potentially weak to nonexistent audit trails to act as a brake on misuse. Perhaps the FTC or some other agency should be given a power to call in and inspect these child safety audits either on their own volition or following a complaint?

It should not be possible for any company to launch a new service or product and walk away from or avoid any potential liability for its actions by the trivial expedient of cutting and pasting a notice saying "This service is only available to persons over the age of 13" or "This service is only available to persons over the age of 18" when they know perfectly well they will make no serious attempt to police or enforce such an age related rule. Some companies do make serious attempts, but few are required to do so so most don't.

There is more than one type of family

We also need to start thinking about the vast range of families and individuals who are already or will soon become internet users or users of specific online services. We need to acknowledge the extremely broad range of competencies, skills and aptitudes that exist among internet users. Companies that accept subscriptions or allow people to start using their service owe a duty of care to every one of them, taking them as they find them. The industry's duty of care is not solely to the notional ideal family of highly literate and numerate engaged, technosavvy communicative parents in the middle of the market. Acres of densely worded legal jargon in contract documents that are never read are an escape route from liability. They do not constitute a reasonable child protection policy or discharge the duty of care.

The chilling effect of the COPPA Rule

We have to find a way to allow adults to continue doing whatever they are currently doing with the internet but also to improve the safety and privacy aspects of the environment in relation to how children and young people have access to it and use it. In that connection we are afraid the operation of the COPPA Rule has had a chilling effect on innovation.

In particular the "actual knowledge" requirement provides US companies with no incentive to improve their ability to determine whether or not the age related rules they appear to espouse are achieving their seemingly intended goals. It creates a legal fiction. This plainly has many advantages for businesses. It has none at all for child protection.

No incentive to change

The "actual knowledge" rule encourages laziness. When companies apply a blanket age limit across all of their services it suggests that every service is equally risky to every child but we know that's not true and it devalues the meaning of the caveat implied by the age limit in the first place. In part we suspect this is also why some parents collude in allowing, perhaps they even encourage, their children to lie about their age to online service providers when, for example, all the parents think they are doing is enabling their children to have an email account to stay in touch with Grandma.

Investing in the development and roll out of a system to make the age rules work better makes no sense if you are never going to have any liability for the ineffectiveness of what you are currently doing. Even if internet companies were to light upon or develop a solution, they might worry that if they were the only ones to deploy it they could lose business to their less fastidious competitors. Everybody has to do it or nobody will.

From a public policy perspective aspects of the current system are a disaster

In the UK, for example, in March 2010 OFCOM, the statutory telecoms regulator, published research showing that 19% of all children aged 8–12 have a social networking profile on either Bebo, Facebook or MySpace, all of which have a policy of not allowing anyone below the age of 13 to be members. This proportion rises to 22% when looking at all social networking sites, most of which also stipulate a minimum age of 13. If you limit the cohort to children of 8–12 who used the internet at home the proportion using Facebook, Bebo or MySpace rises to 25%. 11% of these children have made or left their profiles open for anyone to see or visit. It is great that 89% didn't, but 11% is still far too large a proportion and let's not forget the 89% shouldn't have been there in the first place either.

In the same study OFCOM showed that 37% of 5–7 year olds in the UK who use the internet at home had visited Facebook, although they did not necessarily have or establish a profile. We do not have immediately to hand comparable figures for other countries, but anecdotally from our network of national members we are fairly certain that the UK figures for underage usage are mirrored or exceeded in many other jurisdictions in Europe and further afield.

We have known for a considerable period of time that very substantial numbers of sub–13 year olds are regular users of sites which are not meant to accept anyone below that age and many if not all of these sites adopted 13 as their minimum age rule solely or overwhelmingly because of a simple desire to avoid becoming enmeshed with, as they see it, the offputting and expensive business of seeking verifiable parental consent as required by the COPPA Rule. Had the COPPA Rule specified 12 or 15, that's where they would have pitched their tent.

Of course internet companies are entitled to rely on the research, knowledge and insight that led Congress and the FTC to formulate the rule and set 13 as the limit, and we do not dispute that 13 is probably the right level, but now that we know the operation of the rule is failing on such a significant scale it behoves us all to pitch in and find a better way of doing things. We hope no one will settle for the status quo.

Should the rule be abolished or made to work?

We are almost, stress almost, of the view that you should abolish the legal basis of the 13 rule altogether, and make it clear that it is only advisory. But we would much prefer that a way is found to make the 13 rule truly effective. It cannot be good public policy for children to see or be shown not only that lying works and gets you what you want, but also that lying works and gets you what you want so easily, pretty much immediately and with impunity, even when backed up by the apparent majesty of the law. It discredits not only the rule, but also it discredits the idea of rulemaking and possibly also the rulemaker. It is a very bad example to serve up to young people in whom we are all trying to inculcate a sense of respect for the law and the democratic processes which lie behind law making.

We acknowledge and accept that there are important privacy and other issues raised by this debate but we have never sensed there has ever been any real appetite or determination by any major players in the internet industry to address them. A million alibis for inaction are regularly trotted out, underpinned and comforted by the legal immunity conferred by the current rule. What we need is a high level steely determination to find a solution that works.

Companies sometimes speak of there being little evidence of a demand for this kind of approach by parents. We are not sure we accept that proposition in quite the way it is often intended, not least because it implies the companies themselves are passive, helpless bystanders. However, we know that companies can and often do shape markets and can greatly influence consumer expectations. If the quest for a safer online environment for children and young people had attracted anything like the level of resources that are devoted to some other aspects of internet companies' mainstream activities, we might all be in a very different place today.

Age verification needs to be revisited

The way in which the question of age verification and social networking first presented itself in the USA was in our view very unfortunate. It muddied the waters to a considerable degree. We broadly agreed with the main conclusions of the ISTTF. Age verification systems can never be used to create an environment which is "guaranteed" to contain only persons of a certain age or be guaranteed to be free of paedophiles. But age verification systems can be used to demonstrate that a company has taken reasonable steps to ensure that only persons above a certain age are enabled to access or use particular services or parts of the internet which have some kind of age rule linked to them. This can be done without having to create vast "hackable" databases of children or to create childonly environments which would act as a magnet for paedophiles. It may inconvenience people the first time they go to visit an area of the internet that imposes an age requirement. First time out it could lead to several seconds of delay in them getting what they want, but there is a valuable prize lying beyond that narrow and incredibly selfish horizon. And if everybody did it the potential for any one company to lose business to a rival would vanish.

In the UK, until quite recently, most gambling web sites simply asked their wouldbe customers to tick a box to confirm they were 18 or above. Lots of young people well below that age did just that and were later found to have developed problematic gambling behaviours, in some cases amounting to addiction. The Gambling Act, 2005, changed everything. Now in order to obtain a licence to run an online gambling web site every gambling company must put in place a robust online age verification system to determine that anyone wishing to place a bet with them is at least 18 years old.

Since the law came into effect in September 2007 we are not aware of a single case where a child has beaten the system. Of course we still hear about parents or older siblings who leave their credit cards about the place together with much of their Personal Identifying Information, thus allowing unqualified children to present themselves to gambling or other web sites as being their parent or older sibling. There is little or nothing any legislature can do about that kind of behaviour. But what children in the UK cannot now do is invent an age or a persona for themselves, claim to be over 18 and get away with it. Not on a gambling web site. But they can still do it in a heartbeat on Yahoo and YouTube.

A second working example comes from the way many mobile phone networks now operate. This arose pursuant to an agreement originally negotiated between the EU and the GSMA (the global trade association for mobile phone network operators).

In a number of countries when a new mobile phone network subscription is taken out, the operator automatically assumes that the customer is a child. This means it is impossible for the user of that phone to access straight away any pornography, any dating services, chat services, gambling or other services or content which has been put behind an "adult bar". Premium rate services are also barred and a very wide range of advertisements cannot be presented to the user. If the owner of the mobile phone number is an adult and wants to be able to access any or all of those sites or services, he or she does not have to ring up and ask for the porn to be turned on. All he or she has to do is go through a procedure to establish that they are over 18 then all of the adult services become accessible. Many of the networks apply the same principle to internet content i.e. by default all adult sites and services on the internet are rendered inaccessible through the mobile handset until the adult bar has been lifted.

The introduction of these measures has not led to a fall off in the number of mobile phone users. Nor does it appear to have affected the overall levels of operational efficiency or profitability of the networks. But we do have millions of very grateful parents and children. Again part of the key to this was that in the countries where these measures are now operational the majority of large operators decided to do it more or less together, though each in their own individual way.

The arrival of location aware applications makes this question more urgent

There needs to be a sense of urgency injected into this discussion. "Location aware" applications are starting to come on to the market. They are widely said to be the drivers for a whole new wave of innovation on the internet. Almost universally these applications are being marketed as being for persons aged 18 or above but they are capable of being linked to, for example, social networking sites which specify 13 as the minimum age. See above. All of the location services we know of are free to the end user because they are paid for by advertising. Thus it is clear that anyone below the age of 18 will in fact be able to download and use them. This means children below the age of 13 will be able to use them.

Into a social networking environment which is already well known to generate concerns and anxieties about children's and young people's privacy and safety, parts of the internet industry now seem ready to introduce location based services which clearly bring with them a whole new layer of risk, particularly to those young people who are not mature enough to evaluate or assess the potential consequences of using them.

Location data requires higher standards of security

The standards which should be applied to data about a person's physical whereabouts are, or should be, of a different order of magnitude from those which apply to most other types of data which an internet company might routinely process or allow to be broadcast on their sites. When that location data applies to the physical location of a child, the expectations in relation to the security standards to be observed are that much greater again.

If adults wish to make available information about their whereabouts, that is a matter for them, but companies who provide what is effectively free access to location aware services should find a way to prevent children's naiveté from putting them-selves and others at risk.

If the companies that are sponsoring location applications had had to complete a child safety audit before they sent these applications out on to the internet we are sure they would have tried a great deal harder to find a convincing way of reassuring us that children would not be able to access, download or use them.

Other issues in the COPPA Review

We appreciate that the review of the COPPA rule is looking at many other detailed questions, for example about how the system works in relation to verifying parental consent for children who are acknowledged to be under 13. We have no substantial concrete experience which indicates that there are any pressing or major problems in that area although some of the potential weaknesses are selfevident. For this reason in this submission we have focused on what, to us, seems to be the most glaring deficiencies which urgently require redress. If you mend them in the USA, they will be mended here too.[26]

---

[26] ENASCO LETTER TO FTC RE: SUBMISSION TO THE FTC REVIEW OF THE COPPA RULE (June 29, 2010), http://www.ftc.gov/os/comments/copparulerev2010/547597-00027-54840.pdf (notes omitted).

Ultimately, the FTC has not (as of July 2011) made any further changes to the COPPA regulations to address technological advances, but the possibility remains strong that it will do so.

IV.   CONCLUSION: CHILDREN'S PRIVACY: SIGNIFICANT CHALLENGES AND BEST PRACTICES

Given the additional vulnerability of children, as well as the additional burdens of law, regulation, and public concerns, organizations must exercise special care in their information collection and use practices when the information is provided by (or identifies) younger individuals. Failing to do so could lead to both legal and public relations problems:

[Consumer Reports] Survey: 7.5 Million Facebook Users are Under the Age of 13, Violating the Site's Terms

. . . . Of the 20 million minors who actively used Facebook in the past year, 7.5 million of them were younger than 13, according to projections from Consumer Reports' latest State of the Net survey. Facebook's terms of service require users to be at least 13 years old.

Also among this group of minors using Facebook, more than 5 million were 10 and under. Consumer Reports survey found that their accounts were largely unsupervised by their parents, exposing them to malware or serious threats such as predators or bullies. The report on Internet security, which includes the full survey results and advice for parents of Facebook users, is featured in the June issue of Consumer Reports and on www.ConsumerReports.org.

"Despite Facebook's age requirements, many kids are using the site who shouldn't be," says Jeff Fox, Technology Editor for Consumer Reports. "What's even more troubling was the finding from our survey that indicated that a majority of parents of kids 10 and under seemed largely unconcerned by their children's use of the site."

Using Facebook presents children and their friends and family with safety, security and privacy risks. In the past year, the use of Facebook has exposed more than five million online U.S. households to some type of abuse including virus infections, identity theft, and — for a million children — bullying, the survey shows . . . .[27]

This becomes all the more difficult when one considers that children may be more technically adept than their parents or teachers, including having greater skill at evading age-based restrictions on content access. They are also among the earliest adopters of new communications technologies, so that companies seeking to exploit

---

[27] CR Survey: 7.5 Million Facebook Users are Under the Age of 13, Violating the Site's Terms?: Consumer Reports   http://pressroom.consumerreports.org/pressroom/   (May   10,   2011), http://pressroom.consumerreports.org/pressroom/2011/05/cr-survey-75-million-facebook-users-are-under-t he-age-of-13-violating-the-sites-terms-.html (last visited May 8, 2012).

those technologies may find their audience disproportionately made up of younger people.

Kids Today: How the Class of 2011 Engages with Media

1993 was a big year. The Mosaic Internet Web browser was launched, NAFTA was signed, Seinfeld *won an Emmy for Outstanding Comedy Series and the high school class of 2011 was born. Nielsen congratulates the class of 2011 and takes look at today's American teen, raised in an age dominated by media choices like never before — from the Internet to cable channels to web connected devices galore.*

Kids Today . . .

Are the Heaviest Mobile Video Viewers*: On average, mobile subscribers ages 12–17 watched 7 hours 13 minutes of mobile video a month in Q4 2010, compared to 4 hours 20 minutes for the general population.*

Are More Receptive to Mobile Advertising than their Elders*: More than half (58%) surveyed in September 2010 said they "always" or "sometimes" look at mobile ads.*

Out-Text All Other Age Groups*: In Q1 2011, teens 13–17 sent an average of 3,364 mobile texts per month, more than doubling the rate of the next most active texting demo, 18–24 year olds (1,640 texts per month).*

Talk Less on the Phone*: Besides seniors 65-plus, teens talk the least on their phones, talking an average of 515 minutes per month in Q1 2011 versus more than 750 minutes among 18–24 year olds.*

Grew Up in the Age of Social Media — and It Shows*: While they make up just 7.4 percent of those using social networks, 78.7 percent of 12–17 year olds visited social networks or blogs.*

Watch Less TV than the General Population*: The average American watched 34 hours 39 minutes of TV per week in Q4 2010, a year-over-year increase of two minutes. Teens age 12–17 watch the least amount of TV on average (23 hours 41 minutes per week).*

Spend Less Time on their Computers*: American 18 year olds averaged 39 hours, 50 minutes online from their home computers, of which 5 hours, 26 minutes was spent streaming online video per month.*[28]

Nor can U.S.-based organizations focus solely on domestic risks. As with everything else about the Internet, its borderless nature means that other countries may focus on issues of collection and protection of children's information by American organizations:

---

[28] Kids Today: How the Class of 2011 Engages with Media | Nielsen Wire *(June 8, 2011), http:// blog.nielsen.com/nielsenwire/consumer/kids-today-how-the-class-of-2011-engages-with-media/ (last visited May 8, 2012).*

A-Gs to probe kids' privacy on Facebook

[Australia's] attorneys-general will discuss whether laws should be introduced to allow parents access to their children's Facebook accounts and social networking sites, allowing them to legally breach their privacy.

The Standing Committee of Attorneys-General will focus on social networking and new-media legal issues when it meets in Adelaide today, including discussions on what can be done to crack down on breaches of suppression orders on sites such as Facebook and MySpace.

South Australian Attorney-General John Rau yesterday said there needed to be a discussion on the impact of new technologies on suppression orders.

"Sooner or later there has to be a discussion about what is going to be occurring in the virtual world, because technology has been moving very quickly," Mr Rau told The Australian.

"We need to look at the policing that occurs, who can and should do it and how do you do it." . . .[29]

Accordingly, in addition to the standard best practices that apply to all data collection, organizations should consider the following additional questions with regards to their online operations and children's personally-identifiable information:

- Does the organization operate a Web site or other online community that is focused on, or may be attractive to, children under 18 and especially those under 13?

- Does the organization ask users for their age, age range, or birth year at any point in its online interaction with them?

- Does the Web site reject or segregate Web site submissions indicating the user is under 13?

- Does it also block an under-13 user from merely resubmitting information with a falsified (older) age indicated?

- If the organization maintains an online community such as a message board, is there a moderator who is looking for and able to address potential predatory or other harmful messages to younger participants?

- Are those personnel responsible for receiving and reviewing non-Web site communications from customers or users (such as faxes, letters, e-mail messages, or voicemail) trained to spot and segregate any messages that indicate the sender is under 13 years of age?

---

[29] Verity Edwards, A-Gs to probe kids' privacy on Facebook | The Australian *(July 21, 2011), http://www.theaustralian.com.au/national-affairs/a-gs-to-probe-kids-privacy-on-facebook/story-fn59niix -1226098613068 (last visited May 8, 2012).*

Chapter 5

HEALTH AND MEDICAL PRIVACY: (UN)CONDITIONAL PROTECTION

Health and medical privacy starts with a basic principle: doctors are obligated to keep information confidential. The principle dates back literally to the Hippocratic Oath, the ancient Greek affirmation still influential on (although not mandatory for) modern doctors. The Oath includes the following commitment:

> *Whatever I see or hear in the lives of my patients, whether in connection with my professional practice or not, which ought not to be spoken of outside, I will keep secret, as considering all such things to be private.*[1]

One modern version of this statement, written by then-Academic Dean Louis Lasagna of the Tufts University School of Medicine in 1964, includes the rationale for it:

> *I will respect the privacy of my patients, for their problems are not disclosed to me that the world may know.*[2]

As with similar obligations placed upon clergypeople, attorneys and other professionals, the foundation of the confidentiality obligation for physicians is that doctors must have as complete a set of information as possible to provide effective medical care to their patients:

> *The information disclosed to a physician during the course of the relationship between physician and patient is confidential to the greatest possible degree. The patient should feel free to make a full disclosure of information to the physician in order that the physician may most effectively provide needed services. The patient should be able to make this disclosure with the knowledge that the physician will respect the confidential nature of the communication. The physician should not reveal confidential communications or information without the express consent of the patient, unless required to do so by law.*[3]

This would include behaviors and conditions that patients might find embarrassing

---

[1] GREEK MEDICINE — THE HIPPOCRATIC OATH, *http://www.nlm.nih.gov/hmd/greek/greek_oath.html (last visited May 8, 2012).*

[2] Peter Tyson, NOVA | THE HIPPOCRATIC OATH TODAY, *http://www.pbs.org/wgbh/nova/body/hippocratic-oath-today.html (last visited May 8, 2012).*

[3] Hippocrates to HIPAA: A Foundation for a Federal Physician-Patient Privilege, 77 Temp. L. Rev. 505, citing Codes of Professional Responsibility: Ethics Standards in Business, Health, and Law (Rena A. Gorlin ed., 4th ed. 1999) at 312.

or which might even be illegal, from sexually transmitted diseases to risky behavior to prohibited drug use. If a patient thinks that the doctor might reveal these secrets to law enforcement officials, family members, employers or the general public, she could feel inhibited from telling the doctor in the first place. The doctor might then unknowingly prescribe a medication or treatment that would interact dangerously with other pharmaceuticals or activities the patient had not disclosed, or that might work less well because of those other factors, and overall public health could suffer. As a result, modern medical ethics codes, and evidentiary rules, both prohibit disclosure by physicians and use of any disclosures as evidence (i.e. the physican/patient privilege).[4]

I. HEALTH CONDITIONS AND GENETIC CODE: PREVENTING DISCRIMINATION AND DISCLOSURE

There are consequences beyond embarrassment or even law enforcement for health-related disclosures. Employers may choose not to hire a candidate, or promote an employee, based upon a real or suspected health condition that could raise overall insurance costs or lead to increased absenteeism. Insurers themselves, whether health or other types, may use information beyond that provided by an applicant for coverage to price or approve policies. Home sales could suffer if neighbors' medical conditions were publicized, even when such conditions would have zero impact on the lives or health of the prospective buyers, and so on. With the increased availability and understanding of genetic information, even future possible health issues become potential fodder for improper use if they are disclosed beyond the doctor's office.

The issue of genetic discrimination in employment was the subject of a lawsuit brought by the Equal Employment Opportunity Commission in 2001:

Cases of Genetic Discrimination[5]

Although no genetic-employment discrimination case has been brought before U.S. federal or state courts, in 2001 the U.S. Equal Employment Opportunity Commission (EEOC) [eeoc.gov] settled the first lawsuit alleging this type of discrimination.

EEOC filed a suit against the Burlington Northern Santa Fe (BNSF) Railroad for secretly testing its employees for a rare genetic condition (hereditary neuropathy with liability to pressure palsies — HNPP) that causes carpal tunnel syndrome as one of its many symptoms. BNSF claimed that the testing was a way of determining whether the high incidence of repetitive-stress injuries among its employees was work-related. Besides testing for HNPP, company-paid doctors also were instructed to screen for several other medical conditions such as diabetes and alcoholism. BNSF employees examined by company doctors were not told that they were being genetically tested. One employee who refused testing was threatened with possible termination.

---

[4] *Id.*

[5] National Human Genome Research Institute, National Institutes of Health, CASES OF GENETIC DISCRIMINATION, *http://www.genome.gov/12513976 (last visited May 8, 2012).*

On behalf of BNSF employees, EEOC argued that the tests were unlawful under the Americans with Disabilities Act because they were not job-related, and that any condition of employment based on such tests would be cause for illegal discrimination based on disability. The lawsuit was settled quickly, with BNSF agreeing to everything sought by EEOC.

Besides the BNSF case, the Council for Responsible Genetics [genewatch.org] claims that hundreds of genetic-discrimination cases have been documented and describes select cases in its Genetic Discrimination Position Paper. In one reported case, genetic testing indicated that a young boy had Fragile X Syndrome, an inherited form of mental retardation. The insurance company for the boy's family dropped his health coverage, claiming the syndrome was a preexisting condition. In another case, a social worker lost her job within a week of mentioning that her mother had died of Huntington's disease and that she had a 50 percent chance of developing it.

Despite claims of hundreds of genetic-discrimination incidents, an article from the January 2003 issue of the European Journal of Human Genetics *reports a real need for a comprehensive investigation of these claims. The article warns that many studies rely on unverified, subjective accounts from individuals who believe employers or insurance companies have unfairly subjected them to genetic discrimination. Rarely are these subjective accounts assessed objectively to determine whether actions taken by employers and insurers were truly based on genetic factors or other legitimate concerns.*

Subsequently, the Genetic Information Nondiscrimination Act of 2008 ("GINA")[6] addressed the permissibility of making employment decisions on the basis of genetic testing or results.

§ 2000ff-1: Employer Practices[7]

(a) Discrimination based on genetic information

It shall be an unlawful employment practice for an employer —

(1) to fail or refuse to hire, or to discharge, any employee, or otherwise to discriminate against any employee with respect to the compensation, terms, conditions, or privileges of employment of the employee, because of genetic information with respect to the employee; or

(2) to limit, segregate, or classify the employees of the employer in any way that would deprive or tend to deprive any employee of employment opportunities or otherwise adversely affect the status of the employee as an employee, because of genetic information with respect to the employee.

(b) Acquisition of genetic information

It shall be an unlawful employment practice for an employer to request, require, or

---

[6] 42 U.S.C. 2000ff et seq.

[7] 42 U.S.C. § 2000ff-1.

purchase genetic information with respect to an employee or a family member of the employee except —

(1) where an employer inadvertently requests or requires family medical history of the employee or family member of the employee;

(2) where —

(A) health or genetic services are offered by the employer, including such services offered as part of a wellness program;

(B) the employee provides prior, knowing, voluntary, and written authorization;

(C) only the employee (or family member if the family member is receiving genetic services) and the licensed health care professional or board certified genetic counselor involved in providing such services receive individually identifiable information concerning the results of such services; and

(D) any individually identifiable genetic information provided under subparagraph (C) in connection with the services provided under subparagraph (A) is only available for purposes of such services and shall not be disclosed to the employer except in aggregate terms that do not disclose the identity of specific employees;

(3) where an employer requests or requires family medical history from the employee to comply with the certification provisions of section 2613 of Title 29 or such requirements under State family and medical leave laws;

(4) where an employer purchases documents that are commercially and publicly available (including newspapers, magazines, periodicals, and books, but not including medical databases or court records) that include family medical history;

(5) where the information involved is to be used for genetic monitoring of the biological effects of toxic substances in the workplace, but only if —

(A) the employer provides written notice of the genetic monitoring to the employee;

(B)(i) the employee provides prior, knowing, voluntary, and written authorization; or

(ii) the genetic monitoring is required by Federal or State law;

(C) the employee is informed of individual monitoring results;

(D) the monitoring is in compliance with —

(i) any Federal genetic monitoring regulations, including any such regulations that may be promulgated by the Secretary of Labor pursuant to the Occupational Safety and Health Act of 1970 (29 U.S.C. 651 et seq.), the Federal Mine Safety and Health Act of 1977 (30 U.S.C. 801 et seq.), or the Atomic Energy Act of 1954 (42 U.S.C. 2011 et seq.); or

(ii) State genetic monitoring regulations, in the case of a State that is implementing genetic monitoring regulations under the authority of the Occupational Safety and Health Act of 1970 (29 U.S.C. 651 et seq.); and

(E) the employer, excluding any licensed health care professional or board certified

genetic counselor that is involved in the genetic monitoring program, receives the results of the monitoring only in aggregate terms that do not disclose the identity of specific employees; or

(6) where the employer conducts DNA analysis for law enforcement purposes as a forensic laboratory or for purposes of human remains identification, and requests or requires genetic information of such employer's employees, but only to the extent that such genetic information is used for analysis of DNA identification markers for quality control to detect sample contamination.

(c) Preservation of protections

In the case of information to which any of paragraphs (1) through (6) of subsection (b) applies, such information may not be used in violation of paragraph (1) or (2) of subsection (a) or treated or disclosed in a manner that violates section 2000ff-5 of this title.

Additional section address employment agency,[8] labor organization[9] and training programs.[10] GINA also addresses issues of privacy:

Confidentiality of Genetic Information[11]

(a) Treatment of information as part of confidential medical record

If an employer, employment agency, labor organization, or joint labor-management committee possesses genetic information about an employee or member, such information shall be maintained on separate forms and in separate medical files and be treated as a confidential medical record of the employee or member. An employer, employment agency, labor organization, or joint labor-management committee shall be considered to be in compliance with the maintenance of information requirements of this subsection with respect to genetic information subject to this subsection that is maintained with and treated as a confidential medical record under section 12112(d)(3)(B) of this title.

(b) Limitation on disclosure

An employer, employment agency, labor organization, or joint labor-management committee shall not disclose genetic information concerning an employee or member except —

(1) to the employee or member of a labor organization (or family member if the family member is receiving the genetic services) at the written request of the employee or member of such organization;

(2) to an occupational or other health researcher if the research is conducted in

---

[8] 42 U.S.C. § 2000ff-2.

[9] 42 U.S.C. § 2000ff-3.

[10] 42 U.S.C. § 2000ff-4.

[11] 42 U.S.C. § 2000ff-5.

compliance with the regulations and protections provided for under part 46 of title 45, Code of Federal Regulations;

(3) in response to an order of a court, except that —

(A) the employer, employment agency, labor organization, or joint labor-management committee may disclose only the genetic information expressly authorized by such order; and

(B) if the court order was secured without the knowledge of the employee or member to whom the information refers, the employer, employment agency, labor organization, or joint labor-management committee shall inform the employee or member of the court order and any genetic information that was disclosed pursuant to such order;

(4) to government officials who are investigating compliance with this chapter if the information is relevant to the investigation;

(5) to the extent that such disclosure is made in connection with the employee's compliance with the certification provisions of section 2613 of Title 29 or such requirements under State family and medical leave laws; or

(6) to a Federal, State, or local public health agency only with regard to information that is described in section 2000ff(4)(A)(iii) of this title and that concerns a contagious disease that presents an imminent hazard of death or life-threatening illness, and that the employee whose family member or family members is or are the subject of a disclosure under this paragraph is notified of such disclosure.

(c) Relationship to HIPAA regulations

With respect to the regulations promulgated by the Secretary of Health and Human Services under part C of title XI of the Social Security Act (42 U.S.C. 1320d et seq.) and section 264 of the Health Insurance Portability and Accountability Act of 1996 (42 U. S.C. 1320d-2 note), this chapter does not prohibit a covered entity under such regulations from any use or disclosure of health information that is authorized for the covered entity under such regulations. The previous sentence does not affect the authority of such Secretary to modify such regulations.

There is not, however, any current overall federal privacy protection for genetic information beyond the employment context discussed here, nor does GINA address any overall right to privacy with regard to medical conditions such as HIV/AIDS.

DOE v. BOROUGH OF BARRINGTON[12]

Opinion

BROTMAN, DISTRICT JUDGE.

Presently before the court is the motion of plaintiffs Jane Doe and her children for partial summary judgment against defendants Borough of Runnemede ("Runnemede") and Officer Smith. These defendants have cross-moved for summary judgment. This case presents novel issues concerning the privacy rights of individuals who have contracted Acquired Immune Deficiency Syndrome ("AIDS") and the privacy rights of their family members. For the reasons stated in this opinion, plaintiffs' motion for summary judgment against defendants Runnemede and Smith will be granted. Accordingly, the motion of defendants Runnemede and Smith for summary judgment will be denied.

I. FACTS AND PROCEDURE

The facts are largely undisputed. On March 25, 1987, Jane Doe, her husband, and their friend James Tarvis were traveling in the Doe's pickup truck through the Borough of Barrington ("Barrington"). At approximately 9:00 a.m., a Barrington police officer stopped the truck and questioned the occupants. As a result of the vehicle stop, Barrington officers arrested Jane Doe's husband and impounded the pickup truck. Barrington officers escorted Jane Doe, her husband, and James Tarvis to the Barrington Police Station.

When he was initially arrested, Jane Doe's husband told the police officers that he had tested HIV positive and that the officers should be careful in searching him because he had "weeping lesions." There is some dispute over the exact words used by Jane Doe's husband and about the number of persons present when Jane Doe's husband revealed the information. These disputed facts do not change the outcome here. Barrington police released Jane Doe and James Tarvis from custody, but detained Jane Doe's husband on charges of unlawful possession of a hypodermic needle and a burglary detainer entered by Essex County.

Sometime in the late afternoon of the same day, Jane Doe and James Tarvis drove Tarvis's car to the Doe residence in the Borough of Runnemede ("Runnemede"). The car engine was left running, and the car apparently slipped into gear, rolling down the driveway into a neighbor's fence. The neighbors owning the fence are Michael DiAngelo and defendant Rita DiAngelo. Rita DiAngelo is an employee in the school district in Runnemede.

Two Runnemede police officers, Steven Van Camp and defendant Russell Smith, responded to the radio call about the incident. While they were at the scene, Detective Preen of the Barrington police arrived and, in a private conversation with Van Camp, revealed that Jane Doe's husband had been arrested earlier in the day and had told

---

[12] Doe v. Borough of Barrington, 729 F.Supp. 376 (D.N.J. 1990).

Barrington police officers that he had AIDS. Van Camp then told defendant Smith.

After Jane Doe and Tarvis left the immediate vicinity, defendant Smith told the DiAngelos that Jane Doe's husband had AIDS and that, to protect herself, Rita DiAngelo should wash with disinfectant. There is some dispute about Smith's exact words to the DiAngelos, however this dispute does not change the outcome here. Defendant Rita DiAngelo became upset upon hearing this information. Knowing that the four Doe children attended the Downing School in Runnemede, the school that her own daughter attended, DiAngelo contacted other parents with children in the school. She also contacted the media. The next day, eleven parents removed nineteen children from the Downing School due to a panic over the Doe children's attending the school. The media was present, and the story was covered in the local newspapers and on television. At least one of the reports mentioned the name of the Doe family. Plaintiffs allege that as a result of the disclosure, they have suffered harassment, discrimination, and humiliation. They allege they have been shunned by the community.

Plaintiffs brought this civil rights action against the police officer Smith and the municipalities of Barrington and Runnemede for violations of their federal constitutional rights pursuant to 42 U.S.C. § 1983 (1982). The federal constitutional right is their right to privacy under the fourteenth amendment. The suit contains pendent state claims against defendant DiAngelo for invasion of privacy and intentional infliction of emotional distress. The plaintiffs' motion for summary judgment seeks judgment against only defendants Runnemede and Smith; these defendants filed a cross-motion for summary judgment with their response to plaintiffs' motion.

Plaintiffs maintain that the fourteenth amendment protects them from the government's disclosure of plaintiff Jane Doe's husband's infection with the AIDS virus. Plaintiffs assert that Officer Smith and the Borough of Runnemede are liable under 42 U.S.C. § 1983 (1982) for this violation of their constitutional rights.

Defendants Runnemede and Smith respond by stating:

1. plaintiffs have no standing because only Jane Doe's husband's privacy was invaded, and he is not party to this suit;2. Smith's action was not misconduct, and thus no action can be maintained under section 1983;

3. Jane Doe's husband "published" the information and, therefore, gave up any right to privacy in this information;

4. cases cited by plaintiff are all distinguishable on their facts;

5. there are no conclusive facts about AIDS, thus Smith's warning that DiAngelo might have been exposed through casual contact with Jane Doe was justified; and

6. Runnemede's failure to have an nondisclosure policy for arrestees is not actionable because no other municipality or state agency has a policy in place.

II. DISCUSSION

A. The Summary Judgment Standard.

The standard for granting summary judgment is a stringent one, but it is not insurmountable. A court may grant summary judgment only when the materials of record "show that there is no genuine issue as to any material fact and that the moving party is entitled to judgment as a matter of law." Fed.R.Civ.P. 56(c); see Hersh v. Allen Prods. Co., *789 F.2d 230, 232 (3d Cir.1986);* Lang v. New York Life Ins. Co., *721 F.2d 118, 119 (3d Cir.1983). In deciding whether there is a disputed issue of material fact the court must view all doubt in favor of the nonmoving party.* Meyer v. Riegel Prods. Corp., *720 F.2d 303, 307 n. 2 (3d Cir.1983),* cert. denied, *465 U.S. 1091, 104 S.Ct. 2144, 79 L.Ed.2d 910 (1984);* Smith v. Pittsburgh Gage & Supply Co., *464 F.2d 870, 874 (3d Cir.1972). The threshold inquiry is whether there are "any genuine factual issues that properly can be resolved only by a finder of fact because they may reasonably be resolved in favor of either party."* Anderson v. Liberty Lobby, Inc., *477 U.S. 242, 250, 106 S.Ct. 2505, 2511, 91 L.Ed.2d 202 (1986).*

Recent Supreme Court decisions mandate that "a motion for summary judgment must be granted unless the party opposing the motion can produce evidence which, when considered in light of that party's burden of proof at trial, could be the basis for a jury finding in that party's favor." J.E. Mamiye & Sons, Inc. v. Fidelity Bank, *813 F.2d 610, 618 (3d Cir.1987) (Becker, J., concurring) (citing* Anderson, *477 U.S. 242, 106 S.Ct. 2505, 91 L.Ed.2d 202, and* Celotex Corp. v. Catrett, *477 U.S. 317, 106 S.Ct. 2548, 91 L.Ed.2d 265 (1986)). Moreover, once the moving party has carried its burden of establishing the absence of a genuine issue of material fact, "its opponent must do more than simply show that there is some metaphysical doubt as to material facts."* Matsushita Elec. Indus. Co. v. Zenith Radio Corp., *475 U.S. 574, 586, 106 S.Ct. 1348, 1356, 89 L.Ed.2d 538 (1986). Thus, even if the movant's evidence is merely "colorable" or is "not significantly probative," the court may grant summary judgment.* Anderson, *477 U.S. at 249–50, 106 S.Ct. at 2511.*

B. Facts about AIDS.

AIDS is a viral disease that weakens or destroys the body's immune system. The disease is caused by the presence of the Human Immunodeficiency Virus ("HIV"), which attacks the body's T-lymphocyte cells that are a critical part of the body's immune system. As a result, the body is unable to withstand infections it would normally suppress. These resulting infections, known as "opportunistic diseases," eventually cause permanent disability and death. AIDS is defined by New Jersey health regulations as the presence of both the HIV virus and one or more opportunistic diseases. Thus, a person may test positive for the HIV virus and yet not exhibit any signs of illness; that person is asymptomatic. Persons who exhibit effects of immunodeficiency, such as fever, weight loss, night sweats, or diarrhea, but do not have any opportunistic diseases are described as having AIDS-related Complex ("ARC"). See N.J.A.C. 8:57-1.14(b). AIDS has no known cure.

HIV is transmitted through contact with contaminated blood, semen, or vaginal fluids. The virus is transmitted through activities such as sexual intercourse, anal sex, use of nonsterile hypodermic needles, and transfusions of contaminated blood or blood products. Additionally, women infected with HIV can transmit the virus to their children before or during birth. Although HIV has been detected in other bodily fluids such as saliva and urine, the virus is much less concentrated, and there are no known cases of transmission of the virus by such means. The Centers for Disease Control ("CDC") terms the risk of infection from such fluids as "extremely low or nonexistent." CDC, Update: Universal Precautions for Prevention of Transmission of Human Immunodeficiency Virus, Hepatitis B Virus, and Other Bloodborne Pathogens in Health-Care Settings, *37 MMWR 377, 378 (June 24, 1988);* CDC, Summary: Recommendations for Preventing Transmissions of Infection with Human T-Lymphotropic Virus Type III/Lymphadenopathy-Associated Virus in the Workplace, *34 MMWR 681 (1985) (hereinafter "CDC Summary ").*

In 1986, the Surgeon General announced that HIV is not transmitted through casual contact with an infected person, such as shaking hands, kissing, or contacting an object used by an infected person. United States Public Health Service, Surgeon General's Report on Acquired Immune Deficiency Syndrome *13–14 (1986).* See also CDC Summary, *at 681; Friedland, Saltzman, & Rogers,* Lack of Transmission of HTLV-III/LAV Infection to Household Contacts of Patients with AIDS or AIDS-Related Complex with Oral Candidiasis, *314 New England J.Med. 344 (Feb. 6, 1986); T. Hammett,* AIDS in Correctional Facilities: Issues and Options *7 (1986); Curran, Morgan, Hardy, Jaffe, Darrow & Dowdle,* The Epidemiology of AIDS: Current Status and Future Prospects, *229 Science 1352, 1356 (1985).*

Later reports confirm this fact. Report of the Presidential Commission on the Human Immunodeficiency Virus Epidemic 119 (June 24, 1988); T. Hammett, AIDS and the Law Enforcement Officer: Concerns and Policy Responses *4–5, 17 (1987); M. Rogers,* Transmission of Human Immunodeficiency Virus Infection in the United States, Report of the Surgeon General's Workshop on Children with HIV infection and Their Families *17 (1987); Friedland & Klein,* Transmission of the Human Immunodeficiency Virus, *317 New England J.Med. 1124 (Oct. 29, 1987).*

Defendants assert that there are no conclusive facts about AIDS, therefore, a material issue of fact exists whether warning the DiAngelos was justified. Defendants cite one article to demonstrate that, although no case of AIDS has yet been attributed to casual contact with an infected person, so much is unknown about the disease that infection through casual contact cannot be ruled out. See Heyward & Curran, The Epidemiology of AIDS in the U.S., *Scientific American 72, 80 (Oct. 1988). The Surgeon General of the United States, however, has maintained since 1986 that "AIDS is not spread by common everyday contact but by sexual contact . . . ." United States Department of Health and Human Services,* Surgeon General's Report on Acquired Immune Deficiency Syndrome *5 (1986) (emphasis in original). Defendants ignore the multitude of information, available in 1987, that flatly rejects their argument that AIDS may be spread through casual contact.*

This court must take medical science as it finds it; its decision may not be based on speculation of what the state of medical science may be in the future. Ray v. School District of DeSoto County, *666 F.Supp. 1524, 1529 (M.D.Fla.1987). This court finds that the defendants' argument that the AIDS virus is transmitted by casual contact does not raise an issue of material fact that could "reasonably be resolved in favor of either party."* See Anderson v. Liberty Lobby, Inc., *477 U.S. 242, 250, 106 S.Ct. 2505, 2511, 91 L.Ed.2d 202 (1986). AIDS is not spread by casual contact and this fact was established before March 25, 1987. Other courts considering the question at the time agree.* See Thomas v. Atascadero Unified School District, *662 F.Supp. 376, 380 (C.D.Cal.1987) (decided February 20, 1987);* District 27 Community School Board v. Board of Education, *130 Misc.2d 398, 502 N.Y.S.2d 325 (Sup.Ct.1986) (decided February 11, 1986).*

The opponent to a motion for summary judgment "must do more than simply show that there is some metaphysical doubt as to material facts." Matsushita Elec. Indus. Co. v. Zenith Radio Corp., *475 U.S. 574, 586, 106 S.Ct. 1348, 1356, 89 L.Ed.2d 538 (1986). Defendants' argument that AIDS may be spread by casual contact does not meet this burden, thus, it does not bar summary judgment here.*

C. Plaintiffs' Right to Privacy.

The linchpin here is whether the Constitution protects plaintiffs' confidentiality with respect to Jane Doe's husband's AIDS. If the Constitution does not protect the Does from disclosure of Jane Doe's husband's condition, there is no constitutional violation to support a section 1983 claim against the officer or the municipality. There is no case directly on point. Plaintiffs assert that this privacy right was recognized in Roe v. Wade, *410 U.S. 113, 153, 93 S.Ct. 705, 726, 35 L.Ed.2d 147 (1973) (Constitution protects woman's decision whether or not to terminate pregnancy);* Griswold v. Connecticut, *381 U.S. 479, 483, 85 S.Ct. 1678, 1681, 14 L.Ed.2d 510 (1965) (law prohibiting use of contraceptives violates zone of privacy created by several fundamental constitutional guarantees);* Gillard v. Schmidt, *579 F.2d 825, 829 (3d Cir.1978) (nonconsensual search of teacher's desk by school board member is violation of constitutional rights that states cause of action under section 1983).*

This court finds that the Constitution protects plaintiffs from governmental disclosure of their husband's and father's infection with the AIDS virus. The United States Supreme Court has recognized that the fourteenth amendment protects two types of privacy interests. "One is the individual interest in avoiding disclosure of personal matters, and another is the interest in independence in making certain kinds of important decisions." Whalen v. Roe, *429 U.S. 589, 599–600, 97 S.Ct. 869, 876, 51 L.Ed.2d 64 (1977) (footnotes omitted). Disclosure of a family member's medical condition, especially exposure to or infection with the AIDS virus, is a disclosure of a "personal matter."*

The Third Circuit recognizes a privacy right in medical records and medical information. United States v. Westinghouse, *638 F.2d 570, 577 (3d Cir.1980) (employee medical records clearly within zone of privacy protection).* See also In re Search Warrant (Sealed), *810 F.2d 67, 71 (3d Cir.), cert. denied, 483 U.S. 1007, 107 S.Ct. 3233, 97 L.Ed.2d 739 (1987) (medical records clearly within constitutional sphere of right of privacy);* Trade Waste Management Ass'n, Inc. v. Hughey, *780 F.2d 221, 234 (3d Cir.1985) (personal medical history protected from random governmental intrusion).*

In United States v. Westinghouse, *638 F.2d 570, 577 (3d Cir.1980), the Third Circuit held that the National Institute for Occupational Safety and Health ("NIOSH") could compel the production of employee medical records from a private corporation. The court noted that governmental intrusion into medical records is permitted only after a finding that the societal interest in disclosure outweighs the individual's privacy interest on the specific facts of the case. Id. at 578. The court stated that the factors to be considered include (1) the type of record requested; (2) the information it does or might contain; (3) the potential for harm in any subsequent nonconsensual disclosure; (4) the injury from disclosure to the relationship in which the record was generated; (5) the adequacy of safeguards to prevent unauthorized disclosures; (6) the degree of need for access; and (7) whether there is an express statutory mandate, articulated public policy, or other recognizable public interest militating toward access. Id. In finding that NIOSH could compel production of the documents, the Third Circuit affirmed the trial court's finding that NIOSH's security precautions sufficiently assured nondisclosure by the agency. Id. at 580.*

Westinghouse, *however, addresses compelled disclosure of medical records to the government. This case is somewhat different than* Westinghouse *and its progeny because Jane Doe's husband voluntarily gave the information to the police. See* United States v. Westinghouse, *638 F.2d 570, 577 (3d Cir.1980). See also* In re Search Warrant (Sealed), *810 F.2d 67, 71 (3d Cir.), cert. denied, 483 U.S. 1007, 107 S.Ct. 3233, 97 L.Ed.2d 739 (1987);* Trade Waste Management Ass'n, Inc. v. Hughey, *780 F.2d 221, 234 (3d Cir.1985). Third Circuit precedents are silent on the duty of the government to protect medical information once such confidential information is disclosed to the government.*

The United States Supreme Court has indicated that the government's duty to avoid unwarranted disclosures arguably has its roots in the federal Constitution. In Whalen v. Roe, *429 U.S. 589, 606, 97 S.Ct. 869, 879, 51 L.Ed.2d 64 (1977), the United States Supreme Court held that a New York state statute that required the recording, in a centralized computer, of the names of persons receiving prescriptions for drugs that had a lawful and unlawful market did not contravene the requirements of the fourteenth amendment. The statute expressly prohibited public disclosure of the identity of patients. Id. at 594, 97 S.Ct. at 873. Additionally, the state Department of Health took security measures to prevent unwarranted disclosure of patient information. Id. at 593–95, 97 S.Ct. at 873–74.*

The Court noted that it was not unaware of the threat to privacy implicit in the accumulation of vast amounts of personal information. Moreover, the Court stated that the right to collect and to use such data for public purposes is typically accompanied by a concomitant statutory or regulatory duty to avoid unwarranted disclosure. Id. at 605, 97 S.Ct. at 879. The Court stated that Whalen v. Roe *did not decide whether unwarranted disclosure from a government system without comparable security provisions, made intentionally or unintentionally, would violate the fourteenth amendment. Id. at 605–06, 97 S.Ct. at 879. The Court specifically found that the New York statute evidenced a proper concern with protection of the individual's privacy interest. Id. at 605, 97 S.Ct. at 879. The case suggests that, absent the nondisclosure provisions, the statute might violate the fourteenth amendment.*

Lower courts have held that, once the government has confidential information, it has the obligation to avoid disclosure of the information. In Carter v. Broadlawns Medical Center, *667 F.Supp. 1269, 1282 (S.D.Iowa 1987), cert. denied, 489 U.S. 1096, 109 S.Ct. 1569, 103 L.Ed.2d 935 (1989), the court held that a public hospital had violated plaintiffs' constitutional rights by giving chaplains open access to patient medical records without patient authorization. The court noted that, in permitting free access to medical records, the hospital did not properly respect a patient's confidentiality and privacy as recognized in* Whalen v. Roe, *429 U.S. 589, 599 n. 23, 97 S.Ct. 869, 876 n. 23, 51 L.Ed.2d 64 (1977). The court concluded that a chaplain could review patient medical records only upon prior express approval of the individual patient or his or her guardian. The court noted that this restriction is not so broad as to bar doctors, medical and psychiatric personnel, and nurses from providing basic, unprivileged information to chaplains. The case demonstrates that, not only is the government restricted from collecting personal medical information, it may be restricted from disclosing such private information it lawfully receives.*

At least one court has addressed disclosure of a patient's condition with AIDS. In Woods v. White, *689 F.Supp. 874, 876 (W.D.Wis.1988), the court held that prison officials who discussed the fact that plaintiff had tested positive for AIDS with nonmedical prison personnel and with other inmates violated the inmate's constitutional rights and could be held liable under section 1983. The court recognized plaintiff's privacy interest in the information. The court stated that, to define the scope of the right to privacy in personal information, it must balance the individual's right to confidentiality against the governmental interest in disclosure.* Id. *The court noted that information about one's body and state of health is particularly sensitive, and that such information has traditionally been treated differently from other types of personal information.* Id. *(citing* United States v. Westinghouse Electric Corp., *638 F.2d 570, 577 (3d Cir.1980)). Noting the most publicized aspect of the disease, that it is related more closely than other diseases to sexual activity and intravenous drug use, the court stated that "it is difficult to argue that information about this disease is not information of the most personal kind, or that an individual would not have an interest in protecting against the dissemination of such information."* Id. *The court held that plaintiff had a constitutional right to privacy in his medical records.* Id.

The court then dismissed the need to balance plaintiff's interest against the governmental interest involved because defendants made no claim that any important governmental interest was served by their informal discussion of plaintiff's positive test for the AIDS virus. Recognizing that there might be circumstances that would limit plaintiff's right to privacy of his condition, the court noted that this case did not present such circumstances. This court finds the reasoning employed by the Carter *and* Woods *courts persuasive. The sensitive nature of medical information about AIDS makes a compelling argument for keeping this information confidential. Society's moral judgments about the high-risk activities associated with the disease, including sexual relations and drug use, make the information of the most personal kind. Also, the privacy interest in one's exposure to the AIDS virus is even greater than one's privacy interest in ordinary medical records because of the stigma that attaches with the disease. The potential for harm in the event of a nonconsensual disclosure is substantial; plaintiff's brief details the stigma and harassment that* comes with public knowledge of one's affliction with AIDS. The hysteria surrounding AIDS extends beyond those who have the disease. The stigma attaches not only to the AIDS victim, but to those in contact with AIDS patients, see N.Y. Times, Sept. 8, 1985, at A1, col. 1 (doctor of gay patients threatened with eviction), and to those in high risk groups who do not have the disease. See Poff v. Caro, 228 N.J.Super. 370, 374, 549 A.2d 900, 903 (N.J.Super.Law Div.1987) (landlord refused to rent to three gay men for fear of AIDS); Newsweek, July 1, 1985, at 61 (healthy gay men fired because of AIDS phobia); Nat'l L.J., July 25, 1983, at 3, 11 (California police demand masks and rubber gloves be used when dealing with gays); N.Y. Times, June 28, 1983, at A18, col. 1, 4 (Haitians denied employment because of fear of AIDS). Revealing that one's family or household member has AIDS causes the entire family to be ostracized. The right to privacy in this information extends to members of the AIDS patient's immediate family. Those sharing a household with an infected person suffer from disclosure just as the victim does. Family members, therefore, have a substantial interest in keeping this information confidential. Disclosures about AIDS cause a violation of the family's privacy much greater than simply revealing any other aspect of their family medical history.

An individual's privacy interest in medical information and records is not absolute. The court must determine whether the societal interest in disclosure outweighs the privacy interest involved. United States v. Westinghouse, 638 F.2d at 578. To avoid a constitutional violation, the government must show a compelling state interest in breaching that privacy. McKenna v. Fargo, 451 F.Supp. 1355, 1381 (D.N.J.1978).

The government's interest in disclosure here does not outweigh the substantial privacy interest involved. The government has not shown a compelling state interest in breaching the Does' privacy. The government contends that Officer Smith advised the DiAngelos to wash with disinfectant because of his concern for the prevention and avoidance of AIDS, an incurable and contagious disease. While prevention of this deadly disease is clearly an appropriate state objective, this objective was not served by Smith's statement that the DiAngelos should wash with disinfectant. Disclosure of the Does' confidential information did not advance a compelling governmental interest in preventing the spread of the disease because there was no risk that Mr. or Mrs. DiAngelo might be exposed to the HIV virus through casual contact with Jane Doe. The state of medical knowledge at the time of this incident established that AIDS is not transmitted by casual contact. Smith's statement could not prevent the transmission of AIDS because there was no threat of transmission present.

This court concludes that the Does have a constitutional right of privacy in the information disclosed by Smith and the state had no compelling interest in revealing that information. As such, the disclosure violated the Does' constitutional rights. This conclusion is consistent with the United States Supreme Court's discussion in Whalen v. Roe, 429 U.S. 589, 605, 97 S.Ct. 869, 879, 51 L.Ed.2d 64 (1977) that the government may have a duty to avoid disclosure of personal information. Although sidestepping the question of whether the government had the duty to protect confidential information it lawfully obtains, the Court suggested that such a duty exists. See id. at 605–06, 97 S.Ct. at 879.

1. Defendant Smith.

To maintain an action under 42 U.S.C. § 1983 (1982) against Officer Smith, plaintiffs must show (1) that Smith deprived them of a right secured by the "Constitution and laws of the United States," and (2) that Smith deprived them of this right "under color of any statute, ordinance, regulation, custom, usage, of any State or Territory." Adickes v. S.H. Kress & Co., *398 U.S. 144, 150, 90 S.Ct. 1598, 1604, 26 L.Ed.2d 142 (1970). The second element requires that plaintiffs show that defendant Smith acted "under color of law." Id. Plaintiffs have established that defendant Smith's disclosure violated their constitutional right to privacy. Additionally, Smith was acting in his capacity as a police officer for Runnemede at all times relevant to this case, therefore, he was acting under color of state law within the meaning of section 1983.* See Black v. Stephens, *662 F.2d 181, 188 (3d Cir.1981), cert. denied, 455 U.S. 1008, 102 S.Ct. 1646, 71 L.Ed.2d 876 (1982). Section 1983 liability attaches.*

Defendant Smith did not assert a qualified immunity defense. Officials performing discretionary functions are not liable if their conduct does not violate a clearly established constitutional or statutory right of which a reasonable person should have known. Harlow v. Fitzgerald, *457 U.S. 800, 818, 102 S.Ct. 2727, 2738, 73 L.Ed.2d 396 (1982). Additionally, the contours of the right must be sufficiently clear that a reasonable official would understand that what he or she is doing violates that right.* Anderson v. Creighton, *483 U.S. 635, 107 S.Ct. 3034, 3039, 97 L.Ed.2d 523 (1987). Defendants did not raise the issue in their brief, and when asked at oral argument, counsel for Smith stated that defendants relied on their procedural arguments. Qualified immunity is an affirmative defense that is waived if not pleaded.* Gomez v. Toledo, *446 U.S. 635, 640, 100 S.Ct. 1920, 1923, 64 L.Ed.2d 572 (1980). The court can not consider this defense.*

Defendant Smith raises several other defenses. First, Smith argues that plaintiffs have no standing to bring this action because Smith's statement violated only the privacy rights of Jane Doe's husband. (citing Tyree v. Smith, *289 F.Supp. 174 (E.D.Tenn.1968) (father has no standing to sue for denial of constitutional rights of his children)). The father in* Tyree *filed a section 1983 suit for violations of his son's constitutional rights as guardian for his minor son and individually. The father did not allege violations of his own civil rights. The court found that the father had no standing to sue for violations of his son's civil rights. Id. at 175. The court ordered that the father could not recover damages in his own right, however, the case proceeded against defendants with the father acting as representative for his minor son. Id. at 178.*

Plaintiffs here do not assert the constitutional rights of Jane Doe's husband. Jane Doe sues as guardian for her minor children for the violation of their own rights to privacy. The children have standing to sue for the violation of their right to privacy from governmental disclosure of their father's infection with AIDS. Likewise, Jane Doe individually asserts a violation of her constitutional right to privacy. That the officer did not reveal information about the children's own medical condition is immaterial. A family member's diagnosis with AIDS is a personal matter, as defined in Whalen v. Roe, *429 U.S. 589, 599–600, 97 S.Ct. 869, 876–77, 51 L.Ed.2d 64 (1977), that falls within the protection of the Constitution.*

This court rejects the standing argument because Smith's statement communicated private, confidential information about Jane Doe and her children. The stigma of AIDS extends to all family members, whether or not they actually have the disease. Smith's statement also implicitly suggested that Jane Doe herself might somehow transmit the disease to the DiAngelos. Jane Doe clearly has standing to assert a violation of her right to privacy.

Next, defendant Smith asserts that, because his actions did not amount to misconduct, no action can be maintained under section 1983. While misconduct often accompanies a section 1983 violation, section 1983 does not require misconduct. The plain terms of section 1983 require two allegations to state a cause of action. See *Gomez v. Toledo, 446 U.S. 635, 640, 100 S.Ct. 1920, 1923, 64 L.Ed.2d 572 (1980). The statute provides that "[e]very person who, under color of [state law], subjects, or causes to be subjected, any citizen . . . to the deprivation of any rights . . . secured by the Constitution and laws, shall be liable to the party injured." Civil Rights Act of 1871, 42 U.S.C. § 1983 (1982). Misconduct is not a prerequisite to plaintiffs' prevailing under section 1983. This defense is also rejected.*

Smith asserts that, because Jane Doe's husband told police that he had AIDS, the husband "published" the information, giving up any right to privacy in the information. Defendants do not cite any authority for this premise, but ask the court to use its "common sense." Defendant confuses a federal cause of action under section 1983 for violation of plaintiffs' constitutional right to privacy with a state tort claim for invasion of privacy. The court has found no authority that publication by plaintiff eliminates a cause of action against the government for a federal constitutional violation of one's right to privacy. Additionally, "common sense" requires analysis of the underlying policy supporting Jane Doe's husband's selective disclosure of his condition to police.

Clearly, an arrestee's disclosure to police that he or she has AIDS is preferable to nondisclosure. Police can take whatever precautions are necessary to prevent transmission of the disease. Police have more than "casual contact" with arrestee, increasing the likelihood that the disease can be transmitted. For example, by frisking an arrested person, police may come into contact with hypodermic needles. Thus, disclosure should be encouraged to protect police officers. Common sense demands that persons with AIDS be able to make such disclosures without fear that police will inform neighbors, employers, or the media. Smith's publication argument, therefore, is rejected as contrary to public policy.

Finally, Smith asserts that there are no conclusive facts about AIDS, thus his warning to the DiAngelos was justified. As discussed, supra, *defendant ignores the multitude of information, available in 1987, that flatly rejects his argument that AIDS may be spread through casual contact. This court will not rely on defendant's speculation that further AIDS research may reveal that the virus could be infectious by means currently unknown.*

Defendant additionally has failed to assert a single fact to show that Jane Doe had any physical contact *with the DiAngelos. Thus, his "justification" argument fails. Assuming* arguendo *that the disease could be transmitted by casual contact, defendant has failed to put forth facts to show that the DiAngelos had such contact with Jane Doe.*

Smith does not cite any case to support the contention that justified actions are not actionable under section 1983. Perhaps this contention is defendant's inartful attempt to assert qualified immunity. The defendant, however, has the burden to prove the defense of qualified immunity. Gomez v. Toledo, *446 U.S. 635, 640, 100 S.Ct. 1920, 1923, 64 L.Ed.2d 572 (1980). Because he has not met this burden, Smith has not established that his conduct gives rise to qualified immunity.*

This court rejects the defenses asserted by Smith for his conduct. Smith has failed to produce evidence that, in light of his burden of proof at trial, could be the basis for a jury finding in his favor; thus, summary judgment for plaintiffs is appropriate here.

2. Defendant Borough of Runnemede.

To maintain an action under section 1983 against Runnemede, plaintiffs must show that the unconstitutional actions of a municipal employee were taken pursuant to municipal policy or custom. Monell v. Department of Social Services, *436 U.S. 658, 690–91, 98 S.Ct. 2018, 2035–36, 56 L.Ed.2d 611 (1978). Plaintiffs must also establish a "direct causal link" between the unconstitutional municipal policy or custom and the actions of the municipal employee to establish liability.* City of Canton v. Harris, *489 U.S. 378, 109 S.Ct. 1197, 1203, 103 L.Ed.2d 412 (1989);* Losch v. Borough of Parkesburg, *736 F.2d 903, 910 (3d Cir.1984).*

Plaintiffs assert two theories for municipal liability. Plaintiffs assert that Runnemede's failure to train its employees about AIDS and the need to keep the identity of AIDS carriers confidential caused the constitutional violation of their privacy. Next, plaintiffs assert that Runnemede had a unconstitutional custom or policy of not protecting confidential information as evidenced by its failure to have an affirmative policy on the dissemination of confidential information obtained during investigations.

a. Failure to Train.

The United States Supreme Court recently clarified the standard by which municipalities could be held liable under section 1983 for failure to train. Inadequacy of police training may serve as the basis for section 1983 liability "where the failure to train amounts to deliberate indifference to the rights of the persons with whom the police came into contact." City of Canton v. Harris, *489 U.S. 378, 109 S.Ct. 1197, 1204, 103 L.Ed.2d 412 (1989). Only where a failure to train reflects a "deliberate" or "conscious" choice by municipalities can a city be liable for such a failure under section 1983. Id. 109 S.Ct. at 1205. The municipality's failure to train must be the "moving force [behind] the constitutional violation" for liability under section 1983.* Id.

In City of Canton v. Harris, *police did not summon medical help for an arrestee in their custody. Harris was found sitting on the floor of the police wagon used to transport her to the police station. When asked if she needed medical attention,*

Harris responded with an incoherent remark. Harris slumped to the floor on two occasions while inside the police station for processing; eventually, officers left her lying on the floor to prevent her falling again. After her release from custody, an ambulance took her to a nearby hospital, where she was hospitalized for a week. Id. *at 1200–01.*

The Court noted that the city's policy with respect to medical treatment for detainees was constitutional on its face. It rejected the municipality's contention that liability could attach only if "the policy in question [is] itself unconstitutional." Id. *at 1203. The Court also stated that a city was not automatically liable merely because an employee applied the policy in an unconstitutional manner, for then liability would rest on* respondeat superior. Id.

Reasoning that inadequate training cannot always be said to represent city policy, the Court held that the inadequacy of police training may serve as the basis for section 1983 liability "where the failure to train amounts to deliberate indifference to the rights of the persons with whom the police came into contact." Id. *at 1204. Only where a failure to train reflects a "deliberate" or "conscious" choice by municipalities can a city be liable for such a failure under section 1983.* Id. *at 1205.*

The Court defined "deliberate indifference" as:

[I]n light of the duties assigned to specific officers or employees the need for more or different training is so obvious, and the inadequacy so likely to result in the violation of constitutional rights, that the policymakers of the city can reasonably be said to have been deliberately indifferent to the need. In that event, the failure to provide proper training may fairly be said to represent a policy for which the city is responsible, and for which the city may be held liable if it actually causes injury.

Id.

In a footnote, the Court gave an example of when a municipality could be liable for an unconstitutional failure to train:

[C]ity policy makers know to a moral certainty that their police officers will be required to arrest fleeing felons. The city has armed its officers with firearms, in part to allow them to accomplish this task. Thus, the need to train officers in the constitutional limitations on the use of deadly force can be said to be "so obvious," that failure to do so could properly be characterized as "deliberate indifference" to constitutional rights.

Id. *at 1205 n. 10 (citation omitted).*

City of Canton, *however, offers little guidance to courts applying the "deliberate indifference" standard to specific factual scenarios. Finding that the district court in* City of Canton *used a lesser burden of proof, the Court remanded the case to the court of appeals to determine whether plaintiff should have an opportunity to prove that the deficiency in training actually caused the police officers' indifference to her medical needs.* Id. *at 1207. Justice O'Connor's opinion, concurring in part and dissenting in part, stated that she believed that plaintiff had not and could not satisfy the Court's standard for fault and causation. She suggested that the Court's opinion strongly hinted at this conclusion.* Id. *(O'Connor, J., concurring in part and dissenting in part).*

Applying the City of Canton v. Harris *standard to the instant case, this court finds that defendants can not avoid plaintiffs' motion for summary judgment that their failure to train officers about AIDS caused the violation of the Does' constitutional right to privacy.*

In light of the duties assigned to police officers, the need for police training about AIDS is obvious. Officers frequently come into contact with members of high risk populations, such as intravenous drug users, therefore, police must understand the disease and its transmission to protect themselves and the public. The nature of an officer's duties may bring him or her into contact with bodily fluids, particularly blood, or with nonsterile hypodermic needles.

Additionally, the need for police training to keep confidential one's infection with the AIDS virus is obvious. With the hysteria that surrounds AIDS victims and their families, disclosure clearly has a devastating effect that is easily anticipated. The panic sparked by AIDS was widely known in 1987. The failure to instruct officers to keep information about AIDS carriers confidential was likely to result in disclosure and fan the flames of hysteria. Runnemede's failure to train officers, therefore, was likely to result in a violation of constitutional rights.

The absence of training here is also a deliberate and conscious choice by the municipality. Police Chief James M. Leason testified in his deposition that he knew AIDS was a serious disease, almost always fatal, and prevalent within a population that was a prime target of police operations, that is, intravenous drug users. He also testified in his deposition that, prior to the incident, he had heard from other police chiefs in the county about various precautions being taken to protect police officers from AIDS. Yet, the Borough of Runnemede did not train any officers about AIDS prevention and control. The Borough did not provide an operating procedure or policy to guide officers. The police chief should have known that officers untrained as to the medical facts about AIDS would act out of panic, ignorance, and fear when confronted with a person having or suspected of having AIDS, and that such a confrontation was likely to occur. Knowing that other communities had taken precautions to protect officers from AIDS, Runnemede did not establish its own policy or instruct officers about precautions. As such, Runnemede made a conscious decision not to train its officers about the disease.

The failure to train officers about AIDS and the need to keep confidential the identity of AIDS victims caused the violation of the Does' constitutional rights. Clearly, Officer Smith's ignorance about the disease caused the improper disclosure. Smith's police report to Chief Leason stated his reason for disclosing the information:

Fearing that [Jane Doe] may have had physical contact with Mr. and Mrs. DiAngelo [and acting] in my capacity as a police officer[,] being my responsibility to protect the public, I believe it was my duty to inform the noted parties of the possible hazard that may have been at hand.

An officer trained as to the facts about AIDS would have known that no hazard of transmission of the virus existed under the circumstances, whether or not Jane Doe came into physical contact with the DiAngelos. Failure to train officers on the basic facts about AIDS assured that officers coming into contact with AIDS carriers would be ill-equipped to evaluate the risk of transmission present.

Runnemede's failure to train its officers about AIDS and the need to keep confidential the identity of those known to police to have the disease falls within the Supreme Court's definition of "deliberate indifference" that caused the violation of the Does' constitutional rights. The case is analogous to the Supreme Court's example in City of Canton v. Harris *for the use of deadly force against fleeing felons. See* City of Canton v. Harris, *489 U.S. 378, 109 S.Ct. 1197, 1205 n. 10, 103 L.Ed.2d 412 (1989). City policy makers must know to a moral certainty that their police officers will come into contact with those known or suspected to have AIDS and that transmission of the disease will cause death. The need to train officers about AIDS and its transmission and about the constitutional limitations on the disclosure of the identity of AIDS carriers is so obvious that failure to do so is properly characterized as deliberate indifference to constitutional rights.*

Defendant Runnemede asserts that no other municipality or state agency had a policy in place, and therefore it had no obligation to have a policy in place. Defendant maintains that this comparison to other departments establishes that there was no deliberate indifference. Defendant cites no authority to support this theory.

Municipalities must abide by the Constitution regardless of what other municipalities do or fail to do. That other municipalities do not have policies regarding AIDS is not material to the analysis set forth in City of Canton v. Harris, *489 U.S. 378, 109 S.Ct. 1197, 1205, 103 L.Ed.2d 412 (1989). Section 1983 liability attaches "where the failure to train amounts to deliberate indifference to the rights of the persons with whom the police came into contact." Id. 109 S.Ct. at 1204. Only where a failure to train reflects a "deliberate" or "conscious" choice by municipalities can a city be liable for such a failure under section 1983. Id. at 1205. The standard leaves no room for comparison with the failures of other municipalities. This defense is rejected.*

This court concludes, therefore, that defendant Runnemede has failed to produce evidence that, in light of its burden of proof at trial, could be the basis for a jury finding in its favor. Summary judgment for plaintiffs on their claim against Runnemede that its failure to train officers about AIDS caused the violation of the Does' constitutional right to privacy will be granted.

This court notes that it does not decide whether a municipality may reveal one's affliction with AIDS to those actually at risk of contracting the disease from a known AIDS carrier. Likewise, municipal liability is restricted to failure to train about the disease AIDS. The need for training about AIDS and the need to keep the identity of AIDS carriers confidential satisfies the Supreme Court's standard that the need for training be so obvious that failure to do so amounts to deliberate indifference; training about other confidential matters or their disclosure may not be so obvious. No other disease in recent history has sparked such widespread and publicized panic and hysteria. One's condition with AIDS is a unique personal matter; its disclosure provokes a regrettable, but predictable, response from the community that disclosure of other personal matters would not provoke. Thus, municipal liability for disclosure of this personal matter is appropriate.

b. Unconstitutional Policy.

Plaintiffs' second theory for municipal liability is that Runnemede had an unconstitutional policy of failing to recognize its duty to safeguard private or confidential information. This theory appears to restate plaintiffs' theory of liability for failure to train. The absence of a uniform policy, however, may also be viewed as an affirmative policy leaving decisions about disclosure to the discretion of individual officers. Plaintiffs contend that this policy is unconstitutional.

Defendant asserts that Runnemede merely follows the guidelines promulgated by the Attorney General of New Jersey and the State Police. It contends that absent a federal or state requirement to formulate a policy, it can not be held liable for failure to formulate a policy. This defense is rejected. There is no impediment to Runnemede's formulating its own policy; that it chooses not to do so does not absolve it from liability for its constitutional violations, for example, for failure to train.

The court nonetheless finds that plaintiffs can not prevail on summary judgment on this theory of liability. Plaintiffs have offered no authority that the policy of leaving the disclosure decision to the individual officer is unconstitutional. The municipality can not be found liable under section 1983 if the individual officer makes a decision that results in a constitutional violation unless the officer's action is officially sanctioned or ordered by the municipality. Pembaur v. City of Cincinnati, *475 U.S. 469, 480, 106 S.Ct. 1292, 1298–99, 89 L.Ed.2d 452 (1986). "Official policy" refers to formal rules or understandings that are intended to and do establish fixed plans of action to be followed under similar circumstances consistently and over time.* Id. *at 480–81, 106 S.Ct. at 1298–99. Leaving the disclosure decision to individual officers, by definition, can not rise to the level of official policy because it does not establish a fixed plan of action to be followed under similar circumstances and can not result in consistency. Additionally, in this case, plaintiffs have not offered any evidence that Officer Smith's actions were ordered or sanctioned by Runnemede. Plaintiffs motion for summary judgment based on this theory of liability can not prevail.*

III. CONCLUSION

This court finds that plaintiffs have established that defendants Smith and Runnemede violated their constitutional right to privacy and that defendants are liable under section 1983. Plaintiffs' motion for summary judgment on the issue of liability with respect to defendants Smith and Runnemede will be granted. Likewise, the cross-motion for summary judgment of defendants Smith and Runnemede will be denied.

An appropriate order will be entered.

II.   OBLIGATIONS TO DISCLOSE: CASES AND STATUTES

At the same time, even among physicians, the confidentiality obligation is not absolute. One significant exception is the obligation to report certain public health and safety situations regardless of patient desire. A number of courts have considered the circumstances under which a threat to individual or social safety may overrule the general requirement to keep patient communication and information confidential:

TARASOFF v. REGENTS OF UNIVERSITY OF CALIFORNIA[13]

Opinion

TOBRINER, JUSTICE.

On October 27, 1969, Prosenjit Poddar killed Tatiana Tarasoff. Plaintiffs, Tatiana's parents, allege that two months earlier Poddar confided his intention to kill Tatiana to Dr. Lawrence Moore, a psychologist employed by the Cowell Memorial Hospital at the University of California at Berkeley. They allege that on Moore's request, the campus police briefly detained Poddar, but released him when he appeared rational. They further claim that Dr. Harvey Powelson, Moore's superior, then directed that no further action be taken to detain Poddar. No one warned plaintiffs of Tatiana's peril.

Concluding that these facts set forth causes of action against neither therapists and policemen involved, nor against the Regents of the University of California as their employer, the superior court sustained defendants' demurrers to plaintiffs' second amended complaints without leave to amend. This appeal ensued.

Plaintiffs' complaints predicate liability on two grounds: defendants' failure to warn plaintiffs of the impending danger and their failure to bring about Poddar's confinement pursuant to the Lanterman-Petris-Short Act (Welf. & Inst.Code, s 5000ff.) Defendants, in turn, assert that they owed no duty of reasonable care to Tatiana and that they are immune from suit under the California Tort Claims Act of 1963 (Gov.Code, s 810ff.).

We shall explain that defendant therapists cannot escape liability merely because Tatiana herself was not their patient. When a therapist determines, or pursuant to the standards of his profession should determine, that his patient presents a serious danger of violence to another, he incurs an obligation to use reasonable care to protect the intended victim against such danger. The discharge of this duty may require the therapist to take one or more of various steps, depending upon the nature of the case. Thus it may call for him to warn the intended victim or others likely to apprise the victim of the danger, to notify the police, or to take whatever other steps are reasonably necessary under the circumstances.

In the case at bar, plaintiffs admit that defendant therapists notified the police, but argue on appeal that the therapists failed to exercise reasonable care to protect Tatiana in that they did not confine Poddar and did not warn Tatiana or others likely to apprise her of the danger. Defendant therapists, however, are public employees. Consequently, to the extent that plaintiffs seek to predicate liability upon the therapists' failure to bring about Poddar's confinement, the therapists can claim immunity under Government Code section 856. No specific statutory provision,

---

[13] Tarasoff v. Regents of University of California, 17 Cal.3d 425 (1976) (notes omitted).

however, shields them from liability based upon failure to warn Tatiana or others likely to apprise her of the danger, and Government Code section 820.2 does not protect such failure as an exercise of discretion.

Plaintiffs therefore can amend their complaints to allege that, regardless of the therapists' unsuccessful attempt to confine Poddar, since they knew that Poddar was at large and dangerous, their failure to warn Tatiana or others likely to apprise her of the danger constituted a breach of the therapists' duty to exercise reasonable care to protect Tatiana.

Plaintiffs, however, plead no relationship between Poddar and the police defendants which would impose upon them any duty to Tatiana, and plaintiffs suggest no other basis for such a duty. Plaintiffs have, therefore, failed to show that the trial court erred in sustaining the demurrer of the police defendants without leave to amend.

1. Plaintiffs' complaints.

Plaintiffs, Tatiana's mother and father, filed separate but virtually identical second amended complaints. The issue before us on this appeal is whether those complaints now state, or can be amended to state, causes of action against defendants. We therefore begin by setting forth the pertinent allegations of the complaints. Plaintiffs' first cause of action, entitled 'Failure to Detain a Dangerous Patient,' alleges that on August 20, 1969, Poddar was a voluntary outpatient receiving therapy at Cowell Memorial Hospital. Poddar informed Moore, his therapist, that he was going to kill an unnamed girl, readily identifiable as Tatiana, when she returned home from spending the summer in Brazil. Moore, with the concurrence of Dr. Gold, who had initially examined Poddar, and Dr. Yandell, Assistant to the director of the department of psychiatry, decided that Poddar should be committed for observation in a mental hospital. Moore orally notified Officers Atkinson and Teel of the campus police that he would request commitment. He then sent a letter to Police Chief William Beall requesting the assistance of the police department in securing Poddar's confinement.

Officers Atkinson, Brownrigg, and Halleran took Poddar into custody, but, satisfied that Poddar was rational, released him on his promise to stay away from Tatiana. Powelson, director of the department of psychiatry at Cowell Memorial Hospital, then asked the police to return Moore's letter, directed that all copies of the letter and notes that Moore had taken as therapist be destroyed, and 'ordered no action to place Prosenjit Poddar in 72-hour treatment and evaluation facility.'

Plaintiffs' second cause of action, entitled 'Failure to Warn On a Dangerous Patient,' incorporates the allegations of the first cause of action, but adds the assertion that defendants negligently permitted Poddar to be released from police custody without 'notifying the parents of Tatiana Tarasoff that their daughter was in grave danger from Posenjit Poddar.' Roddar persuaded Tatiana's brother to share an apartment with him near Tatiana's residence; shortly after her return from Brazil, Poddar went to her residence and killed her.

Plaintiffs' third cause of action, entitled 'Abandonment of a Dangerous Patient,' seeks $10,000 punitive damages against defendant Powelson. Incorporating the crucial allegations of the first cause of action, plaintiffs charge that Powelson 'did the *things herein alleged with intent to abandon a dangerous patient, and said acts were done maliciously and oppressively.'*

Plaintiffs' fourth cause of action, for 'Breach of Primary Duty to Patient and the Public,' states essentially the same allegations as the first cause of action, but seeks to characterize defendants' conduct as a breach of duty to safeguard their patient and the public. Since such conclusory labels add nothing to the factual allegations of the complaint, the first and fourth causes of action are legally indistinguishable.

As we explain in part 4 of this opinion, plaintiffs' first and fourth causes of action, which seek to predicate liability upon the defendants' failure to bring about Poddar's confinement, are barred by governmental immunity. Plaintiffs' third cause of action succumbs to the decisions precluding exemplary damages in a wrongful death action. (See part 6 of this opinion.) We direct our attention, therefore, to the issue of whether plaintiffs' second cause of action can be amended to state a basis for recover.

2. Plaintiffs can state a cause of action against defendant therapists for negligent failure to protect Tatiana.

The second cause of action can be amended to allege that Tatiana's death proximately resulted from defendants' negligent failure to warn Tatiana or others likely to apprise her of her danger. Plaintiffs contend that as amended, such allegations of negligence and proximate causation, with resulting damages, establish a cause of action. Defendants, however, contend that in the circumstances of the present case they owed no duty of care to Tatiana or her parents and that, in the absence of such duty, they were free to act in careless disregard of Tatiana's life and safety.

In analyzing this issue, we bear in mind that legal duties are not discoverable facts of nature, but merely conclusory expressions that, in cases of a particular type, liability should be imposed for damage done. As stated in Dillon v. Legg (1968) 68 Cal.2d 728, 734, 69 Cal.Rptr. 72, 76, 441 P.2d 912, 916: 'The assertion that liability must . . . be denied because defendant bears no 'duty' to plaintiff 'begs the essential question — whether the plaintiff's interests are entitled to legal protection against the defendant's conduct . . . (Duty) is not sacrosanct in itself, but only an expression of the sum total of those considerations of policy which lead the law to say that the particular plaintiff is entitled to protection.' (Prosser, Law of Torts (3d ed. 1964) at pp. 332–333.)'

In the landmark case of Rowland v. Christian (1968) 69 Cal.2d 108, 70 Cal.Rptr. 97, 443 P.2d 561, Justice Peters recognized that liability should be imposed 'for an injury occasioned to another by his want of ordinary care or skill' as expressed in section 1714 of the Civil Code. Thus, Justice Peters, quoting from Heaven v. Pender (1883) 11 Q.B.D. 503, 509 stated: "whenever one person is by circumstances placed in such a position with regard to another . . . that if he did not use ordinary care and skill in his own conduct . . . he would cause danger of injury to the person or property of the other, a duty arises to use ordinary care and skill to avoid such danger."

We depart from 'this fundamental principle' only upon the 'balancing of a number of considerations'; major ones 'are the foreseeability of harm to the plaintiff, the degree of certainty that the plaintiff suffered injury, the closeness of the connection between the defendant's conduct and the injury suffered, the moral blame attached to the defendant's conduct, the policy of preventing future harm, the extent of the burden to the defendant and consequences to the community of imposing a duty to exercise care with resulting liability for breach, and the availability, cost and prevalence of insurance for the risk involved.' The most important of these considerations in establishing duty is foreseeability. As a general principle, a 'defendant owes a duty of care to all persons who are foreseeably endangered by his conduct, with respect to all risks which make the conduct unreasonably dangerous.' (Rodriguez v. Bethlehem Steel Corp. (1974) 12 Cal.3d 382, 399, 115 Cal.Rptr. 765, 776, 525 P.2d 669, 680; Dillon v. Legg, Supra, 68 Cal.2d 728, 739, 69 Cal.Rptr. 72, 441 P.2d 912; Weirum v. R.K.O. General, Inc. (1975) 15 Cal.3d 40, 123 Cal.Rptr. 468, 539 P.2d 36; see Civ.Code, s 1714.) As we shall explain, however, when the avoidance of foreseeable harm requires a defendant to control the conduct of another person, or to warn of such conduct, the common law has traditionally imposed liability only if the defendant bears some special relationship to the dangerous person or to the potential victim. Since the relationship between a therapist and his patient satisfies this requirement, we need not here decide whether foreseeability alone is sufficient to create a duty to exercise reasonably care to protect a potential victim of another's conduct.

Although, as we have stated above, under the common law, as a general rule, one person owed no duty to control the conduct of another (Richards v. Stanley (1954) 43 Cal.2d 60, 65, 271 P.2d 23; Wright v. Arcade School Dist. (1964) 230 Cal.App.2d 272, 277, 40 Cal.Rptr. 812; Rest.2d Torts (1965) s 315), nor to warn those endangered by such conduct (Rest.2d Torts, Supra, s 314, com. c Prosser, Law of Torts (4th ed. 1971) s 56, p. 341), the courts have carved out an exception to this rule in cases in which the defendant stands in some special relationship to either the person whose conduct needs to be controlled or in a relationship to the foreseeable victim of that conduct (see Rest.2d Torts, Supra, ss 315–320). Applying this exception to the present case, we note that a relationship of defendant therapists to either Tatiana or Poddar will suffice to establish a duty of care; as explained in section 315 of the Restatement Second of Torts, a duty of care may arise from either '(a) a special relation . . . between the actor and the third person which imposes a duty upon the actor to control the third person's conduct, or (b) a special relation . . . between the actor and the other which gives to the other a right of protection.'

Although plaintiffs' pleadings assert no special relation between Tatiana and defendant therapists, they establish as between Poddar and defendant therapists the special relation that arises between a patient and his doctor or psychotherapist. Such a relationship may support affirmative duties for the benefit of third persons. Thus, for example, a hospital must exercise reasonable care to control the behavior of a patient which may endanger other persons. A doctor must also warn a patient if the patient's condition or medication renders certain conduct, such as driving a car, dangerous to others.Although the California decisions that recognize this duty have involvd cases in which the defendant stood in a special relationship Both to the victim and to the person whose conduct created the danger, we do not think that the duty should logically be constricted to such situations. Decisions of other jurisdictions hold that the single relationship of a doctor to his patient is sufficient to support the duty to exercise reasonable care to rotect others against dangers emanating from the patient's illness. The courts hold that a doctor is liable to persons infected by his patient if he negligently fails to diagnose a contagious disease (Hofmann v. Blackmon (Fla.App.1970) 241 So.2d 752), or, having diagnosed the illness, fails to warn members of the patient's family (Wojcik v. Aluminum Co. of America (1959) 18 Misc.2d 740, 183 N.Y.S2d 351, 357–358; Davis v. Rodman (1921) 147 Ark. 385, 227 S.W. 612; Skillings v. Allen (1919) 143 Minn. 323, 173 N.W. 663; see also Jones v. Stanko (1928) 118 Ohio St. 147, 160 N.E. 456).

Since it involved a dangerous mental patient, the decision in Merchants Nat. Bank & Trust Co. of Fargo v. United States (D.N.D.1967) 272 F.Supp. 409 comes closer to the issue. The Veterans Administration arranged for the patient to work on a local farm, but did not inform the farmer of the man's background. The farmer consequently permitted the patient to come and go freely during nonworking hours; the patient borrowed a car, drove to his wife's residence and killed her. Notwithstanding the lack of any 'special relationship' between the Veterans Administration and the wife, the court found the Veterans Administration liable for the wrongful death of the wife.

In their summary of the relevant rulings Fleming and Maximov conclude that the 'case law should dispel any notion that to impose on the therapists a duty to take precautions for the safety of persons threatened by a patient, where due care so requires, is in any way opposed to contemporary ground rules on the duty relationship. On the contrary, there now seems to be sufficient authority to support the conclusion that by entering into a doctor-patient relationship the therapist becomes sufficiently involved to assume some responsibility for the safety, not only of the patient himself, but also of any third person whom the doctor knows to be threatened by the patient.' (Fleming & Maximov, The Patient or His Victim: The Therapist's Dilemma (1974) 62 Cal.L.Rev. 1025, 1030.)

Defendants contend, however, that imposition of a duty to exercise reasonable care to protect third persons is unworkable because therapists cannot accurately predict whether or not a patient will resort to violence. In support of this argument amicus representing the American Psychiatric Association and other professional societies cites numerous articles which indicate that therapists, in the present state of the art, are unable reliably to predict violent acts; their forecasts, amicus claims, tend consistently to overpredict violence, and indeed are more often wrong than right. Since predictions of violence are often erroneous, amicus concludes, the courts should not render rulings that predicate the liability of therapists upon the validity of such predictions.

The role of the psychiatrist, who is indeed a practitioner of medicine, and that of the psychologist who performs an allied function, are like that of the physician who must conform to the standards of the profession and who must often make diagnoses and predictions based upon such evaluations. Thus the judgment of the therapist in diagnosing emotional disorders and in predicting whether a patient presents a serious danger of violence is comparable to the judgment which doctors and professionals must regularly render under accepted rules of responsibility.

We recognize the difficulty that a therapist encounters in attempting to forecast whether a patient presents a serious danger of violence. Obviously we do not require that the therapist, in making that determination, render a perfect performance; the therapist need only exercise 'that reasonable degree of skill, knowledge, and care ordinarily possessed and exercised by members of (that professional specialty) under similar circumstances.' (Bardessono v. Michels (1970) 3 Cal.3d 780, 788, 91 Cal.Rptr. 760, 764, 478 P.2d 480, 484; Quintal v. Laurel Grove Hospital (1964) 62 Cal.2d 154, 159–160, 41 Cal.Rptr. 577, 397 P.2d 161; see 4 Witkin, Summary of Cal.Law (8th ed. 1974) Torts, s 514 and cases cited.) Within the broad range of reasonable practice and treatment in which professional opinion and judgment may differ, the therapist is free to exercise his or her own best judgment without liability; proof, aided by hindsight, that he or she judged wrongly is insufficient to establish negligence.

In the instant case, however, the pleadings do not raise any question as to failure of defendant therapists to predict that Poddar presented a serious danger of violence. On the contrary, the present complaints allege that defendant therapists did in fact predict that Poddar would kill, but were negligent in failing to warn.

Amicus contends, however, that even when a therapist does in fact predict that a patient poses a serious danger of violence to others, the therapist should be absolved of any responsibility for failing to act to protect the potential victim. In our view, however, once a therapist does in fact determine, or under applicable professional standards reasonably should have determined, that a patient poses a serious danger of violence to others, he bears a duty to exercise reasonable care to protect the foreseeable victim of that danger. While the discharge of this duty of due care will necessarily vary with the facts of each case, in each instance the adequacy of the therapist's conduct must be measured against the traditional negligence standard of the rendition of reasonable care under the circumstances. (Accord Cobbs v. Grant (1972) 8 Cal.3d 229, 243, 104 Cal.Rptr. 505, 502 p.2d 1.) As explained in Fleming and Maximov, The Patient or His Victim: The Therapist's Dilemma (1974) 62 Cal.L.Rev. 1025, 1067: '. . . the ultimate question of resolving the tension between the conflicting interests of patient and potential victim is one of social policy, not professional expertise. . . . In sum, the therapist owes a legal duty not only to his patient, but also to his patient's would-be victim and is subject in both respects to scrutiny by judge and jury.'

Contrary to the assertion of amicus, this conclusion is not inconsistent with our recent decision in People v. Burnick, supra, 14 Cal.3d 306, 121 Cal.Rptr. 488, 535 P.2d 352. Taking note of the uncertain character of therapeutic prediction, we held in Burnick that a person cannot be committed as a mentally disordered sex offender unless found to be such by proof beyond a reasonable doubt. (14 Cal.3d at p. 328, 121 Cal.Rptr. 488, 535 P.2d 352.) The issue in the present context, however, is not whether the patient should be incarcerated, but whether the therapist should take any steps at all to protect the threatened victim; some of the alternatives open to the therapist, such as warning the victim, will not result in the drastic consequences of depriving the patient of his liberty. Weighing the uncertain and conjectural character of the alleged damage done the patient by such a warning against the peril to the victim's life, we conclude that professional inaccuracy in predicting violence cannot negate the therapist's duty to protect the threatened victim.

The risk that unnecessary warnings may be given is a reasonable price to pay for the lives of possible victims that may be saved. We would hesitate to hold that the therapist who is aware that his patient expects to attempt to assassinate the President of the United States would not be obligated to warn the authorities because the therapist cannot predict with accuracy that his patient will commit the crime.

Defendants further argue that free and open communication is essential to psychotherapy (see In re Lifschutz (1970) 2 Cal.3d 415, 431–434, 85 Cal.Rptr. 829, 467 P.2d 557); that 'Unless a patient . . . is assured that . . . information (revealed by him) can and will be held in utmost confidence, he will be reluctant to make the full disclosure upon which diagnosis and treatment . . . depends.' (Sen.Com. on Judiciary, comment on Evid.Code, s 1014.) The giving of a warning, defendants contend, constitutes a breach of trust which entails the revelation of confidential communications.We recognize the public interest in supporting effective treatment of mental illness and in protecting the rights of patients to privacy (see In re Liftschutz, supra, 2 Cal.3d at p. 432, 85 Cal.Rptr. 829, 467 P.2d 557), and the consequent public importance of safeguarding the confidential character of psychotherapeutic communication. Against this interest, however, we must weigh the public interest in safety from violent assault. The Legislature has undertaken the difficult task of balancing the countervailing concerns. In evidence Code section 1014, it established a broad rule of privilege to protect confidential Communications between patient and psychotherapist. In Evidence Code section 1024, the Legislature created a specific and limited exception to the psychotherapist-patient privilege: 'There is no privilege . . . if the psychotherapist has reasonable cause to believe that the patient is in such mental or emotional condition as to be dangerous to himself or to the person or property of another and that disclosure of the communication is necessary to prevent the threatened danger.'We realize that the open and confidential character of psychotherapeutic dialogue encourages patients to express threats of violence, few of which are ever executed. Certainly a therapist should not be encouraged routinely to reveal such threats; such disclosures could seriously disrupt the patient's relationship with his therapist and with the persons threatened. To the contrary, the therapist's obligations to his patient require that he not disclose a confidence unless such disclosure is necessary to avert danger to others, and even then that he do so discreetly, and in a fashion that would preserve the privacy of his patient to the fullest extent compatible with the prevention of the threatened danger. (See Fleming & Maximov, The Patient or His Victim: The Therapist's Dilemma (1974) 62 Cal.L.Rev. 1025, 1065–1066.)The revelation of a communication under the above circumstances is not a breach of trust or a violation of professional ethics; as stated in the Principles of Medical Ethics of the American Medical Association (1957), section 9: 'A physician may not reveal the confidence entrusted to him in the course of medical attendance . . . Unless he is required to do so by law or unless it becomes necessary in order to protect the welfare of the individual or of the community.' (Emphasis added.) We conclude that the public policy favoring protection of the confidential character of patient-psychotherapist communications must yield to the extent to which disclosure is essential to avert danger to others. The protective privilege ends where the public peril begins.

Our current crowded and computerized society compels the interdependence of its members. In this risk-infested society we can hardly tolerate the further exposure to danger that would result from a concealed knowledge of the therapist that his patient was lethal. If the exercise of reasonable care to protect the threatened victim requires the therapist to warn the endangered party or those who can reasonably be expected to notify him, we see no sufficient societal interest that would protect and justify concealment. The containment of such risks lies in the public interest For the foregoing reasons, we find that plaintiffs' complaints can be amended to state a cause of action against defendants Moore, Powelson, Gold, and Yandell and against the Regents as their employer, for breach of a duty to exercise reasonable care to protect Tatiana.Finally, we reject the contention of the dissent that the provisions of the Lanterman-Petris-Short Act which govern the release of confidential information (Welf. & Inst.Code, ss 5328–5328.9) prevented defendant therapists from warning Tatiana. The dissent's contention rests on the assertion that Dr. Moore's letter to the campus police constituted an 'application in writing' within the meaning of Welfare and Institutions Code section 5150, and thus initiates proceedings under the Lanterman-Petris-Short Act. A closer look at the terms of section 5150, however, will demonstrate that it is inapplicable to the present case.

Section 5150 refers to a written application only by a professional person who is '(a) member of the attending staff . . . of an evaluation facility designated by the county,'or who is himself 'designated by the county' as one authorized to take a person into custody and place him in a facility designated by the county and approved by the State Department of Mental Hygiene. The complaint fails specifically to allege that Dr. Moore was so empowered. Dr. Moore and the Regents cannot rely upon any inference to the contrary that might be drawn from plaintiff's allegation that Dr. Moore intended to 'assign' a 'detention' on Poddar; both Dr. Moore and the Regents have expressly conceded that neither Cowell Memorial Hospital nor any member of its staff has ever been designated by the County of Alameda to institute involuntary commitment proceedings pursuant to section 5150.

Furthermore, the provisions of the Lanterman-Petris-Short Act defining a therapist's duty to withhold confidential information are expressly limited to 'information and records Obtained in the course of providing services under Division 5 (commencing with Section 5000), Division 6 (commencing with Section 6000), or Division 7 (commencing with Section 7000)' of the Welfare and Institutions Code (Welf. & Inst. Code, s 5328). (Emphasis added.) Divisions 5, 6 and 7 describe a variety of programs for treatment of the mentally ill or retarded. The pleadings at issue on this appeal, however, state no facts showing that the psychotherapy provided to Poddar by the Cowell Memorial Hospital falls under any of these programs. We therefore conclude that the Lanterman-Petris-Short Act does not govern the release of information acquired by Moore during the course of rendition of those services.

Neither can we adopt the dissent's suggestion that we import wholesale the detailed provisions of the Lanterman-Petris-Short Act regulating the disclosure of confidential information and apply them to disclosure of information Not governed by the act. Since the Legislature did not extend the act to control all disclosures of confidential matter by a therapist, we must infer that the Legislature did not relieve the courts of their obligation to define by reference to the principles of the common law the obligation of the therapist in those situations not governed by the act.

Turning now to the police defendants, we conclude that they do not have any such special relationship to either Tatiana or to Poddar sufficient to impose upon such defendants a duty to warn respecting Poddar's violent intentions. (See Hartzler v. City of San Jose (1975) 46 Cal.App.3d 6, 9–10, 120 Cal.Rptr. 5; Antique Arts Corp. v. City of Torrance (1974) 39 Cal.App.3d 588, 593, 114 Cal.Rptr. 332.) Plaintiffs suggest no theory, and plead no facts that give rise to any duty to warn on the part of the police defendants absent such a special relationship. They have thus failed to demonstrate that the trial court erred in denying leave to amend as to the police defendants. (See Cooper v. Leslie Salt Co. (1969) 70 Cal.2d 627, 636, 75 Cal.Rptr. 766, 451 P.2d 406; Filice v. Boccardo (1962) 210 Cal.App.2d 843, 847, 26 Cal.Rptr. 789.)

3. Defendant therapists are not immune from liability for failure to warn.

We address the issue of whether defendant therapists are protected by governmental immunity for having failed to warn Tatiana or those who reasonably could have been expected to notify her of her peril. We postulate our analysis on section 820.2 of the Government Code. That provision declares, with exceptions not applicable here, that 'a public employee is not liable for an injury resulting from his act or omission where the act or omission was the result of the exercise of the discretion vested in him, whether or not such discretion (was) abused.' Noting that virtually every public act admits of some element of discretion, we drew the line in Johnson v. State of California (1968) 69 Cal.2d 782, 73 Cal.Rptr. 240, 447 P.2d 352, between discretionary policy decisions which enjoy statutory immunity and ministerial administrative acts which do not. We concluded that section 820.2 affords immunity only for 'basic policy decisions.' (Emphasis added.) (See also Elton v. County of Orange (1970) 3 Cal.App.3d 1053, 1057–1058, 84 Cal.Rptr. 27; 4 Cal.Law Revision Com.Rep. (1963) p. 810; Van Alstyne, Supplement to Cal. Government Tort Liability (Cont.Ed.Bar 1969) s 5.54, pp. 16–17; Comment, California Tort Claims Act: Discretionary Immunity (1966) 39 So.Cal.L.Rev. 470, 471; cf. James, Tort Liability of Governmental Units and Their Officers (1955) 22 U.Chi.L.Rev. 610, 637–638, 640, 642, 651.)

We also observed that if courts did not respect this statutory immunity, they would find themselves 'in the unseemly position of determining the propriety of decisions expressly entrusted to a coordinate branch of government.' (Johnson v. State of California, supra, 69 Cal.2d at p. 793, 73 Cal.Rptr. at p. 248, 447 P.2d at p. 360.) It therefore is necessary, we concluded, to 'isolate those areas of quasilegislative policy-making which are sufficiently sensitive to justify a blanket rule that courts will not entertain a tort action alleging that careless conduct contributed to the governmental decision.' (Johnson v. State of California, supra, at p. 794, 73 Cal.Rptr., at p. 248, 447 P.2d, at p. 360.) After careful analysis we rejected, in Johnson, other rationales commonly advanced to support governmental immunity and concluded that the immunity's scope should be no greater than is required to give legislative and executive policymakers sufficient breathing space in which to perform their vital policymaking functions.

Relying on Johnson, we conclude that defendant therapists in the present case are not immune from liability for their failure to warn of Tatiana's peril. Johnson held that a parole officer's determination whether to warn an adult couple that their prospective foster child had a background of violence 'present(ed) no . . . reasons for immunity' (Johnson v. State of California, supra, at p. 795, 73 Cal.Rptr. 240, 447 P.2d 352), was 'at the lowest, ministerial rung of official action' (Id., at p. 796, 73 Cal.Rptr. at p. 250, 447 P.2d at p. 362), and indeed constituted 'a classic case for the imposition of tort liability.' (Id., p. 797, 73 Cal.Rptr. p. 251, 447 P.2d, p. 363; cf. Morgan v. County of Yuba, supra, 230 Cal.App.2d 938, 942–943, 41 Cal.Rptr. 508.) Although defendants in Johnson argued that the decision whether to inform the foster parents of the child's background required the exercise of considerable judgmental skills, we concluded that the state was not immune from liability for the parole officer's failure to warn because such a decision did not rise to the level of a 'basic policy decision.'

We also noted in Johnson that federal courts have consistently categorized failures to warn of latent dangers as falling outside the scope of discretionary omissions immunized by the Federal Tort Claims Act. (See United Air Lines, Inc. v. Wiener (9th Cir. 1964) 335 F.2d 379, 397–398, cert. den. Sub nom. United Air Lines, Inc. v. United States, 379 U.S. 951, 85 S.Ct. 452, 13 L.Ed.2d 549 (decision to conduct military training flights was discretionary but failure to warn commercial airline was not); United States v. Washington (9th Cir. 1965) 351 F.2d 913, 916 (decision where to place transmission lines spanning canyon was assumed to be discretionary but failure to warn pilot was not); United States v. White (9th Cir. 1954) 211 F.2d 79, 82 (decision not to 'dedud' army firing range assumed to be discretionary but failure to warn person about to go onto range of unsafe condition was not); Bulloch v. United States (D.Utah 1955) 133 F.Supp. 885, 888 (decision how and when to conduct nuclear test deemed discretionary but failure to afford proper notice was not); Hernandez v. United States (D.Hawaii 1953) 112 F.Supp. 369, 371 (decision to erect road block characterized as discretionary but failure to warn of resultant hazard was not).

We conclude, therefore, that the therapist defendants' failure to warn Tatiana or those who reasonably could have been expected to notify her of her peril does not fall within the absolute protection afforded by section 820.2 of the Government Code. We emphasize that our conclusion does not raise the specter of therapists employed by the government indiscriminately being held liable for damage despite their exercise of sound professional judgment. We require of publicly employed therapists only that quantum of care which the common law requires of private therapists. The imposition of liability in those rare cases in which a public employee falls short of this standard does not contravene the language or purpose of Government Code section 820.2.

4. Defendant therapists are immune from liability for failing to confine Poddar.

We sustain defendant therapists' contention that Government Code section 856 insulates them from liability under plaintiffs' first and fourth causes of action for failing to confine Poddar. Section 856 affords public entities and their employees absolute protection from liability for 'any injury resulting from determining in accordance with any applicable enactment . . . whether to confine a person for mental illness.' Since this section refers to a determination to confine 'in accordance with any applicable enactment,' plaintiffs suggest that the immunity is limited to persons designated under Welfare and Institutions Code section 5150 as authorized finally to adjudicate a patient's confinement. Defendant therapists, plaintiffs point out, are not among the persons designated under section 5150.

The language and legislative history of section 856, however, suggest a far broader immunity. In 1963, when section 856 was enacted, the Legislature had not established the statutory structure of the Lanterman-Petris-Short Act. Former Welfare and Institutions Code section 5050.3 (renumbered as Welf. & Inst. Code s 5880; repealed July 1, 1969) which resembled present section 5150, authorized emergency detention at the behest only of peace officers, health officers, county physicians, or assistant county physicians; former section 5047 (renumbered as Welf, & Inst. Code s 5551; repealed July 1, 1969), however, authorized a petition seeking commitment by any person, including the 'physician attending the patient.' The Legislature did not refer in section 856 only to those persons authorized to institute emergency proceedings under section 5050.3; it broadly extended immunity to all employees who acted in accord with 'any applicable enactment,' thus granting immunity not only to persons who are empowered to confine, but also to those authorized to request or recommend confinement.

The Lanterman-Petris-Short Act, in its extensive revision of the procedures for commitment of the mentally ill, eliminated any specific statutory reference to petitions by treating physicians, but it did not limit the authority of a therapist in government employ to request, recommend or initiate actions which may lead to commitment of his patient under the act. We believe that the language of section 856, which refers to any action in the course of employment and in accordance with any applicable enactment, protects the therapist who must undertake this delicate and difficult task. (See Fleming & Maximov, The Patient or His Victim: The Therapist's Dilemma (1974) 62 Cal.L.Rev. 1025, 1064.) Thus the scope of the immunity extends not only to the final determination to confine or not to confine the person for mental illness, but to all determinations involved in the process of commitment. (Cf. Hernandez v. State of California (1970) 11 Cal.App.3d 895, 899–900, 90 Cal.Rptr. 205.)

Turning first to Dr. Powelson's status with respect to section 856, we observe that the actions attributed to him by plaintiffs' complaints fall squarely within the protections furnished by that provision. Plaintiffs allege Powelson ordered that no actions leading to Poddar's detention be taken. This conduct reflected Powelson's determination not to seek Poddar's confinement and thus falls within the statutory immunity.

Section 856 also insulates Dr. Moore for his conduct respecting confinement, although the analysis in his case is a bit more subtle. Clearly, moore's decision that Poddar Be confined was not a proximate cause of Tatiana's death, for indeed if Moore's efforts to bring about Poddar's confinement had been successful, Tatiana might still be alive today. Rather, any confinement claim against Moore must rest upon Moore's failure to overcome Powelson's decision and actions opposing confinement.

Such a claim, based as it necessarily would be, upon a subordinate's failure to prevail over his superior, obviously would derive from a rather onerous duty. Whether to impose such a duty we need not decide, however, since we can confine our analysis to the question whether Moore's failure to overcome Powelson's decision realistically falls within the protection afforded by section 856. Based upon the allegations before us, we conclude that Moore's conduct is protected.

Plaintiffs' complaints imply that Moore acquiesced in Powelson's countermand of Moore's confinement recommendation. Such acquiescense is functionally equivalent to determining not to seek Poddar's confinement and thus merits protection under section 856. At this stage we are unaware, of course, precisely how Moore responded to powelson's actions; he may have debated the confinement issue with Powelson, for example, or taken no initiative whatsoever, perhaps because he respected Powelson's judgment, feared for his future at the hospital, or simply recognized that the proverbial handwriting was on the wall. None of these possibilities constitutes, however, the type of careless or wrongful behavior subsequent to a decision respecting confinement which is stripped of protection by the exception in section 856. Rather each is in the nature of a decision not to continue to press for Poddar's confinement. No language in plaintiffs' original or amended complaints suggests that Moore determined to fight Powelson, but failed successfully to do so, due to negligent or otherwise wrongful acts or omissions. Under the circumstances, we conclude that plaintiffs' second amended complaints allege facts which trigger immunity for Dr. Moore under section 856.

5. Defendant police officers are immune from liability for failing to confine Poddar in their custody.

Confronting, finally, the question whether the defendant police officers are immune from liability for releasing Poddar after his brief confinement, we conclude that they are. The source of their immunity is section 5154 of the Welfare and Institutions Code, which declares that: '(t)he professional person in charge of the facility providing 72-hour treatment and evaluation, his designee, And the peace officer responsible for the detainment of the person shall not be held civilly or criminally liable for any action by a person released at or before the end of 72 hours . . . .'(Emphasis added.)

Although defendant police officers technically were not 'peace officers' as contemplated by the Welfare and Institutions Code, plaintiffs' assertion that the officers incurred liability by failing to continue Poddar's confinement clearly contemplates that the officers were 'responsible for the detainment of (Poddar).'We could not impose a duty upon the officers to keep Poddar confined yet deny them the protection furnished by a statute immunizing those 'responsible for . . . (confinement).'Because plaintiffs would have us treat defendant officers as persons who were capable of performing the functions of the 'peace officers' contemplated by the Welfare and Institutions Code, we must accord defendant officers the protections which that code prescribed for such 'peace officers.'

6. Plaintiffs' complaints state no cause of action for exemplary damages.

Plaintiff's third cause of action seeks punitive damages against defendant Powelson. The California statutes and decisions, however, have been interpreted to bar the recovery of punitive damages in a wrongful death action. (See Pease v. Beech Aircraft corp. (1974) 38 Cal.App.3d 450, 460–462, 113 Cal.Rptr. 416, and authorities there cited.)

7. Conclusion

For the reasons stated, we conclude that plaintiffs can amend their complaints to state a cause of action against defendant therapists by asserting that the therapists in fact determined that Poddar presented a serious danger of violence to Tatiana, or pursuant to the standards of their profession should have so determined, but nevertheless failed to exercise reasonable care to protect her from that danger. To the extent, however, that plaintiffs base their claim that defendant therapists breached that duty because they failed to procure Poddar's confinement, the therapists find immunity in Government Code section 856. Further, as to the police defendants we conclude that plaintiffs have failed to show that the trial court erred in sustaining their demurrer without leave to amend.

The judgment of the superior court in favor of defendants Atkinson, Beall, Brownrigg, Hallernan, and Teel is affirmed. The judgment of the superior court in favor of defendants Gold, Moore, Powelson, Yandell, and the Regents of the University of California is reversed, and the cause remanded for further proceedings consistent with the views expressed herein.

* * *

LEONARD v. LATROBE AREA HOSP.[14]

Opinion

CERCONE, JUDGE:

This appeal is from the learned lower court's order granting appellees' motion for summary judgment. The salient question we are asked to discuss and decide is as follows: What is the responsibility of a psychiatrist or psychologist to warn a third person of the violent propensities of a patient who is under his or her care when the patient does not specifically identify the victim whom the patient later harms. In Dunkle v. Food Service East, Inc., 400 Pa.Super. 58, 582 A.2d 1342 (1990), we said "we are cognizant of the extreme importance of this complex issue, as well as the public interest in its resolution." The facts, as disclosed in the pleadings, are as follows. James Gault was admitted to Latrobe Hospital's psychiatric unit after taking an overdose of aspirin on September 10, 1983. He remained there at the hospital for eight days under the care of Dr. George E. Mamo, M.D., Psychiatrist, until September 27, 1983. Two months after his release, Mr. Gault on November 25, 1983 shot and killed his wife Elizabeth. As a result, the children of Elizabeth Gault filed an action against the Latrobe Hospital and Dr. Mamo alleging that their mother's death was the result of the negligent care and treatment of Mr. Gault by the appellees. Appellants further allege that Dr. Mamo, upon release of Mr. Gault, failed to warn them or their mother of his dangerous propensities.

The appellees filed a motion for summary judgment on the premise that no

---

[14]   Leonard v. Latrobe Area Hosp., 425 Pa.Super. 540 (1993) (notes omitted).

common law rule or statutory requirement imposes upon them a duty to warn a non-patient of a patient's dangerous propensities under the circumstances of this case. On the other hand, the appellants contend that issues of fact exist on grounds supporting the claim that the acts of Mr. Gault were foreseeable by Dr. Mamo while he was under the doctor's care. The learned lower court granted appellees' motion for summary judgment and this appeal was subsequently perfected by the children of Mrs. Gault. After careful review of the record, briefs and the learned lower court's opinion, we affirm the judgment of the court.

The trial court below, in commenting on its granting of appellees' motion for summary judgment, said:

> *The defendants maintain that there is no common law rule or statutory requirement which imposes a duty upon a psychiatrist to warn a non-patient of a patient's dangerous propensities. The Plaintiffs respond that an issue of fact exists and liability is dependent upon whether the acts of the patient were foreseeable.*

> *The Defendants' position is that the Plaintiffs have failed to allege facts which would support a finding that the patient threatened to inflict harm on a particular individual. By affidavit, Dr. Mamo has testified that no such communication existed. The Defendants argue that the Plaintiffs have merely alleged that a hostile dependent relationship existed between the decedent and James Gault and that the Defendants were aware of the violent propensities of James Gault through the Plaintiffs.*

> *The undisputed facts in the present matter indicate that the Defendants were aware that the decedent's husband had in the past, abused and threatened the decedent. At the time of the discharge of James Gault, it is also undisputed that there were signs of a hostile dependent relationship with the decedent and James Gault was diagnosed as having an organic brain syndrome with depression. The Plaintiffs have alleged that the Defendants failed to warn the family of James Gault's mental condition, his propensity towards violence, and to explain a "possible" confrontation with his wife.*

Trial court opinion filed May 21, 1992 at 1–2 (citations omitted). Thus, conceding these allegations by appellants, the learned trial court found they were insufficient to present a cognizable claim and granted summary judgment in favor of appellees. Appellants' salient argument on appeal is that the lower court erred in declining to extend to a psychologist a duty to warn a third party of a patient's dangerous propensities and in granting summary judgment in favor of the doctor.

Prior to this court's decision in Dunkle v. Food Service East Inc., *supra, we had no precedential Pennsylvania law which gave guidance into this very important area of social law. In* Dunkle, *in the absence of* stare decisis, *we looked to other jurisdictions which had established views on the subject. In* Tarasoff v. Regents of Univ. of California, 17 Cal.3d 425, 131 Cal.Rptr. 14, 551 P.2d 334 (1976), *the California Supreme Court held that in limited circumstances a psychologist may have a duty to protect an identifiable and foreseeable victim of a patient's dangerous propensities. In that case a patient confided his intention to a psychologist that he intended to kill his girlfriend, Tatiana. The California Supreme Court held that therapists cannot escape a liability merely because the victim is not their patient. "That when a therapist determines, or pursuant to the standards of his profession should determine, that his patient presents a serious danger of violence to another, he incurs an obligation to use reasonable care to protect the intended victim against such danger." Id. at 431, 131 Cal.Rptr. at 20, 551 P.2d at 340.*

Therapists may be required (1) to warn the intended victim or others who are likely to apprise the intended victim of the danger; (2) notify the police, or (3) take whatever steps that our reasonably necessary under the circumstances. Tarasoff explicitly held that where a victim is specifically identified and there is foreseeably a danger to that victim the therapist has the responsibility of notifying that victim concerning the violent propensities of a patient. Id. at 439, 131 Cal.Rptr. at 25, 551 P.2d at 345. By entering into a doctor/patient relationship, the therapist becomes sufficiently involved to assume some responsibility for the safety not only for the patient himself, but also of third parties whom the doctor knows to be threatened by the patient. Id. A therapist must exercise that reasonable degree of skill, knowledge and care ordinarily professed and exercised by members of that professed specialty under similar circumstances. Id.

Tarasoff also held that a patient's right of confidentiality must be weighed against the public interest in safety from violent assault; that there is no privilege of confidentiality after the psychologist has reason to believe that his or her patient is in such mental or emotional condition as to be dangerous to himself or to the person or property of another and that disclosure of the communication is necessary to prevent the threatened danger. See id. In Tarasoff, the court relied upon the fact that the psychiatrist had knowledge that a specific person was targeted for death at the hands of his patient. However, the California Supreme Court has refused to extend this rationale. In Thompson v. County of Alameda, 27 Cal.3d 741, 167 Cal.Rptr. 70, 614 P.2d 728 (1980), the court was confronted with a claim against a county alleging negligence in releasing from custody a juvenile delinquent who was known to have dangerous and violent propensities toward young children and who within 24 hours after being released sexually assaulted and murdered plaintiffs' son who resided in the community into which the juvenile was released. In rejecting the plaintiffs' contention that their complaint stated a cause of action, the Supreme Court of California emphasized that in Tarasoff there was a specifically foreseeable and identifiable victim. While the Thompson court stated that the intended victim need not be specifically named, he must be "readily identifiable." Thompson v. County of Alameda, 27 Cal.3d at 752–53, 167 Cal.Rptr. at 76, 614 P.2d at 734.

The court in Thompson rejected the contention that as a neighborhood child, the plaintiffs' decedent was a foreseeable victim of the released juvenile. Under circumstances in which an individual poses a risk of danger to a significant portion of the community, the court declined to impose any duty to give warnings primarily because it determined that the value of such warnings was not great. In Tarasoff, the warnings were directed at making the victim aware of the danger to which she was "uniquely exposed." The threatened target was "precise." In such a case, "it is fair to conclude that warnings given discreetly and to a limited number of persons would have a greater effect because they would alert those particular targeted individuals of the possibility of a specific threat pointed at them." Id. *at 755, 167 Cal.Rptr. at 78, 614 P.2d at 736.*

In Leedy v. Hartnett, *510 F.Supp. 1125 (M.D.Pa.1981),* aff'd, *676 F.2d 686 (3d Cir.1982), the U.S. District Court for the Middle District of Pennsylvania discussed cases from New Jersey, Florida, North Dakota and Nebraska analyzing the various views of those states, depending upon the facts and circumstances of the cases decided by them. With this assistance we addressed the issue in* Dunkle, supra, *in which we affirmed the trial court's granting summary judgment in favor of the psychiatrist and other professionals. In reviewing* Tarasoff, supra, *we held that the facts of* Dunkle *did not result in the imposition of a duty contemplated by the California court. We stated in* Dunkle:

> *This Commonwealth has never expressly adopted the California opinion in* Tarasoff. *However, even if we were to accept the* Tarasoff *holding as law in this jurisdiction, we would not find that decision determinative of the instant appeal. Conversely, we find that the* Tarasoff *rationale should be confined to a very limited circumstances presented in that case. We narrowly construe the California court's holding. Contrary to the appellants' position in the instant case, we will not interpret* Tarasoff *to mean that, in effect, strict liability should be imposed upon treating physicians for the wrongful acts of their patients where there is any reason to believe that a third party might be endangered by the patient's possible misconduct and the medical professional fails to inform the third party of same. Such a rule would be unworkable and illogical. More importantly, it would infringe upon other well established doctrines in our jurisprudence.*

Dunkle v. Food Service, East, Inc., *400 Pa.Super. at 67–68, 582 A.2d at 1346–47 (footnote omitted).*

The patient in Dunkle *did not communicate any inclination to harm his victim. In the instant case, with all the awareness on the part of Dr. Mamo that Mr. Gault could turn to violence, there was no notice or warning to Dr. Mamo that Mrs. Gault was specifically identified by Mr. Gault as the intended victim. In this case the plaintiffs themselves knew beforehand of Mr. Gault's dangerous inclination. It is a curious lapse in logic on plaintiffs' part to claim that Dr. Mamo should have warned them of information they already had, and with which they were familiar. Under the facts in* Dunkle, supra, *we declined to extend the duty to protect a victim who was non-identifiable in advance of her death and who arguably was a non-foreseeable third party victim. Thus, there is currently no common or statutory law, and no court decision in Pennsylvania, requiring that a psychiatrist or psychologist owes a duty to warn or otherwise protect a non-patient where the patient has not threatened to harm a specific person.*

In Dunkle *we concluded that "a psychologist (or psychiatrist) owes no duty to warn or otherwise protect a non-patient where the patient has not threatened to inflict harm on a particular individual." Id. at 68, 582 A.2d at 1347. Such a conclusion was necessary to support the patient-psychologist relationship and privilege. Id.*

We find no common law rule that imposes a duty on a psychologist or psychiatrist to warn a non-patient of a patient's dangerous propensities. [Nor in Pennsylvania] is there a statutory duty to protect a non-patient from similar potential harm. In the absence of legislative directive or reforms that specifically address this problematic issue, we decline to impose such a stringent legal duty on health care professionals under the fact of this case.

Id. at 69, 582 A.2d at 1347.

The instant case is similar to Dunkle *and* Leedy, supra, *on the issue of a psychiatrist's duty to warn against the dangers of a potentially violent patient. In* Dunkle, *we found no duty when the complainant alleged the following:*

> *(1) Senie Eyer attended "one or more counseling sessions" with Bruce Tindal, provided by Additional Defendants; (2) Bruce Tindal "exhibited signs and symptoms of his deteriorating mental condition, indicating that he presented a danger to himself, and specifically to Senie Eyer;" (3) prior to March 16, 1985, Additional Defendants knew or should have known Bruce Tindal "would present and did present a danger to himself and to Senie Eyer;" (4) Additional Defendants were negligent in failing to warn Senie Eyer of, and protect her from, Bruce Tindal's dangerous propensities; and (5) Senie Eyer was the foreseeable victim of violent behavior on the part of Bruce Tindal.*

Id. at 65, 582 A.2d at 1345 (quoting the trial court opinion).

In Leedy, supra, *the issue was whether the personnel of the Veteran's Administration hospital had a duty to warn the Leedys that Hartnett, a former patient, exhibited violent inclinations when he drank. The personnel, aware that Hartnett would be staying with the Leedys when he left the hospital, failed to inform them of any potential danger. Subsequently, Hartnett attacked the Leedys. The court in* Leedy *held that a victim may not be deemed "readily identifiable" merely because there exists a standard possibility that increased contact between a potentially violent patient and another will yield a higher likelihood of an attack. Thus, it would seem in the above cases, not only foreseeability of a general danger, but the specific identity of an intended victim, must be brought to the attention of the physician before it can be held that a physician has a duty to warn the intended victim. See also* Crosby by Crosby v. Sultz, *405 Pa.Super. 527, 592 A.2d 1337 (1991) and* DiMarco v. Lynch Homes-Chester County, *384 Pa.Super. 463, 559 A.2d 530 (1989), aff'd, 525 Pa. 558, 583 A.2d 422 (1990) (distinguishing similar issues on the facts). Under all the circumstances present in this case, we affirm the learned lower court's grant of a motion for summary judgment.*

Under state ethics laws and rules, doctors and some other health professionals must report gunshot wounds, certain sexually transmitted diseases, and suspicion of physical and sexual abuse. These obligations are not optional (as compared to the permissive disclosure under the model legal ethics rules for impending crime and physical harm), but mandatory, and doctors who fail to report may face sanctions or legal liability, as in this example from New York State:

Persons and officials required to report cases of suspected child abuse or maltreatment

1. (a) The following persons and officials are required to report or cause a report to be made in accordance with this title when they have reasonable cause to suspect that a child coming before them in their professional or official capacity is an abused or maltreated child, or when they have reasonable cause to suspect that a child is an abused or maltreated child where the parent, guardian, custodian or other person legally responsible for such child comes before them in their professional or official capacity and states from personal knowledge facts, conditions or circumstances which, if correct, would render the child an abused or maltreated child: any physician; registered physician assistant; surgeon; medical examiner; coroner; dentist; dental hygienist; osteopath; optometrist; chiropractor; podiatrist; resident; intern; psychologist; registered nurse; social worker; emergency medical technician; licensed creative arts therapist; licensed marriage and family therapist; licensed mental health counselor; licensed psychoanalyst; hospital personnel engaged in the admission, examination, care or treatment of persons; a Christian Science practitioner; school official, which includes but is not limited to school teacher, school guidance counselor, school psychologist, school social worker, school nurse, school administrator or other school personnel required to hold a teaching or administrative license or certificate; social services worker; director of a children's overnight camp, summer day camp or traveling summer day camp, as such camps are defined in section thirteen hundred ninety-two of the public health law; day care center worker; school-age child care worker; provider of family or group family day care; employee or volunteer in a residential care facility defined in subdivision four of section four hundred twelve-a of this title or any other child care or foster care worker; mental health professional; substance abuse counselor; alcoholism counselor; all persons credentialed by the office of alcoholism and substance abuse services; peace officer; police officer; district attorney or assistant district attorney; investigator employed in the office of a district attorney; or other law enforcement official.

(b) Whenever such person is required to report under this title in his or her capacity as a member of the staff of a medical or other public or private institution, school, facility or agency, he or she shall make the report as required by this title and immediately notify the person in charge of such institution, school, facility or agency, or his or her designated agent. Such person in charge, or the designated agent of such person, shall be responsible for all subsequent administration necessitated by the report. Any report shall include the name, title and contact information for every staff person of the institution who is believed to have direct knowledge of the allegations in the report. Nothing in this section or title is intended to require more than one report from any such institution, school or agency.

(c) A medical or other public or private institution, school, facility or agency shall not take any retaliatory personnel action, as such term is defined in paragraph (e) of subdivision one of section seven hundred forty of the labor law, against an employee because such employee believes that he or she has reasonable cause to suspect that a child is an abused or maltreated child and that employee therefore makes a report in accordance with this title. No school, school official, child care provider, foster care

provider, residential care facility provider, hospital, medical institution provider or mental health facility provider shall impose any conditions, including prior approval or prior notification, upon a member of their staff specifically required to report under this title. At the time of the making of a report, or at any time thereafter, such person or official may exercise the right to request, pursuant to paragraph (A) of subdivision four of section four hundred twenty-two of this title, the findings of an investigation made pursuant to this title or section 45.07 of the mental hygiene law.

(d) Social services workers are required to report or cause a report to be made in accordance with this title when they have reasonable cause to suspect that a child is an abused or maltreated child where a person comes before them in their professional or official capacity and states from personal knowledge facts, conditions or circumstances which, if correct, would render the child an abused or maltreated child.

2. Any person, institution, school, facility, agency, organization, partnership or corporation which employs persons mandated to report suspected incidents of child abuse or maltreatment pursuant to subdivision one of this section shall provide consistent with section four hundred twenty-one of this chapter, all such current and new employees with written information explaining the reporting requirements set out in subdivision one of this section and in sections four hundred fifteen through four hundred twenty of this title. The employers shall be responsible for the costs associated with printing and distributing the written information.

3. Any state or local governmental agency or authorized agency which issues a license, certificate or permit to an individual to operate a family day care home or group family day care home shall provide each person currently holding or seeking such a license, certificate or permit with written information explaining the reporting requirements set out in subdivision one of this section and in sections four hundred fifteen through four hundred twenty of this title.

4. Any person, institution, school, facility, agency, organization, partnership or corporation, which employs persons who are mandated to report suspected incidents of child abuse or maltreatment pursuant to subdivision one of this section and whose employees, in the normal course of their employment, travel to locations where children reside, shall provide, consistent with section four hundred twenty-one of this title, all such current and new employees with information on recognizing the signs of an unlawful methamphetamine laboratory. Pursuant to section 19.27 of the mental hygiene law, the office of alcoholism and substance abuse services shall make available to such employers information on recognizing the signs of unlawful methamphetamine laboratories.[15]

III.   THE CHALLENGES OF DIGITAL PERSONAL HEALTH INFORMATION

What works (however well or poorly) on an individual physician-by-physician basis, however, becomes substantially more complicated as the number of providers, and others with access to health-related data, grows. As more people and organizations

---

[15] New York Social Services Law § 413.

become involved in providing and paying for medical care and related products and services, including employers offering benefit plans, the ability to promote and ensure control over patient personal health information ("PHI") becomes significantly more difficult.

A few examples from a single institution provide a useful demonstration of the risks. In 2003, the University of San Francisco Medical Center received an e-mail message from, Lubna Baloch, a woman in Pakistan stating, "Your patient records are out in the open . . . so you better track that person and make him pay my dues." According to published reports, Ms. Baloch was a sub-sub-contractor of UCSF's medical transcription service, Transcription Stat, based in Sausilito, CA, and had not been paid about $500 for her work. Ms. Baloch attached "actual files containing dictation from UCSF doctors . . . . [which] reportedly involved two patients" to prove her claim. Once she was paid at least in part, Ms. Baloch wrote again to retract her threat to release the information.[16]

Five years later, UCSF was once again faced with an unexpected breach of patient information via a third party contractor. In 2008, an outside fundraiser for UCSF, which had been provided former patient records in order to solicit donations from the patients, mistakenly placed the information on a server which was inadequately secured and accessible by the public over the Internet.[17] UCSF subsequently established a number of detailed privacy and security programs covering its faculty and staff.[18]

IV.   FEDERAL STATUTORY DIRECTIVES REGARDING ELECTRONIC MEDICAL RECORDS: HIPAA AND HITECH

The reason that health information has become so widespread, and breaches more common, is the ongoing conversion of health records from analog (i.e., paper) to digital (electronically stored and transmitted) versions. This conversion has been encouraged not only by a general desire for efficiency on the part of healthcare professionals, but a series of statutory mandates whose stated intent has been to improve access to healthcare and health insurance for patients. The primary federal statutory mandate for this transition was the Health Insurance Portability and Accountability Act of 1996 ("HIPAA"),[19] including its subsequent amendment by the Health Information Technology for Economic and Clinical Health Act (HITECH ACT) of 2009.[20]

---

[16] David Lazarus, A TOUGH LESSON ON MEDICAL PRIVACY / PAKISTANI TRANSCRIBER THREATENS UCSF OVER BACK PAY, SFGATE (Oct. 23, 2003), http://www.sfgate.com/cgi-bin/article.cgi?f=/c/a/2003/10/22/MNGCO2FN8G1.DTL (last visited May 8, 2012).

[17] Elizabeth Fernandez, Hospitals, Patients Clash on Privacy Rights, HOSPITALS, PATIENTS CLASH ON PRIVACY RIGHTS, SFGATE (May 27, 2008), http://www.sfgate.com/cgi-bin/article.cgi?f=/c/a/2008/05/26/MNPO10NRC R.DTL (last visited May 8, 2012).

[18] HIPAA HOME, http://hipaa.ucsf.edu/ (last visited May 8, 2012).

[19] PL 104-191.

[20] PL 111-5, Title XIII.

a. Electronic Storage: The HIPAA Statutory Framework

As originally enacted, HIPAA included within it a mandate for shifting to electronic storage of health information:

> *It is the purpose of this subtitle to improve the Medicare program under title XVIII of the Social Security Act, the medicaid program under title XIX of such Act, and the efficiency and effectiveness of the health care system, by encouraging the development of a health information system through the establishment of standards and requirements for the electronic transmission of certain health information.*[21]

Initially, HIPAA placed responsibility for protecting the privacy of electronically transmitted PHI on Congress, with the Department of Health and Human Services ("HHS") mandated to enact regulations if Congress failed to act:

RECOMMENDATIONS WITH RESPECT TO PRIVACY OF CERTAIN HEALTH INFORMATION.

(a) IN GENERAL. — Not later than the date that is 12 months after the date of the enactment of this Act, the Secretary of Health and Human Services shall submit to the Committee on Labor and Human Resources and the Committee on Finance of the Senate and the Committee on Commerce and the Committee on Ways and Means of the House of Representatives detailed recommendations on standards with respect to the privacy of individually identifiable health information.

(b) SUBJECTS FOR RECOMMENDATIONS. — The recommendations under subsection (a) shall address at least the following:

(1) The rights that an individual who is a subject of individually identifiable health information should have.

(2) The procedures that should be established for the exercise of such rights.

(3) The uses and disclosures of such information that should be authorized or required.

(c) REGULATIONS. —

(1) IN GENERAL. — If legislation governing standards with respect to the privacy of individually identifiable health information transmitted in connection with the transactions described in section 1173(a) of the Social Security Act (as added by section 262) is not enacted by the date that is 36 months after the date of the enactment of this Act, the Secretary of Health and Human Services shall promulgate final regulations containing such standards not later than the date that is 42 months after the date of the enactment of this Act. Such regulations shall address at least the subjects described in subsection (b).

(2) PREEMPTION. — A regulation promulgated under paragraph (1) shall not supercede [sic] a contrary provision of State law, if the provision of State law imposes

---

[21] PL 104-191, Sec. 261 (1996).

requirements, standards, or implementation specifications that are more stringent than the requirements, standards, or implementation specifications imposed under the regulation.

(d) CONSULTATION. — In carrying out this section, the Secretary of Health and Human Services shall consult with —

(1) the National Committee on Vital and Health Statistics established under section 306(k) of the Public Health Service Act (42 U.S.C. 242k(k)); and

(2) the Attorney General.[22]

HIPAA additionally required the Secretary of Health and Human Services to enact standards to protect the *security* of electronically stored and transmitted PHI:

SEC. 1173: STANDARDS TO ENABLE ELECTRONIC EXCHANGE

(1) IN GENERAL. — The Secretary shall adopt standards for transactions, and data elements for such transactions, to enable health information to be exchanged electronically, that are appropriate for —

(A) the financial and administrative transactions described in paragraph (2); and

(B) other financial and administrative transactions determined appropriate by the Secretary, consistent with the goals of improving the operation of the health care system and reducing administrative costs.

(2) TRANSACTIONS. — The transactions referred to in paragraph (1)(A) are transactions with respect to the following:

(A) Health claims or equivalent encounter information.

(B) Health claims attachments.

(C) Enrollment and disenrollment in a health plan.

(D) Eligibility for a health plan.

(E) Health care payment and remittance advice.

(F) Health plan premium payments.

(G) First report of injury.

(H) Health claim status.

(I) Referral certification and authorization.

(3) ACCOMMODATION OF SPECIFIC PROVIDERS. — The standards adopted by the Secretary under paragraph (1) shall accommodate the needs of different types of health care providers.

(b) UNIQUE HEALTH IDENTIFIERS. —

---

[22] *Id. § 264.*

(1) IN GENERAL. — The Secretary shall adopt standards providing for a standard unique health identifier for each individual, employer, health plan, and health care provider for use in the health care system. In carrying out the preceding sentence for each health plan and health care provider, the Secretary shall take into account multiple uses for identifiers and multiple locations and specialty classifications for health care providers.

(2) USE OF IDENTIFIERS. — The standards adopted under paragraph (1) shall specify the purposes for which a unique health identifier may be used.

(c) CODE SETS. —

(1) IN GENERAL. — The Secretary shall adopt standards that —

(A) select code sets for appropriate data elements for the transactions referred to in subsection (a)(1) from among the code sets that have been developed by private and public entities; or

(B) establish code sets for such data elements if no code sets for the data elements have been developed.

(2) DISTRIBUTION. — The Secretary shall establish efficient and low-cost procedures for distribution (including electronic distribution) of code sets and modifications made to such code sets under section 1174(b).

(d) SECURITY STANDARDS FOR HEALTH INFORMATION. —

(1) SECURITY STANDARDS. — The Secretary shall adopt security standards that —

(A) take into account —

(i) the technical capabilities of record systems used to maintain health information;

(ii) the costs of security measures;

(iii) the need for training persons who have access to health information;

(iv) the value of audit trails in computerized record systems; and

(v) the needs and capabilities of small health care providers and rural health care providers (as such providers are defined by the Secretary); and

(B) ensure that a health care clearinghouse, if it is part of a larger organization, has policies and security procedures which isolate the activities of the health care clearinghouse with respect to processing information in a manner that prevents unauthorized access to such information by such larger organization.

(2) SAFEGUARDS. — Each person described in section 1172(a) who maintains or transmits health information shall maintain reasonable and appropriate administrative, technical, and physical safeguards —

(A) to ensure the integrity and confidentiality of the information;

(B) to protect against any reasonably anticipated —

(i) threats or hazards to the security or integrity of the information; and

(ii) unauthorized uses or disclosures of the information; and

(C) otherwise to ensure compliance with this part by the officers and employees of such person.

(e) ELECTRONIC SIGNATURE. —

(1) STANDARDS. — The Secretary, in coordination with the Secretary of Commerce, shall adopt standards specifying procedures for the electronic transmission and authentication of signatures with respect to the transactions referred to in subsection (a)(1).

(2) EFFECT OF COMPLIANCE. — Compliance with the standards adopted under paragraph (1) shall be deemed to satisfy Federal and State statutory requirements for written signatures with respect to the transactions referred to in subsection (a)(1).

(f) TRANSFER OF INFORMATION AMONG HEALTH PLANS. — The Secretary shall adopt standards for transferring among health plans appropriate standard data elements needed for the coordination of benefits, the sequential processing of claims, and other data elements for individuals who have more than one health plan.[23]

b.   HIPAA Regulations: The Privacy and Security Rules

Ultimately, HHS did promulgate both privacy and security regulations under HIPAA. The HIPAA Privacy Rule was originally adopted on December 28, 2000,[24] and subsequently modified in 2002.[25] The Privacy Rule went into effect on April 14, 2001, and required compliance for most "covered entities" (see below) by April 14, 2003 (April 14, 2004 for "small health plans).[26] The Security Rule was adopted in February 2003,[27] and covered entities were required to comply with it by April 20, 2005.[28]

As with all regulations, it is crucial to understand the definitions used by the HIPAA rules, to properly comprehend and comply with them:

---

[23] *Id. § 262.*

[24] 45 CFR Part 160.

[25] 45 CFR Part 164, Subparts A and E.

[26] GENERAL   OVERVIEW,   http://www.hhs.gov/ocr/privacy/hipaa/understanding/coveredentities/generaloverview.html (last visited May 8, 2012).

[27] 45 CFR Part 160; Part 164, Subparts A and C.

[28] HIPAA ENFORCEMENT, http://www.hhs.gov/ocr/privacy/hipaa/enforcement/index.html (last visited May 8, 2012).

§ 160.103 Definitions.[29]

Except as otherwise provided, the following definitions apply to this subchapter:

Act means the Social Security Act.

ANSI stands for the American National Standards Institute.

Business associate: (1) Except as provided in paragraph (2) of this definition, business associate means, with respect to a covered entity, a person who:

(i) On behalf of such covered entity or of an organized health care arrangement (as defined in § 164.501 of this subchapter) in which the covered entity participates, but other than in the capacity of a member of the workforce of such covered entity or arrangement, performs, or assists in the performance of:

(A) A function or activity involving the use or disclosure of individually identifiable health information, including claims processing or administration, data analysis, processing or administration, utilization review, quality assurance, billing, benefit management, practice management, and repricing; or

(B) Any other function or activity regulated by this subchapter; or

(ii) Provides, other than in the capacity of a member of the workforce of such covered entity, legal, actuarial, accounting, consulting, data aggregation (as defined in § 164.501 of this subchapter), management, administrative, accreditation, or financial services to or for such covered entity, or to or for an organized health care arrangement in which the covered entity participates, where the provision of the service involves the disclosure of individually identifiable health information from such covered entity or arrangement, or from another business associate of such covered entity or arrangement, to the person.

(2) A covered entity participating in an organized health care arrangement that performs a function or activity as described by paragraph (1)(i) of this definition for or on behalf of such organized health care arrangement, or that provides a service as described in paragraph (1)(ii) of this definition to or for such organized health care arrangement, does not, simply through the performance of such function or activity or the provision of such service, become a business associate of other covered entities participating in such organized health care arrangement.

(3) A covered entity may be a business associate of another covered entity.

CMS stands for Centers for Medicare & Medicaid Services within the Department of Health and Human Services.

Compliance date means the date by which a covered entity must comply with a standard, implementation specification, requirement, or modification adopted under this subchapter.

Covered entity means:

(1) A health plan.

---

[29] 45 CFR § 160.103.

(2) A health care clearinghouse.

(3) A health care provider who transmits any health information in electronic form in connection with a transaction covered by this subchapter.

Disclosure means the release, transfer, provision of, access to, or divulging in any other manner of information outside the entity holding the information.

EIN stands for the employer identification number assigned by the Internal Revenue Service, U.S. Department of the Treasury. The EIN is the taxpayer identifying number of an individual or other entity (whether or not an employer) assigned under one of the following:

(1) 26 U.S.C. 6011(b), which is the portion of the Internal Revenue Code dealing with identifying the taxpayer in tax returns and statements, or corresponding provisions of prior law.

(2) 26 U.S.C. 6109, which is the portion of the Internal Revenue Code dealing with identifying numbers in tax returns, statements, and other required documents.

Electronic media means:

(1) Electronic storage media including memory devices in computers (hard drives) and any removable/transportable digital memory medium, such as magnetic tape or disk, optical disk, or digital memory card; or

(2) Transmission media used to exchange information already in electronic storage media. Transmission media include, for example, the internet (wide-open), extranet (using internet technology to link a business with information accessible only to collaborating parties), leased lines, dial-up lines, private networks, and the physical movement of removable/transportable electronic storage media. Certain transmissions, including of paper, via facsimile, and of voice, via telephone, are not considered to be transmissions via electronic media, because the information being exchanged did not exist in electronic form before the transmission.

Electronic protected health information means information that comes within paragraphs (1)(i) or (1)(ii) of the definition of protected health information as specified in this section.

Employer is defined as it is in 26 U.S.C. 3401(d).

Group health plan (also see definition of health plan in this section) means an employee welfare benefit plan (as defined in section 3(1) of the Employee Retirement Income and Security Act of 1974 (ERISA), 29 U.S.C. 1002(1)), including insured and self-insured plans, to the extent that the plan provides medical care (as defined in section 2791(a)(2) of the Public Health Service Act (PHS Act), 42 U.S.C. 300gg–91(a)(2)), including items and services paid for as medical care, to employees or their dependents directly or through insurance, reimbursement, or otherwise, that:

(1) Has 50 or more participants (as defined in section 3(7) of ERISA, 29 U.S.C. 1002(7)); or

(2) Is administered by an entity other than the employer that established and maintains the plan.

HHS stands for the Department of Health and Human Services.

Health care means care, services, or supplies related to the health of an individual. Health care includes, but is not limited to, the following:

(1) Preventive, diagnostic, therapeutic, rehabilitative, maintenance, or palliative care, and counseling, service, assessment, or procedure with respect to the physical or mental condition, or functional status, of an individual or that affects the structure or function of the body; and

(2) Sale or dispensing of a drug, device, equipment, or other item in accordance with a prescription.

Health care clearinghouse means a public or private entity, including a billing service, repricing company, community health management information system or community health information system, and "value-added" networks and switches, that does either of the following functions:

(1) Processes or facilitates the processing of health information received from another entity in a nonstandard format or containing nonstandard data content into standard data elements or a standard transaction.

(2) Receives a standard transaction from another entity and processes or facilitates the processing of health information into nonstandard format or nonstandard data content for the receiving entity.

Health care provider means a provider of services (as defined in section 1861(u) of the Act, 42 U.S.C. 1395x(u)), a provider of medical or health services (as defined in section 1861(s) of the Act, 42 U.S.C. 1395x(s)), and any other person or organization who furnishes, bills, or is paid for health care in the normal course of business.

Health information means any information, whether oral or recorded in any form or medium, that:

(1) Is created or received by a health care provider, health plan, public health authority, employer, life insurer, school or university, or health care clearinghouse; and

(2) Relates to the past, present, or future physical or mental health or condition of an individual; the provision of health care to an individual; or the past, present, or future payment for the provision of health care to an individual.

Health insurance issuer (as defined in section 2791(b)(2) of the PHS Act, 42 U.S.C. 300gg–91(b)(2) and used in the definition of health plan in this section) means an insurance company, insurance service, or insurance organization (including an HMO) that is licensed to engage in the business of insurance in a State and is subject to State law that regulates insurance. Such term does not include a group health plan.

Health maintenance organization (HMO) (as defined in section 2791(b)(3) of the PHS Act, 42 U.S.C. 300gg–91(b)(3) and used in the definition of health plan in this section) means a federally qualified HMO, an organization recognized as an HMO under State law, or a similar organization regulated for solvency under State law in the same manner and to the same extent as such an HMO.

Health plan means an individual or group plan that provides, or pays the cost of, medical care (as defined in section 2791(a)(2) of the PHS Act, 42 U.S.C. 300gg–91(a)(2)).

(1) Health plan includes the following, singly or in combination:

(i) A group health plan, as defined in this section.

(ii) A health insurance issuer, as defined in this section.

(iii) An HMO, as defined in this section.

(iv) Part A or Part B of the Medicare program under title XVIII of the Act.

(v) The Medicaid program under title XIX of the Act, 42 U.S.C. 1396, et seq.

(vi) An issuer of a Medicare supplemental policy (as defined in section 1882(g)(1) of the Act, 42 U.S.C. 1395ss(g)(1)).

(vii) An issuer of a long-term care policy, excluding a nursing home fixed-indemnity policy.

(viii) An employee welfare benefit plan or any other arrangement that is established or maintained for the purpose of offering or providing health benefits to the employees of two or more employers.

(ix) The health care program for active military personnel under title 10 of the United States Code.

(x) The veterans health care program under 38 U.S.C. chapter 17.

(xi) The Civilian Health and Medical Program of the Uniformed Services (CHAMPUS) (as defined in 10 U.S.C. 1072(4)).

(xii) The Indian Health Service program under the Indian Health Care Improvement Act, 25 U.S.C. 1601, et seq.

(xiii) The Federal Employees Health Benefits Program under 5 U.S.C. 8902, et seq.

(xiv) An approved State child health plan under title XXI of the Act, providing benefits for child health assistance that meet the requirements of section 2103 of the Act, 42 U.S.C. 1397, et seq.

(xv) The Medicare+Choice program under Part C of title XVIII of the Act, 42 U.S.C. 1395w–21 through 1395w–28.

(xvi) A high risk pool that is a mechanism established under State law to provide health insurance coverage or comparable coverage to eligible individuals.

(xvii) Any other individual or group plan, or combination of individual or group plans, that provides or pays for the cost of medical care (as defined in section 2791(a)(2) of the PHS Act, 42 U.S.C. 300gg–91(a)(2)).

(2) Health plan excludes:

(i) Any policy, plan, or program to the extent that it provides, or pays for the cost of, excepted benefits that are listed in section 2791(c)(1) of the PHS Act, 42 U.S.C.

300gg–91(c)(1); and

(ii) A government-funded program (other than one listed in paragraph (1)(i)–(xvi) of this definition):

(A) Whose principal purpose is other than providing, or paying the cost of, health care; or

(B) Whose principal activity is:

(1) The direct provision of health care to persons; or

(2) The making of grants to fund the direct provision of health care to persons.

Implementation specification means specific requirements or instructions for implementing a standard.

Individual means the person who is the subject of protected health information.

Individually identifiable health information is information that is a subset of health information, including demographic information collected from an individual, and:

(1) Is created or received by a health care provider, health plan, employer, or health care clearinghouse; and

(2) Relates to the past, present, or future physical or mental health or condition of an individual; the provision of health care to an individual; or the past, present, or future payment for the provision of health care to an individual; and

(i) That identifies the individual; or

(ii) With respect to which there is a reasonable basis to believe the information can be used to identify the individual.

Modify or modification refers to a change adopted by the Secretary, through regulation, to a standard or an implementation specification.

Organized health care arrangement means:

(1) A clinically integrated care setting in which individuals typically receive health care from more than one health care provider;

(2) An organized system of health care in which more than one covered entity participates and in which the participating covered entities:

(i) Hold themselves out to the public as participating in a joint arrangement; and

(ii) Participate in joint activities that include at least one of the following:

(A) Utilization review, in which health care decisions by participating covered entities are reviewed by other participating covered entities or by a third party on their behalf;

(B) Quality assessment and improvement activities, in which treatment provided by participating covered entities is assessed by other participating covered entities or by a third party on their behalf; or

(C) Payment activities, if the financial risk for delivering health care is shared, in part or in whole, by participating covered entities through the joint arrangement and if protected health information created or received by a covered entity is reviewed by other participating covered entities or by a third party on their behalf for the purpose of administering the sharing of financial risk.

(3) A group health plan and a health insurance issuer or HMO with respect to such group health plan, but only with respect to protected health information created or received by such health insurance issuer or HMO that relates to individuals who are or who have been participants or beneficiaries in such group health plan;

(4) A group health plan and one or more other group health plans each of which are maintained by the same plan sponsor; or

(5) The group health plans described in paragraph (4) of this definition and health insurance issuers or HMOs with respect to such group health plans, but only with respect to protected health information created or received by such health insurance issuers or HMOs that relates to individuals who are or have been participants or beneficiaries in any of such group health plans.

Person means a natural person, trust or estate, partnership, corporation, professional association or corporation, or other entity, public or private.

Protected health information means individually identifiable health information:

(1) Except as provided in paragraph (2) of this definition, that is:

(i) Transmitted by electronic media;

(ii) Maintained in electronic media; or

(iii) Transmitted or maintained in any other form or medium.

(2) Protected health information excludes individually identifiable health information in:

(i) Education records covered by the Family Educational Rights and Privacy Act, as amended, 20 U.S.C. 1232g;

(ii) Records described at 20 U.S.C. 1232g(a)(4)(B)(iv); and

(iii) Employment records held by a covered entity in its role as employer.

Secretary means the Secretary of Health and Human Services or any other officer or employee of HHS to whom the authority involved has been delegated.

Small health plan means a health plan with annual receipts of $5 million or less.

Standard means a rule, condition, or requirement:

(1) Describing the following information for products, systems, services or practices:

(i) Classification of components.

(ii) Specification of materials, performance, or operations; or

(iii) Delineation of procedures; or

(2) With respect to the privacy of individually identifiable health information.

(3) With the exception of operating rules as defined at § 162.103.

Standard setting organization (SSO) means an organization accredited by the American National Standards Institute that develops and maintains standards for information transactions or data elements, or any other standard that is necessary for, or will facilitate the implementation of, this part.

State refers to one of the following:

(1) For a health plan established or regulated by Federal law, State has the meaning set forth in the applicable section of the United States Code for such health plan.

(2) For all other purposes, State means any of the several States, the District of Columbia, the Commonwealth of Puerto Rico, the Virgin Islands, and Guam.

Trading partner agreement means an agreement related to the exchange of information in electronic transactions, whether the agreement is distinct or part of a larger agreement, between each party to the agreement. (For example, a trading partner agreement may specify, among other things, the duties and responsibilities of each party to the agreement in conducting a standard transaction.)

Transaction means the transmission of information between two parties to carry out financial or administrative activities related to health care. It includes the following types of information transmissions:

(1) Health care claims or equivalent encounter information.

(2) Health care payment and remittance advice.

(3) Coordination of benefits.

(4) Health care claim status.

(5) Enrollment and disenrollment in a health plan.

(6) Eligibility for a health plan.

(7) Health plan premium payments.

(8) Referral certification and authorization.

(9) First report of injury.

(10) Health claims attachments.

(11) Health care electronic funds transfers (EFT) and remittance advice.

(12) Other transactions that the Secretary may prescribe by regulation.

Use means, with respect to individually identifiable health information, the sharing, employment, application, utilization, examination, or analysis of such information within an entity that maintains such information.

Workforce means employees, volunteers, trainees, and other persons whose con-

duct, in the performance of work for a covered entity, is under the direct control of such entity, whether or not they are paid by the covered entity.

Although the overall regulations are quite complex, most organizations and individuals whose primary professional focus is healthcare are likely aware of HIPAA and at least the need to comply with its regulations. Non-health businesses, those included in the definition of "business associates," may be entirely unaware that they too are required to obey the requirements of the HIPAA privacy and security rules. HHS, as part of its overall guidance for covered entities,[30] provides some explanation of "Business Associates":

Business Associates[31]

Background

By law, the HIPAA Privacy Rule applies only to covered entities — health plans, health care clearinghouses, and certain health care providers. However, most health care providers and health plans do not carry out all of their health care activities and functions by themselves. Instead, they often use the services of a variety of other persons or businesses. The Privacy Rule allows covered providers and health plans to disclose protected health information to these "business associates" if the providers or plans obtain satisfactory assurances that the business associate will use the information only for the purposes for which it was engaged by the covered entity, will safeguard the information from misuse, and will help the covered entity comply with some of the covered entity's duties under the Privacy Rule. Covered entities may disclose protected health information to an entity in its role as a business associate only to help the covered entity carry out its health care functions — not for the business associate's independent use or purposes, except as needed for the proper management and administration of the business associate.

How the Rule Works

***General Provision.** The Privacy Rule requires that a covered entity obtain satisfactory assurances from its business associate that the business associate will appropriately safeguard the protected health information it receives or creates on behalf of the covered entity. The satisfactory assurances must be in writing, whether in the form of a contract or other agreement between the covered entity and the business associate.*

***What Is a "Business Associate?"** A "business associate" is a person or entity that performs certain functions or activities that involve the use or disclosure of protected health information on behalf of, or provides services to, a covered entity. A member of the covered entity's workforce is not a business associate. A covered health care*

---

[30] For Covered Entities, http://www.hhs.gov/ocr/privacy/hipaa/understanding/coveredentities/index.html(last visited May 8, 2012).

[31] Business Associates, *http://www.hhs.gov/ocr/privacy/hipaa/understanding/coveredentities/business associates.html (last visited May 8, 2012).*

provider, health plan, or health care clearinghouse can be a business associate of another covered entity. The Privacy Rule lists some of the functions or activities, as well as the particular services, that make a person or entity a business associate, if the activity or service involves the use or disclosure of protected health information. The types of functions or activities that may make a person or entity a business associate include payment or health care operations activities, as well as other functions or activities regulated by the Administrative Simplification Rules.

Business associate functions and activities include: claims processing or administration; data analysis, processing or administration; utilization review; quality assurance; billing; benefit management; practice management; and repricing. Business associate services are: legal; actuarial; accounting; consulting; data aggregation; management; administrative; accreditation; and financial. See the definition of "business associate" at 45 CFR 160.103.

Examples of Business Associates.

- *A third party administrator that assists a health plan with claims processing.*

- *A CPA firm whose accounting services to a health care provider involve access to protected health information.*

- *An attorney whose legal services to a health plan involve access to protected health information.*

- *A consultant that performs utilization reviews for a hospital.*

- *A health care clearinghouse that translates a claim from a non-standard format into a standard transaction on behalf of a health care provider and forwards the processed transaction to a payer.*

- *An independent medical transcriptionist that provides transcription services to a physician.*

- *A pharmacy benefits manager that manages a health plan's pharmacist network.*

Business Associate Contracts. *A covered entity's contract or other written arrangement with its business associate must contain the elements specified at 45 CFR 164.504(e). For example, the contract must: Describe the permitted and required uses of protected health information by the business associate; Provide that the business associate will not use or further disclose the protected health information other than as permitted or required by the contract or as required by law; and Require the business associate to use appropriate safeguards to prevent a use or disclosure of the protected health information other than as provided for by the contract. Where a covered entity knows of a material breach or violation by the business associate of the contract or agreement, the covered entity is required to take reasonable steps to cure the breach or end the violation, and if such steps are unsuccessful, to terminate the contract or arrangement. If termination of the contract or agreement is not feasible, a covered entity is required to report the problem to the Department of Health and*

Human Services (HHS) Office for Civil Rights (OCR). Please view our Sample Business Associate Contract.

Transition Provisions for Existing Contracts. *Covered entities (other than small health plans) that have an existing contract (or other written agreement) with a business associate prior to October 15, 2002, are permitted to continue to operate under that contract for up to one additional year beyond the April 14, 2003 compliance date, provided that the contract is not renewed or modified prior to April 14, 2003. This transition period applies only to written contracts or other written arrangements. Oral contracts or other arrangements are not eligible for the transition period. Covered entities with contracts that qualify are permitted to continue to operate under those contracts with their business associates until April 14, 2004, or until the contract is renewed or modified, whichever is sooner, regardless of whether the contract meets the Rule's applicable contract requirements at 45 CFR 164.502(e) and 164.504(e). A covered entity must otherwise comply with the Privacy Rule, such as making only permissible disclosures to the business associate and permitting individuals to exercise their rights under the Rule. See 45 CFR 164.532(d) and (e).*

Exceptions to the Business Associate Standard. *The Privacy Rule includes the following exceptions to the business associate standard. See 45 CFR 164.502(e). In these situations, a covered entity is not required to have a business associate contract or other written agreement in place before protected health information may be disclosed to the person or entity.*

- *Disclosures by a covered entity to a health care provider for treatment of the individual. For example:*

    ○ *A hospital is not required to have a business associate contract with the specialist to whom it refers a patient and transmits the patient's medical chart for treatment purposes.*

    ○ *A physician is not required to have a business associate contract with a laboratory as a condition of disclosing protected health information for the treatment of an individual.*

    ○ *A hospital laboratory is not required to have a business associate contract to disclose protected health information to a reference laboratory for treatment of the individual.*

- *Disclosures to a health plan sponsor, such as an employer, by a group health plan, or by the health insurance issuer or HMO that provides the health insurance benefits or coverage for the group health plan, provided that the group health plan's documents have been amended to limit the disclosures or one of the exceptions at 45 CFR 164.504(f) have been met.*

- *The collection and sharing of protected health information by a health plan that is a public benefits program, such as Medicare, and an agency other than the agency administering the health plan, such as the Social Security Administration, that collects protected health information to determine eligibility or enrollment, or determines eligibility or enrollment, for the government program, where the joint activities are authorized by law.*

Other Situations in Which a Business Associate Contract Is NOT Required.

- *When a health care provider discloses protected health information to a health plan for payment purposes, or when the health care provider simply accepts a discounted rate to participate in the health plan's network. A provider that submits a claim to a health plan and a health plan that assesses and pays the claim are each acting on its own behalf as a covered entity, and not as the "business associate" of the other.*

- *With persons or organizations (e.g., janitorial service or electrician) whose functions or services do not involve the use or disclosure of protected health information, and where any access to protected health information by such persons would be incidental, if at all.*

- *With a person or organization that acts merely as a conduit for protected health information, for example, the US Postal Service, certain private couriers, and their electronic equivalents.*

- *Among covered entities who participate in an organized health care arrangement (OHCA) to make disclosures that relate to the joint health care activities of the OHCA.*

- *Where a group health plan purchases insurance from a health insurance issuer or HMO. The relationship between the group health plan and the health insurance issuer or HMO is defined by the Privacy Rule as an OHCA, with respect to the individuals they jointly serve or have served. Thus, these covered entities are permitted to share protected health information that relates to the joint health care activities of the OHCA.*

- *Where one covered entity purchases a health plan product or other insurance, for example, reinsurance, from an insurer. Each entity is acting on its own behalf when the covered entity purchases the insurance benefits, and when the covered entity submits a claim to the insurer and the insurer pays the claim.*

- *To disclose protected health information to a researcher for research purposes, either with patient authorization, pursuant to a waiver under 45 CFR 164.512(i), or as a limited data set pursuant to 45 CFR 164.514(e). Because the researcher is not conducting a function or activity regulated by the Administrative Simplification Rules, such as payment or health care operations, or providing one of the services listed in the definition of "business associate" at 45 CFR 160.103, the researcher is not a business associate of the covered entity, and no business associate agreement is required.*

- *When a financial institution processes consumer-conducted financial transactions by debit, credit, or other payment card, clears checks, initiates or processes electronic funds transfers, or conducts any other activity that directly facilitates or effects the transfer of funds for payment for health care or health plan premiums. When it conducts these activities, the financial institution is providing its normal banking or other financial transaction services to its customers; it is not performing a function or activity for, or on behalf of, the covered entity.*

c.   The HITECH Act and Revisions to HIPAA

The HITECH Act[32] focused on enhancing both the desired efficiencies and protections related to health technologies and electronically stored PHI (also known as electronic health records or EHR). Subtitle A established the office of National Coordinator for Health Information Technology within HHS, including requiring the appointment of a Chief Privacy Officer for the Office of the National Coordinator,[33] while Subtitle B provides both additional current and proposed grant funding for health information technology structure.

Subtitle D added new provisions to federal law regarding EHR privacy, including strengthening the enforcement regime for breaches of health privacy[34] and extending the applicability of the Privacy and Security Rules to business associates.[35] It also added a specific notification requirement in the event of breaches of PHI.[36]

Notification in the case of breach[37]

(a) In general

A covered entity that accesses, maintains, retains, modifies, records, stores, destroys, or otherwise holds, uses, or discloses unsecured protected health information (as defined in subsection (h)(1)) shall, in the case of a breach of such information that is discovered by the covered entity, notify each individual whose unsecured protected health information has been, or is reasonably believed by the covered entity to have been, accessed, acquired, or disclosed as a result of such breach.

(b) Notification of covered entity by business associate

A business associate of a covered entity that accesses, maintains, retains, modifies, records, stores, destroys, or otherwise holds, uses, or discloses unsecured protected health information shall, following the discovery of a breach of such information, notify the covered entity of such breach. Such notice shall include the identification of each individual whose unsecured protected health information has been, or is reasonably believed by the business associate to have been, accessed, acquired, or disclosed during such breach.

(c) Breaches treated as discovered

For purposes of this section, a breach shall be treated as discovered by a covered entity or by a business associate as of the first day on which such breach is known to such entity or associate, respectively, (including any person, other than the indi-

---

[32] PL 111-5, Title XII.

[33] *Id.* § 3001(e). The first appointee was Joy Pritts. HEALTHIT.HHS.GOV: JOY PRITTS — CHIEF PRIVACY OFFICER, http://healthit.hhs.gov/portal/server.pt?open=512&mode=2&objID=1798 (last visited May 8, 2012).

[34] 42 U.S.C. 17939.

[35] 42 U.S.C. § 17931, § 17934.

[36] See discussion of data breach notification laws in Chapter 8.

[37] 42 U.S.C. § 17932.

vidual committing the breach, that is an employee, officer, or other agent of such entity or associate, respectively) or should reasonably have been known to such entity or associate (or person) to have occurred.

(d) Timeliness of notification

(1) In general

Subject to subsection (g), all notifications required under this section shall be made without unreasonable delay and in no case later than 60 calendar days after the discovery of a breach by the covered entity involved (or business associate involved in the case of a notification required under subsection (b)).

(2) Burden of proof

The covered entity involved (or business associate involved in the case of a notification required under subsection (b)), shall have the burden of demonstrating that all notifications were made as required under this part, including evidence demonstrating the necessity of any delay.

(e) Methods of notice

(1) Individual notice

Notice required under this section to be provided to an individual, with respect to a breach, shall be provided promptly and in the following form:

(A) Written notification by first-class mail to the individual (or the next of kin of the individual if the individual is deceased) at the last known address of the individual or the next of kin, respectively, or, if specified as a preference by the individual, by electronic mail. The notification may be provided in one or more mailings as information is available.

(B) In the case in which there is insufficient, or out-of-date contact information (including a phone number, email address, or any other form of appropriate communication) that precludes direct written (or, if specified by the individual under subparagraph (A), electronic) notification to the individual, a substitute form of notice shall be provided, including, in the case that there are 10 or more individuals for which there is insufficient or out-of-date contact information, a conspicuous posting for a period determined by the Secretary on the home page of the Web site of the covered entity involved or notice in major print or broadcast media, including major media in geographic areas where the individuals affected by the breach likely reside. Such a notice in media or web posting will include a toll-free phone number where an individual can learn whether or not the individual's unsecured protected health information is possibly included in the breach.

(C) In any case deemed by the covered entity involved to require urgency because of possible imminent misuse of unsecured protected health information, the covered entity, in addition to notice provided under subparagraph (A), may provide information to individuals by telephone or other means, as appropriate.

(2) Media notice

Notice shall be provided to prominent media outlets serving a State or jurisdiction, following the discovery of a breach described in subsection (a), if the unsecured protected health information of more than 500 residents of such State or jurisdiction is, or is reasonably believed to have been, accessed, acquired, or disclosed during such breach.

(3) Notice to Secretary

Notice shall be provided to the Secretary by covered entities of unsecured protected health information that has been acquired or disclosed in a breach. If the breach was with respect to 500 or more individuals than such notice must be provided immediately. If the breach was with respect to less than 500 individuals, the covered entity may maintain a log of any such breach occurring and annually submit such a log to the Secretary documenting such breaches occurring during the year involved.

(4) Posting on HHS public website

The Secretary shall make available to the public on the Internet website of the Department of Health and Human Services a list that identifies each covered entity involved in a breach described in subsection (a) in which the unsecured protected health information of more than 500 individuals is acquired or disclosed.

(f) Content of notification

Regardless of the method by which notice is provided to individuals under this section, notice of a breach shall include, to the extent possible, the following:

(1) A brief description of what happened, including the date of the breach and the date of the discovery of the breach, if known.

(2) A description of the types of unsecured protected health information that were involved in the breach (such as full name, Social Security number, date of birth, home address, account number, or disability code).

(3) The steps individuals should take to protect themselves from potential harm resulting from the breach.

(4) A brief description of what the covered entity involved is doing to investigate the breach, to mitigate losses, and to protect against any further breaches.

(5) Contact procedures for individuals to ask questions or learn additional information, which shall include a toll-free telephone number, an e-mail address, Web site, or postal address.

(g) Delay of notification authorized for law enforcement purposes

If a law enforcement official determines that a notification, notice, or posting required under this section would impede a criminal investigation or cause damage to national security, such notification, notice, or posting shall be delayed in the same manner as provided under section 164.528(a)(2) of title 45, Code of Federal Regulations, in the case of a disclosure covered under such section.

(h) Unsecured protected health information

(1) Definition

(A) In general

Subject to subparagraph (B), for purposes of this section, the term "unsecured protected health information" means protected health information that is not secured through the use of a technology or methodology specified by the Secretary in the guidance issued under paragraph (2).

(B) Exception in case timely guidance not issued

In the case that the Secretary does not issue guidance under paragraph (2) by the date specified in such paragraph, for purposes of this section, the term "unsecured protected health information" shall mean protected health information that is not secured by a technology standard that renders protected health information unusable, unreadable, or indecipherable to unauthorized individuals and is developed or endorsed by a standards developing organization that is accredited by the American National Standards Institute.

(2) Guidance

For purposes of paragraph (1) and section 17937(f)(3) of this title, not later than the date that is 60 days after February 17, 2009, the Secretary shall, after consultation with stakeholders, issue (and annually update) guidance specifying the technologies and methodologies that render protected health information unusable, unreadable, or indecipherable to unauthorized individuals, including the use of standards developed under section 300jj-12(b)(2)(B)(vi) of this title, as added by section 13101 of this Act.

(i) Report to Congress on breaches

(1) In general

Not later than 12 months after February 17, 2009 and annually thereafter, the Secretary shall prepare and submit to the Committee on Finance and the Committee on Health, Education, Labor, and Pensions of the Senate and the Committee on Ways and Means and the Committee on Energy and Commerce of the House of Representatives a report containing the information described in paragraph (2) regarding breaches for which notice was provided to the Secretary under subsection (e)(3).

(2) Information

The information described in this paragraph regarding breaches specified in paragraph (1) shall include —

(A) the number and nature of such breaches; and

(B) actions taken in response to such breaches.

(j) Regulations; effective date

To carry out this section, the Secretary of Health and Human Services shall promulgate interim final regulations by not later than the date that is 180 days after February 17, 2009. The provisions of this section shall apply to breaches that are discovered on or after the date that is 30 days after the date of publication of such interim final regulations.

The regulations required under this provision were published by HHS in August 2009.[38] The HHS Web site currently maintains a listing of all reported breaches of unsecured PHI affecting 500 or more individuals, including a single loss of backup tapes by Science Applications International Corp. in Virginia that affected 4,901,432 beneficiaries in the U.S. military's TRICARE health insurance program.[39]

d. HHS Enforcement of the HIPAA Privacy and Security Rules

The HHS Office for Civil Rights ("OCR") is tasked with enforcing the HIPAA Privacy and Security Rules.

How OCR Enforces the HIPAA Privacy Rule[40]

OCR is responsible for enforcing the HIPAA Privacy and Security Rules (45 C.F.R. Parts 160 and 164, Subparts A, C, and E). One of the ways that OCR carries out this responsibility is to investigate complaints filed with it. OCR may also conduct compliance reviews to determine if covered entities are in compliance, and OCR performs education and outreach to foster compliance with requirements of the Privacy and Security Rules.

OCR may only take action on certain complaints. See What OCR Considers During Intake and Review of a Complaint for a description of the types of cases in which OCR cannot take an enforcement action.

If OCR accepts a complaint for investigation, OCR will notify the person who filed the complaint and the covered entity named in it. Then the complainant and the covered entity are asked to present information about the incident or problem described in the complaint. OCR may request specific information from each to get an understanding of the facts. Covered entities are required by law to cooperate with complaint investigations.

If a complaint describes an action that could be a violation of the criminal provision of HIPAA (42 U.S.C. 1320d-6), OCR may refer the complaint to the Department of Justice for investigation.

OCR reviews the information, or evidence, that it gathers in each case. In some cases, it may determine that the covered entity did not violate the requirements of the Privacy or Security Rule. If the evidence indicates that the covered entity was not in compliance, OCR will attempt to resolve the case with the covered entity by obtaining:

- *Voluntary compliance;*

---

[38] 74 FR 42740.

[39] BREACHES AFFECTING 500 OR MORE INDIVIDUALS, http://www.hhs.gov/ocr/privacy/hipaa/administrative/ breachnotificationrule/breachtool.html (last visited May 8, 2012). See also TRICARE BREACH NOTIFICATION IN WORKS — GOVINFOSECURITY, http://www.govinfosecurity.com/tricare-breach-notification-in-works-a-4128 (last visited May 8, 2012).

[40] HOW OCR ENFORCES THE HIPAA PRIVACY RULE, *http://www.hhs.gov/ocr/privacy/hipaa/enforcement/ process/howocrenforces.html (last visited May 8, 2012).*

- *Corrective action; and/or*

- *Resolution agreement.*

Most Privacy and Security Rule investigations are concluded to the satisfaction of OCR through these types of resolutions. OCR notifies the person who filed the complaint and the covered entity in writing of the resolution result.

If the covered entity does not take action to resolve the matter in a way that is satisfactory, OCR may decide to impose civil money penalties (CMPs) on the covered entity. If CMPs are imposed, the covered entity may request a hearing in which an HHS administrative law judge decides if the penalties are supported by the evidence in the case. Complainants do not receive a portion of CMPs collected from covered entities; the penalties are deposited in the U.S. Treasury.

Data on enforcement activities are published on the HHS Web site,[41] broken down by year, state, number of complaints and other criteria.

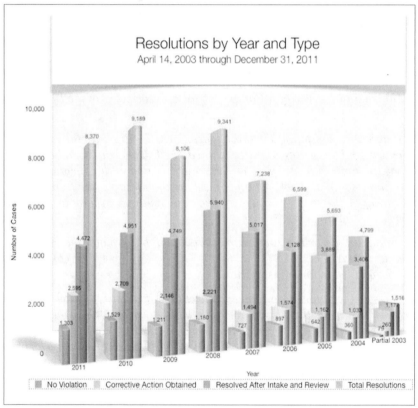

---

[41] ENFORCEMENT DATA, http://www.hhs.gov/ocr/privacy/hipaa/enforcement/data/index.html (last visited May 8, 2012).

Resolutions by Year and Type: April 14, 2003-December 31, 2011[42]

*   *   *

University of California settles HIPAA Privacy and Security case involving UCLA Health System facilities UCLAHS to improve policies and procedures to better safeguard patient information

Following an investigation by the U.S. Department of Health and Human Services (HHS) Office for Civil Rights (OCR), the University of California at Los Angeles Health System (UCLAHS) has agreed to settle potential violations of the Health Insurance Portability and Accountability Act of 1996 (HIPAA) Privacy and Security Rules for $865,500 and has committed to a corrective action plan aimed at remedying gaps in its compliance with the rules.

The resolution agreement resolves two separate complaints filed with OCR on behalf of two celebrity patients who received care at UCLAHS. The complaints alleged that UCLAHS employees repeatedly and without permissible reason looked at the electronic protected health information of these patients. OCR's investigation into the complaints revealed that from 2005–2008, unauthorized employees repeatedly looked at the electronic protected health information of numerous other UCLAHS patients.

Through policies and procedures, entities covered under HIPAA must reasonably restrict access to patient information to only those employees with a valid reason to view the information and must sanction any employee who is found to have violated these policies.

"Covered entities are responsible for the actions of their employees. This is why it is vital that trainings and meaningful policies and procedures, including audit trails, become part of the everyday operations of any health care provider," said OCR Director Georgina Verdugo. "Employees must clearly understand that casual review for personal interest of patients' protected health information is unacceptable and against the law."

The corrective action plan requires UCLAHS to implement Privacy and Security policies and procedures approved by OCR, to conduct regular and robust trainings for all UCLAHS employees who use protected health information, to sanction offending employees, and to designate an independent monitor who will assess UCLAHS compliance with the plan over 3 years.

"Covered entities need to realize that HIPAA privacy protections are real and OCR vigorously enforces those protections. Entities will be held accountable for employees who access protected health information to satisfy their own personal curiosity," said Director Verdugo . . . .[43]

---

[42] Enforcement Results by Year, http://www.hhs.gov/ocr/privacy/hipaa/enforcement/data/historicalnum bers.html#resol (last visited May 8, 2012).

[43] HHS Press Release, University of California Settles HIPAA Privacy and Security Case Involving UCLA Health System Facilities *(July 7, 2011), http://www.hhs.gov/news/press/2011pres/07/20110707a.html (last visited May 8, 2012).*

*   *   *

Rite Aid Agrees to Pay $1 Million to Settle HIPAA Privacy Case
Company agrees to substantial corrective action to safeguard consumer information

Rite Aid Corporation and its 40 affiliated entities (RAC) have agreed to pay $1 million to settle potential violations of the Health Insurance Portability and Accountability Act of 1996 (HIPAA) Privacy Rule, the U.S. Department of Health and Human Services (HHS) announced today. In a coordinated action, RAC also signed a consent order with the Federal Trade Commission (FTC) to settle potential violations of the FTC Act.

Rite Aid, one of the nation's largest drug store chains, has also agreed to take corrective action to improve policies and procedures to safeguard the privacy of its customers when disposing of identifying information on pill bottle labels and other health information. The settlements apply to all of Rite Aid's nearly 4,800 retail pharmacies and follow an extensive joint investigation by the HHS Office for Civil Rights (OCR) and the FTC.

The OCR, which enforces the HIPAA Privacy and Security Rules, opened its investigation of RAC after television media videotaped incidents in which pharmacies were shown to have disposed of prescriptions and labeled pill bottles containing individuals' identifiable information in industrial trash containers that were accessible to the public. These incidents were reported as occurring in a variety of cities across the United States. Rite Aid pharmacy stores in several of the cities were highlighted in media reports.

Disposing of individuals' health information in an industrial trash container accessible to unauthorized persons is not compliant with several requirements of the HIPAA Privacy Rule and exposes the individuals' information to the risk of identity theft and other crimes. This is the second joint investigation and settlement conducted by OCR and FTC. OCR and FTC settled a similar case involving another national drug store chain in February 2009.

"It is critical that companies, large and small, build a culture of compliance to protect consumers' right to privacy and safeguard health information. OCR is committed to strong enforcement of HIPAA," said Georgina Verdugo, director of OCR. "We hope that this agreement will spur other health organizations to examine and improve their policies and procedures for protecting patient information during the disposal process."

The HIPAA Privacy Rule requires health plans, health care clearinghouses and most health care providers (covered entities), including most pharmacies, to safeguard the privacy of patient information, including such information during its disposal.

Among other issues, the reviews by OCR and the FTC indicate that:

Rite Aid failed to implement adequate policies and procedures to appropriately safeguard patient information during the disposal process;

Rite Aid failed to adequately train employees on how to dispose of such information properly; and

Rite Aid did not maintain a sanctions policy for members of its workforce who failed to properly dispose of patient information.

Under the HHS resolution agreement, RAC agreed to pay a $1 million resolution amount to HHS and must implement a strong corrective action program that includes:

Revising and distributing its policies and procedures regarding disposal of protected health information and sanctioning workers who do not follow them;

Training workforce members on these new requirements;

Conducting internal monitoring; and

Engaging a qualified, independent third-party assessor to conduct compliance reviews and render reports to HHS.

Rite Aid has also agreed to external, independent assessments of its pharmacy stores' compliance with the FTC consent order. The HHS corrective action plan will be in place for three years; the FTC order will be in place for 20 years . . .[44]

V. STATE HEALTH PRIVACY LAWS

HIPAA explicitly does not preempt all state health privacy laws.[45] As HHS states,

The HIPAA Privacy Rule provides a Federal floor of privacy protections for individuals' individually identifiable health information where that information is held by a covered entity or by a business associate of the covered entity. State laws that are contrary to the Privacy Rule are preempted by the Federal requirements, unless a specific exception applies. These exceptions include if the State law:

1. *relates to the privacy of individually identifiable health information and provides greater privacy protections or privacy rights with respect to such information,*

2. *provides for the reporting of disease or injury, child abuse, birth, or death, or for public health surveillance, investigation, or intervention, or*

3. *requires certain health plan reporting, such as for management or financial audits. In these circumstances, a covered entity is not required to comply with a contrary provision of the Privacy Rule.*

In addition, the Department of Health and Human Services (HHS) may, upon specific request from a State or other entity or person, determine that a

---

[44] RITE AID AGREES TO PAY $1 MILLION TO SETTLE HIPAA PRIVACY CASE, *http://www.hhs.gov/news/press/2010pres/07/20100727a.html (last visited May 8, 2012).*

[45] PL 104-191, § 264(c).

provision of State law which is "contrary" to the Federal requirements — as defined by the HIPAA Administrative Simplification Rules — and which meets certain additional criteria, will not be preempted by the Federal requirements. Thus, preemption of a contrary State law will not occur if the Secretary or designated HHS official determines, in response to a request, that one of the following criteria apply: the State law:

1. *is necessary to prevent fraud and abuse related to the provision of or payment for health care,*

2. *is necessary to ensure appropriate State regulation of insurance and health plans to the extent expressly authorized by statute or regulation,*

3. *is necessary for State reporting on health care delivery or costs,*

4. *is necessary for purposes of serving a compelling public health, safety, or welfare need, and, if a Privacy Rule provision is at issue, if the Secretary determines that the intrusion into privacy is warranted when balanced against the need to be served; or*

5. *has as its principal purpose the regulation of the manufacture, registration, distribution, dispensing, or other control of any controlled substances (as defined in 21 U.S.C. 802), or that is deemed a controlled substance by State law.*

It is important to recognize that only State laws that are "contrary" to the Federal requirements are eligible for an exemption determination. As defined by the Administrative Simplification Rules, contrary means that it would be impossible for a covered entity to comply with both the State and Federal requirements, or that the provision of State law is an obstacle to accomplishing the full purposes and objectives of the Administrative Simplification provisions of HIPAA . . .[46]

Accordingly, in order to determine the obligations and liabilities of a party with regard to electronically stored PHI, one must analyze HIPAA and its associated regulations as well as any potentially applicable state law, and then determine what (if any) portion of the state law may have in fact been preempted by HIPAA and become unenforceable. This analysis can be fairly complex, especially when multiple state laws may be involved,[47] although the states themselves may provide some helpful (although not necessarily dispositive) information.[48]

---

[46] DOES THE HIPAA PRIVACY RULE PREEMPT STATE LAWS?, *http://www.hhs.gov/hipaafaq/state/399.html (last visited May 8, 2012).*

[47] *See, e.g.*, Beverly Cohen, Reconciling the HIPAA Privacy Rule with State Laws Regulating Ex Parte Interviews of Plaintiffs' Treating Physicians: A Guide to Performing HIPAA Preemption Analysis, 43 Hous. L. Rev. 1091 (Winter 2006).

[48] *See, e.g.*, State of California Office of Health Information Integrity, HIPAA PREEMPTION, http:// ohii.ca.gov/calohi/HIPAA/HIPAAPreemption.aspx (last visited May 8, 2012); New York State Department of Health, HIPAA Preemption Charts, HIPAA PREEMPTION CHARTS, http://www.health.ny.gov/regulations/hipaa/ preemption_charts.htm (last visited May 8, 2012); UTAH ATTORNEY GENERAL — MARK SHURTLEFF — MARK

VI.   PRIVATE ENFORCEMENT OF PHI AND RELATED PRIVACY RIGHTS

Individuals who believe their own or others' PHI may have been improperly protected have a number of potential avenues for recourse. One is through the HHS HIPAA complaint process.[49] Another may be private litigation, based upon theories including negligence and breach of relevant data protection laws.[50]

PHI, however, is not the only possible source of disputes with regard to healthcare and privacy. Healthcare professionals, such as physicians, may have privacy interests with regard to their practices, including their issuance of prescriptions to their patients, which may intersect with questions of free speech and other legal rights:

SORRELL v. IMS HEALTH INC.[51]

Opinion

JUSTICE KENNEDY *delivered the opinion of the Court.*

Vermont law restricts the sale, disclosure, and use of pharmacy records that reveal the prescribing practices of individual doctors. Vt. Stat. Ann., Tit. 18, § 4631 (Supp.2010). Subject to certain exceptions, the information may not be sold, disclosed by pharmacies for marketing purposes, or used for marketing by pharmaceutical manufacturers. Vermont argues that its prohibitions safeguard medical privacy and diminish the likelihood that marketing will lead to prescription decisions not in the best interests of patients or the State. It can be assumed that these interests are significant. Speech in aid of pharmaceutical marketing, however, is a form of expression protected by the Free Speech Clause of the First Amendment. As a consequence, Vermont's statute must be subjected to heightened judicial scrutiny. The law cannot satisfy that standard.

   I

   A

Pharmaceutical manufacturers promote their drugs to doctors through a process called "detailing." This often involves a scheduled visit to a doctor's office to persuade the doctor to prescribe a particular pharmaceutical. Detailers bring drug samples as well as medical studies that explain the "details" and potential advantages of various prescription drugs. Interested physicians listen, ask questions, and receive followup data. Salespersons can be more effective when they know the background and purchasing preferences of their clientele, and pharmaceutical salespersons are no

---

SHURTLEFF — HIPAA, http://attorneygeneral.utah.gov/HIPPA.html (last visited May 8, 2012).

[49] HOW TO FILE A COMPLAINT, http://www.hhs.gov/ocr/privacy/hipaa/complaints/index.html (last visited May 8, 2012).

[50] *See, e.g.,* Deatrick v. Science Applications International Corporation, CV 1055 (N.D. Cal. Filed Mar. 1, 2012) (proposed class action arising out of SAIC TRICARE data breach discussed supra at note 186).

[51] 131 S.Ct. 2653 (2011).

exception. Knowledge of a physician's prescription practices — called "prescriber-identifying information" — enables a detailer better to ascertain which doctors are likely to be interested in a particular drug and how best to present a particular sales message. Detailing is an expensive undertaking, so pharmaceutical companies most often use it to promote high-profit brand-name drugs protected by patent. Once a brand-name drug's patent expires, less expensive bioequivalent generic alternatives are manufactured and sold.

Pharmacies, as a matter of business routine and federal law, receive prescriber-identifying information when processing prescriptions. See 21 U.S.C. § 353(b); see also Vt. Bd. of Pharmacy Admin. Rule 9.1 (2009); Rule 9.2. Many pharmacies sell this information to "data miners," firms that analyze prescriber-identifying information and produce reports on prescriber behavior. Data miners lease these reports to pharmaceutical manufacturers subject to nondisclosure agreements. Detailers, who represent the manufacturers, then use the reports to refine their marketing tactics and increase sales.

In 2007, Vermont enacted the Prescription Confidentiality Law. The measure is also referred to as Act 80. It has several components. The central provision of the present case is § 4631(d).

> *"A health insurer, a self-insured employer, an electronic transmission intermediary, a pharmacy, or other similar entity shall not sell, license, or exchange for value regulated records containing prescriber-identifiable information, nor permit the use of regulated records containing prescriber-identifiable information for marketing or promoting a prescription drug, unless the prescriber consents . . . . Pharmaceutical manufacturers and pharmaceutical marketers shall not use prescriber-identifiable information for marketing or promoting a prescription drug unless the prescriber consents . . . ."*

The quoted provision has three component parts. The provision begins by prohibiting pharmacies, health insurers, and similar entities from selling prescriber-identifying information, absent the prescriber's consent. The parties here dispute whether this clause applies to all sales or only to sales for marketing. The provision then goes on to prohibit pharmacies, health insurers, and similar entities from allowing prescriber-identifying information to be used for marketing, unless the prescriber consents. This prohibition in effect bars pharmacies from disclosing the information for marketing purposes. Finally, the provision's second sentence bars pharmaceutical manufacturers and pharmaceutical marketers from using prescriber-identifying information for marketing, again absent the prescriber's consent. The Vermont attorney general may pursue civil remedies against violators. § 4631(f).

Separate statutory provisions elaborate the scope of the prohibitions set out in § 4631(d). "Marketing" is defined to include "advertising, promotion, or any activity" that is "used to influence sales or the market share of a prescription drug." § 4631(b)(5). Section 4631(c)(1) further provides that Vermont's Department of Health must allow "a prescriber to give consent for his or her identifying information to be used for the purposes" identified in § 4631(d). Finally, the Act's prohibitions on sale, disclosure, and use are subject to a list of exceptions. For example, prescriber-identifying information may be disseminated or used for "health care research"; to enforce "compliance" with health insurance formularies, or preferred drug lists; for "care management educational communications provided to" patients on such matters as "treatment options"; for law enforcement operations; and for purposes "otherwise provided by law." § 4631(e).

Act 80 also authorized funds for an "evidence-based prescription drug education program" designed to provide doctors and others with "information and education on the therapeutic and cost-effective utilization of prescription drugs." § 4622(a)(1). An express aim of the program is to advise prescribers "about commonly used brand-name drugs for which the patent has expired" or will soon expire. § 4622(a)(2). Similar efforts to promote the use of generic pharmaceuticals are sometimes referred to as "counter-detailing." App. 211; see also IMS Health Inc. v. Ayotte, 550 F.3d 42, 91 (C.A.1 2008) *(Lipez, J., concurring and dissenting). The counterdetailer's recommended substitute may be an older, less expensive drug and not a bioequivalent of the brand-name drug the physician might otherwise prescribe. Like the pharmaceutical manufacturers whose efforts they hope to resist, counterdetailers in some States use prescriber-identifying information to increase their effectiveness. States themselves may supply the prescriber-identifying information used in these programs. See App. 313;* id., *at 375 ("[W]e use the data given to us by the State of Pennsylvania . . . to figure out which physicians to talk to"); see also* id., *at 427–429 (Director of the Office of Vermont Health Access explaining that the office collects prescriber-identifying information but "does not at this point in time have a counterdetailing or detailing effort"). As first enacted, Act 80 also required detailers to provide information about alternative treatment options. The Vermont Legislature, however, later repealed that provision. 2008 Vt. Laws No. 89, § 3.*

Act 80 was accompanied by legislative findings. Vt. Acts No. 80, § 1. Vermont found, for example, that the "goals of marketing programs are often in conflict with the goals of the state" and that the "marketplace for ideas on medicine safety and effectiveness is frequently one-sided in that brand-name companies invest in expensive pharmaceutical marketing campaigns to doctors." §§ 1(3), (4). Detailing, in the legislature's view, caused doctors to make decisions based on "incomplete and biased information." § 1(4). Because they "are unable to take the time to research the quickly changing pharmaceutical market," Vermont doctors "rely on information provided by pharmaceutical representatives." § 1(13). The legislature further found that detailing increases the cost of health care and health insurance, § 1(15); encourages hasty and excessive reliance on brand-name drugs, before the profession has observed their effectiveness as compared with older and less expensive generic alternatives, § 1(7); and fosters disruptive and repeated marketing visits tantamount to harassment, §§ 1(27)-(28). The legislative findings further noted that use of prescriber-identifying information "increase[s] the effect of detailing programs" by allowing detailers to target their visits to particular doctors. §§ 1(23)-(26). Use of prescriber-identifying data also helps detailers shape their messages by "tailoring" their "presentations to individual prescriber styles, preferences, and attitudes." § 1(25).

B

The present case involves two consolidated suits. One was brought by three Vermont data miners, the other by an association of pharmaceutical manufacturers that produce brand-name drugs. These entities are the respondents here. Contending that § 4631(d) violates their First Amendment rights as incorporated by the Fourteenth Amendment, the respondents sought declaratory and injunctive relief against the petitioners, the Attorney General and other officials of the State of Vermont.

After a bench trial, the United States District Court for the District of Vermont denied relief. 631 F.Supp.2d 434 (2009). The District Court found that "[p]harmaceutical manufacturers are essentially the only paying customers of the data vendor industry" and that, because detailing unpatented generic drugs is not "cost-effective," pharmaceutical sales representatives "detail only branded drugs." Id., at 451, 442. As the District Court further concluded, "the Legislature's determination that [prescriber-identifying] data is an effective marketing tool that enables detailers to increase sales of new drugs is supported in the record." Id., at 451. The United States Court of Appeals for the Second Circuit reversed and remanded. It held that § 4631(d) violates the First Amendment by burdening the speech of pharmaceutical marketers and data miners without an adequate justification. 630 F.3d 263. Judge Livingston dissented.

The decision of the Second Circuit is in conflict with decisions of the United States Court of Appeals for the First Circuit concerning similar legislation enacted by Maine and New Hampshire. See IMS Health Inc. v. Mills, *616 F.3d 7 (C.A.1 2010) (Maine);* Ayotte, *supra (New Hampshire). Recognizing a division of authority regarding the constitutionality of state statutes, this Court granted certiorari. 562 U.S. ___, 131 S.Ct. 857, 178 L.Ed.2d 623 (2011).*

II

The beginning point is the text of § 4631(d). In the proceedings below, Vermont stated that the first sentence of § 4631(d) prohibits pharmacies and other regulated entities from selling or disseminating prescriber-identifying information for marketing. The information, in other words, could be sold or given away for purposes other than marketing. The District Court and the Court of Appeals accepted the State's reading. See 630 F.3d, at 276. At oral argument in this Court, however, the State for the first time advanced an alternative reading of § 4631(d) — namely, that pharmacies, health insurers, and similar entities may not sell prescriber-identifying information for any purpose, subject to the statutory exceptions set out at § 4631(e). See Tr. of Oral Arg. 19–20. It might be argued that the State's newfound interpretation comes too late in the day. See Sprietsma v. Mercury Marine, *537 U.S. 51, 56, n. 4, 123 S.Ct. 518, 154 L.Ed.2d 466 (2002) (waiver);* New Hampshire v. Maine, *532 U.S. 742, 749, 121 S.Ct. 1808, 149 L.Ed.2d 968 (2001) (judicial estoppel). The respondents, the District Court, and the Court of Appeals were entitled to rely on the State's plausible interpretation of the law it is charged with enforcing. For the State to change its position is particularly troubling in a First Amendment case, where plaintiffs have a special interest in obtaining a prompt adjudication of their rights, despite potential ambiguities of state law. See* Houston v. Hill, *482 U.S. 451, 467–468, and n. 17, 107 S.Ct. 2502, 96 L.Ed.2d 398 (1987);* Zwickler v. Koota, *389 U.S. 241, 252, 88 S.Ct. 391, 19 L.Ed.2d 444 (1967).*

In any event, § 4631(d) cannot be sustained even under the interpretation the State now adopts. As a consequence this Court can assume that the opening clause of § 4631(d) prohibits pharmacies, health insurers, and similar entities from selling prescriber-identifying information, subject to the statutory exceptions set out at § 4631(e). Under that reading, pharmacies may sell the information to private or academic researchers, see § 4631(e)(1), but not, for example, to pharmaceutical marketers. There is no dispute as to the remainder of § 4631(d). It prohibits pharmacies, health insurers, and similar entities from disclosing or otherwise allowing prescriber-identifying information to be used for marketing. And it bars pharmaceutical manufacturers and detailers from using the information for marketing. The questions now are whether § 4631(d) must be tested by heightened judicial scrutiny and, if so, whether the State can justify the law.

A

1

On its face, Vermont's law enacts content-and speaker-based restrictions on the sale, disclosure, and use of prescriber-identifying information. The provision first forbids sale subject to exceptions based in large part on the content of a purchaser's speech. For example, those who wish to engage in certain "educational communications," § 4631(e)(4), may purchase the information. The measure then bars any disclosure when recipient speakers will use the information for marketing. Finally, the provision's second sentence prohibits pharmaceutical manufacturers from using the information for marketing. The statute thus disfavors marketing, that is, speech with a particular content. More than that, the statute disfavors specific speakers, namely pharmaceutical manufacturers. As a result of these content-and speaker-based rules, detailers cannot obtain prescriber-identifying information, even though the information may be purchased or acquired by other speakers with diverse purposes and viewpoints. Detailers are likewise barred from using the information for marketing, even though the information may be used by a wide range of other speakers. For example, it appears that Vermont could supply academic organizations with prescriber-identifying information to use in countering the messages of brand-name pharmaceutical manufacturers and in promoting the prescription of generic drugs. But § 4631(d) leaves detailers no means of purchasing, acquiring, or using prescriber-identifying information. The law on its face burdens disfavored speech by disfavored speakers.

Any doubt that § 4631(d) imposes an aimed, content-based burden on detailers is dispelled by the record and by formal legislative findings. As the District Court noted, "[p]harmaceutical manufacturers are essentially the only paying customers of the data vendor industry"; and the almost invariable rule is that detailing by pharmaceutical manufacturers is in support of brand-name drugs. 631 F.Supp.2d, at 451. Vermont's law thus has the effect of preventing detailers — and only detailers — from communicating with physicians in an effective and informative manner. Cf. Edenfield v. Fane, 507 U.S. 761, 766, 113 S.Ct. 1792, 123 L.Ed.2d 543 (1993) (explaining the "considerable value" of in-person solicitation). Formal legislative findings accompanying § 4631(d) confirm that the law's express purpose and practical effect are to diminish the effectiveness of marketing by manufacturers of brand-name drugs. Just as the "inevitable effect of a statute on its face may render it unconstitutional," a statute's stated purposes may also be considered. United States v. O'Brien, *391 U.S. 367, 384, 88 S.Ct. 1673, 20 L.Ed.2d 672 (1968). Here, the Vermont Legislature explained that detailers, in particular those who promote brand-name drugs, convey messages that "are often in conflict with the goals of the state." 2007 Vt. No. 80, § 1(3). The legislature designed § 4631(d) to target those speakers and their messages for disfavored treatment. "In its practical operation," Vermont's law "goes even beyond mere content discrimination, to actual viewpoint discrimination."* R.A.V. v. St. Paul, *505 U.S. 377, 391, 112 S.Ct. 2538, 120 L.Ed.2d 305 (1992). Given the legislature's expressed statement of purpose, it is apparent that § 4631(d) imposes burdens that are based on the content of speech and that are aimed at a particular viewpoint.*

Act 80 is designed to impose a specific, content-based burden on protected expression. It follows that heightened judicial scrutiny is warranted. See Cincinnati v. Discovery Network, Inc., *507 U.S. 410, 418, 113 S.Ct. 1505, 123 L.Ed.2d 99 (1993) (applying heightened scrutiny to "a categorical prohibition on the use of newsracks to disseminate commercial messages"); id., at 429, 113 S.Ct. 1505 ("[T]he very basis for the regulation is the difference in content between ordinary newspapers and commercial speech" in the form of "commercial handbills . . . . Thus, by any commonsense understanding of the term, the ban in this case is 'content based' " (some internal quotation marks omitted)); see also* Turner Broadcasting System, Inc. v. FCC, *512 U.S. 622, 658, 114 S.Ct. 2445, 129 L.Ed.2d 497 (1994) (explaining that strict scrutiny applies to regulations reflecting "aversion" to what "disfavored speakers" have to say). The Court has recognized that the "distinction between laws burdening and laws banning speech is but a matter of degree" and that the "Government's content-based burdens must satisfy the same rigorous scrutiny as its content-based bans."* United States v. Playboy Entertainment Group, Inc., *529 U.S. 803, 812, 120 S.Ct. 1878, 146 L.Ed.2d 865 (2000). Lawmakers may no more silence unwanted speech by burdening its utterance than by censoring its content. See* Simon & Schuster, Inc. v. Members of N.Y. State Crime Victims Bd., *502 U.S. 105, 115, 112 S.Ct. 501, 116 L.Ed.2d 476 (1991) (content-based financial burden);* Minneapolis Star & Tribune Co. v. Minnesota Comm'r of Revenue, *460 U.S. 575, 103 S.Ct. 1365, 75 L.Ed.2d 295 (1983) (speaker-based financial burden).*

The First Amendment requires heightened scrutiny whenever the government creates "a regulation of speech because of disagreement with the message it conveys." Ward v. Rock Against Racism, *491 U.S. 781, 791, 109 S.Ct. 2746, 105 L.Ed.2d 661 (1989); see also* Renton v. Playtime Theatres, Inc., *475 U.S. 41, 48, 106 S.Ct. 925, 89 L.Ed.2d 29 (1986) (explaining that " 'content-neutral' speech regulations" are "those that are justified without reference to the content of the regulated speech" (internal quotation marks omitted)). A government bent on frustrating an impending demonstration might pass a law demanding two years' notice before the issuance of parade permits. Even if the hypothetical measure on its face appeared neutral as to content and speaker, its purpose to suppress speech and its unjustified burdens on expression would render it unconstitutional. Ibid. Commercial speech is no exception. See* Discovery Network, supra, *at 429–430, 113 S.Ct. 1505 (commercial speech restriction lacking a "neutral justification" was not content neutral). A "consumer's concern for the free flow of commercial speech often may be far keener than his concern for urgent political dialogue.*" Bates v. State Bar of Ariz., *433 U.S. 350, 364, 97 S.Ct. 2691, 53 L.Ed.2d 810 (1977). That reality has great relevance in the fields of medicine and public health, where information can save lives.*

2

The State argues that heightened judicial scrutiny is unwarranted because its law is a mere commercial regulation. It is true that restrictions on protected expression are distinct from restrictions on economic activity or, more generally, on nonexpressive conduct. It is also true that the First Amendment does not prevent restrictions directed at commerce or conduct from imposing incidental burdens on speech. That is why a ban on race-based hiring may require employers to remove " 'White Applicants Only' " signs, Rumsfeld v. Forum for Academic and Institutional Rights, Inc., *547 U.S. 47, 62, 126 S.Ct. 1297, 164 L.Ed.2d 156 (2006); why "an ordinance against outdoor fires" might forbid "burning a flag,"* R.A. V., *supra, at 385, 112 S.Ct. 2538; and why antitrust laws can prohibit "agreements in restraint of trade,"* Giboney v. Empire Storage & Ice Co., *336 U.S. 490, 502, 69 S.Ct. 684, 93 L.Ed. 834 (1949).*

But § 4631(d) imposes more than an incidental burden on protected expression. Both on its face and in its practical operation, Vermont's law imposes a burden based on the content of speech and the identity of the speaker. See supra, at 2663–2665. While the burdened speech results from an economic motive, so too does a great deal of vital expression. See Bigelow v. Virginia, *421 U.S. 809, 818, 95 S.Ct. 2222, 44 L.Ed.2d 600 (1975);* New York Times Co. v. Sullivan, *376 U.S. 254, 266, 84 S.Ct. 710, 11 L.Ed.2d 686 (1964); see also* United States v. United Foods, Inc., *533 U.S. 405, 410–411, 121 S.Ct. 2334, 150 L.Ed.2d 438 (2001) (applying "First Amendment scrutiny" where speech effects were not incidental and noting that "those whose business and livelihood depend in some way upon the product involved no doubt deem First Amendment protection to be just as important for them as it is for other discrete, little noticed groups"). Vermont's law does not simply have an effect on speech, but is directed at certain content and is aimed at particular speakers. The Constitution "does not enact Mr. Herbert Spencer's Social Statics."* Lochner v. New York, *198 U.S. 45, 75, 25 S.Ct. 539, 49 L.Ed. 937 (1905) (Holmes, J., dissenting). It does enact the First Amendment.*

Vermont further argues that § 4631(d) regulates not speech but simply access to information. Prescriber-identifying information was generated in compliance with a legal mandate, the State argues, and so could be considered a kind of governmental information. This argument finds some support in Los Angeles Police Dept. v. United Reporting Publishing Corp., *528 U.S. 32, 120 S.Ct. 483, 145 L.Ed.2d 451 (1999), where the Court held that a plaintiff could not raise a facial challenge to a content-based restriction on access to government held information. Because no private party faced a threat of legal punishment, the Court characterized the law at issue as "nothing more than a governmental denial of access to information in its possession." Id., at 40, 120 S.Ct. 483. Under those circumstances the special reasons for permitting First Amendment plaintiffs to invoke the rights of others did not apply. Id., at 38–39, 120 S.Ct. 483. Having found that the plaintiff could not raise a facial challenge, the Court remanded for consideration of an as-applied challenge. Id., at 41.* United Reporting *is thus a case about the availability of facial challenges. The Court did not rule on the merits of any First Amendment claim.*

United Reporting *is distinguishable in at least two respects. First, Vermont has imposed a restriction on access to information in private hands. This confronts the Court with a point reserved, and a situation not addressed, in* United Reporting. *Here, unlike in* United Reporting, *we do have "a case in which the government is prohibiting a speaker from conveying information that the speaker already possesses."* Id., *at 40, 120 S.Ct. 483. The difference is significant. An individual's right to speak is implicated when information he or she possesses is subjected to "restraints on the way in which the information might be used" or disseminated.* Seattle Times Co. v. Rhinehart, *467 U.S. 20, 32, 104 S.Ct. 2199, 81 L.Ed.2d 17 (1984); see also* Bartnicki v. Vopper, *532 U.S. 514, 527, 121 S.Ct. 1753, 149 L.Ed.2d 787 (2001);* Florida Star v. B.J. F., *491 U.S. 524, 109 S.Ct. 2603, 105 L.Ed.2d 443 (1989);* New York Times Co. v. United States, *403 U.S. 713, 91 S.Ct. 2140, 29 L.Ed.2d 822 (1971) (per curiam). In* Seattle Times, *this Court applied heightened judicial scrutiny before sustaining a trial court order prohibiting a newspaper's disclosure of information it learned through coercive discovery. It is true that the respondents here, unlike the newspaper in* Seattle Times, *do not themselves possess information whose disclosure has been curtailed. That information, however, is in the hands of pharmacies and other private entities. There is no question that the "threat of prosecution . . . hangs over their heads."* United Reporting, *528 U.S., at 41, 120 S.Ct. 483. For that reason* United Reporting *does not bar respondents' facial challenge.*

United Reporting *is distinguishable for a second and even more important reason. The plaintiff in* United Reporting *had neither "attempt [ed] to qualify" for access to the government's information nor presented an as-applied claim in this Court.* Id., *at 40, 120 S.Ct. 483. As a result, the Court assumed that the plaintiff had not suffered a personal First Amendment injury and could prevail only by invoking the rights of others through a facial challenge. Here, by contrast, the respondents claim — with good reason — that § 4631(d) burdens their own speech. That argument finds support in the separate writings in* United Reporting, *which were joined by eight Justices. All of those writings recognized that restrictions on the disclosure of government-held information can facilitate or burden the expression of potential recipients and so transgress the First Amendment. See* id., *at 42, 120 S.Ct. 483 (SCALIA, J., concurring) (suggesting that "a restriction upon access that* allows *access to the press . . . but at the same time* denies *access to persons who wish to use the information for certain speech purposes, is in reality a restriction upon speech");* id., *at 43, 120 S.Ct. 483 (GINSBURG, J., concurring) (noting that "the provision of [government] information is a kind of subsidy to people who wish to speak" about certain subjects, "and once a State decides to make such a benefit available to the public, there are no doubt limits to its freedom to decide how that benefit will be distributed");* id., *at 46, 120 S.Ct. 483 (Stevens, J., dissenting) (concluding that, "because the State's discrimination is based on its desire to prevent the information from being used for constitutionally protected purposes, [i]t must assume the burden of justifying its conduct"). Vermont's law imposes a content-and speaker-based burden on respondents' own speech. That consideration provides a separate basis for distinguishing* United Reporting *and requires heightened judicial scrutiny.*

The State also contends that heightened judicial scrutiny is unwarranted in this case because sales, transfer, and use of prescriber-identifying information are conduct, not speech. Consistent with that submission, the United States Court of Appeals for the First Circuit has characterized prescriber-identifying information as a mere "commodity" with no greater entitlement to First Amendment protection than "beef jerky." Ayotte, 550 F.3d, at 52–53. In contrast the courts below concluded that a prohibition on the sale of prescriber-identifying information is a content-based rule akin to a ban on the sale of cookbooks, laboratory results, or train schedules. See 630 F.3d, at 271–272 ("The First Amendment protects even dry information, devoid of advocacy, political relevance, or artistic expression" (internal quotation marks and alteration omitted)); 631 F.Supp.2d, at 445 ("A restriction on disclosure is a regulation of speech, and the 'sale' of [information] is simply disclosure for profit").

This Court has held that the creation and dissemination of information are speech within the meaning of the First Amendment. See, e.g., Bartnicki, *supra,* at 527, 121 S.Ct. 1753 *("[I]f the acts of 'disclosing' and 'publishing' information do not constitute speech, it is hard to imagine what does fall within that category, as distinct from the category of expressive conduct" (some internal quotation marks omitted));* Rubin v. Coors Brewing Co., 514 U.S. 476, 481, 115 S.Ct. 1585, 131 L.Ed.2d 532 (1995) *("information on beer labels" is speech);* Dun & Bradstreet, Inc. v. Greenmoss Builders, Inc., 472 U.S. 749, 759, 105 S.Ct. 2939, 86 L.Ed.2d 593 (1985) *(plurality opinion) (credit report is "speech"). Facts, after all, are the beginning point for much of the speech that is most essential to advance human knowledge and to conduct human affairs. There is thus a strong argument that prescriber-identifying information is speech for First Amendment purposes.*

The State asks for an exception to the rule that information is speech, but there is no need to consider that request in this case. The State has imposed content-and speaker-based restrictions on the availability and use of prescriber-identifying information. So long as they do not engage in marketing, many speakers can obtain and use the information. But detailers cannot. Vermont's statute could be compared with a law prohibiting trade magazines from purchasing or using ink. Cf. Minneapolis Star, 460 U.S. 575, 103 S.Ct. 1365, 75 L.Ed.2d 295. *Like that hypothetical law, § 4631(d) imposes a speaker-and content-based burden on protected expression, and that circumstance is sufficient to justify application of heightened scrutiny. As a consequence, this case can be resolved even assuming, as the State argues, that prescriber-identifying information is a mere commodity.*

B

In the ordinary case it is all but dispositive to conclude that a law is content-based and, in practice, viewpoint-discriminatory. See R.A. V., 505 U.S., at 382, 112 S.Ct. 2538 *("Content-based regulations are presumptively invalid"); id., at 391–392, 112 S.Ct. 2538. The State argues that a different analysis applies here because, assuming § 4631(d) burdens speech at all, it at most burdens only commercial speech. As in previous cases, however, the outcome is the same whether a special commercial speech inquiry or a stricter form of judicial scrutiny is applied. See, e.g.,* Greater New Orleans Broadcasting Assn., Inc. v. United States, 527 U.S. 173, 184, 119 S.Ct. 1923, 144 L.Ed.2d 161 (1999). *For the same reason there is no need to determine whether all speech hampered by § 4631(d) is commercial, as our cases have used that term. Cf.* Board of Trustees of State Univ. of N.Y. v. Fox, 492 U.S. 469, 474, 109 S.Ct. 3028, 106

L.Ed.2d 388 (1989) (discussing whether "pure speech and commercial speech" were inextricably intertwined, so that "the entirety must . . . be classified as noncommercial").

Under a commercial speech inquiry, it is the State's burden to justify its content-based law as consistent with the First Amendment. Thompson v. Western States Medical Center, *535 U.S. 357, 373, 122 S.Ct. 1497, 152 L.Ed.2d 563 (2002). To sustain the targeted, content-based burden § 4631(d) imposes on protected expression, the State must show at least that the statute directly advances a substantial governmental interest and that the measure is drawn to achieve that interest. See* Fox, supra, *at 480–481, 109 S.Ct. 3028;* Central Hudson Gas & Elec. Corp. v. Public Serv. Comm'n of N.Y., *447 U.S. 557, 566, 100 S.Ct. 2343, 65 L.Ed.2d 341 (1980). There must be a "fit between the legislature's ends and the means chosen to accomplish those ends."* Fox, supra, *at 480, 109 S.Ct. 3028 (internal quotation marks omitted). As in other contexts, these standards ensure not only that the State's interests are proportional to the resulting burdens placed on speech but also that the law does not seek to suppress a disfavored message. See* Turner Broadcasting, *512 U.S., at 662–663, 114 S.Ct. 2445.*

The State's asserted justifications for § 4631(d) come under two general headings. First, the State contends that its law is necessary to protect medical privacy, including physician confidentiality, avoidance of harassment, and the integrity of the doctor-patient relationship. Second, the State argues that § 4631(d) is integral to the achievement of policy objectives — namely, improved public health and reduced healthcare costs. Neither justification withstands scrutiny.

1

Vermont argues that its physicians have a "reasonable expectation" that their prescriber-identifying information "will not be used for purposes other than . . . filling and processing" prescriptions. See 2007 Vt. Laws No. 80, § 1(29). It may be assumed that, for many reasons, physicians have an interest in keeping their prescription decisions confidential. But § 4631(d) is not drawn to serve that interest. Under Vermont's law, pharmacies may share prescriber-identifying information with anyone for any reason save one: They must not allow the information to be used for marketing. Exceptions further allow pharmacies to sell prescriber-identifying information for certain purposes, including "health care research." § 4631(e). And the measure permits insurers, researchers, journalists, the State itself, and others to use the information. See § 4631(d); cf. App. 370–372; id., at 211. All but conceding that § 4631(d) does not in itself advance confidentiality interests, the State suggests that other laws might impose separate bars on the disclosure of prescriber-identifying information. See Vt. Bd. of Pharmacy Admin. Rule 20.1. But the potential effectiveness of other measures cannot justify the distinctive set of prohibitions and sanctions imposed by § 4631(d).

Perhaps the State could have addressed physician confidentiality through "a more coherent policy." Greater New Orleans Broadcasting, supra, *at 195, 119 S.Ct. 1923; see also* Discovery Network, *507 U.S., at 428, 113 S.Ct. 1505. For instance, the State might have advanced its asserted privacy interest by allowing the information's sale or disclosure in only a few narrow and well-justified circumstances. See, e.g.,* Health

Insurance Portability and Accountability Act of 1996, 42 U.S.C. § 1320d–2; 45 CFR pts. 160 and 164 (2010). A statute of that type would present quite a different case than the one presented here. But the State did not enact a statute with that purpose or design. Instead, Vermont made prescriber-identifying information available to an almost limitless audience. The explicit structure of the statute allows the information to be studied and used by all but a narrow class of disfavored speakers. Given the information's widespread availability and many permissible uses, the State's asserted interest in physician confidentiality does not justify the burden that § 4631(d) places on protected expression.

The State points out that it allows doctors to forgo the advantages of § 4631(d) by consenting to the sale, disclosure, and use of their prescriber-identifying information. See § 4631(c)(1). It is true that private decisionmaking can avoid governmental partiality and thus insulate privacy measures from First Amendment challenge. See Rowan v. Post Office Dept., *397 U.S. 728, 90 S.Ct. 1484, 25 L.Ed.2d 736 (1970); cf.* Bolger v. Youngs Drug Products Corp., *463 U.S. 60, 72, 103 S.Ct. 2875, 77 L.Ed.2d 469 (1983). But that principle is inapposite here. Vermont has given its doctors a contrived choice: Either consent, which will allow your prescriber-identifying information to be disseminated and used without constraint; or, withhold consent, which will allow your information to be used by those speakers whose message the State supports. Section 4631(d) may offer a limited degree of privacy, but only on terms favorable to the speech the State prefers. Cf.* Rowan, *supra, at 734, 737, 739, n. 6, 90 S.Ct. 1484 (sustaining a law that allowed private parties to make "unfettered," "unlimited," and "unreviewable" choices regarding their own privacy). This is not to say that all privacy measures must avoid content-based rules. Here, however, the State has conditioned privacy on acceptance of a content-based rule that is not drawn to serve the State's asserted interest. To obtain the limited privacy allowed by § 4631(d), Vermont physicians are forced to acquiesce in the State's goal of burdening disfavored speech by disfavored speakers.*

Respondents suggest that a further defect of § 4631(d) lies in its presumption of applicability absent a physician's election to the contrary. Vermont's law might burden less speech if it came into operation only after an individual choice, but a revision to that effect would not necessarily save § 4631(d). Even reliance on a prior election would not suffice, for instance, if available categories of coverage by design favored speakers of one political persuasion over another. Rules that burden protected expression may not be sustained when the options provided by the State are too narrow to advance legitimate interests or too broad to protect speech. As already explained, § 4631(d) permits extensive use of prescriber-identifying information and so does not advance the State's asserted interest in physician confidentiality. The limited range of available privacy options instead reflects the State's impermissible purpose to burden disfavored speech. Vermont's argument accordingly fails, even if the availability and scope of private election might be relevant in other contexts, as when the statute's design is unrelated to any purpose to advance a preferred message.

The State also contends that § 4631(d) protects doctors from "harassing sales behaviors." 2007 Vt. Laws No. 80, § 1(28). "Some doctors in Vermont are experiencing an undesired increase in the aggressiveness of pharmaceutical sales representatives," the Vermont Legislature found, "and a few have reported that they felt coerced and harassed." § 1(20). It is doubtful that concern for "a few" physicians who may have "felt coerced and harassed" by pharmaceutical marketers can sustain a broad content-based rule like § 4631(d). Many are those who must endure speech they do not like, but that is a necessary cost of freedom. See Erznoznik v. Jacksonville, 422 U.S. 205, 210–211, 95 S.Ct. 2268, 45 L.Ed.2d 125 (1975); Cohen v. California, 403 U.S. 15, 21, 91 S.Ct. 1780, 29 L.Ed.2d 284 (1971). In any event the State offers no explanation why remedies other than content-based rules would be inadequate. See 44 Liquormart, Inc. v. Rhode Island, 517 U.S. 484, 503, 116 S.Ct. 1495, 134 L.Ed.2d 711 (1996) (opinion of Stevens, J.). Physicians can, and often do, simply decline to meet with detailers, including detailers who use prescriber-identifying information. See, e.g., App. 180, 333–334. Doctors who wish to forgo detailing altogether are free to give "No Solicitation" or "No Detailing" instructions to their office managers or to receptionists at their places of work. Personal privacy even in one's own home receives "ample protection" from the "resident's unquestioned right to refuse to engage in conversation with unwelcome visitors." Watchtower Bible & Tract Soc. of N. Y., Inc. v. Village of Stratton, 536 U.S. 150, 168, 122 S.Ct. 2080, 153 L.Ed.2d 205 (2002); see also Bolger, supra, at 72, 103 S.Ct. 2875. A physician's office is no more private and is entitled to no greater protection.

Vermont argues that detailers' use of prescriber-identifying information undermines the doctor-patient relationship by allowing detailers to influence treatment decisions. According to the State, "unwanted pressure occurs" when doctors learn that their prescription decisions are being "monitored" by detailers. 2007 Vt. Laws No. 80, § 1(27). Some physicians accuse detailers of "spying" or of engaging in "underhanded" conduct in order to "subvert" prescription decisions. App. 336, 380, 407–408; see also id., at 326–328. And Vermont claims that detailing makes people "anxious" about whether doctors have their patients' best interests at heart. Id., at 327. But the State does not explain why detailers' use of prescriber-identifying information is more likely to prompt these objections than many other uses permitted by § 4631(d). In any event, this asserted interest is contrary to basic First Amendment principles. Speech remains protected even when it may "stir people to action," "move them to tears," or "inflict great pain." Snyder v. Phelps, 562 U.S. ___, ___, 131 S.Ct. 1207, 1220, 179 L.Ed.2d 172 (2011). The more benign and, many would say, beneficial speech of pharmaceutical marketing is also entitled to the protection of the First Amendment. If pharmaceutical marketing affects treatment decisions, it does so because doctors find it persuasive. Absent circumstances far from those presented here, the fear that speech might persuade provides no lawful basis for quieting it. Brandenburg v. Ohio, 395 U.S. 444, 447, 89 S.Ct. 1827, 23 L.Ed.2d 430 (1969) (per curiam).

2

The State contends that § 4631(d) advances important public policy goals by lowering the costs of medical services and promoting public health. If prescriber-identifying information were available for use by detailers, the State contends, then detailing would be effective in promoting brand-name drugs that are more expensive and less safe than generic alternatives. This logic is set out at length in the legislative findings accompanying § 4631(d). Yet at oral argument here, the State declined to acknowledge that § 4631(d)'s objective purpose and practical effect were to inhibit detailing and alter doctors' prescription decisions. See Tr. of Oral Arg. 5–6. The State's *reluctance to embrace its own legislature's rationale reflects the vulnerability of its position.*

While Vermont's stated policy goals may be proper, § 4631(d) does not advance them in a permissible way. As the Court of Appeals noted, the "state's own explanation of how" § 4631(d) "advances its interests cannot be said to be direct." 630 F.3d, at 277. The State seeks to achieve its policy objectives through the indirect means of restraining certain speech by certain speakers — that is, by diminishing detailers' ability to influence prescription decisions. Those who seek to censor or burden free expression often assert that disfavored speech has adverse effects. But the "fear that people would make bad decisions if given truthful information" cannot justify content-based burdens on speech. Thompson, 535 U.S., at 374, 122 S.Ct. 1497; *see also* Virginia Bd. of Pharmacy v. Virginia Citizens Consumer Council, Inc., 425 U.S. 748, 769–770, 96 S.Ct. 1817, 48 L.Ed.2d 346 (1976). *"The First Amendment directs us to be especially skeptical of regulations that seek to keep people in the dark for what the government perceives to be their own good."* 44 Liquormart, supra, at 503, 116 S.Ct. 1495 *(opinion of Stevens, J.); see also* Linmark Associates, Inc. v. Willingboro, 431 U.S. 85, 97, 97 S.Ct. 1614, 52 L.Ed.2d 155 (1977). *These precepts apply with full force when the audience, in this case prescribing physicians, consists of "sophisticated and experienced" consumers.* Edenfield, 507 U.S., at 775, 113 S.Ct. 1792.

As Vermont's legislative findings acknowledge, the premise of § 4631(d) is that the force of speech can justify the government's attempts to stifle it. Indeed the State defends the law by insisting that "pharmaceutical marketing has a strong influence on doctors' prescribing practices." Brief for Petitioners 49–50. This reasoning is incompatible with the First Amendment. In an attempt to reverse a disfavored trend in public opinion, a State could not ban campaigning with slogans, picketing with signs, or marching during the daytime. Likewise the State may not seek to remove a popular but disfavored product from the marketplace by prohibiting truthful, non-misleading advertisements that contain impressive endorsements or catchy jingles. That the State finds expression too persuasive does not permit it to quiet the speech or to burden its messengers.

The defect in Vermont's law is made clear by the fact that many listeners find detailing instructive. Indeed the record demonstrates that some Vermont doctors view targeted detailing based on prescriber-identifying information as "very helpful" because it allows detailers to shape their messages to each doctor's practice. App. 274; see also id., at 181, 218, 271–272. Even the United States, which appeared here in support of Vermont, took care to dispute the State's "unwarranted view that the dangers of [n]ew drugs outweigh their benefits to patients." Brief for United States as Amicus Curiae 24, n. 4. There are divergent views regarding detailing and the prescription of brand-name drugs. Under the Constitution, resolution of that debate must result from free and uninhibited speech. As one Vermont physician put it: "We have a saying in medicine, information is power. And the more you know, or anyone knows, the better decisions can be made." App. 279. There are similar sayings in law, including that "information is not in itself harmful, that people will perceive their own best interests if only they are well enough informed, and that the best means to that end is to open the channels of communication rather than to close them." Virginia Bd., 425 U.S., at 770, 96 S.Ct. 1817. *The choice "between the dangers of suppressing information, and the dangers of its misuse if it is freely available" is one that "the First Amendment makes for us." Ibid.*

Vermont may be displeased that detailers who use prescriber-identifying information are effective in promoting brand-name drugs. The State can express that view through its own speech. See Linmark, 431 U.S., at 97, 97 S.Ct. 1614; cf. § 4622(a)(1) (establishing a prescription drug educational program). But a State's failure to persuade does not allow it to hamstring the opposition. The State may not burden the speech of others in order to tilt public debate in a preferred direction. "The commercial marketplace, like other spheres of our social and cultural life, provides a forum where ideas and information flourish. Some of the ideas and information are vital, some of slight worth. But the general rule is that the speaker and the audience, not the government, assess the value of the information presented." Edenfield, supra, at 767, 113 S.Ct. 1792.

It is true that content-based restrictions on protected expression are sometimes permissible, and that principle applies to commercial speech. Indeed the government's legitimate interest in protecting consumers from "commercial harms" explains "why commercial speech can be subject to greater governmental regulation than noncommercial speech." Discovery Network, 507 U.S., at 426, 113 S.Ct. 1505; see also 44 Liquormart, 517 U.S., at 502, 116 S.Ct. 1495 (opinion of Stevens, J.). The Court has noted, for example, that "a State may choose to regulate price advertising in one industry but not in others, because the risk of fraud . . . is in its view greater there." R.A.V., 505 U.S., at 388–389, 112 S.Ct. 2538 (citing Virginia Bd., supra, at 771–772, 96 S.Ct. 1817). Here, however, Vermont has not shown that its law has a neutral justification.

The State nowhere contends that detailing is false or misleading within the meaning of this Court's First Amendment precedents. See Thompson, 535 U.S., at 373, 122 S.Ct. 1497. Nor does the State argue that the provision challenged here will prevent false or misleading speech. Cf. post, at 2677–2678 (BREYER, J., dissenting) (collecting regulations that the government might defend on this ground). The State's interest in burdening the speech of detailers instead turns on nothing more than a difference of opinion. See Bolger, 463 U.S., at 69, 103 S.Ct. 2875; Thompson, supra, at 376, 122 S.Ct. 1497.

The capacity of technology to find and publish personal information, including records required by the government, presents serious and unresolved issues with respect to personal privacy and the dignity it seeks to secure. In considering how to protect those interests, however, the State cannot engage in content-based discrimination to advance its own side of a debate.

If Vermont's statute provided that prescriber-identifying information could not be sold or disclosed except in narrow circumstances then the State might have a stronger position. Here, however, the State gives possessors of the information broad discretion and wide latitude in disclosing the information, while at the same time restricting the information's use by some speakers and for some purposes, even while the State itself can use the information to counter the speech it seeks to suppress. Privacy is a concept too integral to the person and a right too essential to freedom to allow its manipulation to support just those ideas the government prefers.

When it enacted § 4631(d), the Vermont Legislature found that the "marketplace for ideas on medicine safety and effectiveness is frequently one-sided in that brand-name companies invest in expensive pharmaceutical marketing campaigns to doctors." 2007 Vt. Laws No. 80, § 1(4). "The goals of marketing programs," the legislature said, "are often in conflict with the goals of the state." § 1(3). The text of § 4631(d), associated legislative findings, and the record developed in the District Court establish that Vermont enacted its law for this end. The State has burdened a form of protected expression that it found too persuasive. At the same time, the State has left unburdened those speakers whose messages are in accord with its own views. This the State cannot do.

The judgment of the Court of Appeals is affirmed.

Chapter 6

FINANCIAL PRIVACY: INFORMATION AND VALUE

The financial industry, and the businesses which depend on it for investment, funding, and payments, face many of the same privacy issues regarding personally identifiable information and behavior monitoring as do other sectors. Finance, though, raises issues unique to itself which make privacy risk assessment and management more difficult, and which have prompted focused legislative and regulatory requirements with regard to user data. Among the added challenges and risks arising out of the financial industry are:

- The need to reliably identify an account holder, payor or payee in almost all circumstances;

- Balancing preferred confidentiality of financial holdings and dealings against a disclosure-based market; and

- Whether, and how, information regarding individuals' purchases should be kept confidential.

These three elements help inform and provide context for the applicable and evolving law regarding financial data privacy.

I. VERIFIABLE IDENTITY FOR FINANCIAL TRANSACTIONS

As with communications, commerce and finance began as local-only efforts. Neighbors would buy from and sell sustenance items to each other for barter or small, easily carried sums, and credit (to the extent it may have existed) was based on personal reputation. Larger equipment and dwellings were personally made or built, not purchased, as were luxury items like art and jewelry. Accordingly, buyers and sellers knew each other, and the major possible fraud was in the quality of the goods or the weighing of merchandise (or currency). Once merchants began venturing to a new town to sell to strangers, customers sought to purchase goods that cost more than they could carry in their money purses, and factors for a distant business traveled to other cities or even countries to acquire inventory, the identity of both merchants and customers became of much greater relevance to promote commerce — as well as avoid abuse. Once the prices for goods went beyond portable sums, and one party did not personally know the other, methods had to be developed to assure payment after purchase and to enable credit based on collateral rather than personal reputation. Sight drafts, personal and bank checks, coins, bank notes, and later innovations such as purchase orders, wire transfers, credit lines and other mechanisms for making large or delayed payments arose to address this new reality.

Accompanying the new power of these large and delayed payment mechanisms was an enhanced capacity for theft and fraud. In the era of small, personal local transactions, a thief could only steal as much property or money as he himself could carry, a similar limitation to that faced by the thief's victims, and the thief could only escape as far from his crimes as transportation allowed and his booty would have value. Perishable goods would spoil before they could be sold in a distant city, and local currency rarely had value elsewhere. (For that matter, the thief could himself be at risk of robbery if he chose to travel far with valuable items or precious metals.) As the new payment and credit instruments evolved, theft became more lucrative: a stolen purse or wallet could contain a bank note or check representing large sums of money, and could be spent or accepted for exchange far beyond the walls or borders of the town from which it was taken. Even when a payment method was authorized for use solely by a specific person, the recipient might not know the designated individual personally, and a thief could impersonate the actual owner (or forge a signature when required) to complete the transaction. Regional and national banks with shared accounts, and credit cards allowing purchases beyond a single local store, added to the potential for fraud and loss, as did the growth of mail-order, telephone, and ultimately Internet-based retailing. The scope of the potential loss to unpaid sellers, as well as the exposure of those whose names (and authority) may be falsely used, are significant.[1]

Because of the need for verifiable identity in order for large and distant financial transactions to work properly, an entire body of law (which is outside the scope of this book) has been created with regard to endorsements, signature obligations, criminalization of identity theft and counterfeiting, and so forth. What is relevant for the study of privacy, however, is that the requirement for verifiable identity means that those who provide financial services and those who benefit from them will more likely collect and retain detailed personally identifiable information than might other businesses for which verifiable identity is less necessary. This has led to a number of federal and local laws focused on protecting the privacy of financial service customers, including provisions of the Right to Financial Privacy Act,[2] the Fair Credit Reporting Act,[3] and the privacy provisions of the Gramm-Leach-Bliley Act,[4] along with the associated regulations. Each of these major laws focuses on different aspects of financial information, its collection, and its use, and is worth discussing in detail.

II.   THE RIGHT TO FINANCIAL PRIVACY ACT

The Right to Financial Privacy Act ("RFPA") addresses the question of whether, and how, *governmental* factors may gain access to individuals' financial information held by financial institutions.[5] The general rule is provided in § 3402:

---

[1] See discussion of data breach and liability in Chapter 8.

[2] 12 U.S.C. § 3401 et seq. (1978).

[3] 15 U.S.C. § 1681 et seq. (1970).

[4] 15 U.S.C. § 6801 et seq. (1999).

[5] The definitions of these various elements are crucial to understanding the RFPA's requirements and exceptions. As provided in relevant part in 12 U.S.C. § 3401:

For the purpose of this chapter, the term —

Except as provided by section 3403(c) or (d), 3413, or 3414 of this title, no Government authority may have access to or obtain copies of, or the information contained in the financial records of any customer from a financial institution unless the financial records are reasonably described and —

(1) such customer has authorized such disclosure in accordance with section 3404 of this title;

(2) such financial records are disclosed in response to an administrative subpoena [sic] or summons which meets the requirements of section 3405 of this title;

---

(1) "financial institution", except as provided in section 3414 of this title, means any office of a bank, savings bank, card issuer as defined in section 1602(n) of Title 15, industrial loan company, trust company, savings association, building and loan, or homestead association (including cooperative banks), credit union, or consumer finance institution, located in any State or territory of the United States, the District of Columbia, Puerto Rico, Guam, American Samoa, or the Virgin Islands;

(2) "financial record" means an original of, a copy of, or information known to have been derived from, any record held by a financial institution pertaining to a customer's relationship with the financial institution;

(3) "Government authority" means any agency or department of the United States, or any officer, employee, or agent thereof;

(4) "person" means an individual or a partnership of five or fewer individuals;

(5) "customer" means any person or authorized representative of that person who utilized or is utilizing any service of a financial institution, or for whom a financial institution is acting or has acted as a fiduciary, in relation to an account maintained in the person's name;

(6) "holding company" means —

(A) any bank holding company (as defined in section 1841 of this title);

(B) any company described in section 1843(f)(1) of this title; and

(C) any savings and loan holding company (as defined in the Home Owners' Loan Act [12 U.S.C.A. § 1461 et seq.]);

(7) "supervisory agency" means with respect to any particular financial institution, holding company, or any subsidiary of a financial institution or holding company, any of the following which has statutory authority to examine the financial condition, business operations, or records or transactions of that institution, holding company, or subsidiary —

(A) the Federal Deposit Insurance Corporation;

(B) Director, Office of Thrift Supervision;

(C) the National Credit Union Administration;

(D) the Board of Governors of the Federal Reserve System;

(E) the Comptroller of the Currency;

(F) the Securities and Exchange Commission;

(G) the Commodity Futures Trading Commission;

(H) the Secretary of the Treasury, with respect to the Bank Secrecy Act (Public Law 91-508, Title I [12 U.S.C.A. § 1951 et seq.]) and subchapter II of chapter 53 of Title 31; or

(I) any State banking or securities department or agency; and

(8) "law enforcement inquiry" means a lawful investigation or official proceeding inquiring into a violation of, or failure to comply with, any criminal or civil statute or any regulation, rule, or order issued pursuant thereto.

(3) such financial records are disclosed in response to a search warrant which meets the requirements of section 3406 of this title;

(4) such financial records are disclosed in response to a judicial subpena [sic] which meets the requirements of section 3407 of this title; or

(5) such financial records are disclosed in response to a formal written request which meets the requirements of section 3408 of this title.

As with many other "rights" enumerated or described by the law, the right to privacy against government access of financial records is quite expressly limited. Consent and standard legal process (warrants and subpoenas) will open up the records, but even absent those, a governmental agency may obtain them via a "formal written request" if it meets the requirements of § 3408:

A Government authority may request financial records under section 3402(5) of this title pursuant to a formal written request only if —

(1) no administrative summons or subpena authority reasonably appears to be available to that Government authority to obtain financial records for the purpose for which such records are sought;

(2) the request is authorized by regulations promulgated by the head of the agency or department;

(3) there is reason to believe that the records sought are relevant to a legitimate law enforcement inquiry; and

(4)(A) a copy of the request has been served upon the customer or mailed to his last known address on or before the date on which the request was made to the financial institution together with the following notice which shall state with reasonable specificity the nature of the law enforcement inquiry:

"Records or information concerning your transactions held by the financial institution named in the attached request are being sought by this (agency or department) in accordance with the Right to Financial Privacy Act of 1978 [12 U.S.C.A. § 3401 et seq.] for the following purpose:

"If you desire that such records or information not be made available, you must:

"1. Fill out the accompanying motion paper and sworn statement or write one of your own, stating that you are the customer whose records are being requested by the Government and either giving the reasons you believe that the records are not relevant to the legitimate law enforcement inquiry stated in this notice or any other legal basis for objecting to the release of the records.

"2. File the motion and statement by mailing or delivering them to the clerk of any one of the following United States District Courts:

"3. Serve the Government authority requesting the records by mailing or delivering a copy of your motion and statement to.

"4. Be prepared to come to court and present your position in further detail.

"5. You do not need to have a lawyer, although you may wish to employ one to represent you and protect your rights.

If you do not follow the above procedures, upon the expiration of ten days from the date of service or fourteen days from the date of mailing of this notice, the records or information requested therein may be made available. These records may be transferred to other Government authorities for legitimate law enforcement inquiries, in which event you will be notified after the transfer;" and

(B) ten days have expired from the date of service or fourteen days from the date of mailing of the notice by the customer and within such time period the customer has not filed a sworn statement and an application to enjoin the Government authority in an appropriate court, or the customer challenge provisions of section 3410 of this title have been complied with.[6]

The remainder of the RFPA includes appeal rights and procedures, restrictions on the right of government agencies receiving financial information to share it with *other* agencies,[7] and some specific exceptions to the general rules.[8] Remember as well that, whenever a governmental body (or a party acting on behalf of the government) undertakes an investigation or intends to disclose financial data, the warrant and other obligations under the U.S. Constitution (and possibly a state equivalent) remain in effect, as may additional criminal or civil legal requirements.[9]

III.   THE FAIR CREDIT REPORTING ACT

The Fair Credit Reporting Act[10] ("FCRA") can be understood at its core to be about privacy: how an individual's credit usage may be tracked, accessed, shared, and used by others. The FCRA's mission statement, however, primarily focuses on the integrity of the financial system rather than the potential risks to those whose information is being collected and used.

The Congress makes the following findings:

(1) The banking system is dependent upon fair and accurate credit reporting. Inaccurate credit reports directly impair the efficiency of the banking system, and unfair credit reporting methods undermine the public confidence which is essential to the continued functioning of the banking system.

---

[6]   12 U.S.C. § 3408 (1978).

[7]   12 U.S.C. § 3412 (2007).

[8]   12 U.S.C. § 3413 (1992).

[9]   See, for example, the general discussion on cybercrime and law enforcement in Chapter 10.

[10]   15 U.S.C. § 1681 et seq. (1970).

(2) An elaborate mechanism has been developed for investigating and evaluating the credit worthiness [sic], credit standing, credit capacity, character, and general reputation of consumers.

(3) Consumer reporting agencies have assumed a vital role in assembling and evaluating consumer credit and other information on consumers.

(4) There is a need to insure that consumer reporting agencies exercise their grave responsibilities with fairness, impartiality, and a respect for the consumer's right to privacy.

(b) Reasonable procedures

It is the purpose of this subchapter to require that consumer reporting agencies adopt reasonable procedures for meeting the needs of commerce for consumer credit, personnel, insurance, and other information in a manner which is fair and equitable to the consumer, with regard to the confidentiality, accuracy, relevancy, and proper utilization of such information in accordance with the requirements of this subchapter.[11]

Nevertheless, privacy issues pervade the FCRA, and not only those related specifically to credit. The definition of "Consumer Report," the central concept of the FCRA, makes this explicit by its broad understanding of the information that may influence credit or employment decisions, and in its inclusion of potential health information sharing as a concern:

(d) Consumer report.

(1) In general.

The term "consumer report" means any written, oral, or other communication of any information by a consumer reporting agency bearing on a consumer's credit worthiness [sic], credit standing, credit capacity, character, general reputation, personal characteristics, or mode of living which is used or expected to be used or collected in whole or in part for the purpose of serving as a factor in establishing the consumer's eligibility for —

(A) credit or insurance to be used primarily for personal, family, or household purposes;

(B) employment purposes; or

(C) any other purpose authorized under section 1681b of this title.

(2) Exclusions.

Except as provided in paragraph (3), the term "consumer report" does not include —

(A) subject to section 1681s-3 of this title, any —

---

[11] *Id.*

(i) report containing information solely as to transactions or experiences between the consumer and the person making the report;

(ii) communication of that information among persons related by common ownership or affiliated by corporate control; or

(iii) communication of other information among persons related by common ownership or affiliated by corporate control, if it is clearly and conspicuously disclosed to the consumer that the information may be communicated among such persons and the consumer is given the opportunity, before the time that the information is initially communicated, to direct that such information not be communicated among such persons;

(B) any authorization or approval of a specific extension of credit directly or indirectly by the issuer of a credit card or similar device;

(C) any report in which a person who has been requested by a third party to make a specific extension of credit directly or indirectly to a consumer conveys his or her decision with respect to such request, if the third party advises the consumer of the name and address of the person to whom the request was made, and such person makes the disclosures to the consumer required under section 1681m of this title; or

(D) a communication described in subsection (o) or (x) of this section.

(3) Restriction on sharing of medical information

Except for information or any communication of information disclosed as provided in section 1681b(g)(3) of this title, the exclusions in paragraph (2) shall not apply with respect to information disclosed to any person related by common ownership or affiliated by corporate control, if the information is —

(A) medical information;

(B) an individualized list or description based on the payment transactions of the consumer for medical products or services; or

(C) an aggregate list of identified consumers based on payment transactions for medical products or services.[12]

Additional definitions address privacy-related matters such as what may be considered "medical information"[13] and fraud arising out of identity theft.[14]

As for potential information sharing, the FCRA provides the exclusive conditions under which a consumer reporting agency is permitted to furnish a consumer report:

(a) In general

Subject to subsection (c) of this section, any consumer reporting agency may furnish a consumer report under the following circumstances and no

---

[12]   15 U.S.C. § 1681a (d) (2004).

[13]   § 1681a (i).

[14]   § 1681a (q).

other:

(1) In response to the order of a court having jurisdiction to issue such an order, or a subpoena issued in connection with proceedings before a Federal grand jury.

(2) In accordance with the written instructions of the consumer to whom it relates.

(3) To a person which it has reason to believe —

(A) intends to use the information in connection with a credit transaction involving the consumer on whom the information is to be furnished and involving the extension of credit to, or review or collection of an account of, the consumer; or

(B) intends to use the information for employment purposes; or

(C) intends to use the information in connection with the underwriting of insurance involving the consumer; or

(D) intends to use the information in connection with a determination of the consumer's eligibility for a license or other benefit granted by a governmental instrumentality required by law to consider an applicant's financial responsibility or status; or

(E) intends to use the information, as a potential investor or servicer, or current insurer, in connection with a valuation of, or an assessment of the credit or prepayment risks associated with, an existing credit obligation; or

(F) otherwise has a legitimate business need for the information —

(i) in connection with a business transaction that is initiated by the consumer; or

(ii) to review an account to determine whether the consumer continues to meet the terms of the account.

(G) executive departments and agencies in connection with the issuance of government-sponsored individually-billed travel charge cards.

(4) In response to a request by the head of a State or local child support enforcement agency (or a State or local government official authorized by the head of such an agency), if the person making the request certifies to the consumer reporting agency that —

(A) the consumer report is needed for the purpose of establishing an individual's capacity to make child support payments or determining the appropriate level of such payments;

(B) the paternity of the consumer for the child to which the obligation relates has been established or acknowledged by the consumer in accordance with State laws under which the obligation arises (if required by those laws);

(C) the person has provided at least 10 days' prior notice to the consumer whose report is requested, by certified or registered mail to the last known address of the consumer, that the report will be requested; and

(D) the consumer report will be kept confidential, will be used solely for a purpose described in subparagraph (A), and will not be used in connection with any other civil, administrative, or criminal proceeding, or for any other purpose.

(5) To an agency administering a State plan under section 654 of Title 42 for use to set an initial or modified child support award.

(6) To the Federal Deposit Insurance Corporation or the National Credit Union Administration as part of its preparation for its appointment or as part of its exercise of powers, as conservator, receiver, or liquidating agent for an insured depository institution or insured credit union under the Federal Deposit Insurance Act or the Federal Credit Union Act, or other applicable Federal or State law, or in connection with the resolution or liquidation of a failed or failing insured depository institution or insured credit union, as applicable.

(b) Conditions for furnishing and using consumer reports for employment purposes

(1) Certification from user

A consumer reporting agency may furnish a consumer report for employment purposes only if —

(A) the person who obtains such report from the agency certifies to the agency that —

(i) the person has complied with paragraph (2) with respect to the consumer report, and the person will comply with paragraph (3) with respect to the consumer report if paragraph (3) becomes applicable; and

(ii) information from the consumer report will not be used in violation of any applicable Federal or State equal employment opportunity law or regulation; and

(B) the consumer reporting agency provides with the report, or has previously provided, a summary of the consumer's rights under this sub-chapter, as prescribed by the Federal Trade Commission under section 1681g(c)(3) of this title.

(2) Disclosure to consumer

(A) In general

Except as provided in subparagraph (B), a person may not procure a consumer report, or cause a consumer report to be procured, for employment purposes with respect to any consumer, unless —

(i) *a clear and conspicuous disclosure has been made in writing to the consumer at any time before the report is procured or caused to be procured, in a document that consists solely of the disclosure, that a consumer report may be obtained for employment purposes; and*

(ii) *the consumer has authorized in writing (which authorization may be made on the document referred to in clause (i)) the procurement of the report by that person.*

(B) Application by mail, telephone, computer, or other similar means

If a consumer described in subparagraph (C) applies for employment by mail, telephone, computer, or other similar means, at any time before a consumer report is procured or caused to be procured in connection with that application —

(i) *the person who procures the consumer report on the consumer for employment purposes shall provide to the consumer, by oral, written, or electronic means, notice that a consumer report may be obtained for employment purposes, and a summary of the consumer's rights under section 1681m(a)(3) of this title; and*

(ii) *the consumer shall have consented, orally, in writing, or electronically to the procurement of the report by that person.*

(C) Scope

Subparagraph (B) shall apply to a person procuring a consumer report on a consumer in connection with the consumer's application for employment only if —

(i) *the consumer is applying for a position over which the Secretary of Transportation has the power to establish qualifications and maximum hours of service pursuant to the provisions of section 31502 of Title 49, or a position subject to safety regulation by a State transportation agency; and*

(ii) *as of the time at which the person procures the report or causes the report to be procured the only interaction between the consumer and the person in connection with that employment application has been by mail, telephone, computer, or other similar means.*

(3) Conditions on use for adverse actions

(A) In general

Except as provided in subparagraph (B), in using a consumer report for employment purposes, before taking any adverse action based in whole or in part on the report, the person intending to take such adverse action shall provide to the consumer to whom the report relates —

(i) *a copy of the report; and*

(ii) *a description in writing of the rights of the consumer under this subchapter, as prescribed by the Federal Trade Commission under section*

1681g(c)(3) of this title.

(B) Application by mail, telephone, computer, or other similar means

(i) If a consumer described in subparagraph (C) applies for employment by mail, telephone, computer, or other similar means, and if a person who has procured a consumer report on the consumer for employment purposes takes adverse action on the employment application based in whole or in part on the report, then the person must provide to the consumer to whom the report relates, in lieu of the notices required under subparagraph (A) of this section and under section 1681m(a) of this title, within 3 business days of taking such action, an oral, written or electronic notification —

(I) that adverse action has been taken based in whole or in part on a consumer report received from a consumer reporting agency;

(II) of the name, address and telephone number of the consumer reporting agency that furnished the consumer report (including a toll-free telephone number established by the agency if the agency compiles and maintains files on consumers on a nationwide basis);

(III) that the consumer reporting agency did not make the decision to take the adverse action and is unable to provide to the consumer the specific reasons why the adverse action was taken; and

(IV) that the consumer may, upon providing proper identification, request a free copy of a report and may dispute with the consumer reporting agency the accuracy or completeness of any information in a report.

(ii) If, under clause (B)(i)(IV), the consumer requests a copy of a consumer report from the person who procured the report, then, within 3 business days of receiving the consumer's request, together with proper identification, the person must send or provide to the consumer a copy of a report and a copy of the consumer's rights as prescribed by the Federal Trade Commission under section 1681g(c)(3) of this title.

(C) Scope

Subparagraph (B) shall apply to a person procuring a consumer report on a consumer in connection with the consumer's application for employment only if —

(i) the consumer is applying for a position over which the Secretary of Transportation has the power to establish qualifications and maximum hours of service pursuant to the provisions of section 31502 of Title 49, or a position subject to safety regulation by a State transportation agency; and

(ii) as of the time at which the person procures the report or causes the report to be procured the only interaction between the consumer and the person in connection with that employment application has been by mail, telephone, computer, or other similar means.

(4) Exception for national security investigations

(A) In general

In the case of an agency or department of the United States Government which seeks to obtain and use a consumer report for employment purposes, paragraph (3) shall not apply to any adverse action by such agency or department which is based in part on such consumer report, if the head of such agency or department makes a written finding that —

(i) the consumer report is relevant to a national security investigation of such agency or department;

(ii) the investigation is within the jurisdiction of such agency or department;

(iii) there is reason to believe that compliance with paragraph (3) will —

(I) endanger the life or physical safety of any person;

(II) result in flight from prosecution;

(III) result in the destruction of, or tampering with, evidence relevant to the investigation;

(IV) result in the intimidation of a potential witness relevant to the investigation;

(V) result in the compromise of classified information; or

(VI) otherwise seriously jeopardize or unduly delay the investigation or another official proceeding.

(B) Notification of consumer upon conclusion of investigation

Upon the conclusion of a national security investigation described in subparagraph (A), or upon the determination that the exception under subparagraph (A) is no longer required for the reasons set forth in such subparagraph, the official exercising the authority in such subparagraph shall provide to the consumer who is the subject of the consumer report with regard to which such finding was made —

(i) a copy of such consumer report with any classified information redacted as necessary;

(ii) notice of any adverse action which is based, in part, on the consumer report; and

(iii) the identification with reasonable specificity of the nature of the investigation for which the consumer report was sought.

(C) Delegation by head of agency or department

For purposes of subparagraphs (A) and (B), the head of any agency or department of the United States Government may delegate his or her authorities under this paragraph to an official of such agency or department who has personnel security responsibilities and is a member of the Senior Executive Service or equivalent civilian or military rank.

(D) Definitions

For purposes of this paragraph, the following definitions shall apply:

(i) Classified information. — The term "classified information" means information that is protected from unauthorized disclosure under Executive Order No. 12958 or successor orders.

(ii) National security investigation. — The term "national security investigation" means any official inquiry by an agency or department of the United States Government to determine the eligibility of a consumer to receive access or continued access to classified information or to determine whether classified information has been lost or compromised.

(c) Furnishing reports in connection with credit or insurance transactions that are not initiated by the consumer

(1) In general

A consumer reporting agency may furnish a consumer report relating to any consumer pursuant to subparagraph (A) or (C) of subsection (a)(3) of this section in connection with any credit or insurance transaction that is not initiated by the consumer only if —

(A) the consumer authorizes the agency to provide such report to such person; or

(B)(i) the transaction consists of a firm offer of credit or insurance;

(ii) the consumer reporting agency has complied with subsection (e) of this section;

(iii) there is not in effect an election by the consumer, made in accordance with subsection (e) of this section, to have the consumer's name and address excluded from lists of names provided by the agency pursuant to this paragraph; and

(iv) the consumer report does not contain a date of birth that shows that the consumer has not attained the age of 21, or, if the date of birth on the consumer report shows that the consumer has not attained the age of 21, such consumer consents to the consumer reporting agency to such furnishing.

(2) Limits on information received under paragraph (1)(B)

A person may receive pursuant to paragraph (1)(B) only —

(A) the name and address of a consumer;

(B) an identifier that is not unique to the consumer and that is used by the person solely for the purpose of verifying the identity of the consumer; and

(C) other information pertaining to a consumer that does not identify the relationship or experience of the consumer with respect to a particular creditor or other entity.

(3) Information regarding inquiries

Except as provided in section 1681g(a)(5) of this title, a consumer reporting agency shall not furnish to any person a record of inquiries in connection with a credit or insurance transaction that is not initiated by a consumer.

(d) Reserved

(e) Election of consumer to be excluded from lists

(1) In general

A consumer may elect to have the consumer's name and address excluded from any list provided by a consumer reporting agency under subsection (c)(1)(B) of this section in connection with a credit or insurance transaction that is not initiated by the consumer, by notifying the agency in accordance with paragraph (2) that the consumer does not consent to any use of a consumer report relating to the consumer in connection with any credit or insurance transaction that is not initiated by the consumer.

(2) Manner of notification

A consumer shall notify a consumer reporting agency under paragraph (1) —

(A) *through the notification system maintained by the agency under paragraph (5); or*

(B) *by submitting to the agency a signed notice of election form issued by the agency for purposes of this subparagraph.*

(3) Response of agency after notification through system

Upon receipt of notification of the election of a consumer under paragraph (1) through the notification system maintained by the agency under paragraph (5), a consumer reporting agency shall —

(A) *inform the consumer that the election is effective only for the 5-year period following the election if the consumer does not submit to the agency a signed notice of election form issued by the agency for purposes of paragraph (2)(B); and*

(B) *provide to the consumer a notice of election form, if requested by the consumer, not later than 5 business days after receipt of the notification of the election through the system established under paragraph (5), in the case of a request made at the time the consumer provides notification through the system.*

(4) Effectiveness of election

An election of a consumer under paragraph (1) —

(A) *shall be effective with respect to a consumer reporting agency beginning 5 business days after the date on which the consumer notifies the agency in accordance with paragraph (2);*

(B) shall be effective with respect to a consumer reporting agency —

(i) subject to subparagraph (C), during the 5-year period beginning 5 business days after the date on which the consumer notifies the agency of the election, in the case of an election for which a consumer notifies the agency only in accordance with paragraph (2)(A); or

(ii) until the consumer notifies the agency under subparagraph (C), in the case of an election for which a consumer notifies the agency in accordance with paragraph (2)(B);

(C) shall not be effective after the date on which the consumer notifies the agency, through the notification system established by the agency under paragraph (5), that the election is no longer effective; and

(D) shall be effective with respect to each affiliate of the agency.

(5) Notification system

(A) In general

Each consumer reporting agency that, under subsection (c)(1)(B) of this section, furnishes a consumer report in connection with a credit or insurance transaction that is not initiated by a consumer, shall —

(i) establish and maintain a notification system, including a toll-free telephone number, which permits any consumer whose consumer report is maintained by the agency to notify the agency, with appropriate identification, of the consumer's election to have the consumer's name and address excluded from any such list of names and addresses provided by the agency for such a transaction; and

(ii) publish by not later than 365 days after September 30, 1996, and not less than annually thereafter, in a publication of general circulation in the area served by the agency —

(I) a notification that information in consumer files maintained by the agency may be used in connection with such transactions; and

(II) the address and toll-free telephone number for consumers to use to notify the agency of the consumer's election under clause (i).

(B) Establishment and maintenance as compliance

Establishment and maintenance of a notification system (including a toll-free telephone number) and publication by a consumer reporting agency on the agency's own behalf and on behalf of any of its affiliates in accordance with this paragraph is deemed to be compliance with this paragraph by each of those affiliates.

(6) Notification system by agencies that operate nationwide

Each consumer reporting agency that compiles and maintains files on consumers on a nationwide basis shall establish and maintain a notification *system for purposes of paragraph (5) jointly with other such consumer reporting agencies.*

(f) Certain use or obtaining of information prohibited

A person shall not use or obtain a consumer report for any purpose unless —

***(1)** the consumer report is obtained for a purpose for which the consumer report is authorized to be furnished under this section; and*

***(2)** the purpose is certified in accordance with section 1681e of this title by a prospective user of the report through a general or specific certification.*

(g) Protection of medical information

(1) Limitation on consumer reporting agencies

A consumer reporting agency shall not furnish for employment purposes, or in connection with a credit or insurance transaction, a consumer report that contains medical information (other than medical contact information treated in the manner required under section 605(a)(6) of this title) about a consumer, unless —

***(A)** if furnished in connection with an insurance transaction, the consumer affirmatively consents to the furnishing of the report;*

***(B)** if furnished for employment purposes or in connection with a credit transaction —*

***(i)** the information to be furnished is relevant to process or effect the employment or credit transaction; and*

***(ii)** the consumer provides specific written consent for the furnishing of the report that describes in clear and conspicuous language the use for which the information will be furnished; or*

***(C)** the information to be furnished pertains solely to transactions, accounts, or balances relating to debts arising from the receipt of medical services, products, or devises, where such information, other than account status or amounts, is restricted or reported using codes that do not identify, or do not provide information sufficient to infer, the specific provider or the nature of such services, products, or devices, as provided in section 1681c(a)(6) of this title.*

(2) Limitation on creditors

Except as permitted pursuant to paragraph (3)(C) or regulations prescribed under paragraph (5)(A), a creditor shall not obtain or use medical information (other than medical information treated in the manner required under section 605(a)(6) of this title) pertaining to a consumer in connection with any determination of the consumer's eligibility, or continued eligibility, for credit.

(3) Actions authorized by Federal law, insurance activities and regulatory determinations

Section 1681a(d)(3) of this title shall not be construed so as to treat information or any communication of information as a consumer report if the information or communication is disclosed —

(A) in connection with the business of insurance or annuities, including the activities described in section 18B of the model Privacy of Consumer Financial and Health Information Regulation issued by the National Association of Insurance Commissioners (as in effect on January 1, 2003);

(B) for any purpose permitted without authorization under the Standards for Individually Identifiable Health Information promulgated by the Department of Health and Human Services pursuant to the Health Insurance Portability and Accountability Act of 1996, or referred to under section 1179 of such Act, or described in section 6802(e) of this title; or

(C) as otherwise determined to be necessary and appropriate, by regulation or order and subject to paragraph (6), by the Commission, any Federal banking agency or the National Credit Union Administration (with respect to any financial institution subject to the jurisdiction of such agency or Administration under paragraph (1), (2), or (3) of section 1681s(b) of this title, [FN1] or the applicable State insurance authority (with respect to any person engaged in providing insurance or annuities).

(4) Limitation on redisclosure of medical information

Any person that receives medical information pursuant to paragraph (1) or (3) shall not disclose such information to any other person, except as necessary to carry out the purpose for which the information was initially disclosed, or as otherwise permitted by statute, regulation, or order.

(5) Regulations and effective date for paragraph (2)

(A) Regulations required

Each Federal banking agency and the National Credit Union Administration shall, subject to paragraph (6) and after notice and opportunity for comment, prescribe regulations that permit transactions under paragraph (2) that are determined to be necessary and appropriate to protect legitimate operational, transactional, risk, consumer, and other needs (and which shall include permitting actions necessary for administrative verification purposes), consistent with the intent of paragraph (2) to restrict the use of medical information for inappropriate purposes.

(B) Final regulations required

The Federal banking agencies and the National Credit Union Administration shall issue the regulations required under subparagraph (A) in final form before the end of the 6-month period beginning on the December 4, 2003.

(6) Coordination with other laws

No provision of this subsection shall be construed as altering, affecting, or superseding the applicability of any other provision of Federal law relating to medical confidentiality.[15]

Subsequent sections address matters including disclosure to government agencies,[16] the consumers to whom the reports pertain,[17] penalties, dispute resolution and jurisdiction,[18] and the priority of enforcement and between FCRA and any relevant state laws,[19] among others.

Note that the FCRA establishes standards and obligations for those who *provide* information for credit reports, not just those who make available or use the reports:

§ 1681s-2. Responsibilities of furnishers of information to consumer reporting agencies

(a) Duty of furnishers of information to provide accurate information

(1) Prohibition

(A) Reporting information with actual knowledge of errors

A person shall not furnish any information relating to a consumer to any consumer reporting agency if the person knows or has reasonable cause to believe that the information is inaccurate.

(B) Reporting information after notice and confirmation of errors

A person shall not furnish information relating to a consumer to any consumer reporting agency if —

(i) the person has been notified by the consumer, at the address specified by the person for such notices, that specific information is inaccurate; and

(ii) the information is, in fact, inaccurate.

(C) No address requirement

A person who clearly and conspicuously specifies to the consumer an address for notices referred to in subparagraph (B) shall not be subject to subparagraph (A); however, nothing in subparagraph (B) shall require a person to specify such an address.

(D) Definition

For purposes of subparagraph (A), the term "reasonable cause to believe that the information is inaccurate" means having specific knowledge, other than solely allegations by the consumer, that would cause a reasonable person to have substantial doubts about the accuracy of the information.

---

[15]   15 U.S.C. § 1681(b) (1970).

[16]   *See, e.g.*, 15 U.S.C. § 1681f (1970), § 1681u-v (2006), § 1681w-x (2003).

[17]   *See, e.g.*, 15 U.S.C. § 1681g (2004), § 1681h (1997).

[18]   *See, e.g.*, 15 U.S.C. § 1681n (2008), § 1681o-p (2004), § 1681q-r (1997), § 1681s (2005).

[19]   15 U.S.C. § 1681t (2003).

(2) Duty to correct and update information

A person who —

(A) regularly and in the ordinary course of business furnishes information to one or more consumer reporting agencies about the person's transactions or experiences with any consumer; and

(B) has furnished to a consumer reporting agency information that the person determines is not complete or accurate,

shall promptly notify the consumer reporting agency of that determination and provide to the agency any corrections to that information, or any additional information, that is necessary to make the information provided by the person to the agency complete and accurate, and shall not thereafter furnish to the agency any of the information that remains not complete or accurate.

(3) Duty to provide notice of dispute

If the completeness or accuracy of any information furnished by any person to any consumer reporting agency is disputed to such person by a consumer, the person may not furnish the information to any consumer reporting agency without notice that such information is disputed by the consumer.

(4) Duty to provide notice of closed accounts

A person who regularly and in the ordinary course of business furnishes information to a consumer reporting agency regarding a consumer who has a credit account with that person shall notify the agency of the voluntary closure of the account by the consumer, in information regularly furnished for the period in which the account is closed.

(5) Duty to provide notice of delinquency of accounts

(A) In general

A person who furnishes information to a consumer reporting agency regarding a delinquent account being placed for collection, charged to profit or loss, or subjected to any similar action shall, not later than 90 days after furnishing the information, notify the agency of the date of delinquency on the account, which shall be the month and year of the commencement of the delinquency on the account that immediately preceded the action.

(B) Rule of construction

For purposes of this paragraph only, and provided that the consumer does not dispute the information, a person that furnishes information on a delinquent account that is placed for collection, charged for profit or loss, or subjected to any similar action, complies with this paragraph, if —

(i) the person reports the same date of delinquency as that provided by the creditor to which the account was owed at the time at which the commence-

ment of the delinquency occurred, if the creditor previously reported that date of delinquency to a consumer reporting agency;

(ii) the creditor did not previously report the date of delinquency to a consumer reporting agency, and the person establishes and follows reasonable procedures to obtain the date of delinquency from the creditor or another reliable source and reports that date to a consumer reporting agency as the date of delinquency; or

(iii) the creditor did not previously report the date of delinquency to a consumer reporting agency and the date of delinquency cannot be reasonably obtained as provided in clause (ii), the person establishes and follows reasonable procedures to ensure the date reported as the date of delinquency precedes the date on which the account is placed for collection, charged to profit or loss, or subjected to any similar action, and reports such date to the credit reporting agency.

(6) Duties of furnishers upon notice of identity theft-related information

(A) Reasonable procedures

A person that furnishes information to any consumer reporting agency shall have in place reasonable procedures to respond to any notification that it receives from a consumer reporting agency under section 1681c-2 of this title relating to information resulting from identity theft, to prevent that person from refurnishing such blocked information.

(B) Information alleged to result from identity theft

If a consumer submits an identity theft report to a person who furnishes information to a consumer reporting agency at the address specified by that person for receiving such reports stating that information maintained by such person that purports to relate to the consumer resulted from identity theft, the person may not furnish such information that purports to relate to the consumer to any consumer reporting agency, unless the person subsequently knows or is informed by the consumer that the information is correct.

(7) Negative information

(A) Notice to consumer required

(i) In general

If any financial institution that extends credit and regularly and in the ordinary course of business furnishes information to a consumer reporting agency described in section 1681a(p) of this title furnishes negative information to such an agency regarding credit extended to a customer, the financial institution shall provide a notice of such furnishing of negative information, in writing, to the customer.

(ii) Notice effective for subsequent submissions

After providing such notice, the financial institution may submit additional negative information to a consumer reporting agency described in *section 1681a(p) of this title with respect to the same transaction, extension of credit, account, or customer without providing additional notice to the customer.*

(B) Time of notice

(i) In general

The notice required under subparagraph (A) shall be provided to the customer prior to, or no later than 30 days after, furnishing the negative information to a consumer reporting agency described in section 1681a(p) of this title.

(ii) Coordination with new account disclosures

If the notice is provided to the customer prior to furnishing the negative information to a consumer reporting agency, the notice may not be included in the initial disclosures provided under section 1637(a) of this title.

(C) Coordination with other disclosures

The notice required under subparagraph (A) —

(i) may be included on or with any notice of default, any billing statement, or any other materials provided to the customer; and

(ii) must be clear and conspicuous.

(D) Model disclosure

(i) Duty of board to prepare

The Board shall prescribe a brief model disclosure a financial institution may use to comply with subparagraph (A), which shall not exceed 30 words.

(ii) Use of model not required

No provision of this paragraph shall be construed as requiring a financial institution to use any such model form prescribed by the Board.

(iii) Compliance using model

A financial institution shall be deemed to be in compliance with subparagraph (A) if the financial institution uses any such model form prescribed by the Board, or the financial institution uses any such model form and rearranges its format.

(E) Use of notice without submitting negative information

No provision of this paragraph shall be construed as requiring a financial institution that has provided a customer with a notice described in subparagraph (A) to furnish negative information about the customer to a consumer reporting agency.

(F) Safe harbor

A financial institution shall not be liable for failure to perform the duties required by this paragraph if, at the time of the failure, the financial institution maintained reasonable policies and procedures to comply with this paragraph or the financial institution reasonably believed that the institution is prohibited, by law, from contacting the consumer.

(G) Definitions

For purposes of this paragraph, the following definitions shall apply:

(i) Negative information

The term "negative information" means information concerning a customer's delinquencies, late payments, insolvency, or any form of default.

(ii) Customer; financial institution

The terms "customer" and "financial institution" have the same meanings as in section 6809 of this title.

(8) Ability of consumer to dispute information directly with furnisher

(A) In general

The Federal banking agencies, the National Credit Union Administration, and the Commission shall jointly prescribe regulations that shall identify the circumstances under which a furnisher shall be required to reinvestigate a dispute concerning the accuracy of information contained in a consumer report on the consumer, based on a direct request of a consumer.

(B) Considerations

In prescribing regulations under subparagraph (A), the agencies shall weigh —

(i) the benefits to consumers with the costs on furnishers and the credit reporting system;

(ii) the impact on the overall accuracy and integrity of consumer reports of any such requirements;

(iii) whether direct contact by the consumer with the furnisher would likely result in the most expeditious resolution of any such dispute; and

(iv) the potential impact on the credit reporting process if credit repair organizations, as defined in section 1679a(3) of this title, including entities that would be a credit repair organization, but for section 1679a(3)(B)(i) of this title, are able to circumvent the prohibition in subparagraph (G).

(C) Applicability

Subparagraphs (D) through (G) shall apply in any circumstance identified under the regulations promulgated under subparagraph (A).

(D) Submitting a notice of dispute

A consumer who seeks to dispute the accuracy of information shall provide a dispute notice directly to such person at the address specified by the person for such notices that —

(i) identifies the specific information that is being disputed;

(ii) explains the basis for the dispute; and

(iii) includes all supporting documentation required by the furnisher to substantiate the basis of the dispute.

(E) Duty of person after receiving notice of dispute

After receiving a notice of dispute from a consumer pursuant to subparagraph (D), the person that provided the information in dispute to a consumer reporting agency shall —

(i) conduct an investigation with respect to the disputed information;

(ii) review all relevant information provided by the consumer with the notice;

(iii) complete such person's investigation of the dispute and report the results of the investigation to the consumer before the expiration of the period under section 1681i(a)(1) of this title within which a consumer reporting agency would be required to complete its action if the consumer had elected to dispute the information under that section; and

(iv) if the investigation finds that the information reported was inaccurate, promptly notify each consumer reporting agency to which the person furnished the inaccurate information of that determination and provide to the agency any correction to that information that is necessary to make the information provided by the person accurate.

(F) Frivolous or irrelevant dispute

(i) In general

This paragraph shall not apply if the person receiving a notice of a dispute from a consumer reasonably determines that the dispute is frivolous or irrelevant, including —

(I) by reason of the failure of a consumer to provide sufficient information to investigate the disputed information; or

(II) the submission by a consumer of a dispute that is substantially the same as a dispute previously submitted by or for the consumer, either directly to the person or through a consumer reporting agency under subsection (b) of this section, with respect to which the person has already performed the person's duties under this paragraph or subsection (b), as applicable.

(ii) Notice of determination

Upon making any determination under clause (i) that a dispute is frivolous or irrelevant, the person shall notify the consumer of such determi-

nation not later than 5 business days after making such determination, by mail or, if authorized by the consumer for that purpose, by any other means available to the person.

(iii) Contents of notice

A notice under clause (ii) shall include —

(I) the reasons for the determination under clause (i); and

(II) identification of any information required to investigate the disputed information, which may consist of a standardized form describing the general nature of such information.

(G) Exclusion of credit repair organizations

This paragraph shall not apply if the notice of the dispute is submitted by, is prepared on behalf of the consumer by, or is submitted on a form supplied to the consumer by, a credit repair organization, as defined in section 1679a(3) of this title, or an entity that would be a credit repair organization, but for section 1679a(3)(B)(i) of this title.

(9) Duty to provide notice of status as medical information furnisher

A person whose primary business is providing medical services, products, or devices, or the person's agent or assignee, who furnishes information to a consumer reporting agency on a consumer shall be considered a medical information furnisher for purposes of this subchapter, and shall notify the agency of such status.

(b) Duties of furnishers of information upon notice of dispute

(1) In general

After receiving notice pursuant to section 1681i(a)(2) of this title of a dispute with regard to the completeness or accuracy of any information provided by a person to a consumer reporting agency, the person shall —

(A) conduct an investigation with respect to the disputed information;

(B) review all relevant information provided by the consumer reporting agency pursuant to section 1681i(a)(2) of this title;

(C) report the results of the investigation to the consumer reporting agency;

(D) if the investigation finds that the information is incomplete or inaccurate, report those results to all other consumer reporting agencies to which the person furnished the information and that compile and maintain files on consumers on a nationwide basis; and

(E) if an item of information disputed by a consumer is found to be inaccurate or incomplete or cannot be verified after any reinvestigation under paragraph (1), for purposes of reporting to a consumer reporting agency only, as appropriate, based on the results of the reinvestigation promptly —

(i) modify that item of information;

(ii) delete that item of information; or

(iii) permanently block the reporting of that item of information.

(2) Deadline

A person shall complete all investigations, reviews, and reports required under paragraph (1) regarding information provided by the person to a consumer reporting agency, before the expiration of the period under section 1681i(a)(1) of this title within which the consumer reporting agency is required to complete actions required by that section regarding that information.

(c) Limitation on liability

Except as provided in section 1681s(c)(1)(B) of this title, sections 1681n and 1681o of this title do not apply to any violation of —

(1) subsection (a) of this section, including any regulations issued thereunder;

(2) subsection (e) of this section, except that nothing in this paragraph shall limit, expand, or otherwise affect liability under section 1681n or 1681o of this title, as applicable, for violations of subsection (b) of this section; or

(3) subsection (e) of section 1681m of this title.

(d) Limitation on enforcement

The provisions of law described in paragraphs (1) through (3) of subsection (c) of this section (other than with respect to the exception described in paragraph (2) of subsection (c) of this section) shall be enforced exclusively as provided under section 1681s of this title by the Federal agencies and officials and the State officials identified in section 1681s of this title.

(e) Accuracy guidelines and regulations required

(1) Guidelines

The Federal banking agencies, the National Credit Union Administration, and the Commission shall, with respect to the entities that are subject to their respective enforcement authority under section 1681m of this title, and in coordination as described in paragraph (2) —

(A) establish and maintain guidelines for use by each person that furnishes information to a consumer reporting agency regarding the accuracy and integrity of the information relating to consumers that such entities furnish to consumer reporting agencies, and update such guidelines as often as necessary; and

(B) prescribe regulations requiring each person that furnishes information to a consumer reporting agency to establish reasonable policies and procedures for implementing the guidelines established pursuant to subparagraph

(A).

(2) Coordination

Each agency required to prescribe regulations under paragraph (1) shall consult and coordinate with each other such agency so that, to the extent possible, the regulations prescribed by each such entity are consistent and comparable with the regulations prescribed by each other such agency.

(3) Criteria

In developing the guidelines required by paragraph (1)(A), the agencies described in paragraph (1) shall —

(A) identify patterns, practices, and specific forms of activity that can compromise the accuracy and integrity of information furnished to consumer reporting agencies;

(B) review the methods (including technological means) used to furnish information relating to consumers to consumer reporting agencies;

(C) determine whether persons that furnish information to consumer reporting agencies maintain and enforce policies to assure the accuracy and integrity of information furnished to consumer reporting agencies; and

(D) examine the policies and processes that persons that furnish information to consumer reporting agencies employ to conduct reinvestigations and correct inaccurate information relating to consumers that has been furnished to consumer reporting agencies.[20]

Note also how, although arranged differently, the information-related provisions of the FCRA address the key Fair Information Practice Principles as described by the FTC among others: notice/awareness; choice/consent; access/participation; integrity/security; and enforcement/redress.[21]

Given that the FCRA applies to any organization creating, adding information to or accessing information from a consumer's credit report, employers, retailers, lenders and government officials, along with the consumers themselves, must be aware of the privacy requirements of the FCRA and how they have been applied. One challenge is that many of those who access credit information are either unaware of the FCRA at all (for example, employers who request credit reports in hiring) or may not be fully informed as to its data use and protection provisions. For its part, the FTC has actively enforced the FCRA:

---

[20] 15 U.S.C. § 1681s-2 (2004).

[21] FAIR INFORMATION PRACTICE PRINCIPLES, http://www.ftc.gov/reports/privacy3/fairinfo.shtm (last visited Jul 27, 2012).

From "40 Years of Experience with the Fair Credit Reporting Act: An FTC Staff Report with Summary of Interpretations"

When it was originally enacted, the FCRA imposed requirements exclusively on CRAs [Consumer Reporting Agencies] such as credit bureaus, except for those sections of the Act requiring users of consumer reports and other third parties to provide certain notices to consumers. The FCRA established the Commission as the primary federal enforcement agency, with jurisdiction over CRAs and all consumer report users (e.g., retailers, finance companies, employers, insurers, and landlords), except for certain entities over which the Commission does not have jurisdiction. Under the FCRA, CRAs are required to establish procedures to ensure that they report consumer information only to those with a legitimate purpose for it and to achieve maximum possible accuracy in the information they report. The FCRA further sought to improve the accuracy of data in CRA files by requiring CRAs to disclose information in their files to consumers and investigate items disputed in good faith by them.

*The Consumer Credit Reporting Reform Act of 1996 made extensive revisions to the FCRA (the "1996 Amendments") in a number of areas. First, it expanded the duties of CRAs, particularly in regard to CRA responses to consumers' disputes — establishing a 30-day time frame for completion of an investigation, mandating written notice to the consumer of the results of the investigation within five days of its completion, and adding restrictions on the reinsertion of items that were deleted following a dispute. The 1996 Amendments also increased the obligations of users of consumer reports, particularly employers. Most significantly, the 1996 Amendments imposed duties on a class of entities not previously treated by the FCRA — **furnishers** of information to CRAs — by including requirements related to accuracy and the handling of disputes by the entities that provided information to CRAs.*

The ensuing seven years brought a number of more modest revisions, the most significant of which was a 1999 amendment that specifically authorized the Board of Governors of the Federal Reserve System, Federal Deposit Insurance Corporation, Office of the Comptroller of the Currency, Office of Thrift Supervision, and National Credit Union Administration (collectively the "federal financial agencies" or "Agencies") to promulgate regulations under the FCRA for the banks and other entities subject to their jurisdiction.

The FACT Act [Fair and Accurate Credit Transactions Act of 2003] was Congress' second major expansion of the FCRA. It added several sections to assist consumers and businesses in combating identity theft and reducing the damage to consumers when that crime occurred. The FACT Act established a national fraud alert system, required merchants to truncate account numbers on electronic credit/debit card receipts, and ordered agencies to promulgate rules on proper disposition of consumer report information and on what companies should do to respond to the "red flag" indicators of identity theft. In addition, it granted consumers the right to request free annual reports from national CRAs, required "blocking" of information placed on a consumer report as a result of identity theft, and required businesses to provide copies of relevant business records to identity theft victims. The Commission, often in conjunction with the federal financial agencies, issued numerous rules to implement the various FACT Act provisions . . . .

During its 40-year history of enforcing the FCRA, the FTC has brought 87 enforcement actions against CRAs, users of consumer reports, and furnishers of information to CRAs. As noted above, the FCRA originally was focused on CRAs and those entities that used consumer reports. As a result, the Commission has extensive enforcement experience against CRAs and users of consumer reports. For example, the Commission has brought a number of cases against CRAs to ensure that consumer reports are only supplied to those with a permissible purpose. The Commission also has enforced these requirements against resellers of consumer reports. In addition, the FTC has brought several enforcement actions against users that failed to provide adverse action notices when required, including creditors and employers.

Following the adoption of the 1996 Amendments, the FTC brought actions against businesses that furnish information to CRAs, primarily debt collectors and mortgage servicers. In many cases, the FTC has enforced important FCRA requirements together with related requirements under the Fair Debt Collection Practices Act ("FDCPA"), the Equal Credit Opportunity Act ("ECOA"), and Section 5 of the FTC Act.[22]

IV. THE GRAMM-LEACH BLILEY ACT

In November 1999, Congress enacted the Gramm-Leach-Bliley Act (the "GLB Act"),[23] a comprehensive set of changes to the laws covering how financial institutions may and may not operate. Title V of the GLB Act[24] established new requirements for the protection of personal information obtained by "financial institutions," defined[25] as institutions engaging in "financial activities." For its part, "financial activities" is further defined elsewhere[26] as activity determined by the Board of Governors of the Federal Reserve System "(A) to be financial in nature or incidental to such financial activity; or (B) [that] is complementary to a financial activity and does not pose a substantial risk to the safety or soundness of depository institutions or the financial system generally." This definition is *extremely* broad and can incorporate many types of business practices not generally considered performed by "financial institutions":

---

[22] FTC, *40 Years of Experience with the Fair Credit Reporting Act: An FTC Staff Report with Summary of Interpretations. July 2011, pp. 2–5 (notes omitted).*

[23] Gramm-Leach-Bliley Financial Modernization Act, Pub. L. No. 106-102, 113 Stat. 1338 (1999).

[24] 15 U.S.C. § 6801 et seq. (1999).

[25] 15 U.S.C. § 6809(3) (1999).

[26] 12 U.S.C. § 1843(k) (2011).

From: The Gramm-Leach-Bliley Act: Privacy of Consumer Financial Information[27]

Financial Institution

Definition: *Any institution the business of which is engaging in* financial activities *as described in* section 4(k) of the Bank Holding Company Act *(12 U.S.C. § 1843(k)). Under the Final Rule promulgated by the Federal Trade Commission (FTC), an institution must be* significantly engaged *in financial activities to be considered a "financial institution."*

A. Financial Activities:

Lending, exchanging, transferring, investing for others, or safeguarding money or securities; insuring, guaranteeing, or indemnifying against loss, harm, damage, illness, disability, or death; providing financial investment or economic advisory services; underwriting or dealing with securities. [§ 4(k)(4)(A-E)]

Engaging in an activity that the Federal Reserve Board has determined to be closely related to banking. [§ 4(k)(4)(F); 12 C.F.R. § 225.28]. For example:

Extending credit and servicing loans

Collection agency services

Real estate and personal property appraising

Check guaranty services

Credit bureau services

Real estate settlement services

Leasing real or personal property (on a nonoperating basis for an initial lease term of at least 90 days)

Engaging in an activity that a bank holding company may engage in outside of the United States. [§ 4(k)(4)(G); 12 C.F.R. § 211.5(d)]. For example:

Operating a travel agency in connection with financial services

Only those activities determined to be financial activities under § 4(k)(1–3) as of November 12, 1999, are covered by the FTC Privacy Rule. While the Federal Reserve Board and the Department of Treasury have authority to add activities that are "incidental" or "complementary" to financial activities, the FTC will review those determinations before proposing to extend coverage of its Rule to such new activities.

B. Examples of businesses that engage in "financial activities" and are "financial institutions" for purposes of the GLB Act(1):

Mortgage lender or broker

Check casher

---

[27] THE GRAMM-LEACH-BLILEY ACT: PRIVACY OF CONSUMER FINANCIAL INFORMATION, *http://ftc.gov/privacy/ glbact/glboutline.htm (last visited May 8, 2012).*

Pay-day lender

Credit counseling service and other financial advisors

Medical-services provider that establishes for a significant number of its patients long-term payment plans that involve interest charges

Financial or investment advisory services including tax planning, tax preparation, and instruction on individual financial management

Retailer that issues its own credit card

Auto dealers that lease and/or finance

Collection agency services

Relocation service that assists individuals with financing for moving expenses and/or mortgages

Sale of money orders, savings bonds, or traveler's checks

Government entities that provide financial products such as student loans or mortgages

C. "Significantly Engaged" in Financial Activities:

Whether a financial institution is "significantly engaged" in financial activities is a flexible standard that takes into account all the facts and circumstances.

Examples of businesses that are not "significantly engaged" for purposes of the GLB Act:

Retailer that does not issue its own credit card (even if it accepts other credit cards)

Grocery store that allows consumers to get cash back by writing a check in an amount higher than the actual purchase price

Merchant who allows an individual to "run a tab"

Retailer that provides occasional "lay-away" and deferred payment plans or accepting payment by means of credit cards issued by others as its only means of extending credit

The GLB Act restricts the ways in which financial institutions may disclose consumers' "nonpublic personal information":

> *(A) The term "nonpublic personal information" means personally identifiable financial information —*
>
> *(i) provided by a consumer to a financial institution;*
>
> *(ii) resulting from any transaction with the consumer or any service performed for the consumer; or*
>
> *(iii) otherwise obtained by the financial institution.*
>
> *(B) Such term does not include publicly available information, as such term is defined by the regulations prescribed under section 6804 of this title.*

(C) Notwithstanding subparagraph (B), such term —

(i) shall include any list, description, or other grouping of consumers (and publicly available information pertaining to them) that is derived using any nonpublic personal information other than publicly available information; but

(ii) shall not include any list, description, or other grouping of consumers (and publicly available information pertaining to them) that is derived without using any nonpublic personal information.[28]

Unlike other federal privacy laws such as COPPA,[29] however, a financial institution need not obtain affirmative consent (i.e., "opt-in") from a consumer prior to making legally permissible disclosures to third parties. Instead, the GLB Act requires institutions to provide "clear and conspicuous" notice of their data practices "[a]t the time of establishing a customer relationship with a consumer and not less than annually during the continuation of such relationship" and, provided they do, allows them to disclose unless consumers request otherwise (i.e. "opt-out").[30] The statute sets out the required contents of this regular notice:

The disclosure required by subsection (a) of this section shall include —

(1) the policies and practices of the institution with respect to disclosing nonpublic personal information to nonaffiliated third parties, other than agents of the institution, consistent with section 6802 of this title, and including —

(A) the categories of persons to whom the information is or may be disclosed, other than the persons to whom the information may be provided pursuant to section 6802(e) of this title; and

(B) the policies and practices of the institution with respect to disclosing of nonpublic personal information of persons who have ceased to be customers of the financial institution;

(2) the categories of nonpublic personal information that are collected by the financial institution;

(3) the policies that the institution maintains to protect the confidentiality and security of nonpublic personal information in accordance with section 6801 of this title; and

(4) the disclosures required, if any, under section 1681a(d)(2)(A)(iii) of this title.[31]

There are a few other important things to note about the GLB Act's disclosure requirements. First, while the Act does permit certain sharing of some non-public

---

[28]   15 U.S.C. § 6809(4) (1999).

[29]   See discussion of COPPA in Chapter 4.

[30]   15 U.S.C. § 6803 (2006).

[31]   *Id.*

information about consumers, account numbers or other access methods to consumers' accounts may not be shared.[32] Next, the statute does permit disclosure to enable consumer-requested transactions, for the protection of the financial institution, as required by other laws and in connection with the sale or merger of the institution, among other exceptions.[33] Finally, the GLB Act restricts further transfers by non-affiliated companies receiving non-public information as permitted.[34] The GLB Act additionally requires its enforcement agencies to enact regulations mandating standards for "administrative, technical and physical safeguards" for customer records and information.[35]

As with other such statutes, companies must comply not only with the formal provisions of the GLB Act itself, but also the regulations enacted pursuant to it. Which regulations apply, and which entity will enforce them, largely depends on the type of organization being regulated.[36] The regulations expand and clarify definitions, as well as providing actual details where Congress has only mandated general requirements such as security, and the agencies may provide guidance to those subject to their regulations about compliance and enforcement.[37] To avoid inconsistency, the various agencies have collaborated on their regulations and guidance.[38]

The FTC in particular has actively enforced the GLB Act, its associated Financial Privacy Rule,[39] and its Safeguards Rule for data security,[40] often in conjunction with other applicable laws such as the FCRA:

Credit Report Resellers Settle FTC Charges; Security Failures Allowed Hackers to Access Consumers' Personal Information

As part of the Federal Trade Commission's ongoing campaign to protect consumers' personal information, three companies whose business is reselling consumers' credit reports have agreed to settle FTC charges that they did not take reasonable steps to protect consumers' personal information, failures that allowed computer hackers to access that data. The settlements require the companies to strengthen their data security procedures and submit to audits for 20 years. These are the FTC's first cases

---

[32] 15 U.S.C. § 6802(d) (1999).

[33] § 6802(e).

[34] § 6802(c).

[35] 15 U.S.C. § 6801(b) (1999).

[36] *See, e.g.*, Regulation P, 12 C.F.R. § 216 (1999) (the Federal Reserve Board); 12 C.F.R. § 573 (1994) (the Department of the Treasury's Office of Thrift Supervision); 12 C.F.R. § 332.1 (2000) (the Federal Deposit Insurance Corporation); 16 C.F.R. § 313 (2000) (the FTC); and Regulations S-P and S-Am, 17 C.F.R. § 248 (2000) (the SEC's version, also called Regulation S-P).

[37] *See, e.g.*, STAFF RESPONSES TO QUESTIONS ABOUT REGULATION S-P, http://www.sec.gov/divisions/investment/guidance/regs2qa.htm (last visited May 8, 2012); FREQUENTLY ASKED QUESTIONS FOR THE PRIVACY REGULATION, http://www.ftc.gov/privacy/glbact/glb-faq.htm (last visited May 8, 2012).

[38] *See, e.g.*, Evolution of a Prototype Financial Privacy Notice, http://ftc.gov/privacy/privacyinitiatives/ftcfinalreport060228.pdf.

[39] 16 C.F.R. § 313 (2000).

[40] 16 C.F.R. § 314 (2002).

against credit report resellers for their clients' data security failures.

"These cases should send a strong message that companies giving their clients online access to sensitive consumer information must have reasonable procedures to secure it," said David Vladeck, Director of the FTC's Bureau of Consumer Protection. "Had these three companies taken adequate steps to ensure the use of basic computer security measures, they might have foiled the hackers who wound up gaining access to extensive personal information in the consumer reporting system."

According to administrative complaints issued by the FTC, the three resellers buy credit reports from the three nationwide consumer reporting agencies (Equifax, Experian, and TransUnion) and combine them into special reports they sell to mortgage brokers and others to determine consumers' eligibility for credit. Due to their lack of information security policies and procedures, the companies allegedly allowed clients without basic security measures, such as firewalls and updated antivirus software, to access their reports. As a result, hackers accessed more than 1,800 credit reports without authorization via the clients' computer networks. In addition, even after becoming aware of the data breaches, the companies did not make reasonable efforts to protect against future breaches.

The resellers are SettlementOne Credit Corporation and its parent company, Sackett National Holdings Inc.; ACRAnet Inc.; Fajilan and Associates Inc., doing business as Statewide Credit Services; and Robert Fajilan. They are charged with violating the Fair Credit Reporting Act by failing to protect their internet portals and thereby furnishing credit reports to hackers who lacked a permissible purpose to have them, failing to maintain reasonable procedures to limit the furnishing of credit reports for such purposes, and furnishing credit reports when they had reasonable grounds for believing the reports would not be used for a permissible purpose. Their failure to protect consumers' personal information also allegedly violated the FTC Act.

In addition, the resellers allegedly violated the Gramm-Leach-Bliley Safeguards Rule by failing to design and implement information safeguards to control the risks to consumer information; to regularly test or monitor the effectiveness of their controls and procedures; to evaluate and adjust their information security programs in light of known or identified risks; and to have comprehensive information security programs.

The proposed consent orders bar the respondents from violating the Safeguards Rule and require them to:

have comprehensive information security programs designed to protect the security, confidentiality, and integrity of consumers' personal information, including information accessible to clients;

obtain independent audits of their security programs, every other year for 20 years;

furnish credit reports only to those with a permissible purpose; and

maintain reasonable procedures to limit the furnishing of credit reports to those with a permissible purpose.

The orders also contain record-keeping provisions to allow the FTC to monitor compliance . . . .[41]

V. OTHER RELEVANT LAWS

While the RFPA, FCRA, and GLB Act are the major federal statutes addressing financial privacy, they are not the only sources of applicable law. For example, the Sarbanes-Oxley Act of 2002,[42] as part of its overall effort to increase transparency and accountability for companies regulated by federal securities laws, makes "the principal executive officer or officers and the principal financial officer or officers" of the company personally certify that they have disclosed to auditors and the audit committee of the board of directors "all significant deficiencies in the design or operation of internal controls which could adversely affect the issuer's ability to record, process, summarize, and report financial data and have identified for the issuer's auditors any material weaknesses in internal controls."[43]

On the state level, while much of the responsibility for regulating financial privacy is retained by the federal government and thus preempts state laws,[44] states retain legislative power over contract and licensing requirements for various industries. Through these areas, and through general local consumer protection authority, companies must still evaluate state-based financial privacy obligations.

VI. PURCHASE PRIVACY: SELF-REGULATION AND INDUSTRY GUIDANCE ON LEGISLATION

While statutes such as the FCRA and the GLB Act provide protection of credit and account information, there are far fewer legal protections applicable to information about a major portion of how consumers *use* their financial resources: their purchases of goods and services. Most such protection, to the extent exists, either arises under the general principles of consumer protection and contract or the few statutes such as the Video Privacy Protection Act[45] discussed in Chapter 4 of this book. For specific industries, however, self-regulation may supplement and inform the requirements to maintain privacy of consumer purchase-related information.

Among the most broadly applicable of the self-regulatory standards is that of the PCI Security Standards ("PCI DSS") Council, a coalition of the five "global payment brands — American Express, Discover Financial Services, JCB International, MasterCard Worldwide, and Visa Inc." to establish and enforce (via contract) data security requirements for the institutions that issue credit cards as well as the merchants that

---

[41] FTC Press Release, Credit Report Resellers Settle FTC Charges; Security Failures Allowed Hackers to Access Consumers' Personal Information *(Feb. 3, 2011), http://ftc.gov/opa/2011/02/settlement.shtm (last visited May 8, 2012).*

[42] Sarbanes-Oxley Act of 2002, Pub. L. No. 107-204, 116 Stat. 745 (2002).

[43] 15 U.S.C. § 7241(5)(A) (2002).

[44] *But see American Bankers Ass'n v. Lockyer,* 541 F.3d 1214 (9th Cir. 2008) (partially reversing previous case ruling FCRA preempted California's Financial Information Privacy Act).

[45] Video Privacy Protection Act, 18 U.S.C. § 2710 (1988).

accept them.[46] Another trade group, the National Association of Insurance Commissioners ("NAIC"), prepared and circulated for state governments a set of draft regulations regarding the privacy of consumer financial and health information which have been adopted in whole or part by various states.[47]

---

[46] PCI Security Standards Council Site - Verify PCI Compliance, Download Data Security and Credit Card Security Standards, https://www.pcisecuritystandards.org/index.php (last visited May 8, 2012).

[47] *See, e.g.*, Kan. Admin Regs. § 40-1-46 (2001) (adopting NAIC regulations except for sections 1 and 24); N.H. Code Admin R. Ins. 3001 (2001) (adopting NAIC form regulations); Utah Admin. R. 590-206 (2002) (adopting and referring to NAIC form regulations).

Chapter 7

WORKPLACE PRIVACY: DIFFERENT NEEDS, DIFFERENT EXPECTATIONS, DIFFERENT RULES

When it comes to the protection of consumer data, the rules and requirements may vary sharply (as seen in the other chapters of this book) depending on the industry, relationships between the organization and individual, the type of information being collected and used, risks involved with misuse of the information, and even the age of the consumer. Beyond concepts such as the Fair Information Practice Principles,[1] it can be difficult to generalize about the requirements for consumer information stewardship.

Whatever their characteristics, though, there is one commonality shared across the various types of organizations: the vast majority of them have, and collect and maintain information about, *employees*. The legal structure and risks regarding managing employee data are quite distinct from those for consumer data, mainly because the expectations, and the underlying rationale for data collection and use, are very different from their consumer data counterparts. So, too, are the respective means and types of information collection in the two contexts.

I. MONITORING WORKERS: PHYSICALLY AND ELECTRONICALLY

a. Reasonable Expectations of Workplace Data Privacy

A key concept in privacy law is the "reasonable expectation of privacy" against monitoring: what it is, whether it exists at all in a given situation, and whether any other factors might outweigh it. If a person lacks a reasonable expectation of privacy in a particular context, the protections of the law may not protect the person from monitoring or data collection by others.[2]

Often, the analysis of whether there is or should be a reasonable expectation of privacy is extremely fact specific. Looking at the physical location, the role played by the individual and anyone else around and the context through which his or her privacy (whether of information or behavior) is being potentially breached.

The workplace represents an odd combination of public and private spheres. On the one hand, from the individual's prospective a workplace is not akin to a home. The

---

[1] See discussion of FIPP in Chapter 2:IV.

[2] *See, e.g.*, Katz v. United States, 88 S.Ct. 507 (1967) (Government found to have illegally monitored defendant's telephone booth conversations without obtaining a warrant).

individual does not own the workplace, and the individual is at work for the overall benefit not of him or herself but of the employer. At the same time, though, there are locations and situations within a workplace where one may reasonably not expect full time complete monitoring. Examples might include a locker room, restrooms or even lockable offices. There could be portions of a work environment that are reasonably expected to be private even when other portions adjacent to them are not. Consider an employee working in a cubicle which lacks walls, a door, or any effective soundproofing. Such employee would not reasonably expect to have his or her conversations, actions or the content shown on a computer screen to be private given that anyone walking by could perceive any of those with little or no effort. The cubicle, however, could include filing cabinets and other lockable storage spaces for which the employee and a limited number of other people in the company might have the key. Information and materials stored within locked storage spaces could, depending on the level of access, have some level of reasonable privacy attached to them:

> Because the reasonableness of an expectation of privacy, as well as the appropriate standard for a search, is understood to differ according to context, it is essential first to delineate the boundaries of the workplace context. The workplace includes those areas and items that are related to work and are generally within the employer's control. At a hospital, for example, the hallways, cafeteria, offices, desks, and file cabinets, among other areas, are all part of the workplace. These areas remain part of the workplace context even if the employee has placed personal items in them, such as a photograph placed in a desk or a letter posted on an employee bulletin board.

> Not everything that passes through the confines of the business address can be considered part of the workplace context, however. An employee may bring closed luggage to the office prior to leaving on a trip, or a handbag or briefcase each workday. While whatever expectation of privacy the employee has in the existence and the outward appearance of the luggage is affected by its presence in the workplace, the employee's expectation of privacy in the contents of the luggage is not affected in the same way. The appropriate standard for a workplace search does not necessarily apply to a piece of closed personal luggage, a handbag or a briefcase that happens to be within the employer's business address . . . .[3]

Another key question in evaluating whether an expectation of privacy at work exists and how reasonable it might be has to do with the purpose of the employer in monitoring, as well as the type of employer. First, employers have traditionally been granted great leeway in their rights to observe and monitor employee behavior provided that that monitoring is done for the purpose of promoting and verifying the purposes for which the business is operated. Although a surveillance camera in a restroom or changing room would not be permissible for the purposes of monitoring those within, placing a camera in a storage room or where sensitive materials are stored would likely be treated very differently given the purpose of protecting the security in deterring and detecting theft from those areas. Even employee telephone

---

[3] O'Connor v. Ortega, 107 S.Ct. 1492, 1496–7 (1987).

calls may be permissibly monitored to the extent that the monitoring is done for the purposes of business.[4]

The type of employer is also a key question. In addition to any other workplace legal requirements, governmental employers (federal, state or local) are subject to the additional obligations and prohibitions of the U.S. Constitution. Of most relevance to employee privacy concerns is the Fourth Amendment:

> *The right of the people to be secure in their persons, houses, papers, and effects, against unreasonable searches and seizures, shall not be violated, and no Warrants shall issue, but upon probable cause, supported by Oath or affirmation, and particularly describing the place to be searched, and the persons or things to be seized.*[5]

In cases where governmental agencies are accused of monitoring employees' work activities, the courts must address the threshold question of whether the employer has violated the Constitution if it failed to obtain a proper warrant before executing the search:

> *The strictures of the Fourth Amendment, applied to the States through the Fourteenth Amendment, have been applied to the conduct of governmental officials in various civil activities.* New Jersey v. T.L.O., *469 U.S. 325, 334–335, 105 S.Ct. 733, 738–739, 83 L.Ed.2d 720 (1985). Thus, we have held in the past that the Fourth Amendment governs the conduct of school officials, see ibid., building inspectors, see* Camara v. Municipal Court, *387 U.S. 523, 528, 87 S.Ct. 1727, 1730, 18 L.Ed.2d 930 (1967), and Occupational Safety and Health Act Inspectors, see* Marshall v. Barlow's, Inc., *436 U.S. 307, 312–313, 98 S.Ct. 1816, 1820–1821, 56 L.Ed.2d 305 (1978). As [the U.S. Supreme Court] observed in T.L.O., "[b]ecause the individual's interest in privacy and personal security 'suffers whether the government's motivation is to investigate violations of criminal laws or breaches of other statutory or regulatory*

---

[4] The Electronic Communications Privacy Act, which generally prohibits interception of wired and wireless communications, provides a relevant exception in its definitions:

> electronic, mechanical, or other device" means any device or apparatus which can be used to intercept a wire, oral, or electronic communication other than —

> (a) any telephone or telegraph instrument, equipment or facility, or any component thereof, (i) furnished to the subscriber or user by a provider of wire or electronic communication service in the ordinary course of its business and being used by the subscriber or user in the ordinary course of its business or furnished by such subscriber or user for connection to the facilities of such service and used in the ordinary course of its business . . . .

18 U.S.C. § 2510(5)(A)(i).

A number of cases have interpreted this exception to permit employers' monitoring of employee telephone calls, at least to the point of determining whether a call was personal or for business purposes. *See, e.g.,* Watkins v. L.M. Berry & Co., 704 F.2d 577, 583 (11th Cir. 1983):

> We hold that a personal call may not be intercepted in the ordinary course of business under the exemption in section 2510(5)(a)(i), except to the extent necessary to guard against unauthorized use of the telephone or to determine whether a call is personal or not. In other words, a personal call may be intercepted in the ordinary course of business to determine its nature but never its contents.

[5] U.S. Const., 4th Amendment.

standards,'. . . it would be 'anomalous to say that the individual and his private property are fully protected by the Fourth Amendment only when the individual is suspected of criminal behavior.' " 469 U.S., at 335, 105 S.Ct., at 739 (quoting Marshall v. Barlow's, Inc., *supra, 436 U.S., at 312–313, 98 S.Ct., at 1820 and* Camara v. Municipal Court, *supra, 387 U.S., at 530, 87 S.Ct., at 1731). Searches and seizures by government employers or supervisors of the private property of their employees, therefore, are subject to the restraints of the Fourth Amendment . . . .*

Within the workplace context, this Court has recognized that employees may have a reasonable expectation of privacy against intrusions by police. See Mancusi v. DeForte, *392 U.S. 364, 88 S.Ct. 2120, 20 L.Ed.2d 1154 (1968). As with the expectation of privacy in one's home, such an expectation in one's place of work is "based upon societal expectations that have deep roots in the history of the Amendment."* Oliver v. United States, *supra, 466 U.S., at 178, n. 8, 104 S.Ct., at 1741, n. 8. Thus, in* Mancusi v. DeForte, *supra, the Court held that a union employee who shared an office with other union employees had a privacy interest in the office sufficient to challenge successfully the warrantless search of that office:*

"It has long been settled that one has standing to object to a search of his office, as well as of his home . . . . [I]t seems clear that if DeForte had occupied a 'private' office in the union headquarters, and union records had been seized from a desk or a filing cabinet in that office, he would have had standing . . . . In such a 'private' office, DeForte would have been entitled to expect that he would not be disturbed except by personal or business invitees, and that records would not be taken except with his permission or that of his union superiors." 392 U.S., at 369, 88 S.Ct., at 2124.

Given the societal expectations of privacy in one's place of work expressed in both Oliver *and* Mancusi, *we reject the contention made by the Solicitor General and petitioners that public employees can never have a reasonable expectation of privacy in their place of work. Individuals do not lose Fourth Amendment rights merely because they work for the government instead of a private employer. The operational realities of the workplace, however, may make some employees' expectations of privacy unreasonable when an intrusion is by a supervisor rather than a law enforcement official. Public employees' expectations of privacy in their offices, desks, and file cabinets, like similar expectations of employees in the private sector, may be reduced by virtue of actual office practices and procedures, or by legitimate regulation. Indeed, in* Mancusi *itself, the Court suggested that the union employee did not have a reasonable expectation of privacy against his union supervisors. 392 U.S., at 369, 88 S.Ct., at 2124. The employee's expectation of privacy must be assessed in the context of the employment relation. An office is seldom a private enclave free from entry by supervisors, other employees, and business and personal invitees. Instead, in many cases offices are continually entered by fellow employees and other visitors during the workday for conferences, consultations, and other work-related visits. Simply put, it is the nature of government offices that others-such as fellow employees, supervisors, consen-*

sual visitors, and the general public-may have frequent access to an individual's office. We agree with Justice [Scalia] that "[c]onstitutional protection against unreasonable searches by the government does not disappear merely because the government has the right to make reasonable intrusions in its capacity as employer," post, at 1505, but some government offices may be so open to fellow employees or the public that no expectation of privacy is reasonable. Cf. Katz v. United States, 389 U.S. 347, 351, 88 S.Ct. 507, 511, 19 L.Ed.2d 576 (1967) ("What a person knowingly exposes to the public, even in his own home or office, is not a subject of Fourth Amendment protection"). Given the great variety of work environments in the public sector, the question whether an employee has a reasonable expectation of privacy must be addressed on a case-by-case basis.[6]

Employers may themselves set or at least affect what expectations of privacy might be reasonable through policies they publish within the company. Such policies represent somewhat of a parallel to the privacy policies published for consumers albeit with a significant difference: where a privacy policy is a disclosure document for the consumer and enforceable generally against the publisher, an employee policy, while a disclosure, is most frequently cast as enforceable by the employee for failure to comply. The policies may be subject to general notions of reasonability as well as labor laws, and may not be necessarily relied upon by employees at least in terms of what companies promise not to do. Still, when a court or counsel evaluates the reasonable expectation of worker privacy, the existence form and terms of any relevant workplace policy especially one that has been signed by employees as many are, will be part of that analysis.

One more element that must be considered in the analysis of whether an employee has a reasonable expectation of privacy from employer monitoring is any obligation of the employer to notify workers of its monitoring practices. Such obligations may arise from applicable state laws, such as that of Connecticut:

§ 31–48d. Employers engaged in electronic monitoring required to give prior notice to employees. Exceptions. Civil penalty

(a) As used in this section:

(1) "Employer" means any person, firm or corporation, including the state and any political subdivision of the state which has employees;

(2) "Employee" means any person who performs services for an employer in a business of the employer, if the employer has the right to control and direct the person as to (A) the result to be accomplished by the services, and (B) the details and means by which such result is accomplished; and

(3) "Electronic monitoring" means the collection of information on an employer's premises concerning employees' activities or communications by any means other than direct observation, including the use of a computer, telephone, wire, radio, camera, electromagnetic, photoelectronic or photo-optical systems, but not including

---

[6] O'Connor v. Ortega, 1496–98.

the collection of information (A) for security purposes in common areas of the employer's premises which are held out for use by the public, or (B) which is prohibited under state or federal law.

(b)(1) Except as provided in subdivision (2) of this subsection, each employer who engages in any type of electronic monitoring shall give prior written notice to all employees who may be affected, informing them of the types of monitoring which may occur. Each employer shall post, in a conspicuous place which is readily available for viewing by its employees, a notice concerning the types of electronic monitoring which the employer may engage in. Such posting shall constitute such prior written notice.

(2) When (A) an employer has reasonable grounds to believe that employees are engaged in conduct which (i) violates the law, (ii) violates the legal rights of the employer or the employer's employees, or (iii) creates a hostile workplace environment, and (B) electronic monitoring may produce evidence of this misconduct, the employer may conduct monitoring without giving prior written notice.

(c) The Labor Commissioner may levy a civil penalty against any person that the commissioner finds to be in violation of subsection (b) of this section, after a hearing . . . . The maximum civil penalty shall be five hundred dollars for the first offense, one thousand dollars for the second offense and three thousand dollars for the third and each subsequent offense.

(d) The provisions of this section shall not apply to a criminal investigation. Any information obtained in the course of a criminal investigation through the use of electronic monitoring may be used in a disciplinary proceeding against an employee.[7]

b. Electronic Monitoring by Private Versus Public Employers: Case Law Counterpoints

One helpful means of understanding the different legal requirements faced by private and public employers seeking to monitor their employees electronically is through some of the key cases in the area. Among the most influential analyses covering private workplaces' rights to monitor employee e-mail is *Smyth v. Pillsbury*:

MICHAEL A. SMYTH v. THE PILLSBURY COMPANY[8]

WEINER, DISTRICT JUDGE.

In this diversity action, plaintiff, an at-will employee, claims he was wrongfully discharged from his position as a regional operations manager by the defendant. Presently before the court is the motion of the defendant to dismiss pursuant to Rule 12(b)(6) of the Federal Rules of Civil Procedure. For the reasons which follow, the motion is granted.

---

[7] Connecticut General Statutes Annoted § 31–48d.

[8] Smyth v. Pillsbury, 914 F.Supp. 97 (E.D. Pa 1996).

A claim may be dismissed under Fed.R.Civ.P. 12(b)(6) only if the plaintiff can prove no set of facts in support of the claim that would entitle him to relief. ALA, Inc. v. CCAIR, Inc., 29 F.3d 855, 859 (3d Cir.1994). The reviewing court must consider only those facts alleged in the Complaint and accept all of the allegations as true. Id. Applying this standard, we find that plaintiff has failed to state a claim upon which relief can be granted.

Defendant maintained an electronic mail communication system ("e-mail") in order to promote internal corporate communications between its employees. Complaint at ¶ 8. Defendant repeatedly assured its employees, including plaintiff, that all e-mail communications would remain confidential and privileged. Complaint at ¶ 9. Defendant further assured its employees, including plaintiff, that e-mail communications could not be intercepted and used by defendant against its employees as grounds for termination or reprimand. Complaint at ¶ 10.

In October 1994, plaintiff received certain e-mail communications from his supervisor over defendant's e-mail system on his computer at home. Complaint at ¶ 11. In reliance on defendant's assurances regarding defendant's e-mail system, plaintiff responded and exchanged e-mails with his supervisor. Id. At some later date, contrary to the assurances of confidentiality made by defendant, defendant, acting through its agents, servants and employees, intercepted plaintiff's private e-mail messages made in October 1994. Complaint at ¶ 12. On January 17, 1995, defendant notified plaintiff that it was terminating his employment effective February 1, 1995, for transmitting what it deemed to be inappropriate and unprofessional comments[9] over defendant's e-mail system in October, 1994. Complaint at ¶¶ 13, 14.

As a general rule, Pennsylvania law does not provide a common law cause of action for the wrongful discharge of an at-will employee such as plaintiff. Borse v. Piece Goods Shop, Inc., 963 F.2d 611, 614 (3d Cir.1992); Paul v. Lankenau Hospital, 524 Pa. 90, 93, 569 A.2d 346, 348 (1990); Geary v. United States Steel Corp., 456 Pa. 171, 319 A.2d 174 (1974). *Pennsylvania is an employment at-will jurisdiction and an employer "may discharge an employee with or without cause, at pleasure, unless restrained by some contract."* Henry v. Pittsburgh & Lake Erie Railroad Co., 139 Pa. 289, 297, 21 A. 157, 157 (1891). See also, Johnson v. Resources for Human Development, Inc., 843 F.Supp. 974, 979 (E.D.Pa.1994); Brown v. Hammond, 810 F.Supp. 644, 645 (E.D.Pa.1993) *(An employer's right to terminate an at-will employee is "virtually absolute".);* Yetter v. Ward Trucking Corp., 401 Pa.Super. 467, 585 A.2d 1022 (1991).

However, in the most limited of circumstances, exceptions have been recognized where discharge of an at-will employee threatens or violates a clear mandate of public policy. Borse, 963 F.2d at 614; Clay v. Advanced Computer Applications, 522 Pa. 86, 88, 559 A.2d 917, 918 (1989) *(If discharge of at-will employee threatens clear mandates of public policy, there is a cause of action against the employer.);* Geary, supra. *A "clear mandate" of public policy must be of a type that "strikes at the heart of a citizen's social right, duties and responsibilities."* Novosel v. Nationwide Insurance Co., 721

---

[9] The footnote in the case states, "Defendant alleges in its motion to dismiss that the e-mails concerned sales management and contained threats to 'kill the backstabbing bastards' and referred to the planned Holiday party as the 'Jim Jones Koolaid affair.' "

F.2d 894, 899 (3d Cir.1983). This recognized public policy exception is an especially narrow one. Burkholder v. Hutchison, *403 Pa.Super. 498, 589 A.2d 721, 724 (1991). To date, the Pennsylvania Superior Court has only recognized three such exceptions.*

First, an employee may not be fired for serving on jury duty. Reuther v. Fowler & Williams, Inc., *255 Pa.Super. 28, 386 A.2d 119 (1978). The Reuther court cited the Pennsylvania constitution as well as the Pennsylvania statutes in concluding that "the necessity of having citizens freely available for jury service is just the sort of 'recognized facet of public policy' alluded to by our Supreme Court in Geary." 386 A.2d at 121.*

Second, an employer may not deny employment to a person with a prior conviction. Hunter v. Port Authority of Allegheny County, *277 Pa.Super. 4, 419 A.2d 631 (1980). The Hunter court relied on federal court decisions as well as Pennsylvania statutes and Pennsylvania court decisions before concluding that the defendant violated the Pennsylvania constitution and "the deeply ingrained public policy of this State . . . to avoid unwarranted stigmatization of and unreasonable restrictions upon former offenders." 419 A.2d at 636, n. 5.*

And finally, an employee may not be fired for reporting violations of federal regulations to the Nuclear Regulatory Commission. Field v. Philadelphia Electric Company, *388 Pa.Super. 400, 565 A.2d 1170, 1180 (1989). That court held that the alleged discharge was against public policy because federal law required the employee to report violations and he was an expert in the area and there was no evidence that he bypassed any internal chain of command. 565 A.2d at 1180.*

As evidenced above, a public policy exception must be clearly defined. See also, McGonagle v. Union Fidelity Corp., 383 Pa.Super. 223, 556 A.2d 878, 885 (1989), *appeal denied, 525 Pa. 584, 575 A.2d 115 (1990) ("Unless an employee identifies a 'specific' expression of public policy violated by his discharge, it will not be labelled as wrongful and within the sphere of public policy"). The sources of public policy can be found in "legislation, administrative rules, regulation, or decision; and judicial decisions . . . Absent legislation, the judiciary must define the cause of action in case by case determinations."* Borse, *963 F.2d at 619, n. 6 (3d Cir.1992)* quoting Cisco v. United Parcel Services, Inc., 328 Pa.Super. 300, 306, 476 A.2d 1340, 1343 (1984); Krajsa v. Keypunch, Inc., *424 Pa.Super. 230, 622 A.2d 355, 358 (1993);* see also, Smith v. Calgon Carbon Corp., 917 F.2d 1338, 1344 (3d Cir.1990), *cert. denied, 499 U.S. 966, 111 S.Ct. 1597, 113 L.Ed.2d 660 (1991) ("[A] 'clear mandate of public policy' [is] embodied in a constitutionally or legislatively established prohibition, requirement, or privilege.").* Whitney v. Xerox, C.A.No. 94-3852, 1994 WL 412429 (E.D.Pa. August 2, 1994) *slip op. at 3–4.*

Plaintiff claims that his termination was in violation of "public policy which precludes an employer from terminating an employee in violation of the employee's right to privacy as embodied in Pennsylvania common law." Complaint at ¶ 15.[10] In

---

[10] The footnote in the case states,

Although plaintiff does not affirmatively allege so in his Complaint or in his memorandum of law in opposition to defendant's motion to dismiss, the allegations in the Complaint might suggest that plaintiff is *support for this proposition, plaintiff directs our attention to a decision by our Court of Appeals in* Borse v. Piece Goods Shop, Inc., *963 F.2d 611 (3d Cir.1992). In* Borse, *the plaintiff sued her employer alleging wrongful discharge as a result of her refusal to submit to urinalysis screening and personal property searches at her work place pursuant to the employer's drug and alcohol policy. After rejecting plaintiff's argument that the employer's drug and alcohol program violated public policy encompassed in the United States and Pennsylvania Constitutions, our Court of Appeals stated "our review of Pennsylvania law reveals other evidence of a public policy that may, under certain circumstances, give rise to a wrongful discharge action related to urinalysis or to personal property searches. Specifically, we refer to the Pennsylvania common law regarding tortious invasion of privacy." Id. at 620.*

The Court of Appeals in Borse, *observed that one of the torts which Pennsylvania recognizes as encompassing an action for invasion of privacy is the tort of "intrusion upon seclusion." As noted by the Court of Appeals, the Restatement (Second) of Torts defines the tort as follows:*

> *One who intentionally intrudes, physically or otherwise, upon the solitude or seclusion of another or his private affairs or concerns, is subject to liability to the other for invasion of his privacy, if the intrusion would be highly offensive to a reasonable person.*

Restatement (Second) of Torts § 652B. Liability only attaches when the "intrusion is substantial and would be highly offensive to the 'ordinary reasonable person.'" Borse, *963 F.2d at 621 (citation omitted). Although the Court of Appeals in* Borse *observed that "[t]he Pennsylvania courts have not had occasion to consider whether a discharge related to an employer's tortious invasion of an employee's privacy violates public policy", the Court of Appeals predicted that in any claim where the employee claimed that his discharge related to an invasion of his privacy "the Pennsylvania Supreme Court would examine the facts and circumstances surrounding the alleged invasion of privacy. If the court determined that the discharge was related to a substantial and highly offensive invasion of the employee's privacy, [the Court of Appeals] believe that it would conclude that the discharge violated public policy." Id. at 622. In determining whether an alleged invasion of privacy is substantial and highly offensive to a reasonable person, the Court of Appeals predicted that Pennsylvania would adopt a balancing test which balances the employee's privacy interest against the employer's interest in maintaining a drug-free workplace. Id. at 625. Because the Court of Appeals in* Borse *could "envision at least two ways in which an employer's drug and alcohol program might violate the public policy protecting individuals from tortious invasion of privacy by private actors" id. at 626, the Court vacated the district court's order dismissing the plaintiff's complaint and remanded the case to the district court with directions to grant* Borse

---

alleging an exception to the at-will employment rule based on estoppel, i.e. that defendant repeatedly assured plaintiff and others that it would not intercept e-mail communications and reprimand or terminate based on the contents thereof and plaintiff relied on these assurances to his detriment when he made the "inappropriate and unprofessional" e-mail communications in October 1994. The law of Pennsylvania is clear, however, that an employer may not be estopped from firing an employee based upon a promise, even when reliance is demonstrated. *Paul v. Lankenau Hospital, 524 Pa. 90, 569 A.2d 346 (1990).*

leave to amend the Complaint to allege how the defendant's drug and alcohol program violates her right to privacy.

Applying the Restatement definition of the tort of intrusion upon seclusion to the facts and circumstances of the case sub judice, *we find that plaintiff has failed to state a claim upon which relief can be granted. In the first instance, unlike urinalysis and personal property searches, we do not find a reasonable expectation of privacy in e-mail communications voluntarily made by an employee to his supervisor over the company e-mail system notwithstanding any assurances that such communications would not be intercepted by management. Once plaintiff communicated the alleged unprofessional comments to a second person (his supervisor) over an e-mail system which was apparently utilized by the entire company, any reasonable expectation of privacy was lost. Significantly, the defendant did not require plaintiff, as in the case of an urinalysis or personal property search to disclose any personal information about himself. Rather, plaintiff voluntarily communicated the alleged unprofessional comments over the company e-mail system. We find no privacy interests in such communications.*

In the second instance, even if we found that an employee had a reasonable expectation of privacy in the contents of his e-mail communications over the company e-mail system, we do not find that a reasonable person would consider the defendant's interception of these communications to be a substantial and highly offensive invasion of his privacy. Again, we note that by intercepting such communications, the company is not, as in the case of urinalysis or personal property searches, requiring the employee to disclose any personal information about himself or invading the employee's person or personal effects. Moreover, the company's interest in preventing inappropriate and unprofessional comments or even illegal activity over its e-mail system outweighs any privacy interest the employee may have in those comments.

In sum, we find that the defendant's actions did not tortiously invade the plaintiff's privacy and, therefore, did not violate public policy. As a result, the motion to dismiss is granted.

Note that the court in *Smyth v. Pillsbury* held that Smyth lacked any reasonable expectation of privacy in the contents of the messages he sent via his work e-mail account; the system belonged to and was run by his employer, and was "apparently utilized by the entire company." The analysis, though, is based entirely on potential state privacy claims; neither the U.S. nor state constitution is evoked, as the employer is a private firm rather than a governmental body.

Additionally, the court denied that Pillsbury's previous "assurance" of its intention not to monitor employee e-mails established any reasonable expectation of privacy. Such policies are established by an employer, and may be revised by that employer at any time, so it would not be reasonable for Smyth or any other worker to rely on the ongoing validity of the non-monitoring policy as a guarantee of e-mail privacy. In other cases, however, where an employer has notified employees that the company can and will monitor e-mails, such a policy has been found to preemptively eliminate any reasonable expectation of privacy in those communications, even to the extent of overriding attorney-client privilege in e-mails sent by an employee from his work e-mail address to his lawyer.[11]

By contrast with the very brief analysis of the existence of a reasonable expectation of privacy for workplace e-mails in *Smyth v. Pillsbury*, the U.S. Supreme Court in *City of Ontario v. Quon* must expend a much greater effort determining whether such an expectation exists when the employer is a city government, because of the Fourth Amendment requirements such an employer faces:

CITY OF ONTARIO v. QUON[12]

Justice Kennedy delivered the opinion of the Court.

This case involves the assertion by a government employer of the right, in circumstances to be described, to read text messages sent and received on a pager the employer owned and issued to an employee. The employee contends that the privacy of the messages is protected by the ban on "unreasonable searches and seizures" found in the Fourth Amendment to the United States Constitution, made applicable to the States by the Due Process Clause of the Fourteenth Amendment. Mapp v. Ohio, *367 U.S. 643, 81 S.Ct. 1684, 6 L.Ed.2d 1081 (1961). Though the case touches issues of farreaching significance, the Court concludes it can be resolved by settled principles determining when a search is reasonable.*

The City of Ontario (City) is a political subdivision of the State of California. The case arose out of incidents in 2001 and 2002 when respondent Jeff Quon was employed by the Ontario Police Department (OPD). He was a police sergeant and member of OPD's Special Weapons and Tactics (SWAT) Team. The City, OPD, and OPD's Chief, Lloyd Scharf, are petitioners here. As will be discussed, two respondents share the last name Quon. In this opinion "Quon" refers to Jeff Quon, for the relevant events mostly revolve around him.

In October 2001, the City acquired 20 alphanumeric pagers capable of sending and receiving text messages. Arch Wireless Operating Company provided wireless service for the pagers. Under the City's service contract with Arch Wireless, each pager was allotted a limited number of characters sent or received each month. Usage in excess of that amount would result in an additional fee. The City issued pagers to Quon and other SWAT Team members in order to help the SWAT Team mobilize and respond to emergency situations.

Before acquiring the pagers, the City announced a "Computer Usage, Internet and E-Mail Policy" (Computer Policy) that applied to all employees. Among other provisions, it specified that the City "reserves the right to monitor and log all network activity including e-mail and Internet use, with or without notice. Users should have no expectation of privacy or confidentiality when using these resources." App. to Pet. for Cert. 152a. In March 2000, Quon signed a statement acknowledging that he had read and understood the Computer Policy.

---

[11] *See* discussion *infra* at Chapter 11, note 16.

[12] 130 S.Ct. 2619 (2011).

The Computer Policy did not apply, on its face, to text messaging. Text messages share similarities with e-mails, but the two differ in an important way. In this case, for instance, an e-mail sent on a City computer was transmitted through the City's own data servers, but a text message sent on one of the City's pagers was transmitted using wireless radio frequencies from an individual pager to a receiving station owned by Arch Wireless. It was routed through Arch Wireless' computer network, where it remained until the recipient's pager or cellular telephone was ready to receive the message, at which point Arch Wireless transmitted the message from the transmitting station nearest to the recipient. After delivery, Arch Wireless retained a copy on its computer servers. The message did not pass through computers owned by the City.

Although the Computer Policy did not cover text messages by its explicit terms, the City made clear to employees, including Quon, that the City would treat text messages the same way as it treated e-mails. At an April 18, 2002, staff meeting at which Quon was present, Lieutenant Steven Duke, the OPD officer responsible for the City's contract with Arch Wireless, told officers that messages sent on the pagers "are considered e-mail messages. This means that [text] messages would fall under the City's policy as public information and [would be] eligible for auditing." App. 30. Duke's comments were put in writing in a memorandum sent on April 29, 2002, by Chief Scharf to Quon and other City personnel.

Within the first or second billing cycle after the pagers were distributed, Quon exceeded his monthly text message character allotment. Duke told Quon about the overage, and reminded him that messages sent on the pagers were "considered e-mail and could be audited." Id., at 40. Duke said, however, that "it was not his intent to audit [an] employee's text messages to see if the overage [was] due to work related transmissions." Ibid. Duke suggested that Quon could reimburse the City for the overage fee rather than have Duke audit the messages. Quon wrote a check to the City for the overage. Duke offered the same arrangement to other employees who incurred overage fees.

Over the next few months, Quon exceeded his character limit three or four times. Each time he reimbursed the City. Quon and another officer again incurred overage fees for their pager usage in August 2002. At a meeting in October, Duke told Scharf that he had become "'tired of being a bill collector.'" Id., at 91. Scharf decided to determine whether the existing character limit was too low-that is, whether officers such as Quon were having to pay fees for sending work-related messages-or if the overages were for personal messages. Scharf told Duke to request transcripts of text messages sent in August and September by Quon and the other employee who had exceeded the character allowance.

At Duke's request, an administrative assistant employed by OPD contacted Arch Wireless. After verifying that the City was the subscriber on the accounts, Arch Wireless provided the desired transcripts. Duke reviewed the transcripts and discovered that many of the messages sent and received on Quon's pager were not work related, and some were sexually explicit. Duke reported his findings to Scharf, who, along with Quon's immediate supervisor, reviewed the transcripts himself. After his review, Scharf referred the matter to OPD's internal affairs division for an investi-

gation into whether Quon was violating OPD rules by pursuing personal matters while on duty.

The officer in charge of the internal affairs review was Sergeant Patrick McMahon. Before conducting a review, McMahon used Quon's work schedule to redact the transcripts in order to eliminate any messages Quon sent while off duty. He then reviewed the content of the messages Quon sent during work hours. McMahon's report noted that Quon sent or received 456 messages during work hours in the month of August 2002, of which no more than 57 were work related; he sent as many as 80 messages during a single day at work; and on an average workday, Quon sent or received 28 messages, of which only 3 were related to police business. The report concluded that Quon had violated OPD rules. Quon was allegedly disciplined.

Raising claims under Rev. Stat. § 1979, 42 U.S.C. § 1983; 18 U.S.C. § 2701 et seq., popularly known as the Stored Communications Act (SCA); and California law, Quon filed suit against petitioners in the United States District Court for the Central District of California. Arch Wireless and an individual not relevant here were also named as defendants. Quon was joined in his suit by another plaintiff who is not a party before this Court and by the other respondents, each of whom exchanged text messages with Quon during August and September 2002: Jerilyn Quon, Jeff Quon's then-wife, from whom he was separated; April Florio, an OPD employee with whom Jeff Quon was romantically involved; and Steve Trujillo, another member of the OPD SWAT Team. Among the allegations in the complaint was that petitioners violated respondents' Fourth Amendment rights and the SCA by obtaining and reviewing the transcript of Jeff Quon's pager messages and that Arch Wireless had violated the SCA by turning over the transcript to the City.

The parties filed cross-motions for summary judgment. The District Court granted Arch Wireless' motion for summary judgment on the SCA claim but denied petitioners' motion for summary judgment on the Fourth Amendment claims. Quon v. Arch Wireless Operating Co., 445 F.Supp.2d 1116 (C.D.Cal.2006). Relying on the plurality opinion in O'Connor v. Ortega, 480 U.S. 709, 711, 107 S.Ct. 1492, 94 L.Ed.2d 714 (1987), the District Court determined that Quon had a reasonable expectation of privacy in the content of his text messages. Whether the audit of the text messages was nonetheless reasonable, the District Court concluded, turned on Chief Scharf's intent: "[I]f the purpose for the audit was to determine if Quon was using his pager to 'play games' and 'waste time,' then the audit was not constitutionally reasonable"; but if the audit's purpose "was to determine the efficacy of the existing character limits to ensure that officers were not paying hidden work-related costs, . . . no constitutional violation occurred." 445 F.Supp.2d, at 1146.

The District Court held a jury trial to determine the purpose of the audit. The jury concluded that Scharf ordered the audit to determine the efficacy of the character limits. The District Court accordingly held that petitioners did not violate the Fourth Amendment. It entered judgment in their favor.

The United States Court of Appeals for the Ninth Circuit reversed in part. 529 F.3d 892 (2008). The panel agreed with the District Court that Jeff Quon had a reasonable expectation of privacy in his text messages but disagreed with the District Court about whether the search was reasonable. Even though the search was conducted for "a legitimate work-related rationale," the Court of Appeals concluded, it "was not reasonable in scope." Id., at 908. The panel disagreed with the District Court's observation that "there were no less-intrusive means" that Chief Scharf could have used "to verify the efficacy of the 25,000 character limit . . . without intruding on [respondents'] Fourth Amendment rights." Id., at 908–909. The opinion pointed to a "host of simple ways" that the chief could have used instead of the audit, such as warning Quon at the beginning of the month that his future messages would be audited, or asking Quon himself to redact the transcript of his messages. Id., at 909. The Court of Appeals further concluded that Arch Wireless had violated the SCA by turning over the transcript to the City.

The Ninth Circuit denied a petition for rehearing en banc. Quon v. Arch Wireless Operating Co., *554 F.3d 769 (2009). Judge Ikuta, joined by six other Circuit Judges, dissented. Id., at 774–779. Judge Wardlaw concurred in the denial of rehearing, defending the panel's opinion against the dissent. Id., at 769–774.*

This Court granted the petition for certiorari filed by the City, OPD, and Chief Scharf challenging the Court of Appeals' holding that they violated the Fourth Amendment. 558 U.S. ___, 130 S.Ct. 1011, ___ L.Ed.2d ___ (2009). The petition for certiorari filed by Arch Wireless challenging the Ninth Circuit's ruling that Arch Wireless violated the SCA was denied. USA Mobility Wireless, Inc. v. Quon, *558 U.S. ___, 130 S.Ct. 1011, ___ L.Ed.2d ___ (2009).*

The Fourth Amendment states: "The right of the people to be secure in their persons, houses, papers, and effects, against unreasonable searches and seizures, shall not be violated . . . ." It is well settled that the Fourth Amendment's protection extends beyond the sphere of criminal investigations. Camara v. Municipal Court of City and County of San Francisco, *387 U.S. 523, 530, 87 S.Ct. 1727, 18 L.Ed.2d 930 (1967). "The Amendment guarantees the privacy, dignity, and security of persons against certain arbitrary and invasive acts by officers of the Government," without regard to whether the government actor is investigating crime or performing another function.* Skinner v. Railway Labor Executives' Assn., *489 U.S. 602, 613–614, 109 S.Ct. 1402, 103 L.Ed.2d 639 (1989). The Fourth Amendment applies as well when the Government acts in its capacity as an employer.* Treasury Employees v. Von Raab, *489 U.S. 656, 665, 109 S.Ct. 1384, 103 L.Ed.2d 685 (1989).*

The Court discussed this principle in O'Connor. *There a physician employed by a state hospital alleged that hospital officials investigating workplace misconduct had violated his Fourth Amendment rights by searching his office and seizing personal items from his desk and filing cabinet. All Members of the Court agreed with the general principle that "[i]ndividuals do not lose Fourth Amendment rights merely because they work for the government instead of a private employer." 480 U.S., at 717, 107 S.Ct. 1492 (plurality opinion); see also id., at 731, 107 S.Ct. 1492 (SCALIA, J., concurring in judgment); id., at 737, 107 S.Ct. 1492 (Blackmun, J., dissenting). A majority of the Court further agreed that " 'special needs, beyond the normal need for law enforcement,' " make the warrant and probable-cause requirement impracticable for government employers. Id., at 725, 107 S.Ct. 1492 (plurality opinion) (quoting* New Jersey v. T.L. O., *469 U.S. 325, 351, 105 S.Ct. 733, 83 L.Ed.2d 720 (1985))*

(Blackmun, J., concurring in judgment); 480 U.S., at 732, 107 S.Ct. 1492 (opinion of SCALIA, J.) (quoting same).

The O'Connor *Court did disagree on the proper analytical framework for Fourth Amendment claims against government employers. A four-Justice plurality concluded that the correct analysis has two steps. First, because "some government offices may be so open to fellow employees or the public that no expectation of privacy is reasonable," id., at 718, 107 S.Ct. 1492, a court must consider "[t]he operational realities of the workplace" in order to determine whether an employee's Fourth Amendment rights are implicated, id., at 717, 107 S.Ct. 1492. On this view, "the question whether an employee has a reasonable expectation of privacy must be addressed on a case-by-case basis." Id., at 718, 107 S.Ct. 1492. Next, where an employee has a legitimate privacy expectation, an employer's intrusion on that expectation "for noninvestigatory, work-related purposes, as well as for investigations of work-related misconduct, should be judged by the standard of reasonableness under all the circumstances." Id., at 725–726, 107 S.Ct. 1492.*

Justice SCALIA, concurring in the judgment, outlined a different approach. His opinion would have dispensed with an inquiry into "operational realities" and would conclude "that the offices of government employees . . . are covered by Fourth Amendment protections as a general matter." Id., at 731, 107 S.Ct. 1492. But he would also have held "that government searches to retrieve work-related materials or to investigate violations of workplace rules-searches of the sort that are regarded as reasonable and normal in the private-employer context-do not violate the Fourth Amendment." Id., at 732, 107 S.Ct. 1492.

Later, in the Von Raab *decision, the Court explained that "operational realities" could diminish an employee's privacy expectations, and that this diminution could be taken into consideration when assessing the reasonableness of a workplace search. 489 U.S., at 671, 109 S.Ct. 1384. In the two decades since O'Connor, however, the threshold test for determining the scope of an employee's Fourth Amendment rights has not been clarified further. Here, though they disagree on whether Quon had a reasonable expectation of privacy, both petitioners and respondents start from the premise that the O'Connor plurality controls. See Brief for Petitioners 22–28; Brief for Respondents 25–32. It is not necessary to resolve whether that premise is correct. The case can be decided by determining that the search was reasonable even assuming Quon had a reasonable expectation of privacy. The two O'Connor approaches-the plurality's and Justice SCALIA's-therefore lead to the same result here.*

Before turning to the reasonableness of the search, it is instructive to note the parties' disagreement over whether Quon had a reasonable expectation of privacy. The record does establish that OPD, at the outset, made it clear that pager messages were not considered private. The City's Computer Policy stated that "[u]sers should have no expectation of privacy or confidentiality when using" City computers. App. to Pet. for Cert. 152a. Chief Scharf's memo and Duke's statements made clear that this official policy extended to text messaging. The disagreement, at least as respondents see the case, is over whether Duke's later statements overrode the official policy. Respondents contend that because Duke told Quon that an audit would be unneces-

sary if Quon paid for the overage, Quon reasonably could expect that the contents of his messages would remain private.

At this point, were we to assume that inquiry into "operational realities" were called for, compare O'Connor, 480 U.S., at 717, 107 S.Ct. 1492 (plurality opinion), with id., at 730–731, 107 S.Ct. 1492 (opinion of SCALIA, J.); see also id., at 737–738, 107 S.Ct. 1492 (BLACKMUN, J., dissenting), it would be necessary to ask whether Duke's statements could be taken as announcing a change in OPD policy, and if so, whether he had, in fact or appearance, the authority to make such a change and to guarantee the privacy of text messaging. It would also be necessary to consider whether a review of messages sent on police pagers, particularly those sent while officers are on duty, might be justified for other reasons, including performance evaluations, litigation concerning the lawfulness of police actions, and perhaps compliance with state open records laws. See Brief for Petitioners 35–40 (citing Cal. Public Records Act, Cal. Govt.Code Ann. § 6250 et seq. (West 2008)). These matters would all bear on the legitimacy of an employee's privacy expectation.

The Court must proceed with care when considering the whole concept of privacy expectations in communications made on electronic equipment owned by a government employer. The judiciary risks error by elaborating too fully on the Fourth Amendment implications of emerging technology before its role in society has become clear. See, e.g., Olmstead v. United States, 277 U.S. 438, 48 S.Ct. 564, 72 L.Ed. 944 (1928), overruled by Katz v. United States, 389 U.S. 347, 353, 88 S.Ct. 507, 19 L.Ed.2d 576 (1967). In Katz, the Court relied on its own knowledge and experience to conclude that there is a reasonable expectation of privacy in a telephone booth. See id., at 360–361, 88 S.Ct. 507 (Harlan, J., concurring). It is not so clear that courts at present are on so sure a ground. Prudence counsels caution before the facts in the instant case are used to establish far-reaching premises that define the existence, and extent, of privacy expectations enjoyed by employees when using employer-provided communication devices.

Rapid changes in the dynamics of communication and information transmission are evident not just in the technology itself but in what society accepts as proper behavior. As one amici brief notes, many employers expect or at least tolerate personal use of such equipment by employees because it often increases worker efficiency. See Brief for Electronic Frontier Foundation et al. 16–20. Another amicus points out that the law is beginning to respond to these developments, as some States have recently passed statutes requiring employers to notify employees when monitoring their electronic communications. See Brief for New York Intellectual Property Law Association 22 (citing Del.Code Ann., Tit. 19, § 705 (2005); Conn. Gen.Stat. Ann. § 31–48d (West 2003)). At present, it is uncertain how workplace norms, and the law's treatment of them, will evolve.

Even if the Court were certain that the O'Connor plurality's approach were the right one, the Court would have difficulty predicting how employees' privacy expectations will be shaped by those changes or the degree to which society will be prepared to recognize those expectations as reasonable. See 480 U.S., at 715, 107 S.Ct. 1492. Cell phone and text message communications are so pervasive that some persons may consider them to be essential means or necessary instruments for self-expression, even self-identification. That might strengthen the case for an expectation of privacy. On the other hand, the ubiquity of those devices has made them generally affordable, so one could counter that employees who need cell phones or similar devices for personal matters can purchase and pay for their own. And employer policies concerning communications will of course shape the reasonable expectations of their employees, especially to the extent that such policies are clearly communicated.

A broad holding concerning employees' privacy expectations vis-à-vis employer-provided technological equipment might have implications for future cases that cannot be predicted. It is preferable to dispose of this case on narrower grounds. For present purposes we assume several propositions arguendo: *First, Quon had a reasonable expectation of privacy in the text messages sent on the pager provided to him by the City; second, petitioners' review of the transcript constituted a search within the meaning of the Fourth Amendment; and third, the principles applicable to a government employer's search of an employee's physical office apply with at least the same force when the employer intrudes on the employee's privacy in the electronic sphere.*

Even if Quon had a reasonable expectation of privacy in his text messages, petitioners did not necessarily violate the Fourth Amendment by obtaining and reviewing the transcripts. Although as a general matter, warrantless searches "are per se *unreasonable under the Fourth Amendment," there are "a few specifically established and well-delineated exceptions" to that general rule.* Katz, supra, *at 357, 88 S.Ct. 507. The Court has held that the " 'special needs' " of the workplace justify one such exception.* O'Connor, 480 U.S., *at 725, 107 S.Ct. 1492 (plurality opinion); id., at 732, 107 S.Ct. 1492 (SCALIA, J., concurring in judgment);* Von Raab, 489 U.S., *at 666–667, 109 S.Ct. 1384.*

Under the approach of the O'Connor *plurality, when conducted for a "noninvestigatory, work-related purpos[e]" or for the "investigatio[n] of work-related misconduct," a government employer's warrantless search is reasonable if it is " 'justified at its inception' " and if " 'the measures adopted are reasonably related to the objectives of the search and not excessively intrusive in light of' " the circumstances giving rise to the search. 480 U.S., at 725–726, 107 S.Ct. 1492. The search here satisfied the standard of the* O'Connor *plurality and was reasonable under that approach.*

The search was justified at its inception because there were "reasonable grounds for suspecting that the search [was] necessary for a noninvestigatory work-related purpose." Id., at 726, 107 S.Ct. 1492. As a jury found, Chief Scharf ordered the search in order to determine whether the character limit on the City's contract with Arch Wireless was sufficient to meet the City's needs. This was, as the Ninth Circuit noted, a "legitimate work-related rationale." 529 F.3d, at 908. The City and OPD had a legitimate interest in ensuring that employees were not being forced to pay out of their own pockets for work-related expenses, or on the other hand that the City was not paying for extensive personal communications.

As for the scope of the search, reviewing the transcripts was reasonable because it was an efficient and expedient way to determine whether Quon's overages were the result of work-related messaging or personal use. The review was also not " 'exces-

sively intrusive.' " O'Connor, *supra, at 726, 107 S.Ct. 1492 (plurality opinion). Although Quon had gone over his monthly allotment a number of times, OPD requested transcripts for only the months of August and September 2002. While it may have been reasonable as well for OPD to review transcripts of all the months in which Quon exceeded his allowance, it was certainly reasonable for OPD to review messages for just two months in order to obtain a large enough sample to decide whether the character limits were efficacious. And it is worth noting that during his internal affairs investigation, McMahon redacted all messages Quon sent while off duty, a measure which reduced the intrusiveness of any further review of the transcripts.*

Furthermore, and again on the assumption that Quon had a reasonable expectation of privacy in the contents of his messages, the extent of an expectation is relevant to assessing whether the search was too intrusive. See Von Raab, *supra, at 671, 109 S.Ct. 1384; cf.* Vernonia School Dist. 47J v. Acton, *515 U.S. 646, 654–657, 115 S.Ct. 2386, 132 L.Ed.2d 564 (1995). Even if he could assume some level of privacy would inhere in his messages, it would not have been reasonable for Quon to conclude that his messages were in all circumstances immune from scrutiny. Quon was told that his messages were subject to auditing. As a law enforcement officer, he would or should have known that his actions were likely to come under legal scrutiny, and that this might entail an analysis of his on-the-job communications. Under the circumstances, a reasonable employee would be aware that sound management principles might require the audit of messages to determine whether the pager was being appropriately used. Given that the City issued the pagers to Quon and other SWAT Team members in order to help them more quickly respond to crises-and given that Quon had received no assurances of privacy-Quon could have anticipated that it might be necessary for the City to audit pager messages to assess the SWAT Team's performance in particular emergency situations.*

From OPD's perspective, the fact that Quon likely had only a limited privacy expectation, with boundaries that we need not here explore, lessened the risk that the review would intrude on highly private details of Quon's life. OPD's audit of messages on Quon's employer-provided pager was not nearly as intrusive as a search of his personal e-mail account or pager, or a wiretap on his home phone line, would have been. That the search did reveal intimate details of Quon's life does not make it unreasonable, for under the circumstances a reasonable employer would not expect that such a review would intrude on such matters. The search was permissible in its scope.

The Court of Appeals erred in finding the search unreasonable. It pointed to a "host of simple ways to verify the efficacy of the 25,000 character limit . . . without intruding on [respondents'] Fourth Amendment rights." 529 F.3d, at 909. The panel suggested that Scharf "could have warned Quon that for the month of September he was forbidden from using his pager for personal communications, and that the contents of all his messages would be reviewed to ensure the pager was used only for work-related purposes during that time frame. Alternatively, if [OPD] wanted to review past usage, it could have asked Quon to count the characters himself, or asked him to redact personal messages and grant permission to [OPD] to review the redacted transcript." Ibid.

This approach was inconsistent with controlling precedents. This Court has "repeatedly refused to declare that only the 'least intrusive' search practicable can be reasonable under the Fourth Amendment."Vernonia, supra, at 663, 115 S.Ct. 2386; see also, e.g., Board of Ed. of Independent School Dist. No. 92 of Pottawatomie Cty. v. Earls, 536 U.S. 822, 837, 122 S.Ct. 2559, 153 L.Ed.2d 735 (2002); Illinois v. Lafayette, 462 U.S. 640, 647, 103 S.Ct. 2605, 77 L.Ed.2d 65 (1983). That rationale "could raise insuperable barriers to the exercise of virtually all search-and-seizure powers," United States v. Martinez-Fuerte, 428 U.S. 543, 557, n. 12, 96 S.Ct. 3074, 49 L.Ed.2d 1116 (1976), because "judges engaged in post hoc evaluations of government conduct can almost always imagine some alternative means by which the objectives of the government might have been accomplished," Skinner, 489 U.S., at 629, n. 9, 109 S.Ct. 1402 (internal quotation marks and brackets omitted). The analytic errors of the Court of Appeals in this case illustrate the necessity of this principle. Even assuming there were ways that OPD could have performed the search that would have been less intrusive, it does not follow that the search as conducted was unreasonable.

Respondents argue that the search was per se unreasonable in light of the Court of Appeals' conclusion that Arch Wireless violated the SCA by giving the City the transcripts of Quon's text messages. The merits of the SCA claim are not before us. But even if the Court of Appeals was correct to conclude that the SCA forbade Arch Wireless from turning over the transcripts, it does not follow that petitioners' actions were unreasonable. Respondents point to no authority for the proposition that the existence of statutory protection renders a search per se unreasonable under the Fourth Amendment. And the precedents counsel otherwise. See Virginia v. Moore, 553 U.S. 164, 168, 128 S.Ct. 1598, 170 L.Ed.2d 559 (2008) (search incident to an arrest that was illegal under state law was reasonable); California v. Greenwood, 486 U.S. 35, 43, 108 S.Ct. 1625, 100 L.Ed.2d 30 (1988) (rejecting argument that if state law forbade police search of individual's garbage the search would violate the Fourth Amendment). Furthermore, respondents do not maintain that any OPD employee either violated the law him or herself or knew or should have known that Arch Wireless, by turning over the transcript, would have violated the law. The otherwise reasonable search by OPD is not rendered unreasonable by the assumption that Arch Wireless violated the SCA by turning over the transcripts.

Because the search was motivated by a legitimate work-related purpose, and because it was not excessive in scope, the search was reasonable under the approach of the O'Connor plurality. 480 U.S., at 726, 107 S.Ct. 1492. For these same reasons-that the employer had a legitimate reason for the search, and that the search was not excessively intrusive in light of that justification-the Court also concludes that the search would be "regarded as reasonable and normal in the private-employer context" and would satisfy the approach of Justice SCALIA's concurrence. Id., at 732, 107 S.Ct. 1492. The search was reasonable, and the Court of Appeals erred by holding to the contrary. Petitioners did not violate Quon's Fourth Amendment rights.

Finally, the Court must consider whether the search violated the Fourth Amendment rights of Jerilyn Quon, Florio, and Trujillo, the respondents who sent text messages to Jeff Quon. Petitioners and respondents disagree whether a sender of a text message can have a reasonable expectation of privacy in a message he knowingly sends to someone's employer-provided pager. It is not necessary to resolve this question in order to dispose of the case, however. Respondents argue that because "the search was unreasonable as to Sergeant Quon, it was also unreasonable as to his correspondents." Brief for Respondents 60 (some capitalization omitted; boldface deleted). They make no corollary argument that the search, if reasonable as to Quon, could nonetheless be unreasonable as to Quon's correspondents. See id., at 65–66. In light of this litigating position and the Court's conclusion that the search was reasonable as to Jeff Quon, it necessarily follows that these other respondents cannot prevail.

Because the search was reasonable, petitioners did not violate respondents' Fourth Amendment rights, and the court below erred by concluding otherwise. The judgment of the Court of Appeals for the Ninth Circuit is reversed, and the case is remanded for further proceedings consistent with this opinion.

As with the *Smith v. Pillsbury* case above, the Supreme Court in *Quon* begins its analysis with the question whether Quon would have a "reasonable expectation of privacy" in his workplace-issued pager. The Court declines to set a general policy with regard to employer-issued technology, choosing instead a fact-based determination of the existence of that expectation. The next stage in the Court's analysis, though, is where the public versus private workplace distinction is critical. In a private workplace, as with Pillsbury, assuming the existence of a reasonable expectation of privacy, that expectation is balanced against the legitimate needs of the company in determining whether the monitoring in question violated employee's privacy. Quon, though, works for a governmental body, which is subject to the restrictions on search and warrant requirements of the Fourth Amendment. As per traditional Fourth Amendment jurisprudence, if the search was unreasonable or, even if reasonable, a warrant were required but not obtained by the body (in this case the employer) performing the search, any evidence obtained through the search would be inadmissible under the Exclusionary Rule.

In the *Quon* case, the Supreme Court notes the existence of and applies an exception to the general warrant requirement: the " 'special needs' of the workplace' " doctrine of the plurality in *O'Connor v. Ortega*.[13] Pursuant to the *O'Connor* analysis, the Court determines that Quon's employer, the Ontario, CA police department, had a legitimate need to determine whether its department-issued and — funded equipment was being used for proper, job-related purposes, and its monitoring of Quon's messages to evaluate whether they were personal or professional. Although the lower courts indicated that there were other, less-intrusive means than that used by the Ontario Police Department (requesting copies of the actual messages from the telecom provider, Arch Wireless), the actions of the department were not "excessive in scope" and were reasonable, and therefore fit within the *O'Connor* exception to the warrant requirement. Having determined that no warrant was needed, the Court overturned the Court of Appeals' decision and rejected Quon's Fourth Amendment claim against the department.

---

[13] 480 U.S. 709 (1987).

c. An Outside View: Monitoring Employees' Personal Activities

Employers have gone beyond monitoring their employees' electronic activities within the work place or using work-issued equipment. In recent years, companies have begun tracking their employees' (and evaluating prospective employees') online behavior outside of the workplace as well. For many companies, the driving concern behind their following workers who are "off the clock" is the possibility that what those employees do in their online personal lives can and will negatively impact on the company itself. The risks to the company may include everything from reputational damage to breaches of confidentiality to regulatory violations to litigation, and certain industries may be more vulnerable to such claims, and therefore more likely to monitor their employees' online actions, than others.

One relatively early, well publicized situation of employer monitoring of personal Internet use involved Michael Hanscom, who in October 2003 was a temporary worker for Microsoft in Redmond, WA. Hanscom was also a blogger and, when he happened to note a shipment of Apple G5 Mac computers outside a Microsoft loading dock, he was sufficiently amused by the seeming irony of Apple computers being purchased by the publisher of Windows that he posted a photo of the shipment on his Eclecticism blog with the title, "Even Microsoft Wants G5s."[14] A few days later, Hanscom was called into a manager's office at Microsoft and, after being asked about and confirming that he had posted the photo to his blog, was summarily fired for violating Microsoft's security policy.[15] Hanscom's experience garnered a great deal of press and attention, as he chronicled in a subsequent blog post.[16] This type of situation has become much more commonplace in recent years,[17] as demonstrated by the number of resources for workers explaining what they should (not) and may (not) do with their personal blogs.[18]

---

[14] Michael Hanscom, Even Microsoft Wants G5s — Eclecticism, http://www.michaelhanscom.com/eclecticism/2003/10/23/even-microsoft-wants-g5s/ (last visited May 8, 2012).

[15] Michael Hanscom, Of Blogging and Unemployment — Eclecticism, http://www.michaelhanscom.com/eclecticism/2003/10/27/of-blogging-and-unemployment/ (last visited May 8, 2012).

[16] Michael Hanscom, Fifteen Minutes of Fame — Eclecticism, http://www.michaelhanscom.com/eclecticism/2003/10/29/fifteen-minutes-of-fame/ (last visited May 8, 2012).

[17] Flight attendant Ellen Simonetti was dismissed by Delta Air Lines in late 2004 for posting "provocative pictures of herself in her Delta uniform" on her personal blog, "Diary of a Flight Attendant." Christine Negroni, The New York Times > Business > Business Travel: Fired Flight Attendant Finds Blogs Can Backfire, The New York Times (Nov. 16, 2004), http://www.nytimes.com/2004/11/16/business/16pose.html (last visited May 8, 2012). In 2008, Chez Pazienza, then a producer for CNN's American Morning, reported that he had been fired after his personal blogging was deemed by CNN to be a violation of its employee handbook's rules about writing for a "non-CNN outlet." Deus Ex Malcontent: Say What You Will (Requiem for a TV News Career), http://www.deusexmalcontent.com/2008/02/say-what-you-will-requiem-for-tv-news.html (last visited May 8, 2012).

[18] See, e.g., How to Blog Safely (About Work or Anything Else) | Electronic Frontier Foundation, https://www.eff.org/wp/blog-safely (last visited May 8, 2012); 10 Ways to Get Fired for Building Your Personal Brand | Personal Branding Blog - Dan Schawbel, http://www.personalbrandingblog.com/10-ways-to-get-fired-for-building-your-personal-brand/ (last visited May 8, 2012); Fired For Blogging | Nolo.com, http://www.nolo.com/legal-encyclopedia/fired-blogging-29762.html (last visited May 8, 2012).

On the social media side, Twitter has been a particularly popular source for employers seeking information on what their employees are saying online, largely because Twitter is almost entirely public: unless a user specifically protects her tweets (making them viewable only to expressly approved followers), they can be readily searched not only through the Twitter site itself but using third-party search engines such as Topsy.com. This enables employers to track employees' Twitter activity without necessarily revealing the monitoring through a follow or friend request. Twitter also provides powerful filtering tools that enable constantly running Boolean searches; a company can use its own brand and product names as search terms and discover not only what customers are saying, but those instances when employees mention their employer or its products in posts. Employers may use this access to discipline or dismiss employees or others associated with the company when their tweets are deemed to damage the business.

Employers, in fact, may feel obligated to monitor their employees off-hour tweets, in order not to be blindsided when others see, and publicize, them first. In 2011, in the aftermath of the devastating Japanese earthquake and subsequent tsunami, the comedian Gilbert Gottfried posted a number of jokes about Japan's experience to Twitter.[19] Unfortunately, Gottfried was a well-known public face (or rather, voice) for the insurance company AFLAC, having done it numerous commercials for the insurer as the voice of the company's "spokesduck." AFLAC, however, does a great deal of its business in Japan and Gottfried's comments were sufficiently disturbing to the company that it fired him from his voiceover role.[20] Similar incidents of embarrassing tweets being publicized and leading to termination in 2011 alone included a profanity-laden message in the official Chrysler Twitter account,[21] three legislative assistance to Democratic Congressman Rick Larsen tweeting negatively about Larsen and their jobs,[22] and Mixed Martial Arts fighter Miguel Torres tweeting, "If a rape van was called a surprise van more women wouldn't mind going for rides in them. Everyone likes surprises."[23] Personal Facebook use has also led to well-publicized terminations.[24]

---

[19] Josh Grossberg, GILBERT GOTTFRIED APOLOGIZES FOR JAPAN CRACK — IS GLENN BECK NEXT? - E! ONLINE (Mar. 15, 2011), http://www.eonline.com/news/gilbert_gottfried_apologizes_japan/231100#ixzz1Ghe6yLB4 (last visited May 8, 2012).

[20] Chloe Albanesius, AFLAC FIRES COMEDIAN GOTTFRIED OVER INSENSITIVE JAPAN TWITTER COMMENTS | NEWS & OPINION | PCMAG.COM (Mar. 15, 2011), http://www.pcmag.com/article2/0,2817,2382040,00.asp (last visited May 8, 2012); PRESS RELEASES, http://www.aflac.com/aboutaflac/pressroom/pressreleasestory.aspx?rid=153 9090 (last visited May 8, 2012).

[21] MAN FIRED OVER OBSCENE CHRYSLER TWEET IS SORRY - BUSINESS — AUTOS — MSNBC.COM, http://www.msnbc.msn.com/id/42132041/ns/business-autos/t/man-fired-over-obscene-chrysler-tweet-sorry/ (last visited May 8, 2012); this incident also led to Chrysler's declining to renew its contract with the media agency that had run its account.

[22] HILL STAFFERS FIRED IN TWITTER FLAP — MARIN COGAN AND JONATHAN ALLEN — POLITICO.COM (Dec. 9, 2011), http://www.politico.com/news/stories/1211/70116.html (last visited May 8, 2012).

[23] Anna North, MMA FIGHTER FIRED FOR TWEETING GROSS "RAPE VAN" JOKE, http://jezebel.com/5866657/mma-fighter-fired-for-tweeting-gross-rape-van-joke (last visited May 8, 2012).

[24] Dylan Love, 17 PEOPLE WHO WERE FIRED FOR USING FACEBOOK — BUSINESS INSIDER (May 11, 2011), http://www.businessinsider.com/facebook-fired-2011-5 (last visited May 8, 2012).

Beyond mere reputational issues, companies may be monitoring employees' tweets and other social media postings to ensure compliance with regulatory requirements. The retention requirements for customer communications in the financial services industry,[25] the healthcare privacy requirements of HIPAA,[26] and the FTC's revised Guides Concerning the Use of Endorsements and Testimonials in Advertising[27] may all impose liability on a company for improper disclosure by employees via social networks; managing these risks includes proactively watching for such disclosures. Businesses may also be required to access employees' home computers and other personal devices in the context of a litigation, if information requested as part of discovery may be found on those devices (as when employees work from home or use personal technology to communicate with the office or customers).[28]

A related question is whether employers may require current or prospective employees to disclose not only the existence of personal social media accounts, but even the passwords to access those accounts. Companies may seek to do so to determine whether there may be content in the accounts that poses a risk to the business and that is initially non-public, available only to approved "friends" or followers, but that could be forwarded by those private connections to the greater public. Although the services themselves may prohibit sharing one's credentials with employers or other third parties,[29] there may be little they can do to detect such sharing, leaving the issue to users to self-administer.

To the extent that an employer accesses a specific employee's personal electronic communications without that employee's consent, it could potentially violate portions of the federal Electronic Communications Privacy Act,[30] as well as collective bargaining and other labor laws. Whether such violations have occurred, though, will depend on relevant facts, including whether the communications were via a shared service to which the employer might have received authorized access from another user:

---

[25] *See supra* Chapter 2, note 140.

[26] *See* Chapter Five:.

[27] FTC, GUIDES CONCERNING THE USE OF ENDORSEMENTS AND TESTIMONIALS IN ADVERTISING, http://www.ftc.gov/os/2009/10/091005revisedendorsementguides.pdf.

[28] *See, e.g.*, Conrad Jacoby, DISCOVERY OF EMPLOYEE-OWNED COMPUTER EQUIPMENT | LLRX.COM, http://www.llrx.com/columns/fios22.htm (last visited May 8, 2012).

[29] *See, e.g.*, FACEBOOK'S LATEST NEWS, ANNOUNCEMENTS AND MEDIA RESOURCES — NEWS — PROTECTING YOUR PASSWORDS AND YOUR PRIVACY — FACEBOOK, http://newsroom.fb.com/News/Protecting-Your-Passwords-and-Your-Privacy-134.aspx (last visited May 8, 2012) (Facebook announcing it has made sharing a password a violation of its Statement of Rights and Responsibilities). *See also* Manuel Valdes & Shannon McFarland, EMPLOYERS ASK JOB SEEKERS FOR FACEBOOK PASSWORDS — BUSINESSWEEK, http://www.businessweek.com/ap/2012-03/D9TKDKIO2.htm (last visited May 8, 2012); BLUMENTHAL, SCHUMER: EMPLOYER DEMANDS FOR FACEBOOK AND EMAIL PASSWORDS AS PRECONDITION FOR JOB INTERVIEWS MAY BE A VIOLATION OF FEDERAL LAW; SENATORS ASK FEDS TO INVESTIGATE | PRESS RELEASES | UNITED STATES SENATOR RICHARD BLUMENTHAL, http://blumenthal.senate.gov/newsroom/press/release/blumenthal-schumer-employer-demands-for-facebook-and-email-passwords-as-precondition-for-job-interviews-may-be-a-violation-of-federal-law-senators-ask-feds-to-investigate (last visited May 8, 2012) (Senators Richard Blumenthal and Charles Schumer requesting investigation of password requests by employers).

[30] See discussion of ECPA in Chapter 3:I.

KONOP v. HAWAIIAN AIRLINES[31]

OPINION

Boochever, Circuit Judge.

Robert Konop brought suit against his employer, Hawaiian Airlines, Inc. ("Hawaiian"), alleging that Hawaiian viewed Konop's secure website without authorization, disclosed the contents of that website, and took other related actions in violation of the federal Wiretap Act, the Stored Communications Act, and the Railway Labor Act. Konop also alleged several state tort claims. The district court granted summary judgment against Konop on all claims, except his retaliation claim under the Railway Labor Act. On the retaliation claim, the district court entered judgment against Konop following a bench trial. Konop appeals the district court's judgement on all claims, except on those brought under state tort law.

On January 8, 2001, we issued an opinion, reversing the district court's decision on Konop's claims under the Wiretap Act and the Stored Communications Act, and on several of his claims under the Railway Labor Act. Konop v. Hawaiian Airlines, Inc., 236 F.3d 1035 (9th Cir.2001). Hawaiian filed a petition for rehearing, which became moot when we withdrew our previous opinion. Konop v. Hawaiian Airlines, Inc., 262 F.3d 972 (9th Cir.2001). We now affirm the judgment of the district court with respect to Konop's Wiretap Act claims and his retaliation claim under the Railway Labor Act. We reverse the district court's judgment with respect to Konop's claims under the Stored Communications Act and his remaining claims under the Railway Labor Act.

FACTS

Konop, a pilot for Hawaiian, created and maintained a website where he posted bulletins critical of his employer, its officers, and the incumbent union, Air Line Pilots Association ("ALPA"). Many of those criticisms related to Konop's opposition to labor concessions which Hawaiian sought from ALPA. Because ALPA supported the concessions, Konop, via his website, encouraged Hawaiian employees to consider alternative union representation.

Konop controlled access to his website by requiring visitors to log in with a user name and password. He created a list of people, mostly pilots and other employees of Hawaiian, who were eligible to access the website. Pilots Gene Wong and James Gardner were included on this list. Konop programmed the website to allow access when a person entered the name of an eligible person, created a password, and clicked the "SUBMIT" button on the screen, indicating acceptance of the terms and conditions of use. These terms and conditions prohibited any member of Hawaiian's management from viewing the website and prohibited users from disclosing the website's contents to anyone else.

In December 1995, Hawaiian vice president James Davis asked Wong for permis-

---

[31] 302 F.3d 868 (9th Cir. 2002).

sion to use Wong's name to access Konop's website. Wong agreed. Davis claimed he was concerned about untruthful allegations that he believed Konop was making on the website. Wong had not previously logged into the website to create an account. When Davis accessed the website using Wong's name, he presumably typed in Wong's name, created a password, and clicked the "SUBMIT" button indicating acceptance of the terms and conditions.

Later that day, Konop received a call from the union chairman of ALPA, Reno Morella.1 Morella told Konop that Hawaiian president Bruce Nobles had contacted him regarding the contents of Konop's website. Morella related that Nobles was upset by Konop's accusations that Nobles was suspected of fraud and by other disparaging statements published on the website. From this conversation with Morella, Konop believed Nobles had obtained the contents of his website and was threatening to sue Konop for defamation based on statements contained on the website.

After speaking with Morella, Konop took his website offline for the remainder of the day. He placed it back online the next morning, however, without knowing how Nobles had obtained the information discussed in the phone call. Konop claims to have learned only later from the examination of system logs that Davis had accessed the website using Wong's name.

In the meantime, Davis continued to view the website using Wong's name. Later, Davis also logged in with the name of another pilot, Gardner, who had similarly consented to Davis' use of his name. Through April 1996, Konop claims that his records indicate that Davis logged in over twenty times as Wong, and that Gardner or Davis logged in at least fourteen more times as Gardner.

Konop filed suit alleging claims under the federal Wiretap Act, the Stored Communications Act, the Railway Labor Act, and state tort law, arising from Davis' viewing and use of Konop's secure website. Konop also alleged that Hawaiian placed him on medical suspension in retaliation for his opposition to the proposed labor concessions, in violation of the Railway Labor Act. The district court granted summary judgment to Hawaiian on all but the retaliatory suspension claim, and entered judgment against Konop on that claim after a short bench trial.

Konop appeals, arguing that the district court erred in granting summary judgment to Hawaiian on his federal claims under the Wiretap Act, Stored Communications Act, and Railway Labor Act. In addition, Konop urges us to reverse the district court's judgment on the retaliation claim following the bench trial, because he claims the district court improperly quashed subpoenas for witnesses Konop sought to have testify at trial.

DISCUSSION

The district court's grant of summary judgment is reviewed de novo. Lopez v. Smith, *203 F.3d 1122, 1131 (9th Cir.2000) (en banc). Viewing the evidence in the light most favorable to Konop, we must determine whether there are any genuine issues of material fact and whether the district court correctly applied the relevant substantive law.* Id.

I. Electronic Communications Privacy Act Claims

We first turn to the difficult task of determining whether Hawaiian violated either the Wiretap Act, 18 U.S.C. §§ 2510-2522 (2000) or the Stored Communications Act, 18 U.S.C. §§ 2701–2711 (2000),2 when Davis accessed Konop's secure website. In 1986, Congress passed the Electronic Communications Privacy Act (ECPA), Pub.L. No. 99-508, 100 Stat. 1848, which was intended to afford privacy protection to electronic communications. Title I of the ECPA amended the federal Wiretap Act, which previously addressed only wire and oral communications, to "address[ ] the interception of . . . electronic communications." S.Rep. No. 99-541, at 3 (1986), reprinted in 1986 U.S.C.C.A.N. 3555, 3557. Title II of the ECPA created the Stored Communications Act (SCA), which was designed to "address[ ] access to stored wire and electronic communications and transactional records." Id.

As we have previously observed, the intersection of these two statutes "is a complex, often convoluted, area of the law." United States v. Smith, 155 F.3d 1051, 1055 (9th Cir.1998). In the present case, the difficulty is compounded by the fact that the ECPA was written prior to the advent of the Internet and the World Wide Web. As a result, the existing statutory framework is ill-suited to address modern forms of communication like Konop's secure website. Courts have struggled to analyze problems involving modern technology within the confines of this statutory framework, often with unsatisfying results. See. e.g., Robert A. Pikowsky, Legal and Technological Issues Surrounding Privacy of Attorney Client Communication Via Email, Advocate, Oct. 2000, at 17–19 (discussing the uncertainty over email privacy caused by the ECPA and judicial interpretations thereof); Lieutenant Colonel LeEllen Coacher, Permitting Systems Protection Monitoring: When the Government Can Look and What It Can See, 46 A.F. L.Rev. 155, 171–74 (1999) (same); Tatsuya Akamine, Note, Proposal for a Fair Statutory Interpretation: E-mail Stored in a Service Provider Computer Is Subject to an Interception Under the Federal Wiretap Act, 7 J.L. Pol'y 519, 521–29, 561–68 (1999) (criticizing the judiciary's interpretation of the ECPA). We observe that until Congress brings the laws in line with modern technology, protection of the Internet and websites such as Konop's will remain a confusing and uncertain area of the law.

A. The Internet and Secure Websites

The Internet is an international network of interconnected computers that allows millions of people to communicate and exchange information. See Reno v. ACLU, 521 U.S. 844, 849–50, 117 S.Ct. 2329, 138 L.Ed.2d 874 (1997); In re DoubleClick Inc. Privacy Litig., 154 F.Supp.2d 497, 501 (S.D.N.Y.2001). The World Wide Web, the best known category of communication over the Internet, consists of a vast number of electronic documents stored in different computers all over the world. Reno v. ACLU, 521 U.S. at 852, 117 S.Ct. 2329. Any person or organization with a computer connected to the Internet can "publish" information on the Web in the form of a "web page" or "website." See id. at 853 & n. 9, 95 S.Ct. 2051. A website consists of electronic information stored by a hosting service computer or "server." The owner of the website may pay a fee for this service. Each website has a unique domain name or web address (e.g., Amazon.com or Lycos.com), which corresponds to a specific location within the server where the electronic information comprising the website is stored. A person who wishes to view the website types the domain name into a computer connected to the Internet. This is essentially a request to the server to make an electronic copy of the website (or at least the first page or "home page") and send it to the user's computer. After this electronic information reaches the user's computer, it is downloaded for viewing on the user's screen. See generally *Preston Gralla,* How the Internet Works *(1999).*

While most websites are public, many, such as Konop's, are restricted. For instance, some websites are password-protected, require a social security number, or require the user to purchase access by entering a credit card number. See Reno, 521 U.S. at 852–53, 856, 117 S.Ct. 2329. The legislative history of the ECPA suggests that Congress wanted to protect electronic communications that are configured to be private, such as email and private electronic bulletin boards. See S.Rep. No. 99-541, at 35–36, 1986 U.S.C.C.A.N. at 3599 ("This provision [the SCA] addresses the growing problem of unauthorized persons deliberately gaining access to . . . electronic or wire communications that are not intended to be available to the public."); H.R.Rep. No. 99-647 at 41, 62–63 (1986) (describing the Committee's understanding that the configuration of the electronic communications system would determine whether or not an electronic communication was readily accessible to the public). The nature of the Internet, however, is such that if a user enters the appropriate information (password, social security number, etc.), it is nearly impossible to verify the true identity of that user. Cf. Reno, 521 U.S. at 855–56, 117 S.Ct. 2329 (discussing the difficulty of verifying the age of a website user by requiring a credit card number or password).

We are confronted with such a situation here. Although Konop took certain steps to restrict the access of Davis and other managers to the website,3 Davis was nevertheless able to access the website by entering the correct information, which was freely provided to Davis by individuals who were eligible to view the website.

B. Wiretap Act

Konop argues that Davis' conduct constitutes an interception of an electronic communication in violation of the

Wiretap Act. The Wiretap Act makes it an offense to "intentionally intercept [ ] . . . any wire, oral, or electronic communication." 18 U.S.C. § 2511(1)(a). We must therefore determine whether Konop's website is an "electronic communication" and, if so, whether Davis "intercepted" that communication.

An "electronic communication" is defined as "any transfer of signs, signals, writing, images, sounds, data, or intelligence of any nature transmitted in whole or in part by a wire, radio, electromagnetic, photoelectronic or photooptical system." Id. § 2510(12). As discussed above, website owners such as Konop transmit electronic documents to servers, where the documents are stored. If a user wishes to view the website, the user requests that the server transmit a copy of the document to the user's computer. When the server sends the document to the user's computer for viewing, a transfer of information from the website owner to the user has occurred. Although the website owner's document does not go directly or immediately to the user, once a user accesses a website, information is transferred from the website owner to the user via one of the specified mediums. We therefore conclude that Konop's website fits the definition of "electronic communication."

The Wiretap Act, however, prohibits only "interceptions" of electronic communications. "Intercept" is defined as "the aural or other acquisition of the contents of any wire, electronic, or oral communication through the use of any electronic, mechanical, or other device." Id. § 2510(4). Standing alone, this definition would seem to suggest that an individual "intercepts" an electronic communication merely by "acquiring" its contents, regardless of when or under what circumstances the acquisition occurs. Courts, however, have clarified that Congress intended a narrower definition of "intercept" with regard to electronic communications.

In Steve Jackson Games, Inc. v. United States Secret Service, *36 F.3d 457 (5th Cir.1994), the Fifth Circuit held that the government's acquisition of email messages stored on an electronic bulletin board system, but not yet retrieved by the intended recipients, was not an "interception" under the Wiretap Act. The court observed that, prior to the enactment of the ECPA, the word "intercept" had been interpreted to mean the acquisition of a communication contemporaneous with transmission. Id. at 460 (citing United States v. Turk, 526 F.2d 654, 658 (5th Cir.1976)). The court further observed that Congress, in passing the ECPA, intended to retain the previous definition of "intercept" with respect to wire and oral communications,4 while amending the Wiretap Act to cover interceptions of electronic communications. See Steve Jackson Games, 36 F.3d at 462; S.Rep. No. 99-541, at 13; H.R.Rep. No. 99-647, at 34. The court reasoned, however, that the word "intercept" could not describe the exact same conduct with respect to wire and electronic communications, because wire and electronic communications were defined differently in the statute. Specifically, the term "wire communication" was defined to include storage of the communication, while "electronic communication" was not.5 The court concluded that this textual difference evidenced Congress' understanding that, although one could "intercept" a* wire *communication in storage, one could not "intercept" an* electronic *communication in storage:*

Critical to the issue before us is the fact that, unlike the definition of "wire communication," the definition of "electronic communication" does not include electronic storage of such communications . . . . Congress' use of the word "transfer" in the definition of "electronic communication," and its omission in that definition of the phrase "any electronic storage of such communication" . . . reflects that Congress did not intend for "intercept" to apply to "electronic communications" when those communications are in "electronic storage."

Steve Jackson Games, *36 F.3d at 461–62*; Wesley Coll. v. Pitts, *974 F.Supp. 375, 386 (D.Del.1997) ("[B]y including the electronic storage of wire communications within the definition of such communications but declining to do the same for electronic communications . . . Congress sufficiently evinced its intent to make acquisitions of electronic communications unlawful under the Wiretap Act only if they occur contemporaneously with their transmissions."), aff'd, 172 F.3d 861 (3d Cir.1998);* United States v. Reyes, *922 F.Supp. 818, 836 (S.D.N.Y.1996) ("Taken together, the definitions thus imply a requirement that the acquisition of[electronic communica-*

tions] be simultaneous with the original transmission of the data."); Bohach v. City of Reno, *932 F.Supp. 1232, 1236–37 (D.Nev.1996) (requiring acquisition during transmission).* The Steve Jackson *Court further noted that the ECPA was deliberately structured to afford electronic communications* in storage *less protection than other forms of communication.* See Steve Jackson Games, *36 F.3d at 462–64.*

The Ninth Circuit endorsed the reasoning of Steve Jackson Games *in* United States v. Smith, *155 F.3d at 1051. The question presented in* Smith *was whether the Wiretap Act covered wire communications in storage, such as voice mail messages, or just wire communications in transmission, such as ongoing telephone conversations. Relying on the same textual distinction as the Fifth Circuit in* Steve Jackson Games, *we concluded that wire communications in storage could be "intercepted" under the Wiretap Act. We found that Congress' inclusion of storage in the definition of "wire communication" militated in favor of a broad definition of the term "intercept" with respect to wire communications, one that included acquisition of a communication subsequent to transmission. We further observed that,* with respect to wire communications only, *the prior definition of "intercept" — acquisition contemporaneous with transmission-had been overruled by the ECPA.* Smith, *155 F.3d at 1057 n. 11. On the other hand, we suggested that the narrower definition of "intercept" was still appropriate with regard to electronic communications:*

[I]n cases concerning "electronic communications" — the definition of which specifically includes "transfers" and specifically excludes "storage" — the "narrow" definition of "intercept" fits like a glove; it is natural to except non-contemporaneous retrievals from the scope of the Wiretap Act. In fact, a number of courts adopting the narrow interpretation of "interception" have specifically premised their decisions to do so on the distinction between § 2510's definitions of wire and electronic communications.

Smith, *155 F.3d at 1057 (citations and alterations omitted).*

We agree with the Steve Jackson *and* Smith *courts that the narrow definition of "intercept" applies to electronic communications. Notably, Congress has since amended the Wiretap Act to eliminate storage from the definition of wire communication, see USA PATRIOT Act § 209, 115 Stat. at 283, such that the textual distinction relied upon by the* Steve Jackson *and* Smith *courts no longer exists. This change, however, supports the analysis of those cases. By eliminating storage from the definition of wire communication, Congress essentially reinstated the pre-ECPA definition of "intercept" — acquisition contemporaneous with transmission-with respect to wire communications. See* Smith, *155 F.3d at 1057 n. 11. The purpose of the recent amendment was to reduce protection of voice mail messages to the lower level of protection provided other electronically stored communications. See H.R. Rep. 107-236(I), at 158–59 (2001). When Congress passed the USA PATRIOT Act, it was aware of the narrow definition courts had given the term "intercept" with respect to electronic communications, but chose not to change or modify that definition. To the contrary, it modified the statute to make that definition applicable to voice mail messages as well. Congress, therefore, accepted and implicitly approved the judicial definition of "intercept" as acquisition contemporaneous with transmission.*

We therefore hold that for a website such as Konop's to be "intercepted" in violation of the Wiretap Act, it must be acquired during transmission, not while it is in electronic storage.6 This conclusion is consistent with the ordinary meaning of "intercept," which is "to stop, seize, or interrupt in progress or course before arrival." Webster's Ninth New Collegiate Dictionary *630 (1985). More importantly, it is consistent with the structure of the ECPA, which created the SCA for the express purpose of addressing "access to stored . . . electronic communications and transactional records." S.Rep. No. 99-541 at 3 (emphasis added). The level of protection provided stored communications under the SCA is considerably less than that provided communications covered by the Wiretap Act. Section 2703(a) of the SCA details the procedures law enforcement must follow to access the contents of stored electronic communications, but these procedures are considerably less burdensome and less restrictive than those required to obtain a wiretap order under the Wiretap Act. See Steve Jackson Games, 36 F.3d at 463. Thus, if Konop's position were correct and acquisition of a stored electronic communication were an interception under the Wiretap Act, the government would have to comply with the more burdensome, more restrictive procedures of the Wiretap Act to do exactly what Congress apparently authorized it to do under the less burdensome procedures of the SCA. Congress could not have intended this result. As the Fifth Circuit recognized in* Steve Jackson Games, *"it is most unlikely that Congress intended to require law enforcement officers to satisfy the more stringent requirements for an intercept in order to gain access to the contents of stored electronic communications." Id.; see also Wesley Coll., 974 F.Supp. at 388 (same).*

Because we conclude that Davis' conduct did not constitute an "interception" of an electronic communication in violation of the Wiretap Act, we affirm the district court's grant of summary judgment against Konop on his Wiretap Act claims.7

C. Stored Communications Act

Konop also argues that, by viewing his secure website, Davis accessed a stored electronic communication without authorization in violation of the SCA. The SCA makes it an offense to "intentionally access[ ] without authorization a facility through which an electronic communication service is provided . . . and thereby obtain[ ] . . . access to a wire or electronic communication while it is in electronic storage in such system." 18 U.S.C. § 2701(a)(1). The SCA excepts from liability, however, "conduct authorized . . . by a user of that service with respect to a communication of or intended for that user." 18 U.S.C. § 2701(c)(2). The district court found that the exception in § 2701(c)(2) applied because Wong and Gardner consented to Davis' use of Konop's website. It therefore granted summary judgment to Hawaiian on the SCA claim.

The parties agree that the relevant "electronic communications service" is Konop's website, and that the website was in "electronic storage." In addition, for the purposes of this opinion, we accept the parties' assumption that Davis' conduct constituted "access without authorization" 8 to "a facility through which an electronic communication service is provided."

We therefore address only the narrow question of whether the district court properly found Hawaiian exempt from liability under § 2701(c)(2). Section 2701(c)(2) allows a person to authorize a third party's access to an electronic communication if the person is 1) a "user" of the "service" and 2) the communication is "of or intended for that user." See 18 U.S.C. § 2701(c)(2). A "user" is "any person or entity who — (A) uses an electronic communications service; and (B) is duly authorized by the provider of such service to engage in such use." 18 U.S.C. § 2510(13).

The district court concluded that Wong and Gardner had the authority under § 2701(c)(2) to consent to Davis' use of the website because Konop put Wong and Gardner on the list of eligible users. This conclusion is consistent with other parts of the Wiretap Act and the SCA which allow intended recipients of wire and electronic communications to authorize third parties to access those communications.9 In addition, there is some indication in the legislative history that Congress believed "addressees" or "intended recipients" of electronic communications would have the authority under the SCA to allow third parties access to those communications. See *H.R.Rep. No. 99-647, at 66–67 (explaining that "an addressee [of an electronic communication] may consent to the disclosure of a communication to any other person" and that "[a] person may be an 'intended recipient' of a communication . . . even if he is not individually identified by name or otherwise").*

Nevertheless, the plain language of § 2701(c)(2) indicates that only a "user" of the service can authorize a third party's access to the communication. The statute defines "user" as one who 1) uses the service and 2) is duly authorized to do so. Because the statutory language is unambiguous, it must control our construction of the statute, notwithstanding the legislative history. See United States v. Daas, *198 F.3d 1167, 1174 (9th Cir.1999). The statute does not define the word "use," so we apply the ordinary definition, which is "to put into action or service, avail oneself of, employ."* Webster's *at 1299;* see Daas, *198 F.3d at 1174 ("If the statute uses a term which it does not define, the court gives that term its ordinary meaning.").*

Based on the common definition of the word "use," we cannot find any evidence in the record that Wong ever used Konop's website. There is some evidence, however, that Gardner may have used the website, but it is unclear when that use occurred. At any rate, the district court did not make any findings on whether Wong and Gardner actually used Konop's website-it simply assumed that Wong and Gardner, by virtue of being eligible to view the website, could authorize Davis' access. The problem with this approach is that it essentially reads the "user" requirement out of § 2701(c)(2). Taking the facts in the light most favorable to Konop, we must assume that neither Wong nor Gardner was a "user" of the website at the time he authorized Davis to view it. We therefore reverse the district court's grant of summary judgment to Hawaiian on Konop's SCA claim.

II. Railway Labor Act Claims

Konop also appeals the district court's grant of summary judgment to Hawaiian on his claims under the Railway Labor Act, 45 U.S.C. §§ 151–188 ("RLA"). The RLA prohibits "interference, influence, or coercion by either party over the designation of representatives by the other." 45 U.S.C. § 152 (Third). It also declares that "it shall be unlawful for any carrier to interfere in any way with the organization of its employees, or to use the funds of the carrier in maintaining or assisting or contributing to any labor organization, labor representative, or other agency of collective bargaining . . . ." Id. at § 152 (Fourth).

Konop asserts three claims under 45 U.S.C. § 152 (Third) and (Fourth) of the RLA. First, Konop alleges that Hawaiian interfered with his organizing efforts by accessing his website under false pretenses. Second, Konop alleges that Hawaiian wrongfully assisted a labor group by disclosing the contents of Konop's website to a union leader who supported the concessionary contract. Third, Konop alleges that Hawaiian engaged in coercion and intimidation by threatening to file a defamation suit against Konop based on statements on the website. The district court dismissed these claims on the alternative grounds that it lacked jurisdiction over the RLA claims, and that Konop failed to support them with evidence sufficient to withstand summary judgment.

A. Subject Matter Jurisdiction

Federal courts lack subject matter jurisdiction over disputes which are "grounded in the [collective bargaining agreement]," Haw. Airlines, Inc. v. Norris, 512 U.S. 246, 256, 114 S.Ct. 2239, 129 L.Ed.2d 203 (1994), and "involve controversies over the meaning of an existing collective bargaining agreement in a particular fact situation," id. at 253, 114 S.Ct. 2239 (internal quotation marks omitted). Such disputes, labeled "minor" disputes under the RLA, are subject to mandatory arbitration. Id. Hawaiian argues, and the district court agreed, that Konop's RLA claims are grounded in the collective bargaining agreement ("CBA") and are therefore subject to mandatory arbitration. We disagree.

In Fennessy v. Southwest Airlines, *91 F.3d 1359 (9th Cir.1996), we addressed whether the district court had jurisdiction over the plaintiff's statutory claim under the RLA. The plaintiff in* Fennessy *alleged that the carrier violated 45 U.S.C. § 152 (Fourth) by terminating his employment in retaliation for his efforts to replace the existing union. Id. at 1360–61. We held that "because his claim is based on a statutory provision rather than on the collective bargaining contract, it is not a minor dispute that must be brought to [arbitration]; it is a statutory claim that he may bring directly in district court." Id. at 1362. The plaintiff's unsuccessful arbitration of a related contractual claim under the CBA did not alter this conclusion. Because the statutory claims were not "grounded in the collective-bargaining agreement," and the statutory rights were "independent of the CBA," we found the district court had jurisdiction. Id.*

Hawaiian argues that, unlike the statutory claim in Fennessy, *Konop's statutory claims are grounded in and dependent on the CBA. To support this position, Hawaiian focuses on conduct which Konop explicitly alleged in his complaint as violating the CBA. Specifically, in the RLA section of the complaint, Konop alleged that Hawaiian violated the CBA by suspending him from work, reducing his employee benefits, requiring him to submit to physical and psychological testing, and giving certain pilots paid opportunities to campaign in favor of the concessionary contract.*

On appeal, however, Konop does not challenge the district court's dismissal of these CBA-related claims. Rather, he objects to the district court's dismissal of his independent RLA claims. Konop claims that Hawaiian violated the RLA by (1) accessing his website under false pretenses, (2) disclosing the website's contents to the rival union faction, and (3) threatening to sue Konop for defamation based on statements on the website. Hawaiian never explains how these RLA claims are grounded in the CBA, except to say that Konop merely presents them as a precursor to the alleged CBA violations. Nothing, however, requires such a narrow reading of Konop's allegations. Konop, like the plaintiff in Fennessy, *presents his statutory claims as independent violations of the RLA. These claims in no way depend upon a finding that Hawaiian, at some later time, violated Konop's contractual rights under the CBA.*

Accordingly, we hold that the RLA claims which Konop presses on appeal are not grounded in the CBA, are not subject to mandatory arbitration and, therefore, fall within the court's jurisdiction.

B. Protected Activity

Hawaiian contends that even if Hawaiian managers accessed Konop's website under false pretenses, conveyed this information to a rival union leader, and threatened to sue Konop for defamation, such conduct did not violate the RLA because it did not interfere with any protected organizing activity. The organizing activity in which Konop engaged principally involved the publication of articles on a secure website. As discussed above, Konop limited access to pilots and other employees on the eligible list and prohibited users from disclosing the contents of the website to others. He also categorically excluded managers. Konop's website publication vigorously criticized Hawaiian management and its proposal for wage concessions in the existing collective bargaining agreement. Because the incumbent union, ALPA, supported the concessionary contract, Konop sought to encourage consideration of alternative union representation.

There is no dispute that Konop's website publication would ordinarily constitute protected union organizing activity under the RLA. Hawaiian argues, however, that Konop forfeited any protection he would otherwise enjoy because his articles contained malicious, defamatory and insulting material known to be false. In Linn v. United Plant Guard Workers, Local 114, *383 U.S. 53, 61, 86 S.Ct. 657, 15 L.Ed.2d 582 (1966), the Supreme Court held that a party forfeits his protection under the National Labor Relations Act (NLRA) by "circulating defamatory or insulting material known to be false." 10 See also* Old Dominion Branch No. 496, Nat'l Ass'n of Letter Carriers v. Austin, *418 U.S. 264, 282–83, 94 S.Ct. 2770, 41 L.Ed.2d 745 (1974);* San Antonio Comm. Hosp. v. S. Cal. Dist. Council of Carpenters, *125 F.3d 1230, 1237 (9th Cir.1997).*

We assume Hawaiian is referring to the alleged defamatory statements contained in the "Facts" section of its brief. There, Hawaiian indicates that Konop published the following false statements: (1) Nobles does his "dirty work . . . like the Nazis during World War II"; (2) "Soviet Negotiating Style Essential to Nobles Plan!"; (3) Nobles is "one incompetent at the top"; (4) Nobles "has little skill and little ability with people . . . . In fact, with as few skills as Nobles possesses, it is difficult to imagine how he got this far"; and (5) "Nobles Suspected in Fraud!" and "Hawaiian Air president,

Bruce Nobles, is the prime suspect in an alleged fraud which took place in 1991."

The first two statements, referencing the Nazis and Soviets, are simply "rhetorical hyperbole" protected by federal labor laws. See Letter Carriers, *418 U.S. at 286, 94 S.Ct. 2770. The second two statements, commenting on Nobles' competence and people skills, are opinions also protected by federal labor laws.* See id. *at 284, 94 S.Ct. 2770;* San Antonio Comm. Hosp., *125 F.3d at 1237. Konop did not forfeit his protection under the Railway Labor Act, as Hawaiian suggests, simply by publishing statements that were critical of and insulting to Nobles. " '[F]ederal law gives a union license to use intemperate, abusive, or* insulting *language without fear of restraint or penalty . . . .' "* San Antonio Comm. Hosp., *125 F.3d at 1235 (quoting* Letter Carriers, *418 U.S. at 283, 94 S.Ct. 2770) (emphasis added);* see also Linn, *383 U.S. at 58, 86 S.Ct. 657 ("[R]epresentation campaigns are frequently characterized by bitter and extreme charges, countercharges, unfounded rumors, vituperations, personal accusations, misrepresentations and distortions.").11*

With respect to the final challenged statement, indicating that Nobles was suspected of fraud, Hawaiian fails to argue or present any evidence that Konop published the statement with knowledge of its falsity or with reckless disregard for the truth. Federal labor law protects even false and defamatory statements unless such statements are made with actual malice-i.e., knowledge of falsity or with reckless disregard for the truth. See Letter Carriers, *418 U.S. at 281, 94 S.Ct. 2770;* Linn, *383 U.S. at 61, 86 S.Ct. 657 (protection under labor law existed "even though the statements [were] erroneous and defame[d] one of the parties to the dispute"). With no evidence or argument that Konop acted with actual malice, Hawaiian cannot demonstrate as a matter of law that Konop forfeited his protection under the RLA.*

NLRB v. Pincus Bros., Inc.-Maxwell, *620 F.2d 367 (3d Cir.1980) (as amended), upon which Hawaiian principally relies, provides little support for Hawaiian's position. In* Pincus Bros., *the Third Circuit, in considering whether the NLRB abused its discretion by declining to defer to an arbitration award, merely concluded it was "at least arguable" that the employee published a defamatory statement known to be false.* Id. *at 376. For Hawaiian to prevail on summary judgment, however, it must do more than show it is "at least arguable" that Konop knew the challenged statement was false. It must demonstrate this as a matter of law. As Hawaiian presents no evidence or argument that Konop acted with the requisite malice, Hawaiian falls short of satisfying this burden.*

Accordingly, we find that Konop has raised a triable issue of fact with respect to whether the development and maintenance of his website constituted protected activity under the RLA.

C. Specific Violations

Konop argues that Hawaiian managers: (1) interfered with Konop's organizing efforts by viewing the website under false pretenses, (2) wrongfully supported one labor group in favor of another by informing the opposing labor faction of the website's contents, and (3) engaged in coercion and intimidation by threatening to sue Konop for defamation, all in violation of the RLA. Hawaiian argues, and the district court agreed, that Konop failed to present sufficient evidence to withstand summary judgment on these claims. We disagree.

1. Access of Website

Konop argues that Davis interfered with Konop's organizing efforts by viewing the website under false pretenses. Absent a legitimate justification, employers are generally prohibited from engaging in surveillance of union organizing activities. Cal. Acrylic Indus. v. NLRB, 150 F.3d 1095, 1099–1100 (9th Cir.1998). The reason for this general proscription is that employer surveillance "tends to create fear among employees of future reprisal" and, thus, "chills an employee's freedom to exercise" his rights under federal labor law. Id. at 1099.

In NLRB v. Unbelievable, Inc., 71 F.3d 1434 (9th Cir.1995), we upheld the Board's finding that the employer "engaged in unfair labor practices by eavesdropping on private conversations between employees and [a] Union representative," which occurred in the employee break room. Id. at 1438–39. We see no principled distinction between the employer's eavesdropping in Unbelievable and Hawaiian's access of Konop's secure website.

Hawaiian suggests that Davis had a legitimate reason to access Konop's website-to identify and correct any false or misleading statements. Assuming such a concern could justify Davis' monitoring of private union organizing activities, Hawaiian has presented little evidence to suggest that any statements on Konop's website were actually defamatory. Moreover, as discussed below, there are triable issues whether Hawaiian used information it obtained from the website to assist one union faction over another, and to coerce and intimidate Konop. Under these circumstances, we conclude that Konop has raised a triable issue that Hawaiian's access of Konop's website was not justified.

Hawaiian also argues that Davis' access did not violate the RLA because it did not appreciably limit Konop's organizing activities. Hawaiian emphasizes that, after learning about Davis' access to the website, Konop restricted access for a mere half-day and declined to temper the language in his articles. Hawaiian, however, presents no authority indicating that employees subject to surveillance or eavesdropping must also demonstrate that they consequently limited their organizing activity. It is the tendency to chill protected activities, not the actual chilling of protected activities, that renders eavesdropping and surveillance generally objectionable under federal labor law. See, e.g., Cal. Acrylic, 150 F.3d at 1099–1100. That a hardy individual might continue his organizing activities undeterred, despite an employer's surveillance, does not render the employer's conduct any less of a violation.12

Accordingly, we find that Konop has raised a triable issue of fact that Hawaiian interfered with Konop's union organizing activity in violation of the RLA by accessing Konop's website.

2. Disclosure to Opposing Union

Konop argues that Nobles unlawfully assisted Reno Morella, the union leader who supported the concessionary contract, by disclosing the contents of Konop's website. Generally, the RLA prohibits employers from providing assistance to a union or labor faction. See Barthelemy v. Air Lines Pilots Ass'n, 897 F.2d 999, 1009 (9th Cir.1990) (per curiam); see also NLRB v. Finishline Indus., 451 F.2d 1280, 1281–82 (9th Cir.1971) (NLRA prohibits employer from telling workers to withdraw from one union and join another); NLRB v. L. Ronney & Sons Furniture Mfg. Co., 206 F.2d 730, 734–35 (9th Cir.1953) (NLRA prohibits employer from initiating membership drive among his employees for employer-favored union).

Konop argues that Nobles disclosed useful intelligence to a rival union faction in an effort to ensure that Konop's faction, which opposed the concessionary contract, would not prevail. Hawaiian does not seriously dispute that disclosure of the contents of Konop's website to Morella would constitute improper assistance. Instead, Hawaiian argues that Konop failed to present sufficient evidence that Nobles made any such disclosure or that Nobles was even familiar with the contents of Konop's website when he spoke to Morella.

Morella, however, states in his declaration that Nobles contacted him on December 14, 1995 and informed him "that he had just reviewed information which was posted on an internet communications system operated by Hawaiian Airlines Pilot Robert Konop." In addition, Morella states that Nobles also "disclosed to me that Konop's internet communications system contained a third written article concerning Konop's efforts to obtain union representation by a labor organization other than the Air Line Pilots Association." This evidence creates a genuine issue of fact whether Nobles was familiar with the contents of Konop's website and whether Nobles disclosed the contents of the website to Morella.

Moreover, Nobles confirmed in his declaration that he contacted Morella because he "felt that Reno Morella, the Chairman of the ALPA Master Executive Council, should be aware of the newsletter because of its inaccurate attack on the proposed labor agreements and the unfair effect it could have on the ratification process." Nobles thus effectively concedes that he interceded to help ensure that Morella's faction-which favored ratification of the concessionary contract-would prevail over Konop's faction, which opposed the agreement.

Accordingly, we find that Konop has raised a triable issue of fact whether Nobles improperly assisted one union faction over another in violation of the RLA.

3. Threat of Defamation Suit

Konop argues that Nobles engaged in unlawful coercion and intimidation by threatening to file a defamation suit against Konop based on statements on Konop's website. An employer's filing or threatened filing of a lawsuit against an employee concerning union organizing activities may, under certain circumstances, violate the RLA. See, e.g., Diamond Walnut Growers, Inc. v. NLRB, 53 F.3d 1085, 1089–90 (9th Cir.1995) (finding employer's defamation lawsuit against union violated NLRA);

GHR Energy Corp., *294 N.L.R.B. 1011, 1014 (1989) (analyzing whether employer's threat to sue employee for defamation violated NLRA)*, aff'd, *924 F.2d 1055 (5th Cir.1991).*

Hawaiian does not argue that Nobles would be justified in threatening to sue Konop for defamation. Instead, Hawaiian contends that Konop failed to present sufficient evidence that Nobles ever made such a threat. Nobles stated in his declaration that he "did mention to Morella that the gross inaccuracies and lies in the newsletter made by Konop amounted to defamation," but that he "never said that[he] intended to file a lawsuit against Konop."

Morella, however, indicates otherwise. Morella states in his declaration, "Nobles advised me that Konop should be cautioned, or informed, of the possibility of a defamation lawsuit by Nobles." Morella also testified, "[I]t was my impression and conclusion that Nobles intended for me to contact Konop, or take other action, for the purpose of opposing Konop's efforts to seek alternative union representation." Morella then "informed Konop of Mr. Nobles' statements . . . regarding caution with respect to a possible lawsuit against Konop for defamation." Konop confirms the same in his declaration. This evidence is sufficient to raise a triable issue of fact whether Nobles threatened to sue Konop for defamation.

Accordingly, we find that Konop has raised a triable issue of fact whether Nobles engaged in coercion and intimidation in violation of the RLA by threatening to sue Konop for defamation.

D. Bench Trial on Retaliation Claim

Konop's retaliation claim under the RLA was tried to the district court. The district court entered judgment against him on this claim, which involved his allegation that Hawaiian violated the RLA when it placed him on sick leave in retaliation for protected labor activities. Konop challenges the district court's judgment on this claim on the ground that his subpoenas for corroborating witnesses were improperly quashed. We review a district court's order quashing subpoenas for an abuse of discretion. United States v. Berberian, *767 F.2d 1324, 1324 (9th Cir.1985). A litigant whose subpoenas have been improperly quashed must also show prejudice.* See Casino Foods Corp. v. Kraftco Corp., *546 F.2d 301, 302 (9th Cir.1976).*

There is some dispute whether the district court's remarks in a pretrial hearing constituted an order to quash subpoenas at all. Assuming, however, that the district court did quash Konop's subpoenas, Konop has not suggested what relevant evidence the subpoenaed witnesses might have provided had they been compelled to testify. Konop has consequently failed to show that he was prejudiced. Accordingly, the district court's judgment against Konop on his retaliation claim under the RLA is affirmed.

CONCLUSION

For the foregoing reasons, we affirm the district court's judgment with respect to Konop's Wiretap Act claims and his retaliation claim under the Railway Labor Act.

We reverse the district court's judgment on Konop's Stored Communications Act claims and his claims under the Railway Labor Act for interference with organizing activities, wrongful support of a union faction, and coercion and intimidation.

As the court notes in *Konop*, beyond the general workplace privacy issues raised by the executives' accessing the message board intended to be for employees only, there were significant labor law issues as well. The right of employees to described under the federal National Labor Relations Act ("NLRA"):[32]

> *§ 157. Right of employees as to organization, collective bargaining, etc.*
>
> *Employees shall have the right to self-organization, to form, join, or assist labor organizations, to bargain collectively through representatives of their own choosing, and to engage in other concerted activities for the purpose of collective bargaining or other mutual aid or protection, and shall also have the right to refrain from any or all of such activities except to the extent that such right may be affected by an agreement requiring membership in a labor organization as a condition of employment as authorized in section 158(a)(3) of this title.*

The National Labor Relations Board ("NLRB"), the federal body tasked with enforcing the NLRA, has had to interpret the right to organize in the context of social media, including the limits of management's right to take action based on employee online activities:

February 8, 2011 NLRB Press Release: Settlement reached in case involving discharge for Facebook comments

A settlement has been reached in a case involving the discharge of a Connecticut ambulance service employee for posting negative comments about a supervisor on her Facebook page.

The NLRB's Hartford regional office issued a complaint against American Medical Response of Connecticut, Inc., on October 27, 2010, alleging that the discharge violated federal labor law because the employee was engaged in protected activity when she posted the comments about her supervisor, and responded to further comments from her co-workers. Under the National Labor Relations Act, employees may discuss the terms and conditions of their employment with co-workers and others.

The NLRB complaint also alleged that the company maintained overly-broad rules in its employee handbook regarding blogging, Internet posting, and communications between employees, and that it had illegally denied union representation to the employee during an investigatory interview shortly before the employee posted the negative comments on her Facebook page.

Under the terms of the settlement approved today by Hartford Regional Director Jonathan Kreisberg, the company agreed to revise its overly-broad rules to ensure that they do not improperly restrict employees from discussing their wages, hours and

---

[32] 29 U.S.C. § 157.

working conditions with co-workers and others while not at work, and that they would not discipline or discharge employees for engaging in such discussions.

The company also promised that employee requests for union representation will not be denied in the future and that employees will not be threatened with discipline for requesting union representation. The allegations involving the employee's discharge were resolved through a separate, private agreement between the employee and the company . . . .[33]

II.   EMPLOYEE PERSONAL INFORMATION: A NON-CONSUMER CONTEXT

Given that most of the law and regulation involving personally identifiable information as well as their enforcement is in the context of consumer protection, the obligations for an employer with regard to data it collects about its employees are not clear. Unlike consumers, the worker is not able to choose whether or not to provide personal information; that generally is both a function and a requirement of employment. It is difficult to imagine a job where the employer does not know the name, address, or other personal information for someone who is providing service on behalf of the company, and who is being paid for that service. Nor are workers protected through the same governmental structures. Consumers are under the oversight of the Federal Trade Commission, State Attorneys General, and similar bodies. Workers' conditions, legal protections, and other issues generally fall under the enforcement of either labor or safety administrators.

Another key distinction between consumers and employees is that while consumers are generally operating only on their own behalf, workers not only share common concerns due to their common workplace, but (as discussed above) they have legally-protected rights of organization which have the power to negotiate collectively on behalf of employees not only for salary and benefits but for other workplace conditions, which could include privacy. Further, the relationship between a worker and a employer is initiated, maintained, and may be terminated very differently from that between a consumer and a marketer. Finally, as has been discussed previously in this chapter, the expectations of privacy that are held to be reasonable in the work environment have different conditions and limitations than those of consumers in an arm's length relationship with a business.

In fact, much of the law of data collection and use with regard to workers in the United States comes from contexts other than traditional privacy. For example, prospective employers are not permitted to make hiring decisions about candidates based upon the candidate's gender, sexual orientation, religious belief or lack thereof, marital status or other specified characteristics. By extension, interviewers are not permitted to ask job candidates questions designed to illicit information that may not be used for job decisions. A female candidate, for example, may not be asked about her

---

[33] Settlement reached in case involving discharge for Facebook comments | NLRB *(Feb. 8, 2011), http://www.nlrb.gov/news/settlement-reached-case-involving-discharge-facebook-comments (last visited May 8, 2012).*

marital status in a job interview or about her plans to have children or current number of children, if any, since neither marital status nor parental obligations are permitted determining factors in employment decisions. To some extent then these prohibitions to limit the permissible information selection of an employer, not for privacy reasons per se but because of laws prohibiting discrimination in employment. In another context, there are statutory restrictions on the right of an employer (either prospective or current) to inquire about an employee's credit history through the solicitation of a credit report. These types of inquiries are generally limited to positions where the employee's or candidate's ability to manage finance is relevant to position either directly or as an indicator of other necessary skills or in order to ensure there are no financial burdens on the employee which could detract from the employee's ability to perform his or her responsibilities. These requirements, contained in the Fair Credit Reporting Act, additionally require that, in situations where a company may request and review a credit report, to the extent that that review results in an adverse decision (either about beginning or maintaining employment or promotion), the employer must provide notice of this adverse decision in writing under the FCRA to the employee. Again, these requirements do not arise out of concerns about employer use and collection of personal information specifically, but rather out of the need to ensure the integrity of and proper functioning of the credit system in the United States. Nevertheless, these requirements result in privacy-related obligations on the part of the company.

If though, there are not specific rules about employer collection of personally identifiable information nor specific prohibitions on employers sharing that information with third parties generally, there are very specific legal obligations with regard to the stewardship (that is the responsible maintenance of integrity and security) of data collected and kept by the employer, under data breach notification laws. As a contrast to consumer privacy rules involving collection, data breach notification requirements rarely if ever, differentiate among the different sources of the personally identifiable information but rather look only to the types of information and how it may or may not have been protected from improper access.[34]

---

[34] For more discussion of data breach notification laws, see Chapter 8.

Chapter 8

DATA BREACH: PREVENTION, DETECTION, AND NOTIFICATION

Throughout this book, we have discussed the laws, regulations, and best practices with regard to collection and purposeful sharing of personally identifiable information, as well as of behavior tracking data. All of these assume that the party collecting the data has control over it, in order to comply with applicable requirements and request and act upon the consent of the person whose information is being collected and used.

It is not, however, always the situation that data are or remain in control of the proper party. As discussed in the introductory chapter, among the biggest changes affecting data privacy in the digital age have been the vast reduction in physical space needed to store a given amount of data,[1] and the speed and ease through which data may be transferred from their original storage location.[2] Add the fact that a digital file may be copied in exact detail once or a million times without the original necessarily being damaged or changed in any way, the substantially increased number of mobile devices containing multiple gigabytes of storage, and the challenges of computer and network security, and the potential for loss of control of stored data, often referred to as a "data breach," becomes that much greater.

The risks from data breach are significant, both for individuals and organizations. Two of the most serious are the loss of the integrity (and therefore reliability) of the stored information and the possibility of "identity theft." A data breach may also violate an organization or professional's obligations to preserve confidentiality, with whatever consequences may arise from such a violation, and even a rumored lapse in responsible data stewardship may hurt a company's reputation and generate signifi-

---

[1] A 2000 Berkeley study estimated that the Library of Congress' 26 million books it then held were the equivalent of 208 terabytes of data. PRINT, http://www2.sims.berkeley.edu/research/projects/how-much-info/print.html (last visited May 8, 2012). The Library has 838 miles of shelves in three buildings (FREQUENTLY ASKED QUESTIONS — ABOUT THE LIBRARY (LIBRARY OF CONGRESS), http://www.loc.gov/about/faqs.html#where_books (last visited May 8, 2012)). By comparison, a ViON HyperStor 6300 solid-state drive has a maximum storage capacity of 10 terabytes, weighs 50 lbs, and fits in a 3U-size standard computer equipment rack (HyperStor Datasheet 6300, http://www.vion.com/images/stories/products/disk-storage/HyperStor%20Datasheet%206300.pdf); and a 3U rack is approximately 5.25" high (DEFINE: RACK UNIT "U" OR "RU" | THE SERVER RACK FAQ, http://www.server-racks.com/rack-unit-u-ru.html (last visited May 8, 2012)). Based on the Berkeley estimate, the content of the print collection of the Library of Congress as of 2000, stored on devices such as the HyperStor 6300, would take up only 109.2 inches of height.

[2] In 2012, Chattanooga, TN, began offering fiber Internet service with a data transfer rate of 1 gigabit-per-second to its residents and businesses. WELCOME TO THE GIG CITY, http://www.thegigcity.com/about (last visited May 8, 2012). At such speeds, the 208 estimated terabytes of data from the Library of Congress in 2000 (see Footnote 280) could potentially be transferred in under 58 hours.

cant expenses.[3]

I.   THE CAUSES AND SCOPE OF DATA BREACHES

Data breaches may arise from a number of different technical and human-driven causes, and from both negligence and malice. The Privacy Rights Clearinghouse ("PRC"),[4] an advocacy group for consumer privacy, maintains a database of reported breaches in the United States categorized by their causes:

> *Unintended disclosure (DISC) — Sensitive information posted publicly on a website, mishandled or sent to the wrong party via email, fax or mail.*

> *Hacking or malware (HACK) — Electronic entry by an outside party, malware and spyware.*

> *Payment Card Fraud (CARD) — Fraud involving debit and credit cards that is not accomplished via hacking. For example, skimming devices at point-of-service terminals.*

> *Insider (INSD) — Someone with legitimate access intentionally breaches information - such as an employee or contractor.*

> *Physical loss (PHYS) — Lost, discarded or stolen non-electronic records, such as paper documents*

> *Portable device (PORT) — Lost, discarded or stolen laptop, PDA, smart-phone, portable memory device, CD, hard drive, data tape, etc*

> *Stationary device (STAT) — Lost, discarded or stolen stationary electronic device such as a computer or server not designed for mobility.*

> *Unknown or other (UNKN)[5]*

Between January 10, 2005 and April 6, 2012, the PRC recorded 3,022 data breaches, encompassing 545,740,085 records, which it assigned to the following causes:[6]

	CARD	DISC	HACK	INSD	PHYS	PORT	STAT	UNKN	Grand Total
2006	3	83	75	32	39	186	48	16	482
2007	2	98	71	23	43	163	36	16	452
2008	5	79	57	31	53	99	22	9	355
2009	4	53	53	30	38	61	10	4	253
2010	13	97	97	104	103	142	37	12	605

---

[3] Cindy Chick, FEATURES — LEXIS/NEXIS HELD HOSTAGE BY THE INTERNET: THE P-TRAK DEBACLE | LLRX.COM, http://www.llrx.com/features/ptrak.htm (last visited May 8, 2012).

[4] PRIVACY RIGHTS CLEARINGHOUSE | EMPOWERING CONSUMERS. PROTECTING PRIVACY., http://www.privacyrights.org/ (last visited May 8, 2012).

[5] CHRONOLOGY OF DATA BREACHES | PRIVACY RIGHTS CLEARINGHOUSE, *http://www.privacyrights.org/data-breach (last visited May 8, 2012).*

[6] Chart created by Jonathan I. Ezor based on data derived from *Id.*

	CARD	DISC	HACK	INSD	PHYS	PORT	STAT	UNKN	Grand Total
2011	14	80	143	92	87	119	28	27	590
2012	2	33	40	13	21	30	2	8	149
Grand Total	43	543	584	335	392	838	193	94	3022

It is also instructive to view the same data in terms of the percentage of each cause per year:

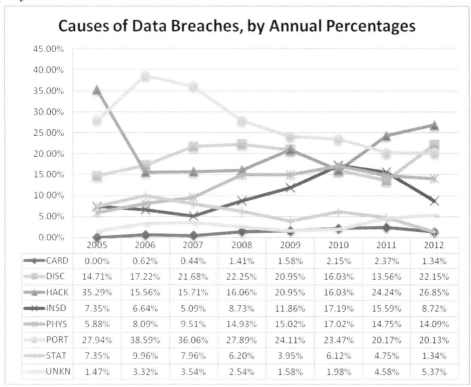

	2005	2006	2007	2008	2009	2010	2011	2012
CARD	0.00%	0.62%	0.44%	1.41%	1.58%	2.15%	2.37%	1.34%
DISC	14.71%	17.22%	21.68%	22.25%	20.95%	16.03%	13.56%	22.15%
HACK	35.29%	15.56%	15.71%	16.06%	20.95%	16.03%	24.24%	26.85%
INSD	7.35%	6.64%	5.09%	8.73%	11.86%	17.19%	15.59%	8.72%
PHYS	5.88%	8.09%	9.51%	14.93%	15.02%	17.02%	14.75%	14.09%
PORT	27.94%	38.59%	36.06%	27.89%	24.11%	23.47%	20.17%	20.13%
STAT	7.35%	9.96%	7.96%	6.20%	3.95%	6.12%	4.75%	1.34%
UNKN	1.47%	3.32%	3.54%	2.54%	1.58%	1.98%	4.58%	5.37%

Note the steady increase in the percentage of incidents ascribed by the PRC to hacking or malware between 2006 (15.56%) and 2012 (26.85% as of April), after a sharp drop from 35.29% in 2005. By contrast, the percentage of data breaches from portable devices peaked at 38.59% in 2006, then has consistently dropped. These trends likely suggest the interplay among the level of technological adoption, sophistication of users, availability and use of data protection tools, and (particularly in the first instance) the growing ability of malicious hackers to circumvent efforts to prevent access, although it may also be the case that self-caused losses may be underreported in some instances.[7] Another source, a 2012 joint report study conducted with a different methodology by the Verizon RISK Team with cooperation from the Austra-

---

[7] In its January 2012 report, The Human Factor in Data Protection, the Ponemon Institute (a

lian Federal Police, Dutch National High Tech Crime Unit, Irish Reporting and Information Security Service, Police Central e-Crime Unit, and United States Secret Service, reported at least 855 incidents throughout the world, involving 174 million compromised records, in 2011 alone.[8]

The international factor should not be overlooked. With the growth of compatible and connected networks throughout the world has come the ability for malicious hackers to access U.S.-based systems from far beyond our borders. Finding and prosecuting cybercriminals who access databases filled with personal information can be extremely difficult for U.S. law enforcement officials, who must first establish jurisdiction and verify that a particular law is applicable to the circumstance before seeking appropriate remedies or punishment from a court.

UNITED STATES V. IVANOV[9]

THOMPSON, DISTRICT JUDGE.

Defendant Aleksey Vladimirovich Ivanov ("Ivanov") has been indicted, in a superseding indictment, on charges of conspiracy, computer fraud and related activity, extortion and possession of unauthorized access devices. Ivanov has moved to dismiss the indictment on the grounds that the court lacks subject matter jurisdiction. Ivanov argues that because it is alleged that he was physically located in Russia when the offenses were committed, he can not be charged with violations of United States law. For the reasons set forth below, the defendant's motion is being denied.

I. Background

Online Information Bureau, Inc. ("OIB"), the alleged victim in this case, is a Connecticut corporation based in Vernon, Connecticut. It is an "e-commerce" business which assists retail and Internet merchants by, among other things, hosting their websites and processing their credit card data and other financial transactions. In this capacity, OIB acts as a financial transaction "clearinghouse", by aggregating

---

privacy-focused research body) described the results of its having surveyed 709 IT practitioners in the United States about data breach issues:

> According to 78 percent of respondents, their organizations have experienced a data breach as a result of negligent or malicious employees or other insiders. Employees losing laptops or other mobile devices, mishandling of data at rest and in motion and malicious employees or other insiders are the root causes of many of these data breaches in organizations . . . . Unfortunately, it seems that even when employees make unintentional mistakes most of these breaches are only discovered accidentally. Rarely do employees self-report the incident. While technologies are important in data protection, so is it critical for organizations to reduce the risk of employee negligence or maliciousness through policies, training, monitoring and enforcement.

www.trendmicro.com/cloud-content/us/pdfs/security-intelligence/reports/rpt_trend-micro_ponemon-survey -2012.pdf, p. 1.

[8] 2012 DATA BREACH INVESTIGATIONS REPORT, http://www.verizonbusiness.com/resources/reports/rp_data-breach-investigations-report-2012_en_xg.pdf.

[9] 175 F.Supp.2d 367 (D. Ct. 2001) [notes omitted].

and assisting in the debiting or crediting of funds against each account for thousands of retail and Internet purchasers and vendors. In doing so, OIB collects and maintains customer credit card information, merchant account numbers, and related financial data from credit card companies and other financial institutions.

The government alleges that Ivanov "hacked" into OIB's computer system and obtained the key passwords to control OIB's entire network. The government contends that in late January and early February 2000, OIB received from Ivanov a series of unsolicited e-mails indicating that the defendant had obtained the "root" passwords for certain computer systems operated by OIB. A "root" password grants its user access to and control over an entire computer system, including the ability to manipulate, extract, and delete any and all data. Such passwords are generally reserved for use by the system administrator only.

The government claims that Ivanov then threatened OIB with the destruction of its computer systems (including its merchant account database) and demanded approximately $10,000 for his assistance in making those systems secure. It claims, for example, that on February 3, 2000, after his initial solicitations had been rebuffed, Ivanov sent the following e-mail to an employee of OIB:

[name redacted], now imagine please Somebody hack you network (and not notify you about this), he download Atomic software with more than 300 merchants, transfer money, and after this did 'rm-rf/' and after this you company be ruined. I don't want this, and because this i notify you about possible hack in you network, if you want you can hire me and im allways be check security in you network. What you think about this?The government contends that Ivanov's extortionate communications originated from an e-mail account at Lightrealm.com, an Internet Service Provider based in Kirkland, Washington. It contends that while he was in Russia, Ivanov gained access to the Lightrealm computer network and that he used that system to communicate with OIB, also while he was in Russia. Thus, each e-mail sent by Ivanov was allegedly transmitted from a Lightrealm.com computer in Kirkland, Washington through the Internet to an OIB computer in Vernon, Connecticut, where the e-mail was opened by an OIB employee.The parties agree that the defendant was physically located in Russia (or one of the other former Soviet Bloc countries) when, it is alleged, he committed the offenses set forth in the superseding indictment.

The superseding indictment comprises eight counts. Count One charges that beginning in or about December 1999, or earlier, the defendant and others conspired to commit the substantive offenses charged in Counts Two through Eight of the indictment, in violation of 18 U.S.C. § 371. Count Two charges that the defendant, knowingly and with intent to defraud, accessed protected computers owned by OIB and by means of this conduct furthered a fraud and obtained something of value, in violation of 18 U.S.C. §§ 2, 1030(a)(4) and 1030(c)(3)(A). Count Three charges that the defendant intentionally accessed protected computers owned by OIB and thereby obtained information, which conduct involved interstate and foreign communications and was engaged in for purposes of financial gain and in furtherance of a criminal act, in violation of 18 U.S.C. §§ 2, 1030(a)(2)(C) and 1030(c)(2)(B). Counts Four and Five do not pertain to this defendant.

Count Six charges that the defendant transmitted in interstate and foreign commerce communications containing a threat to cause damage to protected computers owned by OIB, in violation of 18 U.S.C. §§ 1030(a)(7) and 1030(c)(3)(A). Count Seven charges that the defendant obstructed, delayed and affected commerce, and attempted to obstruct, delay and affect commerce, by means of extortion by attempting to obtain property from OIB with OIB's consent, inducing such consent by means of threats to damage OIB and its business unless OIB paid the defendant money and hired the defendant as a security consultant, in violation of 18 U.S.C. § 1951(a). Count Eight charges that the defendant, knowingly and with intent to defraud, possessed unauthorized access devices, which conduct affected interstate and foreign commerce, in violation of 18 U.S.C. §§ 1029(a)(3).

II. Discussion

The defendant and the government agree that when Ivanov allegedly engaged in the conduct charged in the superseding indictment, he was physically present in Russia and using a computer there at all relevant times. Ivanov contends that for this reason, charging him under the Hobbs Act, 18 U.S.C. § 1951, under the Computer Fraud and Abuse Act, 18 U.S.C. § 1030, and under the access device statute, 18 U.S.C. § 1029, would in each case require extraterritorial application of that law and such application is impermissible. The court concludes that it has jurisdiction, first, because the intended and actual detrimental effects of Ivanov's actions in Russia occurred within the United States, and second, because each of the statutes under which Ivanov was charged with a substantive offense was intended by Congress to apply extraterritorially.

A. The Intended and Actual Detrimental Effects of the Charged Offenses Occurred Within the United States

As noted by the court in United States v. Muench, *694 F.2d 28 (2d Cir.1982), "[t]he intent to cause effects within the United States . . . makes it reasonable to apply to persons outside United States territory a statute which is not expressly extraterritorial in scope." Id. at 33. "It has long been a commonplace of criminal liability that a person may be charged in the place where the evil results, though he is beyond the jurisdiction when he starts the train of events of which that evil is the fruit."* United States v. Steinberg, *62 F.2d 77, 78 (2d Cir.1932). "[T]he Government may punish a defendant in the same manner as if [he] were present in the jurisdiction when the detrimental effects occurred."* Marc Rich & Co., A.G. v. United States, *707 F.2d 663, 666 (2d Cir.1983).*

The Supreme Court has quoted with approval the following language from Moore's International Law Digest:

The principle that a man, who outside of a country willfully puts in motion a force to take effect in it, is answerable at the place where the evil is done, is recognized in the criminal jurisprudence of all countries. And the methods which modern invention has furnished for the performance of criminal acts in that manner has made this principle one of constantly growing importance and of increasing frequency of application.

Ford v. United States, *273 U.S. 593, 623, 47 S.Ct. 531, 71 L.Ed. 793 (1927). Moreover, the court noted in* Rich *that:*

> [I]t is certain that the courts of many countries, even of countries which have given their criminal legislation a strictly territorial character, interpret criminal law in the sense that offences, the authors of which at the moment of commission are in the territory of another State, are nevertheless to be regarded as having been committed in the national territory, if one of the constituent elements of the offence, and more especially its effects, have taken place there. The S.S. Lotus, *1927 P.C.I.J., ser. A, No. 10, at 23,* reprinted in *2 Hudson,* World Court Reports, *23, 38 (1935).*

Rich, *707 F.2d at 666.*

Here, all of the intended and actual detrimental effects of the substantive offenses Ivanov is charged with in the indictment occurred within the United States. In Counts Two and Three, the defendant is charged with accessing OIB's computers. Those computers were located in Vernon, Connecticut. The fact that the computers were accessed by means of a complex process initiated and controlled from a remote location does not alter the fact that the accessing of the computers, i.e. part of the detrimental effect prohibited by the statute, occurred at the place where the computers were physically located, namely OIB's place of business in Vernon, Connecticut.

Count Two charges further that Ivanov obtained something of value when he accessed OIB's computers, that "something of value" being the data obtained from OIB's computers. In order for Ivanov to violate § 1030(a)(4), it was necessary that he do more than merely access OIB's computers and view the data. See United States v. Czubinski, *106 F.3d 1069, 1078 (1st Cir.1997) ("[M]erely viewing information cannot be deemed the same as obtaining something of value for purposes of this statute." . . . "[T]his section should apply to those who steal information through unauthorized access . . . ."). The indictment charges that Ivanov did more than merely gain unauthorized access and view the data. Ivanov allegedly obtained root access to the OIB computers located in Vernon, Connecticut. Once Ivanov had root access to the computers, he was able to control the data, e.g., credit card numbers and merchant account numbers, stored in the OIB computers; Ivanov could copy, sell, transfer, alter, or destroy that data. That data is intangible property of OIB.* See Carpenter v. United States, *484 U.S. 19, 25, 108 S.Ct. 316, 98 L.Ed.2d 275 (1987) (noting that the "intangible nature [of confidential business information] does not make it any less 'property' protected by the mail and wire fraud statutes."). "In determining where, in the case of intangibles, possession resides, the measure of control exercised is the deciding factor."* New York Credit Men's Ass'n v. Mfrs. Disc. Corp., *147 F.2d 885, 887 (2d Cir.1945).*

At the point Ivanov gained root access to OIB's computers, he had complete control over that data, and consequently, had possession of it. That data was in OIB's computers. Since Ivanov possessed that data while it was in OIB's computers in Vernon, Connecticut, the court concludes that he obtained it, for purposes of § 1030(a)(4), in Vernon, Connecticut. The fact that Ivanov is charged with obtaining OIB's valuable data by means of a complex process initiated and controlled from a remote location, and that he subsequently moved that data to a computer located in Russia, does not alter the fact that at the point when Ivanov first possessed that data, it was on OIB's computers in Vernon, Connecticut.

Count Three charges further that when he accessed OIB's computers, Ivanov obtained information from protected computers. The analysis as to the location at which Ivanov obtained the information referenced in this count is the same as the analysis as to the location at which he obtained the "something of value" referenced in Count Two. Thus, as to both Counts Two and Three, it is charged that the balance of the detrimental effect prohibited by the pertinent statute, i.e., Ivanov's obtaining something of value or obtaining information, also occurred within the United States.

Count Six charges that Ivanov transmitted a threat to cause damage to protected computers. The detrimental effect prohibited by § 1030(a)(7), namely the receipt by an individual or entity of a threat to cause damage to a protected computer, occurred in Vernon, Connecticut because that is where OIB was located, where it received the threat, and where the protected computers were located. The analysis is the same as to Count Seven, the charge under the Hobbs Act.

Count Eight charges that Ivanov knowingly and with intent to defraud possessed over ten thousand unauthorized access devices, i.e., credit card numbers and merchant account numbers. For the reasons discussed above, although it is charged that Ivanov later transferred this intangible property to Russia, he first possessed it while it was on OIB's computers in Vernon, Connecticut. Had he not possessed it here, he would not have been able to transfer it to his computer in Russia. Thus, the detrimental effect prohibited by the statute occurred within the United States.

Finally, Count One charges that Ivanov and others conspired to commit each of the substantive offenses charged in the indictment. The Second Circuit has stated that "the jurisdictional element should be viewed for purposes of the conspiracy count exactly as we view it for purposes of the substantive offense . . . ." United States v. Blackmon, 839 F.2d 900, 910 (2d Cir.1988) (internal citations and quotation marks omitted). See also United States v. Kim, 246 F.3d 186, 191, n. 2 (2d Cir.2001) (noting that jurisdiction over a conspiracy charge depends upon jurisdiction over the underlying substantive charge). Federal jurisdiction over a conspiracy charge "is established by proof that the accused planned to commit a substantive offense which, if attainable, would have violated a federal statute, and that at least one overt act has been committed in furtherance of the conspiracy." United States v. Giordano, 693 F.2d 245, 249 (2d Cir.1982). Here, Ivanov is charged with planning to commit substantive offenses in violation of federal statutes, and it is charged that at least one overt act was committed in furtherance of the conspiracy. As discussed above, the court has jurisdiction over the underlying substantive charges. Therefore, the court has jurisdiction over the conspiracy charge, at a minimum, to the extent it relates to Counts Two, Three, Six, Seven or Eight.

Accordingly, the court concludes that it has subject matter jurisdiction over each of the charges against Ivanov, whether or not the statutes under which the substantive offenses are charged are intended by Congress to apply extraterritorially, because the intended and actual detrimental effects of the substantive offenses Ivanov is charged with in the indictment occurred within the United States.

B. Intended Extraterritorial Application

The defendant's motion should also be denied because, as to each of the statutes under which the defendant has been indicted for a substantive offense, there is clear evidence that the statute was intended by Congress to apply extraterritorially. This fact is evidenced by both the plain language and the legislative history of each of these statutes.

There is a presumption that Congress intends its acts to apply only within the United States, and not extraterritorially. However, this "presumption against extraterritoriality" may be overcome by showing "clear evidence of congressional intent to apply a statute beyond our borders . . . ." U.S. v. Gatlin, 216 F.3d 207, 211 (2d Cir.2000). "Congress has the authority to enforce its laws beyond the territorial boundaries of the United States. Whether Congress has in fact exercised that authority in [a particular case] is a matter of statutory construction." Equal Employment Opportunity Comm. v. Arabian American Oil Co., *499 U.S. 244, 248, 111 S.Ct. 1227, 113 L.Ed.2d 274 (1991) (internal citations omitted)* ("ArAmCo").

The defendant is charged with substantive offenses in violation of 18 U.S.C. § 1951, 18 U.S.C. § 1030 and 18 U.S.C. § 1029, and with conspiracy in violation of 18 U.S.C. § 371.

1. 18 U.S.C. § 1951: The Hobbs Act

The Hobbs Act provides, in pertinent part, as follows:

Whoever in any way or degree obstructs, delays, or affects commerce or the movement of any article or commodity in commerce, by robbery or extortion or attempts or conspires so to do, or commits or threatens physical violence to any person or property in furtherance of a plan or purpose to do anything in violation of this section shall be fined under this title or imprisoned not more than twenty years, or both.

18 U.S.C. § 1951(a) (West 2000).

The Supreme Court has stated that the Hobbs Act "speaks in broad language, manifesting a purpose to use all the constitutional power Congress has to punish interference with interstate commerce by extortion, robbery or physical violence." Stirone v. United States, *361 U.S. 212, 215, 80 S.Ct. 270, 4 L.Ed.2d 252 (1960). The Court has not had occasion to decide whether the "broad language" of the Hobbs Act expresses a congressional intent to apply the statute extraterritorially. However, the Third Circuit, relying in part on* Stirone, *concluded that:*

[E]ven if none of the [defendants'] overt acts had occurred in this country . . . Congress could give the district court jurisdiction under the commerce clause so long as [the defendants'] activities affected [the victim's] commercial ventures in interstate commerce within the United States. See Stirone v. United States, 361 U.S. 212, 215, 80 S.Ct. 270, 272, 4 L.Ed.2d 252 (1960) (Hobbs Act utilizes all of Congress's commerce clause power and reaches even a minimal interference with commerce) . . . ."

United States v. Inigo, *925 F.2d 641, 648 (3d Cir.1991).*

Based on the foregoing, this court concludes that the Hobbs Act encompasses not only all extortionate interference with interstate commerce by means of conduct occurring within the United States, but also all such conduct which, although it occurs outside the United States, affects commerce within the borders of the United States. Therefore, it is immaterial whether Ivanov's alleged conduct can be said to have taken place entirely outside the United States, because that conduct clearly constituted "interference with interstate commerce by extortion", Stirone, 361 U.S. at 215, 80 S.Ct. 270, in violation of the Hobbs Act. Consequently, the court has jurisdiction over this charge against him.

2. 18 U.S.C. § 1030: The Computer Fraud and Abuse Act

The Computer Fraud and Abuse Act ("CFAA") was amended in 1996 by Pub.L. No. 104-294, 110 Stat. 3491, 3508. The 1996 amendments made several changes that are relevant to the issue of extraterritoriality, including a change in the definition of "protected computer" so that it included any computer "which is used in interstate or foreign commerce or communication." 18 U.S.C. § 1030(e)(2)(B) (emphasis added). The 1996 amendments also added subsections (a)(2)(C) and (a)(7), which explicitly address "interstate or foreign commerce", and subsection (e)(9), which added to the definition of "government entity" the clause "any foreign country, and any state, province, municipality or other political subdivision of a foreign country". The plain language of the statute, as amended, is clear. Congress intended the CFAA to apply to computers used "in interstate or foreign commerce or communication." The defendant argues that this language is ambiguous. The court disagrees. The Supreme Court has often stated that "a statute ought, upon the whole, to be so construed that, if it can be prevented, no clause, sentence, or word shall be superfluous, void, or insignificant." Regions Hosp. v. Shalala, 522 U.S. 448, 467, 118 S.Ct. 909, 139 L.Ed.2d 895 (1998) (internal citations and quotation marks omitted). In order for the word "foreign" to have meaning, and not be superfluous, it must mean something other than "interstate". In other words, "foreign" in this context must mean international. Thus, Congress has clearly manifested its intent to apply § 1030 to computers used either in interstate or in foreign commerce.

The legislative history of the CFAA supports this reading of the plain language of the statute. The Senate Judiciary Committee issued a report explaining its reasons for adopting the 1996 amendments. S.Rep. No. 357, 104th Congr., 2d Sess. (1996). In that report, the Committee specifically noted its concern that the statute as it existed prior to the 1996 amendments did not cover "computers used in foreign communications or commerce, despite the fact that hackers are often foreign-based." Id. at 4. The Committee cited two specific cases in which foreign-based hackers had infiltrated computer systems in the United States, as examples of the kind of situation the amendments were intended to address:

For example, the 1994 intrusion into the Rome Laboratory at Grifess Air Force Base in New York, was perpetrated by a 16-year-old hacker in the United Kingdom. More recently, in March 1996, the Justice Department tracked down a young Argentinean man who had broken into Harvard University's computers from Buenos Aires and used those computers as a staging ground to hack into many other computer sites, including the Defense Department and NASA.

Id. *at 4–5. Congress has the power to apply its statutes extraterritorially, and in the case of 18 U.S.C. § 1030, it has clearly manifested its intention to do so.*

3. 18 U.S.C. § 1029: The Access Device Statute

Section 1029 of Title 18 of the United States Code provides for the imposition of criminal sanctions on any person who uses, possesses or traffics in a counterfeit access device "if the offense affects interslale or foreign commerce." 18 U.S.C. § 1029 (2000). As noted above, there is a centuries old canon of statutory construction to the effect that a statute should be construed so that no word or phrase is rendered superfluous. See, e.g., Platt v. Union Pac. R.R. Co., 99 U.S. 48, 58, 9 Otto 48, 25 L.Ed. 424 (1878) (noting that the "rules of statutory construction declare that a legislature is presumed to have used no superfluous words."). Therefore, based on the same reasoning applied above in the discussion of § 1030, the court concludes that the plain language of § 1029 indicates a congressional intent to apply the statute extraterritorially.

The parties agreed at oral argument that the legislative history of 18 U.S.C. § 1029 mirrors that of § 1030. Therefore, the discussion above of the congressional intent behind § 1030 also applies to § 1029. Accordingly, the court finds that this section, too, was intended to apply extraterritorially.

4. 18 U.S.C. § 371: The Conspiracy Statute

The Second Circuit has recently noted that where the court has jurisdiction over the underlying substantive criminal counts against a defendant, the court also has jurisdiction over the conspiracy counts. See Kim, 246 F.3d at 191, n. 2. A court may "infer[ ] the extra-territorial reach of conspiracy statutes on the basis of a finding that the underlying substantive statute reached extra-territorial offenses, even though the conspiracy charges came under separate code sections . . . ." United States v. Evans, 667 F.Supp. 974, 981 (S.D.N.Y.1987) (internal quotation marks and citations omitted). See also United States v. Yousef, 927 F.Supp. 673, 682 (S.D.N.Y.1996) ("Extraterritorial jurisdiction over a conspiracy charge depends on whether extraterritorial jurisdiction exists as to the underlying substantive crime.") Because the court finds that each of the underlying substantive statutes in this case was intended by Congress to apply extraterritorially, it also finds that it has jurisdiction over the conspiracy charge.

IV. Conclusion

For the reasons set forth above, the defendant's Motion to Dismiss for Lack of Subject Matter Jurisdiction [Doc. #34] is hereby DENIED.

It is so ordered.

II. LEGAL OBLIGATIONS TO PREVENT DATA BREACH

Given how many ways electronically stored information may be accessed, transmitted and transported both with and without authorization, and the ever-evolving challenges of both physical and computer security, it is essentially impossible to prevent all possible data breaches from occurring. That does not, though, mean that there may not be legal obligations to do so (or at least to attempt to do so), nor that there are not consequences not only for a breach but for the failure in advance to prevent it.

a. Self-Imposed Obligations: Contracts, Disclosure and Internal Policies

One means by which a party may become obligated to attempt to or actually prevent data breaches is through a self-imposed mandate. This can occur in the context of a contract, whose terms can include specific data security obligations and/or more broad confidentiality commitments. Especially when a party or its counsel do not understand the technical requirements and challenges of data breach prevention, they may agree to or even volunteer contractual language beyond the party's ability to perform fully, with absolute statements about securing data from any unauthorized access. Instead, it is preferable to craft language about data breach prevention in terms of reasonable efforts, and to be as specific as possible about both the measures to be taken and the limits of those measures to protect the information.

An organization may also impose data protection liability on itself through its public disclosures, whether in the context of a privacy policy, a securities-related filing or merely a statement to the press or consumers about practices. In such contexts, particularly where disclosure is viewed as a means for consumer protection, overpromising or inaccurate statements may themselves lead to liability, even where the party did not violate actual statute or regulation through its failures to protect the data it held consistent with its disclosures.[10]

Public scrutiny as well as public disclosure may increase exposure for an organization, especially a governmental body, with regard to data protection practices and lapses. In such circumstances, there could be political as well as financial consequences for such lapses, and the confidence of the population in the integrity of the body (and especially the willingness to take guidance from the body on issues of data security) may seriously suffer when the practices are disclosed.

The U.S. Government Accountability Office ("GAO"), the chief auditor for the U.S. government, has evaluated and reported on poor data protection practices within a number of federal agencies in recent years, including the National Archives and Records Administration,[11] the Internal Revenue Service,[12] and the Securities and

---

[10] See discussion of liability for broken promises regarding encryption and other data protection methods in Chapter 2:IV.a.

[11] GAO-11-20, INFORMATION SECURITY: NATIONAL ARCHIVES AND RECORDS ADMINISTRATION NEEDS TO IMPLEMENT KEY PROGRAM ELEMENTS AND CONTROLS, http://www.gao.gov/assets/320/311584.html (last visited May 8, 2012).

[12] GAO-11-308, INFORMATION SECURITY: IRS NEEDS TO ENHANCE INTERNAL CONTROL OVER FINANCIAL REPORT-

Exchange Commission.[13] Given the SEC's role in supervising both financial services companies and the disclosure practices of publicly traded firms, both of which may be subject to substantial regulation on issues of data protection, the SEC's own failures are especially significant.

United States Government Accountability Office:

Washington, DC 20548:

April 13, 2012:

The Honorable Mary L. Schapiro:

Chairman:

U.S. Securities and Exchange Commission:

Subject: Management Report: Improvements Needed in SEC's Internal

Controls and Accounting Procedures:

Dear Ms. Schapiro:

On November 15, 2011, we issued our opinion on the U.S. Securities and Exchange Commission's (SEC) and its Investor Protection Fund's (IPF) fiscal years 2011 and 2010 financial statements. We also issued our opinion on the effectiveness of SEC's internal controls over financial reporting as of September 30, 2011, and our evaluation of SEC's compliance with selected provisions of laws and regulations during fiscal year 2011. In that report, we identified significant deficiencies in SEC's internal control over financial reporting.

The purpose of this report is to (1) present new recommendations related to the significant deficiencies we identified in our November 2011 report; (2) communicate less significant internal control issues we identified during our fiscal year 2011 audit of SEC's internal controls and accounting procedures, along with our related recommended corrective actions; and (3) summarize information on the status of the recommendations reported as open in our March 29, 2011, management report (see enclosure I).

Results in Brief:

In our audit of SEC's fiscal years 2011 and 2010 financial statements, we identified four significant deficiencies in internal control as of September 30, 2011. These significant internal control deficiencies represent continuing deficiencies concerning controls over (1) information systems, (2) financial reporting and accounting processes, (3) budgetary resources, and (4) registrant deposits and filing fees. These significant control deficiencies may adversely affect the accuracy and completeness of information used and reported by SEC's management. We are making a total of 10 new recommen-

---

ING AND TAXPAYER DATA, http://www.gao.gov/assets/320/316573.html (last visited May 8, 2012).

[13] GAO-12-424R, MANAGEMENT REPORT: IMPROVEMENTS NEEDED IN SEC'S INTERNAL CONTROLS AND ACCOUNTING PROCEDURES, http://www.gao.gov/assets/600/590122.txt (last visited May 8, 2012).

dations to address these continuing significant internal control deficiencies.

We also identified other internal control issues that although not considered material weaknesses or significant control deficiencies, nonetheless warrant SEC management's attention. These issues concern SEC's controls over:

* *payroll monitoring,*

* *implementation of post-judgment interest accounting procedures,*

* *accounting for disgorgement and penalty transactions, and:*

* *the government purchase card program.*

We are making a total of 9 new recommendations related to these other internal control deficiencies.

We are also providing summary information on the status of SEC's actions to address the recommendations from our prior audits as of the conclusion of our fiscal year 2011 audit. By the end of our fiscal year 2011 audit, we found that SEC took action to fully address 38 of the 66 recommendations from our prior audits, subsequent to our March 29, 2011, management report.

Lastly, we found that SEC took action to address and resolve all four weaknesses in information systems controls that we identified in public and "Limited Official Use Only" reports issued in 2008 through 2009 that were reported as open at the time of our March 29, 2011, management report.

In providing written comments on a draft of this report, the SEC Chairman stated that continued improvement in the agency's internal control structure, particularly in the areas of information security, financial reporting and accounting processes, budgetary resources, and registrant deposits and filing fees, is a top priority. The Chairman stated that the centerpiece of SEC's effort to strengthen financial controls is to migrate SEC's core financial system and transaction processing to a federal shared service provider. We will evaluate SEC's actions, strategies, and plans as part of our fiscal year 2012 audit. SEC's written comments are reprinted in enclosure II. SEC also provided technical comments, which we considered and incorporated as appropriate.

Scope and Methodology:

As part of our audit of SEC's fiscal years 2011 and 2010 financial statements, we evaluated SEC's internal controls over financial reporting and tested its compliance with selected provisions of laws and regulations. We designed our audit procedures to test relevant controls over financial reporting, including those designed to provide reasonable assurance that transactions are properly recorded, processed, and summarized to permit the preparation of financial statements in conformity with U.S. generally accepted accounting principles, and that assets are safeguarded against loss from unauthorized acquisition, use, or disposition. As part of our audit, we considered and evaluated the work performed and conclusions reached by SEC management in its internal control assessment. Further details on our scope and methodology are included in our November 2011 report on our audit of SEC's fiscal years 2011 and 2010 financial statements and are summarized in enclosure III.

We conducted our audit of SEC's fiscal years 2011 and 2010 financial statements in accordance with U.S. generally accepted government auditing standards. We believe our audit provided a reasonable basis for our conclusions in this report.

Significant Deficiency over Information Security:

As we reported in our report on our audit of SEC's fiscal years 2011 and 2010 financial statements, SEC has made progress in strengthening internal control over its financial information systems. However, despite this progress, we identified new weaknesses in information security controls regarding (1) incomplete implementation of SEC's information security program and (2) inadequate review of service auditors' reports that jeopardized the confidentiality and integrity of SEC's financial information, as discussed below.

Incomplete Implementation of SEC's Information Security Program:

During our audit, we identified new deficiencies that limited the effectiveness of information security controls protecting the confidentiality and integrity of key financial systems and databases that support financial reporting. Specifically, SEC had not consistently or fully implemented controls for identifying and authenticating users, authorizing access to resources, ensuring that sensitive data are encrypted, or auditing actions taken on its systems. In addition, SEC had not installed patch updates on its software, exposing it to known vulnerabilities, which could jeopardize data integrity and confidentiality.

* Controls were not consistently implemented for identifying and authenticating users. A computer system needs to be able to identify and authenticate each user so that activities on the system can be linked and traced to a specific individual. An organization does this by assigning a unique user account to each user, and because of this, the system is able to distinguish one user from another — a process called identification. The system also needs to establish the validity of a user's claimed identity by requesting some kind of information, such as a password, that is known only by the user — a process known as authentication. The combination of identification and authentication — such as user account password combinations — provides the basis for establishing individual accountability and for controlling access to the system. SEC policy requires password controls such as complex passwords and account lockout after unsuccessful log-in attempts, as well as disabling inactive accounts. However, the commission had not enforced complex passwords or account lockout for certain servers supporting key financial applications, nor had it disabled inactive accounts on one server. As a result, SEC is at increased risk that accounts could be compromised and used by

unauthorized individuals to access sensitive information.

* *Weaknesses in authorization controls limited their effectiveness. Authorization is the process of granting or denying access rights and permissions to a protected resource, such as a network, a system, an application, a function, or a file. A key component of granting or denying access rights is the concept of "least privilege." Least privilege is a basic principle for securing computer resources and data that means that users are granted only those access rights and permissions that they need to perform their official duties. SEC policy requires that each user or process be assigned only those privileges or functions needed to perform authorized tasks. However, SEC did not always employ the principle of least privilege when authorizing access permissions. Specifically, it did not appropriately restrict security-related parameters and users' rights and privileges for certain network devices, databases, and servers supporting key financial applications. As a result, users have excessive levels of access that were not required to perform their jobs. This could lead to data being inappropriately modified, either inadvertently or deliberately.*

* *Certain sensitive data were transmitted unencrypted. Cryptography underlies many of the mechanisms used to enforce the confidentiality and integrity of critical and sensitive information. A basic element of cryptography is encryption, which is used to transform plain text into cipher text using a special value known as a key and a mathematical process known as an algorithm. According to the National Institute of Standards and Technology (NIST), employing encryption protects the confidentiality and integrity of transmitted data. However, SEC did not configure servers supporting key financial applications to use encryption when transmitting data. As a result, increased risk exists that transmitted data can be intercepted, viewed, and modified.*

* *Certain systems were not configured to maintain audit trails of security-relevant events. To establish individual accountability, monitor compliance with security policies, and investigate security violations, organizations need to determine what, when, and by whom specific actions have been taken on a system. Organizations accomplish this by implementing system or security software that provides an audit trail — a log of system activity — that they can use to determine the source of a transaction or attempted transaction and to monitor users' activities. The way in which organizations configure system or security software determines the nature and extent of information that can be provided by the audit trail. To be effective, organizations should configure their software to collect and maintain audit trails that are sufficient to track security-relevant events. Accordingly, SEC requires the enforcement of auditing and accountability by configuring information systems to produce, store, and retain audit records of system, application, network, and user activity. However, SEC had not consistently configured certain servers supporting key financial applications to maintain audit trails for all security-relevant events. As a result, increased risk exists that the commission will be unable to determine (1) if certain*

malicious incidents have occurred and (2) who or what caused them.

* *Systems were not routinely and consistently patched. Configuration management involves, among other things, (1) verifying the correctness of the security settings in the operating systems, applications, or computing and network devices and (2) obtaining reasonable assurance that systems are configured and operating securely and as intended. Patch management, a component of configuration management, is an important element in mitigating the risks associated with software vulnerabilities. When a software vulnerability is discovered, the software vendor may develop and distribute a patch or work-around to mitigate the vulnerability. Without the patch, an attacker can exploit a software vulnerability to read, modify, or delete sensitive information; disrupt operations; or launch attacks against systems at another organization. SEC policy requires remediation efforts, such as patching, to be implemented within 7 days or less for those vulnerabilities deemed of high importance or critical. However, the commission did not routinely and consistently patch servers supporting key financial applications in a timely manner. Failing to apply critical patches increases the risk of exposing SEC systems to vulnerabilities that could be exploited.*

An underlying reason for these deficiencies is that SEC has not fully implemented elements of its information security program. Specifically, SEC did not consistently take the following actions:

* *Develop baselines and guidance for securely configuring systems. NIST guidance recommends developing, documenting, and maintaining a baseline configuration of information systems. In addition, the United States Government Configuration Baseline provides the baseline security settings that federal agencies are required by the Office of Management and Budget (OMB) to implement, for platforms such as Windows, to improve information security and reduce overall information technology (IT) operating costs. Also, SEC policy requires that it establish and maintain baseline configuration standards for its systems. However, SEC management did not develop or maintain baseline configurations of security settings or associated guides for configuring several of its systems and devices. In addition, in its fiscal year 2011 Federal Information Security Management Act of 2002 (FISMA) reporting, the commission reported that it did not have an automated capability that provided visibility into the system configurations of any of its IT assets. As a result, SEC risks not being able to ensure that its systems are securely configured in accordance with federal and commission policies.*

* *Document security requirements for an SEC subsystem in a system security plan. According to NIST, organizations should document security requirements for information systems — and any subsystems they contain — as part of the process of certifying a system to operate. However, SEC did not document security requirements for its EDGAR/Fee Momentum subsystem in its security plan for EDGAR. Without documenting these requirements, SEC risks not effectively securing the EDGAR/Fee Momentum subsystem.*

* Scan for vulnerabilities in all its systems and applications. NIST recommends that organizations implement a vulnerability management program that includes (1) scanning for vulnerabilities, (2) employing scanning tools and techniques that promote interoperability and automation, (3) analyzing vulnerability reports and results, and (4) sharing information obtained from the scanning process and assessments with appropriate personnel throughout the organization. However, SEC had not developed a comprehensive vulnerability management strategy, including a scanning schedule; performed compliance and vulnerability scans on its applications, databases, and network devices; or provided evidence of analysis and actions taken based on scan results. By not implementing a comprehensive vulnerability management scanning program, SEC is at increased risk of not being able to detect vulnerabilities that could jeopardize the security of its systems.

SEC officials stated that they had taken actions to correct several of the weaknesses we identified in the agency's security controls, but we have not yet verified the extent or effectiveness of SEC's actions as they occurred subsequent to the completion of our fiscal year 2011 financial audit.

Nevertheless, although SEC has made progress in strengthening information security controls intended to protect key financial information, control weaknesses continue to jeopardize the confidentiality and integrity of that information. These include deficiencies in SEC's controls for identifying and authenticating users, authorizing access to resources, ensuring that sensitive data are encrypted, and monitoring actions taken on its systems, as well as inconsistent patching of software. These increase the risk that unauthorized individuals could gain access to critical systems and intentionally or inadvertently access, alter, or delete sensitive data or computer programs. Until SEC mitigates its control deficiencies and fully implements its information security program, it will continue to be at risk of ongoing deficiencies in the security controls over its financial and support systems and the information they contain.

Recommendations for Executive Action:

To address the deficiencies in internal control over information security, we recommend that the Chairman direct the Chief Operating Officer (COO) and Chief Information Officer (CIO) to take the following specific actions:

1. Establish configuration baselines and related guidance for securing systems and monitoring system configuration baseline implementation.

2. Enhance the EDGAR security plan to document security requirements for the EDGAR/Fee Momentum subsystem.

3. Develop and implement a comprehensive vulnerability management strategy that includes routine scanning of SEC's systems and evaluation of such scanning to provide for any needed corrective actions.

In a separate report designated "Limited Official Use Only," we are also making 27 recommendations to enhance SEC's internal control over infor-

mation security.

Inadequate Review of Service Auditors' Reports:

During our audit, we found that SEC did not take appropriate action to address the audit reports of SEC's external service providers although a significant portion of SEC's collections, payroll, and investment transaction processing is performed by U.S. Bancorp (for the Department of the Treasury's (Treasury) CA$HLINK system), the Department of the Interior's National Business Center, and the Bureau of the Public Debt's Federal Investments Branch, respectively. As such, SEC places significant reliance on these service providers to determine whether its collections, payroll, and investment transactions are complete, valid, accurate, and timely.

In fiscal year 2011, each of these service providers contracted with an independent auditor to perform an audit of controls related to its service operations under Statement on Standards for Attestation Engagements (SSAE) No. 16, Reporting on Controls at a Service Organization. SSAE No. 16 provides authoritative guidance for service auditors to report on the design and operating effectiveness of controls at organizations that provide services to user entities when those controls are likely to be relevant to user entities' internal control over financial reporting. The issuance of a service auditor's report prepared in accordance with SSAE No. 16 signifies that a service organization has had its control objectives and control activities examined by an independent auditing firm. The service auditor's report includes valuable information regarding the service organization's controls and the effectiveness of those controls and also identifies complementary user entity controls that should be implemented by the user entity to ensure that its control objectives are met.

NIST recommends that organizations that authorize connections from systems outside of their authorization boundary should monitor these connections on an ongoing basis to ensure that security measures are in place. In accordance with OMB Circular No. A-123 agency management should review the scope of the SSAE No. 16 service auditor's report (SSAE No. 16 report) in the context of the agency's overall internal control assessment and take timely and effective actions to address any deficiencies identified. Moreover, according to Standards for Internal Control in the Federal Government, management should comprehensively identify risks and consider all significant interactions between the entity and other parties as well as internal factors at both the entitywide and activity levels.

In fiscal year 2011, based on our review of SEC's risk assessment of internal controls over financial reporting and its SSAE No. 16 report review process, we found that management did not develop an understanding of its complete financial reporting control environment sufficient to identify all relevant risks and effectively plan and test controls and mitigate for any control deficiencies of its service provider that affected the integrity and availability of SEC's information. Specifically, we found that SEC did not do the following:

* Have a documented process in place to review SSAE No. 16 reports from its lockbox service provider to determine whether the service organization's controls were suitably designed and operating effectively. The SSAE No.16 report we were provided noted exceptions in user access privileges and shared administrative user identification and passwords.

* Timely evaluate or test the effectiveness of complementary user entity controls identified by the SSAE No. 16 report from its payroll service provider. The service provider's processing of transactions and controls over the processing were designed under the assumption that these complementary user entity controls would be placed in operation by its clients to ensure that control objectives were met. As a result, we concluded that SEC was unable to fully consider these controls as part of its assessment of the effectiveness of its internal control over financial reporting as of September 30, 2011. SEC completed its assessment of complementary user controls from its payroll service provider after the end of fiscal year 2011 and did not review the SSAE No. 16 report from its investments service provider. Consequently, SEC did not evaluate and test the design and operating effectiveness of the complementary user controls the service providers' auditors recommended.

As a result, SEC is at risk that it may not be aware of deficiencies in security controls that could affect SEC data. Further, as a result of these weaknesses in SEC's risk assessment and control monitoring process, SEC did not consider the complete financial reporting control environment for the areas evaluated and management did not identify all risks or test all of the key controls that drive a significant portion of its cash collections; payroll, which accounts for over 69 percent of gross costs in its statement of net cost; and investment operations.

Recommendation for Executive Action:

To address the deficiencies in internal control over review of service auditors' reports, we recommend that the Chairman direct the COO and Chief Financial Officer (CFO) to take the following action:

4. As part of the risk assessment process, include steps for reviewing the SSAE No. 16 reports from all service organizations key to SEC's financial reporting control environment in time to allow appropriate actions to be taken before the end of the fiscal year to address any identified deficiencies in the design and operating effectiveness of service organization or user entity controls . . . .[14]

---

[14] *Id. (footnotes omitted).*

b. Spotting Potential Data Breach Vulnerability: The FTC's Red Flags Rule

Beyond the FTC's role in enforcing violations of consumer protection statutes and its own regulations, it may also take a proactive role in preventing, or at least reducing the chance, of harm to consumers. One such effort is the Red Flags Rule, enacted by the FTC together with other federal agencies pursuant to a mandate in the Fair Credit Reporting Act to create guidelines for identifying potential risk factors (i.e. "red flags") for identity theft vulnerability.[15]

In response to the statutory requirement, the FTC, the Federal Reserve, the Federal Deposit Insurance Corporation, the Department of the Treasury, the National Credit Union and Administration jointly enacted the Red Flags Rule, with each agency responsible for those elements within its jurisdiction.[16] The first section of the FTC's version of the Rule[17] provides:

> *(a) Scope. This section applies to financial institutions and creditors that are subject to administrative enforcement of the FCRA by the Federal Trade Commission pursuant to 15 U.S.C. 1681s(a)(1).*
>
> *(b) Definitions. For purposes of this section, and Appendix A, the following definitions apply:*
>
> *(1) Account means a continuing relationship established by a person with a financial institution or creditor to obtain a product or service for personal, family, household or business purposes. Account includes:*
>
> *(i) An extension of credit, such as the purchase of property or services involving a deferred payment; and*
>
> *(ii) A deposit account.*
>
> *(2) The term board of directors includes:*
>
> *(i) In the case of a branch or agency of a foreign bank, the managing official in charge of the branch or agency; and*
>
> *(ii) In the case of any other creditor that does not have a board of directors, a designated employee at the level of senior management.*
>
> *(3) Covered account means:*
>
> *(i) An account that a financial institution or creditor offers or maintains, primarily for personal, family, or household purposes, that involves or is designed to permit multiple payments or transactions, such as a credit card account, mortgage loan, automobile loan, margin account, cell phone account, utility account, checking account, or savings account; and*

---

[15] 15 U.S.C. § 1681m(e).

[16] 72 FR 63718-01, Nov. 9, 2007; revised, 74 FR 22644, May 14, 2009.

[17] 16 CFR § 681.1.

(ii) Any other account that the financial institution or creditor offers or maintains for which there is a reasonably foreseeable risk to customers or to the safety and soundness of the financial institution or creditor from identity theft, including financial, operational, compliance, reputation, or litigation risks.

(4) Credit has the same meaning as in 15 U.S.C. 1681a(r)(5).

(5) Creditor has the same meaning as in 15 U.S.C. 1681a(r)(5)[18], and includes lenders such as banks, finance companies, automobile dealers, mortgage brokers, utility companies, and telecommunications companies.

(6) Customer means a person that has a covered account with a financial institution or creditor.

(7) Financial institution has the same meaning as in 15 U.S.C. 1681a(t).

(8) Identity theft has the same meaning as in 16 CFR 603.2(a).

(9) Red Flag means a pattern, practice, or specific activity that indicates the possible existence of identity theft.

(10) Service provider means a person that provides a service directly to the financial institution or creditor.

(c) Periodic Identification of Covered Accounts. Each financial institution or creditor must periodically determine whether it offers or maintains covered accounts. As a part of this determination, a financial institution or creditor must conduct a risk assessment to determine whether it offers or maintains covered accounts described in paragraph (b)(3)(ii) of this section, taking into consideration:

(1) The methods it provides to open its accounts;

(2) The methods it provides to access its accounts; and

(3) Its previous experiences with identity theft.

(d) Establishment of an Identity Theft Prevention Program —

(1) Program requirement. Each financial institution or creditor that offers or maintains one or more covered accounts must develop and implement a written Identity Theft Prevention Program (Program) that is designed to detect, prevent, and mitigate identity theft in connection with the opening of a covered account or any existing covered account. The Program must be appropriate to the size and complexity of the financial institution or creditor and the nature and scope of its activities.

---

[18] This statute in turn refers to the definition of credit and creditor contained in 15 U.S.C. § 1691a; that definition of "creditor" provides, "[t]he term "creditor" means any person who regularly extends, renews, or continues credit; any person who regularly arranges for the extension, renewal, or continuation of credit; or any assignee of an original creditor who participates in the decision to extend, renew, or continue credit." 15 U.S.C. § 1691a(e).

(2) Elements of the Program. The Program must include reasonable policies and procedures to:

(i) Identify relevant Red Flags for the covered accounts that the financial institution or creditor offers or maintains, and incorporate those Red Flags into its Program;

(ii) Detect Red Flags that have been incorporated into the Program of the financial institution or creditor;

(iii) Respond appropriately to any Red Flags that are detected pursuant to paragraph (d)(2)(ii) of this section to prevent and mitigate identity theft; and

(iv) Ensure the Program (including the Red Flags determined to be relevant) is updated periodically, to reflect changes in risks to customers and to the safety and soundness of the financial institution or creditor from identity theft.

(e) Administration of the Program. Each financial institution or creditor that is required to implement a Program must provide for the continued administration of the Program and must:

(1) Obtain approval of the initial written Program from either its board of directors or an appropriate committee of the board of directors;

(2) Involve the board of directors, an appropriate committee thereof, or a designated employee at the level of senior management in the oversight, development, implementation and administration of the Program;

(3) Train staff, as necessary, to effectively implement the Program; and

(4) Exercise appropriate and effective oversight of service provider arrangements.

(f) Guidelines. Each financial institution or creditor that is required to implement a Program must consider the guidelines in appendix A of this part[19] and include in its Program those guidelines that are appropriate.

Although the FTC's Red Flags Rule was initially promulgated in 2007, and was originally to go into effect on November 1, 2008, its enforcement was delayed repeatedly by the FTC until December 31, 2010,[20] largely because of concern that the definition of "creditor" was overbroad and would require more companies than

---

[19] The interagency guidelines may be found at 16 C.F.R. pt. 681, App. A.

[20] FTC WILL GRANT SIX-MONTH DELAY OF ENFORCEMENT OF "RED FLAGS" RULE REQUIRING CREDITORS TO HAVE IDENTITY THEFT PREVENTION PROGRAMS (Oct. 22, 2008), http://www.ftc.gov/opa/2008/10/redflags.shtm (last visited May 8, 2012); FTC WILL GRANT THREE-MONTH DELAY OF ENFORCEMENT OF "RED FLAGS" RULE REQUIRING CREDITORS AND FINANCIAL INSTITUTIONS TO ADOPT IDENTITY THEFT PREVENTION PROGRAMS (Apr. 30, 2009), http://www.ftc.gov/opa/2009/04/redflagsrule.shtm (last visited May 8, 2012); FTC ANNOUNCES EXPANDED BUSINESS EDUCATION CAMPAIGN ON "RED FLAGS" RULE (July 29, 2009), http://www.ftc.gov/opa/2009/07/redflag.shtm (last visited May 8, 2012); FTC EXTENDS ENFORCEMENT DEADLINE FOR IDENTITY THEFT RED FLAGS RULE (May 28, 2010), http://www.ftc.gov/opa/2010/05/redflags.shtm (last visited May 8, 2012).

intended to comply with its obligations.[21] In response to this concern, a definition of creditor in the underlying FCRA statute specific to the Red Flags Rule was added:

> *(4) Definitions*
>
> *As used in this subsection, the term "creditor" —*
>
> *(A) means a creditor, as defined in section 1691a of this title, that regularly and in the ordinary course of business —*
>
> *(i) obtains or uses consumer reports, directly or indirectly, in connection with a credit transaction;*
>
> *(ii) furnishes information to consumer reporting agencies, as described in section 1681s-2 of this title, in connection with a credit transaction; or*
>
> *(iii) advances funds to or on behalf of a person, based on an obligation of the person to repay the funds or repayable from specific property pledged by or on behalf of the person;*
>
> *(B) does not include a creditor described in subparagraph (A)(iii) that advances funds on behalf of a person for expenses incidental to a service provided by the creditor to that person; and*
>
> *(C) includes any other type of creditor, as defined in that section 1691a of this title, as the agency described in paragraph (1) having authority over that creditor may determine appropriate by rule promulgated by that agency, based on a determination that such creditor offers or maintains accounts that are subject to a reasonably foreseeable risk of identity theft.*[22]

The FTC also provides guidance to businesses on complying with the Red Flags Rule,[23] offers articles for republication,[24] and has joined with the other agencies sharing enforcement authority in publishing a frequently asked questions ("FAQ") document on the Rule.[25]

III.   POST-BREACH: DISCLOSURE AND LIABILITY

What if, despite all precautions and legal obligations, a business' records are breached (either through malice or negligence)? This raises two major concerns: any legal obligation to disclose the breach, and potential exposure to litigation arising out of the breach.

---

[21] FTC Extended Enforcement Policy: Identity Theft Red Flags Rule, http://www.ftc.gov/os/2010/05/100528redflagsrule.pdf.

[22] 15 U.S.C. 1681m(e)(4).

[23] Fighting Fraud with the Red Flags Rule, http://www.ftc.gov/bcp/edu/microsites/redflagsrule/index.shtml (last visited May 8, 2012).

[24] Fighting Fraud with the Red Flags Rule, http://www.ftc.gov/bcp/edu/microsites/redflagsrule/publish-articles.shtm (last visited May 8, 2012).

[25] Frequently Asked Questions: Identity Theft Red Flags and Address Discrepancies, http://www.ftc.gov/os/2009/06/090611redflagsfaq.pdf.

a.   Breach Notification Laws: State and Potential Federal Requirements

While breaches may occur in a single location (especially if the data are located on a single physical server or other digital storage device), the impact and exposure may extend not only to that location but any other states in which the company, the victims or even the party responsible for the breach are located. While there have been numerous efforts in Congress to enact an overall federal data breach notification law,[26] as of the date of publication of this work none has become a statute. It has been left, therefore, to the individual states to consider and adopt mandatory disclosure laws, and more than 40 have done so.[27]

California was among the first to enact laws that both mandated proper stewardship of consumer data and required notice to consumers if their information was improperly released. Its statute has become a model for some other states' laws:

§ 1798.81.5. Security procedures and practices with respect to personal information about California residents

(a) It is the intent of the Legislature to ensure that personal information about California residents is protected. To that end, the purpose of this section is to encourage businesses that own or license personal information about Californians to provide reasonable security for that information. For the purpose of this section, the phrase "owns or licenses" is intended to include, but is not limited to, personal information that a business retains as part of the business' internal customer account or for the purpose of using that information in transactions with the person to whom the information relates.

(b) A business that owns or licenses personal information about a California resident shall implement and maintain reasonable security procedures and practices appropriate to the nature of the information, to protect the personal information from unauthorized access, destruction, use, modification, or disclosure.

(c) A business that discloses personal information about a California resident pursuant to a contract with a nonaffiliated third party shall require by contract that the third party implement and maintain reasonable security procedures and practices appropriate to the nature of the information, to protect the personal information from unauthorized access, destruction, use, modification, or disclosure.

(d) For purposes of this section, the following terms have the following meanings:

(1) "Personal information" means an individual's first name or first initial and his or her last name in combination with any one or more of the following data elements, when either the name or the data elements are not encrypted or redacted:

---

[26] See, e.g., the Data Breach Notification Act of 2011, S. 1408 (112th Congress).

[27] According to the National Conference of State Legislatures, as of February 6, 2012, "[f]orty-six states, the District of Columbia, Puerto Rico and the Virgin Islands have enacted legislation requiring notification of security breaches involving personal information." Security Breach Notification Laws, http://www.ncsl.org/issues-research/telecom/security-breach-notification-laws.aspx (last visited May 8, 2012).

(A) Social security number.

(B) Driver's license number or California identification card number.

(C) Account number, credit or debit card number, in combination with any required security code, access code, or password that would permit access to an individual's financial account.

(D) Medical information.

(2) "Medical information" means any individually identifiable information, in electronic or physical form, regarding the individual's medical history or medical treatment or diagnosis by a health care professional.

(3) "Personal information" does not include publicly available information that is lawfully made available to the general public from federal, state, or local government records.

(e) The provisions of this section do not apply to any of the following:

(1) A provider of health care, health care service plan, or contractor regulated by the Confidentiality of Medical Information Act (Part 2.6 (commencing with Section 56) of Division 1).

(2) A financial institution as defined in Section 4052 of the Financial Code and subject to the California Financial Information Privacy Act (Division 1.2 (commencing with Section 4050) of the Financial Code.

(3) A covered entity governed by the medical privacy and security rules issued by the federal Department of Health and Human Services, Parts 160 and 164 of Title 45 of the Code of Federal Regulations, established pursuant to the Health Insurance Portability and Availability Act of 1996 (HIPAA).

(4) An entity that obtains information under an agreement pursuant to Article 3 (commencing with Section 1800) of Chapter 1 of Division 2 of the Vehicle Code and is subject to the confidentiality requirements of the Vehicle Code.

(5) A business that is regulated by state or federal law providing greater protection to personal information than that provided by this section in regard to the subjects addressed by this section. Compliance with that state or federal law shall be deemed compliance with this section with regard to those subjects. This paragraph does not relieve a business from a duty to comply with any other requirements of other state and federal law regarding the protection and privacy of personal information.

§ 1798.82. Civil actions; violation of title

(a) Any person or business that conducts business in California, and that owns or licenses computerized data that includes personal information, shall disclose any breach of the security of the system following discovery or notification of the breach in the security of the data to any resident of California whose unencrypted personal information was, or is reasonably believed to have been, acquired by an unauthorized person. The disclosure shall be made in the most expedient time possible and without unreasonable delay, consistent with the legitimate needs of law enforcement, as *provided in subdivision (c), or any measures necessary to determine the scope of the breach and restore the reasonable integrity of the data system.*

(b) Any person or business that maintains computerized data that includes personal information that the person or business does not own shall notify the owner or licensee of the information of any breach of the security of the data immediately following discovery, if the personal information was, or is reasonably believed to have been, acquired by an unauthorized person.

(c) The notification required by this section may be delayed if a law enforcement agency determines that the notification will impede a criminal investigation. The notification required by this section shall be made after the law enforcement agency determines that it will not compromise the investigation.

(d) Any person or business that is required to issue a security breach notification pursuant to this section shall meet all of the following requirements:

(1) The security breach notification shall be written in plain language.

(2) The security breach notification shall include, at a minimum, the following information:

(A) The name and contact information of the reporting person or business subject to this section.

(B) A list of the types of personal information that were or are reasonably believed to have been the subject of a breach.

(C) If the information is possible to determine at the time the notice is provided, then any of the following: (i) the date of the breach, (ii) the estimated date of the breach, or (iii) the date range within which the breach occurred. The notification shall also include the date of the notice.

(D) Whether notification was delayed as a result of a law enforcement investigation, if that information is possible to determine at the time the notice is provided.

(E) A general description of the breach incident, if that information is possible to determine at the time the notice is provided.

(F) The toll-free telephone numbers and addresses of the major credit reporting agencies if the breach exposed a social security number or a driver's license or California identification card number.

(3) At the discretion of the person or business, the security breach notification may also include any of the following:

(A) Information about what the person or business has done to protect individuals whose information has been breached.

(B) Advice on steps that the person whose information has been breached may take to protect himself or herself.

(e) A covered entity under the federal Health Insurance Portability and Accountability Act of 1996 (42 U.S.C. Sec. 1320d et seq.) will be deemed to have complied with the notice requirements in subdivision (d) if it has complied completely with Section

13402(f) of the federal Health Information Technology for Economic and Clinical Health Act (Public Law 111-5). However, nothing in this subdivision shall be construed to exempt a covered entity from any other provision of this section.

(f) Any person or business that is required to issue a security breach notification pursuant to this section to more than 500 California residents as a result of a single breach of the security system shall electronically submit a single sample copy of that security breach notification, excluding any personally identifiable information, to the Attorney General. A single sample copy of a security breach notification shall not be deemed to be within subdivision (f) of Section 6254 of the Government Code.

(g) For purposes of this section, "breach of the security of the system" means unauthorized acquisition of computerized data that compromises the security, confidentiality, or integrity of personal information maintained by the person or business. Good faith acquisition of personal information by an employee or agent of the person or business for the purposes of the person or business is not a breach of the security of the system, provided that the personal information is not used or subject to further unauthorized disclosure.

(h) For purposes of this section, "personal information" means an individual's first name or first initial and last name in combination with any one or more of the following data elements, when either the name or the data elements are not encrypted:

(1) Social security number.

(2) Driver's license number or California Identification Card number.

(3) Account number, credit or debit card number, in combination with any required security code, access code, or password that would permit access to an individual's financial account.

(4) Medical information.

(5) Health insurance information.

(i)(1) For purposes of this section, "personal information" does not include publicly available information that is lawfully made available to the general public from federal, state, or local government records.

(2) For purposes of this section, "medical information" means any information regarding an individual's medical history, mental or physical condition, or medical treatment or diagnosis by a health care professional.

(3) For purposes of this section, "health insurance information" means an individual's health insurance policy number or subscriber identification number, any unique identifier used by a health insurer to identify the individual, or any information in an individual's application and claims history, including any appeals records.

(j) For purposes of this section, "notice" may be provided by one of the following methods:

(1) Written notice.

(2) Electronic notice, if the notice provided is consistent with the provisions regarding electronic records and signatures set forth in Section 7001 of Title 15 of the United States Code.

(3) Substitute notice, if the person or business demonstrates that the cost of providing notice would exceed two hundred fifty thousand dollars ($250,000), or that the affected class of subject persons to be notified exceeds 500,000, or the person or business does not have sufficient contact information. Substitute notice shall consist of all of the following:

(A) E-mail notice when the person or business has an e-mail address for the subject persons.

(B) Conspicuous posting of the notice on the Internet Web site page of the person or business, if the person or business maintains one.

(C) Notification to major statewide media and the Office of Privacy Protection within the State and Consumer Services Agency.

(k) Notwithstanding subdivision (j), a person or business that maintains its own notification procedures as part of an information security policy for the treatment of personal information and is otherwise consistent with the timing requirements of this part, shall be deemed to be in compliance with the notification requirements of this section if the person or business notifies subject persons in accordance with its policies in the event of a breach of security of the system.

There are a few particular noteworthy elements in California's law. First, the main provision applies to "[a]ny person or business that conducts business in California, and that owns or licenses computerized data that includes personal information," which, given the borderless nature of the Internet and the potential definitions of conducting business, effectively includes a vast number of people and companies that are not physically located in California. It is also crucial to note that California's law contains a significant "safe harbor" exemption to its obligations: by defining "personal information" as "an individual's first name or first initial and last name in combination with any one or more of the following data elements, *when either the name or the data elements are not encrypted*" [emphasis added], the statute excuses those entities that store those data in an *encrypted* form from having to provide notice of any breach. The reason for this differentiation is that, even if encrypted data are accessed without authorization, they are not usable for identity theft or other malicious purposes unless the party gaining access also has the means to decrypt them. Thus, although it does not mandate encryption of personal information stored by a business, California strongly incentivizes doing so in order to avoid the potential liability and reputational damage associated with both breaches and the obligation to notify those affected about them.[28]

---

[28] California's approach, and its inclusion of encryption in its definition of "personal information," has been followed by states including Maryland (MD Code, Commercial Law, § 14-3501(d)(1)); New Hampshire (N.H. Rev. Stat. § 359-B:22(I)); Nevada (N.R.S. 603A.040); Illinois (815 ILCS 530/5) and others.

b. Litigation Arising out of Data Breach

Depending on the circumstances and the relevant jurisdiction, a single data breach may generate law enforcement actions by state and federal consumer protection officials, either separately or working in cooperation:

Agency Announces Settlement of Separate Actions Against Retailer TJX, and Data Brokers Reed Elsevier and Seisint for Failing to Provide Adequate Security for Consumers' Data

In two unrelated Federal Trade Commission actions, discount retailer TJX and data brokers Reed Elsevier and Seisint have agreed to settle charges that each engaged in practices that, taken together, failed to provide reasonable and appropriate security for sensitive consumer information. The settlements will require that the companies implement comprehensive information security programs and obtain audits by independent third-party security professionals every other year for 20 years.

"By now, the message should be clear: companies that collect sensitive consumer information have a responsibility to keep it secure," said FTC Chairman Deborah Platt Majoras. "These cases bring to 20 the number of complaints in which the FTC has charged companies with security deficiencies in protecting sensitive consumer information. Information security is a priority for the FTC, as it should be for every business in America."

According to the FTC complaint, TJX, with over 2,500 stores worldwide, failed to use reasonable and appropriate security measures to prevent unauthorized access to personal information on its computer networks. An intruder exploited these failures and obtained tens of millions of credit and debit payment cards that consumers used at TJX's stores, as well as the personal information of approximately 455,000 consumers who returned merchandise to the stores. Banks have claimed that tens of millions of dollars in fraudulent charges have been made on the cards and millions of cards have been cancelled and reissued.

Specifically, the agency charged that TJX:

- *Created an unnecessary risk to personal information by storing it on, and transmitting it between and within, its various computer networks in clear text;*

- *Did not use readily available security measures to limit wireless access to its networks, thereby allowing an intruder to connect wirelessly to its networks without authorization;*

- *Did not require network administrators and others to use strong passwords or to use different passwords to access different programs, computers, and networks;*

- *Failed to use readily available security measures, such as firewalls, to limit access among its computers and the Internet; and*

- *Failed to employ sufficient measures to detect and prevent unauthorized access to computer networks or to conduct security investigations, such as patching or updating anti-virus software.*

In the FTC's action against data brokers Reed Elsevier (REI) and Seisint, the complaint alleges that REI — through its LexisNexis data broker business — and Seisint collect and store in databases information about millions of consumers, including names, current and prior addresses, dates of birth, drivers license numbers and Social Security numbers. They obtain information about consumers from credit reporting agencies and other sources, and sell products customers use online to find and retrieve the information from their databases. The companies relied on user IDs and passwords (or "user credentials") to control customer access to consumer information in their databases.

The complaint alleges that, among other security failures, they allowed customers to use easy-to-guess passwords to access Seisint's "Accurint" databases. The databases contained sensitive consumer information, including drivers license numbers and Social Security numbers. Identity thieves exploited these security failures, and through multiple breaches obtained access to sensitive information about at least 316,000 consumers from Accurint databases. The identity thieves used the information to activate credit cards and open new accounts, and made fraudulent purchases on the cards and new accounts. REI acquired Seisint in late 2004, and the breaches continued for at least nine months afterward, during which time REI controlled Seisint's practices.

The agency charged that Seisint and REI:

- *Failed to make Seisint user credentials hard to guess;*

- *Failed to require periodic changes of Seisint user credentials;*

- *Failed to suspend credentials after a certain number unsuccessful log-in attempts;*

- *Allowed Seisint customers to store their credentials in a vulnerable format in cookies on their computers;*

- *Failed to require Seisint customers to encrypt or protect credentials, search queries or search results in transit between customer computers and Seisint Web sites;*

- *Allowed customers to create new user credentials without confirming that the new credentials were created by customers rather than identity thieves;*

- *Permitted users to share credentials;*

- *Did not adequately assess the vulnerability of Seisint's Web applications and computer network to commonly known attacks; and*

- *Did not implement simple, low-cost, and readily available defenses to such attacks.*

The settlement with TJX requires it to establish and maintain a comprehensive security program reasonably designed to protect the security, confidentiality, and integrity of personal information it collects from or about consumers. The settlement with REI and Seisint requires them to establish and maintain comprehensive security programs to protect personal information that is in whole or part nonpublic information. The settlements require the programs to contain administrative, technical, and physical safeguards appropriate to each company's size, the nature of its activities, and the sensitivity of the personal information it collects. Specifically, the companies must:

- *Designate an employee or employees to coordinate the information security program;*

- *Identify internal and external risks to the security and confidentiality of personal information and assess the safeguards already in place;*

- *Design and implement safeguards to control the risks identified in the risk assessment and monitor their effectiveness;*

- *Develop reasonable steps to select and oversee service providers that handle the personal information they receive from the companies; and*

- *Evaluate and adjust their information security programs to reflect the results of monitoring, any material changes to their operations, or other circumstances that may impact the effectiveness of their security programs;*

The settlements require the companies to retain independent, third-party security auditors to assess their security programs on a biennial basis for the next 20 years. The auditors will be required to certify that the companies' security programs meet or exceed the requirements of the FTC's orders and are operating with sufficient effectiveness to provide reasonable assurance that the security of consumers' personal information is being protected.

The settlements also contain bookkeeping and record keeping provisions to allow the agency to monitor compliance with its orders.

The FTC coordinated its investigation of TJX with 39 state Attorneys General, lead by the office of the Massachusetts Attorney General, and acknowledges the invaluable assistance of the states in the agency's investigation.

The FTC acknowledges the invaluable assistance of the Hayward, California Police Department and the REACT (Rapid Enforcement Allied Computer Team) Task Force in the agency's investigation of Seisint and REI . . . .[29]

Beyond governmental action, data breaches may generate private litigation, often as class action suits, brought on behalf of the individuals whose personal identity was improperly accessed or businesses that suffered damages arising out of the breach, and may be brought under specific (and multiple) state laws.

---

[29] FTC Press Release, AGENCY ANNOUNCES SETTLEMENT OF SEPARATE ACTIONS AGAINST RETAILER TJX, AND DATA BROKERS REED ELSEVIER AND SEISINT FOR FAILING TO PROVIDE ADEQUATE SECURITY FOR CONSUMERS' DATA (Mar. 27, 2008), http://www.ftc.gov/opa/2008/03/datasec.shtm (last visited May 8, 2012).

IN RE HANNAFORD BROS. CO. CUSTOMER DATA SECURITY BREACH LITIGATION[30]

Opinion

JABAR, J.

The United States District Court for the District of Maine (Hornby, J.), acting pursuant to 4 M.R.S. § 57 (2009) and M.R.App. P. 25, has certified two questions of state law to this Court for review. These questions arise from a multi-count complaint filed against Hannaford Bros. Co. by customers whose financial information was stolen during a breach of Hannaford's computer system and who expended time and effort to identify and remediate fraudulent charges on their credit and debit card accounts. The questions certified are:

(1) "In the absence of physical harm or economic loss or identity theft, do time and effort alone, spent in a reasonable effort to avoid or remediate reasonably foreseeable harm, constitute a cognizable injury for which damages may be recovered under Maine law of negligence and/or implied contract?"

(2) "If the answer to question #1 is yes under a negligence claim and no under an implied contract claim, can a plaintiff suing for negligence recover damages under Maine law for purely economic harm absent personal injury, physical harm to property, or misrepresentation?"

We answer the federal court's first question in the negative and accordingly do not address the second question.

I. CASE HISTORY

Between December 2007 and March 2008, data thieves breached Hannaford's computer system and stole up to 4.2 million debit and credit card numbers, expiration dates, security codes, PINs, and other information belonging to customers who had used Hannaford's electronic payment processing services. Visa, Inc., notified Hannaford of the breach in late February of 2008. Hannaford discovered the means of the thieves' access on March 8, 2008, contained it, notified financial institutions on March 10, 2008, and publicly disclosed the breach on March 17, 2008.

Due to the data theft, a number of Hannaford customers initially experienced fraudulent and unauthorized charges on their credit card accounts or bank accounts. These customers expended time and effort identifying the fraudulent charges and convincing their banks and credit card companies that the charges should be reversed. By October 10, 2008, when a group of twenty-one representative plaintiffs filed a complaint in the United States District Court for the District of Maine, only one named plaintiff had outstanding fraudulent charges on her account. The other named plaintiffs had already been reimbursed by their banks or credit card companies.

---

[30] 4 A.3d 492 (Supreme Judical Ct. Maine 2010) (notes omitted).

The plaintiffs' complaint alleged breach of implied contract (Count 1), breach of implied warranty (Count 2), breach of a confidential relationship (Count 3), failure to advise customers of the data theft (Count 4), strict liability (Count 5), negligence (Count 6), and unfair trade practices (Count 7). The plaintiffs sought damages to compensate them for the expenditure of time and effort necessary to remedy the disruption of their financial affairs and for various fees, charges, and lost reward points.

Hannaford filed a motion to dismiss the plaintiffs' consolidated complaint for failure to state a claim upon which relief may be granted, pursuant to Fed.R.Civ.P. 12(b)(6). After a hearing, the court granted the motion to dismiss in part and denied it in part. In re Hannaford Bros. Co. Customer Data Sec. Breach Litig., 613 F.Supp.2d 108, 136 (D.Me.2009). The court dismissed Counts 2, 3, 4, and 5 as to all plaintiffs. Id. at 119–26, 136. For the remaining counts, the court determined that dismissal was dependent upon whether the plaintiffs had suffered an injury for which Maine law would grant relief. Id. at 131.

To make this determination, the court identified three categories of plaintiffs: (1) those who had never experienced a fraudulent charge; (2) the sole plaintiff who still had outstanding fraudulent charges; and (3) those who had fraudulent charges that had been reversed. Id. at 131–35. Citing numerous data-breach cases from other jurisdictions, the court determined that the first category of plaintiffs experienced only a risk of injury and therefore had no recoverable damages. Id. at 131–33. For the plaintiff in the second category, the court found that the fraudulent charges on her account were a cognizable injury. Id. at 133. Finally, the court found that for those plaintiffs who had already been reimbursed, their claims for various consequential losses, such as the loss of accumulated reward points and the time spent identifying and persuading financial institutions to reverse fraudulent charges, failed because the losses were "too remote, not reasonably foreseeable, and/or speculative." Id. at 134. Specifically, the court concluded that there was "no way to value and recompense . . . time and effort," noting that "[t]hose are the ordinary frustrations and inconveniences that everyone confronts in daily life with or without fraud or negligence." Id.

Based on this reasoning, the court granted Hannaford's motion to dismiss the claims of all the plaintiffs except Counts 1, 6, and 7 made by the plaintiff with recoverable damages. Id. at 136. However, after the court's ruling, the remaining plaintiff's bank fully reimbursed all contested charges. In re Hannaford Bros. Co. Customer Data Sec. Breach Litig., 660 F.Supp.2d 94, 97 (D.Me.2009). The parties filed a stipulation to this effect with the court, effectively ending the litigation. Id. Shortly thereafter, the plaintiffs moved for reconsideration and for certification of questions of law to this Court. Id. Relying on the Restatement (Second) of Torts § 919 (1979), the plaintiffs asserted that time and effort expended to avoid or remediate harm from fraudulent charges was a cognizable loss, regardless of whether they suffered other losses. In re Hannaford Bros. Co. Customer Data Sec. Breach Litig., 660 F.Supp.2d at 101. The court agreed that Maine law regarding recoverability of damages for time and effort alone was uncertain and, as a result, it certified the first question. See In re Hannaford Bros. Co. Customer Data Sec. Breach Litig., 671 F.Supp.2d 198, 201 (D.Me.2009). Because, depending upon our answer to the first question, the economic loss doctrine would be dispositive of the plaintiffs' claim, the court also certified a *second question to be answered if we concluded that time and effort alone was a cognizable injury only under Maine law of negligence.* See id. *The court stayed further briefing on the motion for reconsideration pending an answer from us on the certified questions.* In re Hannaford Bros. Co. Customer Data Sec. Breach Litig., *660 F.Supp.2d at 103.*

II. DISCUSSION

The plaintiffs here have suffered no physical harm, economic loss, or identity theft. As the federal district court recognized, actual injury or damage is an element of both negligence and breach of contract claims. See Estate of Cilley v. Lane, *2009 ME 133, ¶ 10, 985 A.2d 481, 485;* Me. Energy Recovery Co. v. United Steel Structures, Inc., *1999 ME 31, ¶ 7, 724 A.2d 1248, 1250. We, therefore, are asked to determine whether time and effort alone, spent in a reasonable effort to avoid reasonably foreseeable harm, is a cognizable injury under Maine law of negligence or implied contract. We conclude that it is not.*

A. Recovery for Time and Effort in Negligence

The tort of negligence does not compensate individuals for the typical annoyances or inconveniences that are a part of everyday life. See W. Page Keeton et al., *Prosser & Keeton on the Law of Torts § 30, at 165 (W. Page Keeton ed., 5th ed. 1984) ("Negligent conduct in itself is not such an interference with the interests of the world at large that there is any right to complain of it, or to be free from it, except in the case of some individual whose interests have suffered."). Liability in negligence, therefore, ordinarily requires proof of personal injury or property damage.* See Simmons, Zillman & Gregory, *Maine Tort Law § 19.02 at 19–8 to 19–11 (2004 ed.). An individual's time, alone, is not legally protected from the negligence of others.*

When personal injury is established, loss of time is a cognizable harm as it is related to loss of earning capacity or wages. See, e.g., Snow v. Villacci, *2000 ME 127, ¶¶ 9–12, 754 A.2d 360, 363–64;* Fotter v. Butler, *145 Me. 266, 272, 75 A.2d 160, 163 (1950). Similar types of financial recovery are permissible in connection with property damage.* See Walters v. Petrolane — Ne. Gas Serv., Inc., *425 A.2d 968, 973–74 (Me.1981) (approving damages for harm to property and lost profits in a negligence action). In each of these cases, because the time in question could be assigned a value reflecting a loss of earnings or earning opportunities resulting from personal injury or property damage, loss of time was a harm cognizable in negligence.* See Snow, *2000 ME 127, ¶¶ 9–12, 754 A.2d at 363–64;* Fotter, *145 Me. at 272, 75 A.2d at 163.*

Our case law, therefore, does not recognize the expenditure of time and effort alone as a harm. The plaintiffs contend that because their time and effort represented reasonable efforts to avoid reasonably foreseeable harm, it is compensable. However, we do not attach such significance to mitigation efforts.

The doctrine of mitigation of damages, or avoidable consequences, encourages plaintiffs to take reasonable steps to minimize losses caused by a defendant's negligence by prohibiting recovery for any damages that the plaintiff could reasonably have avoided. See Walter v. Wal — Mart Stores, Inc., *2000 ME 63, ¶ 24, 748 A.2d 961,*

970. A corollary of the mitigation doctrine permits the plaintiff to recover for costs and harms incurred during a reasonable effort to mitigate. See Marchesseault v. Jackson, 611 A.2d 95, 99 (Me.1992); Restatement (Second) of Torts § 919(1) (1979); Dan B. Dobbs, Law of Remedies § 3.9 (2d ed.1993). However, it must still be established that the time and effort expended constitute a legal injury rather than an inconvenience or annoyance.

*Unless the plaintiffs' loss of time reflects a corresponding loss of earnings or earning opportunities, it is not a cognizable injury under Maine law of negligence. See Snow, 2000 ME 127, ¶¶ 9–12, 754 A.2d at 363–64. The cases cited by the plaintiffs do not compel a contrary conclusion. In many of those cases, the party seeking recovery for time and effort expended had alleged at least one claim of intentional tort. See Craddock v. Jones, 143 So. 529, 531 (La.Ct.App.1932); McDonald v. North, 47 Barb. 530 (N.Y.Sup.Ct.1867); Bennett v. Lockwood & Carter, 20 Wend. 223, 224 (N.Y.Sup.Ct.1838); EMC Mortg. Corp. v. Jones, 252 S.W.3d 857, 868–69, 871, 872 (Tex.Ct.App.2008). Because liability is often more extensive in cases of intentional torts than those in negligence, intentional tort cases recognizing recovery for time and effort have little bearing on our analysis. Cf. Picher v. Roman Catholic Bishop of Portland, 2009 ME 67, ¶¶ 9–10, 29, 974 A.2d 286, 290, 295 (noting, in the context of a charitable immunity analysis, that recovery for intentional torts may be broader than it is for negligence claims); Garland v. Roy, 2009 ME 86, ¶ 26, 976 A.2d 940, 948. In other cases, a passing mention of loss of time without adequate facts to demonstrate how those damages were being measured is insufficient to persuade us that the expenditure of time and effort alone is a harm recoverable in negligence. See Kuhn v. Capital One Fin. Corp., No. 05-P-810, 2006 WL 3007931, at *3 (Mass.App.Ct. Oct. 23, 2006); Freeman v. Missouri Pac. Ry. Co., 101 Kan. 516, 167 P. 1062, 1063–65 (1917).*

Contrary to the plaintiffs' contention, our case law does not recognize time and effort as a compensable injury in the context of the plaintiffs' negligence claim. We decline to expand recovery in negligence in these circumstances.

B. Recovery for Time and Effort in Contract

Not every consequence of a breach of contract is a cognizable injury. See Rubin v. Matthews Int'l Corp., 503 A.2d 694, 696 (Me.1986); see also Cherny v. Emigrant Bank, 604 F.Supp.2d 605, 609 (S.D.N.Y.2009) (concluding that the receipt of unwanted spam after the plaintiff's personal e-mail address was disclosed did not constitute compensable harm). Generally, contract damages are more restricted than compensatory damages for a tort. Stull v. First Am. Title Ins. Co., 2000 ME 21, ¶ 17, 745 A.2d 975, 981. For example, emotional distress suffered as a result of breach of contract is ordinarily not recoverable unless it is accompanied by physical injury or it results in serious emotional disturbance due to the nature of the contract. Marquis v. Farm Family Mut. Ins. Co., 628 A.2d 644, 651 (Me.1993); Rubin, 503 A.2d at 696–98; cf. Gayer v. Bath Iron Works Corp., 687 A.2d 617, 621 n. 3 (Me.1996) (listing specific types of contracts for which emotional distress damages may be available).

As the federal district court pointed out, the time and effort expended by the plaintiffs here represent "the ordinary frustrations and inconveniences that everyone confronts in daily life." In re Hannaford Bros. Co. Customer Data Sec. Breach Litig.,

613 F.Supp.2d at 134. Accordingly, we conclude that the expenditure of time and effort alone does not represent a cognizable injury recoverable in implied contract.

The entry is:

We answer certified question (1): "No, Maine law of negligence and implied contract does not recognize time and effort alone, spent in a reasonable effort to avoid or remediate reasonably foreseeable harm, as a cognizable injury in the absence of physical harm or economic loss or identity theft." We do not address certified question (2).

* * * * *

IN RE: HEARTLAND PAYMENT SYSTEMS, INC. CUSTOMER DATA SECURITY BREACH LITIGATION[31]

Lee H. Rosenthal, District Judge.

In January 2009, Heartland Payment Systems, Inc. ("Heartland") publicly disclosed that hackers had breached its computer systems and obtained access to confidential payment-card information for over one hundred million consumers. Consumers and financial institutions filed suits across the nation. The Judicial Panel on Multidistrict Litigation consolidated those cases before this court. The cases have proceeded on two tracks, one for the Consumer Plaintiffs and one for the Financial Institution Plaintiffs.

The Financial Institution Plaintiffs filed a master complaint asserting causes of action for breach of contract and implied contract, negligence and negligence per se, negligent and intentional misrepresentation, and violations of consumer-protection statutes in New Jersey and other states. (Docket Entry No. 32). Heartland moved to dismiss. (Docket Entry No. 39). After this court dismissed claims filed by some of the Financial Institution Plaintiffs against the banks that contracted with Heartland, (Docket Entry No. 117), the parties supplemented their briefs. (Docket Entry Nos. 122, 124, 127, 131, 133–35). Based on the master complaint, the motion, the extensive briefing, and the relevant law, this court grants the motion to dismiss in part and denies it in part . . . .

I. Background

Every day, merchants swipe millions of customers' payment cards. In the seconds that pass between the swipe and approval (or disapproval), the transaction information goes from the point of sale, to an acquirer bank, across the credit-card network, to the issuer bank, and back. Acquirer banks contract with merchants to process their transactions, while issuer banks provide credit to consumers and issue payment cards. The acquirer bank receives the transaction information from the merchant and

---

[31] 2011 WL 6012598 (S.D. Texas 2011) (notes omitted).

forwards it over the network to the issuer bank for approval. If the issuer bank approves the transaction, that bank sends money to cover the transaction to the acquirer bank. The acquirer bank then forwards payment to the merchant. A bank often acts as both an issuer and an acquirer. Banks frequently outsource the processing functions to companies specializing in that service.

Visa and MasterCard are two of the largest credit-card networks. They neither issue cards nor contract with merchants to process transactions. Instead, acquirer and issuer banks contract with them for access to the Visa and MasterCard networks. Visa and MasterCard, like the other credit-card networks, impose extensive regulations on acquirer and issuer banks. Visa and MasterCard require the banks they contract with to impose these regulations on the merchants who submit transactions for processing and on the entities that process the transactions.

The Financial Institution Plaintiffs are nine banks suing as issuer banks. Heartland, the defendant, processes merchant transactions on behalf of two acquirer banks, Heartland Bank and KeyBank, N.A. (Docket Entry No. 42, Exs. 4, 5). Heartland's contracts with KeyBank and Heartland Bank required Heartland to comply with Visa and MasterCard network regulations. (Id., Ex. 4, ¶ 1.1(f); Ex. 5, ¶ 1.1(f)). To the extent that the terms of Heartland's contracts with these and other banks differed from the Visa and MasterCard regulations, the regulations governed. (Id., Ex. 4, ¶ 1.1(h); Ex. 5, ¶ 1.1(i)).

Beginning at least as early as December 2007, three hackers — an American, Albert Gonzalez, and two unknown Russians — infiltrated Heartland's computer systems. (Docket Entry No. 32, ¶¶ 35, 63–64). The hackers installed programs that allowed them to capture some of the payment-card information stored on the Heartland computer systems. (Id., ¶ 65). In late October 2008, Visa alerted Heartland to suspicious account activity. Heartland, with Visa and MasterCard and others, investigated. (Id., ¶ 35). Heartland discovered suspicious files in its systems on January 12, 2009. A day later, Heartland uncovered the program creating those files. (Id., ¶ 37). That program provided the hackers with access to data on the systems. (Id., ¶¶ 41–42). On January 20, Heartland publicly announced the data breach. (Id., ¶ 38). The hackers obtained payment-card numbers and expiration dates for approximately 130 million accounts. (Id., ¶ 5). For some of these accounts, the hackers also obtained cardholder names. (Id., ¶ 44). They did not obtain any cardholder addresses, however, which meant that the stolen card information generally could be used only for in-person transactions. (Id., ¶ 70).

The Financial Institution Plaintiffs allege that this data breach resulted from Heartland's failure to follow industry security standards known as PCI — DSS. (See id., ¶¶ 53–62). After the breach, the Financial Institution Plaintiffs incurred signifi-cant expenses replacing payment cards and reimbursing fraudulent transactions. (Id., ¶ 78). The master complaint asserts ten causes of action:

(I) breach of Heartland's contracts with Heartland Bank, KeyBank, and its merchants, to which the Financial Institution Plaintiffs are third-party beneficiaries;

(II) negligence;

(III) breach of an implied contract to the Financial Institution Plaintiffs;

(IV) negligence per se;

(V) negligent misrepresentation;

(VI) intentional misrepresentation;

(VII) violations of the New Jersey Consumer Fraud Act; and

(VIII, IX, and X) violations of other states' consumer-protection laws.

The complaint seeks class certification.

Heartland has moved to dismiss the complaint in its entirety. (Docket Entry No. 39). Its arguments, and the Financial Institution Plaintiffs' responses, are addressed in detail below.

II. Rule 12(b)(6)

A complaint may be dismissed when the plaintiff fails "to state a claim upon which relief can be granted." FED. R. CIV. P. 12(b)(6). In Bell Atlantic Corp. v. Twombly, *550 U.S. 544, 555, 127 S.Ct. 1955, 167 L.Ed.2d 929 (2007), and* Ashcroft v. Iqbal, *556 U.S. 662, 129 S.Ct. 1937, 1949–50, 173 L.Ed.2d 868 (2009), the Supreme Court confirmed that Rule 12(b)(6) must be read in conjunction with Rule 8(a), which requires "a short and plain statement of the claim showing that the pleader is entitled to relief." FED. R. CIV. P. 8(a)(2). A complaint must contain "enough facts to state a claim to relief that is plausible on its face" to withstand a Rule 12(b)(6) motion.* Iqbal, *129 S.Ct. at 1949. "A claim has facial plausibility when the plaintiff pleads factual content that allows the court to draw the reasonable inference that the defendant is liable for the misconduct alleged."* Id. *Facial plausibility "does not require 'detailed factual allegations,' but it demands more than an unadorned, the-defendant-unlawfully-harmed-me accusation."* Id. *(quoting* Twombly, *550 U.S. at 555, 127 S.Ct. 1955). Nor is facial plausibility "akin to a 'probability requirement' "; rather, "it asks for more than a sheer possibility that a defendant has acted unlawfully."* Iqbal, *129 S.Ct. at 1949 (quoting* Twombly, *550 U.S. at 556, 127 S.Ct. 1955). Facial plausibility requires "the plaintiff [to] plead[ ] factual content that allows the court to draw the reasonable inference that the defendant is liable for the misconduct alleged."* Iqbal, *129 S.Ct. at 1949. "Where a complaint pleads facts that are 'merely consistent with' a defendant's liability, it 'stops short of the line between possibility and plausibility of entitlement to relief.' "* Id. *(quoting* Twombly, *550 U.S. at 557, 127 S.Ct. 1955).*

When a plaintiff's complaint fails to state a claim, a district court generally should provide the plaintiff at least one chance to amend the complaint under Rule 15(a) before dismissing the action with prejudice. See Great Plains Trust Co. v. Morgan Stanley Dean Witter & Co., *313 F.3d 305, 329 (5th Cir.2002) ("district courts often afford plaintiffs at least one opportunity to cure pleading deficiencies before dismissing a case"); see also* United States ex rel. Adrian v. Regents of the Univ. of Cal., *363 F.3d 398, 403 (5th Cir.2004) ("Leave to amend should be freely given, and outright refusal to grant leave to amend without a justification . . . is considered an abuse of discretion." (internal citation omitted)). "Denial of leave to amend may be warranted for undue delay, bad faith or dilatory motive on the part of the movant, repeated failure to cure deficiencies, undue prejudice to the opposing party, or futility of a proposed amendment.*" United States ex rel. Steury v. Cardinal Health, Inc., *625 F.3d 262, 270 (5th Cir.2010) (emphasis added). A district court has broad discretion to dismiss a complaint without leave to amend "where the plaintiff has previously been granted leave to amend [to cure pleading deficiencies] and has subsequently failed to add the requisite particularity to its claims[.]"* Zucco Partners, LLC v. Digimarc Corp., *552 F.3d 981, 1007 (9th Cir.2009); see also Carroll v. Fort James Corp., 470 F.3d 1171, 1175 (5th Cir.2006) (affirming a district court's dismissal for failure to state a claim without leave to amend after the court "instructed [the plaintiffs] to plead their fraud claim with greater particularity, but the amended complaint was still woefully inadequate").*

III. Analysis

A. The Contract and Implied Contract Claims

The master complaint asserts claims for breach of contract and breach of implied contract. The Financial Institution Plaintiffs base these claims, "without limitation," on Heartland's contracts with: (1) its merchants; (2) Heartland Bank and KeyBank; and (3) Visa and MasterCard. (Docket Entry No. 32, ¶ 95). They allege that the contracts create duties to safeguard payment-card information. (Id., ¶ 96). The Financial Institution Plaintiffs assert that they are intended third-party beneficiaries of those contracts and that, "[u]nder the circumstances, recognition of a right to performance by [the Financial Institution Plaintiffs] is appropriate to effectuate the intentions of the parties to these contracts." (Id., ¶ 97). They contend that Heartland breached the contracts by "failing to adequately safeguard . . . sensitive financial information" of their customers, resulting in the Financial Institution Plaintiffs' financial harm. (Id., ¶ 98).

Heartland notes that the master complaint does not precisely identify the allegedly breached contracts. Heartland submits what it contends to be the relevant contracts: its contracts with Heartland Bank and KeyBank and an "exemplar" of a contract with a merchant. (Docket Entry No. 40, at 35, 41; Docket Entry No. 42, Exs. 4–6). An affidavit from a Heartland attorney states that these were the only types of contracts in effect at the time of the data breach. (See Docket Entry No. 41, ¶¶ 6–8).

A court ordinarily may not go outside the pleadings in considering a motion to dismiss. Scanlan v. Tex. A & M Univ., 343 F.3d 533, 536 (5th Cir.2003). The Fifth Circuit "recognize[s] one limited exception" for documents attached to a motion to dismiss "that are referred to in the plaintiff's complaint and are central to the plaintiff's claim." Id.; accord, e.g., Rodriguez v. Rutter, 310 Fed.Appx. 623, 626 (5th Cir.2009). The contracts on which Heartland relies meet this standard.

1. The Contracts with the Acquirer Banks

The Financial Institution Plaintiffs allege that Heartland's contracts with Heartland Bank and KeyBank required Heartland to take "appropriate steps to safeguard the sensitive financial information" of the Financial Institution Plaintiffs' custom-

ers. *(Docket Entry No. 32, ¶ 96). The Financial Institution Plaintiffs assert that they are intended third-party beneficiaries to these contracts. (Id., ¶ 97). Heartland disagrees. According to Heartland, the contracts do not show an intent primarily to benefit the Financial Institution Plaintiffs. Even if the contracts showed such an intent, Heartland argues, the Financial Institution Plaintiffs still cannot recover because they are not creditor or donee beneficiaries of the contracts. Heartland further contends that the incorporated Visa and MasterCard regulations preclude third-party claims. Finally, Heartland argues that even if the Financial Institution Plaintiffs are third-party beneficiaries of the contracts, the allegations are too conclusory to state a plausible breach of contract claim. (See Docket Entry No. 40, at 37–39).*

a. The Heartland Bank Contract

Heartland's contract with Heartland Bank contains a choice-of-law provision specifying Missouri law. (Docket Entry No. 42, Ex. 4, ¶ 4.11). The parties do not dispute that Missouri law applies. Under Missouri law, "[o]nly parties to a contract and any third-party beneficiaries of a contract have standing to enforce that contract." Verni v. Cleveland Chiropractic Coll., 212 S.W.3d 150, 153 (Mo.2007). *Intended beneficiaries qualify as third-party beneficiaries, but incidental beneficiaries do not.* See id. *A third party is an intended beneficiary only when "the contract clearly express[es] intent to benefit that party or an identifiable class of which the party is a member."* Id. *(internal quotation marks omitted). Absent such express language, "there is a strong presumption . . . that the parties contracted only to benefit only themselves."* Id. *(internal quotation marks omitted).*

In recent cases, the Missouri Supreme Court has held that a court must limit itself to examining the contract language in determining third-party beneficiary status. In Nitro Distributing, Inc. v. Dunn, 194 S.W.3d 339 (Mo.2006), *the court explained that, "[t]o be bound as a third-party beneficiary, the terms of the contract must clearly express intent to benefit that party or an identifiable class of which the party is a member."* Id. at 345 *(emphasis added). Looking only to the contract, and not to extrinsic evidence, the court concluded that the contract "expresse[d] no intent whatsoever to benefit" the asserted third parties.* Id. *In* Netco, Inc. v. Dunn, 194 S.W.3d 353 (Mo.2006), *decided on the same day, the state supreme court again limited its consideration to the contract language.* See id. at 358. *In that case, the defendant, an Amway distributor, argued that the plaintiff was bound to the Amway franchise contract as a third-party beneficiary because the plaintiff conceded that "it relied on and profited from [the] relationship, a relationship predicated on the Amway Rules of Conduct and [the defendant's] status as an Amway distributor[.]"* Id. *(internal quotation marks omitted). The court found this concession irrelevant, explaining that "the mere fact [of] a mutually beneficial relationship . . . does not make [the plaintiff] a third-party beneficiary."* Id. *The court once again considered only the contract language and found no express statement of intent to make the plaintiff a third-party beneficiary.* See id.

The Missouri Supreme Court recently reaffirmed its narrow focus on contract language in determining third-party beneficiary status. In Verni v. Cleveland Chiropractic College, *a student — upset with his college after it fired a favorite professor — argued that he was a third-party beneficiary of the professor's employ-ment contract with the college. 212 S.W.3d at 152–53. The court quoted* Nitro Distributing *'s requirement that the contract clearly state the parties' intent to confer third-party beneficiary status. Id. at 153. The court emphasized its resolution of the issue "by examining the contract's language," id., citing* OFW Corporation v. City of Columbia, *893 S.W.2d 876, 879 (Mo.Ct.App.1995). In* OFW, *the Missouri Court of Appeals held that, "[i]n determining whether plaintiff was a third-party beneficiary to the contract, the question of intent is paramount and is to be gleaned from the four corners of the contract." Id. (internal quotation marks and alterations omitted; emphasis added). The* Verni *court succinctly applied this rule to the professor's employment contract:*

> *The contract is a one-page document providing that [the professor] would be a full-time faculty member . . . for one year. The contract required him to be on campus a certain amount of time each week and outlined his teaching duties. In return, the contract provided . . . salary and employment benefits. Although the contract might incidentally provide a benefit to . . . students, it does not clearly express any intent that [the professor] was undertaking a duty to benefit [the plaintiff] or a class of students.*

212 S.W.3d at 153. The court considered no extrinsic evidence. It concluded that the student was not entitled to third-party beneficiary status because the contract did not "directly and clearly express the intent to benefit [the plaintiff] or any class of which [he] claims to be a member." Id.

Under Missouri law, this court must look only to the contract terms in determin-ing whether there was a direct and clear expression of intent to benefit the third party — in this case, the Financial Institution Plaintiffs. The contract between Heartland and Heartland Bank states:

> *[Heartland] will safeguard, and hold confidential from disclosure to unauthorized persons, all data relating to Bank business received by [Heartland] pursuant to this Agreement to the same extent that [Heartland] safeguards data relating to its own business[.]*

(Docket Entry No. 42, Ex. 4, ¶ 4.3(b)). The contract contains an identical promise by Heartland Bank to Heartland. (Id., ¶ 4.3(a)). This exchange of promises does not state an intent to benefit anyone other than the contracting parties. There is no clearly expressed intent to convey any enforceable right to the Financial Institution Plaintiffs or to any class to which they belong.

The contract refers to data relating to the business of the contracting parties, indicating an intent to protect the contracting parties' businesses from unauthorized disclosures. The Financial Institution Plaintiffs acknowledge that Heartland's failure to protect consumer payment-card data would harm Heartland's own business. (See Docket Entry No. 32, ¶¶ 57–60). The Financial Institution Plaintiffs cite the contract's requirement that Heartland indemnify Heartland Bank's "affili-ates[.]" (Docket Entry No 42, Ex. 4, ¶ 4.5(a)). But this indemnification clause does not show an intent primarily to benefit the Financial Institution Plaintiffs. The term "affiliate" means "[a] corporation that is related to another corporation by sharehold-

*ings or other means of control; a subsidiary, parent, or sibling corporation."
BLACK'S LAW DICTIONARY 63 (8th ed. 2004); see also Nitro Distrib., 194 S.W.3d at
349 ("courts will enforce contracts according to their plain meaning"). The Financial
Institution Plaintiffs are not "affiliates" of Heartland Bank within the word's
common meaning.*

*Heartland's motion to dismiss based on the Heartland Bank contract is granted
with prejudice and without leave to amend because amendment would be futile. The
Financial Institution Plaintiffs emphasize that they have not had a chance to conduct
discovery into whether there are other contracts in this category with provisions
expressly and directly stating an intent to make them third-party beneficiaries.
(Docket Entry No. 50, at 42–43, 45). Leave to amend is granted only insofar as the
Financial Institution Plaintiffs are able to plead plausibly that they are third-party
beneficiaries to other contracts between Heartland and Heartland Bank.*

b. The KeyBank Contract

*This court previously reviewed Ohio law on third-party beneficiaries in the related
case against KeyBank and found the complaint insufficient to state a claim that the
issuer banks were third-party beneficiaries to the contract between KeyBank and
Heartland. The contract language itself did not show an intent to benefit third parties.
Because Ohio law, unlike Missouri law, allows consideration of evidence beyond the
contract terms to determine third-party beneficiary status, it was appropriate to grant
the issuer banks leave to amend. This court also found that the Financial Institution
Plaintiffs had failed to identify any provision of the KeyBank contract that Heartland
had breached. (Docket Entry No. 117, at 27–32). For essentially the same reasons set
out in the March 31, 2011 memorandum and order, 2011 WL 1232352, the claims based
on the KeyBank contract asserted by the Financial Institution Plaintiffs in this case
must also be dismissed.*

*Heartland advances an additional reason to dismiss in this case. The damages the
Financial Institution Plaintiffs seek are consequential damages, which the KeyBank
contract excludes absent a willful breach. (Docket Entry No. 40, at 40–41). The
KeyBank contract states that "damages will be limited to general money damages in
an amount not to exceed the actual damages of the party. In no case will the other
party be responsible for special, incidental, consequential or exemplary damages,
except for willful breach of this Agreement." (Docket Entry No. 42, Ex. 5, ¶ 4.7).
Damages-limitation clauses are generally enforceable under Ohio law.* E.g., Skurka
Aerospace, Inc. v. Eaton Aerospace, L.L.C., 781 F.Supp.2d 561, 571–72 (N.D.Ohio
2011); TLC Healthcare Servs., L.L.C. v. Enhanced Billing Servs., L.L.C., No.
L-08-1121, 2008 WL 3878349, at *3 (Ohio Ct.App. Aug. 22, 2008); Morantz v. Ortiz, No.
07AP-597, 2008 WL 642630, at *7 (Ohio Ct.App. Mar. 11, 2008) (collecting cases).

*When a contract limits recovery to direct damages, a plaintiff may recover only the
difference between the amount paid and the value received.* See Nat'l Mulch & Seed,
Inc. v. Rexius Forest By — Products Inc., No. 2:02-cv-1288, 2007 WL 894833, at *6 n.
3 (S.D.Ohio Mar. 22, 2007); see also Wartsila NSD N. Am., Inc. v. Hill Int'l, Inc., 530
F.3d 269, 278 (3d Cir.2008) (limiting recovery for a breach in a service contract that
excluded consequential damages to "the amount paid . . . for [the] services, less the

actual value, if any, of those services"); Reynolds Metals Co. v. Westinghouse Elec. Corp., *758 F.2d 1073, 1080 (5th Cir.1985) (same). The damages the Financial Institution Plaintiffs seek are not the difference between the contract price and the value of the payment-card services. Instead, the Financial Institution Plaintiffs seek the costs they incurred in covering fraudulent transactions and replacing payment cards after the hacker intrusion into the Heartland computer systems. These costs are consequential damages, available only if the contract breach is willful. The master complaint alleges insufficient facts to assert a willful breach. See, e.g.,* Said v. SBS Elecs., Inc., *No. CV 08-3067(RJD)(JO), 2010 WL 1265186, at *8 (E.D.N.Y. Feb. 24, 2010) (dismissing a complaint containing conclusory allegations of willfulness),* adopted as modified on other grounds in *2010 WL 1287080 (E.D.N.Y. Mar. 31, 2010).*

The breach of contract allegations based on the KeyBank contract are dismissed, without prejudice and with leave to amend.

2. The Merchant Processing Agreements

Heartland argues that its Merchant Processing Agreements ("Agreements"), an exemplar of which it has produced, do not provide a basis for recovery for breach of contract. The Agreements provide that New Jersey law applies. (Docket Entry No. 42, Ex. 6, ¶ 14.12). The parties do not dispute the application of New Jersey law.

Heartland contends that the Financial Institution Plaintiffs cannot state a claim for breach of contract because: (1) they are not intended third-party beneficiaries of the Agreements; (2) they have not sufficiently pleaded a breach of those Agreements; and (3) the Agreements do not allow recovery for consequential damages. (Docket Entry No. 40, at 41–44). The third contention is dispositive.

Under the Agreements, Heartland's "sole liability . . . shall be to correct . . . any data in which errors have been caused by [Heartland.]" (Docket Entry No. 42, Ex. 6, ¶ 8.5). The Agreements state that "Heartland shall have no other liability whatsoever to Merchant, and Merchant hereby expressly wa[i]ves any claim against [Heartland] for indirect, special, exemplary, incidental or consequential damages or lost profits or interest." (Id., ¶ 8.7). New Jersey generally enforces damages-limitation clauses between businesses. 66 VMD Assocs., LLC v. Melick — Tully & Assocs., P.C., *No. L-6584-07, 2011 WL 3503160, at *3 (N.J.Super.Ct.App.Div. Aug. 11, 2011);* Marbro, Inc. v. Borough of Tinton Falls, *297 N.J.Super. 411, 688 A.2d 159, 162 (N.J.Super.Ct. Law Div.1996);* see also Jasphy v. Osinsky, *364 N.J.Super. 13, 834 A.2d 426, 431 (N.J.Super.Ct.App.Div.2003). The damages the Financial Institution Plaintiffs seek are consequential damages.*

The Financial Institution Plaintiffs do not assert that the damages-limitation clauses are unenforceable. Instead, they contend that these clauses only limit a merchant's *ability to recover for consequential damages. These clauses, they say, do not apply to their claim as third-party beneficiaries to the Agreements. This contention is unpersuasive. "It is black letter law that a third-party beneficiary is not entitled to any more rights than the actual contracting party."* Merchants Mut. Ins. Co. v. Monmouth Truck Equip., Inc., *Civ. A. No. 06-cv-05395 (FLW), 2008 WL 65109, at *5 (D.N.J. Jan. 4, 2008) (citing, for example,* United Steelworkers of Am. v. Rawson,

495 U.S. 362, 375, 110 S.Ct. 1904, 109 L.Ed.2d 362 (1990); and Allgor v. Travelers Ins. Co., *280 N.J.Super. 254, 654 A.2d 1375, 1379 (N.J.Super.Ct.App.Div.1995)). The Financial Institution Plaintiffs' breach of contract claim under the Agreements containing the damages-limitation clauses is dismissed, with prejudice. The Financial Institution Plaintiffs may assert a breach of contract claim based on the Agreements only insofar as they have a good-faith basis to believe that: (1) there are Agreements to which they are third-party beneficiaries; and (2) these Agreements do not contain damages-limitation clauses.*

3. The Implied Contract Claim

Under New Jersey law, "[a]n implied-in-fact contract is a true contract arising from mutual agreement and intent to promise, but where the agreement and promise have not been verbally expressed." S. Jersey Hosp., Inc. v. Corr. Med. Servs., *Civ. No. 02-2619(JBS), 2005 WL 1410860, at *4 (D.N.J. June 15, 2005) (quoting* In re Penn Cent., *831 F.2d 1221, 1228 (3d Cir.1987)). "[C]ontracts implied in fact are no different than express contracts, although they exhibit a different way or form of expressing assent than through statements or writings."* Wanaque Borough Sewerage Auth. v. Twp. of W. Milford, *144 N.J. 564, 677 A.2d 747, 752 (1996). Courts look to the parties' "word[s] and conduct in light of the surrounding circumstances." Id. (citing RE-STATEMENT (SECOND) OF CONTRACTS §§ 4 cmt. a, 5 cmt. a (1979)).*

The Financial Institution Plaintiffs rely on In re Hannaford Brothers Co. Customer Data Security Breach Litigation, *613 F.Supp.2d 108 (D.Me.2009),* aff'd in part, rev'd in part sub nom. Anderson v. Hannaford Brothers Co., *659 F.3d 151 (1st Cir.2011). In* Hannaford Brothers, *customers used payment cards to pay for groceries. A third party breached the grocer's information-technology systems, gaining access to stored payment-card information. See 613 F.Supp.2d at 116. The customers filed a class-action lawsuit against the grocer for the unauthorized access to their payment-card information, claiming breach of implied contract. The district court first noted the existence of a direct contract relationship between the grocer and the customers: a contract to buy groceries. Id. at 118. Because that contract required payment, the court held that a customer's use of a payment card would allow a jury to*

> *find certain other implied terms in the grocery purchase contract: for example, that the merchant will not use the card data for other people's purchases, will not sell or give the data to others (except in completing the payment process), and* will take reasonable measures to protect the information (which might include meeting industry standards), *on the basis that these are implied commitments that are "absolutely necessary to effectuate the contract," and "indispensable to effectuate the intention of the parties."*

Id. *at 119 (emphasis in original) (quoting* Seashore Performing Arts Ctr., Inc. v. Town of Old Orchard Beach, *676 A.2d 482, 484–85 (Me.1996)). The court found that the customers had sufficiently stated a claim for breach of implied contract under Maine law. But the starting point for the court's analysis is the parties' direct contractual relationship. See* Hannaford Brothers, *613 F.Supp.2d at 118. That is not true in the present case.A case with facts more similar to those at issue here is* Hammond v. The Bank of New York Mellon Corporation, *No. 08 Civ. 6060(RMB)(RLE), 2010 WL*

2643307 (S.D.N.Y. June 25, 2010). In Hammond, *a company owned by the defendant lost computer-backup tapes that contained the payment-card data of 12.5 million individuals. Id. at *4. A class action against the defendant claimed breach of implied contract. The court emphasized that there was no direct relationship between the individuals whose data was released and the defendant. The court explained:*

> *Rather, Plaintiffs had relationships (only) with institutional clients of Defendant, such as the Walt Disney Company . . . . Plaintiffs gave their personal data over to these entities, which, in turn, forwarded the data to Defendant (which stored the data on the tapes that ultimately were lost or stolen).*

Id. at *9. Applying New York law, the court concluded that, absent evidence of "any direct dealings" between the individuals and the defendant, there was no basis to find the mutual assent necessary for an implied contract. Id. at *11.

Unlike the plaintiffs in Hannaford Brothers, *and like those in* Hammond, *the Financial Institution Plaintiffs do not allege a direct contract relationship with Heartland that would plausibly suggest the mutual assent necessary for an implied contract. The Financial Institution Plaintiffs' contracts are with Heartland's clients, not Heartland. The pleadings allege that the Financial Institution Plaintiffs have at most an indirect relationship with Heartland through Heartland's processing of transactions made with payment cards that they issued. The implied contract claim is dismissed. The Financial Institution Plaintiffs may replead this claim, but only insofar as they have a good-faith basis to allege the existence of a direct contractual relationship between them and Heartland.*

B. The Negligence Claims

1. Negligence Per Se

The Financial Institution Plaintiffs have withdrawn their negligence per se claim based on Heartland's alleged failure to follow the security protocols set out in the Visa and MasterCard regulations. (Docket Entry No. 50, at 23 n. 14).

2. Negligence

The Financial Institution Plaintiffs allege that Heartland breached three duties: "a duty to exercise reasonable care in safeguarding and protecting [payment-card] information from being compromised and/or stolen," (Docket Entry No. 32, ¶ 101); a seemingly related "duty to put into place internal policies and procedures designed to detect and prevent the unauthorized dissemination of [the Financial Institution Plaintiffs'] customers' private, non-public, sensitive financial information," (id., ¶ 103); and "a duty to timely disclose to [the Financial Institution Plaintiffs'] customers that the Data Breach had occurred and the private, non-public, sensitive financial information of [the Financial Institution Plaintiffs'] customers" may have been compromised, (id., ¶ 102).

Suits by issuer banks against other participants in the credit-card processing chain are "of fairly recent vintage." Rebecca Hatch Weston, Liability of Retailer and Its Affiliate Bank to Credit Card Issuer for Costs Arising out of Breach of Retailer's Computer Security, *51 A.L.R.6th 311, § 2 (2010) (noting that the first published decision appeared in 2005). Courts addressing such claims have generally found that the economic-loss doctrine prevents recovery. Id. at § 5; cf. Juliet M. Moringiello,* Warranting Data Security, *5 BROOK. J. CORP. FIN. & COM. L. 63, 71 (2010) (calling the economic-loss doctrine a "major impediment[ ]" to consumer tort actions against payment-card processors). It is instructive to review the cases.*

In Banknorth, N.A. v. BJ's Wholesale Club, Inc., *394 F.Supp.2d 283 (D.Me.2005), an issuer bank sued a retailer and an acquiring bank after the retailer's computer systems, which contained customers' payment-card information, were breached. Id. at 284. The issuer bank alleged that the retailer and acquiring bank negligently breached a duty "to safeguard cardholder information from thieves." Id. at 286. The retailer and acquirer bank argued that the economic-loss doctrine barred recovery on this claim. Id. The court observed that, under Maine law, it was unclear how the doctrine applied outside the products liability context. Id. at 287. The court noted the "complex web of relationships involving numerous players governed by both individual contracts and exhaustive regulations promulgated by Visa and other card networks." Id. The court reasoned that although there might be a duty of care among the members of the credit-card network, "this web of relationships may or may not render Plaintiff's negligence claim susceptible to the economic loss doctrine." Id. Because the issuer bank's ability to recover would turn on the specific facts of each case, the court concluded that dismissal was inappropriate. Id.*

Another court applying Maine law reached the opposite conclusion. In a case raising the same claims, brought in Pennsylvania federal court, the court found that the economic-loss doctrine precluded liability for negligence. See Banknorth N.A. v. BJ's Wholesale Club, Inc., *442 F.Supp.2d 206, 211–14 (M.D.Pa.2006). In* In re TJX Companies Retail Security Breach Litigation, *564 F.3d 489 (1st Cir.2009), the First Circuit considered a negligence claim by issuer banks against a merchant and an acquirer bank for losses stemming from a data breach. Recognizing that "purely economic losses are unrecoverable [under Massachusetts law] in tort and strict liability actions in the absence of personal injury or property damage," the court affirmed the district court's dismissal of the negligence claim. Id. at 498–99 (quoting* Aldrich v. ADD Inc., *437 Mass. 213, 770 N.E.2d 447, 454 (2002)). The court rejected the issuer banks' argument that they suffered compensable property loss. Massachusetts law, the court emphasized, required physical property damage for a negligence claim. Id. at 498. The Massachusetts Supreme Judicial Court reached the same result in* Cumis Insurance Society, Inc. v. BJ's Wholesale Club, Inc., *455 Mass. 458, 918 N.E.2d 36 (2009). The issuer banks' insurer attempted to avoid the economic-loss doctrine by arguing that "the plastic credit cards [were] tangible personal property and their damages included physical harm to the plastic cards that had to be canceled following the thefts." Id. at 46. The court rejected this argument, noting that the relevant issue was not "whether the credit cards are tangible property, but rather the nature of the damages sought by the plaintiffs." Id.*

The Third Circuit reached the same conclusion under Pennsylvania law in

Sovereign Bank v. BJ's Wholesale Club, Inc., *533 F.3d 162 (3d Cir.2008). In that case, an issuer bank sued a merchant after a data breach. The court reviewed Pennsylvania cases applying the economic-loss doctrine and dismissed the bank's negligence claim. Id. at 175–78. In rejecting the bank's argument that its loss of money was a loss of property, the court reasoned that accepting "the argument would totally eviscerate the economic loss doctrine because any economic loss would morph into the required loss of property and thereby furnish the damages required for a negligence claim." Id. at 176.*

The Iowa Supreme Court recently rejected a similar negligence claim under the economic-loss doctrine. In Annett Holdings, Inc. v. Kum & Go, L.C., 801 N.W.2d 499 (Iowa 2011), a trucking company's employee used a card issued by the company to make unauthorized purchases at a gas station. Id. at 501. The trucking company sued the gas station. Id. at 502. The Iowa Supreme Court noted that although the trucking company and the gas station lacked privity of contract, the gas station had contracted with the company's credit-card network. "When parties enter into a chain of contracts, even if the two parties at issue have not actually entered into an agreement with each other, courts have applied the 'contractual economic loss rule' to bar tort claims for economic loss, on the theory that tort law should not supplant a consensual network of contracts." Id. at 504; see also Robins Dry Dock & Repair Co. v. Flint, 275 U.S. 303, 308–09, 48 S.Ct. 134, 72 L.Ed. 290 (1927) (applying the economic-loss doctrine to a chain of contracts). The court pointed out that the trucking company would be "fully responsible" for fraudulent charges under its agreement with the network; that the company knew that the network contracted with service centers like the gas station; and that the network would reimburse those service centers, with the expectation that the company would reimburse the network under the terms of the agreement. Annett Holdings, 801 N.W.2d at 505. "It is difficult to see why a tort remedy is needed here," the court concluded, because the trucking company "contracted to assume certain risks of financial loss and had the ability to minimize these risks." Id. The court dismissed the negligence claim.

Heartland argues that this court must dismiss the negligence claim because Texas law does not allow tort claims for purely economic loss. See Memorial Hermann Healthcare Sys., Inc. v. Eurocopter Deutschland, GMBH, 524 F.3d 676, 678 (5th Cir.2008) (citing Hou — Tex, Inc. v. Landmark Graphics, 26 S.W.3d 103, 107 (Tex.App.-Houston [14th Dist.] 2000, no pet.)). The Financial Institution Plaintiffs do not dispute Heartland's characterization of Texas law. They instead contend that New Jersey law applies. Under New Jersey law, they state, a plaintiff may recover for economic losses resulting from negligence without physical or property injury. Heartland responds that even if New Jersey law applies, it owed no duty to the Financial Institution Plaintiffs to protect cardholder data and therefore cannot be liable for negligence. New Jersey law, however, would not recognize a duty owing by Heartland to the Financial Institution Plaintiffs to protect cardholder data. Even assuming that New Jersey law applies, the Financial Institution Plaintiffs' negligence claim must be dismissed. The elements of negligence under New Jersey law are (1) a duty of care, (2) a breach of that duty, (3) proximate cause, and (4) damages. Brunson v. Affinity Fed. Credit Union, 199 N.J. 381, 972 A.2d 1112, 1122–23 (2009); Polzo v. Cnty. of Essex, 196 N.J. 569, 960 A.2d 375, 384 (2008). "The New Jersey

Supreme Court has long been a leader in expanding tort liability." Hakimoglu v. Trump Taj Mahal Assocs., *70 F.3d 291, 295 (3d Cir.1995) (Becker, J., dissenting). In* People Express Airlines, Inc. v. Consolidated Rail Corp., *100 N.J. 246, 495 A.2d 107 (1985), the New Jersey Supreme Court abandoned the rule that economic losses, unaccompanied by physical or property damage, are never compensable in tort.* See id. *at 114–15. In* People Express, *an airline sued various defendants for business-interruption damages after a volatile chemical caught fire in a rail yard adjacent to the Newark Airport. An evacuation of a one-mile radius closed the airport's northern terminal for 12 hours. That terminal housed the airline's business operations. The evacuation forced the airline to cancel flights and prevented its employees from booking flights for customers.* Id. *at 108–09. The defendants moved for summary judgment that the economic-loss doctrine prohibited recovery for purely economic loss. The New Jersey Supreme Court concluded that the traditional reasons for prohibiting recovery for economic loss, including fears of unbounded liability and fraudulent claims, were unpersuasive. The court held that a duty generally exists "to take reasonable measures to avoid the risk of causing economic damages, aside from physical injury, to particular plaintiffs or plaintiffs comprising an identifiable class with respect to whom defendant knows or has reason to know are likely to suffer such damages from its conduct."* Id. *at 116. Whether a duty exists depends in part on the foreseeability of such damages. "The more particular is the foreseeability that economic loss will be suffered by the plaintiff as the result of the defendant's negligence, the more just is it that liability be imposed and recovery allowed."* Id. *The "class of plaintiffs must be particularly foreseeable in terms of the type of persons or entities comprising the class, the certainty or predictability of their presence, the approximate numbers of those in the class, as well as the type of economic expectations disrupted."* Id. *The court recognized a "spectrum [of foreseeability] ranging from the general to the particular," allowing a court to "limit otherwise boundless liability and define an identifiable class of plaintiffs that may recover."* Id. *at 115, 116. In holding that the defendants owed a duty to the plaintiffs, the* People Express *court identified the close proximity of the north terminal to the accident; the "obvious nature" of the airline's presence and operations that made the asserted economic harm foreseeable; the rail company's knowledge of the chemical's volatility; and the existence of an emergency-response plan established with the participation of some of the defendants that called for evacuating the terminal.* Id. *at 118. Although the airline could seek its economic losses, an example of a class that could not seek such losses was drivers on a highway delayed by a negligently caused accident. The drivers may be a foreseeable class, the court acknowledged, but they were not an identifiable one. Rather, the presence of any particular driver — and therefore the economic injury of that driver — was merely "fortuitous."* Id. *at 116.*

People Express *recognizes that "a plaintiff [can] bring an action for purely economic losses, regardless of any accompanying physical harm or property damage, if the plaintiff [is] a member of an identifiable class that the defendant should have reasonably foreseen was likely to be injured by the defendant's conduct[.]"* Carter Lincoln — Mercury, Inc., Leasing Div. v. EMAR Grp., Inc., *135 N.J. 182, 638 A.2d 1288, 1294 (1994). But* People Express *equally acknowledges that the foreseeability standard will not always adequately guide a court's evaluation of tort duties. In certain cases, "the courts will be required to draw upon notions of fairness, common sense and morality to fix the line limiting liability as a matter of public policy, rather than an uncritical application of particular foreseeability." People Express, 495 A.2d at 116. The New Jersey Supreme Court has emphasized in decisions since People Express that the "[a]bility to foresee injury to a potential plaintiff does not in itself establish the existence of a duty [.]" Carter Lincoln — Mercury, 638 A.2d at 1294 (citing Goldberg v. Housing Auth. of City of Newark, 38 N.J. 578, 186 A.2d 291, 293 (1962)); see also Clohesy v. Food Circus Supermarkets, Inc., 149 N.J. 496, 694 A.2d 1017, 1020 (1997) ("Foreseeability of harm alone is not dispositive of whether a duty exists."). Rather, "[o]nce the foreseeability of an injured party is established, [a court] must decide whether considerations of fairness and policy warrant the imposition of a duty." Carter Lincoln — Mercury, 638 A.2d at 1294.*

New Jersey has exhibited a "strong resistance to the usurpation of contract law by tort law[.]" Travelers Indem. Co. v. Dammann & Co., 594 F.3d 238, 248 (3d Cir.2010). "New Jersey courts have consistently held that contract law is better suited to resolve disputes where a plaintiff alleges direct and consequential losses that were within the contemplation of sophisticated business entities that could have been the subject of their negotiations." Id.; see also Arcand v. Brother Int'l Corp., 673 F.Supp.2d 282, 308 (D.N.J.2009); (Docket Entry No. 117, at 40–43 (discussing cases)). The New Jersey cases repeatedly emphasize that respecting the parties' voluntary agreements to allocate risk best serves the public interest. See Spring Motors Distributors, Inc. v. Ford Motor Co., 98 N.J. 555, 489 A.2d 660, 671 (1985) ("As between commercial parties, [ ] the allocation of risks in accordance with their agreement better serves the public interest than an allocation achieved as a matter of policy without reference to that agreement."). The decisions represent a "clear rejection of an approach that would allow tort law to substitute for contract law in cases involving sophisticated parties with equal bargaining power[.]" Travelers Indem., 594 F.3d at 251. This court previously concluded that, under New Jersey law, Heartland owed no duty to the issuer banks because "relationships among issuers, acquirers, and their contractors — such as Heartland Payment Systems — are governed by the Visa and MasterCard regulations," not tort law. (Docket Entry No. 117, at 44). The court dismissed vicarious liability claims against an acquirer bank that hired Heartland to process payment-card transactions. In supplemental briefing following that order, the Finan- cial Institution Plaintiffs argue that the economic-loss doctrine does not apply to them because Heartland, unlike the acquirer banks, is not a member of the Visa and MasterCard networks. (Docket Entry No. 124, at 1). The Financial Institution Plaintiffs note that no New Jersey case has applied the economic-loss doctrine to bar tort recovery absent a direct contractual relationship. The Financial Institution Plaintiffs cite Consult Urban, 2009 WL 1969083, in which a district court held that a series of contracts did not preclude recovery in tort. This argument and citation are unpersuasive. An issuer bank's decision to issue payment cards is, of course, a voluntary choice. To participate, issuer banks must accept the Visa and MasterCard regulations. By participating in the Visa and MasterCard networks, the Financial Institution Plaintiffs entered into the web of contractual relationships that included not only issuer and acquirer banks but also third-party businesses, such as Heartland, that process transactions for network members. Heartland agreed to follow the Visa and MasterCard regulations. (Docket Entry No. 32, ¶ 96; Docket Entry No. 42, Ex. 4, ¶ 1.1(f) (requiring Heartland to "comply fully with all by-laws and regulations of Visa and MasterCard, including but not limited to, rules regarding independent sales organizations and member service providers"); id., Ex. 5, ¶ 1.1(f) (same)). The regulations specifically contemplate the possibility of a data breach. They specify procedures for issuer banks to make claims when such data breaches occur through private dispute-resolution systems. (Docket Entry No. 124, Exs. 1, 2); see also Sovereign Bank, *533 F.3d at 165 (describing the "comprehensive provisions for resolving disputes between Visa members," which allowed Visa to decide disputes "in accordance with risk allocation judgments made by Visa");* Cumis Ins. Soc'y, Inc. v. BJ's Wholesale Club, *No. 20051158J, 2008 WL 2345865, at *4 (Mass.Super. Ct. June 4, 2008) (noting that the Visa and MasterCard regulations "provide for an elaborate dispute resolution procedure and for fines for non-compliance"),* aff'd, *455 Mass. 458, 918 N.E.2d 36 (2009). Although Heartland is not a direct member of the Visa and MasterCard networks, it was subject to the network regulations. The complaint highlights Visa's investigation into Heartland, alleging that Visa both found Heartland to be "in violation of the Visa operating regulations" and banned network members from using Heartland to process transactions for approximately one week. (Docket Entry No. 32, ¶ 57). Visa also "put Heartland on probationary status," which "subjected Heartland to more-stringent security assessments, monitoring and reporting[.]" (Id., ¶ 58). Visa and MasterCard fined Heartland Bank and KeyBank, the network members that had retained Heartland. The banks passed those fines to Heartland under their contracts with Heartland and the Visa and MasterCard networks, the network regulations, not tort law, are the appropriate means for the Financial Institution Plaintiffs to seek relief.*

Additionally, the damages the Financial Institution Plaintiffs seek — the costs of covering fraudulent charges and of reissuing cards — are the kinds of damages ordinarily expected to flow from a data breach, damages that can be addressed in the parties' contractual arrangements. These damages are not the type of injuries for which tort law is appropriate. Arcand, *673 F.Supp.2d at 308;* Kearney & Trecker Corp. v. Master Engraving Co., *107 N.J. 584, 527 A.2d 429, 437 (1987) (declining to impose a tort duty between businesses for damages that were not "highly unusual or unforeseeable" in the kind of transaction covered by the parties' contract, and quoting* Chatlos Sys., Inc. v. Nat'l Cash Register Corp., *635 F.2d 1081, 1087 (3d Cir.1980));* see also Annett Holdings, *801 N.W.2d at 504–05 (holding that tort law should not displace the risks and responsibilities allocated through a system of contracts for payment cards). The New Jersey Supreme Court's recognition that an "allocation of risks in accordance with [a voluntary] agreement better serves the public interest than an allocation achieved as a matter of policy without reference to that agreement" also weighs against creating a tort duty between payment processors and issuer banks to protect payment-card information from unauthorized access.* Spring Motors, *489 A.2d at 671. This result also is consistent with the approach of the federal government and most states, which generally have avoided regulating risk allocations in the payment-card industry except to cap consumers' liability. Federal legislation and regulations address consumer-protection concerns, not "further allocation of fraud liability after shifting responsibility from the cardholder to the card insurer."* Douglass, *supra, at 45;* see also *Ballen & Fox, supra, at 939 (noting that federal regulations "do not generally address the interbank payment systems and the liabilities that flow into the interbank system"). The states' approaches are similar. Like most states, New Jersey regulates payment-card privacy. In particular, New Jersey regulates how merchants handle payment-card information and requires businesses holding personal information to notify the public when a data breach occurs. N.J. STAT. §§ 56:8–163; 56:11–17, –21, –24, –25, –42; see also Abraham Shaw,* Data Breach: From Notification to Prevention Using PCI DSS, *43 COLUM. J.L. & SOC. PROBS. 517, 524 n. 36 (listing states with notification laws) (2010). Only Minnesota has statutorily shifted the risk of loss arising from a data breach between the businesses involved in the Visa and MasterCard networks. See Mark MacCarthy,* What Payment Intermediaries Are Doing about Online Liability and Why It Matters, *25 BERKELEY TECH. L.J. 1037, 1044 n. 25 (2010) (discussing MINN.STAT. § 325E.64, which "holds merchants liable for the costs associated with a breach when they failed to take specific precautions that are part of an industry data security standard"). The fact that New Jersey regulates data-security measures, but does not address risk allocation, weighs against imposing a common-law duty between these entities. See Hojnowski v. Vans Skate Park, 187 N.J. 323, 901 A.2d 381, 389 (2006) (concluding that a New Jersey statute conferring immunity from suit upon certain volunteers but not businesses weighed against recognizing a minor's waiver of liability against a business); Hannaford Bros., 613 F.Supp.2d at 125 (observing that a Maine law requiring notification of a data breach "give[s the court] reason to be wary of creating any new state standards where the Maine Law Court has not already clearly provided a remedy").*

Relying on Dynalectric Company v. Westinghouse Electric Corporation, *803 F.Supp. 985 (D.N.J.1992), and* Consult Urban, *2009 WL 1969083, the Financial Institution Plaintiffs argue that the economic-loss doctrine does not apply because the "Visa and MasterCard regulations do not and cannot provide the alternative means of redress requisite to the application of the economic loss doctrine under New Jersey law." (Docket Entry No. 124, at 8 (emphasis omitted)). In* Dynalectric, *the plaintiff pursued tort claims against the defendant in federal court while simultaneously pursuing identical breach of contract claims against the defendant in arbitration. Applying New Jersey law, the district court concluded that "when a party has suffered economic loss because of the negligent actions of another, and the party has another means of redress against the alleged tortfeasor, that party may not assert the identical claims for identical damages under tort theories." 803 F.Supp. at 991. The court refused to hear the tort claim because of the ongoing arbitration. Id. at 991, 993. The court did not address whether a tort duty would exist absent the other avenue of redress against the plaintiff. In* Consult Urban, *a contractor asserted a negligence claim against a company that a subcontractor had retained to inspect modular housing units for compliance with New Jersey law. 2009 WL 1969083, at *1. The court rejected the company's argument that it owed no duty, noting that the contractor "had no opportunity to negotiate the terms of the agreement or the amount of risk it would accept." Id. at *4. Neither* Dynalectric *nor* Consult Urban Renewal *involved a comprehensive risk-allocation arrangement like the contracts and network regulations in this case. To the extent that the Visa and MasterCard regulations do not allow the Financial Institution Plaintiffs to recover damages directly from Heartland, New Jersey law disfavors a sophisticated business entity's efforts to use tort law "to obtain a better bargain than it made." Spring Motors, 489 A.2d at 671.The negligence claim is dismissed with prejudice and without leave to amend because amendment would be futile.*

C. The Misrepresentation Claims

The Financial Institution Plaintiffs allege fraud and negligent misrepresentation under New Jersey law. According to the complaint, numerous statements by Heartland — in S.E.C. filings; in analyst calls; on Heartland's logo; and on Heartland's web site, before and after the data breach — suggested that Heartland's security measures were better than they actually were. The complaint also faults Heartland for failing to disclose information about its security flaws. It additionally asserts that Heartland, by participating in the Visa and MasterCard networks, effectively represented that it would follow the network security regulations. Heartland argues that, even assuming New Jersey law applies, the allegations are insufficient to state a claim. Heartland contends that the complaint does not allege the material falsity of the statements; that the Financial Institution Plaintiffs were neither intended recipients (as required for fraud) nor reasonably foreseeable recipients (as required for negligent misrepresentation) of those statements; that Heartland had no duty to disclose; that participation in the Visa and MasterCard networks is not an actionable misrepresentation; and that causation is insufficiently alleged. (Docket Entry No. 40, at 18–28).

Under New Jersey law, common-law fraud has five elements: "(1) a material misrepresentation of a presently existing or past fact; (2) knowledge or belief by the defendant of its falsity; (3) an intention that the other person rely on it; (4) reasonable reliance thereon by the other person; and (5) resulting damages." Banco Popular N. Am. v. Gandi, *184 N.J. 161, 876 A.2d 253, 260 (2005) (quoting* Gennari v. Weichert Co. Realtors, *148 N.J. 582, 691 A.2d 350, 367 (1997)). Negligent misrepresentation differs only in that it requires neither intent to deceive nor knowledge that the statement is false.* See Kaufman v. i-Stat Corp., *165 N.J. 94, 754 A.2d 1188, 1195–96 (2000).*

Federal Rule of Civil Procedure 9(b) applies to fraud allegations. Under the rule, "a party must state with particularity the circumstances constituting fraud or mistake. Malice, intent, knowledge, and other conditions of a person's mind may be alleged generally." FED. R. CIV. P. 9(b). "Put simply, Rule 9(b) requires 'the who, what, when, where, and how' to be laid out." Shandong Yinguang Chem. Indus. Joint Stock Co. v. Potter, *607 F.3d 1029, 1032 (5th Cir.2010) (internal quotation marks omitted). The plaintiff "must specify the statements contended to be fraudulent, identify the speaker, state when and where the statements were made, and explain why the statements were fraudulent."* Southland Secs. Corp. v. INSpire Ins. Solutions, Inc., *365 F.3d 353, 362 (5th Cir.2004) (internal quotation marks omitted). At the same time, "Rule 9(b)'s ultimate meaning is context-specific, and thus there is no single construction of Rule 9(b) that applies in all contexts."* United States ex rel. Grubbs v. Kanneganti, *565 F.3d 180, 188 (5th Cir.2009) (internal quotation marks omitted).*

The parties dispute whether the complaint's negligent misrepresentation allegations must comply with Rule 9(b). It is unnecessary to resolve this dispute, for the allegations of negligent misrepresentation fail to meet Rule 8's basic pleading standard.

1. Misrepresentation

Heartland asserts that many of the alleged misrepresentations are not the kinds of statements that give rise to liability under either a fraud or negligence theory. New Jersey law distinguishes between factual misrepresentations and "puffery." It is reasonable to rely on the first but not the second. E.g., Lieberson v. Johnson & Johnson Consumer Cos., ___ F.Supp.2d ___, ___, 2011 WL 4414214, at *7 (D.N.J.2011). "Advertising that amounts to 'mere' puffery is not actionable because no reasonable consumer relies on puffery. The distinguishing characteristics of puffery are vague, highly subjective claims as opposed to specific, detailed factual assertions." Id. (quoting In re Toshiba Am. HD DVD Mktg. & Sales Practices Litig., Civ. No. 08-939(DRD), MDL No.1956, 2009 WL 2940081, at *10 (D.N.J. Sep. 11, 2009)). For example, the New Jersey Supreme Court held that Allstate Insurance's slogan, "You're in good hands with Allstate," was not an actionable misrepresentation. "However persuasive, [the slogan] is nothing more than puffery." Rodio v. Smith, 123 N.J. 345, 587 A.2d 621, 623 (1991). By contrast, specific factual misrepresentations are actionable. In Gennari v. Weichert Company Realtors, for example, the New Jersey Supreme Court allowed homeowners' suits against a realtor who made "affirmative misrepresentations about the builder's experience and qualifications as well as the quality of his homes," 691 A.2d at 366, such as that the builder "had built hundreds of homes," id. at 357. Similarly, in Lieberson v. Johnson & Johnson Consumer Companies, a federal district court found actionable a defendant's representation of its products as " 'clinically proven' to help babies sleep better" because stating that a product is "clinically proven" to achieve a result is " 'both specific and measurable.' " ___ F.Supp.2d at ___, 2011 WL 4414214, at *7 (quoting Castrol Inc. v. Pennzoil Co., 987 F.2d 939, 946 (3d Cir.1993)).

Certain statements alleged in the master complaint are not actionable misrepresentations, as a matter of law. To the extent that the Financial Institution Plaintiffs argue that Heartland's statements and conduct amounted to a guarantee of absolute data security, reliance on that statement would be unreasonable as a matter of law. Cf. Hannaford Bros., 613 F.Supp.2d at 119 (dismissing under Rule 12(b)(6) a claim for breach of implied contract to keep customer data completely safe because "in today's known world of sophisticated hackers, data theft, software glitches, and computer viruses, a jury could not reasonably find an implied merchant commitment against every intrusion under any circumstances whatsoever" (emphasis in original)). Heartland's slogans —" "The Highest Standards" and "The Most Trusted Transactions" — are puffery on which the Financial Institution Plaintiffs could not reasonably rely. Similarly, the following statements relied on by the Financial Institution Plaintiffs are not actionable representations: that Heartland used "layers of state-of-the-art security, technology and techniques to safeguard sensitive credit and debit card account information"; that it used the "state-of-the-art [Heartland] Exchange"; and that its "success is the result of the combination of a superior long-term customer relationship sales model and the premier technology processing platform in the industry today." (Docket Entry No. 32, ¶¶ 47, 48). See, e.g., Toshiba Am. HD DVD, 2009 WL 2940081, at *10 ("best of high-definition television and DVD" is not an actionable misrepresentation); Bubbles N' Bows, LLC v. Fey Pub'g Co., No. 06-5391(FLW), 2007 WL 2406980, at *9 (D.N.J. Aug. 20, 2007) ("high importance is *placed on personal relationships"; "the success of this business always has and always will rely on the satisfaction of our clients"; "if the customer isn't smiling, fix it" are not actionable); N.J. Citizen Action v. Schering — Plough Corp., 367 N.J.Super. 8, 842 A.2d 174, 177 (N.J.Super.Ct.App.Div.2003) ("you . . . can lead a normal nearly symptom-free life again" is not actionable (ellipsis in original)). The master complaint also lists one alleged misrepresentation by Heartland after it publicly disclosed the data breach. According to the complaint:*

> *Even after the Data Breach occurred, [Heartland] continued to provide . . . assurances that it was adequately protecting the sensitive financial information with which it was entrusted. For example, the website that Heartland created in connection with its disclosure of the Data Breach claims that "Heartland is deeply committed to maintaining the security of card-holder data, and we will continue doing everything reasonably possible to achieve this objective."*

(Docket Entry No. 32, ¶ 50). Statements after the data breach was announced cannot form the basis of a misrepresentation claim because they could not have been material to the banks' and merchants' decisions to contract with Heartland. See, e.g., Prezant v. Jegou, L-819-07, 2010 WL 2556882, at *5 (N.J.Super.Ct.App.Div. June 23, 2010) (per curiam) (holding that a list of inflated antique-furniture values "could not have been material to the [ ] decision to purchase because the list was prepared after the transactions were complete"); Cole v. Laughrey Funeral Home, 376 N.J.Super. 135, 869 A.2d 457, 462–63 (N.J.Super.Ct.App.Div.2005) (alleged misrepresentations were not material because they "were all acts done after the contract for funeral services was entered into").

The master complaint also alleges representations about Heartland's information-sharing practices. The statements include that "we have limited our use of consumer information solely to providing services to other businesses and financial institutions," and that "[w]e limit sharing of non-public personal information to that necessary to complete the transactions on behalf of the consumer and the merchant and to that permitted by federal and state laws." (Docket Entry No. 32, ¶ 45). These are not statements about Heartland's data-security practices. Instead, these statements are promises that Heartland will not intentionally share consumers' personal information with others. The Financial Institution Plaintiffs have not alleged that Heartland intentionally shared information beyond the limits it stated.

On the other hand, some alleged statements are factual representations that are sufficiently definite to support a claim for negligent misrepresentation. According to the master complaint, Heartland stated that "[w]e maintain current updates of network and operating system security releases and virus definitions, and have engaged a third party to regularly test our systems for vulnerability to unauthorized access." Heartland also stated that "we encrypt the cardholder numbers that are stored in our databases using triple-DES protocols, which represent the highest commercially available standard for encryption." (Id., ¶ 45). These statements are factually concrete and verifiable. Similarly, Heartland's statement that its "Exchange has passed an independent verification process validating compliance with VISA requirements for data security" is susceptible to proof. (Id., ¶ 46). Either Heartland's

Exchange passed the independent verification process, or it did not.

Heartland argues that even assuming that some of the alleged misrepresentations are actionable, the master complaint insufficiently alleges reliance. The complaint's allegations of reliance are wholly conclusory. (Docket Entry No. 32, ¶¶ 125 (alleging that the Financial Institution Plaintiffs "justifiably relied"), 129 (alleging that they "reasonably relied")). It is unclear, for example, if the issuer banks' reliance was through their joining, remaining in, or withdrawing from the Visa and MasterCard networks, or what relationship the statements have to any such actions. See, e.g., Cumis Ins. Soc'y, 918 N.E.2d at 49 ("Because the plaintiff credit unions have presented no evidence that any representations by the defendants induced them to become or remain issuers in the Visa and MasterCard system, or that they have withdrawn from or altered their participation in the system after becoming aware of the defendants' breach, the defendants' motions for summary judgment on the fraud claims were properly allowed."). Because the complaint does not give sufficient notice of the Financial Institution Plaintiffs' misrepresentation claims either to determine their entitlement to relief or to allow Heartland to prepare its defense, the claims must be dismissed. See FED. R. CIV. P. 8(a)(2).

It is unnecessary to address the remaining arguments at this time. Dismissal is without prejudice and with leave to amend.

2. Implied Misrepresentation

The Financial Institution Plaintiffs allege that "by accepting and agreeing to process the credit cards and/or debit cards issued by [the Financial Institution Plaintiffs], Heartland impliedly agreed that it would adequately protect the sensitive information contained in these cards, as well as comply with applicable standards to safeguard data." (Docket Entry No. 32, ¶ 52). The Financial Institution Plaintiffs allege that "Heartland knew that by virtue of their membership in the Visa and MasterCard Networks, [they] relied on Heartland to employ appropriate data security measures." (Id., ¶ 123). The Massachusetts Supreme Judicial Court rejected the same theory of negligent implied misrepresentation in litigation arising out of a similar data breach. In Cumis Insurance Society v. BJ's Wholesale Club, *an insurance company (acting on behalf of 69 issuer banks) and numerous issuer banks sued an acquirer bank and a retailer that allegedly retained payment-card information in a manner that violated the Visa and MasterCard regulations. Hackers obtained information for approximately 9.2 million credit cards from the retailer's database. The plaintiffs alleged both fraud and negligent misrepresentation, "based only on the requirements in the Visa and MasterCard operating regulations and the defendants' contracts with each other that require the defendants to abide by these regulations." 918 N.E.2d at 48. The plaintiffs conceded that they had not seen the contracts between the defendants before the lawsuit. Id. The court dismissed the claims. It first explained that the plaintiffs had presented "no evidence or contention . . . that the defendants never intended to perform their contractual obligations to comply with the operating regulations at the time they entered into the contracts." Id. at 49. The court next rejected any suggestion that the plaintiffs could reasonably rely on an implied representation of compliance with the Visa and MasterCard regulations during each payment-card transaction. These regulations "explicitly provide for fines for breach of regulations such as storage of magnetic stripe data," which in turn shows "that the system is designed with the expectation that breaches will occur." Id. at 50. In fact, issuer banks, in insuring themselves against fraudulent charges through companies like Cumis, anticipated that breaches of the regulations might occur. Id. Additionally, the plaintiffs admitted that before the breach leading to their lawsuit, they had "received numerous and repeated alerts from Visa and MasterCard concerning specific instances of improper storage of magnetic stripe data," a violation of the regulations. Id. The plaintiffs knew that data breaches could occur, notwithstanding the defendants' contractual obligation to follow the Visa and MasterCard regulations. Id. The same reasons and reasoning require dismissal in this case. Under New Jersey law, it is unreasonable to rely on a representation when, as here, a financial arrangement exists to provide compensation if circumstances later prove that representation false.* See Russell — Stanley Corp. v. Plant Indus., Inc., *250 N.J.Super. 478, 595 A.2d 534, 549 (N.J.Super.Ct. Ch. Div.1991) (describing as "completely untenable" the plaintiff's claim that it relied on a land seller's statements about environmental damage when the sale contract created an escrow to fund environmental liability). Additionally, the Financial Institution Plaintiffs do not allege that Heartland never intended to follow the Visa and MasterCard regulations. They merely argue that it is premature to dismiss under Rule 12(b)(6). The master complaint, however, alleges no facts suggesting a plausible claim. Dismissal is appropriate, with prejudice, because amendment would be futile.*

3. Nondisclosure

For their third theory of misrepresentation, the Financial Institution Plaintiffs allege that Heartland failed to disclose weaknesses in its data security. "The deliberate suppression of a material fact is equivalent to a material misrepresentation if the party has a duty to disclose the fact." Maertin v. Armstrong World Indus. Inc., *241 F.Supp.2d 434, 461 (D.N.J.2002) (citing* N.J. Econ. Dev. Auth. v. Pavonia Rest., Inc., *319 N.J.Super. 435, 725 A.2d 1133, 1139 (N.J.Super.Ct.App.Div.1998)). "The concealed facts must be material facts[.]"* Maertin, *241 F.Supp.2d at 461. A concealed, or undisclosed, fact is material if the plaintiff would not have entered the contract had he known that fact.* See id. *A duty may arise whenever "good faith and common decency require it."* Id. *(quoting* City Check Cashing, Inc. v. Mfrs. Hanover Trust, *166 N.J. 49, 764 A.2d 411, 417 (2001)). "There are three general types of transactions where the duty to disclose arises: (1) where a fiduciary relationship exists between the parties, (2) where the transaction itself calls for perfect good faith and full disclosure, or (3) where one party expressly reposes a trust and confidence in the other."* Maertin, *241 F.Supp.2d at 461 (internal quotation marks omitted). In addition, a party has a duty to disclose whenever necessary to correct a material misrepresentation.* See id. *at 462 (citing* Strawn v. Canuso, *271 N.J.Super. 88, 638 A.2d 141, 149 (N.J.Super.Ct.App.Div.1994)). Whether a party has a duty to disclose is a question of law.* Maertin, *241 F.Supp.2d at 461 (citing* United Jersey Bank v. Kensey, *306 N.J.Super. 540, 704 A.2d 38, 43 (N.J.Super.Ct.App.Div.1997)).*

To the extent the Financial Institution Plaintiffs allege that Heartland had a duty to disclose corrective information unrelated to any material misrepresentation, the *complaint alleges insufficient facts to find such a duty. There is no fiduciary relationship alleged. Businesses rarely owe each other fiduciary duties in arms-length business transactions.* See City of Millville v. Rock, *683 F.Supp.2d 319, 330 (D.N.J.2010);* Maksin Mgmt. Corp. v. Roy A. Rapp, Inc., *No. L-4633-03, 2008 WL 3165465, at *8 (N.J.Super.Ct.App.Div. Aug. 8, 2008) (per curiam);* Pavonia Rest., *725 A.2d at 1139;* Berman v. Gurwicz, *189 N.J.Super. 89, 458 A.2d 1311, 1313–14 (N.J.Super.Ct. Ch. Div.1981). The Financial Institution Plaintiffs have not pleaded facts or presented argument demonstrating why their indirect relationship with Heartland, as one of many payment processors, presents an exception to the general rule.*

Although the allegations supporting the duty to disclose are thin, the Financial Institution Plaintiffs' briefing clarifies that the basis of the alleged duty is that "Heartland held itself out to the [Financial Institution Plaintiffs] and the public at large as having adequate system security measures in place." (Docket Entry No. 50, at 33). "Even where no duty to speak exists, one who elects to speak must tell the truth when it is apparent that another may reasonably rely on the statements made." Voilas v. Gen. Motors Corp., *170 F.3d 367, 378 (3d Cir.1999) (quoting* Strawn, *638 A.2d at 149). Some of the statements identified in the complaint are verifiable factual statements that can give rise to a negligent misrepresentation claim. The Financial Institution Plaintiffs argue that if those statements were material misrepresentations, then Heartland had a duty to correct them. Because the claims based on those alleged misrepresentations have been dismissed, the failure to disclose claim based on the same alleged misrepresentations is also dismissed. The Financial Institution Plaintiffs may amend their negligent misrepresentation claim based on this nondisclosure theory, but only as to the failure to correct verifiable factual statements that are actionable misrepresentations and on which the Financial Institution Plaintiffs relied.*

D. The Consumer — Protection Claims

The Financial Institution Plaintiffs allege violations of 23 states' consumer-protection laws. Heartland argues that the Financial Institution Plaintiffs lack standing to bring claims under the laws of states where neither they nor Heartland are located. (Docket Entry No. 56, at 15 n. 25). The Financial Institution Plaintiffs do not dispute this argument. The state-law claims at issue are those brought under the laws of California, Colorado, Florida, Illinois, New Jersey, New York, Texas, and Washington.

Heartland argues that this court should consider only the claims under New Jersey law, and that the claims under the remaining states' laws should be dismissed. Heartland contends that multiple states' laws cannot apply to the same set of misrepresentations. It further asserts that the Financial Institution Plaintiffs should not be allowed to plead the application of different states' law so that they can strategically choose which law to apply after seeing which claims survive a motion to dismiss. These arguments are unpersuasive. Courts have applied multiple states' laws in consumer protection cases when choice-of-law rules require doing so. See In re Pharm. Indus. Average Wholesale Price Litig., *252 F.R.D. 83, 93–96 (D.Mass.2008) (considering the appropriate approach to certifying a consumer class action involving multiple states' laws). Even if only one state's law could apply, Rule 8 allows a plaintiff to "set out 2 or more statements of a claim . . . alternatively[.]" FED. R. CIV. P. 8(d)(2). The rule applies equally to contentions regarding the applicable law. See, e.g., Zabors v. Chatsworth Data Corp., 735 F.Supp.2d 1010, 1013–14 (N.D.Ill.2010); see also Levin v. Dalva Bros., Inc., 459 F.3d 68, 73 (1st Cir.2006) (explaining that there is no "definitive point by which a litigant must raise a choice-of-law argument").*

*The cases on which Heartland relies to argue that only New Jersey law applies are distinguishable. In a separate Hannaford Brothers opinion, the district court had certified a question to the Maine Law Court based on the defendant's concession that Maine law applied. Judicial estoppel prevented the defendant from later arguing that a different state's law applied. MDL No. 2:08-MD-1954, 2009 WL 3824393, at *3 (D.Me. Nov. 16, 2009). Similarly, in Lott v. Levitt, 556 F.3d 564 (7th Cir.2009), the Seventh Circuit held that the plaintiff had waived his argument that Virginia law applied after having "agreed with Defendants that Illinois law governs this dispute, made no separate choice-of-law analysis, and cited no Virginia cases." Id. at 567 (internal quotation marks and alteration omitted). The cases do not stand for the proposition that the Financial Institution Plaintiffs, at this stage of the litigation, are limited to pleading the application of only one state's law.*

Neither side has briefed the choice-of-law issue. This court will not conduct such an analysis before the parties have done so. The arguments about each state's law instead are analyzed below.

1. The New Jersey Consumer Fraud Act

The parties focus primarily on the New Jersey Consumer Fraud Act ("NJCFA"), N.J. STAT. § 56:8–1 et seq. The NJCFA prohibits

[t]he act, use or employment by any person of any unconscionable commercial practice, deception, fraud, false pretense, false promise, misrepresentation, or the knowing, concealment, suppression, or omission of any material fact with intent that others rely upon such concealment, suppression or omission, in connection with the sale or advertisement of any merchandise or real estate, or with the subsequent performance of such person as aforesaid, whether or not any person has in fact been misled, deceived or damaged thereby, is declared to be an unlawful practice[.]

Id. § 56:8–2. The NJCFA creates a private right of action for "[a]ny person who suffers any ascertainable loss of moneys or property, real or personal, as a result of the use or employment by another person of any method, act, or practice" prohibited under the NJCFA. Id. § 56:8–19. Under the NJCFA, "merchandise" includes "any objects, wares, goods, commodities, services or anything offered, directly or indirectly to the public for sale[.]" Id. § 56:8–1(c). The NJCFA includes business entities in the definition of "person." Id. § 56:8–1(d); see also Finderne Mgmt. Co. v. Barrett, 402 N.J.Super. 546, 955 A.2d 940, 954 (N.J.Super.Ct.App.Div.2008) (noting that "[u]nlawful practices . . . can victimize business entities as well as individual consumers" (internal quotation marks omitted)). The three elements of an NJCFA claim are: "1) unlawful conduct by defendant; 2) an ascertainable loss by plaintiff; and 3) a causal relationship between the unlawful conduct and the ascertainable loss." Bosland v. Warnock Dodge, Inc., *197 N.J. 543, 964 A.2d 741, 749 (2009);* accord Lee v. Carter — Reed Co., *203 N.J. 496, 4 A.3d 561, 576 (2010).*

"Because it is remedial legislation, the [NJ]CFA is construed liberally to accomplish its broad purpose of safeguarding the public." Lee, *4 A.3d at 577 (internal quotation marks and alterations omitted). One early state case observed that "the entire thrust of the [NJCFA] is pointed to products and services sold to consumers in the popular sense. . . . The legislative language throughout the statute and the evils sought to be eliminated point to an intent to protect the consumer in the context of the ordinary meaning of that term in the market place."* Neveroski v. Blair, *141 N.J.Super. 365, 358 A.2d 473, 480 (N.J.Super.Ct.App.Div.1976) (per curiam),* superseded by statute on other grounds as recognized in Lee v. First Union Nat. Bank, *199 N.J. 251, 971 A.2d 1054, 1059–60 (2009);* accord Shogen v. Global Aggressive Growth Fund, Ltd., *Civ. A. No. 04-5695(SRC), 2007 WL 1237829, at *7–8 (D.N.J. Apr. 26, 2007) (quoting* Neveroski *and citing* J & R Ice Cream Corp. v. Cal. Smoothie Licensing Corp., *31 F.3d 1259, 1272 (3d Cir.1994)). The NJCFA "does not cover every sale in the marketplace."* Papergraphics Int'l Inc. v. Correa, *389 N.J.Super. 8, 910 A.2d 625, 628 (N.J.Super.Ct.App.Div.2006) (citing cases). The New Jersey Supreme Court has emphasized that "the strongest case for relief. . . is presented by the poor, the naive and the uneducated consumers [.]"* Kugler v. Romain, *58 N.J. 522, 279 A.2d 640, 649 (1971).*

State and federal courts have recognized that a business may sue under the NJCFA. J & R Ice Cream, *31 F.3d at 1273–74 (collecting cases). An early case analyzing whether a business could invoke the NJCFA was* Hundred East Credit Corporation v. Eric Schuster Corporation, *212 N.J.Super. 350, 515 A.2d 246 (N.J.Super.Ct.App.Div.1986). The plaintiff business purchased computer peripherals to upgrade its computer. When that sale occurred, the defendant, the peripherals manufacturer, knew that the computers for which the peripherals were designed would be discontinued that year. Id. at 247. The manufacturer argued that the NJCFA did not apply to merchandise sales for use in business operations. The court first noted that the statutory language expressly encompassed business entities and defined " 'merchandise' without regard to its intended use or the nature of the buyer." Id. at 248. The court acknowledged that the NJCFA was concerned primarily with consumers, but pointed out that "a business entity can be, and frequently is, a consumer in the ordinary meaning of that term. Since a business entity is also a 'person' entitled to recover under the Act, there is no sound reason to deny it the protection of the Act." Id. (internal citations omitted). The court acknowledged that the purpose of the NJCFA limited the Act's reach, but explained that in many cases a business needs protection from unfair practices just as much as an individual consumer:*

Business entities, like individual consumers, cover a wide range. Some are poor, some wealthy; some are naive, some sophisticated; some are required to submit, some are able to dominate. Even the most world-wise business entity can be inexperienced and uninformed in a given consumer transaction. Unlawful practices thus can victimize business entities as well as individual consumers. It may well be, of course, that certain practices unlawful in a sale of personal goods to an individual consumer would not be held unlawful in a transaction between particular business entities; the

Act largely permits the meaning of "unlawful practice" to be determined on a case-by-case basis.

Id. at 249. *Subsequent state and federal courts have agreed that a case-by-case approach to NJCFA claims asserted by businesses is appropriate.* Papergraphics, *910 A.2d at 628–29 (collecting cases).*

Courts generally have limited NJCFA claims by businesses to "consumer oriented situations." J & R Ice Cream, *31 F.3d at 1273 (citing cases);* BOC Grp., Inc. v. Lummus Crest, Inc., *251 N.J.Super. 271, 597 A.2d 1109, 1112 (N.J.Super.Ct. Law Div.1990) (same). Under this approach, "it is the character of the transaction rather than the identity of the purchaser which determines if the [NJCFA] is applicable."* J & R Ice Cream, *31 F.3d at 1273;* accord In re Schering — Plough Corp. Intron/Temodar Consumer Class Action, *No. 2:06-cv-5774 (SRC), 2009 WL 2043604, at *31 (D.N.J. July 10, 2009) (quoting* J & R Ice Cream*);* Marascio v. Campanella, *298 N.J.Super. 491, 689 A.2d 852, 857–58 (N.J.Super.Ct.App.Div.1997) (explaining that "the focus of the Act is on the nature of the goods and services being sold, and not the nature of the buyer or the buyer's intended use of the goods or services").*

Only a "bona fide consumer" may bring a claim under the NJCFA. Smith v. Trusted Universal Standards in Elec. Transactions, Inc., *Civ. No. 09-4567 (RBK/ KMW), 2010 WL 1799456, at *4 (D.N.J. May 4, 2010) ("The NJCFA only creates a cause of action for 'bona fide consumers of a product.'" (quoting* Grauer v. Norman Chevrolet Geo, *321 N.J.Super. 547, 729 A.2d 522, 524 (N.J.Super. Ct. Law Div.1998)));* DIRECTV, Inc. v. Marino, *No. Civ. 03-5606(GEB), 2005 WL 1367232, at *3 (D.N.J. June 8, 2005) (citing* Grauer*). "The absence of a consumer transaction is fatal to a[n] NJCFA claim."* Smith, *2010 WL 1799456, at *4 (citing* DIRECTV*). Business "competitors, direct or otherwise, suffering non-consumer like injuries [lack] standing to sue under the NJCFA."* Church & Dwight Co. v. SPD Swiss Precision Diagnostics, GmBH, *Civ. A. No. 10-453, 2010 WL 5239238, at *10 (D.N.J. Dec. 16, 2010). Courts also have held that insurers and assignees lack standing to sue under the NJCFA.* Standard Fire Ins. Co. v. MTU Detroit Diesel, Inc., *Civ. A. No. 07-3827(GEB), 2009 WL 2568199, at *5 (D.N.J. Aug. 13, 2009) (insurer);* Taylor v. Foulke Mgmt. Corp., *No. L-1502-08, 2011 WL 10050, at *2 (N.J.Super.Ct.App.Div. Oct. 14, 2010) (per curiam) (assignee) (citing* Levy v. Edmund Buick — Pontiac, Ltd., *270 N.J.Super. 563, 637 A.2d 600, 602 (N.J.Super.Ct. Law Div.1993)).*

Courts uniformly have excluded wholesalers from the NJCFA's protection, because they themselves do not consume merchandise; rather, they pass merchandise along to consumers. See, e.g., Diamond Life Lighting MFG (HK) Ltd. v. Picasso Lighting, Inc., *Civ. A. No. 10-161(PGS), 2010 WL 5186168, at *6 (D.N.J. Dec. 14, 2010) (wholesaler of lighting);* City Check Cashing, Inc. v. Nat'l State Bank, *244 N.J.Super. 304, 582 A.2d 809, 811 (N.J.Super.Ct.App.Div.1990) (analogizing a check-cashing business's claim against a bank to a wholesaler and denying the claim);* Arc Networks, Inc. v. Gold Phone Card Co., *333 N.J.Super. 587, 756 A.2d 636, 638–39 (N.J.Super.Ct. Law Div.2000) (reseller of bulk phone services in the form of phone cards)* cf. Viking Yacht Co. v. Composites One LLC, *496 F.Supp.2d 462, 474–75 (D.N.J.2007) (holding that a boat manufacturer that used defective marine gel in its manufacturing process could sue under the NJCFA). Privity is not a requirement, so long as the plaintiff is a* *consumer of the merchandise.* Gonzalez v. Wilshire Credit Corp., *411 N.J.Super. 582, 988 A.2d 567, 574 n. 9 (N.J.Super.Ct.App.Div.2010);* Marrone v. Greer & Polman Constr., Inc., *405 N.J.Super. 288, 964 A.2d 330, 335 (N.J.Super.Ct.App.Div.2009),* abrogated on other grounds by Dean v. Barrett Homes, Inc., *204 N.J. 286, 8 A.3d 766 (2010);* Katz v. Schachter, *251 N.J.Super. 467, 598 A.2d 923, 926 (N.J.Super.Ct.App.Div.1991);* Perth Amboy Iron Works, Inc. v. Am. Home Assur. Co., *226 N.J.Super. 200, 543 A.2d 1020, 1026 (N.J.Super.Ct.App.Div.1988),* aff'd, *118 N.J. 249, 571 A.2d 294 (1990);* Neveroski, *358 A.2d at 479.*

Even when a business is a consumer of merchandise, other factors may exclude it from NJCFA protection. The NJCFA applies only to "goods or services generally sold to the public at large." Cetel v. Kirwan Fin. Grp., Inc., *460 F.3d 494, 514 (3d Cir.2006) (quoting* Marascio, *689 A.2d at 857);* see also *Prof'l Cleaning & Innovative Bldg. Servs., Inc. v. Kennedy Funding Inc., 408 Fed.Appx. 566, 570 (3d Cir.2010) (per curiam) (describing this requirement as the "touchstone for the statute's applicability"). Businesses that have purchased yachts, computer peripherals, cranes, concrete, and commercial-renovation services have brought successful NJCFA claims. But courts have excluded sales of complex business franchises and custom services targeted to businesses. See* Prof'l Cleaning, *408 Fed.Appx. at 570–71 (credit services offered by lender of last resort to distressed businesses);* Cetel, *460 F.3d at 514–15 (tax shelters sold to businesses);* BOC Grp., *597 A.2d at 1113–14 (research and development services). The presence of large transactions or sophisticated business plaintiffs is a factor weighing against the NJCFA's applicability. See* Prof'l Cleaning, *408 Fed.Appx. at 571–72;* Diamond Life Lighting, *2010 WL 5186168, at *5;* Papergraphics, *910 A.2d at 629;* BOC Grp., *597 A.2d at 1113–14.*

The master complaint alleges that the Financial Institution Plaintiffs are "consumers in the marketplace for, inter alia, credit card and/or debit card transaction processing services, and have been injured in this capacity." (Docket Entry No. 32, ¶ 133). The complaint describes representations and services offered to merchants and members of the Visa and MasterCard networks, including the Financial Institution Plaintiffs. The complaint does not, however, allege that the Financial Institution Plaintiffs purchased any services from Heartland. The Financial Institution Plaintiffs' relationship with Heartland exists only by virtue of their participation in the Visa and MasterCard networks. This relationship is far different from the direct, downstream relationship between a consumer of a good and its manufacturer or seller. Cf., e.g., Diamond Life Lighting, *2010 WL 5186168, at *6. As noted above, the Visa and MasterCard regulations explicitly contemplate the presence of third-party processors, and there is no suggestion that the Financial Institution Plaintiffs had any control over who would perform those tasks. Cf.* Messeka Sheet Metal Co. v. Hodder, *368 N.J.Super. 116, 845 A.2d 646, 655 (N.J.Super.Ct.App.Div.2004) (holding that a homeowner could not sue a subcontractor under the NJCFA because the homeowner "left it to the general contractor to make the choices as to who would perform" each task on the project).*

Additionally, payment-card processing services are not offered to the general public. Instead, such services are provided by specific entities for members of the Visa and MasterCard networks. Heartland promises in its contracts to comply with the networks' regulations. These regulations significantly protect the Financial Institu-

tion Plaintiffs through loss-allocation rules and a cost-recovery process. In turn, issuer banks such as the Financial Institution Plaintiffs are required to maintain fraud-detection programs. These aspects of the Visa and MasterCard networks, along with the Financial Institution Plaintiffs' status as sophisticated financial institutions, set the Financial Institution Plaintiffs apart from the type of consumer protected under the NJCFA. The NJCFA claim is dismissed with prejudice and without leave to amend because amendment would be futile.

2. The California Unfair Competition Law

The Financial Institution Plaintiffs allege that Heartland violated the California Unfair Competition Law, CAL. BUS. & PROF. CODE § 17200 et seq. "A UCL plaintiff with standing is a person who '[1] has suffered injury in fact and [2] has lost money or property as a result of the unfair competition.'" Degelmann v. Advanced Med. Optics, Inc., *659 F.3d 835, 839 (9th Cir.2011) (quoting CAL. BUS. & PROF. CODE § 17204). Through the phrase "as a result of," the second element "requires a showing of a causal connection or reliance on the alleged misrepresentation."* Kwikset Corp. v. Superior Court, *51 Cal.4th 310, 120 Cal.Rptr.3d 741, 246 P.3d 877, 887 (2011) (quoting* Hall v. Time, Inc., *158 Cal.App.4th 847, 70 Cal.Rptr.3d 466, 471–72 (2008)). In* Kwikset, *the California Supreme Court held that the plaintiffs had sufficiently pleaded standing by alleging that the "plaintiffs saw and relied on the [false] labels for their truth in purchasing Kwikset's locksets, and [the] plaintiffs would not have bought the locksets otherwise." 120 Cal.Rptr.3d 741, 246 P.3d at 889. The Financial Institution Plaintiffs, by contrast, conclusorily assert reliance. As with the New Jersey misrepresentation claim, they do not explain the nature or form of their reliance. The claim is dismissed, without prejudice and with leave to amend.*

3. The Colorado Consumer Protection Act

The complaint alleges that Heartland violated the subsection of the Colorado Consumer Protection Act that prohibits, as a deceptive trade practice, "false or misleading statements of fact concerning the price of goods, services, or property or the reasons for, existence of, or amounts of price reductions." COLO. REV. STAT. § 6-1-105(1)(l). As Heartland points out, there are no allegations in the complaint about pricing. The Financial Institution Plaintiffs contend that Heartland selectively quotes from the Colorado Act, given that it contains "approximately 45 different categories of conduct that are considered deceptive trade practices." (Docket Entry No. 64, at 14). The complaint, however, refers only to subsection (1)(l). This claim is dismissed, without prejudice and with leave to amend.

4. The Florida Deceptive and Unfair Trade Practices Act

The Financial Institution Plaintiffs claim a violation of the Florida Deceptive and Unfair Trade Practices Act ("FDUTPA"), FLA. STAT. § 501.201 et seq. Heartland argues that this claim must be dismissed because only consumers, as the word is traditionally used, may assert claims under the FDUTPA. The Financial Institution

Plaintiffs respond that the Act's definition of "consumer" is broad enough to include them.

The FDUTPA prohibits "[u]nfair methods of competition, unconscionable acts or practices, and unfair or deceptive acts or practices in the conduct of any trade or commerce[.]" Id. § 501.204(1). The Act's purpose is "[t]o protect the consuming public and legitimate business enterprises from those who engage in unfair methods of competition, or unconscionable, deceptive, or unfair acts or practices in the conduct of any trade or commerce." Id. § 501.202(2). A practice is unfair if it "offends established public policy" or is "immoral, unethical, oppressive, unscrupulous, or substantially injurious to consumers." PNR, Inc. v. Beacon Prop. Mgmt., Inc., 842 So.2d 773, 777 (Fla.2003) (internal quotation marks omitted). Courts are to construe the FDUTPA liberally. FLA. STAT. § 501.202.

Before 2001, the FDUTPA allowed "a consumer who has suffered a loss as a result of a violation" of the FDUTPA to bring a cause of action. Am. Honda Motor Co. v. Motorcycle Info. Network, Inc., 390 F.Supp.2d 1170, 1176 (M.D.Fla.2005) (quoting FLA. STAT. § 501.211(2) (2000)) (emphasis in original). The Florida Legislature amended § 501.211(2) to replace "consumer" with "person" in 2001. Id.; see also FLA. STAT. § 501.211(2) ("a person who has suffered a loss as a result of a violation"). Since that amendment, courts have disagreed as to whether nonconsumers may bring a private action under the FDUTPA. See, e.g., Intercoastal Realty, Inc. v. Tracy, 706 F.Supp.2d 1325, 1334–35 (S.D.Fla.2010). Heartland relies on Kertesz v. Net Transactions, Ltd., 635 F.Supp.2d 1339 (S.D.Fla.2009), in which a Florida federal district court held that the amendment did not broaden the FDUTPA's private right of action. Id. at 1350. The court concluded that the Florida Legislature intended this amendment "to clarify that businesses, just like individuals, could obtain monetary damages in FDUTPA cases," but that only consumers could bring a private cause of action under the Act. Id. at 1349. Another Florida federal district court reached the opposite conclusion, holding that nonconsumers could sue under the FDUTPA. Kelly v. Palmer, Reifler, & Assocs., P.A., 681 F.Supp.2d 1356, 1373–74 (S.D.Fla.2010). The Kelly court explained:

[I]n 2001, the Legislature made two changes to FDUTPA that are relevant to the issue before us. As noted, the Legislature replaced the word "consumer" with "person." (The term "person," the Committee Staff noted, "is understood to include a business." See Senate Staff Analysis[, CS/SB 208, Mar. 22, 2001,] at 6.) The Legislature also amended the definition of "consumer" in § 501.203(7) to add "business" and "any commercial entity, however denominated." See Laws of Fla. Ch. 2001–39 § 1 (amending § 501.203(7) as described). So at the same time the Legislature expanded the definition of "consumer," it replaced the term "consumer" with "person" in the section providing for monetary remedies for a violation of the statute. To us, this evinces an intent to expand the applicability of the remedies provision to more than just consumers. If the purpose had been to assure that businesses could avail themselves of the remedies under § 501.211(2), given "inconsistent court interpretations" in which "remedies available to individual consumers have not always been available to business consumers," see Senate Staff Analysis at 4, that purpose could have been accomplished by the change to the definition of "consumer" (in § 501.203(7)), such that the term "consumer" did not have to be replaced with "person" in § 501.211(2). Thus

a non-consumer (like a competitor, either individually or through a corporate form) could seek relief under the statute so long as the trade or commerce element of the statute was satisfied.

Id. *at 1373 n. 9;* cf. Hetrick v. Ideal Image Dev. Corp., *372 Fed.Appx. 985, 990 (11th Cir.2010) (per curiam) (allowing individuals who "formed and funded a corporation on the basis of misrepresentations" to proceed with an FDUTPA claim because standing under the Act "is available to any person who was subject to an unfair or deceptive trade practice").*

The question is a close one. The Act's purpose is "[t]o protect the consuming public and legitimate business enterprises." *FLA. STAT. § 501.202(2) (emphasis added). It is unclear if the word "consuming" applies to only "public" or also to "legitimate business enterprises." The more natural reading is that this clause lists two independent groups that the Act seeks to protect: first, "the consuming public," and second, "legitimate business enterprises."* See Akzo Nobel Coatings, Inc. v. Auto Paint & Supply of Lakeland, Inc., *No. 8:09-cv-2453-T-30TBM, 2011 WL 5597364, at *3 (M.D.Fla. Nov. 17, 2011) (holding that "whether or not an individual non-consumer plaintiff has standing [under the Act], a legitimate business enterprise* does" *(emphasis in original));* Tracy, *706 F.Supp.2d at 1335 (allowing a claim by a "legitimate business enterprise" without regard to whether the business was a consumer);* Kertesz, *635 F.Supp.2d at 1349 (emphasizing only the word "consuming"). Limiting the private right of action to consumers also overlooks that even after the FDUTPA was amended to replace the word "consumer" with "person" in § 501.211(2), the Act continues to include a definition for "consumer,"* id. *§ 501.203(7), and to use that word in other provisions. For example, the Florida state attorney or Department of Legal Affairs may bring "[a]n action on behalf of one or more consumers . . . for the actual damages caused by an act or practice in violation" of the FDUTPA.* Id. *§ 501.207(c). The Florida Legislature's use of the word "person" in creating a private right of action suggests a broader reach than the word "consumer."* See Fla. Dep't of Revenue v. Cent. Dade Malpractice Trust Fund, *673 So.2d 899, 901 (Fla.Dist.Ct.App.1996) (noting that "legislative intent may be discerned from the Legislature's election to use different words to convey different meanings within a statute") (citing* Dep't of Prof'l Regulation v. Durrani, *455 So.2d 515, 518 (Fla.Dist.Ct.App.1984)).*

The motion to dismiss the FDUTPA claim on the basis of lack of standing is denied.

5. The Illinois Consumer Fraud and Deceptive Business Practices Act

Heartland argues that the Financial Institution Plaintiffs' claim under the Illinois Consumer Fraud and Deceptive Business Practices Act, 815 ILL. COMP. STAT. § 505/1 et seq., must be dismissed because the master complaint neither "relate[s] to consumer protection issues" nor alleges reliance. (Docket Entry No. 56, at 15–16). The Illinois statute prohibits "[u]nfair methods of competition and unfair or deceptive acts or practices, including but not limited to the use or employment of any deception, fraud, false pretense, false promise, misrepresentation or the concealment, suppression or omission of any material fact, with intent that others rely upon the concealment, suppression or omission of such material fact[.]" 815 ILL. COMP. STAT. § 505/2. There are four elements of a claim under the Illinois Act: (1) a deceptive act or practice; (2) the intent that the plaintiff rely on the deception; (3) the deception occurred in the course of conduct involving trade or commerce; and (4) the deceptive act proximately caused the plaintiff's injury. Cozzi Iron & Metal, Inc. v. U.S. Office Equipment, Inc., *250 F.3d 570, 575–76 (7th Cir.2001) (citing* Connick v. Suzuki Motor Co., *174 Ill.2d 482, 221 Ill.Dec. 389, 675 N.E.2d 584, 593 (1996)). "[A] statutory consumer fraud claim must be pled with specificity[.]"* Avery v. State Farm Mut. Auto. Ins. Co., *216 Ill.2d 100, 296 Ill.Dec. 448, 835 N.E.2d 801, 843 (2005).*

The master complaint does not adequately allege that Heartland intended the Financial Institution Plaintiffs to rely on any of its statements. The alleged misstatements in the S.E.C. filings, analyst calls, and the Merchant's Bill of Rights were not directed to issuer banks. Because issuers have no direct dealings with payment-card processors, it is implausible that Heartland intended statements in documents not directed to the Financial Institution Plaintiffs to be relied on by them or by any issuer banks. The master complaint conclusorily alleges reliance, insufficient to state a claim.

Heartland correctly states that under Illinois law, nonconsumers must show that "the complained-of conduct implicates consumer protection concerns." Speakers of Sport, Inc. v. ProServ, Inc., *178 F.3d 862, 868 (7th Cir.1999) (internal quotation marks omitted); accord, e.g.,* Gen. Ins. Co. of Am. v. Clark Mali Corp., *No. 08 C 2787, 2010 WL 1286076, at *6 (N.D.Ill. Mar. 30, 2010). In light of the sparse briefing on this issue, this court declines to address it at this time. The Illinois claim is dismissed, but without prejudice and with leave to amend.*

6. The New York Consumer — Protection Law

The Financial Institution Plaintiffs allege violations of New York's consumer-protection statute, which prohibits "[d]eceptive acts or practices in the conduct of any business, trade or commerce or in the furnishing of any service [.]" N.Y. GEN. BUS. LAW § 349(a). "Generally, claims under the statute are available to an individual consumer who falls victim to misrepresentations made by a seller of consumer goods through false or misleading advertising." Eaves v. Designs for Fin., Inc., *785 F.Supp.2d 229, 265 (S.D.N.Y.2011) (quoting* Small v. Lorillard Tobacco Co., *94 N.Y.2d 43, 698 N.Y.S.2d 615, 720 N.E.2d 892, 897 (1999)); accord, e.g.,* Waverly Props., LLC v. KMG Waverly, LLC, *___ F.Supp.2d ___, ___, 2011 WL 4472284, at *18 (S.D.N.Y.2011). "Courts have repeatedly held that a consumer, for § 349 purposes, is one who purchases goods and services for personal, family or household use."* Eaves, *785 F.Supp.2d at 265 (quoting* Exxonmobil Inter — America, Inc. v. Advanced Info. Eng'g Servs., Inc., *328 F.Supp.2d 443, 448 (S.D.N.Y.2004) (internal alteration omitted)).*

"To maintain a cause of action under § 349, a plaintiff must show: (1) that the defendant's conduct is 'consumer-oriented'; (2) that the defendant is engaged in a 'deceptive act or practice'; and (3) that the plaintiff was injured by this practice." Wilson v. Nw. Mut. Ins. Co., *625 F.3d 54, 64 (2d Cir.2010) (citing* Oswego Laborers' Local 214 Pension Fund. v. Marine Midland Bank, N.A., *85 N.Y.2d 20, 623 N.Y.S.2d*

529, 647 N.E.2d 741, 744 (1995)). Consumer-oriented conduct is defined as "acts or practices [that] have a broader impact on consumers at large. Private contract disputes, unique to the parties . . . would not fall within the ambit of the statute[.]" Oswego, *623 N.Y.S.2d 529, 647 N.E.2d at 744;* see also, e.g., N.Y. Workers' Comp. Bd. v. 26–28 Maple Avenue, Inc., *80 A.D.3d 1135, 915 N.Y.S.2d 744, 745 (2011) (defining consumer-oriented conduct as "an act having the potential to affect the public at large, as distinguished from merely a private contractual dispute" (internal quotation marks omitted)). "When more complex claims are asserted under [N.Y. GEN. BUS. LAW] § 349, courts have looked to the identity of the parties, their sophistication and experience, and the contract type and amount to determine whether the statute applies."* Wells Fargo Bank Nw., N.A. v. Am. Gen. Life Ins. Co., *Civ. A. No. 10-1327(FLW), 2011 WL 1899338, at *6 (D.N.J. May 19, 2011);* see also Exxonmobil Inter — America, *328 F.Supp.2d at 449 (explaining that "transactions involving complex arrangements, knowledgeable and experienced parties and large sums of money are different in kind and degree from those that confront the average consumer who requires the protection of a statute against fraudulent practices" (internal quotation marks and alteration omitted)). As one New York federal district court has explained, "While the 'consumer-orient[ed] act' prong does not preclude the application of § 349 to disputes between businesses per se, it does severely limit it. Contracts to provide commodities that are available only to businesses do not fall within the parameters of § 349."* Exxonmobil Inter — America, *328 F.Supp.2d at 449 (citing* Cruz v. NYNEX Info. Res., *263 A.D.2d 285, 703 N.Y.S.2d 103, 107 (2000)). When the parties are "both sophisticated contracting entities with equal bargaining power, and the contract between them was for a business-only commodity, not a common consumer good," § 349 is inapplicable.* Exxonmobil Inter — America, *328 F.Supp.2d at 450. The act "was designed to protect 'the little guy' from false advertising, pyramid schemes, bait-and-switch sales tactics, and other mischievous machinations by swindlers and scallywags."* Id. *(citing generally* Teller v. Bill Hayes, Ltd., *213 A.D.2d 141, 630 N.Y.S.2d 769 (1995)). If the product or service is not "for 'personal, family or household use' and the deceptive conduct alleged by Plaintiffs was not directed at non-business consumers," the claim does not fall within § 349.* Eaves, *785 F.Supp.2d at 266 (citing cases).*

Even assuming that the Financial Institution Plaintiffs had adequately pleaded that Heartland engaged in deceptive practices and that those practices injured them, the Financial Institution Plaintiffs are not "consumers." Nor is the conduct "consumer-oriented" under § 349. The Financial Institution Plaintiffs are far removed from an individual "who purchases goods and services for personal, family or household use," the paradigmatic § 349 plaintiff. Id. *at 265 (quoting* Exxonmobil Inter — America, *328 F.Supp.2d at 448 (internal alteration omitted)). To the extent that the Financial Institution Plaintiffs even "purchase" a service from Heartland — questionable, given the nature of their relationship with Heartland — their purchase is solely for commercial use and not personal, family or household use.*

Moreover, Heartland's allegedly deceptive representations — whether made in S.E.C. filings, to acquiring banks, or to merchants — do not qualify as "consumer-oriented conduct," as required to state a claim under § 349. Heartland made statements to acquiring banks and merchants about card-processing services. Such services are neither marketed nor offered to consumers, but only to specific types of commercial entities. Even assuming that the Financial Institution Plaintiffs can plausibly plead that they were injured by statements not directed toward them, the deceptive conduct they allege was not directed at "non-business consumers." Eaves, 785 F.Supp.2d at 266. The Financial Institution Plaintiffs' New York claim is dismissed, with prejudice because amendment would be futile.

7. The Texas Deceptive Trade Practices — Consumer Protection Act

The complaint alleges violations of the Texas Deceptive Trade Practices — Consumer Protection Act ("TDTPA"), TEX. BUS. & COM. CODE § 17.41 et seq. Heartland argues that the master complaint fails to state a claim because it does not allege: (1) that Lone Star National Bank, the only Texas plaintiff, has less than $25 million in assets, see id. § 17.45(4) (excluding business entities with more than $25 million in assets from the term "Consumer"); (2) misrepresentations made "in connection with *the [Financial Institution Plaintiffs'] transaction in goods or services,"* Amstadt v. U.S. Brass Corp., *919 S.W.2d 644, 650 (Tex.1996) (emphasis in original); and (3) that the Financial Institution Plaintiffs relied on a misrepresentation. (Docket Entry No. 56, at 16).*

Like the misrepresentation claim, the TDTPA claim must be dismissed because the conclusory allegation of reliance is insufficient under Rule 8. See, e.g., Rice v. Metro. Life Ins. Co., *324 S.W.3d 660, 676 (Tex.App.-Fort Worth 2010, no pet.) (explaining that reliance is a required element of a TDTPA claim). This claim is dismissed, without prejudice and with leave to amend.*

8. The Washington Consumer Protection Act

The complaint alleges that Heartland violated Washington's Consumer Protection Act, WASH. REV.CODEE[sic] § 19.86.010 et seq. "To prevail in a private CPA claim, the plaintiff must prove (1) an unfair or deceptive act or practice, (2) occurring in trade or commerce, (3) affecting the public interest, (4) injury to a person's business or property, and (5) causation." Panag v. Farmers Ins. Co. of Wash., *166 Wash.2d 27, 204 P.3d 885, 889 (2009); see also* Segal Co. (E. States), Inc. v. Amazon.Com, *280 F.Supp.2d 1229, 1232 (W.D.Wash.2003) (citing* Hangman Ridge Training Stables, Inc. v. Safeco Title Ins. Co., *105 Wash.2d 778, 719 P.2d 531, 535 (1986)). Heartland argues that the complaint insufficiently alleges an effect on the public interest. When a case involves a private dispute, as opposed to an ordinary consumer transaction, the plaintiff must show "a likelihood that additional persons have been or will be injured in the same fashion."* A.G. & Design Assocs., LLC v. Trainman Lantern Co., *No. C07-5158RBL, 2009 WL 230083, at *6 (W.D.Wash. Jan. 30, 2009) (citing* Goodyear Tire & Rubber Co. v. Whiteman Tire, Inc., *86 Wash.App. 732, 935 P.2d 628, 635 (1997)). "It is the likelihood that additional plaintiffs have been or will be injured in exactly the same fashion that changes a factual pattern from a private dispute to one that affects the public interest."* Michael v. Mosquera — Lacy, *165 Wash.2d 595, 200 P.3d 695, 700 (2009) (internal quotation marks and alteration omitted). The conduct must have "the capacity to deceive a substantial portion of the public."* Columbia Physical Therapy, Inc. v. Benton Franklin Orthopedic Assocs., P.L.L.C., *168 Wash.2d 421, 228 P.3d 1260,*

1270 (2010) (internal quotations marks and emphasis omitted). "Where the complaint involves essentially a private dispute such as the provision of professional services," courts consider four nonexclusive factors:

(1) Were the alleged acts committed in the course of defendant's business? (2) Did defendant advertise to the public in general? (3) Did defendant actively solicit this particular plaintiff, indicating potential solicitation of others? (4) Did plaintiff and defendant occupy unequal bargaining positions?

Stephens v. Omni Ins. Co., *138 Wash.App. 151, 159 P.3d 10, 24 (2007) (quoting* Hangman Ridge, *719 P.2d at 538);* accord, e.g., Hambleton Bros. Lumber Co. v. Balkin Enters., Inc., *397 F.3d 1217, 1234 (9th Cir.2005). Courts have dismissed cases under the public-interest element under Rule 12(b)(6). See, e.g.,* Swartz v. KPMG, LLC, *401 F.Supp.2d 1146, 1150, 1153–54 (W.D.Wash.2004),* aff'd in part, rev'd in part, *476 F.3d 756 (9th Cir.2007).*

The master complaint fails to allege sufficient facts suggesting that the Financial Institution Plaintiffs' claim affects the public interest. The only group likely to be injured in the same fashion — incurring expenses for replacement cards and fraudulent transactions — consists of other issuer banks. Such a group is both too small and too specialized to constitute a substantial portion of the public. See Swartz, *401 F.Supp.2d at 1153–54 (W.D.Wash.2004) ("The number of consumers who could conceivably find themselves in plaintiff's circumstances — looking for a tax savings on millions of dollars of capital gains — is extremely small and unable to qualify as a 'substantial portion of the public' under any reasonable definition of that term.");* Goodyear Tire & Rubber Co., *935 P.2d at 635 (finding that a company's representations to its dealers "had no deceptive capacity affecting the public in general");* see also Columbia Physical Therapy, *228 P.3d at 1270 (holding that the complained-of conduct must have "the capacity to deceive a substantial portion of the public" (quoting* Hangman Ridge, *719 P.2d at 535)). The Financial Institution Plaintiffs and other issuer banks have "sufficient sophistication to remove them from the class of bargainers subject to exploitation."* Segal Co., *280 F.Supp.2d at 1234 n. 5 (quoting* Pac. Nw. Life Ins. Co. v. Turnbull, *51 Wash.App. 692, 754 P.2d 1262, 1269 (1988));* see also Fleetwood v. Stanley Steemer Int'l, Inc., *725 F.Supp.2d 1258, 1276 (E.D.Wash.2010) (explaining that "parties with 'a history of business experience' cannot claim a CPA violation because they are 'not representative of bargainers who are subject to exploitation and unable to protect themselves' " (quoting* Hangman Ridge, *719 P.2d at 540 (alteration omitted)));* Swartz, *401 F.Supp.2d at 1154 (noting, in the context of tax products, that, "as a (very small) group, the extremely wealthy [multimillionaires] are neither unsophisticated nor easily subject to chicanery");* Hangman Ridge, *719 P.2d at 540 (noting that the plaintiffs were "not representative of bargainers subject to exploitation and unable to protect themselves").*

The master complaint vaguely alleges that Heartland intended its statements to lull the public into believing that its data security was better than it actually was. That allegation is insufficient to show that a dispute between sophisticated banks that issue payment cards and the company hired by other banks to process payments for merchants affects the public interest. The WCPA claim is dismissed, with prejudice and without leave to amend because amendment would be futile.

IV. Conclusion

Heartland's motion to dismiss, (Docket Entry No. 39), is granted in part and denied in part. All claims except that under the FDUTPA are dismissed. Leave to amend is granted only as to the following claims: breach of contract and implied contract (both under the limited circumstances described above); express misrepresentation; negligent misrepresentation based on nondisclosure; and violations of the California Unfair Competition Law, the Colorado Consumer Protection Act, the Illinois Consumer Fraud and Deceptive Business Practices Act, and the Texas Deceptive Trade Practices — Consumer Protection Act.

Chapter 9

INTERNATIONAL PRIVACY LAW: A WORLD OF DIFFERENT APPROACHES

The laws, regulations and practices described throughout this book arise out of, and are based within, the legal and cultural foundations of the United States. Other countries, though, have their own foundations, including those which impact on data privacy laws. Often, these variations result in privacy regimes which are not only different but directly conflicting with that of the United States.

With the expansion and integration of the Internet into all aspects of business and government, the variations among countries' privacy laws have become much more relevant, since data, including personally identifiable information, are crossing borders literally at light speed. Further, even small and mid-sized organizations are able to seek and exploit the opportunities of a multinational market, which can also open them up to multinational compliance.

I. JURISDICTION: WHAT LAWS APPLY?

While it is unrealistic for a business of any size to research every country's laws, and comply with all of them, there are certain factors which can help an organization determine which countries' requirements it should prioritize; essentially, it should first consider those nations in which it may most readily be subject to enforcement actions. Some of the factors include:

- Where the company maintains physical offices

- Where it keeps significant financial assets (i.e. local banks and financial institutions)

- The location of its most important and active strategic partner or supplier companies

- Where a substantial number of its customers reside

- Regions to which its employees may travel

The last is among the least anticipated or addressed, but it can have serious implications. Even in a country where a company does not maintain offices or personnel regularly, its employees may be subject to arrest or other legal action should the company be deemed to be violating local law, and the employees then travel to (or even through) that country. This has occurred in the context of local obscenity law[1] and

---

[1] *See* UCLA Online Institute for Cyberspace Law and Policy, COMPUSERVE GERMANY CASE — MAY 1998,

online gambling;[2] it has also happened in the area of privacy law. In September 2006, teenagers in Turin, Italy, posted to Google Video a recording of their bullying an autistic classmate, which was a violation of Italian privacy law. Two months later, Google received a request, and promptly removed the video. In January 2008, Peter Fleischer, Google's senior Privacy Officer in Europe, traveled from his office in Paris to speak at a conference in Italy. As he wrote in his own blog:

> . . . . *It began in January 2008 when I was invited to speak at a privacy conference at the University of Milan. I was approaching the University on foot, when I heard someone call my name. I turned around, and saw a guy in plain clothes, who told me to wait a minute, while he spoke into a cell phone, and within seconds, I found myself on the sidewalk surrounded by 5 Italian policemen. I had no idea what was going on. I was scared. I couldn't understand much, but I did understand that they wanted to take my passport, asked me to sign some documents, and wanted to escort me to a judge. I was allowed to put a call into my Italian colleagues at Google, who thankfully were able to rush to the scene and talk to the policemen. I was escorted by the policemen on foot through central Milan, with tourists and locals alike stopping to stare at the scene. My colleagues told the group of policemen that I was supposed to deliver a speech at the privacy conference shortly. After much discussion, it was agreed that I would be allowed to deliver the speech, after providing my passport and signing various documents that were being served on me, and that I would be interrogated by the Public Prosecutor afterwards.*[3]

Fleischer, along with three other Google executives, were ultimately arrested and charged under privacy laws because of the posted video. None of the executives charged, including Fleischer, had had any connection with either the posting of the video nor the process of its removal. Nevertheless, in February 2010, Fleischer, David Carl Drummond (a senior vice president) and George De Los Reyes (a retired financial executive) were convicted of violating privacy laws and given a six-month suspended sentence; the fourth executive was acquitted.[4] As of late 2011, the case was under appeal.[5]

---

http://legacy.gseis.ucla.edu/iclp/fsomm.html (last visited May 8, 2012) (CompuServe official in German arrested and convicted of pornography charges because employer connected service to Internet).

[2] *See*, 11 Charged In Web Gambling Crackdown — CBS News (Feb. 11, 2009), http://www.cbsnews.com/2100-201_162-1812590.html (last visited May 8, 2012) (BetOnSportsUK CEO David Carruthers arrested by U.S. officials in Texas airport during stopover between UK and Costa Rica).

[3] Peter Fleischer, Peter Fleischer: Privacy . . . ?: On Trial in Italy (Nov. 23, 2009), http://peterfleischer.blogspot.com/2009/11/on-trial-in-italy.html (last visited May 8, 2012).

[4] Nick Pisa, Google Italy ruling "threat to internet freedom" — Telegraph (Feb. 24, 2010), http://www.telegraph.co.uk/technology/google/7308384/Google-Italy-ruling-threat-to-internet-freedom.html (last visited May 8, 2012).

[5] Chronicle News Services, Google to appeal Italian conviction of 3 workers, SFGate (Dec. 1, 2011), http://www.sfgate.com/cgi-bin/article.cgi?f=/c/a/2011/11/30/BUT61M68A2.DTL (last visited May 8, 2012).

II. TWO MAJOR RELEVANT REGIMES: THE EU DATA PROTECTION DIRECTIVE AND PIPEDA

For organizations based in the United States, the two other privacy legal structures that are likely to be most relevant are the Data Protection Directive of the European Union, and Canada's Personal Information Protection and Electronic Documents Act ("PIPEDA"). Each takes a substantially different approach from U.S. law, one less reliant on the self-regulatory framework common in the United States, and the differences may lead to significant compliance challenges for businesses whose exposure crosses into either or both of those other regions

a. The EU Data Protection Directive and the U.S. Safe Harbor

The European Union's legal structure seeks to address the differences in laws within member states and establish basic universality by promulgating directives:

> *EU directives lay down certain end results that must be achieved in every Member State. National authorities have to adapt their laws to meet these goals, but are free to decide how to do so. Directives may concern one or more Member States, or all of them.*
>
> *Each directive specifies the date by which the national laws must be adapted — giving national authorities the room for manoeuvre within the deadlines necessary to take account of differing national situations.*
>
> *Directives are used to bring different national laws into line with each other, and are particularly common in matters affecting the operation of the single market (e.g. product safety standards).*[6]

i. The EU Data Protection Directive

In the area of data privacy, the key legislative mandate is the Data Protection Directive, first enacted in 1995.[7] While many areas of the Data Protection Directive parallel the issues raised by the FTC in its Fair Information Practice Principles,[8] there are a few key requirements that do not have U.S. counterparts. One involves the obligation of the party collecting personal information (known as a "controller") to register with the data privacy supervisory authority of the applicable national government:

---

[6] APPLICATION OF EU LAW — WHAT ARE EU DIRECTIVES?, *http://ec.europa.eu/eu_law/introduction/what_directive_en.htm (last visited May 8, 2012).*

[7] European Union, DIRECTIVE 95/46/EC OF THE EUROPEAN PARLIAMENT AND OF THE COUNCIL OF 24 OCTOBER 1995 ON THE PROTECTION OF INDIVIDUALS WITH REGARD TO THE PROCESSING OF PERSONAL DATA AND ON THE FREE MOVEMENT OF SUCH DATA, http://eur-lex.europa.eu/LexUriServ/LexUriServ.do?uri=CELEX:31995L0046:EN:HTML (last visited May 7, 2012).

[8] See discussion of FIPP in Chapter 2, Section IV.

SECTION IX: NOTIFICATION

Obligation to notify the supervisory authority

1. Member States shall provide that the controller or his representative, if any, must notify the supervisory authority referred to in Article 28 before carrying out any wholly or partly automatic processing operation or set of such operations intended to serve a single purpose or several related purposes.

2. Member States may provide for the simplification of or exemption from notification only in the following cases and under the following conditions:

— where, for categories of processing operations which are unlikely, taking account of the data to be processed, to affect adversely the rights and freedoms of data subjects, they specify the purposes of the processing, the data or categories of data undergoing processing, the category or categories of data subject, the recipients or categories of recipient to whom the data are to be disclosed and the length of time the data are to be stored, and/or

— where the controller, in compliance with the national law which governs him, appoints a personal data protection official, responsible in particular:

— for ensuring in an independent manner the internal application of the national provisions taken pursuant to this Directive

— for keeping the register of processing operations carried out by the controller, containing the items of information referred to in Article 21 (2),

thereby ensuring that the rights and freedoms of the data subjects are unlikely to be adversely affected by the processing operations.

3. Member States may provide that paragraph 1 does not apply to processing whose sole purpose is the keeping of a register which according to laws or regulations is intended to provide information to the public and which is open to consultation either by the public in general or by any person demonstrating a legitimate interest.

4. Member States may provide for an exemption from the obligation to notify or a simplification of the notification in the case of processing operations referred to in Article 8 (2) (d).

5. Member States may stipulate that certain or all non-automatic processing operations involving personal data shall be notified, or provide for these processing operations to be subject to simplified notification.

Article 19

Contents of notification

1. Member States shall specify the information to be given in the notification. It shall include at least:

(a) the name and address of the controller and of his representative, if any;

(b) the purpose or purposes of the processing;

(c) a description of the category or categories of data subject and of the data or categories of data relating to them;

(d) the recipients or categories of recipient to whom the data might be disclosed;

(e) proposed transfers of data to third countries;

(f) a general description allowing a preliminary assessment to be made of the appropriateness of the measures taken pursuant to Article 17 to ensure security of processing.

2. Member States shall specify the procedures under which any change affecting the information referred to in paragraph 1 must be notified to the supervisory authority.

Article 20

Prior checking

1. Member States shall determine the processing operations likely to present specific risks to the rights and freedoms of data subjects and shall check that these processing operations are examined prior to the start thereof.

2. Such prior checks shall be carried out by the supervisory authority following receipt of a notification from the controller or by the data protection official, who, in cases of doubt, must consult the supervisory authority.

3. Member States may also carry out such checks in the context of preparation either of a measure of the national parliament or of a measure based on such a legislative measure, which define the nature of the processing and lay down appropriate safeguards.

Article 21

Publicizing of processing operations

1. Member States shall take measures to ensure that processing operations are publicized.

2. Member States shall provide that a register of processing operations notified in accordance with Article 18 shall be kept by the supervisory authority.

The register shall contain at least the information listed in Article 19 (1) (a) to (e).

The register may be inspected by any person.

3. Member States shall provide, in relation to processing operations not subject to notification, that controllers or another body appointed by the Member States make available at least the information referred to in Article 19 (1) (a) to (e) in an appropriate form to any person on request.

Member States may provide that this provision does not apply to processing whose sole purpose is the keeping of a register which according to laws or regulations is intended to provide information to the public and which is open to consultation either by the public in general or by any person who can provide proof of a legitimate interest.[9]

An additional significant provision of the EU Data Protection Directive restricts "outward transfer"; that is, transferring collected personal information outside the EU:

Chapter IV: Transfer of Personal Data to Third Countries

Article 25

Principles

1. *The Member States shall provide that the transfer to a third country of personal data which are undergoing processing or are intended for processing after transfer may take place only if, without prejudice to compliance with the national provisions adopted pursuant to the other provisions of this Directive, the third country in question ensures an adequate level of protection.*

2. *The adequacy of the level of protection afforded by a third country shall be assessed in the light of all the circumstances surrounding a data transfer operation or set of data transfer operations; particular consideration shall be given to the nature of the data, the purpose and duration of the proposed processing operation or operations, the country of origin and country of final destination, the rules of law, both general and sectoral, in force in the third country in question and the professional rules and security measures which are complied with in that country.*

3. *The Member States and the Commission shall inform each other of cases where they consider that a third country does not ensure an adequate level of protection within the meaning of paragraph 2.*

4. *Where the Commission finds, under the procedure provided for in Article 31 (2), that a third country does not ensure an adequate level of protection within the meaning of paragraph 2 of this Article, Member States shall take the measures necessary to prevent any transfer of data of the same type to the third country in question.*

5. *At the appropriate time, the Commission shall enter into negotiations with a view to remedying the situation resulting from the finding made pursuant to paragraph 4.*

6. *The Commission may find, in accordance with the procedure referred to in Article 31 (2), that a third country ensures an adequate level of protection within the meaning of paragraph 2 of this Article, by reason of its domestic law or of the international commitments it has entered into, particularly upon conclusion of the negotiations referred to in paragraph 5, for the protection of the private lives and basic freedoms and rights of individuals.*

Member States shall take the measures necessary to comply with the Commission's decision.

---

[9] DIRECTIVE 95/46/EC at Chapter 2, Section IX.

Article 26

Derogations

1. By way of derogation from Article 25 and save where otherwise provided by domestic law governing particular cases, Member States shall provide that a transfer or a set of transfers of personal data to a third country which does not ensure an adequate level of protection within the meaning of Article 25 (2) may take place on condition that:

(a) the data subject has given his consent unambiguously to the proposed transfer; or

(b) the transfer is necessary for the performance of a contract between the data subject and the controller or the implementation of precontractual measures taken in response to the data subject's request; or

(c) the transfer is necessary for the conclusion or performance of a contract concluded in the interest of the data subject between the controller and a third party; or

(d) the transfer is necessary or legally required on important public interest grounds, or for the establishment, exercise or defence of legal claims; or

(e) the transfer is necessary in order to protect the vital interests of the data subject; or

(f) the transfer is made from a register which according to laws or regulations is intended to provide information to the public and which is open to consultation either by the public in general or by any person who can demonstrate legitimate interest, to the extent that the conditions laid down in law for consultation are fulfilled in the particular case.

2. Without prejudice to paragraph 1, a Member State may authorize a transfer or a set of transfers of personal data to a third country which does not ensure an adequate level of protection within the meaning of Article 25 (2), where the controller adduces adequate safeguards with respect to the protection of the privacy and fundamental rights and freedoms of individuals and as regards the exercise of the corresponding rights; such safeguards may in particular result from appropriate contractual clauses.

3. The Member State shall inform the Commission and the other Member States of the authorizations it grants pursuant to paragraph 2.

If a Member State or the Commission objects on justified grounds involving the protection of the privacy and fundamental rights and freedoms of individuals, the Commission shall take appropriate measures in accordance with the procedure laid down in Article 31 (2).

Member States shall take the necessary measures to comply with the Commission's decision.

4. Where the Commission decides, in accordance with the procedure referred to in Article 31 (2), that certain standard contractual clauses offer sufficient safeguards as required by paragraph 2, Member States shall take the necessary measures to comply with the Commission's decision.[10]

ii. The U.S. Safe Harbor

Note that, under these provisions, member states must prohibit data transfers to any country that does not "[ensure] an adequate level of protection." One such country is the United States, whose largely self-regulatory framework, lacking the overall data protection requirements such as those mandated by the EU, is deemed inadequate. This created a significant potential problem for the numerous organizations with both EU and US operations, which might not be able to move personal information (whether of consumers or even employees) out of the EU to the United States under the Data Protection Directive. As a result, the U.S. Department of Commerce, specifically the Export Division, negotiated the so-called "Safe Harbor Framework" through which U.S. companies could self-certify their compliance with a greater level of privacy protection than they were obligated to provide under U.S. law, and thereby qualify to transfer personal information out of Europe:

U.S.-EU Safe Harbor Overview

The European Commission's Directive on Data Protection went into effect in October 1998, and would prohibit the transfer of personal data to non-European Union countries that do not meet the European Union (EU) "adequacy" standard for privacy protection. While the United States and the EU share the goal of enhancing privacy protection for their citizens, the United States takes a different approach to privacy from that taken by the EU. The United States uses a sectoral approach that relies on a mix of legislation, regulation, and self-regulation. The EU, however, relies on comprehensive legislation that requires, among other things, the creation of independent government data protection agencies, registration of databases with those agencies, and in some instances prior approval before personal data processing may begin. As a result of these differences, the Directive could have significantly hampered the ability of U.S. organizations to engage in a range of trans-Atlantic transactions.

In order to bridge these differences and provide a streamlined and cost-effective means for U.S. organizations to satisfy the Directive's "adequacy" requirement, the U.S. Department of Commerce in consultation with the European Commission developed a "safe harbor" framework. The U.S.-EU Safe Harbor Framework, which was approved by the EU in 2000, is an important way for U.S. organizations to avoid experiencing interruptions in their business dealings with the EU or facing prosecution by EU member state authorities under EU member state privacy laws. Self-certifying to the U.S.-EU Safe Harbor Framework will ensure that EU organizations know that your organization provides "adequate" privacy protection, as defined by the Directive.

---

[10] *Id. Chapter IV, Arts. 25–26.*

U.S.-EU SAFE HARBOR BENEFITS

The U.S.-EU Safe Harbor program provides a number of important benefits to U.S. and EU organizations.

Benefits for participating U.S. organizations include:

- *All 27 Member States of the European Union will be bound by the European Commission's finding of "adequacy";*

- *Participating organizations will be deemed to provide "adequate" privacy protection;*

- *Member State requirements for prior approval of data transfers either will be waived or approval will be automatically granted;*

- *Claims brought by EU citizens against U.S. organizations will be heard, subject to limited exceptions, in the U.S.; and*

- *Compliance requirements are streamlined and cost-effective, which should particularly benefit small and medium enterprises.*

An EU organization can ensure that it is sending information to a U.S. organization participating in the U.S.-EU Safe Harbor program by viewing the public list of Safe Harbor organizations posted on this website. This list contains the names of all U.S. organizations that have self-certified to the U.S.-EU Safe Harbor Framework. This list will be regularly updated, so that it is clear which organizations are assured of Safe Harbor benefits.

HOW DOES AN ORGANIZATION JOIN?

The decision by U.S. organizations to enter the U.S.-EU Safe Harbor program is entirely voluntary. Organizations that decide to participate in the U.S.-EU Safe Harbor program must comply with the U.S.-EU Safe Harbor Framework's requirements and publicly declare that they do so. To be assured of Safe Harbor benefits, an organization must self-certify annually to the Department of Commerce in writing that it agrees to adhere to the U.S.-EU Safe Harbor Framework's requirements, which includes elements such as notice, choice, access, and enforcement. It must also state in its published privacy policy statement that it adheres to the Safe Harbor Privacy Principles.

To qualify for the U.S.-EU Safe Harbor program, an organization can (1) join a self-regulatory privacy program that adheres to the U.S.-EU Safe Harbor Framework's requirements; or (2) develop its own self-regulatory privacy policy that conforms to the U.S.-EU Safe Harbor Framework.

WHAT DO THE SAFE HARBOR PRIVACY PRINCIPLES REQUIRE?

Organizations must comply with the seven Safe Harbor Privacy Principles, which require the following:

Notice

Organizations must notify individuals about the purposes for which they collect and use information about them. They must provide information about how individuals can contact the organization with any inquiries or complaints, the types of third parties to which it discloses the information and the choices and means the organization offers for limiting its use and disclosure.

Choice

Organizations must give individuals the opportunity to choose (opt out) whether their personal information will be disclosed to a third party or used for a purpose incompatible with the purpose for which it was originally collected or subsequently authorized by the individual. For sensitive information, affirmative or explicit (opt in) choice must be given if the information is to be disclosed to a third party or used for a purpose other than its original purpose or the purpose authorized subsequently by the individual.

Onward Transfer (Transfers to Third Parties)

To disclose information to a third party, organizations must apply the notice and choice principles. Where an organization wishes to transfer information to a third party that is acting as an agent, it may do so if it makes sure that the third party subscribes to the Safe Harbor Privacy Principles or is subject to the Directive or another adequacy finding. As an alternative, the organization can enter into a written agreement with such third party requiring that the third party provide at least the same level of privacy protection as is required by the relevant principles.

Access

Individuals must have access to personal information about them that an organization holds and be able to correct, amend, or delete that information where it is inaccurate, except where the burden or expense of providing access would be disproportionate to the risks to the individual's privacy in the case in question, or where the rights of persons other than the individual would be violated.

Security

Organizations must take reasonable precautions to protect personal information from loss, misuse and unauthorized access, disclosure, alteration and destruction.

Data integrity

Personal information must be relevant for the purposes for which it is to be used. An organization should take reasonable steps to ensure that data is reliable for its intended use, accurate, complete, and current.

Enforcement

In order to ensure compliance with the safe harbor principles, there must be (a) readily available and affordable independent recourse mechanisms so that each individual's complaints and disputes can be investigated and resolved and damages awarded where the applicable law or private sector initiatives so provide; (b) procedures for verifying that the commitments companies make to adhere to the safe harbor principles have been implemented; and (c) obligations to remedy problems arising out of a failure to comply with the principles. Sanctions must be sufficiently rigorous to ensure compliance by the organization. Organizations that fail to provide annual self certification letters will no longer appear in the list of participants and safe harbor benefits will no longer be assured.

To provide further guidance, the Department of Commerce has issued a set of frequently asked questions and answers (FAQs) that clarify and supplement the Safe Harbor Privacy Principles.

HOW AND WHERE WILL THE U.S.-EU SAFE HARBOR BE ENFORCED?

In general, enforcement of the U.S.-EU Safe Harbor will take place in the United States in accordance with U.S. law and will be carried out primarily by the private sector. Private sector self-regulation and enforcement will be backed up as needed by government enforcement of the federal and state unfair and deceptive statutes. The effect of these statutes is to give an organization's U.S.-EU Safe Harbor commitments the force of law vis a vis that organization.

Private Sector Enforcement

As part of their U.S.-EU Safe Harbor program obligations, organizations are required to have in place a dispute resolution system that will investigate and resolve individual complaints and disputes and procedures for verifying compliance. They are also required to remedy problems arising out of a failure to comply with the principles. Sanctions that dispute resolution bodies can apply must be severe enough to ensure compliance by the organization; they must include publicity for findings of non-compliance and deletion of data in certain circumstances. They may also include suspension from membership in a privacy program (and thus effectively suspension from the U.S.-EU Safe harbor program) and injunctive orders.

The dispute resolution, verification, and remedy requirements can be satisfied in different ways. An organization could meet the requirements by complying with a private sector developed privacy seal program that incorporates and satisfies the Safe Harbor Privacy Principles. If the seal program, however, only provides for dispute resolution and remedies but not verification, then the organization would have to satisfy the verification requirement in an alternate way. An organization could also meet the requirements by complying with government supervisory authorities or by committing to cooperate with the EU data protection authorities.

Government Enforcement

Depending on the industry sector, the Federal Trade Commission, comparable U.S. government agencies, and/or the states may provide overarching government enforcement of the Safe Harbor Privacy Principles. Where an organization relies in whole or in part on self-regulation in complying with the Safe Harbor Privacy Principles, its failure to comply with such self-regulation must be actionable under federal or state law prohibiting unfair and deceptive acts or it is not eligible to join the safe harbor. At present, U.S. organizations that are subject to the jurisdiction of either the Federal Trade Commission or the Department of Transportation with respect to air carriers and ticket agents may participate in the U.S.-EU Safe Harbor program. The Federal Trade Commission and the Department of Transportation have both stated in letters to the European Commission that they will take enforcement action against organizations that state that they are in compliance with the U.S.-EU Safe Harbor Framework, but then fail to live up to their statements.

Under the Federal Trade Commission Act, for example, an organization's failure to abide by commitments to implement the Safe Harbor Privacy Principles might be considered deceptive and actionable by the Federal Trade Commission. This is the case even where an organization adhering to the Safe Harbor Privacy Principles relies entirely on self-regulation to provide the enforcement required by the Safe Harbor enforcement principle. The FTC has the power to rectify such misrepresentations by seeking administrative orders and civil penalties of up to $12,000 per day for violations.

Failure to Comply with the U.S.-EU Safe Harbor Framework Requirements: If an organization persistently fails to comply with the U.S.-EU Safe Harbor Framework requirements, it is no longer entitled to benefit from the U.S.-EU Safe Harbor. Persistent failure to comply arises where an organization refuses to comply with a final determination by any self-regulatory or government body or where such a body determines that an organization frequently fails to comply with the requirements to the point where its claim to comply is no longer credible. In these cases, the organization must promptly notify the Department of Commerce of such facts. Failure to do so may be actionable under the False Statements Act (18 U.S.C. § 1001).

The Department of Commerce will indicate on the public list it maintains of organizations self-certifying adherence to the U.S.-EU Safe harbor Framework requirements any notification it receives of persistent failure to comply and will make clear which organizations are assured and which organizations are no longer assured of U.S.-EU Safe Harbor benefits.

An organization applying to participate in a self-regulatory body for the purposes of re-qualifying for the U.S.-EU Safe Harbor program must provide that body with full information about its prior participation in the U.S.-EU Safe Harbor program.[11]

---

[11] U.S. Dept. of Commerce, Export.gov — Safe Harbor Overview, *http://export.gov/safeharbor/eu/eg_main_018476.asp (last visited May 8, 2012).*

iii.   Safe Harbor Enforcement

There has not been significant enforcement of the U.S.-E.U. Safe Harbor. The FTC has, though, taken action to protect U.S. consumers from a U.S. company with European-based online business, even when that company has no U.S. operations:

Court Halts U.S. Internet Seller Deceptively Posing as U.K. Home Electronics Site

In the wake of a Federal Trade Commission complaint against a company that deceptively sold electronics to hundreds of British consumers, the company has agreed to stop its allegedly illegal tactics until the case is decided in federal court.

Using the Web site names www.bestpricedbrands.co.uk and www.bite-sizedeals.co.uk, the California company tricked consumers into believing that they were buying from a company operating in the United Kingdom and were protected by manufacturer warranties that were valid there, according to the FTC complaint. When consumers received the cameras, video games, and other electronic goods, they discovered they had been charged unexpected import duties, were left with invalid warranties, and would be charged draconian cancellation and refund fees if they attempted to send the merchandise back, the complaint stated.

This is the first case the FTC has brought against a U.S. company exclusively doing business abroad. The U.S. SAFE WEB Act of 2006 gave the FTC the authority to sue U.S. companies deceiving foreign consumers, and was part of a strategy to prevent the United States from becoming a haven for fraud.

The Pasadena, California-based defendants charged in the case are Balls of Kryptonite, doing business as Best Priced Brands and Bite Size Deals, and its owner, Jaivin Karnani. Due in part to the defendants' deceptive use of Web sites ending in ".uk", the complaint alleges that consumers in the United Kingdom were duped into purchasing goods that carried no manufacturer warranties, were misled about their rights to return or exchange goods under U.K. regulations, were denied the option of cancelling orders, and were sent goods that were different from those depicted on the defendants' Web sites — and in some cases were unusable.

The FTC also charged the defendants with deceiving consumers about their participation in a program in which U.S. companies assure customers in the European Union that they secure the customers' personal information, as required by European law. Known as the EU/U.S. Safe Harbor program, it is administered by U.S. Department of Commerce. The complaint alleges that although the defendants claimed to participate in the EU/U.S. Safe Harbor program, they did not.

European consumers who want to know whether a U.S. company believes it is complying with European law by participating in the Safe Harbor program can go to http://export.gov/safeharbor to see if the company has self-certified.

The FTC was assisted in its investigation by the U.K. Office of Fair Trading, one of the FTC's principal international law enforcement partners. Many consumers in the United Kingdom registered complaints with the FTC by using the Web site www.econsumer.gov. Established by consumer protection agencies from 25 countries, this Web site collects consumers' complaints about problems in other countries, and facilitates international enforcement cooperation by making the complaints available to international consumer protection agencies through the FTC's Consumer Sentinel Network.[12]

The FTC has brought a number of other complaints alleging violations of the EU/U.S. Safe Harbor as well.[13]

iv. Proposed Updates to the EU Data Protection Directive

Since the original Data Protection Directive was enacted in 1995, both technology and the way consumers and businesses use the Internet and other data channels have substantially evolved. Accordingly, the EU has proposed revisions to the Data Protection Directive to address these new challenges:

Commission proposes a comprehensive reform of data protection rules to increase users' control of their data and to cut costs for businesses

. . . . *Technological progress and globalisation have profoundly changed the way our data is collected, accessed and used. In addition, the 27 EU Member States have implemented the 1995 rules differently, resulting in divergences in enforcement. A single law will do away with the current fragmentation and costly administrative burdens, leading to savings for businesses of around €2.3 billion a year. The initiative will help reinforce consumer confidence in online services, providing a much needed boost to growth, jobs and innovation in Europe.*

"17 years ago less than 1% of Europeans used the internet. Today, vast amounts of personal data are transferred and exchanged, across continents and around the globe in fractions of seconds," said EU Justice Commissioner Viviane Reding, the Commission's Vice-President. "The protection of personal data is a fundamental right for all Europeans, but citizens do not always feel in full control of their personal data. My proposals will help build trust in online services because people will be better informed about their rights and in more control of their information. The reform will accomplish this while making life easier and less costly for businesses. A strong, clear and uniform legal framework at EU level will help to unleash the potential of the Digital Single Market and foster economic growth, innovation and job creation."

The Commission's proposals update and modernise the principles enshrined in the 1995 Data Protection Directive to guarantee privacy rights in the future. They include a policy Communication setting out the Commission's objectives and two legislative proposals: a Regulation setting out a general EU framework for data protection and

---

[12] FTC Press Release, Court Halts U.S. Internet Seller Deceptively Posing as U.K. Home Electronics Site *(Aug. 6, 2009), http://www.ftc.gov/opa/2009/08/bestpriced.shtm (last visited May 8, 2012); see also FTC Press Release, FTC Settlement Bans Online U.S. Electronics Retailer from Deceiving Consumers with Foreign Website Names (June 9, 2011), http://ftc.gov/opa/2011/06/bestbrands.shtm (last visited May 8, 2012).*

[13] *See, e.g.,* FTC Press Release, FTC Settles with Six Companies Claiming to Comply with International Privacy Framework (Oct. 6, 2009), http://www.ftc.gov/opa/2009/10/safeharbor.shtm (last visited May 8, 2012).

a Directive on protecting personal data processed for the purposes of prevention, detection, investigation or prosecution of criminal offences and related judicial activities.

Key changes in the reform include:

- *A single set of rules on data protection, valid across the EU. Unnecessary administrative requirements, such as notification requirements for companies, will be removed. This will save businesses around €2.3 billion a year.*

- *Instead of the current obligation of all companies to notify all data protection activities to data protection supervisors — a requirement that has led to unnecessary paperwork and costs businesses €130 million per year, the Regulation provides for increased responsibility and accountability for those processing personal data.*

- *For example, companies and organisations must notify the national supervisory authority of serious data breaches as soon as possible (if feasible within 24 hours).*

- *Organisations will only have to deal with a single national data protection authority in the EU country where they have their main establishment. Likewise, people can refer to the data protection authority in their country, even when their data is processed by a company based outside the EU. Wherever consent is required for data to be processed, it is clarified that it has to be given explicitly, rather than assumed.*

- *People will have easier access to their own data and be able to transfer personal data from one service provider to another more easily (right to data portability). This will improve competition among services.*

- *A 'right to be forgotten' will help people better manage data protection risks online: people will be able to delete their data if there are no legitimate grounds for retaining it.*

- *EU rules must apply if personal data is handled abroad by companies that are active in the EU market and offer their services to EU citizens.*

- *Independent national data protection authorities will be strengthened so they can better enforce the EU rules at home. They will be empowered to fine companies that violate EU data protection rules. This can lead to penalties of up to €1 million or up to 2% of the global annual turnover of a company.*

- *A new Directive will apply general data protection principles and rules for police and judicial cooperation in criminal matters. The rules will apply to both domestic and cross-border transfers of data.*

The Commission's proposals will now be passed on to the European Parliament and EU Member States (meeting in the Council of Ministers) for discussion. They will take effect two years after they have been adopted . . .[14]

---

[14] Press Release, European Commission, Jan 25, 2012, EUROPA — *Press Releases — Commission*

b. PIPEDA

The overall Canadian data privacy law commonly known as PIPEDA went into partial effect in January 2001, with additional portions becoming effective in subsequent years.[15] While not as restrictive as the EU Data Protection Directive, it too has unique elements that must be addressed by companies doing business both in the U.S. and Canada.

The guiding principle of PIPEDA may be found in Division 1, Section 5, paragraph 3: "An organization may collect, use or disclose personal information only for purposes that a reasonable person would consider are appropriate in the circumstances."[16] PIPEDA further provides guidance as to the standards to be applied to data collection in its Schedule 1, which incorporates the Model Code for the Protection of Personal Information published by the not-for-profit Canadian Standards Association.[17] This Model Code offers principles similar to those of the FIPP, although structured somewhat differently:

> *Principle 1 — Accountability*
>
> *Principle 2 — Identifying Purposes*
>
> *Principle 3 — Consent*
>
> *Principle 4 — Limiting Collection*
>
> *Principle 5 — Limiting Use, Disclosure, and Retention*
>
> *Principle 6 — Accuracy*
>
> *Principle 7 — Safeguards*
>
> *Principle 8 — Openness*
>
> *Principle 9 — Individual Access*
>
> *Principle 10 — Challenging Compliance*[18]

Industry Canada, the governmental department responsible for economic development, publishes a frequently asked questions ("FAQ") list to assist businesses in complying with PIPEDA and its related laws.[19] Canada has also established the Office

---

PROPOSES A COMPREHENSIVE REFORM OF DATA PROTECTION RULES TO INCREASE USERS' CONTROL OF THEIR DATA AND TO CUT COSTS FOR BUSINESSES, *http://europa.eu/rapid/pressReleasesAction.do?reference=IP/12/46&format=HTML&aged=1&language=EN&guiLanguage=en (last visited May 8, 2012). The proposed revisions may be found at http://eur-lex.europa.eu/LexUriServ/LexUriServ.do?uri=COM:2012:0010:FIN :EN:HTML.*

[15] PERSONAL INFORMATION PROTECTION AND ELECTRONIC DOCUMENTS ACT, Part 6, http://laws-lois.justice.gc.ca/eng/acts/P-8.6/FullText.html.

[16] *Id.* at Div. 1, Sec. 5, Para. 3.

[17] Canadian Standards Association, VIEW PRIVACY CODE | PUBLICATIONS | CSA, http://www.csa.ca/cm/ca/en/privacy-code/publications/view-privacy-code (last visited May 8, 2012).

[18] *Id.*

[19] Industry Canada, FREQUENTLY ASKED QUESTIONS — ELECTRONIC COMMERCE IN CANADA, http://www.ic.gc.ca/eic/site/ecic-ceac.nsf/eng/gv00466.html (last viewed May 7, 2012).

of the Privacy Commissioner, with official responsibility for advocating for the privacy rights of Canadians, including under PIPEDA.[20]

c. Other International Privacy Regimes: The APEC Framework, Pathfinder and Cross-Border Enforcement Arrangement.

Although the EU Directive and PIPEDA are the major international privacy regimes with which most U.S. companies must be concerned, others may be relevant as well. One important body in particular is the Privacy Framework of the Asia-Pacific Economic Cooperation ("APEC") forum.[21] APEC has established a number of privacy-related efforts, one of which is the 2005 Privacy Framework, a set of principles for both internal practices and international cooperation among members on privacy issues.[22] Based upon the Framework, APEC's Electronic Commerce Steering Group[23] developed its Data Privacy Pathfinder[24] and a Cross-Border Privacy Enforcement Arrangement which the United States joined in July 2012:

Acting U.S. Commerce Secretary Rebecca Blank Announces U.S. Participation in APEC's Cross Border Privacy Rules System

Acting U.S. Commerce Secretary Rebecca Blank today announced the United States' participation in the Asia-Pacific Economic Cooperation's (APEC) Cross Border Privacy Rules (CBPR) system. This voluntary system promotes a baseline set of data privacy practices for companies doing business in participating APEC economies. The goal of the system is to enhance electronic commerce, facilitate trade and economic growth, and strengthen consumer privacy protections across the Asia Pacific region.

> *"U.S. participation in APEC's Cross Border Privacy Rules system is a significant milestone in international data protection and is an important step in the implementation of the global privacy strategy outlined in the Obama administration's February 2012 Data Privacy Blueprint," said Acting Secretary Rebecca Blank. "This system will enable participating companies in the United States and other APEC member economies to more efficiently exchange data in a secure manner and will enhance consumer*

---

[20] Office of the Privacy Commissioner of Canada, http://www.priv.gc.ca/index_e.asp (last visited May 8, 2012).

[21] Asia-Pacific Economic Cooperation — Asia-Pacific Economic Cooperation, http://www.apec.org/ (last visited Jul 30, 2012).

[22] APEC Privacy Framework — Asia-Pacific Economic Cooperation, http://www.apec.org/About-Us/About-APEC/Fact-Sheets/APEC-Privacy-Framework.aspx (last visited Jul 30, 2012).

[23] Electronic Commerce Steering Group — Asia-Pacific Economic Cooperation, http://www.apec.org/Groups/Committee-on-Trade-and-Investment/Electronic-Commerce-Steering-Group.aspx (last visited Jul 30, 2012).

[24] APEC Electronic Commerce Steering Group, *APEC Data Privacy Pathfinder Projects Implementation Work Plan — Revised*(2009), at http://aimp.apec.org/Documents/2009/ECSG/SEM1/09_ecsg_sem1_027.doc.

data privacy by establishing a consistent level of protection and accountability in the APEC region. The CBPR system directly supports the president's National Export Initiative goal of doubling U.S. exports by the end of 2014 by decreasing regulatory barriers to trade and commerce, and creating more export opportunities for American companies, and more American jobs. We are committed to working with our trading partners in APEC to help maximize its implementation throughout the region."

The 21 member economies in APEC comprise a market of 2.7 billion consumers, and account for 55 percent of world real gross domestic product, as well as 44 percent of world trade. On November 13, 2011, President Obama and representatives from the other APEC economies endorsed the CBPR system at the APEC Leaders Summit in Honolulu, Hawaii. In the APEC Leaders' Declaration, President Obama and his counterparts committed to implementing the CBPR system to further open markets and facilitate regional trade. The United States plans to work with APEC to launch the system in the next six months. . . .[25]

* * *

FTC Becomes First Enforcement Authority in APEC Cross-Border Privacy Rules System

The Federal Trade Commission welcomed the approval of the United States' participation in the Asia-Pacific Economic Cooperation (APEC) Cross-Border Privacy Rules system, which was announced by the U.S. Department of Commerce today. The APEC privacy system is a self-regulatory initiative to enhance the protection of consumer data that moves between the United States and other APEC members through a voluntary but enforceable code of conduct implemented by participating businesses. President Obama and representatives from the other APEC economies endorsed the system in November 2011. On July 25, the United States was approved as the first formal participant in the system and the FTC as the system's first privacy enforcement authority.

FTC Commissioner Edith Ramirez, who has been active in the FTC effort within APEC, applauded the development on behalf of the agency. "The APEC privacy rules offer the promise of significant benefits to companies, consumers and privacy regulators, and the FTC is pleased to be the first privacy enforcement authority in the Cross-Border Privacy Rules system," Ramirez said. "We hope that many more APEC economies will soon join and help realize the system's potential as a model for global interoperability among privacy regimes."

The FTC, the Department of Commerce, U.S. corporations, and privacy advocacy organizations worked together with their counterparts in other APEC economies to formulate the APEC privacy rules. In addition to the United States, the 21 APEC

---

[25] U.S. Dept. of Commerce Press Release, July 26, 2012, ACTING U.S. COMMERCE SECRETARY REBECCA BLANK ANNOUNCES U.S. PARTICIPATION IN APEC'S CROSS BORDER PRIVACY RULES SYSTEM | DEPARTMENT OF COMMERCE, *http://www.commerce.gov/news/press-releases/2012/07/26/acting-us-commerce-secretary-rebecca-blank-announces-us-participation (last visited Jul 30, 2012).*

members include Australia, Brunei, Canada, Chile, China, Hong Kong, Indonesia, Japan, Korea, Malaysia, Mexico, New Zealand, Papua New Guinea, Peru, the Philippines, Russia, Singapore, Taiwan, Thailand, and Vietnam. . . .[26]

---

[26] FTC Press Release, July 26, 2012, FTC Becomes First Enforcement Authority in APEC Cross-Border Privacy Rules System, *http://www.ftc.gov/opa/2012/07/apec.shtm (last visited Jul 30, 2012).*

Chapter 10

PRIVACY AND CYBERCRIME INVESTIGATIONS: THE FOURTH AMENDMENT AND ECPA

Discussions of privacy in the context of the state and federal governments can encompass a wide range of topics and concerns. For example, the "right to privacy" under constitutional jurisprudence often refers to disputes regarding governmental control over citizens' bodily integrity and access to reproductive services (contraception, abortion) that are the subject of landmark Supreme Court cases such as *Griswold v. Connecticut*[1] and *Roe v. Wade*.[2] These issues, while very important in themselves, are nevertheless largely out of the scope of the questions of personally identifiable and behavioral information collection, use and protection that are the subject of this book (although they are addressed to some extent in the discussion of health privacy in Chapter Five).

When it comes to law enforcement, however, matters of obtaining, using and protecting identity and behavior information are significant. Police have long created and utilized their own collections of information about actual and potential criminals to assist in investigations and prosecutions. From the earliest use by Parisian police of photographs (or mugshots) of criminals,[3] to the adoption and growth of anecdotal forensic tools of varying reliability such as fingerprints, bitemarks and even phrenology[4] to modern DNA databases like the FBI's Combined DNA Index System ("CODIS"),[5] law enforcement agencies have sought to empower victims, witnesses and investigators with greater tools to identify perpetrators.

Beyond their own resources, though, police and other law enforcement officials understand that their investigations may be aided via access to third party collections of identifying and behavioral tracking information. As the various chapters of this book describe, Internet service providers, Web site operators, social media services, employers, non-law enforcement governmental bodies and other organizations are amassing their own substantial stores of data from and about individuals. Even where such databases have nothing to do directly with criminal law or enforcement, they may provide extremely valuable evidence to help prove that a particular suspect was (or

---

[1] 381 U.S. 479 (1965).

[2] 410 U.S. 113 (1973).

[3] A SHORT HISTORY OF MUG SHOTS, FROM LEON TROTSKY TO JOHNNY CASH. — SLATE MAGAZINE, http://www.slate.com/articles/arts/gallery/2010/10/a_short_history_of_mug_shots.html (last visited Jul 6, 2012)

[4] D. L. Faigman, *Anecdotal Forensics, Phrenology, and Other Abject Lessons from the History of Science*, 59 HASTINGS LJ 979 (2007).

[5] FBI — CODIS, http://www.fbi.gov/about-us/lab/codis/ (last visited Jul 6, 2012)

was not) involved in a crime.[6]

One major concern with the use by law enforcement officers of third-party databases is that those data were almost certainly collected without explicit notice of, or consent to, such uses, making self-enforcement a poor method for privacy protection in this context. Even where a well-drafted and thought-out privacy policy may mention disclosure in response to governmental request,[7] such a mention is rarely if ever prominent, and both the collecting organization and information-providing user will likely be focusing on the expected and more frequent uses to which the information will be put in connection with the specific transaction or relationship between them. In many other information collection contexts, such as the recording of incoming and outgoing calls by a cellphone company for billing purposes, there may be little or no standard disclosure of either the expected or rarer disclosures, including those to law enforcement agencies.

Rather than depending on disclosure and consent as the primary means of regulating personal and behavior data use by the police, explicit statutes and constitutional law play a primary role in the preservation of privacy during criminal investigations and prosecutions. Depending on the type of information, and intended use, law enforcement officials as well as those from whom they wish to obtain information may need to consider, and comply with, multiple overlapping requirements.

I. THE FOURTH AMENDMENT AND DATA SEARCHES

The primary source of law and analysis for governmental collection of personal data and monitoring behavior, particularly in the law enforcement context, is very clear: the Fourth Amendment to the U.S. Constitution:

> *The right of the people to be secure in their persons, houses, papers, and effects, against unreasonable searches and seizures, shall not be violated, and no Warrants shall issue, but upon probable cause, supported by Oath or affirmation, and particularly describing the place to be searched, and the persons or things to be seized.*[8]

The original focus of this amendment was physical, in-person searches and seizures of physical goods (and themselves) by police and other law enforcement officials, and the vast majority of past and ongoing judicial analysis of the Fourth Amendment remains within this context. As technology has advanced, both as it is used by (alleged) criminals and those seeking to apprehend and interrogate them, the applicability of the Fourth Amendment has become less clear, requiring both judicial interpretation and new statutory frameworks to supplement its protections and restrictions.

---

[6] See, e.g., MARKEY: LAW ENFORCEMENT COLLECTING INFORMATION ON MILLIONS OF AMERICANS FROM MOBILE PHONE CARRIERS | CONGRESSMAN ED MARKEY, MASSACHUSETTS 7TH DISTRICT, http://markey.house.gov/press-release/markey-law-enforcement-collecting-information-millions-americans-mobile-phone-carriers (last visited Jul 9, 2012).

[7] *See generally* the discussion of privacy policies in Chapter Two.

[8] U.S. Const., 4th Amend.

To understand the difference, compare a police investigation of a bank robbery in 1912 with that of a 2012 cybercrime equivalent: maliciously hacking into a bank computer and changing account ownership information. The 1912 investigation would require detectives to examine the physical setting of the bank, to interview actual in-person eyewitnesses, and potentially to enter the suspected criminal's home or other location (likely requiring a search warrant) to seek the stolen currency. Being 1912, there would be no security film footage to examine; all evidence would be physical or testimonial. In contrast, a cybercrime investigation can largely be performed from the detectives' desks, using forensic computer programs to examine access logs, and the stolen "funds" might still be in place in the victim bank's computers or, if not, will likely be stored in another bank's electronic records. Tracking the alleged perpetrator will require not eyewitness testimony but IP address records, which are matched to particular user accounts by an Internet service provider. There may never be any need to enter the alleged thief's home or office until and unless the police wish to make an arrest; a search of the premises might produce no relevant evidence if the thief used an outside computer or network to perform the theft. That analysis in turn assumes a single thief in a single location, but in reality cybercrimes may be committed remotely (if the thief writes software that infects others' computers to perform the actual malicious hacking automatically) and the thief could be located literally anywhere in the world.

With any situation in which a warrant may be required, the validity will depend on whether the requesting official fulfilled the constitutional requirements of probable cause and specificity. The latter requirement can be of a particular challenge in circumstances where the search in question is for electronically stored information. Among the potential specificity problems in a digital data-related warrant request are:

- Technical description: must the warrant name the devices and file locations on which the data that are sought are stored? What if the officer or issuing court does not understand differences between, for example, a computer versus a smartphone, a disk drive versus a memory card, and so forth?

- Location of the data: Where are they physically located? This can raise not only warrant language but jurisdictional questions.[9]

- Proper identification of the suspect: Often, potential criminals are only identifiable by the IP address of the computer used in the incident, which may be traceable to an account holder but not necessarily to an individual. "Drive-by" uses of unsecured wireless networks or even inaccurate records of IP address allocations by ISPs can lead to wrong identifications and therefore improper searches.[10]

---

[9] See, e.g., Orin Kerr, THE VOLOKH CONSPIRACY DOES THE FOURTH AMENDMENT ALLOW EXTRATERRITORIAL STATE SEARCH WARRANTS? (Jan 8, 2010), http://volokh.com/2010/01/08/does-the-fourth-amendment-allow-extraterritorial-state-search-warrants/ (last visited May 8, 2012).

[10] See, e.g., Jeffrey Brown, NAAG | UNSECURED WIRELESS NETWORKS STILL AN ISSUE, http://www.naag.org/unsecured-wireless-networks-still-an-issue.php (last visited May 8, 2012), citing *United States v. Ahrndt*, 2010 U.S. Dist. LEXIS 7821 (D. Or. 2010).

Even assuming that a search is properly requested and conducted, the question of what constitutes a "seizure" of data remains. Given that a copy can be made of electronically stored information while the original remains intact, would that constitute a seizure? What if the process of copying altered the "metadata," the information stored with the data being copied which describes their characteristics (including when last they may have been accessed or modified)? Would that be considered a legal seizure? For that matter, the metadata themselves may turn out to be the relevant information for the case, although they might not have been included in the original warrant. In such an instance, the metadata and any evidence derived from them might fall under the Exclusionary Rule and be inadmissible, unless the officer could show that the accessing of metadata fell under an existing exception to the warrant requirement such as the presence of exigent circumstances. There is also the potential for the party possessing the data (such as an Internet service provider or an online retailer) to be held liable for improperly releasing the data if the warrant or other request documentation are legally invalid, or if any relevant privacy policy does not provide an exception to non-disclosure obligations for requests from law enforcement officials.

GUEST v. LEIS[11]

ALAN E. NORRIS, *Circuit Judge.*

In 1995, the Hamilton County, Ohio, Regional Electronic Computer Intelligence Task Force (RECI) was investigating on-line obscenity and seized two computer bulletin board systems. The first system seized was the Cincinnati Computer Connection Bulletin Board System (CCC BBS). Several users of the system filed a class action on behalf of subscribers against RECI, the sheriff, and his department alleging violations of the First and Fourth Amendments, the Electronic Communications Privacy Act (ECPA), and the Privacy Protection Act (PPA), and setting out state law and common law claims. The second system seized in the same general investigation was the Spanish Inquisition Bulletin Board System (SI BBS). The system's users, operator, and computer owner brought suit against the same defendants alleging the same violations as in the CCC BBS suit.

The district court granted summary judgment for defendants in each case, and plaintiffs appeal. We affirm.

I. Background

A. Cincinnati Computer Connection Bulletin Board System

In early 1995, there was a complaint lodged with the Hamilton County Sheriff's Department about on-line obscenity, and RECI, a division of the sheriff's department, began investigating several electronic bulletin board systems, including the CCC BBS. The CCC BBS computers were operated by Robert Emerson in Union

---

[11] 255 F.3d 325 (2001) [notes omitted].

Township (Clermont County), Ohio. The system, according to plaintiffs, included "thousands of subscribers from the Greater Cincinnati area, the United States and even overseas." Guest Brief at 5. Users could, with a password, send e-mail to subscribers or to others on the internet. They could also participate in chat room conversations, on-line games, and conferences, where they could post or read messages on many topics, and they could download files such as computer programs and pictures.

RECI officers assumed an undercover identity and obtained access to the adult part of the bulletin board system, where they downloaded sample images. A detective presented more than one hundred of these images to a Hamilton County municipal court judge, who determined that forty-five of them were obscene. RECI officers then prepared a search warrant, which identified the forty-five obscene images. The affidavit attached to the warrant listed the offenses in question as pandering obscenity (Ohio Rev.Code § 2907.32) and possessing criminal tools (Ohio Rev.Code § 2923.24). RECI showed the warrant to attorneys in the Hamilton County prosecutor's office and edited it after this meeting. The revised warrant authorized the search and seizure of computer hardware, software, financial and computer records, and personal communications, limiting the items searched or seized to those that had been used in the offense. RECI officers then presented the warrant to a Clermont County municipal court judge, who signed the warrant, directing it to the police chief of Union Township, located in Clermont County.

On June 16, 1995, members of RECI and the Union Township Police Department went to the home of Robert Emerson to execute the warrant. The officers asked Emerson to locate the obscene images on his system so that they could seize only those files; Emerson denied knowledge of obscene images on the computer and placed a call to his lawyer. While everyone waited for the attorney to return the call, the Union Township officers left the house. Emerson eventually stated that he did not know where the images were on the computer. Several hours after the police's arrival, with still no word from the lawyer, the RECI officers began dismantling the computer system to take it away; Emerson then said that the images were on the large file server. The officers, skeptical of his statement, seized the large and small file servers and took them to the police station.

Deputy Sheriff Ausdenmoore explained the way the computer search proceeded at the station. He said that he used a computer program to locate the forty-five obscene files according to the file names listed in the warrant, and he also searched for unlicenced software. He testified that once he had located the image files, he did not review the rest of the seized property. Plaintiffs, on the other hand, allege that defendants read e-mail on the seized system.

On August 7, 1995, plaintiffs filed this suit against the Hamilton County Sheriff's Department, RECI, Hamilton County Sheriff Simon Leis, and Deputy Sheriffs Dale Menkhaus, James Nerlinger, and David Ausdenmoore. The class of CCC BBS users was certified on July 5, 1996. Sometime during the pendency of the suit, defendants returned the computer equipment to Emerson. On March 31, 1998, the magistrate judge issued a report and recommendation to grant the defendants' motions for summary judgment on the ECPA, Fourth Amendment, and corollary Ohio constitu-

tional claims, and to grant qualified immunity to the individual defendants on the Fourth Amendment claim. The district court adopted the recommendation on September 30, 1996, and later granted defendants' renewed motion for qualified immunity and summary judgment on the remaining claims, dismissing the case on August 5, 1999.

B. Spanish Inquisition Bulletin Board System

The SI BBS was a smaller bulletin board system than the CCC BBS, and it was run by a teenager on his father's home computer. Only one user could log on at a time, and the connection to the internet was more rudimentary than the CCC BBS's connection. The SI BBS included a posted disclaimer on privacy:

Pursuant to the Electronic and Communications Privacy Act of 1986, Title 18 U.S.Code 2510 and following, all users are hereby notified that there are NO provisions for private messages on this board. This is TRUE notwithstanding the fact that the system software indicates to the user that he or she may and can make a message "private." All messages may be read by the SysOp [systems operator] and his assigns[.]

O'Brien *Joint Appendix (J.A.) at 655 (Nerlinger Dep. at 237).*

The SI BBS investigation began after a parent reported to police that his son and a friend were viewing child pornography. RECI officials interviewed several of the juveniles implicated and analyzed their computers, which disclosed child and adult pornography and files indicating unauthorized access to computer systems. RECI traced the latter files, called HPACV (hacker/phreaker/anarchy/cracking/virus) files, to the SI BBS, but the detectives were unable to gain access to the bulletin board system. They obtained a warrant on the basis of their interviews with the juveniles and examination of their computers, which indicated that the SI BBS was used to tap phone lines, recover debit card numbers, acquire pirated software, and download child pornography. The warrant borrowed the CCC BBS warrant language authorizing the seizure of all equipment, documentation, and personal communications that were used in the offenses listed. The supporting affidavit listed three offenses: illegal use of a minor in nudity-oriented material (Ohio Rev.Code § 2907.323), unauthorized use of property (Ohio Rev.Code § 2913.04), and possessing criminal tools (Ohio Rev.Code § 2923.24). The warrant for a search of the owner's home in Butler County was issued by the Butler County Court of Common Pleas and directed to the Police Chief of Union Township.

On August 31, 1995, RECI executed the search warrant for the SI BBS. After unsuccessful attempts to contact the computer's owner, defendants removed computer equipment and disks. Union Township police accompanied RECI officials and remained present until RECI officials left the premises.

This lawsuit was filed on March 6, 1996, by four individual members of the SI BBS, the operator of the SI BBS, and the owner of the computer that housed the system. Plaintiffs alleged the same violations of law in this suit as in the CCC BBS suit, but the court denied class certification. On November 5, 1998, the district court granted summary judgment on the ECPA, Fourth Amendment, and corresponding Ohio constitutional claims and found the individual defendants entitled to qualified immunity on the constitutional claims. On August 5, 1999, the court granted defendants' motion for qualified immunity and summary judgment on the remaining claims.

II. Fourth Amendment

Plaintiffs argue that the district court erred in granting qualified immunity and summary judgment to the defendants on the Fourth Amendment claims. We review a grant of summary judgment, including summary judgment on the grounds of qualified immunity, de novo. McCloud v. Testa, 97 F.3d 1536, 1541 (6th Cir.1996). Summary judgment is appropriate where, viewing the evidence in the light most favorable to the non-moving party, there is "no genuine issue as to any material fact and . . . the moving party is entitled to a judgment as a matter of law." Fed.R.Civ.P. 56(c); Birgel v. Bd. of Comm'rs, 125 F.3d 948, 950 (6th Cir.1997).

Qualified immunity shields government officials from liability, as well as from suit, if their official conduct "does not violate clearly established statutory or constitutional rights of which a reasonable person would have known." Harlow v. Fitzgerald, 457 U.S. 800, 818, 102 S.Ct. 2727, 73 L.Ed.2d 396 (1982). We review issues of qualified immunity using a two-step inquiry. First, we determine whether the plaintiff has demonstrated the violation of a constitutionally protected right. Brennan v. Township of Northville, 78 F.3d 1152, 1154 (6th Cir.1996). If there is such a violation, then we examine "whether the right is so 'clearly established' that a 'reasonable official would understand that what he is doing violates that right.' " Id. (quoting Anderson v. Creighton, 483 U.S. 635, 640, 107 S.Ct. 3034, 97 L.Ed.2d 523 (1987)).

Plaintiffs argue that defendants did not have the legal authority to conduct a search and seizure outside of their (Hamilton County) jurisdiction; that defendants exceeded the scope of the warrants; that the search warrants were not sufficiently particularized; that the warrants did not state probable cause for the seizure of e-mail and subscriber information; and that defendants were not entitled to qualified immunity because they were governmental units. Defendants challenge plaintiffs' standing to assert the Fourth Amendment claims.

A. Standing

Defendants argue that plaintiffs do not have standing to assert Fourth Amendment claims in these cases. In order to challenge a search or seizure as a violation of the Fourth Amendment, a person must have had a subjective expectation of privacy in the place or property to be searched which was objectively reasonable. Minnesota v. Olson, 495 U.S. 91, 95–96, 110 S.Ct. 1684, 109 L.Ed.2d 85 (1990). Home owners would of course have a reasonable expectation of privacy in their homes and in their belongings — including computers — inside the home. Bulletin board users would not share the same interest in someone else's house or computer, so they would not be able to challenge the search of the homes and the seizure of the computers as physical objects. Their interest in the computer content presents a different question and would depend on their expectations of privacy in the materials. In the O'Brien case, the SI

BBS posted a disclaimer stating that personal communications were not private. This disclaimer defeats claims to an objectively reasonable expectation of privacy for the SI BBS users. See United States v. Simons, 206 F.3d 392, 398 (4th Cir.2000) (finding no privacy interest in an employee's internet search records when an employer posted a privacy disclaimer regarding computer files). Accordingly, the O'Brien *user-plaintiffs do not have standing to assert Fourth Amendment claims.*

The Guest *user-plaintiffs' standing would turn on the materials they had on the CCC BBS. Users would logically lack a legitimate expectation of privacy in the materials intended for publication or public posting. See United States v. Maxwell, 45 M.J. 406, 417–19 (C.A.A.F.1996). They would lose a legitimate expectation of privacy in an e-mail that had already reached its recipient; at this moment, the e-mailer would be analogous to a letter-writer, whose "expectation of privacy ordinarily terminates upon delivery" of the letter. United States v. King, 55 F.3d 1193, 1196 (6th Cir.1995) (citations omitted); see also Maxwell, 45 M.J. at 418. Whether the users had more private material on the system that entitled them to standing is not a question we must reach since we conclude below that there was no Fourth Amendment violation in this case.*

B. Legal Authority

Plaintiffs allege that defendants were outside of their jurisdiction and therefore did not have the legal authority to conduct the search or seizure in question. Such an extra-legal seizure, say plaintiffs, was a Fourth Amendment violation, and defendants were not entitled to qualified immunity because their lack of jurisdiction rendered them private citizens.

Ohio law does not permit a police officer to execute a search warrant outside his jurisdiction unless an officer of the jurisdiction where the warrant is executed "accompanies the other officers and remains present at all times." State v. Miller, No. 12198, 1986 WL 1127, at (Ohio Ct.App. Jan. 22, 1986) (unpublished opinion); see also State v. Harrison, 20 Ohio Misc. 282, 287, 251 N.E.2d 521, 525 (Ct. Comm. Pleas 1969). In the O'Brien *case, the warrant was directed to Union Township police, who accompanied the defendants during the entire search and seizure at the* O'Brien *home. There was therefore no violation of the search rule in the* O'Brien *case.*

In the Guest *case, the home to be searched was in Union Township, the search warrant was addressed to Union Township officials, and Union Township police accompanied the defendants but left before the actual seizure of the computer equipment occurred. Although their departure violated the rule stated in* Miller *and* Harrison, *this conclusion does not end our inquiry. We must still ask whether the failure to comply with a state rule rises to the level of a constitutional violation.*

The Fourth Amendment protects against unreasonable searches and seizures. See, e.g., United States v. Ramirez, 523 U.S. 65, 71, 118 S.Ct. 992, 140 L.Ed.2d 191 (1998) (stating that a reasonableness standard governs the execution of warrants). The Ohio Court of Appeals declined to find a constitutional violation under similar circumstances in State v. Klemm, 41 Ohio App.3d 382, 383, 536 N.E.2d 14, 16 (Ct.App.1987). In Klemm, *the court considered the application of the exclusionary rule when*

Cincinnati police conducted a search outside of their jurisdiction. Even though the police violated state law, the violation did not make the search unreasonable in a constitutional sense because the search warrant was supported by probable cause. Id.; see also United States v. Green, *178 F.3d 1099, 1106 (10th Cir.1999) ("The Fourth Amendment is satisfied where, as here, officers obtain a warrant, grounded in probable cause and phrased with sufficient particularity, from a magistrate of the relevant jurisdiction authorizing them to search a particular location, even if those officers are acting outside their jurisdiction as defined by state law"). The technical violation that occurred in the* Guest *case when the Union Township officers decided to leave the home did not render the search and seizure unreasonable in constitutional terms.*

C. Exceeding the Scope of the Warrant

Plaintiffs claim that defendants exceeded the scope of the warrant by seizing and reading e-mail and members' subscriber information. The warrants authorized the search and seizure of:

[a]ny documentation and/or notations referring to the computer, the contents of the computer, the use of the computer or any computer software and/or communications. All information within the above listed items including but not limited to machine readable data, all previously erased data, and any personal communications including but not limited to e-mail, chat capture, capture files, correspondence stored in electronic form, and/or correspondence exchange in electronic form. . . . All items to be searched and/or seized having been used in the obtaining, maintenance, and/or as evidence of said offense.

Guest *J.A. at 69–70;* O'Brien *J.A. at 242–43.*

1. Seizure of Computer Contents

The warrant authorized the seizure of personal communications related to the offense. Although there were presumably communications on the computers that did not relate to the offenses, "[a] search does not become invalid merely because some items not covered by a warrant are seized." United States v. Henson, *848 F.2d 1374, 1383 (6th Cir.1988). In* Henson, *a case affirming convictions involving false odometer statements, we rejected a Fourth Amendment challenge to the seizure of documents and computer files that were unrelated to the offenses because we concluded that it would have been unreasonable to require police to sort through extensive files in a suspect's office in order to separate out those items that were outside the warrant. Id. at 1383–84;* see also Davis v. Gracey, *111 F.3d 1472, 1481 (10th Cir.1997) (finding no Fourth Amendment violation when defendants seized a bulletin board system computer that contained personal communications unrelated to the crime under investigation);* United States v. Hay, *231 F.3d 630, 637–38 (9th Cir.2000) (finding no Fourth Amendment violation in the search and seizure of a computer system in a child pornography investigation);* United States v. Upham, *168 F.3d 532, 536 (1st Cir.1999) (same). In the instant cases, when the seizures occurred, defendants were unable to separate relevant files from unrelated files, so they took the computers to be able to sort out the documents off-site. Because of the technical difficulties of conducting a computer search in a suspect's home, the seizure of the computers, including their content, was reasonable in these cases to allow police to locate the offending files.*

2. E-mail Search

Plaintiffs also allege that defendants read their e-mail, an allegation defendants deny. Plaintiffs rely for evidence on the following. A plaintiff testified as an expert witness that certain log records were missing from the Guest *CCC BBS computers when the computers were returned; these logs normally keep a record of the use of the computer, and the expert testified that defendants must have deleted the log files or prevented them from generating. The* Guest *plaintiffs also refer to a paper printout of the computer directories, which showed defendants' check marks next to several directory names, including a directory labeled "e-mail."*

The printout and absence of log files are not evidence that the defendants read private communications. Plaintiffs are essentially relying on an assumption that because defendants could have read e-mail, there is evidence that they did read e-mail. Defendants may legitimately have checked to see that the contents of the directories corresponded to the labels placed on the directories. Suspects would otherwise be able to shield evidence from a search simply by "misfiling" it in a directory labeled "e-mail." In the Guest *case, defendants had a list of file names and thus could conduct their search by reviewing the file names in a directory, without actually opening the files and viewing the contents. While we construe the facts on summary judgment in the light most favorable to the nonmoving party, "[t]he mere existence of a scintilla of evidence in support of the plaintiff's position will be insufficient; there must be evidence on which the jury could reasonably find for the plaintiff."* Mitchell v. Toledo Hosp., *964 F.2d 577, 581 (6th Cir.1992) (quoting* Anderson v. Liberty Lobby, Inc., *477 U.S. 242, 252, 106 S.Ct. 2505, 91 L.Ed.2d 202 (1986)). Plaintiffs' assumptions are insufficient to establish a genuine issue of fact regarding an e-mail search.*

3. Search of Subscriber Information

Plaintiffs argue that defendants violated the Fourth Amendment by accessing bulletin board subscriber information. These records include information such as subscribers' names, addresses, birthdates, and passwords. As we have noted above, a person must have a reasonable expectation of privacy in the matter searched in order to challenge a search under the Fourth Amendment. Individuals generally lose a reasonable expectation of privacy in their information once they reveal it to third parties. See United States v. Miller, *425 U.S. 435, 443, 96 S.Ct. 1619, 48 L.Ed.2d 71 (1976), limited by statute. A bank customer, for instance, does not have a legitimate expectation of privacy in the information that he or she has conveyed to the bank; by placing the information under control of a third party, the customer assumes the risk that the bank will convey the information to the government. Id. Courts have applied this principle to computer searches and seizures to conclude that computer users do not have a legitimate expectation of privacy in their subscriber information because they have conveyed it to another person — the system operator. See* Maxwell, *45 M.J.*

at 418; United States v. Kennedy, *81 F.Supp.2d 1103, 1110 (D.Kan.2000) (rejecting a privacy interest in subscriber information communicated to an internet service provider);* United States v. Hambrick, *No. 99–4793, 2000 WL 1062039, at 4th Cir. Aug.3, 2000) (unpublished) (holding that defendant destroyed any privacy interest in his subscriber information when he conveyed it to an internet service provider) (citing* Miller, *425 U.S. at 442, 96 S.Ct. 1619). We conclude that plaintiffs in these cases lack a Fourth Amendment privacy interest in their subscriber information because they communicated it to the systems operators. In addition, in the* O'Brien *case, subscriber information would be that of the users, who do not have Fourth Amendment standing.*

4. Software Search

Plaintiffs also assert that defendants exceeded the scope of the warrant when they searched for unlicensed software. The only individual with a privacy interest in the software would be the person possessing the software, i.e., the computer's owner or the system operator. In the Guest *case, the owner and bulletin board operator, Robert Emerson, is not a party to the case. In the* O'Brien *case, although the owner and operator are parties, the warrant listed the offense of "possession of unlicensed property," so the search for unlicensed software in that case was clearly authorized by the warrant.*

D. Particularity

Plaintiffs argue that the warrant failed to describe with sufficient particularity the things to be seized. They seem to base this argument on the warrant's failure to particularly identify communications or subscriber information. A search warrant must particularly describe the things to be seized, but the description, whose specificity will vary with the circumstances of the case, will be "valid if it is as specific as the circumstances and the nature of the activity under investigation permit." Henson, *848 F.2d at 1383 (quoting* United States v. Blum, *753 F.2d 999, 1001 (11th Cir.1985)).*

In the instant cases, the warrants required that the communications and computer records pertain to the listed offenses. Defendants could not have obtained more specific identification of e-mails and subscriber data, which were not accessible to them. The description was thus particular enough as the circumstances permitted for these items. Moreover, since plaintiffs have not established that their communications were searched, there would be no harm from an alleged defect in the warrant regarding any of the communications.

E. Probable Cause

Plaintiffs assert that the warrants did not state "probable cause to believe that the Plaintiffs' public and private communications, and their subscriber information, was evidence of a crime." Guest Brief *at 43. Plaintiffs do not dispute in their briefs that defendants had probable cause to search for evidence of crimes on the computers. As we have already determined, the difficulty of locating and extracting these images meant that a seizure of the whole computer system was not unreasonable, so long as there was probable cause to conclude that evidence of a crime would be found on the computer. An analysis of probable cause to search the materials is unnecessary since plaintiffs have failed to establish that their communications were searched, and they lack a privacy interest in their subscriber information.*

F. Qualified Immunity

According to plaintiffs, "Defendants Leis, Hamilton County Sheriff's Department and RECI cannot assert qualified immunity" as "political subdivisions." Guest Br. at 46. Qualified immunity may be asserted by government officials sued in their individual capacity. Harlow, 457 U.S. at 807, 102 S.Ct. 2727. As the district court granted qualified immunity only to the individual defendants, plaintiffs' objections about immunity for the sheriff's department and RECI are unfounded. Sheriff Leis was sued in his individual capacity (as well as in his official capacity), so he may properly assert the defense in his individual capacity. Because we have concluded that there were no Fourth Amendment violations, the individual defendants are all entitled to qualified immunity on the Fourth Amendment claims asserted against them in their individual capacities.

III. First Amendment

Plaintiffs allege that the defendants violated their First Amendment rights by seizing and shutting down the bulletin board systems, thus effecting a prior restraint on speech. They rely on two Supreme Court cases which established a general rule that police cannot make mass seizures of allegedly obscene material without a prior adversarial judicial determination of obscenity. See A Quantity of Copies of Books v. Kansas, *378 U.S. 205, 84 S.Ct. 1723, 12 L.Ed.2d 809 (1964);* Marcus v. Search Warrants, *367 U.S. 717, 81 S.Ct. 1708, 6 L.Ed.2d 1127 (1961). In* A Quantity of Copies, *police seized 1,715 copies of 31 novels after ex parte judicial examination of seven of the allegedly obscene books.* A Quantity of Copies, *378 U.S. at 208–09, 84 S.Ct. 1723. In* Marcus, *police seized approximately 11,000 copies of 280 publications, without a prior judicial determination of obscenity.* Marcus, *367 U.S. at 723, 81 S.Ct. 1708. Such seizures violated the First Amendment because the lack of a pre-seizure hearing risked the "abridgment of the right of the public in a free society to unobstructed circulation of nonobscene books."* A Quantity of Copies, *378 U.S. at 213, 84 S.Ct. 1723.*

There is not, however, an absolute right to a prior adversarial hearing in cases where allegedly obscene material is seized to preserve evidence in a criminal prosecution. Heller v. New York, *413 U.S. 483, 488, 93 S.Ct. 2789, 37 L.Ed.2d 745 (1973). Police are permitted to seize evidence of a crime — even expressive materials — if the seizure is pursuant to a valid warrant. In* Heller, *police with a warrant seized one copy of an allegedly obscene film. The Supreme Court did not find a First Amendment violation, holding that*

[i]f such a seizure is pursuant to a warrant, issued after a determination of probable cause by a neutral magistrate, and, following the seizure, a prompt judicial determination of the obscenity issue in an adversary proceeding is available at the

request of any interested party, the seizure is constitutionally permissible.

Id. *at 492, 93 S.Ct. 2789. The Court emphasized that* Marcus *and* A Quantity of Copies *"concerned the seizure of large quantities of books for the sole purpose of their destruction." Id. at 491, 84 S.Ct. 1723. "[W]here allegedly obscene material is seized, pursuant to a warrant, to preserve the material as evidence in a criminal prosecution," there is no absolute First or Fourteenth Amendment right to a prior adversary hearing. Id. at 488, 93 S.Ct. 2789. In dicta, the Court warned that if the exhibitor made a showing to the trial court that he did not have other copies of the film available, "the court should permit the seized film to be copied so that showing can be continued pending a judicial determination of the obscenity issue in an adversary proceeding. Otherwise, the film must be returned." Id. at 492–93, 93 S.Ct. 2789 (footnotes omitted).*

In the instant cases, RECI took the computers to establish evidence of criminal violations, as in Heller. *They operated with a warrant and a prior determination of obscenity by a magistrate, unlike the* Marcus *case. There was no mass seizure of books, and no showing that the seizure was designed to halt the distribution of materials. Courts have not required adversarial determinations of obscenity to precede similar computer searches. See, e.g., United States v. Hall, 142 F.3d 988, 996 (7th Cir.1998) (rejecting a First Amendment challenge to a search of defendant's computer because the warrant limited the search to items related to child pornography).*

Although dicta in the Heller *case suggest that police must return material if the seizure would otherwise impede publication, the Supreme Court noted that it was up to the materials' owner to request the return of the materials and to make a showing to the trial court that the seizure prevented a First Amendment activity. Plaintiffs in this case have failed to establish that they requested return of their materials. In fact, the district court concluded in the* Guest *case that the materials had been returned, and in the* O'Brien *case that "Plaintiffs [did] not allege that defendants continue[d] to hold materials that belong to them." (O'Brien Dist. Ct. Order, Nov. 5, 1998, at 31.) While the* O'Brien *plaintiffs chose to contest that conclusion at oral argument on appeal, they have not alleged that they presented the claim to the district court or requested their materials from the defendants. We leave the question suggested by* Heller's *dicta for another case where plaintiffs have made a showing that they requested and were refused return of expressive materials. We find no First Amendment violation in these cases because defendants seized materials as evidence in criminal prosecutions pursuant to valid warrants.*

IV. Electronic Communications Privacy Act

Plaintiffs assert that RECI searched their electronic communications and subscriber information and thus violated the Electronic Communications Privacy Act (ECPA). Title II of the ECPA regulates the disclosure of electronic communications and subscriber information. 18 U.S.C. §§ 2701–2711. Section 2707 provides a civil cause of action against a person who is "aggrieved by any violation of this chapter." 18 U.S.C. § 2707(a). The same section provides a statutory good faith defense; a defendant's "good faith reliance on . . . a court warrant or order" provides "a complete defense to any civil or criminal action brought under this chapter or any other law." 18 U.S.C. § 2707(e).

In their complaint, plaintiffs alleged violations of the ECPA requirements for access to stored communications and subscriber information, as set forth in 18 U.S.C. § 2703(a), (b), and (c). Subsection (a) provides that the government may have access to the contents of electronic communications that have been stored 180 days or less only by using a warrant. Subsection (b) allows the government to access contents that have been stored more than 180 days if the government uses a warrant, subpoena, or a court order. Subsection (c) is directed to the provider of an electronic communication service (not to the government) and states that such a provider may only give subscriber information to the government if the government has a warrant, court order, or subscriber consent (with an exception for telemarketing fraud).

We conclude that plaintiffs have not stated a claim under the ECPA. There is no violation of § 2703(a), (b), or (c) if access is pursuant to a warrant, and the officials in this case had a valid warrant. Moreover, § 2703(c) applies to the service provider and not to the government. See Tucker v. Waddell, 83 F.3d 688, 693 (4th Cir.1996) ("[T]he language of § 2703(c) does not prohibit any governmental conduct, and thus a governmental entity may not violate that subsection by simply accessing information improperly").

In their brief, plaintiffs mention in passing 18 U.S.C. § 2701, which prohibits intentional unlawful access to an electronic communication service if the offender "obtains, alters, or prevents authorized access to a wire or electronic communication while it is in electronic storage." 18 U.S.C. § 2701(a). Such access is again excused if it occurs pursuant to the approved procedures, which include the use of a warrant. There was no violation of the ECPA in these cases.

V. Privacy Protection Act

A. The Statute

Plaintiffs claim that the defendants seized materials intended for publication and thus violated the Privacy Protection Act (PPA), an act prohibiting police searches for certain types of documents intended for publication. The statute was passed in response to Zurcher v. Stanford Daily, 436 U.S. 547, 98 S.Ct. 1970, 56 L.Ed.2d 525 (1978), in which the Supreme Court held that the Fourth Amendment did not prohibit police from undertaking searches and seizures of documentary evidence held by innocent third parties, such as the newspaper whose records were searched in the case. Id. at 567–68, 98 S.Ct. 1970. According to the Senate Report, the PPA was enacted to afford "the press and certain other persons not suspected of committing a crime with protections not provided currently by the Fourth Amendment." S.Rep. No. 96–874, at 4 (1980), reprinted in 1980 U.S.C.C.A.N. 3950.

The PPA prohibits the government from seizing certain materials, called "work product materials," that are intended for publication:

Notwithstanding any other law, it shall be unlawful for a government officer or employee, in connection with the investigation or prosecution of a criminal offense, to search for or seize any work product materials possessed by a person reasonably believed to have a purpose to disseminate to the public a newspaper, book, broadcast, or other similar form of public communication, in or affecting interstate or foreign commerce.

42 U.S.C. § 2000aa(a).

Work product material means materials (other than property used to commit a criminal offense) that are to be communicated to the public and contain the authors' impressions, opinions, conclusions, or theories. The act also bars seizure of "documentary materials," which include materials like notes, photographs, or tapes, other than things possessed for use in a criminal offense. The police may still access documentary materials with a subpoena, an option not available for work product materials. See 42 U.S.C. § 2000aa(b)(3).

The police can avoid the constraints of the act in some circumstances when the person possessing the materials is a criminal suspect, rather than an innocent third party. The materials exempted by this "suspect exception" must relate to the offense and the offense must not involve the communication of the materials.

B. Discussion

Defendants argue that most of the plaintiffs lack standing in these cases because only the operator of the bulletin board systems "possessed" the materials at issue in these cases. However, the statute creates a cause of action for any "aggrieved person": "A person aggrieved by a search for or seizure of materials in violation of this chapter shall have a civil cause of action for damages for such search or seizure. . . ." 42 U.S.C. § 2000aa 6(a); cf. 18 U.S.C. § 2510(11) (defining "aggrieved person" under ECPA Title I as "a person who was a party to any intercepted wire, oral, or electronic communication or a person against whom the interception was directed"). Accordingly, plaintiffs had standing to bring a PPA claim because they were "aggrieved" by the seizure of their communications.

The statute's protection of documents held by publishers such as mainstream newspapers may be straightforward, but interpretation of the act presents particular challenges in a situation unforeseen by the drafters, that of a computer search. As we have explained, when police execute a search warrant for documents on a computer, it will often be difficult or impossible (particularly without the cooperation of the owner) to separate the offending materials from other "innocent" material on the computer. The PPA does not explicitly address the question of liability for a seizure of communicative material that is technically difficult to separate from the evidence of a crime whose seizure is authorized by a valid warrant.

If we were to understand the statute to mean that the presence of some protected materials on the computer extends the PPA protections to all materials, even evidence of a crime, located on the computer, the statute would prevent police in many cases from seizing evidence located on a computer. Criminals would be able to insulate any of their electronically-held criminal records or evidence by including on their computer communicative materials that qualify as work product or documentary materials under the PPA. We hold that when protected materials are commingled on a criminal suspect's computer with criminal evidence that is unprotected by the act, we will not find liability under the PPA for seizure of the PPA-protected materials. We emphasize, though, that police may not then search the PPA-protected materials that were seized incidentally to the criminal evidence.

In the instant cases, we will assume without deciding that there were PPA-protected materials on the systems. The targeted files — obscene images or pirated software — would not qualify as protected work product or documentary material because both definitions exclude "property designed or intended for use, or which is or has been used as, the means of committing a criminal offense." 42 U.S.C. § 2000aa–7(a) & (b). The arguably PPA-protected materials were commingled with this criminal evidence on computers whose owner or operator was a criminal suspect. The seizure of the PPA materials occurred incidentally to the seizure of this evidence pursuant to a valid warrant, and plaintiffs have not shown that the protected materials were searched. We will not find liability under the PPA under these circumstances.

VI. Conclusion

For the foregoing reasons, the judgments of the district court are affirmed.

* * *

Remember, as well, that in determining whether a warrant is needed to search and seize electronically stored data, the general obligations and requirements for warrants in criminal investigations must also be observed in addition to anything specifically related to digital information. This can include issues of consent: whether the party consenting to a warrantless search has the right to do so, or whether instead a warrant must be obtained to search the particular location or resource. This can be a challenging analysis, particularly when computers may be shared by multiple users. In such an instance, the police officer considering whether a warrant is needed (and the court that may be evaluating the officer's decision after the fact) may need to look not only at physical ownership of the computer, but whether and how individual files and directories may be shared or kept separate and private, to evaluate the reasonable expectation of privacy the user has in the information.

* * *

UNITED STATES v. ADJANI[12]

FISHER, *Circuit Judge:*

While executing a search warrant at the home of defendant Christopher Adjani to obtain evidence of his alleged extortion, agents from the Federal Bureau of Investigation seized Adjani's computer and external storage devices, which were later

---

[12] 452 F.3d 1140 (9th Cir. 2006) (notes omitted).

searched at an FBI computer lab. They also seized and subsequently searched a computer belonging to defendant Jana Reinhold, who lived with Adjani, even though she had not at that point been identified as a suspect and was not named as a target in the warrant. Some of the emails found on Reinhold's computer chronicled conversations between her and Adjani that implicated her in the extortion plot. Relying in part on the incriminating emails, the government charged both Adjani and Reinhold with conspiring to commit extortion in violation of 18 U.S.C. § 371 and transmitting a threatening communication with intent to extort in violation of 18 U.S.C. § 875(d).

The defendants brought motions to suppress the emails, arguing that the warrant did not authorize the seizure and search of Reinhold's computer and its contents; but if it did, the warrant was unconstitutionally overbroad or, alternatively, the emails fell outside the scope of the warrant. The district court granted the defendants' motion to suppress the email communications between Reinhold and Adjani, finding that the agents did not have sufficient probable cause to search Reinhold's computer, and that once they discovered information incriminating her, the agents should have obtained an additional search warrant. The government appeals this evidentiary ruling, but only with respect to three emails dated January 12, 2004.

The district court's ruling on the motion to suppress is subject to de novo review. United States v. Vargas-Castillo, 329 F.3d 715, 722 (9th Cir.2003). *We review de novo a district court's determination regarding the specificity of a warrant, including whether it is overbroad or not sufficiently particular.* United States v. Wong, 334 F.3d 831, 836-37 (9th Cir.2003). *We hold that the government had probable cause to search Reinhold's computer, the warrant satisfied our test for specificity and the seized e-mail communications fell within the scope of the properly issued warrant. Accordingly, we reverse the district court's order suppressing the January 12, 2004 email communications between Reinhold and Adjani.*

I. Background

A. The Extortion Scheme

Adjani was once employed by Paycom Billing Services Inc. (formerly Epoch), which facilitates payments from Internet users to its client websites. As a payment facilitator, Paycom receives and stores vast amounts of data containing credit card information. On January 8, 2004, a woman (later identified as Reinhold) delivered envelopes to three Paycom partners, Christopher Mallick, Clay Andrews and Joel Hall. Each envelope contained a letter from Adjani advising that he had purchased a copy of Paycom's database containing its clients' sensitive financial information. The letter threatened that Adjani would sell the Paycom database and master client control list if he did not receive $3 million. To prove his threats were real, Adjani included samples of the classified data. He directed the Paycom partners to sign an enclosed agreement attesting to the proposed quid pro quo and fax it back to him by January 12. The letter included Adjani's email address, cadjani@mac.com, and a fax number. Agents later learned that Adjani's email address was billed to Reinhold's account.

Evidence suggested that Adjani left Los Angeles on January 9, 2004, and ultimately ended up in Zurich, Switzerland. From Switzerland, Adjani sent an email on January 12 to Joel Hall to confirm that Hall and the others had received the envelopes. Adjani followed up on this email on January 13 by instructing Hall to contact him through AOL/Mac iChat instant messaging if he wanted to discuss the settlement agreement. With the FBI monitoring, Hall conversed several times with Adjani on the Internet and over the telephone. In spite of Adjani's insistence that he remain overseas, Hall convinced him to come to Los Angeles on January 26 to pick up $2.5 million in exchange for the database.

Adjani returned to Los Angeles on January 22, under FBI surveillance. Reinhold, driving in a car that the FBI had earlier identified as Adjani's, was observed leaving Adjani's residence in Venice, California, picking him up from the airport and returning to his residence. The FBI also observed Reinhold using an Apple computer, the same brand of computer Adjani used to email and chat with Paycom.

B. Obtaining and Executing the Search Warrant

On January 23, 2004, based on the facts recited above and attested to in FBI Agent Cloney's affidavit (which was affixed to the warrant), a federal magistrate judge granted the government an arrest warrant for Adjani and a search warrant covering Adjani's Venice residence, his vehicle, his person and the residence of the individual who had stolen the confidential information from Paycom. The warrant specifically sought "evidence of violations of [18 U.S.C. § 875(d)]: Transmitting Threatening Communications With Intent to Commit Extortion." Further, the warrant expressly authorized seizure of:

5g. Records, documents and materials containing Paycom's or Epoch's master client control documents, Paycom's or Epoch's email database, or other company information relating to Paycom or Epoch.

5h. Records, documents and materials which reflect communications with Christopher Mallick, Clay Andrews, Joel Hall or other employees or officers of Paycom or Epoch.

5i. Any and all evidence of travel, including hotel bills and receipts, gasoline receipts, plane tickets, bus tickets, train tickets, or any other documents related to travel from January 8, 2004 to the present.

. . . .

5k. Computer, hard drives, computer disks, CD's, and other computer storage devices.

With respect to the computer search, the warrant prescribed the process to be followed: "In searching the data, the computer personnel will examine all of the data contained in the computer equipment and storage devices to view their precise contents and determine whether the data falls within the items to be seized as set forth herein." Additionally, it noted that "[i]n order to search for data that is capable of being read or intercepted by a computer, law enforcement personnel will need to seize and search . . . . [a]ny computer equipment and storage device capable of being used to commit, further, or store evidence of the offense listed above."

On January 26, 2004, agents observed Reinhold driving Adjani, in a car registered to him, to his meeting with Paycom. While Adjani went into a hotel, Reinhold slipped into the backseat of his car, placing curtains over the windows. at this point, agents proceeded to search Adjani's car. That same day, agents executed the search warrant for Adjani's Venice residence. There they found and seized various computers and hard drives, including Reinhold's computer, which were later sent to an FBI computer lab to be searched. During that search process, the hard drive from Reinhold's computer revealed certain email correspondence between Reinhold and Adjani, implicating Reinhold in the extortion plot and supporting a charge of conspiracy against both of them.

The defendants successfully sought suppression of these seized email communications in the district court. This appeal requires us to determine whether the agents permissibly searched Reinhold's computer; whether the warrant satisfied our specificity standards; and whether the emails seized fell within the scope of the otherwise properly issued warrant.

II. Analysis

A. Probable Cause

The government principally argues that contrary to the district court's finding and the defendants' assertions, the search warrant affidavit established probable cause to search all instrumentalities that might contain "evidence of violations of" 18 U.S.C. § 875(d), including Reinhold's computer and emails. Reinhold counters that the affidavit may have generally established probable cause, but did not do so with respect to her computer, because "[i]n the affidavit, Reinhold was not labeled as a target, suspect, or co-conspirator."

1. Probable cause to issue the warrant

"A search warrant . . . is issued upon a showing of probable cause to believe that the legitimate object of a search is located in a particular place, and therefore safeguards an individual's interest in the privacy of his home and possessions against the unjustified intrusion of the police." Steagald v. United States, 451 U.S. 204, 213, 101 S.Ct. 1642, 68 L.Ed.2d 38 (1981). *As the Supreme Court has explained, the "probable cause standard . . . is a practical, nontechnical conception."* Illinois v. Gates, 462 U.S. 213, 231, 103 S.Ct. 2317, 76 L.Ed.2d 527 (1983) *(quoting* Brinegar v. United States, 338 U.S. 160, 176, 69 S.Ct. 1302, 93 L.Ed. 1879 (1949)). *Furthermore, "probable cause is a fluid concept-turning on the assessment of probabilities in particular factual contexts-not readily, or even usefully, reduced to a neat set of legal rules."* Id. at 232, 103 S.Ct. 2317; *see also* United States v. Gourde, 440 F.3d 1065, 1071 (9th Cir.2006) (en banc) *("Employing the principles of* Gates-*practicality, common sense, a fluid and nontechnical conception of probable cause, and deference to the magistrate's determination-we conclude that the search warrant was supported by*

probable cause."). The warrant here was supported by probable cause, because the affidavit submitted to the magistrate judge established that "there [was] a fair probability that contraband or evidence of a crime [would] be found in" computers at Adjani's residence. See Gates, 462 U.S. at 238, 103 S.Ct. 2317. The extensive 24-page supporting affidavit described the extortion scheme in detail, including that Adjani possessed a computer-generated database and communicated with Paycom over email, requiring the use of a computer. Cf. Gourde, 440 F.3d at 1072 ("The details provided on the use of computers by child pornographers and the collector profile strengthen th[e] inference [that probable cause supported the warrant] and help 'provide[ ] context' for the 'fair probability' that Gourde received or downloaded images." (internal citation omitted)). Furthermore, the agent's affidavit explained the need to search computers, in particular, for evidence of the extortion scheme: "I know that considerable planning is typically performed to construct and consummate an extortion. The plan can be documented in the form of a simple written note or more elaborate information stored on computer equipment."

"Probable cause exists if 'it would be reasonable to seek the evidence in the place indicated in the affidavit.'" United States v. Wong, 334 F.3d 831, 836 (9th Cir.2003) (quoting United States v. Peacock, 761 F.2d 1313, 1315 (9th Cir.1985)). The crime contemplated by the warrant was transmitting a threatening communication with intent to extort. See 18 U.S.C. § 875(d). To find evidence of extortion, the government would have probable cause to search for and seize instrumentalities likely to have been used to facilitate the transmission. The magistrate judge could rightfully assume that there was a "fair probability" that such evidence could be contained on computers or storage devices found in Adjani's residence.

2. Probable cause to search "Reinhold's computer"

Having held that the affidavit supporting the warrant established probable cause to search for and seize instrumentalities of the extortion (including records, files and computers) in Adjani's residence, we turn to Reinhold's contention that the probable cause for the Adjani warrant did not extend so far as to permit a search of her property. We disagree. The agents, acting pursuant to a valid warrant to look for evidence of a computer-based crime, searched computers found in Adjani's residence and to which he had apparent access. That one of the computers actually belonged to Reinhold did not exempt it from being searched, especially given her association with Adjani and participation (however potentially innocuous) in some of his activities as documented in the agent's supporting affidavit. The officers therefore did not act unreasonably in searching Reinhold's computer as a source of the evidence targeted by the warrant. See Illinois v. Rodriguez, 497 U.S. 177, 185, 110 S.Ct. 2793, 111 L.Ed.2d 148 (1990) (holding Fourth Amendment requires officers to act reasonably in executing a search warrant); Brinegar v. United States, 338 U.S. 160, 176, 69 S.Ct. 1302, 93 L.Ed. 1879 (1949).

Reinhold's argument that there was no probable cause to search her computer, a private and personal piece of property, because the warrant failed to list her as a "target, suspect, or co-conspirator" misunderstands Fourth Amendment jurisprudence. Although individuals undoubtedly have a high expectation of privacy in the files stored on their personal computers, we have never held that agents may establish probable cause to search only those items owned or possessed by the criminal suspect. The law is to the contrary. "The critical element in a reasonable search is not that the owner of the property is suspected of crime but that there is reasonable cause to believe that the specific 'things' to be searched for and seized are located on the property to which entry is sought." Zurcher v. Stanford Daily, 436 U.S. 547, 556, 98 S.Ct. 1970, 56 L.Ed.2d 525 (1978); cf. United States v. Ross, 456 U.S. 798, 820-21, 102 S.Ct. 2157, 72 L.Ed.2d 572 (1982) ("A lawful search of fixed premises generally extends to the entire area in which the object of the search may be found and is not limited by the possibility that separate acts of entry or opening may be required to complete the search.").

In United States v. Hay, *231 F.3d 630 (9th Cir.2000), the defendant made an argument similar to Reinhold's, challenging the district court's ruling allowing evidence of child pornography found on his computer to be used against him at trial. Hay claimed that the affidavit submitted by officers to obtain a warrant did not establish probable cause to engage in a search of Hay's computer because "there was no evidence that he fell within a class of persons likely to collect and traffic in child pornography because the affidavit does not indicate that he was a child molester, pedophile, or collector of child pornography and sets forth no evidence that he solicited, sold or transmitted child pornography." Id. at 635. We rejected Hay's challenge, holding that "[i]t is well established that a location can be searched for evidence of a crime even if there is no probable cause to arrest the person at the location." Id. (citing Zurcher, 436 U.S. at 556, 98 S.Ct. 1970). See also United States v. Taketa, 923 F.2d 665, 674 (9th Cir.1991) ("[T]he correct inquiry is whether there was reasonable cause to believe that evidence of . . . misconduct was located on the property that was searched."); United States v. Tehfe, 722 F.2d 1114, 1118 (3d Cir.1983) ("Property owned by a person absolutely innocent of any wrongdoing may nevertheless be searched under a valid warrant."); United States v. Melvin, 596 F.2d 492, 496 (1st Cir.1979) (holding the Zurcher rule applies to "a person who the police do indeed suspect but do not have probable cause to arrest; such a person's property may be searched upon probable cause to believe that fruits, instrumentalities, or evidence of the crime are present, even though the products of the search may implicate him.").*

Likewise, there was no need here for the agents expressly to claim in the affidavit that they wanted to arrest Reinhold, or even that Reinhold was suspected of any criminal activity. The government needed only to satisfy the magistrate judge that there was probable cause to believe that evidence of the crime in question-here extortion-could be found on computers accessible to Adjani in his home, including-as it developed-Reinhold's computer. By setting forth the details of the extortion scheme and the instrumentalities of the crime, augmented by descriptions of Reinhold's involvement with Adjani, the government satisfied its burden. The magistrate judge therefore properly approved the warrant, which in turn encompassed all the computers found at Adjani's residence.

B. Specificity Requirement

The defendants argue that if the warrant did authorize a search that properly included Reinhold's computer, the warrant was fatally overbroad, justifying the district court's exclusion of the Reinhold emails. The government counters that the warrant satisfied the particularity standards articulated by this court, so exclusion was improper.

The Fourth Amendment's specificity requirement prevents officers from engaging in general, exploratory searches by limiting their discretion and providing specific guidance as to what can and cannot be searched and seized. See United States v. McClintock, 748 F.2d 1278, 1282 (9th Cir.1984) ("[G]eneral warrants are prohibited." (internal quotation marks omitted)); United States v. Cardwell, 680 F.2d 75, 77 (9th Cir.1982) ("Nothing is left to the discretion of the officer executing the warrant." (internal quotation marks and citation omitted)). However, the level of detail necessary in a warrant is related to the particular circumstances and the nature of the evidence sought. See United States v. Spilotro, 800 F.2d 959, 963 (9th Cir.1986). "Warrants which describe generic categories of items are not necessarily invalid if a more precise description of the items subject to seizure is not possible." Id.

In determining whether a warrant is sufficiently particular, we consider one or more of the following factors:

(1) whether probable cause exists to seize all items of a particular type described in the warrant; (2) whether the warrant sets out objective standards by which executing officers can differentiate items subject to seizure from those which are not; and (3) whether the government was able to describe the items more particularly in light of the information available to it at the time the warrant was issued.

Id. *at 963 (internal citations omitted).*

Spilotro *involved a warrant issued against individuals suspected of loan sharking and gambling activities. See id. at 960. The warrant authorized "the seizure of address books, notebooks, notes, documents, records, assets, photographs, and other items and paraphernalia evidencing violations of the multiple criminal statutes listed." Id. at 964. It failed, however, to state the "precise identity, type, or contents of the records sought." Id. Partly because of this reason, we held that the warrant was not sufficiently specific to pass muster under the Fourth Amendment. More could have been done to tie the documents sought to the crimes alleged by, for example, stating that the police were searching for "records relating to loan sharking and gambling, including pay and collection sheets, lists of loan customers, loan accounts and telephone numbers. . . ." Id. (internal quotation marks and citation omitted).*

In contrast to Spilotro, *the warrant to search Adjani's residence satisfied our specificity criteria. First, we have already held that there was probable cause to search the computers. As to the second factor, the warrant objectively described the items to be searched and seized with adequate specificity and sufficiently restricted the discretion of agents executing the search. The warrant affidavit began by limiting the search for evidence of a specific crime-transmitting threatening communications with intent to commit extortion. See id. ("Reference to a specific illegal activity can, in appropriate cases, provide substantive guidance for the officer's exercise of discretion in executing the warrant.");* see also United States v. Wong, *334 F.3d 831, 837-38 (9th Cir.2003) ("The specificity of the items listed in the warrant combined with the language . . . directing officers to 'obtain data as it relates to this case' from the computers is sufficiently specific to focus the officer's search.");* Cardwell, *680 F.2d at 76-77 (holding impermissibly general a warrant where "the only limitation on the search and seizure of appellants' business papers was the requirement that they be the instrumentality or evidence of violation of the general tax evasion statute," but noting that if the warrant is cabined by a "preambulatory statement limiting the search to evidence of particular criminal episodes," it may fulfill the particularity requirement). Further, unlike in* Spilotro, *the Adjani warrant provided the "precise identity" and nature of the items to be seized.* Spilotro, *800 F.2d at 964. For example, paragraph 5h of the warrant instructed agents to search for documents reflecting communications with three individuals or other employees of a specific company. Also, paragraph 5i authorized seizure of "any" evidence of travel but provided a specific, though not exhaustive, list of possible documents that fell within this category and temporally restricted the breadth of the search. Cf.* United States v. Abrams, *615 F.2d 541, 543 (1st Cir.1980) (cited favorably in* Cardwell, *680 F.2d at 77-78) (holding a warrant was not sufficiently particular because "[t]he officers' discretion was unfettered, there is no limitation as to time and there is no description as to what specific records are to be seized."). Moreover, the extensive statement of probable cause in the affidavit detailed the alleged crime and Adjani's unlawful scheme. See* Spilotro, *800 F.2d at 964 (considering favorably warrants "describing the criminal activit[y] . . . rather than simply referring to the statute believed to have been violated.").*

With respect to the final Spilotro *factor, we conclude that the government described the items to be searched and seized as particularly as could be reasonably expected given the nature of the crime and the evidence it then possessed. The Adjani warrant "describe[d] in great[ ] detail the items one commonly expects to find on premises used for the criminal activities in question. . . ."* Spilotro, *800 F.2d at 964;* see also United States v. Mann, *389 F.3d 869, 877 (9th Cir.2004) ("While a search warrant must describe items to be seized with particularity sufficient to prevent a general, exploratory rummaging in a person's belongings, it need only be reasonably specific, rather than elaborately detailed.") (internal quotation marks and citation omitted).*

Center Art Galleries-Hawaii, Inc. v. United States, *875 F.2d 747 (9th Cir.1989), the principal case defendants rely upon in making their overbreadth argument, is distinguishable. In that case, we held that a warrant providing for "the almost unrestricted seizure of items which are 'evidence of violations of federal criminal law' without describing the specific crimes suspected is constitutionally inadequate." Id. at 750 (quoting* Spilotro, *800 F.2d at 964). In contrast, the government here did describe at some length both the nature of and the means of committing the crime. Further, unlike in* Center Art Galleries, *the affidavit was expressly incorporated into the warrant. Id. ("An affidavit can cure the overbreadth of a warrant if the affidavit is 'attached to and incorporated by reference in' the warrant.") (quoting* Spilotro, *800 F.2d at 967, and citing* United States v. Leary, *846 F.2d 592, 603 (10th Cir.1988)).*

We understand the heightened specificity concerns in the computer context, given the vast amount of data they can store. As the defendants urge, the warrant arguably might have provided for a "less invasive search of Adjani's [email] 'inbox' and 'outbox' for the addressees specifically cited in the warrant, as opposed to the wholesale search of the contents of all emails purportedly looking for evidence' reflecting' communications with those individuals." Avoiding that kind of specificity and limitation was not unreasonable under the circumstances here, however. To require such a pinpointed computer search, restricting the search to an email program or to specific search terms, would likely have failed to cast a sufficiently wide net to capture the evidence sought. Cf. Ross, 456 U.S. at 821, 102 S.Ct. 2157 ("When a legitimate search is under way, and when its purpose and its limits have been precisely defined, nice distinctions between closets, drawers, and containers, in the case of a home, or between glove compartments, upholstered seats, trunks, and wrapped packages, in the case of a vehicle, must give way to the interest in the prompt and efficient completion of the task at hand."). Moreover, agents are limited by the longstanding principle that a duly issued warrant, even one with a thorough affidavit, may not be used to engage in a general, exploratory search. See United States v. Rettig, 589 F.2d 418, 423 (9th Cir.1978) ("Where evidence is uncovered during a search pursuant to a warrant, the threshold question must be whether the search was confined to the warrant's terms. . . . [T]he search must be one directed in good faith toward the objects specified in the warrant or for other means and instrumentalities by which the crime charged had been committed. It must not be a general exploratory search . . . ." (internal quotation marks and alterations omitted)); see also Franklin v. Foxworth, 31 F.3d 873, 875 (9th Cir.1994) ("[T]he reasonableness of a search or seizure depends not only on when it is made, but also on how it is carried out." (internal quotation marks omitted and emphasis in original)).

Computer files are easy to disguise or rename, and were we to limit the warrant to such a specific search protocol, much evidence could escape discovery simply because of Adjani's (or Reinhold's) labeling of the files documenting Adjani's criminal activity. The government should not be required to trust the suspect's self-labeling when executing a warrant. See Guest v. Leis, 255 F.3d 325, 335 (6th Cir.2001) ("Defendants may legitimately have checked to see that the contents of the directories corresponded to the labels placed on the directories. Suspects would otherwise be able to shield evidence from a search simply by 'misfiling' it in a directory labeled 'e-mail.' "); cf. United States v. Tamura, 694 F.2d 591, 595 (9th Cir.1982) ("[A]ll items in a set of files may be inspected during a search, provided that sufficiently specific guidelines for identifying the documents sought are provided in the search warrant and are followed by the officers conducting the search.").

C. Scope of the Warrant

Even assuming that the warrant was supported by probable cause and was adequately specific such that a search of Reinhold's computer and emails were permissible, Reinhold argues that the actual emails sought to be introduced into evidence were outside the scope of the warrant. Again, we disagree.

The three seized emails the government seeks to admit clearly fall within the scope of paragraph 5h of the warrant affidavit, authorizing seizure of "[r]ecords, documents and materials which reflect communications with Christopher Mallick, Clay An-

drews, Joel Hall or other employees or officers of Paycom or Epoch," which are relevant evidence of violations of 18 U.S.C. § 875(d). Each email specifically refers to communication with Joel Hall or one of the stated companies (identifying them by name). Reinhold's argument that the term "reflect communications with" should be read narrowly to cover only those emails sent between one of the named Paycom employees and Adjani is nonsensical. The government already had the emails sent between the victims of the extortion and Adjani-obtained from the victims themselves. The purpose of the warrant was to obtain further and corroborating evidence of the extortion scheme and Adjani's criminal intent in communicating with the victims, and the three emails plainly "reflect" the relevant communications specified in paragraph 5h.

To the extent Reinhold argues that the emails were outside the scope of the warrant because they implicated her in the crime and supported a charge of conspiracy to commit extortion (a crime not specifically mentioned in the warrant), we reject the argument. There is no rule, and Reinhold points to no case law suggesting otherwise, that evidence turned up while officers are rightfully searching a location under a properly issued warrant must be excluded simply because the evidence found may support charges for a related crime (or against a suspect) not expressly contemplated in the warrant.

In United States v. Beusch, 596 F.2d 871 (9th Cir.1979), the defendants argued that certain seized items, including two ledgers and a file, should be excluded because they contained information unrelated to the suspect identified in the warrant. The defendants claimed that the officers impermissibly engaged in a general search by not segregating out those items implicating a third individual in the crime. We rejected this proposition and refused to impose the burden of segregation on the police. In so doing we held,

All three items admittedly contained information seizable under the terms of the warrant and they therefore met the particularity requirement of the Fourth Amendment. As long as an item appears, at the time of the search, to contain evidence reasonably related to the purposes of the search, there is no reason absent some other Fourth Amendment violation to suppress it. The fact that an item seized happens to contain other incriminating information not covered by the terms of the warrant does not compel its suppression, either in whole or in part. In so holding we are careful to point out that we are discussing single files and single ledgers, i.e., single items which, though theoretically separable, in fact constitute one volume or file folder.

Id. *at 877 (internal citation omitted). Beusch is analogous to the situation at hand. The agents were rightfully searching Reinhold's computer for evidence of Adjani's crime of extortion. They were looking in Reinhold's email program when they came across information that was both related to the purposes of their search and implicated Reinhold in the crime. That the evidence could now support a new charge against a new (but already identified) person does not compel its suppression. On these facts, we disagree with the district court's conclusion that the officers should have obtained a new search warrant when they came across the incriminating emails. In so concluding, we are careful to note that in this case the evidence discovered was clearly related to the crime referred to in the warrant. We need not decide to what extent the government would be able to introduce evidence discovered that the police knew, at the time of discovery, was not related to the crime cited in the warrant. Cf. United States v. Carey, 172 F.3d 1268, 1272-73 (10th Cir.1999) (excluding certain evidence of child pornography where the warrant authorized only seizure of drug evidence and the detective knew he was expanding the scope of the warrant, and holding that the officer should have stopped the search and obtained a new warrant.).*

III. Conclusion

"The Fourth Amendment incorporates a great many specific protections against unreasonable searches and seizures." Beusch, 596 F.2d at 876-77. The contours of these protections in the context of computer searches pose difficult questions. Computers are simultaneously file cabinets (with millions of files) and locked desk drawers; they can be repositories of innocent and deeply personal information, but also of evidence of crimes. The former must be protected, the latter discovered. As society grows ever more reliant on computers as a means of storing data and communicating, courts will be called upon to analyze novel legal issues and develop new rules within our well established Fourth Amendment jurisprudence. See Eric L. Probst and Kerri A. Wright, Using Their E-Words Against Them, NEW JERSEY LAW JOURNAL, Jan. 30, 2006, at S1 (noting that tens of billions of emails are sent daily). The fact of an increasingly technological world is not lost upon us as we consider the proper balance to strike between protecting an individual's right to privacy and ensuring that the government is able to prosecute suspected criminals effectively. In this era of rapid change, we are mindful of Justice Brandeis's worry in Olmstead v. United States,

Ways may some day be developed by which the Government, without removing papers from secret drawers, can reproduce them in court, and by which it will be enabled to expose to a jury the most intimate occurrences of the home. . . . Can it be that the Constitution affords no protection against such invasions of individual security?

277 U.S. 438, 474, 48 S.Ct. 564, 72 L.Ed. 944 (1928) (BRANDEIS, J., dissenting).

We do not now have occasion to address the myriad complex issues raised in deciding when a court should exclude evidence found on a computer, but are satisfied that the agents in this case acted properly in searching Reinhold's computer and seizing the emails in question here. The district court erred in excluding these emails. Therefore, the district court's ruling on the motion to suppress is reversed, and this matter is remanded for further proceedings consistent with this opinion.

REVERSED and REMANDED.

*   *   *

U.S. v. HOROWITZ[13]

Donald Russell, Circuit Judge:

The defendant, Richard I. Horowitz, appeals from the trial court's denial of his pre-trial motion to suppress evidence obtained by authorities pursuant to an authorized search of the premises of Electro-Methods, Inc. (EMI), a Connecticut corporation which contracted for defendant's services. The defendant was employed by Pratt & Whitney Aircraft (Pratt) as supervisor of pricing in its Government Products Division in North Palm Beach, Florida. In this role the defendant oversaw preparation of sealed bids which Pratt submitted to the Air Force for supplying spare parts for the F-100 jet engine. EMI was among several companies competing with Pratt for the Air Force contract.

In 1978, unbeknownst to Pratt, the defendant, while still employed by Pratt, established an independent consulting firm, Sandrich Associates, Inc., which was operated from his Florida home and which advised clients on government contracting and on pricing of aircraft parts. Two of these clients were Perry Oceanographics and Lenzar Optics. The defendant's primary client, however, was EMI, which was owned by Alfred Stanger. Stanger also owned Turbo Tech, Inc., which represented Fabrique Nationale and N.V. Philips in their efforts to compete with Pratt for the Air Force F-100 spare parts contracts. The defendant, until 1982, failed to report the existence of his consulting contracts to Pratt on the conflict of interest statements Pratt annually required of its employees.

In his role as "consultant" to EMI, the defendant sold to Alfred Stanger confidential Pratt pricing information which EMI used to underbid Pratt on the Air Force contracts. Stanger paid the defendant as much as $5,000 per month for his so-called "consulting services", reaching a total of $260,000. In 1982, Stanger installed a computer terminal and telephone modem in the defendant's Florida home to facilitate communication between the defendant and EMI's Connecticut office. The defendant transmitted the pricing information to EMI's computer terminal where the information was then stored on EMI's tapes.

On June 8, 1983, agents of the FBI executed a search warrant at EMI, having alleged in an affidavit probable cause to believe that Pratt pricing information was held by EMI on computer magnetic storage devices. The warrant authorized the agents to search a one-story industrial-commercial building housing EMI and to seize property listed on an attached schedule including computer magnetic storage devices, computer keypunch cards and computer print-outs containing Pratt pricing material. The agents, to prevent erasure of on-line tapes and discs (tapes), seized all of the tapes in EMI's computer room, including stored back-ups, and later examined them on outside compatible computer terminals with the aid of an expert. The contents of a tape could not be discerned from visual inspection but required specialized programming to review and record the information contained on the tapes. The agents looked specifically for a file designated RER which they believed

---

[13] 806 F.2d 1222 (4th Cir. 1986).

contained the price data and for files containing messages between Stanger and the defendant.

In a subsequent proceeding brought by the government to suspend EMI from bidding on Air Force contracts, the defendant filed two sworn affidavits before the Air Force Debarment, Suspension and Review Board stating that he did not supply EMI with secret Pratt pricing information. Those affidavits conflicted with the evidence seized at EMI and the defendant was indicted on two counts of making false statements to the board in violation of 18 U.S.C. 1001 (1982 & Supp. III 1985). Prior to trial, the defendant challenged the admissibility of the seized evidence on fourth amendment grounds. The trial judge denied his motion to suppress the evidence for lack of standing to contest the search and the defendant was convicted. On appeal the defendant challenges only the court's denial of his motion to suppress.

The defendant can contest the search and seizure on fourth amendment grounds only if "the disputed search and seizure has infringed an interest of the defendant which the fourth amendment was designed to protect." Rakas v. Illinois, 439 U.S. 128, 140, 99 S.Ct. 421, 428, 58 L.Ed.2d 387 (1978). The Supreme Court has articulated the appropriate inquiry to be whether the individual had a reasonable expectation of privacy in the area searched, not merely in the items found, Rawlings v. Kentucky, 448 U.S. 98, 104-106, 100 S.Ct. 2556, 2561-62, 65 L.Ed.2d 633 (1980) and the burden is upon the defendant to prove his reasonable expectation of privacy. Rakas, 439 U.S. at 130, n. 1, 99 S.Ct. at 424, n. 1.

The defendant claims he had a reasonable expectation of privacy in the seized tapes storing the information he supplied to EMI. He alleges that for purposes of his fourth amendment challenge the search at issue was not the search of EMI's building, but was the search of the "intangible space where images and sounds are recorded in a computer memory disc or tape." Appellant's brief at 12. The defendant relies on Supreme Court decisions finding reasonable expectations of privacy in one's office, Mancusi v. DeForte, 392 U.S. 364, 88 S.Ct. 2120, 20 L.Ed.2d 1154 (1968), and in other areas beyond the home, United States v. Chadwick, 433 U.S. 1, 97 S.Ct. 2476, 53 L.Ed.2d 538 (1977) (footlocker transported by rail), to support his novel argument that certain tapes seized on EMI's premises constituted his "electronic file cabinet," an extension of his private home office, and that the government agents violated his reasonable expectation of privacy in the tapes by playing them without obtaining a second search warrant. The government contends that the tapes were EMI's electronic records properly seized and later inspected pursuant to the search warrant. The government argues that the defendant had no reasonable and legitimate expectation of privacy in either the tapes or in EMI's premises.

The factors we must use to determine whether the defendant retained a reasonable expectation of privacy in the computer tapes can be stated generally as an analysis of the defendant's interest in and control of the area searched, his subjective expectation of privacy in the area as evidenced by his efforts to ensure that privacy, and society's willingness to recognize his expectation as reasonable. See Rakas v. Illinois, 439 U.S. 128, 99 S.Ct. 421, 58 L.Ed.2d 387 (1978); United States v. Manbeck, 744 F.2d 360 (4th Cir.1984), cert. denied, 469 U.S. 1217, 105 S.Ct. 1197, 84 L.Ed.2d 342 (1985); United States v. Dart, 747 F.2d 263 (4th Cir.1984); United States v. Torch, 609

F.2d 1088 (4th Cir.1979), cert. denied, 446 U.S. 957, 100 S.Ct. 2928, 64 L.Ed.2d 815 (1980). We agree with the trial court that the defendant had no reasonable expectation of privacy either in EMI's premises or in the tapes seized and played by the government.

The defendant claims that he had a privacy interest in the tapes storing the information he had transmitted to EMI because they constituted his workplace in that he maintained an ongoing relationship with EMI and a continuing interest in the material on the tapes, his work product. We disagree. The tapes may indeed have constituted an "electronic filing cabinet," but that filing cabinet belonged to EMI and was maintained by EMI for its own use. The defendant sold information to EMI and, once paid for, that information belonged to EMI, as did the tapes upon which the information was stored and the building in which the tapes were kept. "Property rights, while not determinative, remain conceptually relevant to whether one's expectations are legitimate or 'reasonable.' " United States v. Givens, *733 F.2d 339, 341 (4th Cir.1984). And as the Supreme Court reiterated in* Rakas, *"[a] person who is aggrieved by an illegal search and seizure only through the introduction of damaging evidence secured by a search of a third person's premises or property has not had any of his Fourth Amendment rights infringed."* Id. at 134, 99 S.Ct. at 425, *citing* Alderman v. United States, *394 U.S. 165, 174, 89 S.Ct. 961, 966, 22 L.Ed.2d 176 (1969). The defendant has failed to show even a tenuous privacy interest in the tapes for he never owned or possessed them, was rarely if ever physically present at EMI, was assigned no office at EMI's headquarters, and was hundreds of miles away when the search and seizure took place. See* United States v. Torch, *609 F.2d 1088 (4th Cir.1979), cert. denied, 446 U.S. 957, 100 S.Ct. 2928, 64 L.Ed.2d 815 (1980).*

The tapes merely stored for EMI's benefit, information transmitted by the defendant which, once recorded, could not be further manipulated by the defendant, albeit he could review the information from his home terminal. The defendant did not have an indelible privacy interest in the information. Having sold the information, the defendant lost any interest in it and EMI could use the information for any business purpose it pleased. Thus, the defendant's claim that the tapes were merely an electronic extension of his office fails because he cannot demonstrate a sufficient nexus *between the area searched and his workplace in Florida,* United States v. Britt, *508 F.2d 1052, 1056 (5th Cir.1975), cert. denied, 423 U.S. 825, 96 S.Ct. 40, 46 L.Ed.2d 42 (1975).*

Since the defendant has proved no interest in the tapes, the information recorded on them, or in the premises upon which the tapes were stored, for this reason alone the defendant's claim must fail. But the defendant has also failed to prove that he had any control over the tapes. Control is measured by physical presence in, or access to the area to be searched, Torch, *609 F.2d at 1091, and by the ability to exclude others.* Givens, *733 F.2d at 342. Although an individual need not maintain absolute personal control (exclusive use) over an area to support his expectation of privacy, "occasional presence, without any right to exclude others, is not enough."* Torch, *609 F.2d at 1091. The defendant lacked any ability to exclude others from the tapes; on the contrary, his own access was controlled by EMI. The defendant had no keys to either EMI's building or EMI's computer room. His only access to the RER file was by an electronic hookup through the use of a password. But employees of EMI could bar his access simply by removing the tapes from the computer or by changing the password. The defendant could not effectively exclude anyone from access to the tapes since any of several EMI employees knowing the password could give it to others and any employee with a key to the computer room could remove the tapes. Indeed, the defendant's very purpose in making the transmissions to EMI was to enable the employees of EMI to use the information in preparation of EMI's bids so that EMI could unfairly compete with Pratt, the defendant's employer. Thus, the information was necessarily disseminated to others within EMI and any security measures taken by EMI to restrict access primarily benefitted EMI and only incidentally the defendant.*

The defendant's reliance on Mancusi v. DeForte, *392 U.S. 364, 88 S.Ct. 2120, 20 L.Ed.2d 1154 (1968) is misplaced. In* Mancusi, *the Court determined that a union official had a reasonable expectation of privacy in his work office even though he shared the office with other union officials and even though the files seized by the government belonged to the union rather than to Mancusi. But unlike the defendant in the case before us, Mancusi was present in his office when the search occurred and only he and a few co-officials had access to the seized files. Thus, for the reasons stated earlier, Mancusi is inapposite to the case before us. In short, the defendant has shown neither an interest in nor control over the area searched.*

Although the defendant may well have wished to conceal his egregious perfidy from his employer, as would any person wrongfully selling his employer's secrets, his willful disclosure to EMI vitiates any reasonable expectation of privacy he may have once had. Assurances by Stanger as to EMI's limited use of the information could not sustain a Fourth Amendment interest. See United States v. Miller, *425 U.S. 435, 443, 96 S.Ct. 1619, 48 L.Ed.2d 71 (1973). "Legitimation of expectations of privacy by law must have a source outside of the Fourth Amendment, either by reference to concepts of real or personal property law or to understandings that are recognized and permitted by society."* Rakas, *439 U.S. at 144, n. 12, 99 S.Ct. at 430, n. 12. The defendant has failed to show any source of legitimation in this case; therefore, we affirm the decision of the trial court.*

Since we agree with the trial court that the defendant had no reasonable expectation of privacy in EMI's tapes nor in the premises searched, we, like the trial judge, need not consider whether the warrant was sufficient to encompass the seizure and search of the tapes. We do, however, believe that it was adequate.

Accordingly, the judgment of the district court is

AFFIRMED.

II. THE ELECTRONIC COMMUNICATIONS PRIVACY ACT AND LAW ENFORCEMENT

In addition to constitutional requirements, requests by law enforcement officials for personal information may be subject to the requirements of the Electronic Communications Privacy Act ("ECPA"),[14] or more specifically its three major components: the Wiretap Act,[15] the Pen Register Statute,[16] and the Stored Communications Act.[17] It is critical to note that all of these statutes *only* apply when the data in question are contained within or otherwise form part of a communication; data which do not fall within that category are excluded from ECPA's requirements. ECPA generally addresses both the obligations of parties (private and governmental) to keep undisclosed different elements of communications during and after transmission; it also provides for exceptions, and relevant procedure, through which the possessing party may access or share the data. In the case of law enforcement, the various sections of ECPA establish standards and requirements when court orders, subpoenas or warrants may be required before an Internet service provider or network administrator may release data. The requirements of ECPA are separate from those arising out the Fourth Amendment, and depending on the circumstance, either or both may apply.

*   *   *

PEOPLE v. HARRIS[18]

Matthew A. Sciarrino JR., J.

Twitter, Inc. ("Twitter") seeks to quash the January 26, 2012 subpoena issued by the New York County District Attorney's Office and upheld by this court's April 20, 2012 order. That order required Twitter to provide any and all user information, including email addresses, as well as any and all tweets posted for the period of September 15, 2011 to December 31, 2011, from the Twitter account @destructuremal, which was allegedly used by Malcolm Harris. This is a case of first impression, distinctive because it is a criminal case rather than a civil case, and the movant is the corporate entity (Twitter) and not an individual (Harris). It also deals with tweets that were publicly posted rather than an e-mail or text that would be directed to a single person or a select few.

On October 1, 2011, the Defendant, Malcolm Harris, was charged with Disorderly Conduct (Penal Law § 240.20[5]) after allegedly marching on the roadway of the Brooklyn Bridge. On January 26, 2012, the People sent a subpoena duces tecum to Twitter seeking the defendant's account information and tweets for their relevance in

---

[14] PL No. 99-508, as revised.

[15] 18 U.S.C. §§ 2510-22.

[16] 18 U.S.C. §§ 3121-27.

[17] 18 U.S.C. §§ 2701-11.

[18] 2012 N.Y. Misc. LEXIS 3076; 2012 NY Slip Op 22175 (N.Y.Crim.Ct. June 30, 2012) (notes omitted).

the ongoing criminal investigation (CPL 610; Stored Communications Act [18 USC § 2703(c)(2)]). On January 30, 2012, Twitter, after conferring with the District Attorney's office, informed the defendant that the Twitter account @destructuremal had been subpoenaed. On January 31, 2012, the defendant notified Twitter of his intention to file a motion to quash the subpoena. Twitter then took the position that it would not comply with the subpoena until the court ruled on the defendant's motion to quash the subpoena and intervened.

On April 20, 2012, this court held that the defendant had no proprietary interest in the user information on his Twitter account, as he lacked standing to quash the subpoena (See CPLR 1012[a], 1013; People v. Harris, 945 N.Y.S.2d 505, 2012 N.Y. Slip Op 22109 [Crim Ct, N.Y. County 2012]). This court ordered Twitter to provide certain information to the court for in camera review to safeguard the privacy rights of Mr. Harris.

On May 31, 2012 David Rosenblatt, a member of Twitter's Board of Directors, was personally served within New York County with a copy of this Court's April 20, 2012 order, a copy of the January 26, 2012 trial subpoena, and a copy of the March 8, 2012 trial subpoena. Twitter subsequently moved to quash the April 20, 2012 court order. To date, Twitter has not complied with this court's order.

Discussion:

Twitter is a public, real-time social and information network that enables people to share, communicate, and receive news. Users can create a Twitter profile that contains a profile image, background image, and status updates called tweets, which can be up to 140 — characters in length on the website. Twitter provides its services to the public at large. Anyone can sign up to use Twitter's services as long as they agree to Twitter's terms. Twitter is a Delaware corporation with its principal place of business in California.

The Stored Communications Act ("SCA") (18 USC § 2701 et seq.) defines and makes distinctions between Electronic Communication Service ("ECS") versus Remote Computing Service ("RCS"), and content information versus non-content information. ECS is defined as "any service that provides the user thereof the ability to send or receive wire or electronic communication." (See 18 USC § 2510[15]). RCS is defined as "the provision to the public of computer storage or processing services by means of an electronic communications system." (see 18 USC § 2711[2]). The Wire Tap Act (18 USC § 2510[8]) defines content information as "contents, when used with respect to any wire, oral or electronic communication, includes any information concerning the substance, purport, or meaning of that communication." In contrast, logs of account usage, mailer header information (minus the subject line), list of outgoing e-mail addresses sent from an account, and basic subscriber information are all considered to be non-content information.

While Twitter is primarily an ECS (as discussed in Harris, ___ N.Y.S.2d ___, at 6), it also acts as a RCS. It collects and stores both non-content information such as IP addresses, physical locations, browser type, subscriber information, etc. and content information such as tweets. The SCA grants greater privacy protections to content information because actual contents of messages naturally implicate greater privacy concerns than network generated information about those communications.

1.Twitter Users and Standing to Challenge Third — Party Disclosure Request

Twitter argues that users have standing to quash the subpoena. The issue is whether Twitter users have standing to challenge third-party disclosure requests under the terms of service that existed during the dates in question. In Harris, *(id. at 7) the New York City Criminal Court held that a criminal defendant did not have standing to quash a subpoena issued to a third-party online social networking service because the defendant has no proprietary interest. The court's decision was partially based on Twitter's then terms of service agreement. After the April 20, 2012 decision, Twitter changed its terms and policy effective May 17, 2012. The newly added portion states that: "You Retain Your Right To Any Content You Submit, Post Or Display On Or Through The Service." (See* Twitter, Terms of Service, *https://twitter.com/tos/ [accessed June 11, 2012]).*

Twitter argues that the court's decision to deny the defendant standing places an undue burden on Twitter. It forces Twitter to choose between either providing user communications and account information in response to all subpoenas or attempting to vindicate its users' rights by moving to quash these subpoenas itself. However, that burden is placed on every third-party respondent to a subpoena (see In Re Verizon, *257 F Supp 2d 244, 257–258 [2003];* United States v. Kennedy, *81 F Supp 2d 1103, 1110 [2000]) and cannot be used to create standing for a defendant where none exists.*

The Stored Communications Act (18 USC § 2703[d]) states:

A court issuing an order pursuant to this section, on a motion made promptly by the service provider, may quash or modify such order, *if the information or records requested are unusually voluminous in nature or compliance with such order otherwise would cause an undue burden on such provider.* (Emphasis added).

In the defense motion they also reference a concurrence by J. Sotomayor who said that "it may be necessary for the court to reconsider the premise that an individual has no reasonable expectation of privacy in information voluntarily disclosed to third parties" (see United States v. Jones, *565 U.S. ——, 132 S Ct 957 [2012]). Publication to third parties is the issue. Tweets are not e-mails sent to a single party. At best, the defense may argue that this is more akin to an e-mail that is sent to a party and carbon copied to hundreds of others. There can be no reasonable expectation of privacy in a tweet sent around the world. The court order is not unreasonably burdensome to Twitter, as it does not take much to search and provide the data to the court. So long as the third party is in possession of the materials, the court may issue an order for the materials from the third party when the materials are relevant and evidentiary (18 USC § 2703[d];* People v. Carassavas, *103 Misc.2d 562 [Saratoga County Ct 1980]).*

Consider the following: a man walks to his window, opens the window, and screams down to a young lady, "I'm sorry I hit you, please come back upstairs." At trial, the People call a person who was walking across the street at the time this occurred. The prosecutor asks, "What did the defendant yell?" Clearly the answer is relevant and the witness could be compelled to testify. Well today, the street is an online, information superhighway, and the witnesses can be the third party providers like Twitter, Facebook, Instragram, Pinterest, or the next hot social media application.

2. The Court Order, Federal Law and New York State Law

The second issue is whether the court order was a violation of the Fourth Amendment, the Federal Stored Communications Act, or any other New York law.

The Fourth Amendment

To establish a violation of the Fourth Amendment, the defendant must show either (1) a physical intrusion onto defendant's personal property; or (2) a violation of a defendant's reasonable expectation of privacy. (see United States v. Jones *(132 S Ct 945, 950 [2012];* Kyllo v. United States, *533 U.S. 27, 33 [2001].)* In Jones *(id. at 949), the U.S. Supreme Court held that the government's installation of a Global Positioning System ("GPS") tracking device on a target's vehicle to obtain information was a physical intrusion on a constitutionally protected area. In* People v. Weaver *(12 NY3d 433 [2009]) the New York Court of Appeals held that the placing of a GPS tracking device inside the bumper of the defendant's vehicle, by a state police investigator, was a physical intrusion. However, in this case there was no physical intrusion into the defendant's Twitter account. The defendant had purposely broadcast to the entire world into a server 3,000 miles away. Therefore, the defendant's account is protected by the Fourth Amendment only if "the government violated a subjective expectation of privacy that society recognizes as reasonable." (see* Kyllo v. United States, *533 U.S. 27, 33 [2001], citing* Katz v. United States, *389 U.S. 347, 361 [1967]).*

The Supreme Court has repeatedly held that the Fourth Amendment does not protect information revealed by third parties. (see United States v. Miller, 425 U.S. 435, 443 [1976].) Several courts have applied this rationale and held that internet users do not retain a reasonable expectation of privacy. In Romano v. Steelcase Inc., *(30 Misc.3d 426 [Sup Ct, N.Y. County 2010]) the court held that "users would logically lack a legitimate expectation of privacy in materials intended for publication or public posting."*

If you post a tweet, just like if you scream it out the window, there is no reasonable expectation of privacy. There is no proprietary interest in your tweets, which you have now gifted to the world. This is not the same as a private email, a private direct message, a private chat, or any of the other readily available ways to have a private conversation via the internet that now exist. Those private dialogues would require a warrant based on probable cause in order to access the relevant information.

Interestingly, in 2010, Twitter signed an agreement with the Library of Congress providing that every public tweet from Twitter's inception and beyond would be archived by the Library of Congress. Also, Twitter's Privacy Policy states in part:

Our Services are primarily designed to help you share information with the world. Most of the information you provide us is information you are asking us to make public. This includes not only the messages you Tweet and the metadata provided with Tweets, such as when you Tweeted, but also the lists you create, the people you follow, the Tweets you mark as favorites or Retweet, and many other bits of information that result from your use of the Services. (see Twitter, Twitter Privacy Policy https://twitter.com/privacy [accessed June 11, 2012].)

There is no reasonable expectation of privacy for tweets that the user has made public. It is the act of tweeting or disseminating communications to the public that controls. Even when a user deletes his or her tweets there are search engines available such as "Untweetable", "Tweleted" and "Politwoops" that hold users accountable for everything they had publicly tweeted and later deleted.

Therefore, the defendant's Fourth Amendment rights were not violated because there was no physical intrusion of the defendant's tweets and the defendant has no reasonable expectation of privacy in the information he intentionally broadcast to the world.

Stored Communications Act *The SCA's requirements for a court order states that:*

A court order for disclosure under subsection (b) or (c) . . . . shall be issued only if the government entity offers specific and articulate facts showing that there are reasonable grounds to believe that the contents of a wire or electronic communication, or the records or other information sought, are relevant and materials to an ongoing criminal investigation. (Emphasis added) (see 18 USC § 2703[d]).

The defendant's anticipated trial defense is that the police either led or escorted him onto the non-pedestrian part of the Brooklyn Bridge, a defense allegedly contradicted by his publicly posted tweets around the time of the incident. In Harris, *(id . at 7–8) the court held that the information sought was relevant. The April 20, 2012 court order was issued to comply with the January 26, 2012 subpoena.*

The People are seeking two types of information, non-content information such as subscriber information, e-mail addresses, etc. and content information such as tweets. The SCA protects only private communications and allows disclosure of electronic communication when it's not overbroad.

In general, court orders have no limitations on the types of information to be disclosed (18 USC § 2703[d]). The SCA mandates different standards that the government must satisfy to compel a provider to disclose various types of information (18 USC § 2703). To compel a provider of ECS to disclose contents of communication in its possession that are in temporary "electronic storage" for 180 days or less, the government must obtain a search warrant (18 USC § 2703[a]). A court order must compel a provider of ECS to disclose contents in electronic storage for greater than 180 days or to compel a provider of RCS to disclose its contents (18 USC § 2703[a], [b], and [d]). The law governing compelled disclosure also covers the above mentioned non-content records. The rules are the same for providers of ECS and RCS and the government can obtain a § 2703(d) order to compel such non-content information (18 USC § 2703[c][1][B]).

The non-content records such as subscriber information, logs maintained by the network server, etc. and the September 15, 2011 to December 30, 2011 tweets are covered by the court order. However, the government must obtain a search warrant for the December 31, 2011 tweets.

New York State Law

The scope of a subpoena duces tecum *is sufficiently circumscribed when: (1) the materials are relevant and evidentiary; (2) the request is specific; (3) the materials are not otherwise procurable reasonably in advance of trial by the exercise of due diligence; (4) the party cannot properly prepare for trial without such a production and inspection in advance of trial and the failure to obtain such inspection may tend unreasonably to delay the trial; and (5) the application is made in good faith and is not intended as a general "fishing expedition" (*People v. Carassavas, *103 Misc.2d 562 [Saratoga County Ct 1980], citing *People v. Price, *100 Misc.2d 372, 379 [1979]). The District Attorney seeks the subpoenaed information to refute Harris's anticipated trial defense. In *Harris, (id. at 7–8) the court agreed that the* subpoena duce tecum *was sufficiently circumscribed and a court order was issued on April 20, 2012 to comply with the subpoena.*

On May 31, 2012 David Rosenblatt, a member of Twitter's Board of Directors, was personally served within New York County with a copy of this court's April 20, 2012 order, a copy of the January 26, 2012 trial subpoena, and a copy of the March 8, 2012 trial subpoena. There are no jurisdictional issues and there are no violations of the New York Constitution.

Conclusion:

*In dealing with social media issues, judges are asked to make decisions based on statutes that can never keep up with technology. In some cases, those same judges have no understanding of the technology themselves (*Stephanie Rabiner, Esq., Technologist, Do Judges Really Understand Social Media? *http://blogs.findlaw.com/tec hnologist/2012/05/do-judges-really-understandsocial-media.html [May 9, 2012]). Judges must then do what they have always done-balance the arguments on the scales of justice. They must weigh the interests of society against*

*The world of social media is evolving, as is the law around it. Society struggle with policies, whether they are between student and teacher (*N.Y.C Department of Education, NYC Department of Education Social Media Guidelines), *or the right of a company to examine an applicant's Facebook page as part of the interview process (*Bill Chappell, State Approves Bill to Ban Employers From Seeking Facebook Login Info, *http:// www.npr.org/blogs/the two-way/2012/04/10/150354579/state-approves-billto-ban-employers-from-seeking-facebook-login-info). As the laws, rules and societal norms evolve and change with each new advance in technology, so too will the decisions of our courts. While the U.S. Constitution clearly did not take into consideration any tweets by our founding fathers, it is probably safe to assume that Samuel Adams, Benjamin Franklin, Alexander Hamilton and Thomas Jefferson would have loved to tweet their opinions as much as they loved to write for the newspapers of their day (sometimes under anonymous pseudonyms similar to today's twitter user names). Those men, and countless soldiers in service to this nation, have risked their lives for our right to tweet or to post an article on Facebook; but that is not the same as arguing that those public tweets are protected. The Constitution gives you the right to post, but as numerous people have learned, there* *are still consequences for your public posts. What you give to the public belongs to the public. What you keep to yourself belongs only to you.*

Accordingly, the motion to quash is granted in part and denied in part. The court finds in favor of the People for all non-content information and content information in ECS and RCS from September 15, 2011 to December 30, 2011. However, ECS content information less than 180 days old (tweeted on December 31, 2011) may only be disclosed pursuant to a search warrant, and the court decision in People v. Harris *is so modified. That search warrant should be requested of a judge of competent jurisdiction. However, to avoid any issue of alleged non-impartiality, that warrant should be made to another judge of this court.*

Accordingly, it is hereby:

ORDERED, that Twitter disclose all non-content information and content information from September 15, 2011 to December 30, 2011; and it is further

ORDERED, that the materials be provided to this court for in camera *inspection. The relevant portions thereof will be provided to the office of the District Attorney, who will provide copies to the defense counsel as part of discovery; and it is further*

ORDERED, that the clerk of this court notify the Presiding Judge of Jury 2 of the receipt of the materials.

This opinion shall constitute the decision and order of the Court.

III. EYES IN THE GROUND AND SKY: THE USE OF GPS TRACKING AND DRONES IN LAW ENFORCEMENT

Just as databases can boost the efficiency and maximize the resources available to investigators seeking identifying information, so too can automated and unmanned devices enable police officers to track suspects' behavior and activities with little or no personnel risk or expense. Global positioning system ("GPS") receivers, which are present in every cellular phone to fulfill the FCC's "enhanced 911" requirements regarding emergency call location,[19] allow cellular carriers to know (and potentially reveal to police) the location and movement histories of their subscribers (or at least their subscribers' devices), raising potential privacy concerns.[20] Similar capabilities contained within automotive "telematics" services, although intended to enhance convenience, have also raised consumer worries about the potential sharing of tracking data with third parties including law enforcement agencies.[21]

---

[19] See, e.g., WIRELESS 911 SERVICES | FCC.GOV, http://www.fcc.gov/guides/wireless-911-services/ (last visited Jul 20, 2012).

[20] AARON FUTCH AND CHRISTINE SOARES, *ENHANCED 911 TECHNOLOGY AND PRIVACY CONCERNS: HOW HAS THE BALANCE CHANGED SINCE SEPTEMBER 11?*, 2001 Duke Law & Technology Review 38(2001).

[21] CHANGES TO ONSTAR'S PRIVACY TERMS RILE SOME USERS — NYTIMES.COM, http://wheels.blogs.nytimes.com/2011/09/22/changes-to-onstars-privacy-terms-rile-some-users/ (last visited Jul 20, 2012); SCHUMER SEEKS FTC PROBE OF ONSTAR PRIVACY POLICY — COMPUTERWORLD, http://www.computerworld.com/s/article/9220310/Schumer_seeks_FTC_probe_of_OnStar_privacy_policy (last visited Jul 20, 2012); GM'S ONSTAR REVERSES

Law enforcement departments have also sought to expand their own surveillance capabilities by installing their own GPS trackers on suspects' vehicles, rather than using officers to follow them (which can be timeconsuming, expensive, potentially hazardous to the officers if they are detected and opposed). The Supreme Court, however, has ruled that such tracking represents a Fourth Amendment search and thus requires a warrant:

U.S. v. JONES[22]

JUSTICE SCALIA delivered the opinion of the Court.

We decide whether the attachment of a Global — Positioning — System (GPS) tracking device to an individual's vehicle, and subsequent use of that device to monitor the vehicle's movements on public streets, constitutes a search or seizure within the meaning of the Fourth Amendment.

I

In 2004 respondent Antoine Jones, owner and operator of a nightclub in the District of Columbia, came under suspicion of trafficking in narcotics and was made the target of an investigation by a joint FBI and Metropolitan Police Department task force. Officers employed various investigative techniques, including visual surveillance of the nightclub, installation of a camera focused on the front door of the club, and a pen register and wiretap covering Jones's cellular phone.

Based in part on information gathered from these sources, in 2005 the Government applied to the United States District Court for the District of Columbia for a warrant authorizing the use of an electronic tracking device on the Jeep Grand Cherokee registered to Jones's wife. A warrant issued, authorizing installation of the device in the District of Columbia and within 10 days.

On the 11th day, and not in the District of Columbia but in Maryland, agents installed a GPS tracking device on the undercarriage of the Jeep while it was parked in a public parking lot. Over the next 28 days, the Government used the device to track the vehicle's movements, and once had to replace the device's battery when the vehicle was parked in a different public lot in Maryland. By means of signals from multiple satellites, the device established the vehicle's location within 50 to 100 feet, and communicated that location by cellular phone to a Government computer. It relayed more than 2,000 pages of data over the 4 — week period.

The Government ultimately obtained a multiple-count indictment charging Jones and several alleged co-conspirators with, as relevant here, conspiracy to distribute and possess with intent to distribute five kilograms or more of cocaine and 50 grams or more of cocaine base, in violation of 21 U.S.C. §§ 841 and 846. Before trial, Jones

POLICY THAT RAISED PRIVACY ALARMS, http://content.usatoday.com/communities/driveon/post/2011/09/gm-general-motors-onstar-privacy-sell-data-charles-schumer/1 (last visited Jul 20, 2012).

[22] 132 S.Ct. 945 (2012) (notes omitted).

filed a motion to suppress evidence obtained through the GPS device. The District Court granted the motion only in part, suppressing the data obtained while the vehicle was parked in the garage adjoining Jones's residence. 451 F.Supp.2d 71, 88 (2006). It held the remaining data admissible, because " '[a] person traveling in an automobile on public thoroughfares has no reasonable expectation of privacy in his movements from one place to another.' " Ibid. (quoting United States v. Knotts, *460 U.S. 276, 281, 103 S.Ct. 1081, 75 L.Ed.2d 55 (1983)). Jones's trial in October 2006 produced a hung jury on the conspiracy count.*

In March 2007, a grand jury returned another indictment, charging Jones and others with the same conspiracy. The Government introduced at trial the same GPS-derived locational data admitted in the first trial, which connected Jones to the alleged conspirators' stash house that contained $850,000 in cash, 97 kilograms of cocaine, and 1 kilogram of cocaine base. The jury returned a guilty verdict, and the District Court sentenced Jones to life imprisonment.

The United States Court of Appeals for the District of Columbia Circuit reversed the conviction because of admission of the evidence obtained by warrantless use of the GPS device which, it said, violated the Fourth Amendment. United States v. Maynard, *615 F.3d 544 (2010). The D.C. Circuit denied the Government's petition for rehearing en banc, with four judges dissenting. 625 F.3d 766 (2010). We granted certiorari, 564 U.S. ——, 131 S.Ct. 3064, 180 L.Ed.2d 885 (2011).*

II

A

The Fourth Amendment provides in relevant part that "[t]he right of the people to be secure in their persons, houses, papers, and effects, against unreasonable searches and seizures, shall not be violated." It is beyond dispute that a vehicle is an "effect" as that term is used in the Amendment. United States v. Chadwick, *433 U.S. 1, 12, 97 S.Ct. 2476, 53 L.Ed.2d 538 (1977). We hold that the Government's installation of a GPS device on a target's vehicle, and its use of that device to monitor the vehicle's movements, constitutes a "search."*

It is important to be clear about what occurred in this case: The Government physically occupied private property for the purpose of obtaining information. We have no doubt that such a physical intrusion would have been considered a "search" within the meaning of the Fourth Amendment when it was adopted. Entick v. Carrington, *95 Eng. Rep. 807 (C.P. 1765), is a "case we have described as a 'monument of English freedom' 'undoubtedly familiar' to 'every American statesman' at the time the Constitution was adopted, and considered to be 'the true and ultimate expression of constitutional law' " with regard to search and seizure.* Brower v. County of Inyo, *489 U.S. 593, 596, 109 S.Ct. 1378, 103 L.Ed.2d 628 (1989) (quoting* Boyd v. United States, *116 U.S. 616, 626, 6 S.Ct. 524, 29 L.Ed. 746 (1886)). In that case, Lord Camden expressed in plain terms the significance of property rights in search-and-seizure analysis:*

"[O]ur law holds the property of every man so sacred, that no man can set his foot

upon his neighbour's close without his leave; if he does he is a trespasser, though he does no damage at all; if he will tread upon his neighbour's ground, he must justify it by law." Entick, supra, at 817.

The text of the Fourth Amendment reflects its close connection to property, since otherwise it would have referred simply to "the right of the people to be secure against unreasonable searches and seizures"; the phrase "in their persons, houses, papers, and effects" would have been superfluous.

Consistent with this understanding, our Fourth Amendment jurisprudence was tied to common-law trespass, at least until the latter half of the 20th century. Kyllo v. United States, *533 U.S. 27, 31, 121 S.Ct. 2038, 150 L.Ed.2d 94 (2001);* Kerr, The Fourth Amendment and New Technologies: Constitutional Myths and the Case for Caution, *102 Mich. L.Rev. 801, 816 (2004). Thus, in* Olmstead v. United States, *277 U.S. 438, 48 S.Ct. 564, 72 L.Ed. 944 (1928), we held that wiretaps attached to telephone wires on the public streets did not constitute a Fourth Amendment search because "[t]here was no entry of the houses or offices of the defendants," id., at 464, 48 S.Ct. 564.*

Our later cases, of course, have deviated from that exclusively property-based approach. In Katz v. United States, *389 U.S. 347, 351, 88 S.Ct. 507, 19 L.Ed.2d 576 (1967), we said that "the Fourth Amendment protects people, not places," and found a violation in attachment of an eavesdropping device to a public telephone booth. Our later cases have applied the analysis of Justice Harlan's concurrence in that case, which said that a violation occurs when government officers violate a person's "reasonable expectation of privacy," id., at 360, 88 S.Ct. 507. See, e.g.,* Bond v. United States, *529 U.S. 334, 120 S.Ct. 1462, 146 L.Ed.2d 365 (2000);* California v. Ciraolo, *476 U.S. 207, 106 S.Ct. 1809, 90 L.Ed.2d 210 (1986);* Smith v. Maryland, *442 U.S. 735, 99 S.Ct. 2577, 61 L.Ed.2d 220 (1979).*

The Government contends that the Harlan standard shows that no search occurred here, since Jones had no "reasonable expectation of privacy" in the area of the Jeep accessed by Government agents (its underbody) and in the locations of the Jeep on the public roads, which were visible to all. But we need not address the Government's contentions, because Jones's Fourth Amendment rights do not rise or fall with the Katz *formulation. At bottom, we must "assur[e] preservation of that degree of privacy against government that existed when the Fourth Amendment was adopted."* Kyllo, *supra, at 34, 121 S.Ct. 2038. As explained, for most of our history the Fourth Amendment was understood to embody a particular concern for government trespass upon the areas ("persons, houses, papers, and effects") it enumerates.* Katz *did not repudiate that understanding. Less than two years later the Court upheld defendants' contention that the Government could not introduce against them conversations between other people obtained by warrantless placement of electronic surveillance devices in their homes. The opinion rejected the dissent's contention that there was no Fourth Amendment violation "unless the conversational privacy of the homeowner himself is invaded."* Alderman v. United States, *394 U.S. 165, 176, 89 S.Ct. 961, 22 L.Ed.2d 176 (1969). "[W]e [do not] believe that* Katz, *by holding that the Fourth Amendment protects persons and their private conversations, was intended to withdraw any of the protection which the Amendment extends to the home. . . ."* Id., *at 180, 89 S.Ct. 961.*

More recently, in Soldal v. Cook County, *506 U.S. 56, 113 S.Ct. 538, 121 L.Ed.2d 450 (1992), the Court unanimously rejected the argument that although a "seizure" had occurred "in a 'technical' sense" when a trailer home was forcibly removed, id., at 62, 113 S.Ct. 538, no Fourth Amendment violation occurred because law enforcement had not "invade[d] the [individuals'] privacy," id., at 60, 113 S.Ct. 538.* Katz, *the Court explained, established that "property rights are not the sole measure of Fourth Amendment violations," but did not "snuf[f] out the previously recognized protection for property." 506 U.S., at 64, 113 S.Ct. 538. As Justice Brennan explained in his concurrence in* Knotts, Katz *did not erode the principle "that, when the Government does engage in physical intrusion of a constitutionally protected area in order to obtain information, that intrusion may constitute a violation of the Fourth Amendment." 460 U.S., at 286, 103 S.Ct. 1081 (opinion concurring in judgment). We have embodied that preservation of past rights in our very definition of "reasonable expectation of privacy" which we have said to be an expectation "that has a source outside of the Fourth Amendment, either by reference to concepts of real or personal property law or to understandings that are recognized and permitted by society."* Minnesota v. Carter, *525 U.S. 83, 88, 119 S.Ct. 469, 142 L.Ed.2d 373 (1998) (internal quotation marks omitted).* Katz *did not narrow the Fourth Amendment's scope. The Government contends that several of our post-*Katz *cases foreclose the conclusion that what occurred here constituted a search. It relies principally on two cases in which we rejected Fourth Amendment challenges to "beepers," electronic tracking devices that represent another form of electronic monitoring. The first case,* Knotts, *upheld against Fourth Amendment challenge the use of a "beeper" that had been placed in a container of chloroform, allowing law enforcement to monitor the location of the container. 460 U.S., at 278, 103 S.Ct. 1081. We said that there had been no infringement of* Knotts' *reasonable expectation of privacy since the information obtained — the location of the automobile carrying the container on public roads, and the location of the off-loaded container in open fields near* Knotts' *cabin — had been voluntarily conveyed to the public. Id., at 281–282, 103 S.Ct. 1081. But as we have discussed, the* Katz *reasonable-expectation-of-privacy test has been* added to, *not substituted for, the common-law trespassory test. The holding in* Knotts *addressed only the former, since the latter was not at issue. The beeper had been placed in the container before it came into* Knotts' *possession, with the consent of the then-owner. 460 U.S., at 278, 103 S.Ct. 1081.* Knotts *did not challenge that installation, and we specifically declined to consider its effect on the Fourth Amendment analysis. Id., at 279, n. **, 103 S.Ct. 1081* Knotts *would be relevant, perhaps, if the Government were making the argument that what would otherwise be an unconstitutional search is not such where it produces only public information. The Government does not make that argument, and we know of no case that would support it.*

The second "beeper" case, United States v. Karo, *468 U.S. 705, 104 S.Ct. 3296, 82 L.Ed.2d 530 (1984), does not suggest a different conclusion. There we addressed the question left open by* Knotts, *whether the installation of a beeper in a container amounted to a search or seizure. 468 U.S., at 713, 104 S.Ct. 3296. As in* Knotts, *at the time the beeper was installed the container belonged to a third party, and it did not come into possession of the defendant until later. 468 U.S., at 708, 104 S.Ct. 3296. Thus, the specific question we considered was whether the installation "with the consent of the original owner constitute[d] a search or seizure . . . when the container is delivered to a buyer having no knowledge of the presence of the beeper." Id., at 707, 104 S.Ct. 3296 (emphasis added). We held not. The Government, we said, came into physical contact with the container only before it belonged to the defendant Karo; and the transfer of the container with the unmonitored beeper inside did not convey any information and thus did not invade Karo's privacy. See id., at 712, 104 S.Ct. 3296. That conclusion is perfectly consistent with the one we reach here. Karo accepted the container as it came to him, beeper and all, and was therefore not entitled to object to the beeper's presence, even though it was used to monitor the container's location. Cf.* On Lee v. United States, *343 U.S. 747, 751–752, 72 S.Ct. 967, 96 L.Ed. 1270 (1952) (no search or seizure where an informant, who was wearing a concealed microphone, was invited into the defendant's business). Jones, who possessed the Jeep at the time the Government trespassorily inserted the information-gathering device, is on much different footing.*

The Government also points to our exposition in New York v. Class, *475 U.S. 106, 106 S.Ct. 960, 89 L.Ed.2d 81 (1986), that "[t]he exterior of a car . . . is thrust into the public eye, and thus to examine it does not constitute a 'search.' " Id., at 114, 106 S.Ct. 960. That statement is of marginal relevance here since, as the Government acknowledges, "the officers in this case did* more *than conduct a visual inspection of respondent's vehicle," Brief for United States 41 (emphasis added). By attaching the device to the Jeep, officers encroached on a protected area. In* Class *itself we suggested that this would make a difference, for we concluded that an officer's momentary reaching into the interior of a vehicle did constitute a search. 475 U.S., at 114–115, 106 S.Ct. 960.*

Finally, the Government's position gains little support from our conclusion in Oliver v. United States, *466 U.S. 170, 104 S.Ct. 1735, 80 L.Ed.2d 214 (1984), that officers' information-gathering intrusion on an "open field" did not constitute a Fourth Amendment search even though it was a trespass at common law, id., at 183, 104 S.Ct. 1735. Quite simply, an open field, unlike the curtilage of a home, see* United States v. Dunn, *480 U.S. 294, 300, 107 S.Ct. 1134, 94 L.Ed.2d 326 (1987), is not one of those protected areas enumerated in the Fourth Amendment.* Oliver, supra, *at 176–177, 104 S.Ct. 1735. See also* Hester v. United States, *265 U.S. 57, 59, 44 S.Ct. 445, 68 L.Ed. 898 (1924). The Government's physical intrusion on such an area — unlike its intrusion on the "effect" at issue here — is of no Fourth Amendment significance.*

B

The concurrence begins by accusing us of applying "18th-century tort law." Post, at 957. That is a distortion. What we apply is an 18th-century guarantee against unreasonable searches, which we believe must provide at a minimum the degree of protection it afforded when it was adopted. The concurrence does not share that belief. It would apply exclusively Katz 's reasonable-expectation-of-privacy test, even when that eliminates rights that previously existed.

The concurrence faults our approach for "present[ing] particularly vexing problems" in cases that do not involve physical contact, such as those that involve the transmission of electronic signals. Post, at 962. We entirely fail to understand that point. For unlike the concurrence, which would make Katz the exclusive test, we do not make trespass the exclusive test. Situations involving merely the transmission of electronic signals without trespass would remain *subject to* Katz *analysis.*

In fact, it is the concurrence's insistence on the exclusivity of the Katz *test that needlessly leads us into "particularly vexing problems" in the present case. This Court has to date not deviated from the understanding that mere visual observation does not constitute a search. See* Kyllo, *533 U.S., at 31–32, 121 S.Ct. 2038. We accordingly held in* Knotts *that "[a] person traveling in an automobile on public thoroughfares has no reasonable expectation of privacy in his movements from one place to another." 460 U.S., at 281, 103 S.Ct. 1081. Thus, even assuming that the concurrence is correct to say that "[t]raditional surveillance" of Jones for a 4 — week period "would have required a large team of agents, multiple vehicles, and perhaps aerial assistance," post, at 963, our cases suggest that such visual observation is constitutionally permissible. It may be that achieving the same result through electronic means, without an accompanying trespass, is an unconstitutional invasion of privacy, but the present case does not require us to answer that question.*

And answering it affirmatively leads us needlessly into additional thorny problems. The concurrence posits that "relatively short-term monitoring of a person's movements on public streets" is okay, but that "the use of longer term GPS monitoring in investigations of most offenses" is no good. Post, at 964 (emphasis added). That introduces yet another novelty into our jurisprudence. There is no precedent for the proposition that whether a search has occurred depends on the nature of the crime being investigated. And even accepting that novelty, it remains unexplained why a 4 — week investigation is "surely" too long and why a drug-trafficking conspiracy involving substantial amounts of cash and narcotics is not an "extraordinary offens[e]" which may permit longer observation. See post, at 964. What of a 2 — day monitoring of a suspected purveyor of stolen electronics? Or of a 6 — month monitoring of a suspected terrorist? We may have to grapple with these "vexing problems" in some future case where a classic trespassory search is not involved and resort must be had to Katz *analysis; but there is no reason for rushing forward to resolve them here.*

III

The Government argues in the alternative that even if the attachment and use of the device was a search, it was reasonable — and thus lawful — under the Fourth Amendment because "officers had reasonable suspicion, and indeed probable cause, to believe that [Jones] was a leader in a large-scale cocaine distribution conspiracy." Brief for United States 50–51. We have no occasion to consider this argument. The Government did not raise it below, and the D.C. Circuit therefore did not address it. See 625 F.3d, at 767 (Ginsburg, Tatel, and Griffith, JJ., concurring in denial of rehearing en banc). We consider the argument forfeited. See Sprietsma v. Mercury Marine, *537 U.S. 51, 56, n. 4, 123 S.Ct. 518, 154 L.Ed.2d 466 (2002).*

*   *   *

The judgment of the Court of Appeals for the D.C. Circuit is affirmed.

Another recent development in law enforcement with substantial potential privacy implications is the adoption and use of unmanned aerial vehicles ("UAVs"), also known as drones. UAVs, which may take winged, rotor or lighter-than-air forms and may also carry (and fire) weapons, began being used by the U.S. military on an experimental basis in World War I.[23] Since then, UAV military utilization has expanded substantially, since their flexibility in size, lower cost, enhanced information gathering potential and reduced risk of (pilot) injury or death when compared to manned aircraft make them a desirable tool for both surveillance and active engagement of strategic targets.[24]

The same combination of cost, operator safety and surveillance capabilities has led domestic law enforcement agencies to pursue adoption of UAVs as well. While the Federal Aviation Administration exercises supervisory air traffic control authority over all non-military UAV use, whether by law enforcement, private industry or hobbyists (radio-controlled model aircraft),[25] the permissibility of, and limitations on, use by law enforcement of the surveillance data drones collect is a more complicated matter. One essential question is whether use by UAV for law enforcement purposes requires a warrant under the Fourth Amendment. On the one hand, the "take" (or information received) from a UAV's cameras (at least if they are using visible light only) could be covered by the "plain view" exception to the general warrant requirement, since the drone would only be recording what was ordinarily visible. The exception is described by the Supreme Court in *Coolidge v. New Hampshire*:[26]

> *It is well established that under certain circumstances the police may seize evidence in plain view without a warrant. But it is important to keep in mind that, in the vast majority of cases, any evidence seized by the police will be in plain view, at least at the moment of seizure. The problem with the 'plain view' doctrine has been to identify the circumstances in which plain view has legal significance rather than being simply the normal concomitant of any search, legal or illegal.*
>
> *An example of the applicability of the 'plain view' doctrine is the situation in which the police have a warrant to search a given area for specified objects, and in the course of the search come across some other article of incriminating character. Cf. Go-Bart Importing Co. v. United States, 282 U.S. 344, 358, 51 S.Ct. 153, 158, 75 L.Ed. 374; United States v. Lefkowitz, 285 U.S. 452, 465, 52 S.Ct. 420, 423, 76 L.Ed. 877; Steele v. United States, 267 U.S. 498, 45 S.Ct. 414, 69 L.Ed. 757; Stanley v. Georgia, 394 U.S. 557, 571, 89 S.Ct. 1243, 1251, 22 L.Ed.2d 542 (Stewart, J., concurring in result). Where the initial intrusion that brings the police within plain view of such an article is supported, not by a warrant, but by one of the recognized exceptions to the warrant require-*

---

[23] MILITARY UNMANNED AERIAL VEHICLES — NATIONAL AIR AND SPACE MUSEUM EXHIBITION HOME PAGE, http://airandspace.si.edu/exhibitions/gal104/uav.cfm (last visited Jul 9, 2012).

[24] See, e.g., MICRODRONES, SOME AS SMALL AS BUGS, ARE POISED TO ALTER WAR — NYTIMES.COM, http://www.nytimes.com/2011/06/20/world/20drones.html?_r=1&ref=unmannedaerialvehicles (last visited Jul 9, 2012).

[25] FACT SHEET — UNMANNED AIRCRAFT SYSTEMS (UAS), http://www.faa.gov/news/fact_sheets/news_story.cfm?newsid=6287 (last visited Jul 9, 2012).

[26] 403 U.S. 443 (1971).

ment, the seizure is also legitimate. Thus the police may inadvertently come across evidence while in 'hot pursuit' of a fleeing suspect. Warden v. Hayden, supra; cf. Hester v. United States, 265 U.S. 57, 44 S.Ct. 445, 68 L.Ed. 898. *And an object that comes into view during a search incident to arrest that is appropriately limited in scope under existing law may be seized without a warrant.* Chimel v. California, 395 U.S., at 762–763, 89 S.Ct., at 2039–2040. *Finally, the 'plain view' doctrine has been applied where a police officer is not searching for evidence against the accused, but nonetheless inadvertently comes across an incriminating object.* Harris v. United States, 390 U.S. 234, 88 S.Ct. 992, 19 L.Ed.2d 1067; Frazier v. Cupp, 394 U.S. 731, 89 S.Ct. 1420, 22 L.Ed.2d 684; Ker v. California, 374 U.S., at 43, 83 S.Ct., at 1635. *Cf.* Lewis v. United States, 385 U.S. 206, 87 S.Ct. 424, 17 L.Ed.2d 312.

What the 'plain view' cases have in common is that the police officer in each of them had a prior justification for an intrusion in the course of which he came inadvertently across a piece of evidence incriminating the accused. The doctrine serves to supplement the prior justification — whether it be a warrant for another object, hot pursuit, search incident to lawful arrest, or some other legitimate reason for being present unconnected with a search directed against the accused — and permits the warrantless seizure. Of course, the extension of the original justification is legitimate only where it is immediately apparent to the police that they have evidence before them; the 'plan view' doctrine may not be used to extend a general exploratory search from one object to another until something incriminating at last emerges. Cf. Stanley v. Georgia, supra, at 571–572, 89 S.Ct., at 1251 *(Stewart, J., concurring in result).*

The rationale for the 'plain view' exception is evident if we keep in mind the two distinct constitutional protections served by the warrant requirement. First, the magistrate's scrutiny is intended to eliminate altogether searches not based on probable cause. The premise here is that any intrusion in the way of search or seizure is an evil, so that no intrusion at all is justified without a careful prior determination of necessity. See, e.g., McDonald v. United States, 335 U.S. 451, 69 S.Ct. 191, 83 L.Ed. 153; Warden v. Hayden, 387 U.S. 294, 87 S.Ct. 1642, 18 L.Ed.2d 782; Katz v. United States, 389 U.S. 347, 88 S.Ct. 507, 19 L.Ed.2d 576; Chimel v. California, 395 U.S., at 761–762, 89 S.Ct., at 2039. *The second, distinct objective is that those searches deemed necessary should be as limited as possible. Here, the specific evil is the 'general warrant' abhorred by the colonists, and the problem is not that of intrusion per se, but of a general, exploratory rummaging in a person's belongings. See, e.g.,* Boyd v. United States, 116 U.S., at 624–630, 6 S.Ct., at 528–532; Marron v. United States, 275 U.S. 192, 195–196, 48 S.Ct. 74, 75–76, 72 L.Ed. 231; Stanford v. Texas, 379 U.S. 476, 85 S.Ct. 506, 13 L.Ed.2d 431. *The warrant accomplishes this second objective by requiring a 'particular description' of the things to be seized.*

The 'plain view' doctrine is not in conflict with the first objective because plain view does not occur until a search is in progress. In each case, this initial intrusion is justified by a warrant or by an exception such as 'hot pursuit' or search incident to a lawful arrest, or by an extraneous valid reason for the officer's presence. And, given the initial intrusion, the seizure of an object in plain view is consistent with the second objective, since it does not convert the search into a general or exploratory one. As against the minor peril to Fourth Amendment protections, there is a major gain in effective law enforcement. Where, once an otherwise lawful search is in progress, the police inadvertently come upon a piece of evidence, it would often be a needless inconvenience, and sometimes dangerous — to the evidence or to the police themselves — to require them to ignore it until they have obtained a warrant particularly describing it.

The limits on the doctrine are implicit in the statement of its rationale. The first of these is that plain view alone is never enough to justify the warrantless seizure of evidence. This is simply a corollary of the familiar principle discussed above, that no amount of probable cause can justify a warrantless search or seizure absent 'exigent circumstances.' Incontrovertible testimony of the senses that an incriminating object is on premises belonging to a criminal suspect may establish the fullest possible measure of probable cause. But even where the object is contraband, this Court has repeatedly stated and enforced the basic rule that the police may not enter and make a warrantless seizure. Taylor v. United States, 286 U.S. 1, 52 S.Ct. 466, 76 L.Ed. 951; Johnson v. United States, 333 U.S. 10, 68 S.Ct. 367, 92 L.Ed. 436; McDonald v. United States, 335 U.S. 451, 69 S.Ct. 191, 93 L.Ed. 153; Jones v. United States, 357 U.S. 493, 497–498, 78 S.Ct. 1253, 1256–1257, 2 L.Ed.2d 1514; Chapman v. United States, 365 U.S. 610, 81 S.Ct. 776, 5 L.Ed.2d 828; Trupiano v. United States, 334 U.S. 699, 68 S.Ct. 1229, 92 L.Ed. 1663.

The second limitation is that the discovery of evidence in plain view must be inadvertent. The rationale of the exception to the warrant requirement, as just stated, is that a plain-view seizure will not turn an initially valid (and therefore limited) search into a 'general' one, while the inconvenience of procuring a warrant to cover an inadvertent discovery is great. But where the discovery is anticipated, where the police know in advance the location of the evidence and intend to seize it, the situation is altogether different. The requirement of a warrant to seize imposes no inconvenience whatever, or at least none which is constitutionally cognizable in a legal system that regards warrantless searches as 'per se unreasonable' in the absence of 'exigent circumstances.'[27]

Subsequent cases have held that the "plain view" exception applies when police view potential evidence from helicopters and other aircraft operating in public airspace.[28]

On the other hand, though, the use by law enforcement agencies of UAVs without warrants is new enough, and arrests based on such use still rare enough, that courts are only beginning to consider whether such use in a civilian context is itself

---

[27] *Id. pp. 465-69.*

[28] *See, e.g., Florida v. Riley, 488 U.S. 445 (1989).*

unreasonable, which might make any evidence obtained from such flights inadmissible in resulting court proceedings:

From "Did a Surveillance Drone Help in the Arrest of a North Dakota Farmer?"

Alleging "outrageous governmental conduct," the first American arrested with the help of a surveillance drone attended a court hearing yesterday as part of an effort to have the charges against him dismissed.

In the small town of Lakota, N.D., farmer Rodney Brossart appeared before a district judge with his wife and their four children over a bizarre sequence of events that occurred last year — beginning with accusations of cattle theft and ending with a military-style Predator spy drone being deployed alongside an elite SWAT team.

Brossart and his family face various criminal charges that relate to a conflict they got into with law enforcement officers after six cows from a neighboring farm wandered onto their land. Brossart declined to return the cattle to their owner until he was paid for the feed they had consumed. When police got involved, three of Brossart's sons allegedly chased the officers away with guns. In the end, a drone was deployed, Rodney Brossart was repeatedly tased and then arrested, and the cows were handed over . . . .[29]

---

[29] RODNEY BROSSART, NORTH DAKOTA FARMER ARRESTED IN CASE INVOLVING PREDATOR SURVEILLANCE DRONE., http://www.slate.com/blogs/future_tense/2012/06/12/ rodney_brossart_north_dakota_farmer_arrested_in_case_involving_predator_surveillance_drone_.html (last visited Jul 20, 2012).

Chapter 11

ATTORNEYS: CLIENT PRIVACY AND ETHICS

Elsewhere in this work, we have examined the legal and other obligations with regard to privacy on those who work in the healthcare context: doctors, hospitals, insurance providers, pharmacies, and others. Those obligations arise out of the unique characteristics of health-related information, and are in addition to any obligations those professionals may face generally in connection with privacy. It is worthwhile to examine another industry, one in which the character of information collected as well as the type of relationship between professional and consumer, raises some unique privacy questions. That industry is the practice of law.

I. APPLICABILITY OF PRIVACY LAWS AND REGULATIONS TO ATTORNEYS

Initially, one might expect that attorneys face fewer legal obligations with regard to privacy. After all, an attorney's obligation to keep her clients' information strictly confidential is both well known and well enforced.[1] Further, unlike in the health context (in which there may be similar confidentiality obligations cased by doctors at least) the type of information maintained by attorneys may not immediately strike an

---

[1] Rule 1.6 of the ABA's Model Rules of Professional Conduct, titled "Confidentiality of Information," states:

> (a) A lawyer shall not reveal information relating to the representation of a client unless the client gives informed consent, the disclosure is impliedly authorized in order to carry out the representation or the disclosure is permitted by paragraph (b).

> (b) A lawyer may reveal information relating to the representation of a client to the extent the lawyer reasonably believes necessary:

> (1) to prevent reasonably certain death or substantial bodily harm;

> (2) to prevent the client from committing a crime or fraud that is reasonably certain to result in substantial injury to the financial interests or property of another and in furtherance of which the client has used or is using the lawyer's services;

> (3) to prevent, mitigate or rectify substantial injury to the financial interests or property of another that is reasonably certain to result or has resulted from the client's commission of a crime or fraud in furtherance of which the client has used the lawyer's services;

> (4) to secure legal advice about the lawyer's compliance with these Rules;

> (5) to establish a claim or defense on behalf of the lawyer in a controversy between the lawyer and the client, to establish a defense to a criminal charge or civil claim against the lawyer based upon conduct in which the client was involved, or to respond to allegations in any proceeding concerning the lawyer's representation of the client; or

> (6) to comply with other law or a court order.

RULE 1.6: CONFIDENTIALITY OF INFORMATION | THE CENTER FOR PROFESSIONAL RESPONSIBILITY, http://www.americanbar.org/groups/professional_responsibility/publications/model_rules_of_professional_conduct/rule_1_6_confidentiality_of_information.html (last visited May 8, 2012).

observer as being overly sensitive in the way health information is. Attorneys deal with the full range of matters and questions on behalf of their clients whether in litigation or transactional context.

This overall obligation of confidentiality, though, did not prevent both the New York State Bar Association and the American Bar Association from having to bring federal lawsuits against the FTC to determine the applicability of the Gramm-Leach-Bliley Act's privacy and reporting obligations[2] on attorneys who counsel on financial matters.[3] At issue in both cases (which were combined by the Court of Appeals) was the definition of the "financial activities" which triggered the Gramm-Leach-Bliley requirements:

AMERICAN BAR ASS'N v. F.T.C.[4]

SENTELLE, CIRCUIT JUDGE.

The Federal Trade Commission ("FTC" or "the Commission") appeals from an order of the District Court granting summary judgment in consolidated cases brought by the appellees American Bar Association and the New York State Bar Association (collectively, "ABA" or "the Bar Associations"). The Bar Associations sought a declaratory judgment that the FTC's decision that attorneys engaged in the practice of law are covered by the Gramm-Leach-Bliley Act ("GLBA" or "the Act") exceeded the statutory authority of the Commission and was therefore invalid as a matter of law. Because we agree with the District Court that the Commission's attempt to regulate the practice of law under the Act fell outside its statutory authority, we affirm the judgment under review.

I. Background

A. Statutory Framework

Effective November 12, 1999, Congress enacted the Gramm-Leach-Bliley Financial Modernization Act, Pub.L. No. 106-102, 113 Stat. 1338. The Act declared it to be "the policy of the Congress that each financial institution has an affirmative and continuing obligation to respect the privacy of its customers and to protect the security and confidentiality of those customers' nonpublic personal information." 15 U.S.C. § 6801(a). To further that goal, Congress enacted broad privacy protective provisions, described by one Member of the House of Representatives as "represent-[ing] the most comprehensive federal privacy protections ever enacted by Congress." 145 Cong. Rec. H11,544 (daily ed. Nov. 4, 1999) (statement of Rep. Sandlin).

---

[2] For a more detailed discussion of the Gramm-Leach-Bliley requirements and other financial privacy laws and regulations, see Chapter 6.

[3] N.Y. State Bar Ass'n v. FTC, 276 F. Supp. 2d 110 (D.D.C. 2003), and *sub nom.* 2004 WL 964173 (D.D.C. 2004), jointly affirmed, Am. Bar Ass'n v. FTC, 430 F.3d 457 (D.D.C. 2005).

[4] Am. Bar Ass'n, 430 F.3d 457 (some notes omitted).

The privacy provisions empowered the Federal Trade Commission, along with other federal regulatory agencies, to "prescribe . . . such regulations as may be necessary to carry out the purposes of this subchapter with respect to the financial institutions subject to their jurisdiction under section 6805 of this title." 15 U.S.C. § 6804(a)(1). The cited section, 6805, outlines the institutions and persons subject to the jurisdiction of "Federal functional regulators," and in section 6805(a)(7) assigns enforcement "[u]nder the Federal Trade Commission Act . . . [to] the Federal Trade Commission for any other financial institution or other person that is not subject to the jurisdiction of any agency or authority under" the preceding paragraphs of the subsection. The definitional section of the statute, section 6809, defines "financial institution" as "any institution the business of which is engaging in financial activities as described in section 1843(k) of Title 12." Id. § 6809(3)(A). Other subsections of section 6809 create exceptions and modifications to the general definition of "financial institution." See id. § 6809(3)(B)-(D).

Title 12 U.S.C. § 1843(k), referenced in section 6809(a), is a part of the Bank Holding Company Act of 1956, Pub.L. No. 109-41, 70 Stat. 133 (codified as amended at 12 U.S.C. §§ 1971–1978, 1841–1850) ("BHCA"). The BHCA, in section 1843, limits the ability of the bank holding companies regulated under that statutory scheme to hold interests in nonbanking organizations. Specifically, section 1843(a) provides that

[e]xcept as otherwise provided in this chapter, no bank holding company shall . . . retain direct or indirect ownership or control of any voting shares of any company which is not a bank or bank holding company or engage in any activities other than (A) those of banking or of managing or controlling banks and other subsidiaries authorized under this chapter or of furnishing services to or performing services for its subsidiaries, and (B) those permitted under [other subsections of the statute].12 U.S.C. § 1843(a). However, section 1843(k) limits the effect of the general prohibition created by section 1843(a) by providing that

[n]otwithstanding subsection (a) of this section, a financial holding company may engage in any activity, and may acquire and retain the shares of any company engaged in any activity, that the [Federal Reserve] Board . . . determines (by regulation or order)-(A) to be financial in nature or incidental to such financial activity; or (B) is complementary to a financial activity and does not pose a substantial risk to the safety or soundness of depository institutions or the financial system generally.

Id. *§ 1843(k)(1).*

The BHCA declares to be financial in nature activities listed in section 1843(k)(4), to wit:

(A) Lending, exchanging, transferring, investing for others, or safeguarding money or securities.

(B) Insuring, guaranteeing, or indemnifying against loss, harm, damage, illness, disability, or death, or providing and issuing annuities, and acting as principal, agent, or broker for purposes of the foregoing, in any State.

(C) Providing financial, investment, or economic advisory services, including

advising an investment company (as defined in [section 80a-3 of Title 15]).

(D) Issuing or selling instruments representing interests in pools of assets permissible for a bank to hold directly.

(E) Underwriting, dealing in, or making a market in securities.

Id. *§ 1843(k)(4).*

Following the list of activities that "shall be considered" financial in nature, the BHCA enacted the following category of activity, which is most pertinent to the current case:

(F) Engaging in any activity that the Board has determined, by order or regulation that is in effect on November 12, 1999, to be so closely related to banking or managing or controlling banks as to be a proper incident thereto (subject to the same terms and conditions contained in such order or regulation, unless modified by the [Federal Reserve] Board).

The phrase "order or regulation that is in effect on November 12, 1999" adopts a Federal Reserve Board ("Board") regulation published at 12 C.F.R. § 225.28 (2000), commonly known as Regulation Y. Regulation Y, as is to be expected, deals with the subject matter of section 1843(k), that is, "nonbanking activities and acquisitions by bank holding companies": It lists "permissible nonbanking activities." That list is described in the regulation as activities that are

(a) Closely related nonbanking activities. The activities listed in paragraph (b) of this section are so closely related to banking or managing or controlling banks as to be a proper incident thereto, and may be engaged in by a bank holding company or its subsidiary in accordance with the requirements of this regulation.

12 C.F.R. § 225.28(a). We set forth the entire text of the relevant subsection in the footnote below[5] not because it is all in itself relevant, but in order to demonstrate the depths plumbed by the Commission in order to find authority to undertake the regulation of the practice of law, which we will discuss further, infra.[5]

---

[5] The original footnote from the case reads:

In paragraph (b), referenced above, Regulation Y sets forth the following list:

(1) Extending credit and servicing loans. Making, acquiring, brokering, or servicing loans or other extensions of credit (including factoring, issuing letters of credit and accepting drafts) for the company's account or for the account of others.

(2) Activities related to extending credit. Any activity usual in connection with making, acquiring, brokering or servicing loans or other extensions of credit, as determined by the Board. The Board has determined that the following activities are usual in connection with making, acquiring, brokering, or servicing loans or other extensions of credit:

(i) Real estate and personal property appraising. Performing appraisals of real estate and tangible and intangible personal property, including securities.

(ii) Arranging commercial real estate equity financing. Acting as intermediary for the financing of commercial or industrial income-producing real estate by arranging for the transfer of the title, control, and risk of such a real estate project to one or more investors, if the bank holding company and its affiliates do not have an interest in, or participate in managing or developing, a real estate project for which it arranges equity financing, and do not promote or sponsor the development of the property.

(iii) Check-guaranty services. Authorizing a subscribing merchant to accept personal checks tendered by the merchant's customers in payment for goods and services, and purchasing from the merchant validly authorized checks that are subsequently dishonored.

(iv) Collection agency services. Collecting overdue accounts receivable, either retail or commercial.

(v) Credit bureau services. Maintaining information related to the credit history of consumers and providing the information to a credit grantor who is considering a borrower's application for credit or who has extended credit to the borrower.

(vi) Asset management, servicing, and collection activities. Engaging under contract with a third party in asset management, servicing, and collection of assets of a type that an insured depository institution may originate and own, if the company does not engage in real property management or real estate brokerage services as part of these services.

(vii) Acquiring debt in default. Acquiring debt that is in default at the time of acquisition, if the company:

(A) Divests shares or assets securing debt in default that are not permissible investments for bank holding companies, within the time period required for divestiture of property acquired in satisfaction of a debt previously contracted under § 225.12(b);

(B) Stands only in the position of a creditor and does not purchase equity of obligors of debt in default (other than equity that may be collateral for such debt); and

(C) Does not acquire debt in default secured by shares of a bank or bank holding company.

(viii) Real estate settlement servicing. Providing real estate settlement services.

(3) Leasing personal or real property. Leasing personal or real property or acting as agent, broker, or adviser in leasing such property if:

(i) The lease is on a nonoperating basis;

(ii) The initial term of the lease is at least 90 days;

(iii) In the case of leases involving real property:

(A) At the inception of the initial lease, the effect of the transaction will yield a return that will compensate the lessor for not less than the lessor's full investment in the property plus the estimated total cost of financing the property over the term of the lease from rental payments, estimated tax benefits, and the estimated residual value of the property at the expiration of the initial lease; and

(B) The estimated residual value of property for purposes of paragraph (b)(3)(iii)(A) of this section shall not exceed 25 percent of the acquisition cost of the property to the lessor.

(4) Operating nonbank depository institutions —

(i) Industrial banking. Owning, controlling, or operating an industrial bank, Morris Plan bank, or industrial loan company, so long as the institution is not a bank.

(ii) Operating savings association. Owning, controlling, or operating a savings association, if the savings association engages only in deposit-taking activities, lending, and other activities that are permissible for bank holding companies under this subpart C.

(5) Trust company functions. Performing functions or activities that may be performed by a trust company (including activities of a fiduciary, agency, or custodial nature), in the manner authorized by federal or state law, so long as the company is not a bank for purposes of section 2(c) of the Bank Holding Company Act.

(6) Financial and investment advisory activities. Acting as investment or financial advisor to any person, including (without, in any way, limiting the foregoing):

(i) Serving as investment adviser (as defined in section 2(a)(20) of the Investment Company Act of 1940, 15 U.S.C. 80a-2(a)(20)), to an investment company registered under that act, including sponsoring, organizing, and managing a closed-end investment company;

(ii) Furnishing general economic information and advice, general economic statistical forecasting services, and industry studies;

(iii) Providing advice in connection with mergers, acquisitions, divestitures, investments, joint ventures, leveraged buyouts, recapitalizations, capital structurings, financing transactions and similar transactions, and conducting financial feasibility studies;

(iv) Providing information, statistical forecasting, and advice with respect to any transaction in foreign exchange, swaps, and similar transactions, commodities, and any forward contract, option, future, option on a future, and similar instruments;

(v) Providing educational courses, and instructional materials to consumers on individual financial management matters; and

(vi) Providing tax-planning and tax-preparation services to any person.

(7) Agency transactional services for customer investments —

(i) Securities brokerage. Providing securities brokerage services (including securities clearing and/or securities execution services on an exchange), whether alone or in combination with investment advisory services, and incidental activities (including related securities credit activities and custodial services), if the securities brokerage services are restricted to buying and selling securities solely as agent for the account of customers and do not include securities underwriting or dealing.

(ii) Riskless principal transactions. Buying and selling in the secondary market all types of securities on the order of customers as a "riskless principal" to the extent of engaging in a transaction in which the company, after receiving an order to buy (or sell) a security from a customer, purchases (or sells) the security for its own account to offset a contemporaneous sale to (or purchase from) the customer. This does not include:

(A) Selling bank-ineligible securities at the order of a customer that is the issuer of the securities, or selling bank-ineligible securities in any transaction where the company has a contractual agreement to place the securities as agent of the issuer; or

(B) Acting as a riskless principal in any transaction involving a bank-ineligible security for which the company or any of its affiliates acts as underwriter (during the period of the underwriting or for 30 days thereafter) or dealer.

(iii) Private placement services. Acting as agent for the private placement of securities in accordance with the requirements of the Securities Act of 1933 (1933 Act) and the rules of the Securities and Exchange Commission, if the company engaged in the activity does not purchase or repurchase for its own account the securities being placed, or hold in inventory unsold portions of issues of these securities.

(iv) Futures commission merchant. Acting as a futures commission merchant (FCM) for unaffiliated persons in the execution, clearance, or execution and clearance of any futures contract and option on a futures contract traded on an exchange in the United States or abroad if:

(A) The activity is conducted through a separately incorporated subsidiary of the bank holding company, which may engage in activities other than FCM activities (including, but not limited to, permissible advisory and trading activities); and

(B) The parent bank holding company does not provide a guarantee or otherwise become liable to the exchange or clearing association other than for those trades conducted by the subsidiary for its own account or for the account of any affiliate.

(v) Other transactional services. Providing to customers as agent transactional services with respect to swaps and similar transactions, any transaction described in paragraph (b)(8) of this section, any transaction that is permissible for a state member bank, and any other transaction involving a forward contract, option, futures, option on a futures or similar contract (whether traded on an exchange or not) relating to a commodity that is traded on an exchange.

(8) Investment transactions as principal —

(i) Underwriting and dealing in government obligations and money market instruments. Underwriting and dealing in obligations of the United States, general obligations of states and their political subdivisions, and other obligations that state member banks of the Federal Reserve System may be authorized to underwrite and deal in under 12 U.S.C. 24 and 335, including banker's acceptances and certificates of deposit, under the same limitations as would be applicable if the activity were performed by the bank holding company's subsidiary member banks or its subsidiary nonmember banks as if they were member banks.

(ii) Investing and trading activities. Engaging as principal in:

(A) Foreign exchange;

(B) Forward contracts, options, futures, options on futures, swaps, and similar contracts, whether traded on exchanges or not, based on any rate, price, financial asset (including gold, silver, platinum, palladium, copper, or any other metal approved by the Board), nonfinancial asset, or group of assets, other than a bank-ineligible security, if:

(1) A state member bank is authorized to invest in the asset underlying the contract;

(2) The contract requires cash settlement; or

(3) The contract allows for assignment, termination, or offset prior to delivery or expiration, and the company makes every reasonable effort to avoid taking or making delivery; and

(C) Forward contracts, options, futures, options on futures, swaps, and similar contracts, whether traded on exchanges or not, based on an index of a rate, a price, or the value of any financial asset, nonfinancial asset, or group of assets, if the contract requires cash settlement.

(iii) Buying and selling bullion, and related activities. Buying, selling and storing bars, rounds, bullion, and coins of gold, silver, platinum, palladium, copper, and any other metal approved by the Board, for the company's own account and the account of others, and providing incidental services such as arranging for storage, safe custody, assaying, and shipment.

(9) Management consulting and counseling activities —

(i) Management consulting.

(A) Providing management consulting advice:

(1) On any matter to unaffiliated depository institutions, including commercial banks, savings and loan associations, savings banks, credit unions, industrial banks, Morris Plan banks, cooperative banks, industrial loan companies, trust companies, and branches or agencies of foreign banks;

(2) On any financial, economic, accounting, or audit matter to any other company.

(B) A company conducting management consulting activities under this subparagraph and any affiliate of such company may not:

(1) Own or control, directly or indirectly, more than 5 percent of the voting securities of the client institution; and

(2) Allow a management official, as defined in 12 CFR 212.2(h), of the company or any of its affiliates to serve as a management official of the client institution, except where such interlocking relationship is permitted pursuant to an exemption granted under 12 CFR 212.4(b) or otherwise permitted by the Board.

(C) A company conducting management consulting activities may provide management consulting services to customers not described in paragraph (b)(9)(i)(A)(1) of this section or regarding matters not described in paragraph (b)(9)(i)(A)(2) of this section, if the total annual revenue derived from those management consulting services does not exceed 30 percent of the company's total annual revenue derived from management consulting activities.

(ii) Employee benefits consulting services. Providing consulting services to employee benefit, compensation and insurance plans, including designing plans, assisting in the implementation of plans, providing administrative services to plans, and developing employee communication programs for plans.

(iii) Career counseling services. Providing career counseling services to:

(A) A financial organization and individuals currently employed by, or recently displaced from, a financial organization;

(B) Individuals who are seeking employment at a financial organization; and

(C) Individuals who are currently employed in or who seek positions in the finance, accounting, and audit departments of any company.

(10) Support services —

(i) Courier services. Providing courier services for:

(A) Checks, commercial papers, documents, and written instruments (excluding currency or bearer-type negotiable instruments) that are exchanged among banks and financial institutions; and

(B) Audit and accounting media of a banking or financial nature and other business records and documents used in processing such media.

(ii) Printing and selling MICR-encoded items. Printing and selling checks and related documents, including corporate image checks, cash tickets, voucher checks, deposit slips, savings withdrawal packages, and other forms that require Magnetic Ink Character Recognition (MICR) encoding.

(11) Insurance agency and underwriting —

(i) Credit insurance. Acting as principal, agent, or broker for insurance (including home mortgage redemption insurance) that is:

(A) Directly related to an extension of credit by the bank holding company or any of its subsidiaries; and

(B) Limited to ensuring the repayment of the outstanding balance due on the extension of credit in the event of the death, disability, or involuntary unemployment of the debtor.

(ii) Finance company subsidiary. Acting as agent or broker for insurance directly related to an extension of credit by a finance company that is a subsidiary of a bank holding company, if:

(A) The insurance is limited to ensuring repayment of the outstanding balance on such extension of credit in the event of loss or damage to any property used as collateral for the extension of credit; and

(B) The extension of credit is not more than $10,000, or $25,000 if it is to finance the purchase of a residential manufactured home and the credit is secured by the home; and

(C) The applicant commits to notify borrowers in writing that:

(1) They are not required to purchase such insurance from the applicant;

(2) Such insurance does not insure any interest of the borrower in the collateral; and

(3) The applicant will accept more comprehensive property insurance in place of such single-interest insurance.

(iii) Insurance in small towns. Engaging in any insurance agency activity in a place where the bank holding company or a subsidiary of the bank holding company has a lending office and that:

(A) Has a population not exceeding 5,000 (as shown in the preceding decennial census); or

(B) Has inadequate insurance agency facilities, as determined by the Board, after notice and opportunity for hearing.

(iv) Insurance-agency activities conducted on May 1, 1982. Engaging in any specific insurance-agency activity if the bank holding company, or subsidiary conducting the specific activity, conducted such activity on May 1, 1982, or received Board approval to conduct such activity on or before May 1, 1982. A bank holding company or subsidiary engaging in a specific insurance agency activity under this clause may:

(A) Engage in such specific insurance agency activity only at locations:

(1) In the state in which the bank holding company has its principal place of business (as defined in 12 U.S.C. 1842(d));

(2) In any state or states immediately adjacent to such state; and

(3) In any state in which the specific insurance-agency activity was conducted (or was approved to be conducted) by such bank holding company or subsidiary thereof or by any other subsidiary of such bank holding company on May 1, 1982; and

(B) Provide other insurance coverages that may become available after May 1, 1982, so long as those coverages insure against the types of risks as (or are otherwise functionally equivalent to) coverages sold or approved to be sold on May 1, 1982, by the bank holding company or subsidiary.

(v) Supervision of retail insurance agents. Supervising on behalf of insurance underwriters the activities of retail insurance agents who sell:

(A) Fidelity insurance and property and casualty insurance on the real and personal property used in the operations of the bank holding company or its subsidiaries; and

(B) Group insurance that protects the employees of the bank holding company or its subsidiaries.

(vi) Small bank holding companies. Engaging in any insurance-agency activity if the bank holding company has total consolidated assets of $50 million or less. A bank holding company performing insurance-agency activities under this paragraph may not engage in the sale of life insurance or annuities except as provided in paragraphs (b)(11)(i) and (iii) of this section, and it may not continue to engage in insurance-agency activities pursuant to this provision more than 90

To recapitulate: The GLBA contains extensive privacy protection provisions that apply to "financial institutions." In section 6809, the Act defines "financial institution" as "any institution the business of which is engaging in financial activities as described in section 1843(k) of Title 12." The referenced section of Title 12 is contained in the BHCA. Specifically, that section identifies institutions engaged in nonbanking activities that are financial in nature, such that bank holding companies may retain ownership interests in institutions engaged in their pursuit. The section of the BHCA defining those activities incorporates by reference Regulation Y, which offers an extensive list of examples of such "financial activities" so closely related to banking as to be permissible.

B. The Commission's Interpretation

Upon the passage of the Act, the FTC, pursuant to the authority granted it in 15 U.S.C. § 6805(a)(7), undertook a rulemaking. In May 2000, the FTC concluded the rulemaking and issued regulations published at 65 Fed.Reg. 33,646 (codified at 16 C.F.R. pt. 313). Although the FTC relied in the first instance on Congress's definition of "financial institution" as "an institution the business of which is engaging in financial activities," the Commission restated the definition: "An institution that is

---

days after the end of the quarterly reporting period in which total assets of the holding company and its subsidiaries exceed $50 million.

(vii) Insurance-agency activities conducted before 1971. Engaging in any insurance-agency activity performed at any location in the United States directly or indirectly by a bank holding company that was engaged in insurance-agency activities prior to January 1, 1971, as a consequence of approval by the Board prior to January 1, 1971.

(12) Community development activities —

(i) Financing and investment activities. Making equity and debt investments in corporations or projects designed primarily to promote community welfare, such as the economic rehabilitation and development of low-income areas by providing housing, services, or jobs for residents.

(ii) Advisory activities. Providing advisory and related services for programs designed primarily to promote community welfare.

(13) Money orders, savings bonds, and traveler's checks. The issuance and sale at retail of money orders and similar consumer-type payment instruments; the sale of U.S. savings bonds; and the issuance and sale of traveler's checks.

(14) Data processing.

(i) Providing data processing and data transmission services, facilities (including data processing and data transmission hardware, software, documentation, or operating personnel), data bases, advice, and access to such services, facilities, or data bases by any technological means, if:

(A) The data to be processed or furnished are financial, banking, or economic; and

(B) The hardware provided in connection therewith is offered only in conjunction with software designed and marketed for the processing and transmission of financial, banking, or economic data, and where the general purpose hardware does not constitute more than 30 percent of the cost of any packaged offering.

(ii) A company conducting data processing and data transmission activities may conduct data processing and data transmission activities not described in paragraph (b)(14)(i) of this section if the total annual revenue derived from those activities does not exceed 30 percent of the company's total annual revenues derived from data processing and data transmission activities.

Id. § 225.28(b) (footnotes omitted).

Id. at 464.

significantly engaged in financial activities is a financial institution." 16 C.F.R. § 313.3(k)(1).

Like the statute, the regulations at no point describe the statutory or regulatory scheme as governing the practice of law as such. Indeed, the phrase "practice of law" never appears in part 313, and the word "attorneys," while present in two places, appears in the context of describing persons to whom financial institutions can make release of customer information, if authorized, not in the context of defining "financial institutions" as including attorneys. Nonetheless, the breadth of the FTC's regulation, apparently taken in conjunction with statements to or by news media, caused concern among representatives of the bar. Therefore, various bar associations, including the American Bar Association, made inquiry of the Commission as to whether the Commission was taking a position that privacy provisions of the GLBA and the regulations made pursuant thereto governed attorneys engaged in the practice of law.

On April 8, 2002, the Director of the Bureau of Consumer Protection at the Commission sent a letter to the President and the Director of Governmental Affairs of the ABA "in response to your correspondence regarding the application of Title V, Subtitle A, of the Gramm-Leach-Bliley Act, 15 U.S.C. 6801 et seq . . . . and the Federal Trade Commission's Rule, Privacy of Consumer Financial Information . . . to attorneys at law." (Citations omitted.) As part of the inquiry, the ABA had also requested exemption from the Act if the Commission purported to regulate the practice of law under the Act. That position has been abandoned by the bar associations during the course of this litigation, but was still a live question between the parties at the time of the FTC's communication to the ABA. Although recognizing that the bar associations' letters had "question[ed] the appropriateness and utility of applying the GLB Act's privacy provisions to attorneys engaged in the practice of law," the Director only directly addressed the ABA's request for exemption. However, in rejecting that request, the Director made it plain that the Commission was purporting to regulate attorneys engaged in the practice of their profession and asserted that "the GLB Act itself states that entities *engaged in 'financial activities' are subject to the Act." (emphasis supplied).*

After some further negotiation, the bar associations brought the present litigation.

II. The Litigation

The New York State Bar Association and the American Bar Association separately filed actions for declaratory judgment. While the prayers for relief in the two complaints are differently worded, the gist is the same, in that each seeks, inter alia, *a declaratory order that, in the words of the ABA complaint:*

(a) Congress did not in the GLBA confer authority on the FTC to regulate the confidentiality, privacy and security of information disclosed by clients to their attorneys;

(b) The FTC's decision that attorneys engaged in the practice of law are covered by the GLBA is unlawful and hereby set aside; . . . .

Although the district judge never formally ordered the two actions consolidated, he dealt with them together and ultimately disposed of them in a single opinion and order. The FTC moved to dismiss the actions under Federal Rule of Civil Procedure 12(b)(6), on the theory that the complaints failed to state a claim for relief. The District Court denied the motion. N.Y. State Bar Ass'n v. FTC, 276 F.Supp.2d 110 (D.D.C.2003). *In that opinion, the court reasoned that Congress did not intend GLBA's privacy provisions to apply to attorneys. Further, the court reasoned, even if the GLBA were ambiguous on that point, the court should not defer to the FTC's interpretation applying the Act to attorneys because the interpretation was not the product of notice and comment rulemaking, did not appear to have been made with any degree of deliberation, and was supported only by* post hoc *rationalization. The court held that the Commission's attempt to regulate attorneys under the privacy provisions of the GLBA was not only inconsistent with the statute, but also arbitrary and capricious in violation of the Administrative Procedure Act.*

After the denial of the motion to dismiss, the parties proceeded with cross-motions for summary judgment. The District Court found no genuine issues as to any material fact and, incorporating its earlier decision on the motion to dismiss, again held that Congress in 5 U.S.C. § 706(2)(C) did not intend the GLBA's privacy provisions to apply to attorneys engaged in the practice of law.

The current appeal followed.

III. Analysis

As we analyze the FTC's arguments for the proposition that Congress in the privacy provisions of the GLBA enabled the Commission to regulate the practice of law, we are reminded repeatedly of a recent admonition from the Supreme Court: "[Congress] does not . . . hide elephants in mouseholes." Whitman v. Am. Trucking Ass'ns, 531 U.S. 457, 468, 121 S.Ct. 903, 149 L.Ed.2d 1 (2001). *The FTC begins its defense of its attempted turf expansion in the correct place, that is, by recognizing that "the starting point in any case involving the meaning of a statute[ ] is the language of the statute itself."* Group Life & Health Ins. Co. v. Royal Drug Co., 440 U.S. 205, 210, 99 S.Ct. 1067, 59 L.Ed.2d 261 (1979). *The Commission argues, as it did before the District Court, that the language of the statute evidences a congressional intent to empower the Commission to regulate attorneys engaged in certain types of law practice as "financial institutions" under the privacy regulations promulgated pursuant to the GLBA privacy provisions. More specifically, the Commission notes that the legislation defines "financial institution" quite broadly as "any institution the business of which is engaging in financial activities as described in section 1843(k) of Title 12." The statute in turn deems as "financial in nature" various listed activities, together with those not expressly listed but theretofore listed by the Federal Reserve Board in Regulation Y. Regulation Y, set forth at its staggering full-length above, includes the activities "[p]roviding real estate settlement services," and "[p]roviding tax-planning and tax-preparation services to any person." 12 C.F.R. § 225.28(b)(2)(viii), (b)(6)(vi) (2001). The Commission then asserts, "[t]hus, under the terms of the statute, any institution that is in the business of engaging in a financial activity listed in section 4(k) of the BHCA, including those set forth in Regulation Y, qualifies as a 'financial institution.'* " *Appellant's Brief at 16. That statement by the Commission is unassailable: Indeed, it does no more than restate the provisions of that statute. That is precisely the problem. The Commission's reasoning, doing no more than restating the statute, leaves as open as ever the question of whether an attorney practicing law is an "institution engaging in the business of financial activities."*

    The statute certainly does not so plainly grant the Commission the authority to regulate attorneys engaged in the practice of law as to entitle the Commission to what is called a "Chevron One" disposition. That is, rather simply we cannot hold that Congress has directly and plainly granted the Commission the authority to regulate practicing attorneys as the Commission attempts. See Chevron U.S.A. Inc. v. Natural Res. Def. Council, Inc., *467 U.S. 837, 842–43, 104 S.Ct. 2778, 81 L.Ed.2d 694 (1984). Indeed, such professionals are subject to regulation under the words of the statute only if they are "institutions" and if they are "engaged in the business of financial activity." It is not plain at all to us that Congress has entered such a direct regulatory command by plain language of a statute, a lengthy statute incorporated by reference, and an even more lengthy and detailed regulation incorporated by reference in the second statute, none of which ever mentioned attorneys engaged in the practice of law. Therefore, if the Commission is to prevail, it must do so under a deferential standard of review. That is, to uphold the Commission's regulatory decision, we must conclude first that the words of the statute are ambiguous in such a way as to make the Commission's decision worthy of deference under the second step of* Chevron. *Id. at 843, 104 S.Ct. 2778. If we so hold, we will then uphold the agency's interpretation of the ambiguous statute if that interpretation is "permissible," that is, if it is "reasonable."* Id. *at 845, 104 S.Ct. 2778.*

A. Chevron *Step One*

    The first question, whether there is such an ambiguity, is for the court, and we owe the agency no deference on the existence of ambiguity. Deference to the agency's interpretation under Chevron *is warranted only where "Congress has left a gap for the agency to fill pursuant to an express or implied 'delegation of authority to the agency.'* " *Ry. Labor Exec. Ass'n v. Nat'l Mediation Bd., 29 F.3d 655, 671 (D.C.Cir.1994) (en banc) (internal citation omitted). The Commission argues along the line suggested by the scant reasoning in the letter announcing its decision. The opinion letter had directed its language principally toward the question of whether the Commission should "exempt attorneys at law from the application of the Privacy Rule." True, the Bar Association had requested such an exemption, but only as a conditional request if the Commission held in the first instance that the privacy provisions of the GLBA covered attorneys engaged in the practice of law, a proposition that the association resisted. The Commission's letter, while claiming that "[w]e have carefully considered your concerns, and recognize the issues you have raised regarding the application of the GLB Act to attorneys at law," addressed only the "significant questions as to the legal authority of the Commission to grant the exemption you request."*

    The Commission apparently assumed-without reasoning-that it could extend its regulatory authority over attorneys engaged in the practice of law with no other basis than the observation that the Act did not provide for an exemption. Before the District Court and before us, the Commission has persisted in this style of reasoning. While there is limited post hoc *rationalization in the Commission's brief addressing the inclusion of attorneys in the definition of "financial institution," which we will discuss* infra, *the Commission repeatedly repairs to the position that no language in the statute exempts attorneys from regulation. That is not the question. As we have often cautioned, "[t]o suggest, as the [Commission] effectively does, that* Chevron *step two is implicated any time a statute does not expressly* negate *the existence of a claimed administrative power . . . is both flatly unfaithful to the principles of administrative law . . . and refuted by precedent."* Ry. Labor Exec. Ass'n, *29 F.3d at 671 (emphasis in original). Plainly, if we were "to* presume *a delegation of power" from the absence of "an express* withholding *of such power, agencies would enjoy virtually limitless hegemony . . . ."* Id. *(emphasis in original). Therefore, if there is the sort of ambiguity that supports an implicit congressional delegation of authority to the agency to make a deference-worthy interpretation of the statute, we must look elsewhere than the failure to negate regulation of attorneys. That failure does not advance the Commission's cause at all. Otherwise put, the question is not whether the statute permits exemption from regulation for attorneys, but whether it supports such regulation at all. We will defer to the agency's interpretation on that subject only if the statute "is silent or ambiguous with respect to the specific issue."* Barnhart v. Walton, *535 U.S. 212, 218, 122 S.Ct. 1265, 152 L.Ed.2d 330 (2002) (internal quotation marks and citation omitted).*

We further recognize that the existence of ambiguity is not enough per se to warrant deference to the agency's interpretation. The ambiguity must be such as to make it appear that Congress either explicitly or implicitly delegated authority to cure that ambiguity. "Mere ambiguity in a statute is not evidence of congressional delegation of authority." Michigan v. EPA, *268 F.3d 1075, 1082 (D.C.Cir.2001) (citations omitted). The deference mandated in* Chevron *"comes into play, of course, only as a consequence of statutory ambiguity, and then only if the reviewing court finds an implicit delegation of authority to the agency."* Sea-Land Serv., Inc. v. Dep't of Transp., *137 F.3d 640, 645 (D.C.Cir.1998) (emphasis added). When we examine a scheme of the length, detail, and intricacy of the one before us, we find it difficult to believe that Congress, by any remaining ambiguity, intended to undertake the regulation of the profession of law-a profession never before regulated by "federal functional regulators" — and never mentioned in the statute. To find this interpretation deference-worthy, we would have to conclude that Congress not only had hidden a rather large elephant in a rather obscure mousehole, but had buried the ambiguity in which the pachyderm lurks beneath an incredibly deep mound of specificity, none of which bears the footprints of the beast or any indication that Congress even suspected its presence. We therefore seriously doubt that Congress intended to empower the Commission to undertake that regulation, and we are reluctant to even afford the regulation the deference due agency action that survives the analysis at the first step of* Chevron. See FDA v. Brown & Williamson Tobacco Corp., *529 U.S. 120, 160–61, 120 S.Ct. 1291, 146 L.Ed.2d 121 (2000).*

By way of comparison, in California Independent System Operator Corp. v.

FERC, *372 F.3d 395 (D.C.Cir.2004)* (*"CAISO"*), *we reviewed an order of the Federal Energy Regulatory Commission ("FERC") purporting to replace the governing board of a nonprofit, "public benefit" corporation created by the State of California pursuant to statutes of that state. FERC claimed* Chevron *deference for its action, pointing specifically to the language of 16 U.S.C. § 824e(a), which empowered FERC, upon a finding that "any rule, regulation, practice, or contract affecting [a] rate, charge, or classification is unjust, unreasonable, unduly discriminatory or preferential," to "determine the just and reasonable rate, charge, classification, rule, regulation, practice, or contract to be thereafter observed and in force . . . ." FERC construed the word "practice" to be sufficiently ambiguous to allow it, under the deferential formula of* Chevron, *to set aside and replace the state-imposed method for selecting the corporation's board.*

On review, we noted that the sort of ambiguity giving rise to Chevron *deference " 'is a creature not of definitional possibilities, but of statutory context.' " 372 F.3d at 400 (quoting* Brown v. Gardner, *513 U.S. 115, 118, 115 S.Ct. 552, 130 L.Ed.2d 462 (1994)). In granting review and setting aside the FERC order, we concluded,* inter alia, *that the intent of Congress in the statutory section before us was "actually quite plain: the grant of authority to regulate rates, charges, classifications, and closely related matters." Id. We further concluded that it was "quite a leap to move" from the context of transactional terms used in the statute to an implication that, by the ambiguity inherent in the word "practice," Congress intended to grant to the Commission not merely the power "to effect a reformation of some 'practice' in a more traditional sense," but also "to reform completely the governing structure of the utility . . . ." Id.*

We further held that such an extraordinary construction of "practice" in such a discrete regulatory context was a "sufficiently poor fit with the apparent meaning of the statute that the statute is not ambiguous on the very question before us," as would be necessary to afford Chevron *deference at the first step of the two-step inquiry. Id. at 401.*

We were instructed in our CAISO reasoning by the Supreme Court's decision in Brown v. Gardner, *513 U.S. 115, 115 S.Ct. 552, 130 L.Ed.2d 462 (1994). In* Gardner, *the Court considered an interpretation by the Veterans Administration of statutory language requiring the VA to compensate for "an injury, or an aggravation of an injury," that occurs "as a result of" VA treatment. 38 U.S.C. § 1151(a) (1994) (amended 1996). The Veterans Administration, in 38 C.F.R. § 3.358(c)(3), interpreted the compensation requirement as covering an injury only if it resulted from negligent treatment by the VA or an accident occurring during treatment. The lower courts held that the statute imposed no such fault-or-accident requirement and found the regulation invalid. The Supreme Court affirmed and, in language followed by us in* CAISO, *noted the "poor fit of this language with any implicit requirement of VA fault . . . ." 513 U.S. at 120, 115 S.Ct. 552. We find a similarly poor fit between the statutory language and the Commission's interpretation in this case.*

Lest it be forgotten, the basic language in which the Commission finds the ambiguity permitting it to regulate the practice of law is that of § 6805 empowering the Federal Trade Commission and other "federal functional regulators" to enforce the statute and regulations prescribed under it with respect to "financial institutions and

*other persons subject to [the Commission's] jurisdiction . . . ." 15 U.S.C. § 6805(a).
That language, even with-perhaps especially with-the layers of incorporated statutory
and regulatory language describing financial institutions makes an exceptionally
poor fit with the FTC's apparent decision that Congress, after centuries of not doing
so, has suddenly decided to regulate the practice of law. This fit is helped but little, if
at all, by the congressional definition of "financial institution" as "an institution the
business of which is engaging in financial activity." 15 U.S.C. § 6809(3)(A). An
attorney, or even a law firm, does not fit very neatly into the niche of a "financial
institution." Even if one concedes-and it is quite a concession-that Congress would
have intended the word "institution" to include an attorney, or even a law firm, it still
requires quite a stretch to conclude that such an institution is a "financial institution." It trims the stretch little, if at all, to read the entire statutory definition of
"financial institution" as "any institution the business of which is engaging in
financial activities as described in section 1843(k) of Title 12" (set forth above).
Without reiterating the language of the incorporated statute, attorneys and law firms,
even if viewed as "institutions," are not institutions "the business of which is engaging
in financial activities," as defined in the statute. The Commission itself seems to
recognize the improbability of Congress's having intended to include law firms within
the designation "institutions" in the letter under review, in which it conspicuously
substituted the word "entities" for "institutions." Such a dramatic rewriting of the
statute is not mere interpretation. Even if we accept the inclusion of "entities" such
as law firms within the meaning of "institutions," the "business" of a law firm (if the
practice of a profession is properly viewed as business is the practice of the profession
of law.*

*The Commission distorts the definition slightly but improves the fit but little by its
regulatory definition that a financial institution is "an institution that is significantly engaged in financial activities," as opposed to requiring that the institution
must be one the business of which is engaging in financial activities. Building on this
stretch, the Commission, in its brief, supplies reasoning conspicuously lacking from
the letter of determination that we review. Although we cannot affirm an agency's
actions based on the* post hoc *rationale of its litigating position, see, e.g., Motor
Vehicle Mfrs. Ass'n v. State Farm Mut. Auto. Insurance Co., 463 U.S. 29, 50, 103 S.Ct.
2856, 77 L.Ed.2d 443 (1983), even if we charitably construe the letter to imply the
reasoning, it is still inadequate.*

*The reasoning in the brief relies on the language of Regulation Y, the second tier
incorporation. As noted above, Regulation Y, in its original application, described the
"closely related nonbanking activities" in which a bank holding company or its
subsidiaries might engage. Within that voluminous listing, the regulation included
two activities, "[p]roviding real estate settlement services," and "[p]roviding tax-
planning and tax-preparation services," in which attorneys sometimes, and apparently in the view of the Commission, significantly engage. See 16 C.F.R. § 313.3(k)(1).
Again, if Congress intended to empower a federal financial regulator to undertake
regulation of the practice of law, this seems a strangely unclear method of doing so.
The statute after all defined a "financial institution" as "an institution the business
of which is engaging in financial activities." Congress did not adopt the approach of
the Commission by covering "an institution that is significantly engaged in financial*

activities." Certainly it did not extend that definition to cover all "entities." In sum, Congress did not leave an ambiguity on the question before us that is, the power of the Commission to regulate the practice of law-sufficient to compel deference to the Commission's determination to do so. We further determine that even if we err in our conclusion that the regulation fails at Chevron Step One, *we are satisfied that the interpretation afforded by the Commission is not sufficiently reasonable to survive that deference at Step Two.*

B. Chevron *Step Two*

All the reasons set forth above for our determination that Congress did not intend to leave sufficient ambiguity to support deferential review return to convince us that the interpretation is not reasonable even if we afford it deference. But our analysis under Chevron Step Two *need not end there. It is undisputed that the regulation of the practice of law is traditionally the province of the states. Federal law "may not be interpreted to reach into areas of State sovereignty unless the language of the federal law compels the intrusion."* City of Abilene v. FCC, *164 F.3d 49, 52 (D.C.Cir.1999). Otherwise put, "if Congress intends to alter the 'usual constitutional balance between the States and the Federal Government,' it must make its intention to do so 'unmistakably clear in the language of the statute.'"* Will v. Michigan Dep't of State Police, *491 U.S. 58, 65, 109 S.Ct. 2304, 105 L.Ed.2d 45 (1989) (quoting* Atascadero State Hospital v. Scanlon, *473 U.S. 234, 242, 105 S.Ct. 3142, 87 L.Ed.2d 171 (1985)). By now it should be abundantly plain that Congress has not made an intention to regulate the practice of law "unmistakably clear" in the language of the GLBA. In* Gregory v. Ashcroft, *501 U.S. 452, 111 S.Ct. 2395, 115 L.Ed.2d 410 (1991), citing,* inter alia, Will *and* Atascadero State Hospital, *the Supreme Court held that*

[t]his plain statement rule is nothing more than an acknowledgment that the States retain substantial sovereign powers under our constitutional scheme, powers with which Congress does not readily interfere.

501 U.S. at 461, 111 S.Ct. 2395.

The Commission contends that this plain statement rule of Gregory *is not applicable, arguing that* Gregory, *which concerns a determination of qualification for state officials, involved a "decision of the most fundamental sort for a sovereign entity." Id. at 460, 111 S.Ct. 2395. According to the Commission, the present regulation, "by contrast . . . regulates the conduct of private entities or individuals; there is no regulation of States or state officials." Reply Brief at 27. This response does not pass muster.* Gregory *itself quoted from* Will *the language in which the Supreme Court rejected an argument that the plain statement rule applied only in an Eleventh Amendment context. "'Atascadero was an Eleventh Amendment case, but a similar approach is applied in other contexts.'"* Gregory, *501 U.S. at 461, 111 S.Ct. 2395 (quoting* Will, *491 U.S. at 65, 109 S.Ct. 2304). We see no reason why the reasoning should not apply in the present context. The states have regulated the practice of law throughout the history of the country; the federal government has not. This is not to conclude that the federal government could not do so. We simply conclude that it is not reasonable for an agency to decide that Congress has chosen such a course of action in language that is, even charitably viewed, at most ambiguous.*

Finally, the original context of the language of Regulation Y argues against the Commission's application in the present context. That regulation sets out the "[c]losely related nonbanking activities," which "are so closely related to banking or managing or controlling banks as to be a proper incident thereto." (emphasis added). The effect of the regulation was to establish what activities "may be engaged in by a bank holding company or its subsidiary in accordance with the requirements of this regulation." Granted, banks and bank holding companies may at times engage in "providing real estate settlement services, and providing tax planning and tax preparation services." We know of no instance in which banks or bank holding companies have engaged in the practice of law. We know of no state in which state bar regulations would permit such practice. We know of no instances in which the Commission has approved a bank holding company owning a law firm as its subsidiary. We are not prepared to hold on the basis of the present record that it would be lawful for a bank or a bank holding company to do so; nonetheless, that result would seem to flow from the holding the Commission seeks to have us enter today. We cannot hold that an interpretation compelling that result is reasonable, even if the Commission's letter order survives Chevron *Step One and earns deference.*

IV. Conclusion

For the reasons set forth above, we hold that the Commission's interpretation is not entitled to Chevron *deference. We further hold that, even if we afford the interpretation deference, the Commission's interpretation is not a reasonable one. We therefore conclude and hold that the judgment appealed from is affirmed.*

Another privacy-related concern is whether a law firm must comply with the FTC's Red Flags Rule, which mandates certain practices designed to identify and reduce potential avenues of consumer information breaches that can lead to identity theft.[6] Although this regulation is intended to apply to businesses such as telecommunications companies that maintain and regularly bill customer accounts, its obligations could bind law firms as well under certain circumstances, as noted in the FTC's Frequently Asked Questions for the Rule:

> *. . . .Our clients pay a retainer before we provide services. Although we may send an invoice for our charges, we satisfy it by drawing on the retainer. Does this make us a creditor under the Red Flags Rule?*

> *No, an arrangement like that wouldn't make your business a creditor. Many businesses require a payment before work begins. For example, a law firm may require clients to pay a retainer. Some medical practices charge patients monthly fixed fees for unlimited services. They may send their clients or patients invoices each month, but draw payment from the money they've already received. The Red Flags Rule applies to businesses that regularly defer payment until* after *services have been performed. Because the law firm or medical practice in this example is paid* before *they provide services, these arrangements aren't "credit," as the law defines that word.*

---

[6] 16 C.F.R. pt. 681 (2011). The Red Flags Rule is discussed at greater length in Chapter 8.

*** My law firm brings cases on a contingency basis. Does this type of fee arrangement make me a creditor under the Red Flags Rule?*

No. Generally, under a contingency fee arrangement, a law firm will not earn its fee unless and until it wins a recovery for its client. Therefore, this arrangement is not a credit relationship, and the law firm would not be a creditor under the Red Flags Rule. If, however, the client is responsible for certain litigation expenses regardless of the outcome of the case, the firm would have to consider whether there is a deferral of payment that would meet the definition of "credit . . . ."[7]

In fact, though, attorneys' unique status within the law (a status often limited by rules passed by other attorneys) and especially the near-universal confidentiality obligations for the lawyers can lead to an unintentionally lax view of privacy that may yield more data loss than from other professions. The risks here are not so much in the use and misuse of the information by the attorneys themselves, given that lawyers generally aren't utilizing their clients' information for their own purposes. Nevertheless, there are, though, some specific situations where an attorney can misuse his clients' non-public information in violation of the law, as when corporate counsel with knowledge of client business and securities plans make illegal insider trades based upon that knowledge:

Lawyer for preeminent firms pleads guilty in $37 million insider trading scheme using information stolen from employers

Illicit Trades Ahead of More than 30 Different Corporate Transactions Over 17 Years Netted More than $37 Million in Profits

NEWARK, N.J. — A corporate lawyer who previously worked at four prominent, international law firms admitted today to participating in an insider trading scheme that lasted for 17 years, relied on information he stole from his law firms and their clients and netted more than $37 million in illicit profits, New Jersey U.S. Attorney Paul J. Fishman announced.

Matthew Kluger, 50, of Oakton, Va., pleaded guilty to all four counts charged in the Information against him: conspiracy to commit securities fraud, securities fraud, conspiracy to commit money laundering and obstruction of justice. Kluger entered his guilty plea before U.S. District Judge Katharine S. Hayden in Newark federal court.

"Not only did Matthew Kluger defraud the investing public, he betrayed the colleagues and clients who depended on his confidentiality in some of the biggest deals of the last decade," said U.S. Attorney Fishman. "In order to be confident in our markets, investors must have comfort that those with inside information won't abuse positions of trust for personal gain."

---

[7] Fighting Fraud with the Red Flags Rule, *http://www.ftc.gov/bcp/edu/microsites/redflagsrule/faqs.shtm* *(last visited May 8, 2012).*

"In this time of economic uncertainty, securities fraud remains a top investigative priority for the FBI," said Michael B. Ward, Special Agent In Charge of the Newark Division of the FBI. "Millions of investors have entrusted their life savings to the integrity of the financial markets and the belief of a level playing field. Insider trading, such as the conduct attributable to Matthew Kluger, corrupts the process and tilts the playing field in favor of those privileged few with access to information not available to the public, and at the expense of unsuspecting and unknowing investors."

According to documents filed in this case and statements made in court:

Kluger and two coconspirators — Garrett D. Bauer, 44, of New York, and Kenneth Robinson, 45, of Long Beach, N.Y. — engaged in an insider trading scheme that began in 1994. Kluger admitted that he passed inside information to Bauer and Robinson that the men used to trade ahead of more than 30 different corporate transactions.

During the scheme, Kluger worked at four of the nation's premier mergers and acquisitions law firms. From 1994 to 1997, he worked first as a summer associate and later as a corporate associate at Cravath Swaine & Moore in New York. From 1998 to 2001, he worked at Skadden, Arps, Slate, Meagher & Flom in New York and Palo Alto, Calif., as an associate in their corporate department. From 2001 to 2002, Kluger worked as a corporate associate at Fried, Frank, Harris, Shriver & Jacobson LLP in New York. From December 5, 2005, to March 11, 2011, Kluger worked at Wilson Sonsini Goodrich & Rosati ("Wilson Sonsini") as a senior associate in the Mergers & Acquisitions department of the firm's Washington office.

While at the firms, Kluger regularly stole and disclosed to Robinson material, nonpublic information regarding anticipated corporate mergers and acquisitions on which his firms were working. Early in the scheme, Kluger disclosed information relating to deals on which he personally worked. As the scheme developed, and in an effort to avoid law enforcement detection, Kluger took information which he found primarily by viewing documents on his firms' computer systems.

Kluger admitted that once he provided the inside information to Robinson, Robinson passed it to Bauer. Bauer then purchased shares for himself, Kluger, and Robinson in Bauer's trading accounts, then sold them once the relevant deal was publicly announced and the stock price rose. Bauer gave Robinson and Kluger their shares of the illicit profits in cash — often tens or hundreds of thousands of dollars per deal — that Bauer withdrew in multiple transactions from ATM machines.

The three conspirators took greater efforts to prevent detection of their insider trading scheme after Kluger joined Wilson Sonsini. Among other techniques, they used pay phones and prepaid cellular phones that they referred to as "throwaway phones" to discuss the scheme.

Kluger also admitted that, after Robinson told him that the FBI and IRS had searched Robinson's house and had asked questions about the illicit scheme, Kluger destroyed multiple pieces of evidence, including an iPhone and a computer. Kluger also instructed Robinson to destroy a prepaid phone.

As part of his guilty plea, Kluger agreed to forfeit $415,000, which is the *approximate amount that he obtained from recent transactions in the scheme . . . .*[8]

II. CLIENT CONFIDENTIAL INFORMATION: UNINTENTIONAL DISCLOSURE BY LAWYERS

The vast majority of legal professionals will not seek personal benefit from misuse of information belonging to (or about) their clients that they collect in the course of their practices. Attorneys will, however, possess client information in paper and electronic files, e-mail messages, documents, and other forms, and may also be transporting or transmitting the information in the course of performing legal services. In such circumstances, the broad scope of information held and used on behalf of clients by lawyers may lead to heightened risk of identity theft.

As one example, consider a trusts and estates attorney who is helping a client manage the affairs of a recently deceased relative. Among the tasks that the attorney may perform on his client's behalf could be filing a will for probate, requesting access to bank accounts, filing tax forms, and other tasks where account numbers, Social Security numbers, and other financially powerful data are included. If, in the course of preparing those documents, the attorney takes them out of the office on a laptop or even in paper form and loses them, or attaches them to an e-mail message accidentally sent to the wrong recipient, those records (whether of the deceased or the living relative) may be misused for theft or fraud purposes.

The risk, though, does not just come with errors made by the attorney. Many jurisdictions have adopted electronic filing ("e-filing") regimes, which either require or permit lawyers to serve and file documentation via e-mail or uploads.[9] In these systems, exhibits such as account statements, Social Security cards and the like, are scanned and then attached to the filings as they would be in a paper filing. The difference, though, is that unlike a paper filing system, many electronic filing regimes allow members of the public to obtain copies of the document without appearing in person before a court clerk to request them. This can lead to a situation where documents and other data that are appropriately part of legal filings can be accessed and misused by those without an interest in the case. While there are provisions in court rules for sealing sensitive documents (as with identification of sexual abuse

---

[8] Press Release, U.S. Department of Justice, USDOJ: US Attorney's Office — District of New Jersey (Dec. 14, 2011), http://www.justice.gov/usao/nj/Press/files/Kluger,%20Matthew%20Plea%20News%20 Release.html (last visited May 8, 2012).

[9] The mandatory Case Management/Electronic Case Files system of the U.S. federal court system was gradually introduced in bankruptcy courts beginning in 2001 and subsequently to district and appellate courts. About CM/ECF, http://www.uscourts.gov/FederalCourts/CMECF/AboutCMECF.aspx (last visited May 8, 2012). State courts have also moved toward electronic filing of court papers; see, e.g., the New York State Courts Electronic Filing system (New York State Courts Electronic Filing, https:// iapps.courts.state.ny.us/nyscef/HomePage (last visited May 8, 2012)); the Judiciary Electronic Filing System in New Jersey (Judiciary Electronic Filing System (JEFIS), http://www.judiciary.state.nj.us/jefis/ index.htm (last visited May 8, 2012)); the Electronic Filing pilot projects in Illinois (Illinois E-Filing, http://www.state.il.us/court/ebusiness/efiling.asp (last visited May 8, 2012)); and Texas' eFiling for Courts (Texas.gov | Efiling for Courts, http://www.texas.gov/en/tx-efiling/Pages/default.aspx (last visited May 8, 2012)).

victims, minors, and other similar situations) much of the information that can be part of legal filings and can in the wrong hands lead to identity theft is not generally eligible for sealing under traditional off-line filing regimes. That information is protected from improper access through the physical presence and judgment of a court clerk, who might as part of her responsibilities watch out for frequent requesters who seem to be seeking much more information than is customary or could inquire as to the purpose of a document request before filing it. In the electronic filings, by contrast, much of the document requesting happens without any human intervention or monitoring, and these risks are heightened. This reality, which arises out of e-filing, places a unique burden on an attorney to think not only whether information for a particular case or matter should be sealed, but whether some level or redaction might be needed even of otherwise innocuous information in order to prevent identity theft.[10]

Setting aside the questions of identity theft, though, one must consider that in fact some of the information maintained by attorneys as part of their representation could itself cause damage to the client if improperly released. Such damage could be as minor as difficulties in completing transactions if statements that are not meant for the other side are publicized, or as literally life-threatening as information regarding guilt or innocence in a capital defense case. Law firm data breaches could even raise issues of national security.[11] While court rules may limit the admissibility of accidentally released information if otherwise covered by the attorney-client privilege or similar protections,[12] that may not avoid the damage. Sometimes, the risks do not involve the proceedings but financial or personal interactions where admissibility is irrelevant.

---

[10] In her June 2011 report on eFiling in the New York State Courts, Chief Administrative Judge Ann Pfau discusses how New York has addressed the security concerns arising out of electronic filing:

> Apart from the proven security of the NYSCEF system itself, there are robust protections in place for confidential information in documents filed in the system. First, statute provides that attorneys filing documents with the clerk of a court shall not, with narrow exceptions, reveal social security numbers. Further, the e-filing rules promulgated by the Chief Administrative Judge provide protection for the health information of individuals and other sensitive personal information. An e-filer filing a document containing such information need only note that the document should be treated as secure, which can easily be done in NYSCEF. A document in secure status is accessible online only to another attorney or other filer participating in the e-filed case although, as with any document in paper form, it is available for inspection at the courthouse or County Clerk's Office unless it has been sealed pursuant to court order. E-filing allows the court clerk or the County Clerk to easily seal a document or a file as directed by the court.

http://www.courts.state.ny.us/whatsnew/pdf/eFiling-Report_6-2011.pdf.

As Judge Pfau notes, it is up to the e-filer (generally the attorney) to designate a document to be treated as secure in order for it to be made unavailable to those not involved in the case. Attorneys unfamiliar with the openness of e-filing, or who fail to carefully review court documents for sensitive information, may well disclose these data to anyone with an Internet connection.

[11] In February 2012, the law firm of Puckett Faraj, which had represented Marine Staff Sergeant Frank Wuterich against accusations of leading a massacre of 24 unarmed Iraqis at Haditha in November 2005, had 2.6 gigabytes of its files and e-mails accessed, downloaded, and publicly distributed by the hacker collective Anonymous. When the Gawker blog analyzed the data, it discovered not only information about Wuterich but other firm clients, including explicit witness statements from a rape case against one client. John Cook, ANONYMOUS' LATEST RELEASE INCLUDES PRIVATE INFO ABOUT SEXUAL ASSAULT VICTIMS AND GUANTANAMO LAWYERS (Feb. 3, 2012), http://gawker.com/5882150/anonymous-latest-release-includes-private-info-about-sexual-assault-victims-and-guantanamo-lawyers (last visited May 8, 2012).

[12] Under the Federal Rules of Civil Procedure, attorneys who accidentally provide privileged material to opposing counsel during discovery may retroactively withdraw that material

Because lawyers are so used to the protections of attorney-client privilege and are so comfortable with their own understanding of their confidentiality obligations, they may not take the type of precautions that other business people might in their everyday work. An attorney accustomed to the protections of privilege may not automatically think to password-protect client communications stored on a smartphone through which she sends and receives client e-mails, since disclosure would not be admissible against her client in court. Similarly, an executive working on documents for an especially sensitive transaction could be more likely to take precautions against accidental revelation than a lawyer for whom confidentiality is required for even the most mundane project. Even where attorneys have attempted to protect client confidentiality, unfamiliarity with the use and limitations of their electronic tools can mean that the information is nonetheless disclosed by the lawyers.[13]

In 1999, the American Bar Association issued Formal Ethics Opinion 99-413, which analyzed whether ethics obligations including Model Rule 1.6 would require lawyers to encrypt (scramble) e-mail messages to and from clients in order to adequately establish the expectation of privacy necessary to preserve the attorney/client privilege. In summary, the ABA stated:

> *The Committee believes that e-mail communications, including those sent unencrypted over the Internet, pose no greater risk of interception or disclosure than other modes of communication commonly relied upon as having a reasonable expectation of privacy. The level of legal protection accorded e-mail transmissions, like that accorded other modes of electronic communication, also supports the reasonableness of an expectation of privacy for unenerypted [sic] e-mail transmissions. The risk of unauthorized interception and disclosure exists in every medium of communication, including e-mail. It is not, however, reasonable to require that a mode of communicating information must be avoided simply because interception is technologically possible, especially when unauthorized interception or dissemination of the information is a violation of law . . . . The Committee concludes, based upon current technology and law as we are informed of it, that a lawyer sending confidential client information by unencrypted e-mail does not violate Model Rule 1.6(a) in choosing that mode to communicate. This is principally because there is a reasonable expectation of privacy in its*

If information produced in discovery is subject to a claim of privilege or of protection as trial-preparation material, the party making the claim may notify any party that received the information of the claim and the basis for it. After being notified, a party must promptly return, sequester, or destroy the specified information and any copies it has; must not use or disclose the information until the claim is resolved; must take reasonable steps to retrieve the information if the party disclosed it before being notified; and may promptly present the information to the court under seal for a determination of the claim. The producing party must preserve the information until the claim is resolved.

Fed. R. Civ. P. 26(b)(5)(B).

[13] See, e.g., Thomas Claburn, THINGS FACEBOOK COULDN'T KEEP SECRET IN COURT — SECURITY — PRIVACY — INFORMATIONWEEK (Feb. 12, 2009), http://www.informationweek.com/news/security/privacy/214000046 (last visited May 8, 2012); REDACTION OF INFORMATION, https://ecf.cand.uscourts.gov/cand/faq/tips/redacting.htm (last visited May 8, 2012).

use.[14]

While the general understanding supporting the ABA's viewpoint appears to remain current, and is supported by state and federal legislative and procedural materials,[15] preservation of privilege is not an absolute certainty. There have been cases in which privilege was denied for unencrypted e-mail messages between lawyers and their clients, when (a) the case was brought against the client's (former) employer, (b) the messages had been sent via the then-employer's internal e-mail system, and (c) the employer maintained a formal policy stating it reserved the right to read employee e-mails to ensure they were for business rather than personal use.[16]

One other practical privacy challenge for attorneys is their access to information technology ("IT") resources, especially for those who may be engaged in solo or small-firm practice. Again, while all businesses have IT needs, legal practice adds ethical requirements not only for confidentiality but document management, conflict checks, file retention, detailed billing and other practical concerns. It can be difficult enough for lawyers who are not well-versed in technology to specify, locate and manage (by themselves or using service providers) the systems they need just to practice efficiently and effectively; many may not know the right questions to ask, let alone what they need, when it comes to ensuring the privacy of their client data. Further, even when the attorney selects an IT provider whose services are specifically designed for legal professionals, the provider may not offer the full range of advice and systems design, including addressing mobile and home office work environments, to ensure (or at least promote) confidentiality.

---

[14] American Bar Association Standing Committee on Ethics and Professional Responsibility, Formal Opinion 99-413, Protecting the Confidentiality of Unencrypted E-Mail, Mar. 10, 1999.

[15] See, e.g., Cal. Evid. Code § 917(b) (Deering ?YEAR?) ("A [privileged] communication . . . does not lose its privileged character for the sole reason that it is communicated by electronic means or because persons involved in the delivery, facilitation, or storage of electronic communication may have access to the content of the communication.") See also N.Y. C.P.L.R. 4548 ("No communication privileged under this article shall lose its privileged character for the sole reason that it is communicated by electronic means or because persons necessary for the delivery or facilitation of such electronic communication may have access to the content of the communication.").

[16] See, e.g., *Scott v. Beth Isr. Med. Ctr.*, 847 N.Y.S.2d 436 (Sup. Ct. 2007); *In re Asia Global Crossing, Ltd. et al, Debtors*, 322 B.R. 247 (2008) (S.D.NY Bankr. Ct. 2008). But see *Stengart v. Loving Care*, 200 N.J. 300 (2010) (privilege preserved where former employee used employer computer but personal, third-party e-mail system to communicate with counsel).

TABLE OF CASES

[References are to pages]

INDEX

[References are to sections.]

[References are to sections.]